ASHGATE
RESEARCH
COMPANION

THE ASHGATE RESEARCH COMPANION TO ISLAMIC LAW

ASHGATE
RESEARCH
COMPANION

The *Ashgate Research Companions* are designed to offer scholars and graduate students a comprehensive and authoritative state-of-the-art review of current research in a particular area. The companions' editors bring together a team of respected and experienced experts to write chapters on the key issues in their speciality, providing a comprehensive reference to the field.

The Ashgate Research Companion to Islamic Law

Edited by

Rudolph Peters
University of Amsterdam

and

Peri Bearman
Harvard University, USA

Routledge
Taylor & Francis Group
LONDON AND NEW YORK

First published 2014 by Ashgate Publishing

2 Park Square, Milton Park, Abingdon, Oxfordshire OX14 4RN
52 Vanderbilt Avenue, New York, NY 10017

Routledge is an imprint of the Taylor & Francis Group, an informa business

First issued in paperback 2018

British Library Cataloguing in Publication Data
A catalogue record for this book is available from the British Library

Library of Congress Cataloging-in-Publication Data
The Ashgate research companion to Islamic law / by Rudolph Peters and Peri Bearman.
pages cm. – (Ashgate research companion)
Includes bibliographical references and index.
ISBN 978-1-4094-3893-9 (hardback)
1. Islamic law. I. Peters, Rudolph, editor of compilation. II. Bearman, P. J. (Peri J.) editor of compilation.
KBP144.A839 2014
340.5'9–dc23

2013045815

ISBN 978-1-4094-3893-9 (hbk)
ISBN 978-0-367-19662-2 (pbk)

ASHGATE
RESEARCH
COMPANION

Contents

Part II Substantive Islamic Law

Part III Islamic Law through the Prism of the Modern State

PART IV PRESENT-DAY DISCUSSIONS ABOUT SHARIA

Preface

This volume on Islamic law was solicited by Ashgate in the fall of 2010 for its ever-expanding series of *Research Companions*. Although there was no paucity of introductions to Islamic law preceding it, nor will this one be the last, we felt that an approach like the one we envisaged was altogether missing. We proposed to Ashgate to present classical Islamic law through a historiographical introduction to and analysis of the Western scholarship and key debates that have formed the field and continue to provoke new ways of thinking about long-standing issues in this increasingly relevant and popular discipline. By teaching the basics of the history of Islamic law through a linear study of the research that unearthed it, we wanted to provide for both the student and advanced scholar a real research companion, in the very sense of the word. Our Companion is meant to open their eyes to the challenges posed by past, sometimes flawed scholarship, to the magnitude of milestones that have been achieved in reinterpreting and revising at one time current ideas, and ultimately to a thorough conceptual understanding of the subject at hand.

Chapter 1 comprises an introduction that defines the nature of the Sharia in comparison and contrast to Western law, explaining the moral, religious, and cultural aspects that stand in the way of Islamic law being seen as a veritable legal system in the family of laws. It is followed by seven historiographical chapters that survey secondary literature on the biggest questions that have animated the field of Islamic law since its beginnings—Chapter 2 treats the question of its origins; Chapter 3, its divine sources, their authenticity and historicity; Chapter 4, the singular Islamic school of jurisprudence (*madhhab*) and its development; Chapter 5, the emergence and genre of legal theory (*uṣūl al-fiqh*); Chapter 6, the role of the Islamic judge and jurist; and Chapters 7 and 8, the relationship between the state and Sharia, in early and Ottoman times respectively. Combined, these seven chapters present an introduction to the history of the Islamic legal system and to the imperfect or pioneering studies that unearthed it, uncovering and resolving the dichotomies of applied vs ideal, secular vs religious, human vs divine that characterize the last century of thinking in the field (and can still be found fallaciously today).

Following the historiographical first section, the next six chapters delve into an exposition of the substantive law. The rules relating to legal status, family law, socio-economic justice, penal law, constitutional authority, and the law of war are presented and discussed in the context of premodern juristic thinking. This section is followed by three chapters that treat the appropriation of Sharia after the advent of the colonial enterprise—a chapter on the colonial state, one on the nation state, and a final one on the re-Islamization process of national legal systems, as ongoing in, for example, northern Nigeria today. A final section contains four chapters devoted to contemporary debates on the relevance and role of Sharia relating to finance, Muslims living in non-Muslim-majority countries, modern governance, and the sphere of medical ethics, bringing the reader up to the present day.

The volume is rounded off with a clarion call by Abdullahi An-Naʿim, one of our most celebrated advocates for Sharia reform, for Muslims to restore the normative relevance—and confirm the legal irrelevance—of Sharia in their everyday lives. Sharia, he argues, is religion, and religious ideas and norms must not be imposed upon believers, or non-believers. Legislation inspired by the Sharia can be enacted by the state through a democratic constitutional process; but above all, it should comply with the principles of human rights and the rights of minorities. With this final chapter, which captures the struggle over the role of Sharia in the lives of Muslims from the perspective of one Muslim intellectual, the Research Companion has brought the study of Islamic law from the year 622, through the medium of twentieth- and twenty-first-century scholarship, into the future.

Some points of style used in the volume are in order. We attempted to keep undefined non-English technical terms to a minimum, but for instances where a term ventured into the text unaccompanied, the Glossary at the back of the volume hopefully provides sufficient recourse. The diacritical marks that differentiate Arabic letters in English were used sparingly, only in names and italicized terms. Thus, Abbasid instead of ʿAbbāsid, Sharia instead of Sharīʿa, Hanafi instead of Ḥanafī, etc. In the same vein, all dates are given as Christian-era dates except for death dates, when hijri dates precede the Christian date, as in al-Shāfiʿī (d. 204/819). The death dates of Western scholars mentioned throughout the text are also added to their entries in the index. Finally, the singular form of an individual account of Prophetic custom, hadith (Ar. *ḥadīth*), has been used as well for the collective.

Lastly, our thanks go to the contributors whose selfless efforts can be found in these pages. Our hair is grayer than when we started, but it is very likely that theirs is as well. They put up with a lengthy process and at times cruel edits. And we would like to salute our friend and colleague Lutz Wiederhold, whose very untimely death in March 2012 brought his collaboration with this volume to a shocking and infinitely sad end.

Ruud Peters
Peri Bearman

Introduction: The Nature of the Sharia

Rudolph Peters and Peri Bearman

It should be said at the outset that the term "Islamic law," with which this volume is concerned, is not unequivocal. It denotes at least two different concepts. On the one hand it can stand for Islamic normativity in the fields of ritual, morality, and law—in other words, Sharia in its totality. As such Islamic law is then used in the same way one speaks of, for example, Jewish law. On the other hand Islamic law can refer only to the legal normativity of Sharia—Sharia in a narrow sense. In this Research Companion the latter use is paramount but not exclusively so (see, for instance, Part IV). In general the context will make clear in what sense the term is used.

Our point of departure for the concept of Sharia is the definition found in the standard works of Islamic jurisprudence as the set of divine injunctions (*aḥkām*, sg. *ḥukm*) revealed to humanity through God's messenger Muḥammad. God has communicated these injunctions through His words as recorded in the Quran and through the Prophet's divinely inspired sayings and exemplary behavior (Sunna), as recorded in the hadith compilations. The texts of Quran and Sunna, however, are the raw material of the Sharia and not immediately ready for use. They need interpretation and reasoning in order to formulate the rules that they were meant to convey. This human activity is called *fiqh*, jurisprudence, which term in practice is extended to the rulings derived by the jurists from the two foundational texts. Strictly speaking, the Sharia is the set of divine commands, transmitted by God through the foundational sources of Quran and Sunna, and fiqh is the human endeavor to identify and elucidate these divine injunctions. Often, however, the terms Sharia and fiqh are used indiscriminately and interchangeably.

The divine instructions addressed to mankind are commands or prohibitions regarding human behavior; obeying or disobeying God's instructions (*taklīf*, obligation or duty) entails reward or punishment in the hereafter. The acts that are the object of the instructions are sorted into one of five categories (*al-aḥkām al-sharʿiyya*): they are either obligatory (*wājib*) or forbidden (*ḥarām*), meaning that obedience is rewarded and disobedience is punished; recommended (*mandūb*) or reprehensible (*makrūh*), meaning that compliance is rewarded but non-compliance is not punished; or they are

Rudolph (Ruud) Peters is Emeritus Professor of Islamic Law at the University of Amsterdam. He is the author of *Islamic Criminal Law in Nigeria* (2003), *Jihad in Classical and Modern Islam* (updated 2nd ed., 2005), *Crime and Punishment in Islamic Law: Theory and Practice from the Sixteenth to the Twenty-first Century* (2005), and *Wathāʾiq madīnat al-Qaṣr bi-l-wāḥāt al-Dākhila maṣdaran li-tārīkh Miṣr fī l-ʿaṣr al-ʿuthmānī* (2011), as well as many articles on Sharia and on the nineteenth-century legal history of Egypt. Peri Bearman is the former Associate Director of the Islamic Legal Studies Program at Harvard Law School. She is the Sectional Editor for Islamic Studies of the *Journal of the American Oriental Society* and the co-editor of a number of publications, among which the *Encyclopaedia of Islam*, 2nd edition; *The Law Applied: Contextualizing the Islamic Shariʿa* (2008); and *The Islamic School of Law: Evolution, Devolution, and Progress* (2005).

neutral (*mubāḥ*)—they offer neither reward nor punishment in the hereafter and believers are free to perform or not to perform the act.

The Sharia, then, is God's prescription for a life of submission (*islām*) to Him (Weiss 1998: 18), serving as the normative guide for Muslim behavior. The Sharia is also the basis and the reference point for the Islamic law and legal system. As a code animated by rules believed to be set forth by a divine lawgiver, the Sharia embodies normative and legal domains that transcend temporal and state-appointed ones. For Muslims, the Sharia is morality, law, etiquette, and religion in one. In order to fully capture the nature of the Sharia, in particular its multifold understanding in contemporary times, a description must branch out to include all of its components.

This broad nature of Sharia gives rise to a different experience of law than that understood by subjects of a common-law or civil-law system. The criterion to establish whether a Sharia rule is legal is whether its compliance can be enforced by the judiciary or by executive state organs. If this is not the case, such rule is not legal, but religious or moral. These latter sets of rules are complied with voluntarily or by virtue of social pressure, and the consequences of disobedience have, theoretically, only ramifications in the hereafter. Although the boundaries sometimes overlap, Muslim jurists separated the rules of worship (*ʿibādāt*) from the norms of social conduct, or the civil obligations (*muʿāmalāt*), which then were further divided between the domain of adjudication (*qaḍāʾ*), that is, enforceable in this world, and the domain of conscience (*diyāna*), their compliance only affecting the relationship between the believer and God.

Sharia, the Religious Law

The Sharia can be labeled as religious law for two reasons. First, because of its theological foundation: Muslims hold that the Sharia is what God revealed—in word and by mediation of His messenger Muḥammad—to lead the believer on the straight and narrow path to salvation; and second, because it contains rules that are primarily meaningful in the relationship between a believer and his or her Creator, such as those defining practices of worship (*ʿibādāt*).

The significance of this aspect of the Sharia is affirmed in that the ritual duties of Islam, the five pillars, are traditionally spelled out in the opening chapters of the handbooks on legal doctrine (*fiqh*), preceding all other rules. Here are found, for instance, detailed instructions on ritual purity and cleansing, on performing the ritual prayer (*ṣalāt*), on fasting during the month of Ramadan, on calculating, collecting, and distributing the religious taxes (*zakāt*), and on performing the pilgrimage to Mecca (*ḥajj*). In other chapters one finds instructions as to what food and drinks may or may not be consumed, how people ought to dress, how young boys must be circumcised. There are also rules about playing music and listening to it, wearing jewelry, defining the parts of the body that may be visible in public, ways of salutation, accepting or not accepting invitations to dinner, furnishing rooms, and proper greetings. Many of these straddle the line between religion and good manners. Some religious rules overlap with enforceable law: one of the pillars of Islam, the *zakāt*, is a property tax collected by the state and distributed to special groups, such as the poor.[1] The rules regarding this tax constitute legal norms both enforceable in this world and rewarded or punished in the next.

The religious character of the Sharia is often used in the West to disparage it as being irrational and unadaptable, lacking the properties that ideally are supposed to characterize viable legal systems. One of the first to formulate this and underpin it with an academic discourse was the renowned sociologist

1 See Q 9:60: "The freewill offerings are for the poor and needy, those who work to collect them; those whose hearts are brought together; the ransoming of slaves, debtors, in God's way, and the traveller; so God ordains; God is All-knowing, All-wise." Translations are those of Arberry 1955. For more on *zakāt*, see Chapter 11, below.

Max Weber (d. 1920). He argued that religious law in general cannot be rational since its lawmaking is grounded in revelation and not in rational decision-making, and its adjudication allows non-legal considerations to be taken into account and magic or supernatural procedural elements to be used. Being a religious law, Islamic law must therefore be irrational, both procedurally and substantively, and because it is based on fixed revealed texts, rigid and not adaptive (Crone 1987). Weber borrowed the notion of the rigidity of Islamic law from the Dutch scholar (and colonial official) Christiaan Snouck Hurgronje (d. 1936), who asserted that fiqh was a theoretical construct and could hardly work in practice. Weber contrasted Islamic law (as well as other religious laws) with Roman law, the foundation of most Western legal systems, which he regarded as showing the highest degree of legal rationality. Weber's ideas were adopted by many subsequent scholars and were used to establish the inferiority of Islamic law compared to Western legal systems (for Weber's typification of qadi justice, see Chapter 6, below). This characterization of Islamic law, which overlooked any empirical research into Sharia practice, became the authoritative Western view of Islamic law until the 1970s, when researchers began studying Islamic law in action from judicial records (Johansen 1999: 46–54).

Sharia, the Moral Law

As befits rules revealed to believers to keep them on the right path toward a sinless life in this world and toward eternal bliss in the next, God's ordinances encompass a set of moral qualifications of all human acts. This forms such a large part of the Sharia that Western pioneers of the study of fiqh, such as Snouck Hurgronje, denied it its legal character, preferring to call it a "deontology," a system of moral obligations rather than law. More recently, while acknowledging the legal elements of the Sharia, Kevin Reinhart (2010: 220 n. 5) suggested that it can best be translated with "morality" instead of "law" to emphasize how much the Sharia constitutes a moral basis for the Muslim community and how much of it is regulated by the pious conscience.[2] Indeed, Sharia governs a spectrum of moral, religious, and social behavior denied to the reach of law by a secularist or positivist view, famously defined by the distinguished legal philosopher H.L.A. Hart (d. 1992) as "the simple contention that it is in no sense a necessary truth that laws reproduce or satisfy certain demands of morality" (Hart 1994: 184–5).

The fact that Muslims regard morality and law as part of one single ideational institution and derived from the same foundational texts is contrary to the Western perception of the contrast between law and morality, which are seen to have separate domains. Many Western scholars have criticized the intimate connection between morality and law in the Sharia, just as they criticized its religious character. Noel Coulson, for example, qualified the Sharia as "a rigid and immutable system, embodying norms of an absolute and eternal validity, which are not susceptible to modification by any legislative authority" (Coulson 1964: 5), thus blaming the Sharia's alleged rigidity on the "failure" to distinguish between law and morality. The connection between law and morality, however, may well be one of the strengths of the Sharia and enhance its efficacy, for its transcendental properties could incline Muslims to comply with the law also in worldy, legal affairs. In other words, the fact that fasting during the month of Ramadan and paying a worker's wages as contracted belong to the same divine normative system could enhance compliance with the mundane obligations of daily life. Wael Hallaq (2005/2006: 152) argues that this intimate connection between morality and law equipped the law

2 This moral aspect of the Sharia should be distinguished from ethics (*ʿilm al-akhlāq*), the object of which—ethical values and ideals—is more often studied from a philosophical perspective (Walzer and Gibb 1960).

> with efficient, communally based, socially embedded, bottom-top methods of control that earned it remarkably willing obedience and—as another consequence—made it less coercive than any church or imperial law Europe introduced since the fall of the Roman Empire.

In fact, the connection between law and morality in the Sharia is not very different from that proposed by Western legal philosophers, as we shall see.

Western philosophers and jurists have debated the link between law and morality for centuries. Fundamentally distinguishing between man-made law and morality, they explored the connection in order to find criteria for good laws. Advocates of the theory of natural law, such as Thomas Aquinas (d. 1274) and his followers, held that there is an ideal type of law, based on reason and morality, and that it is part of the natural order and consistent with the purposes of nature. In order for man-made law to be valid and binding, it must be in conformity with natural law—and thus morality. On the other side of the debate are legal positivists such as John Austin (d. 1859), who argued that the connection between law and morality is loose and accidental and that law can be defined without having recourse to morality (Murphy and Coleman 1990: 37). Finally, philosophers such as Hart maintain that there must be an overlap between law and morality because both regulate human conduct with respect to central human values and are about the same issues (Hart 1994: 193–200).

In the standard fiqh works, moral and legal rules are not presented separately, but are distinguished by being qualified either as belonging to the domain of adjudication (legal rules) or the domain of conscience (moral rules), as described above. Most Sharia rules are moral, categorized thus not only by Muslim scholars but also by present-day (Western) philosophy in that they satisfy its formal criteria of morality. These criteria are: (1) moral rules address significant issues (such as those related to human life, property, sexuality); (2) they cannot or can hardly be changed deliberately (a point to which we will return); (3) they only judge voluntary behavior; and (4) they are complied with by virtue of individual conscience and social pressure, not by force (Hart 1994: 173–80). However, because many of these rules are enforceable by the judiciary or the executive, which thus form a normative coercive system to uphold the social order, they have a double character, moral and legal. Not complying with legal obligations by, for example, killing someone, violating sexual prohibitions, not paying debts, or inflicting damage on a person's property are not only punished or redressed by law in this world, but are also sins in the sight of God and entail sanctions in the hereafter. Indeed, the administration of justice shares this double character since it is regarded as divinely commanded and divinely inspired.[3]

Nevertheless, law and morality in Islam do not overlap in every instance. There are legal rules that do not address significant issues and are thus not moral, as, for instance, the requirement that a marriage must be witnessed by two men (and not three or four) or that not more than one-third of an estate may be bequeathed. Other legal rules cannot be qualified as moral because they are based on strict liability, that is, liability for acts committed beyond one's control—as, for instance, the liability of the insane for damage they have caused or the liability of the owner of land for the blood money of a person who was found killed by a person or persons unknown on his land.[4] Likewise there are moral rules that are not enforceable as law. The Sharia acts in the recommended, reprehensible, or permitted categories—referred to above—are a case in point.[5] Despite there being no temporal

3 See, for example, Q 3:18: "God bears witness that there is no God but He—and the angels and men possessed of knowledge—upholding justice"; Q 6:115: "Perfect are the words of thy Lord in truthfulness and justice"; Q 4:58: "God commands […] when you judge between the people, that you judge with justice"; Q 16:90: "God bids to justice and good-doing and giving to kinsmen."

4 After the completion of the *qasāma* procedure, that is, the swearing of 50 oaths by the owner of the land to the effect that he or she is innocent and does not know the killer.

5 The section on the law of marriage in the books of fiqh often includes passages discussing the moral dimensions of concluding a marriage (addressed to men) depending on certain circumstances: "Marriage

authority imposing any consequences on acts of these categories, they are integral to Sharia as moral code, and they possess an authority that can only be circumvented by political or administrative means. Thus, the permissibility (*ibāḥa*) of marrying up to four wives at a time is only bypassed in the modern state by regulatory obstacles that encumber the husband; permitted by the Quran, it cannot, or can only with difficulty, be prescribed by law.[6]

Finally, there is a distinction between legal and moral rules deriving from the validity of proof. The jurists are well aware of this and describe the cases in which law and morality take a different course, as when a judge finds for one of the parties on the strength of valid testimonies that the winning party knows are false, the party can legally enforce the judgment but is morally bound not to do so (Johansen 1999: 35–7).

Sharia, the Law

As we have seen, the Sharia deals with mankind's obligations to God; it is a guide for the believer, serving as a template on how to live a moral life and thereby attain eternal salvation after death. However, the Sharia that is the focus of this volume is also the sum of enforceable legal norms dealing with obligations and rights between humans. If law is a binding custom or practice of a community, requiring people to perform or abstain from certain actions, and if law is a system that resolves conflicts and makes rules, applies, and enforces them, then the Sharia is as much a law and legal system as the next one. The Sharia as law is positivist, pragmatic, and dynamic, despite its canonical beginnings and bases. These bases were fleshed out over centuries by legal scholars, but jurisprudence on its own would be a sterile corpus without the legal institutions provided by the governing body, for example the judiciary and executive body, to apply it. The Sharia became a full-fledged legal system when Islamic fiqh interacted with Islamic rules and principles for governance (*siyāsa*).[7]

The legal domain of the Sharia includes all fields known in Western law, such as marriage, inheritance, contracts, penal law, evidence, and procedure, and defines the obligations and rights of the parties concerned. Moreover, the Sharia as law recognizes the same types of rules as are found in Western law (see below), and within its own established limits it was anchored in communities by the recognition of local customary practice. For instance, if spouses had a dispute about when payment of the bride price (*mahr*) was due and the marriage contract provided no answer, the judge took recourse in the local custom. Customary practice that contravened the Sharia, however, such as the acceptance of usurious commerce, would not prevail.

So far the discussion has centered on the contents of the obligations and their sanctions, both in this world and the next. These are rules of conduct, such as that a Muslim pray five times a day or that a husband provide for his wife. However, both Muslim and Western jurists accounted for rules determining the beginning, the end, and the change of obligations. In Western legal philosophy these are referred to as rules conferring legal power. They determine, for example, the legal capacity of the actors, the formalities of a legal act, and the duration of the legal powers that were

is obligatory for a man who yearns for it if he is afraid of committing fornication […]. If he is not afraid of committing fornication, marriage is commendable for him, unless he has to provide for his wife's maintenance by illicit methods, in which case marriage is forbidden for him. For a man who does not yearn for it, it is reprehensible if being married would result in giving up commendable acts." Dardīr n.d.: 214–5.

6 To date, polygynous marriages have been banned in very few Muslim countries; examples are Turkey (where the Sharia has been abolished altogether), Tunisia, and Albania.

7 This is also illustrated by the fact that the Sharia as law applies not only to Muslims, but to all subjects of Islamic states, regardless of their religion. Religious courts in the field of family law for non-Muslims did not issue enforceable judgments (except through social pressure or ecclesiastical sanctions). If non-Muslims required one, they would have recourse to Sharia courts (Gradeva 1997: 68–9).

transferred (Hart 1994: 27–8). Muslim jurists distinguish between *ḥukm taklīfī*, a prescriptive rule establishing that an act is mandatory, forbidden, or neutral, and *ḥukm waḍ'ī*, usually translated as a declaratory rule, regulating the implementation of the former, similar to the rules conferring legal power identified in Western law. The declaratory rules specify the event or legal act that is the cause, condition, and impediment affecting the creating, transferring, modifying, or extinguishing of an obligation (Kamali 1991: 335–42). Thus, certain rules only apply if there is a cause: a death entails the application of the rules of succession; a validly concluded contract of lease creates the obligation to pay rent. A condition for performing a legal act that has legal force is to be of sound mind—a contract of sale concluded by an insane person is null and void and does not create any obligation or right. Finally, an impediment is a situation that precludes the validly carrying out of a religious or legal act, for instance an impediment for marriage is a close blood relationship between the bride and groom, as, for example, a brother and sister or a father and daughter; if such a marriage is concluded and all the formalities have been observed, the marriage is nevertheless void, that is, there is no marriage. In the same vein, if a person performs the ritual prayer but is not ritually pure, the prayer is void and the obligation has not been discharged.[8]

A legal system includes more than rules commanding conduct (primary rules): there must also be rules, known as secondary rules, by which it can be recognized what a valid legal rule is (rules of recognition); rules empowering individuals to determine authoritatively that in a special case a primary rule has been broken (adjudication); and, finally, rules of change. As society develops, the law must adapt to it (Hart 1994: 94–8).

In Western legal systems there is usually a complex set of rules of recognition, including, for instance, rules regarding lawmaking, the hierarchy between the rules issued by different legislative bodies, the binding character of judicial decisions, and the status of customary law. A test for a valid rule is that a court of law or an official applies it. It is less complex in the Islamic legal system—the state never acquired the authority to create the Sharia or to issue authoritative interpretations. That was in the hands of the jurists. The simple version of the rule of recognition is that a valid rule is one given by God, through His revealed sources. However, since these foundational texts are often equivocal and/or contradictory, they require interpretation. To manage this, a separate legal discipline, the principles of jurisprudence (*uṣūl al-fiqh*, or legal epistemology, for which see Chapter 5, below), which contains the rules for deriving legal (and religious) injunctions from the sources (*ijtihād*), was developed by jurists during the first centuries of Islam. The Sharia rule of recognition became that a legal norm must be derived from the sources by a qualified jurist in accordance with the principles of jurisprudence.

Since there was no central authority deciding on the correctness of an interpretation, this did not guarantee uniformity. Different interpretations abounded. In the early development of the law, jurists who shared interpretations and methods coalesced in doctrinal circles, which eventually developed into the schools of jurisprudence (sg. *madhhab*, for which see Chapter 4, below), each deriving its name from its alleged founder, a prominent jurist from an earlier generation. Adhering to a school, which in the course of time became mandatory, meant that a jurist's autonomy in exercising *ijtihād*—the independent effort to derive a legal rule—was gradually restricted; the school doctrine, originating in the opinions of the jurists from previous generations, prevailed and had to be followed (*taqlīd*) by the jurists. As a result of the crystallization of the school doctrines, the fiqh of each school became more homogeneous (Fadel 1996), yet between the schools there remained a great deal of variety, and the Sharia continued on its pluralistic path, accommodating conflicting opinions. The rule of recognition, therefore, taking into account the existing pluralism, can only be formulated with regard to one specific school: a valid and enforceable norm is the one that is regarded as authoritative by the jurists following that particular school.

Since judges as a rule followed the madhhab to which they were affiliated in their decisions, the crystallization of the school doctrine helped create a measure of uniformity and legal certainty in

8 Muslim jurists use the categories of valid (*ṣaḥīḥ, jā'iz*) and void (*bāṭil*) both for religious and legal acts.

the administration of justice, aided by the large body of authoritative juridical literature developed by each school. In the early years, the legal opinions of the founders and their students were orally transmitted, but in the course of time their legacy, sometimes in various standard versions, became canonical literature containing the doctrinal bases of each madhhab. To facilitate teaching, summaries (sg. *mukhtaṣar*) of the doctrine were written as early as the second half of the ninth century. These presented systematically both the school's legal opinions and the debates swirling around them, and as time went on, their authors would indicate which opinions were authoritative and which were not, thus standardizing the doctrine. The jurists who used these for teaching would often compose commentaries (sg. *sharḥ*) and glosses (sg. *ḥāshiya*), adding to the bulk of writings. In addition to this growing fiqh corpus, the fatwas issued by renowned muftis were collected, and specialized works catering to certain professions were composed, for example manuals for procedure intended for judges and formularies for the use of notaries.

A second type of secondary rules are "the rules empowering individuals to determine authoritatively that in a special case a primary rule may have been broken" (Hart 1994: 96). These rules determine the who and how of adjudication—who can be a judge and what is the legal procedure. The Islamic fiqh books devote several chapters to these matters (see Chapter 6, below). The actual appointment of judges fell to the ruler. This is the window through which the state had some impact on the Sharia, since the state, or rather the head of state, could impose certain conditions. Thus, he could limit the judge's jurisdiction in terms of territory, types of cases, and statute of limitations. He could instruct the judge to adjudicate according to a certain school, or even according to certain authorities within the school (Peters 2005). What the state could not do was interfere with the rules of the Sharia (see Chapter 7, below).

Theoretically lacking in Islamic law is the third type of secondary rules, those governing change. Muslims believe that God, the Lawgiver (*shāriʿ*), revealed a perfect set of rules (Q 6:154),[9] and after the death of His messenger Muḥammad ceased communicating with mankind. Thus, clear rules in the source texts cannot be altered, except by interpretation. The jurist practicing *ijtihād* (a *mujtahid*) could propose new opinions, but not as an overt response to social change, rather as a more correct presentation of the divine ideal. As noted above, *ijtihād* became restricted, no matter how learned the jurist was, and abiding by previously formulated rules was enjoined. Nevertheless, from time to time an entirely new phenomenon had to be assessed by the Sharia, as, for instance, in the sixteenth century upon the introduction of coffee and tobacco and in the nineteenth century when Muslim merchants began to enter into contracts of insurance with Western companies. The doctrine of *taqlīd* made legal change theoretically impossible; however, by exploiting the pluralistic character of the legal system and by picking and choosing one school's opinion over another, the law could be changed. Another method was to classify facts in different ways so as to apply different rules to them. Thus, although there was no formal set of rules of change, in practice fiqh was sufficiently flexible to construct a viable legal order, adaptable to social change (Johansen 1988).

Sharia Today

A main difference between the Sharia and Western law, as we have seen, is that the Sharia is conceived by Muslims to be divine law, a communication from God, whereas the present-day Western conception of law is that it is secular and created by humans. The Sharia includes religious and moral obligations, obedience of which is enforced by the notion of sanctions in the hereafter. Some of its rules are also enforced in this world by judges and state authorities. A second crucial difference is that the law was made not by the state but by religious scholars without any centralized authority to unify the legal

9 "Then We gave Moses the Book, complete for him who does good, and distinguishing every thing, and as a guidance and a mercy; haply they would believe in the encounter with their Lord."

doctrine. Locally the judiciary could be and often was restricted by instructions from the head of state regarding application of the Sharia, which created, within one polity, more homogeneity in the administration of justice and a greater legal certainty.

Such was the state of affairs until the late nineteenth century when the legal paradigm underlying the Sharia began to be eroded. Through much of the Muslim world a concept of law was adopted that had heretofore been unknown: the notion of the state being the sole legislator, creating law in the form of enacted codes. Such a codification of legislation, exhaustively regulating a certain domain of the law to the exclusion of all other types of law previously applicable in that field (unless the codification itself confers force of law on them, as is sometimes done in the case of custom), implies that only the state determines what law is and that the law it enacts is the highest form of law (see Chapter 16, below). This notion of codification had its origins in the European civil code tradition of the early nineteenth century.

The issuing of state law would prima facie seem to be contradictory to and incompatible with the notion of the Sharia as a divine law monopolized by the ulema. However, the areas of law that had always been left to the rulers to legislate in the Islamic legal system facilitated its reception. From the fifteenth century on, Ottoman sultans had begun to enact regulations (sg. *qānūn*, for which see Chapter 8, below) dealing with land law and fiscal and criminal law. These regulations did not replace Sharia rules, rather they supplemented them where the Sharia was silent or not precise. This legislation was always regarded as part of the Islamic legal order and as not being in conflict with the Sharia. Although the enactment of these statutes did not imply that the state had a monopoly on lawmaking or that state-enacted law was of a higher order than other types of law, the existence of Ottoman state legislation within a Sharia-dominant legal system helped pave the way for the codification movement of the nineteenth century.

The adoption of the notion that law must come from the state required that the Sharia became part of the national legal order—subordinate to national law and operating only by virtue of a legal provision issued by the national legislator, either by codification of parts of the Sharia or by referring the judiciary to the Sharia for adjudicating cases in certain domains. This drastically changed the rule of recognition in the Muslim world. The criterion for valid legal rules was no longer that they had been derived by Islamic scholars from the foundational sources according to the principles of Islamic jurisprudence, but that they were grounded in the constitutional rules of each state regarding the composition of the national legal system. Moreover, the law could now more easily be changed through the legislature.

Codification took place both in regions colonized by Western powers and in those that were (still) independent in the late nineteenth century. This was done to meet the needs of the expanded administrative duties of the state but also to introduce Western law (see Chapter 15, below). As a result, the domain in which the Sharia was applied was reduced to family law, which gradually was itself codified during the late nineteenth and twentieth centuries. Codification, however, was not only a matter of the form in which the law was presented, but also a matter of content: the Sharia was excised of all religious and moral elements. Moreover, whereas fiqh texts are discursive and include various, often contradictory opinions on an issue, the provisions of a law code are authoritative, clear, and unequivocal. Codifying the Sharia, therefore, required making choices between the various interpretations (Peters 2002). As a result of the Westernization of the law, the power of the religious scholars diminished; although they retained their authority in the fields of worship and morality, they lost their monopoly on controlling the content of Sharia as enforced law. They had to relinquish their position to the legislature of the state and their role was relegated to legitimate reforms of the Sharia initiated by the state.

By the mid-twentieth century most Muslim countries had hybrid legal systems, consisting of a mix of Western- and Sharia-inspired law. As a rule family law and the law of succession were governed by the latter. After the 1970s the balance between both types of law shifted in a number of countries where Islamist political forces acquired more power. As a result, these countries re-Islamized some domains of the law that were previously dominated by Western-inspired law (see Chapter 17, below).

They introduced Sharia penal codes and a few of them also adopted *zakāt* taxation and banned interest on loans. These innovations were not introduced by referring the judiciary to the classical fiqh books, however, but by codification by the state.

In almost all Muslim countries today, however, Sharia or "the rules of the religion" are still upheld as the formal motivation for the law of the land. Many constitutions include a clause stipulating that the Sharia or the principles of the Sharia are the basis of legislations (Brown and Sherif 2004). The legal implications of such clauses vary from country to country. With the law and the religion having become increasingly dissociated, much of the contemporary appeal of Sharia for Muslims is its centrality to their Muslim identity. By recourse, however formal, to Sharia law, the belief endures that the character of their modern-day state is governed by their faith. For those who view contemporary Muslim societies as abnegating their proper Muslim identity by the loss of Sharia law—disregarding the fact that law is the product of the society whose law it is (Voegelin 1991)—and call for its re-establishment, an understanding of the interpretive role that fiqh played in producing the legal system and of the innate pluralistic and non-codified nature of Sharia is generally lacking.

In conformity with the words of the legal philosopher Robert Cover (d. 1986) that "the creation of legal meaning takes place always through an essentially cultural medium" (Cover 1993: 103), the Sharia today is also a cultural phenomenon. It is necessarily viewed through socio-cultural norms. Thus, often understood by Muslims today in the light of their own customary background, it is sometimes said to incorporate values and practices that are in fact alien to prescriptions of Sharia law. In a number of areas of the Muslim world, for example, customs such as enforcing a strict dress code for women, upholding a family's honor by retribution, or undergoing legal procedures that are purely customary in nature are considered erroneously to be in conformity with Sharia. On the other hand, the few binding rules in the revealed texts and the overarching conciliatory nature of Islamic legal methodology lead to a law that is valid for and characteristic of Muslims, the society, and the age in which it applies.

References

Brown, Nathan J., and Adel Omar Sherif. 2004. Inscribing the Islamic Shari'a in Arab Constitutional Law. In *Islamic Law and the Challenges of Modernity*, ed. Y.Y. Haddad and B.F. Stowasser, pp. 55–81. Walnut Creek, CA: AltaMira Press.

Coulson, Noel J. 1964. *A History of Islamic Law*. Edinburgh: Edinburgh University Press.

Cover, Robert. 1993. Nomos and Narrative. In *Narrative, Violence, and the Law: The Essays of Robert Cover*, ed. M. Minow et al., pp. 95–172. Ann Arbor: University of Michigan Press.

Crone, Patricia. 1987. Max Weber, das islamische Recht, und die Entstehung des Kapitalismus. In *Max Webers Sicht des Islams: Interpretation und Kritik*, ed. W. Schluchter, pp. 294–335. Frankfurt am Main: Suhrkamp.

Dardīr, Aḥmad. n.d. *Al-Sharḥ al-kabīr ʿalā Mukhtaṣar Khalīl ibn Isḥāq*. In *Ḥāshiyat al-Dasūqī ʿalā l-Sharḥ al-kabīr*. Vol. 2. Cairo: Dār Iḥyāʾ al-Kutub al-ʿArabiyya.

Fadel, Mohammad. 1996. The Social Logic of *Taqlīd* and the Rise of the *Mukhtaṣar*. *Islamic Law and Society* 3(2): 193–233.

Gradeva, Rossitsa. 1997. Orthodox Christians in the Kadi Courts: The Practice of the Sofia Sheriat Courts, Seventeenth Century. *Islamic Law and Society* 4(1): 37–69.

Hallaq, Wael B. 2005/2006. What is Shariʿa? *Yearbook of Islamic and Middle Eastern Law* 12: 151–80.

Hart, H.L.A. 1994. *The Concept of Law*. 2nd ed. Oxford: Clarendon Press.

Johansen, Baber. 1988. *The Islamic Law on Land Tax and Rent*. London: Croom Helm.

———. 1999. *Contingency in a Sacred Law: Legal and Ethical Norms in the Muslim* Fiqh. Leiden: Brill.

Kamali, Mohammad Hashim. 1991. *Principles of Islamic Jurisprudence*. Cambridge: Islamic Texts Society.

Murphy, Jeffrie G., and Jules L. Coleman. 1990. *Philosophy of Law: An Introduction to Jurisprudence*. Rev. ed. Boulder: Westview Press.

Peters, Rudolph. 2002. From Jurists' Law to Statute Law or What Happens When the Shariʿa is Codified. *Mediterranean Politics* 7(3): 82–95.

———. 2005. What Does It Mean to Be an Official Madhhab? Hanafism and the Ottoman Empire. In *The Islamic School of Law: Evolution, Devolution, and Progress*, ed. P. Bearman et al., pp. 147–58. Cambridge, MA: ILSP, Harvard Law School.

Reinhart, A. Kevin. 2010. Law. In *Key Themes for the Study of Islam*, ed. J.J. Elias, pp. 220–44. Oxford: Oneworld.

Voegelin, Eric. 1991. *The Collected Works of Eric Voegelin*, vol. 27, *The Nature of the Law and Related Legal Writings*, ed. R.A. Pascal et al. Baton Rouge: Louisiana State University Press.

Walzer, Richard, and H.A.R. Gibb. 1960. Akhlāḳ. In *Encyclopaedia of Islam*, 2nd ed. Vol. 1: 325–7. Leiden: E.J. Brill.

Weiss, Bernard G. 1998. *The Spirit of Islamic Law*. Athens, GA: University of Georgia Press.

Part I

The Historical Islamic Law

The Origins of the Sharia

Knut S. Vikør

Few topics in the history of Islamic law have been more hotly debated than the question of its origins. All scholars, Muslim and non-Muslim, agree that the Sharia gained in detail and sophistication during the first few centuries of Islam, but there is considerable diversity of viewpoints as to when this process began and what components or influences came into play, particularly during the first two or three generations after the Prophet's death. While standard Muslim chronology identifies the Prophet's example, supported and enhanced by the transmissions of his Companions, as being decisive, whereupon it was collected, systematized, and theorized in the later formulations of classical law, some Western scholars proposed revisionist views that downgrade the continuity from the Prophet's example and place greater emphasis on the adoption of non-Islamic legal practices in the regions the Muslims came to conquer in the Near East.

The Early Orientalists

Such views were proposed by several European authors in the course of the nineteenth century. They were particularly developed by the Hungarian orientalist Ignaz Goldziher (d. 1921). His thoughts on the role of foreign influence can perhaps best be seen in a short article he wrote for *The Historians' History of the World* (Goldziher 1904, also 1913)[1] in which he describes what happened when the doors to the Roman and Persian worlds, previously closed to the Arabs, were opened upon the Muslim conquest. According to Goldziher, the first Umayyad caliphs, little concerned with religious edicts, had initially issued judgments on the basis of pre-Islamic custom (*sunna*), but this soon showed itself to be inadequate for the demands that ruling the new provinces required of the caliphs. Nor were the few specific rules found in the Quran and the legal decisions issued by the first four caliphs and the Prophet's Companions sufficient. It was thus "impossible that contact with foreign elements should fail to implant fresh ideas in the Semitic mind, singularly receptive as it is" (1904: 296). Stemming from the more unrefined conditions of the desert, Arab society had no choice but to leave the legal institutions of the conquered territories much as they had found them, although Islam molded these elements as far as possible "into harmony with its own religious sentiment."

While the religion had been influenced by Greek philosophy, Goldziher asserted that it was Rome's heritage that influenced the law. Even the Arabic legal terms were mere translations from Latin—fiqh being a translation of *(juris)prudentia*; *ʿilla* (the core term in *qiyās*, analogy) of *ratio*

Knut Vikør, Professor of the History of the Middle East and Muslim Africa at the University of Bergen, Norway, is the author of eight books and numerous papers in English and Norwegian, among which most recently the monograph *Between God and the Sultan: A History of Islamic Law* (London: Hurst, 2005).

1 See also his more general theory in Goldziher 1971, 1981.

legis; *ra'y* of *opinio*; and *maṣlaḥa* of *utilitas publica* (1904: 296–7). The dualism between "written law" (*naṣṣ*) and "unwritten law" was taken from *leges scriptæ* and *leges non scriptæ*, but was also taken over in Jewish legal theory as a distinction between "written" and "oral" law.[2] Islamic legal reasoning borrowed from Roman "scientific jurisprudence" in Syria.

But as the center of the empire moved to Mesopotamia in 750 CE and came under Persian influence, "sectarianism, pietism, harsh dogmatism, and [...] the persecuting spirit" came to prevail. The Abbasid dynasty was the Sasanid spirit in Islamic garb. Under this influence the great legal scholars of Iraq developed "into practical juridical systems the suggestions in the department of jurisprudence derived in earlier days from Roman law" (1904: 299). From this joint history, then, came the "glory of the scholarly world of Mesopotamia"—the golden age of Islamic legal elaboration.

Goldziher's theory was opposed by the Italian orientalist Carlo Nallino, who did not believe in any considerable Roman influence on Muslim law (Nallino 1940–42; also pp. 7, 101).[3] He argued that, clearly, the pre-Islamic Arabs already had a developed law, not just from the South Arabian kingdoms, but also necessitated by the interregional trade that they carried out. The "germs" of large parts of the later Islamic law can thus be found in pre-existing Arabian law. The first Muslim community continued practicing this law, except where the Prophetic revelation caused Muḥammad to explicitly change the established practice. As the Muslims spread out of Arabia, they met new challenges in the new societies, and to solve these, the legal scholars began the process of developing their existing laws by interpreting the Quranic injunctions and the example of the Prophet. The sources for Islamic law were therefore almost purely Arab, either pre-Islamic Arab law or based on Prophetic practice, but all from the time before the great Muslim conquests.

Nallino acknowledged that scholars' understanding of this period was mostly conjectural, and that his main argument was essentially a logical inference. We can see, he wrote, that all the basic principles of Islamic law are the same for all the legal doctrines, whether Sunni, Shi'i, or Ibadi, which means that these principles must have been in place before the doctrinal divisions occurred, that is, during the period of the first generation of Muslims before 650. If Shi'i law had developed after the division, then it would have shown an independent development rather than imitating the law of the Sunnis in all but a few aspects, and similarly with the other branches (1940–42: 87).

Later, the German scholar Joseph Schacht discussed this argument at some length, claiming that the later "sects" in fact did copy these basic principles of law from the established Sunni law when that was developed (Schacht 1950a: 12; 1950b: 260–8; 1964: 14–15). Schacht did not, however, challenge the chronology of Shi'i separation from Sunnism itself. The problem Nallino raised, he opined, could probably be solved more easily if one deconstructed the meaning of "sectarian divisions" and saw it as a process stretched out over several centuries, taking place thus in parallel or even in interplay with the legal developments.

Nallino did not exclude, at least hypothetically, some foreign influence, but he allowed for it indirectly, possibly by way of pre-Islamic Arabs being acquainted with some specific Roman rules, or through the medium of Sasanid law, which would have been influenced by Roman law. He accepted that the second caliph 'Umar (r. 634–44) borrowed some technical terms from Sasanid land law and that Persian irrigation regulations were already well known in pre-Islamic Arabia, as the Arabs had no reason to develop such laws independently in the desert. But he considered absurd the idea that Arab scholars spent any time studying Roman legal theory (Nallino 1940–42: 90, 92).

---

2 It is not obvious from the passage what Goldziher meant by Islamic "unwritten law"; possibly he refers to the distinction of *qāṭi'*, a rule that is clear-cut in the revealed text, *naṣṣ*, and is thus indisputable, and *ẓann*, a rule based on inference that can be subject to discussion.

3 Nallino traced the first claims of Roman influence to Domenico Gatteschi in 1865.

Schacht's History

Goldziher's basic understanding of the development of early Islamic law was followed by the above-mentioned Joseph Schacht, who probably gave the most elaborate version of what we might call the "revisionist" approach to the early history of Islamic law in his *Origins of Muhammadan Jurisprudence* and other works. His chronology of events can briefly be summarized as follows:

The Prophet and the early caliphs did not practice what we could call a systematic law, but continued the legal practices of pre-Islamic society except when these flatly contradicted a direct and unambiguous prescription in the Quran. Their motives were ethical rather than legal; their emphasis was on prohibition more than punishment. While the pre-Islamic Arabs must have had knowledge of some of the laws and practices of the neighboring Roman or Persian empires, none of it had entered Arab customary law (Schacht 1964: 8, 12–13). Thus, "law" in the first decades was pre-Islamic customary law plus the direct, literal commands contained in the Quran.

When the Umayyad caliphate transferred its seat of power to Syria in 661, however, this customary law was not sufficient to run the new and expanded territory. The caliphs therefore adopted the legal and administrative practices of those regions, for purely practical reasons, again tempered by Quranic injunctions, but the direct Quranic text had already at this early stage begun to be modified in practice.

At this point, there was no "Islamic law" as such, and the administrative practice was only in the hands of the ruler—the caliph—and his functionaries (1964: 15). But in the course of this first century, scholars with such interests began to systematize the rules of behavior. Their raw material for this were the actual administrative practices of the Umayyads as well as the customs of the locality they lived in, including the Quranic prescriptions that had entered into this custom.[4] Slowly—Schacht dated it to the end of the Umayyad period and into the Abbasid reign—the scholars developed methods of analysis and systematization using a new Arabic vocabulary but to a large extent borrowing concepts from the various legal traditions in the region, such as Jewish, Roman, and Sasanid law. Schacht calls these the "ancient schools of law," which worked from the "living tradition," by which he meant the continuity of practice of the community defined by the consensus of the scholars. This systematic law thus partly accepted, partly rejected, or redefined the Umayyads' actual legal practices (1950a: 13; 1950b: 58, 70, 98, 190–213; 1964: 8, 29).

While there was thus no "Islamic" law as such in the first century, the scholars' rules went through a process of systematization in the gradual process of Islamization. The ancient schools based their law on practice, *ʿamal* or *al-sunna al-māḍiya* (past custom). This could be bolstered by referring to the practice of the Companions of the Prophet, although this was not at this stage a final authority. Companion reports were used if they supported the living tradition, and ignored if they did not. The original center for this development was in Iraq (1950b: 30, 222–3). Later, Medina and Syria began to develop their own way of thinking, thus their own ancient schools, but these grew out of an original common basis that was in Iraq, not in the Hijaz. Thus, the introduction of foreign elements of Roman, Jewish, or other law into the "living tradition" took place in Iraq.

In the second century the process of Islamization began to dominate debates between scholars, propelled by the pressure of groups that wanted to base all law on Prophetic traditions, redefining past custom (*al-sunna al-māḍiya*) to mean only the custom of the Prophet (Sunna). Only now had hadith begun to be used systematically as a source for legal rules. Schacht puts al-Shāfiʿī (d. 204/820) at the center of this transition; but still the rules and systematizations of the living tradition remain a basis for this Islamized law.

4 However, using scholarly interpretations of Quranic verses as a basis for legal rules was, according to Schacht, only a later occurrence.

In this way the actual historical roots that rules and legal principles had in the earlier legal practice were covered over and severed, and they were instead artificially attached to the Islamic revelation of the Prophetic practice and to interpretations of the Quran (1950a: 11).[5] But by comparing these apparently revealed rules with pre-conquest law in the Near East, Schacht claimed that we can still see their genealogy. There is not always a direct correspondence between old and new, because the Arab jurists did not necessarily study or apply the formal Roman law and legal theory, relying instead on the more rudimentary practice of these laws in the provinces, the law that any well-informed citizen of the Roman Near East would know. Instead of the pristine law of Rome, the Arabs picked up "well-worn coins," as Schacht phrased it (1950a: 11, 14; 1964: 20), viz., legal rules that had taken on local forms, but where we can clearly see their Roman or Jewish origin.[6] Schacht acknowledged that Roman law was not in use in Iraq, then under Persian rule, but Iraq was "deeply imbued with the spirit of Hellenistic civilization" and was a center of Jewish learning—this was the avenue for importing elements of Roman and Jewish law into the ancient schools' "living tradition," some of which survived into classical law, other elements being forced out in the later process of transformation from ancient law to classical Sharia (1950a: 13). Schacht listed a number of examples of borrowed law, such as the principle that a child born in wedlock is presumed to be the child of the husband unless something else is proven (*al-walad li-l-firāsh*, from *pater est quem nuptiae demonstrant*), a rule that "has no real part to play" in Islamic law. The well-known fixed punishment (*ḥadd*) rule of cutting off the hand of a thief is a Quranic innovation that has no precedent in Arab law, which had no punishment for theft. If this particular punishment could not be applied, early Muslim law held that the thief had to pay twice the value of the stolen object, a rule unknown to the Arabs and inconsistent with the Quran. Its origin must therefore be the Roman law called *furtum*, even if the two are far from identical. The Roman rule was not consciously adopted by the Umayyads or ancient lawyers, but it had become a "general idea" in Syria and Iraq, and was thus taken over by the Muslims when they sought a legal response to theft (1950a: 15). However, this element of "ancient Muslim law" went against the inclinations of the Islamizers, who over time interpreted it to refer not to theft, but only to the marginal case of someone concealing a stray camel he had found. This Roman borrowing was thus squeezed out of the classical law and disappeared.

Another typical case of borrowing by changing the meaning of established terms concerned security, *rahn*. In pre-Islamic Arabia *rahn* referred to a sum given to guarantee the conclusion of an unwritten contract, and the Quran refers to it in this meaning. In ancient law it still meant "security" but for a debt, not for a contract. Since this meaning was neither Arab nor Quranic, it must have been borrowed, and the "obvious model" was a Roman concept called *pignus* (1950a: 16; 1950b: 186; 1964: 138–40). What *rahn* did mean, however, was a point of discussion among the schools; al-Shāfiʿī and the classical law weakened the *rahn* security to a point where the Roman element was no longer present.

An element borrowed from Sasanid law was that of the court clerk, *kātib* (1950a: 14–17; 1964: 21–2), while Jewish law evidently had an enormous impact on the rules of ritual in the Sharia.[7] This was also shown in legal theory. To Schacht one of the most fundamental principles in Islamic systematic law, analogy (*qiyās*), was an adoption of the Jewish term *hiqqīsh*, which like *qiyās* means legal analogy based on the establishment of an essential common feature (*ʿilla*) (1950a: 14; 1950b: 21, 99–100). Its origin may, however, have been Greek. It clearly survived into classical law where the further sophistication of the *qiyās* rules, such as analogizing "from the stronger to the weaker" and "from the weaker to the stronger," is also found in the earlier Jewish legal theory but is present as well in almost

5 The Islamization of the law did, of course, also occasion great changes where the "living tradition" had to cede to opposing views backed by hadith, a process that will be discussed in later chapters. Here we are concerned with what remained of the pre-classical or "ancient" law, which is where Schacht expected to find the elements of foreign borrowing.

6 Schacht also assumed that there must have been a Sasanid influence, but knowledge of this law was insufficient to trace it in detail. Another possible source he mentioned was canon law (1950a: 10).

7 Thus, the idea that the dog is an unclean animal came from Jewish law (1950b: 216).

literally identical form in classical Roman legal literature.[8] Other basic elements of legal theory in the ancient schools, such as *istiḥsān* and *istiṣḥāb*, also originate in Greek logic and Roman law, and were borrowed into Islamic law either directly or via Jewish law (1950b: 100; 1964: 21). Law in the ancient schools was established by the consensus, *ijmāʿ*, of the majority of scholars in each location. This corresponds, stated Schacht, to the *opinio prudentium* of Roman law, again a general concept of which the scholars of Iraq would have been aware (1950a: 14).

Muslim Anti-Revisionism

Schacht's and Goldziher's views clearly undermined the foundation of the traditional legitimation of the Sharia, and indeed much of Muslim theology and practice, since this was primarily grounded in its historicity of the Prophet's practice and of the revelation. Thus, it is no wonder that Muslims criticized these revisionist views.

The most extensive attack was carried out by Muhammad Mustafa al-Azami (Muḥammad Muṣṭafā al-Aʿẓamī, b. ca. 1932) who wrote *On Schacht's Origins of Muhammadan Jurisprudence*, in refutation of Schacht and in defense of the classical Muslim view. Al-Azami's point of departure is Schacht's claim that there was not only no Islamic law, but no (systematic) law at all in the first century, only ad hoc decisions and an "administrative practice" of the new rulers. Such a legal vacuum is prima facie inconceivable, al-Azami wrote (1985: 19)—common sense and rational analysis dictate that a society cannot survive without a law. Reciting from the Quran—the authenticity of which, he noted, Schacht did not deny—he pointed out (1985: 11, 13) that we can read there already who has given us the law, it is God who has given us the law (Q 4:105, "Lo! We reveal unto thee the Scripture with the truth, that thou mayest judge between mankind by that which Allah makes clear to thee"). God also appointed the Prophet as lawgiver (Q 7:157, "He [the Prophet] will make lawful for them all good things and prohibit for them only the foul").[9] Thus, in these and many other verses it is clear that for the Quran, law is integral to Islam and was not "outside the sphere of religion," as Schacht claimed for the early period, as it is clear that there was no aspect of behavior that was not intended to be covered by the revealed law (1985: 15).

If we follow Schacht's argument, al-Azami continued (1985: 16–17), as well as that of other revisionists such as Fazlur Rahman, that the Prophet did not have any systematic legal activity, then there was no Sunna of the Prophet, and it thus has no validity for later Muslims, contrary to what Fazlur Rahman himself argued. Although other historians of law, such as Noel Coulson disagreed,[10] Schacht had indeed no hesitation in drawing this conclusion, al-Azami pointed out.

Clearly the validity of the Prophet's Sunna was the main sticking point for al-Azami and other Muslim critics, and most of al-Azami's book is taken up with refuting Schacht's attack on hadith, to be discussed in Chapter 3. This probably led him to overly hone Schacht's argument. As we have seen, Schacht never denied that the direct and literal commands cited in the Quran were put into practice from the very beginning, although he argued that some were reinterpreted to fit with the "living tradition." Thus, the Quranic injunction to follow God's commands and the direct instructions of the Prophet is not at issue. But al-Azami assumed that these commands include "every aspect" of Muslim behavior, which is not stated directly in the verses that he cited—the verses state only that a Muslim should follow the Quran and the Prophet as to the commands that they have (been) given. Schacht

8 In Latin, *a maiore ad minus* and *a minore ad maius*.

9 Thus, arguably denying the idea that God is the only legislator.

10 Al-Azami here cites Coulson (1965: 20), where Coulson states that the principle of God as the only lawgiver had been established, but—not quoted by al-Azami—there was no "complete or comprehensive charter" or law at this point in time.

and other revisionists were concerned with the rest of legal behavior, in areas where there are no unequivocal commands; al-Azami's assertion that this, too, must be based on extrapolations from the Quranic text and Prophetic Sunna was in opposition to the revisionists' view that this was the dogma of later classical Islam.

The problem may have lain in Schacht's use of the word "systematic." He asserted that the development of a consistent legal theory and systematic set of rules only appeared a century after the rise of Islam, which al-Azami seemed to understand to mean that there was for that period of time a "legal vacuum," that is, no laws and no legal authority. This is not an accurate reading of Schacht, who identified the development of a legal—he calls it administrative—practice among the Umayyads based on the combination of Arab customary law, existing customs in the provinces, and, then, direct Quranic injunctions. It was not the law but the systematization of it that in his view began in the second century.

Roman or Provincial Law?

Both Goldziher and Schacht were primarily concerned with the historicity of hadith. Neither actually delved into the corresponding problem of exactly what role the assumed, or postulated, foreign influences played or how they came about, summarizing their arguments on this point in fairly short articles. A more thorough study of the topic was made by the historian Patricia Crone in *Roman, Provincial and Islamic Law* (1987), in which she did not fundamentally challenge Schacht's chronology but took issue with a number of his assertions. She rejected completely his insistence that Roman law entered Islamic law in the Persian province of Iraq rather than in the former Roman provinces; this somewhat peculiar claim was necessary for Schacht to make so as to agree with his more important assertion that the early development of Islamic law took place in Iraq and not in the Hijaz or Syria. Furthermore, and this is her major point, she qualified the term "Roman law" by distinguishing between formal Roman law, including Roman legal theory and rhetoric, from the law that was practiced in the Roman provinces of the Near East, which is what she (and Schacht) called "provincial law."

Crone contended that Schacht's claim that Iraq was the arena for Roman influence was extremely unlikely as there was no Roman law in Iraq, and little to no knowledge of it (1987: 10–11). Schacht's and Goldziher's unsubstantiated assumptions of such borrowing were only possible, according to her, because they paid attention solely to the Arab and Muslim contexts, having little real knowledge of the law of the pre-Islamic Near East; had they made a comparison, they would have noticed the lack of similarity. None of the elements that the two listed as borrowings from Roman law have been proven to have such origins, while some clearly do not. Schacht based his assumptions on the presence of concepts similar to the Islamic ones in Roman legal rhetoric, but the Islamic concepts he mentioned, such as *istiṣlāḥ*, *istiṣḥāb*, and *ijmāʿ*, are in fact quite different from the very Roman concepts that Schacht linked them to, and are not related to them.

Crone argued that Islamic law was certainly influenced by the law of the regions that the Muslims conquered. But this law was not Roman law in the sense of the formalized law of Justinian. Those who practiced it probably believed that it was; there was no conscious attempt to draft a "Syrian" or "Egyptian" law different from that of the empire—the law of the land was the law of Rome (1987: 14). However, "familiar ways died hard," and what was practiced in the region shows a much older and deeper heritage than that of Rome. It was a mixture of customary law and established practices borrowed from other legal practice in the area along with the Roman input which was also there. The sources of this "Oriental" law could be Sasanid or other local traditions, but the most important element was Greek law. This amalgam, the practiced law of Syria and Egypt at the end of the Roman period, is the "provincial law," and when Crone looked at the differences between it and Roman law, it was primarily the Greek influence that she saw in the Near Eastern provincial law.

This, then, was the law that the Arab conquerors met and it was the law that came to mark the Umayyad period. Like Schacht, Crone traced the legal functions of the Umayyad period to "the administrative practices" of the nascent state (1987: 15–16). She asserted it more forcefully, however—Umayyad law was caliphal law. The Umayyad caliphs saw themselves as the representatives of God on earth, and as such they were thus themselves the authority for the law. This allowed them to incorporate foreign borrowings much more readily than the religious scholars, who later took over this position of authority over the law.

In Crone's chronology the history of Islamic law consisted of several layers. Classical law was developed by the scholars over the centuries as they amended and changed earlier rules and linked them to the revelation through hadith. They based this effort on a foundation of earlier Umayyad caliphal law, which in turn relied in part on the existing Near Eastern provincial law, in particular that of Syria. This provincial legal practice, although proclaiming Roman provenance, was in fact an amalgamation of many pre-Islamic and also pre-Roman legal practices, on which Greek law was heavily influential. However, our knowledge of both this provincial and the pre-classical Umayyad Islamic law is at best fragmentary. It may only be through a critical analysis of developed Islamic law that we can unearth the remnants of the pre-classical law, and through that, of the provincial Near Eastern law.

To illustrate—or prove—her point, Crone used the example of a legal issue that was politically controversial at the time—how to integrate non-Arab Muslims into the Arab and Muslim community (1987: 35–6). As a universal religion, Islam could not discourage conquered peoples from joining the religion and thus the community. But the conquerors constituted a tribal society and needed a method for assimilating new members into that society. That became known as the client (*mawlā*) system which lasted for about a century. Clientship forced the new Muslims into a second-class status that they increasingly abhorred as their numbers grew, and the *mawlā* status for converts was abolished with the Abbasid revolution in 749–50 (Crone 1991).

But where did this institution come from? Crone argued that while the "context"—that is, the idea of assimilating outsiders through a form of clientship—came from pre-Islamic Arabia, the form it took was borrowed from Roman law, first through a process that was widespread in the Near Eastern provincial law, and in a later, second shift, by borrowing more directly from Roman law proper (1987: 41).

The term *mawlā*, and its verbal form *walāʾ*, was well known in pre-Islamic Arabia, but was used for many different types of relationship, most commonly for *ḥilf*, a contractual and collective relationship between two tribal groups, or between a newcomer and a patron tribal group (1987: 51–63). While it could also accommodate non-Arabs, such as Persians, these, too, tended to become independent sub-groups, and the *ḥilf* did not in any way change kinship relations. It is thus not the source for the Islamic *mawlā* relationship, which is an individual relationship between a patron and the individual client, where the latter is removed from his original (or non-existent) kinship group and attached as a subaltern member to the patron's kinship group.

On the other hand, it displays some similarities with the process for freed slaves, although they, too, often formed quasi-tribal groups (1987: 63). But upon being freed, it was common for ex-slaves to then owe services or a monetary debt to their former master for a specific number of years. This ensuing relationship, *kitāba*, is an unclear term in Islamic law, but bears very close resemblance with the Roman practice of *paramonē*, whereby also a freed slave owed service or other compensation to his former master. It was not a form of kinship tie, but rather an obligation that could be renounced, sold, or bequeathed.

This seems also to have been the basis for the early conception of *mawlā* in the "pre-classical"—that is, caliphal—Umayyad period. It was probably the first Umayyad caliph Muʿāwiya (r. 661–80) who instituted this system, adopting the method for integration of former slaves as a model for how to incorporate non-Arab outsiders into the Muslim community (1987: 91). Thus, it was both an innovation, a new system imposed by caliphal authority (without recourse to the scholars, *ʿulamāʾ*),

and a borrowing, in that it was based on a practice that was common throughout the Roman Near East. As well as Muslim, it was "Roman," as it followed Roman law, but only in the sense that it continued existing "provincial" practice that went much further back than any direct transfer from Roman to Islamic law. The Roman understanding of the manumission system contained many elements that differed from the Greek or provincial *paramonē*, and the early, pre-classical Islamic system followed the provincial and not the scholarly Roman precedent.

Finally, Crone argued, with the fall of the Umayyads and the increasing influence of the ulema who claimed legal authority based on hadith, the *mawlā* system went through another change (1987: 79–80). The concept of *mawlā* itself survived, but as the legal distinction between Arab and non-Arab Muslims disappeared, it was no longer linked to the assimilation of converts. In Islamic legal theory the concept of *walā'* as a limited obligation that could be disposed of in different ways morphed into the perception of clientship as a fictional kinship tie, one between the individual *mawlā* and his patron. The latter could inherit from his *mawlā*, and the *mawlā* could even inherit from his patron in the absence of close agnatic relatives (that is, to the exclusion of the *dhawū l-arḥām*, uterine heirs). This was unknown in the provincial *paramonē*, but it can be found in Roman practice, where the freedman was part of the household led by a *pater familias* and could inherit as an agnatic relative (1987: 77). Thus, Roman influence (as distinct from Roman Near Eastern provincial practice) was less part of the origins of the law than a source that was used in the later development of it in the classical period.

Crone's argument is more sophisticated than that of those who preceded her, but it is not as comprehensive as it might first appear. Her basic point is that there was a more or less universal legal culture in the Near East, at least from Egypt through the Greco-Roman Levant to Persia, which shared many features. The Arabian peninsula was also part of that culture, and Islamic law, stemming from this existing legal culture, had roots in pre-Islamic Arab practice as it had roots in Justinian's Roman law. But all of these were part of a greater whole, and as the formal legal culture in the Roman provinces deteriorated after the fall of the empire, it was local practices that constituted the "law" that the Umayyad caliphs reshaped, with the help of Jewish legal concepts, into the first Muslim law.

Her primary method for this argument is one of similarities. When two practices share many features, the younger practice is most likely borrowed from the older; if there are distinct differences between them, then the younger must have taken its inspiration from somewhere else. However, given that our understanding for what is "younger" and "older" in Islamic legal history may often be conjectural and the source material inevitably thin, arguments like these are often open to criticism.

Indeed, three years later (1990) the legal historian Wael Hallaq published a blistering attack on Crone's thesis, which he claimed was grounded in her inability to accept that the "uncivilized Arabs" could create a sophisticated legal instrument as that found in the Sharia. He did not necessarily disagree with her conclusion that the Sharia was influenced by the practices of the areas it came to govern, but he did take issue with the importance she gave to such an influence. His assessment (1990: 81–3) was that when Crone saw similarities between the Arab *kitāba* system and the Greek *paramonē* (1987: 64–76), she assumed that the Arab conquerors must have taken it from the superior Greeks, ignoring the importance of the cultured pre-Islamic Arabs living in Syria and their close relations with the peninsula.

Hallaq also claimed that Crone had misunderstood some of the sources, and that the patronage system, which was not recognized by the majority of the legal schools, was of little importance. The gap that Crone claimed between the pre-Islamic "Arab" form of clientship and the later "Roman borrowing" form is not there, he wrote, or at least cannot be proven by what she presented as evidence. On the other hand, differences between Roman and Islamic clientship, which Crone saw as minor adjustments to the new situation of the Muslim empire, appeared to Hallaq to be major and decisive. He concluded that the fact that the Muslim empire was familiar with the legal tradition in Syria "does not in itself constitute evidence for borrowing" (1990: 90). The Sharia is a result of assimilation, systematization, and Islamicization, which created something quite new and quite different from what was there before, in particular due to the necessity to make the rules conform to the laws of the Quran.

A Near Eastern Law

Hallaq is one of the most prolific authors on the history of Islamic law and legal theory, and in a number of books, among them a survey entitled *The Origins and Evolution of Islamic Law* (2005), he has given a detailed presentation of both the history and the theorization of Islamic law. While his description of events may appear to share many features with that of the revisionist authors,[11] he profoundly disagrees with how they define these legal developments and with their attempt to dissociate the early law of the Muslims from religion. His chronology (2005: 8–79; 2009a: 28–34)[12] can be summarized as follows:

There was no specific "Arab law" in the pre-Islamic period. There was instead a general legal culture that spanned the Near East from North Africa to Iraq and Iran, of which the Arabs were part and parcel. Arab nomads had their own criminal procedures, but old and established urban centers such as Mecca and Yathrib were strongly influenced by the commercial law of Mesopotamia and other regions with which they traded. As a trader, Muḥammad was, of course, fully familiar with this general legal culture.

When Muḥammad became the leader of the nascent Muslim community in Medina, he therefore maintained most of the pre-existing practices. Nevertheless, the law he imposed on the Muslims was undeniably an Islamic law, based on a new ethic provided by the Quran. The reason earlier scholars have ignored this is because they draw a distinction between law and morality. This separation is a modern and Western conceit, and was unimaginable to the early Muslims. "Islamic law" was rather a "moral-legal system" (2009b; 2011: 428). Even though most of the effective rules were known from before, they were imbued with a new and Quranic ethic, one that was consciously and specifically Muslim.

This is also reflected in the Quran itself in the form of very clear statements that the Quran is a legal source. It contains a considerable number of clear and specific legal rules, which were implemented from the beginning and formed the basis for the conscious attempt to build a legal system for the Muslim community.[13] In terms of legal rules beyond those drawn directly from the Quran, Muḥammad relied on existing laws and practices as he knew them, that is, on this wider Near Eastern legal culture, but he began to amend them in line with the Quranic morality.[14] Thus, in his lifetime we can already see adjustments, for example, of the economic status of women—giving them economic independence in marriage. We can clearly see how some of these laws have roots in the wider Near East; thus the conceptual basis for the dower, *mahr*—the assumption that the father of the bride should give the dower to her rather than keep it for himself—is of Mesopotamian origin (2005: 23). Some rules were given new meaning—*zakāt* is a concept known from pre-Islamic South Arabia, which the Muslims reintroduced carrying a new understanding. Much of this Near Eastern—and that also means Arab—law has survived into the classical Sharia. However, there was no particular influence from "Roman" or "Sasanid" law, nor did the Arabs "borrow" from these sources. The Arabs were simply equal participants in this wider regional legal culture.

As the Muslims spread out of Arabia, they settled in a number of garrison towns that were first organized according to tribal structures; each group thus followed its established tribal practices. However, these divisions among the settled Arabs soon became blurred, and ʿUmar, the first caliph to face this situation, saw the need to unify the settlements around a single identity (2005: 29–34; 2009a: 34–6). He thus began the "Islamization" of the Arabs in the garrisons, first by building mosques and focusing on religious observance, but soon also by promulgating new laws and practices. These were again

11 See David Powers's critical survey of Hallaq's works on early law (2010), strongly refuted by Hallaq (2011).

12 See also Hallaq's 2002–3 criticism of earlier scholarship.

13 Hallaq (2005: 21) follows S.D. Goitein (1960) in dating this consciously Islamic legal effort to when Muḥammad's message was rejected by the Medina Jews in AH 5. Later (2009b: 272; 2011: 424) he revises this effort to comprise all of the Quranic period, that is, already in Mecca before the *hijra*.

14 According to Hallaq, it is thus meaningless to discuss when the Muslims began assigning legislative authority to God. In this Near Eastern culture it was self-evident that all laws were given by God; it was just a matter of which god (2009b: 273).

based on the Quran and on interpretations of religious morality, even though ʿUmar, too, relied for many of his rulings on existing Arab practice. His and the later caliphs' legal efforts only concerned the Muslims of the garrison towns or in Arabia proper; the non-Muslim original inhabitants played no role in these developments and their laws were left untouched by the Muslims.

To administer the law the governors appointed "proto-*qāḍīs*." They continued the traditional role of mediator (*ḥākim*) between conflicting parties and were mostly administrators, but also took on new tasks, such as relating stories from the Prophet (2005: 34–40; 2009a: 36–44). These stories did not yet have any definitive legal authority, but informed the judges' decisions that were made. In the last quarter of the first Muslim century, that is, around 700–20, some of the more established new settlers began to take a scholarly interest in legal studies and became the first legal experts of Islam. They began formulating correct practice on the basis of, first, Quranic rules, second, established practice (or *sunna māḍiya*, which could be either the practice of the caliphs or of the community before them, including the Prophet's practice), and, third, lacking any other source, their own considered opinion (*raʾy*).

Thus, according to Hallaq (2005: 68), early Islamic law was in one sense caliphal—it was defined and imposed by the caliphs but not on their personal authority. The caliphs' laws had to be based either on the practice and precedence of the Muslim community or on religious argumentation. The caliphs were therefore not insulated from the debates of the legal scholars, but they were increasingly influenced by them as they were elaborated and refined. The views of the revisionists that there were two legal developments—one caliphal and non-religious, stemming from Roman administrative practice, and the other a scholar's law that later became bound to religion through the imposition of Prophetic authority—can only be right if it is assumed that the earlier, non-Prophetic meaning of *sunna* was not religiously based (2009a: 46). But it clearly was, Hallaq concluded; it included the practice of the Prophet himself, of his Companions, and of the early caliphs, all imbued with religious legitimacy. It was clearly an Islamic law that from the beginning took form in the practice of the caliphs and the proto-qadis and in the scholarly debates of the early legal experts.

Scholarship on the Early Period

Harald Motzki has raised perhaps the most methodical opposition to Schacht's historicization of the early law (2002: 287–97), although he also does not accept the traditional presentation of the law unfolding immediately from Prophetic precedence. The truth is "in the middle," he says—according to Motzki, Schacht postdated the actual events by about 50 to 75 years (2002: 296). Motzki offers the following timeline:

The discussion of proper behavior for Muslims was begun by some of the Prophet's Companions already. The most prominent of these, and the earliest figure in Islamic law, was ʿAbd Allāh ibn ʿAbbās (d. 68/687), who was close to the fourth caliph ʿAlī (r. 656–61). When Muʿāwiya established the Umayyad caliphate in 661, Ibn ʿAbbās was estranged from the political leadership, but he continued to teach in Mecca and his students, such as ʿAṭāʾ b. Abī Rabāḥ (d. ca. 114/734), carried on his work. Their views may have constituted a "common doctrine," in Schacht's terms, but if so it originated in Mecca, not in Iraq. These early scholars formulated their views based on the Quran and on opinions of the Prophet and the Companions. They did relate the views of the Prophet (in spite of Schacht's assumptions), but their conclusions were pure *raʾy*, that is, based on their own authority.

Their main concern were issues within the sphere of private law, which shows little or no influence from Umayyad administrative practice. Umayyad influence may be more marked on public law, but Motzki disagrees with Schacht's view that the "ancient schools" were primarily based on the Umayyad rulers' practices. The influence was probably of greater consequence in the opposite direction, Motzki asserts. Since he emphasizes the importance of Meccan and scholarly Islamic dominance over the development of the law, Motzki also does not accept (or at least discuss) any significant Roman or other foreign influence on Islamic law. Schacht's proposal that the *walad li-l-firāsh* rule is of Roman origin is pure speculation, Motzki contends (2002: 129–30), based on the dubious assertion that the rule is inconsistent with Quranic logic. On the contrary, it is perfectly suited to the Quran's main concern for clarity regarding custody and paternity issues. Motzki allows that the rule might stem from pre-Islamic practices (which could lead to the suggestion of shared Jewish or Near Eastern Roman norms if the pre-Islamic customs were at all similar).

Divergent Views

Schacht's theories and the scholars who reject, support, or develop them are not the only currents of tradition in the Western study of early Islamic law. Noel Coulson published his *History of Islamic Law* in the same year as Schacht's *Introduction* (1964). He presented a chronology that diverges less from the classical Muslim one as that of Schacht. In his view, the Umayyads were primarily pragmatic administrators who preserved the existing practices of the provinces. This allowed for a "wider reception of foreign elements in substantive law proper." The status of *dhimma* as elaborated by the Umayyads, for example, embodied the Roman concept of *fides*, while *waqf* stemmed largely from the Byzantine *piae causae* (1964: 27–8). Within this general framework the new judges were given considerable leeway to find practical solutions, thus leading to a diversity in private law in particular. Toward the end of the Umayyad century of rule, this open practice led to a religious as well as a political opposition, giving rise to the class of legal scholars. Islamic jurisprudence thus grew as a movement of opposition to the existing legal practice, and the legal scholars were more interested in religion and ritual practices than in the law of the courts (1964: 37). In contrast to Umayyad pragmatic practice, Coulson asserted, classical law was primarily an academic speculation.

The German Islamicist Tilman Nagel (2001: 174–200) emphasized the distinction between the concepts of Sharia, which appears later, and the term fiqh, which has its roots already in the Prophet's time. By fiqh was meant primarily a religious endeavor to seek to act according to the principles of revelation. During the reign of ʿUmar II the jurist (*faqīh*) was already a model of behavior, but he could have a presence as well in the courtroom from his having been consulted by the judge. Thus, Nagel also lowered the bar between law and morality, but unlike Schacht did not fully collapse the former into the latter.

Finally, a recent work by another German author, Benjamin Jokisch, takes a dramatically different and controversial view of the genesis of Islamic law than the other authors mentioned here, who consider the development of the classical law primarily to be the result of an independent class of religious and legal scholars. Jokisch argues that it was the result of a basically secular imperial law "produced on the drawing board by a couple of state jurists in Baghdad" (2007: 3)—more precisely, by a commission set up by the early Abbasid caliph Hārūn (r. 786–809) composed of Muslim, Christian, and Jewish scholars. The dominant figure in this group was Muḥammad b. al-Ḥasan al-Shaybānī (d. 189/805), generally known as one of the leading figures of the early Hanafi school; but to Jokisch the founder of this imperial law code (2007: 52).[15] This law, which Jokisch claims is found in "Shaybānī's Codex" (a combination of eight of his major works), came under attack by the scholars, and in 848[16] the caliph had to abandon his attempt to have the codex implemented under caliphal authority. Instead, Jokisch alleges, the legitimation of the law was transferred to scholarly consensus, in the form we know as classical law and which Jokisch calls the "post-imperial law." The classical

15 Al-Shaybānī's near-contemporary Abū Yūsuf, the third founding figure of the Hanafi school, was also closely attached to the project; the legal school's eponym Abū Ḥanīfa himself (who was mostly active before the Abbasid take-over) was not primarily concerned with law, according to Jokisch.

16 The year is noteworthy as the final year of the *miḥna* (trial), an inquisition initiated by Hārūn's son, the Abbasid caliph al-Maʾmūn (r. 813–33), against traditionalist religious scholars; it did not achieve its purpose of subjugating the scholars to caliphal authority in religion and was dispensed with in 848.

law took over most of the content of the imperial law and what we now know as Islamic law is in fact a modified continuation of Hārūn's and al-Shaybānī's imperial law.

Muslim legal history before the Abbasids is of no concern to Jokisch, who says only that it was then "heterogeneous." To Jokisch, the origins of Islamic law do not lie there but in the sources the imperial scholars used for their effort, which were primarily in Byzantine Greek. Thus, much of the theory and rules of Islamic law is a continuation of Byzantine law. Byzantine converts, in many cases adherents of minority Christian sects who fled to the Abbasid capital and converted to Islam but continued as separate sects or politico-religious groups within Islam (2007: 19, 321), brought the Byzantine law with them and translated it into Arabic. Only later were Byzantine legal concepts, such as *qiyās*, *ijtihād*, and *kharāj*, translated from Greek and given an invented Arabic and Islamic etymology (2007: 4f.).[17]

A Debate over Concepts or Methods?

Much of the diversity of opinion concerning the early period and the origins of Islamic law clearly stems from the scarcity of incontrovertible source material and methodological differences about how to treat unconfirmed sources—always ignore them (which leaves us with no knowledge), always accept them (which provides very shaky history), or accept them only if they fit our theory (a charge often raised against Schacht). Interpretations of early history may therefore often seem impressionistic, deduced from logical inferences of "how it must have been" for the early Muslims based on whatever biographical or historical sources pass muster with the individual historian.

Much of the discussion also seems to stem as much from a disagreement about the concepts as about the empirical data, for example, what do we mean by "law" in this formative period—a systematized and coherent structure or ad hoc legal practices found on the ground? What is required to use the qualifier "Islamic" for these practices? What is actually "Roman" or "Greek" law in the pre-Islamic Near East?

There is also another methodological issue involved that is well known to anthropologists: When the same idea or practice can be found in two different societies, does this mean that it spread from one to the other (diffusionism) or could it have come about independently due to similar factors in both societies generating such a practice? Goldziher, Schacht, and Crone clearly assume diffusion, which was a common anthropological theory in Goldziher's time but less so today.

If we move beyond these conceptual disagreements, however, a picture of the early development of law emerges that many of these scholars actually seem to share, but call by a different name. The rapid expansion of their empire clearly left the Arabs with little time to prepare for legal administration. The unambiguous commands of the Quran were heeded and they provided an "Islamic" continuity through the Umayyad period and beyond. But when it came to private conflicts between Arabs, whether in the new towns or on the peninsula, the early administrators settled them according to a custom which they did not necessarily distinguish as "Arab," "Muslim," or "Meccan" law, as long as the tribal structure was determinant. When they were forced to innovate, they sought solutions in Arab legal logic and what they found in the new lands—whether it is called "Roman," "Provincial," or "Generic Near Eastern including Arab." At a certain point in time—most seem to agree that it was toward the end of the Umayyad period—specialist scholars began to appear from whom individuals sought advice about contentious private or commercial issues, perhaps because traditional and tribal Arab methods of conflict resolution were fading away. These ad hoc decisions then became the subject of debates and increasing systematization, which eventually led to the formulation of principles regarding the sources on which the rules should be based and the methods to be used to develop the rules. This process led to the developments that are the focus of subsequent chapters.

17 As we have seen, Schacht and other proponents of Roman borrowing follow similar reasoning on the issue of Islamic terminology.

References

al-Azami, Muhammad M. 1985. *On Schacht's Origins of Muhammadan Jurisprudence*. New York: John Wiley and Sons.

Coulson, Noel J. 1964. *A History of Islamic Law*. Edinburgh: Edinburgh University Press.

Crone, Patricia. 1980. *Slaves on Horses: The Evolution of the Islamic Polity*. Cambridge: Cambridge University Press.

———. 1987. *Roman, Provincial and Islamic Law: The Origins of the Islamic Patronate*. Cambridge: Cambridge University Press.

———. 1991. Mawlā. In *Encyclopaedia of Islam*, 2nd ed. Vol. 6: 874–80. Leiden: E.J. Brill.

Goitein, S.D. 1960. The Birth-Hour of Muslim Law? *The Muslim World* 50: 23–9.

Goldziher, Ignaz. 1904. The Principles of Law in Islam. In *The Historians' History of the World*, ed. H.S. Williams. Vol. 8: 294–304. New York and London: Encyclopaedia Britannica.

———. 1913. Fiḳh. In *Encyclopaedia of Islam*, 1st ed. Vol. 3: 101–5. Leiden: E.J. Brill.

———. 1971. *Muslim Studies*, ed. S.M. Stern, tr. C.R. Barber and S.M. Stern. 2 vols. London: George Allen and Unwin; trans. of *Muhammedanische Studien*. Halle: M. Niemeyer, 1888–90.

———. 1981. *Introduction to Islamic Theology and Law*. Princeton: Princeton University Press; trans. of *Vorlesungen über den Islam*. Heidelberg: C. Winter, 1910.

Hallaq, Wael B. 1990. The Use and Abuse of Evidence: The Question of Provincial and Roman Influences on Early Islamic Law. *Journal of the American Oriental Society* 110: 79–91.

———. 1999. The Authenticity of Prophetic Ḥadîth: A Pseudo-Problem. *Studia Islamica* 89: 75–90.

———. 2002–3. The Quest for Origins or Doctrine? Islamic Legal Studies as Colonialist Discourse. *UCLA Journal of Islamic and Near Eastern Law* 2: 1–31.

———. 2005. *The Origins and Evolution of Islamic Law*. Cambridge: Cambridge University Press.

———. 2009a. *Sharīʿa: Theory, Practice, Transformations*. Cambridge: Cambridge University Press.

———. 2009b. Groundwork of the Moral Law: A New Look at the Qurʾān and the Genesis of the Sharīʿa. *Islamic Law and Society* 16: 239–79.

———. 2011. On Orientalism, Self-Consciousness and History. *Islamic Law and Society* 18: 389–439.

Jokisch, Benjamin. 2007. *Islamic Imperial Law: Harun-al-Rashid's Codification Project*. Berlin: Walter De Gruyter.

Motzki, Harald. 2002. *The Origins of Islamic Jurisprudence: Meccan Fiqh before the Classical Schools*, tr. M.H. Katz. Leiden: Brill; trans. of *Die Anfänge der islamischen Jurisprudenz: Ihre Entwicklung in Mekka bis zur Mitte des 2./8. Jahrhunderts*. Stuttgart: Deutsche Morgenländische Gesellschaft, 1991.

Nagel, Tilman. 2001. *Das islamische Recht: Eine Einführung*. Westhofen: WVA-Verlag Skulima.

Nallino, Carlo. 1940–42. Considerazioni sui rapporti fra diritto romano e diritto musulmano. In *Raccolta di scritti, editi e inediti*, ed. M. Nallino. Vol. 4: 85–94. Rome: Istituto per l'Oriente.

Powers, David S. 2010. Wael B. Hallaq on the Origins of Islamic Law: A Review Essay. *Islamic Law and Society* 17: 126–57.

Schacht, Joseph. 1950a. Foreign Elements in Ancient Islamic Law. *Journal of Comparative Legislation and International Law* 32: 9–17. Reprinted in *The Formation of Islamic Law*, ed. W.B. Hallaq, pp. 59–67. Aldershot: Ashgate, 2004.

———. 1950b. *The Origins of Muhammadan Jurisprudence*. Oxford: Clarendon Press.

———. 1964. *An Introduction to Islamic Law*. Oxford: Clarendon Press.

The Divine Sources

Herbert Berg

The primary sources for Sharia are the Quran and the Sunna. The Quran is believed to be the speech of God revealed to Muḥammad, so to obey God, as the Quran itself commands, is to follow the precepts provided in the Quran. Its status as a "divine source" for the Sharia seems obvious. The Quran also repeatedly commands Muslims to obey God's Messenger. As God's chosen messenger, Muḥammad understood the Quran the best and most perfectly exemplified its teachings through his activities and words. Thus, his example, Sunna, is also an obvious source for Sharia, and a divine one in that it is prescribed by God in the Quran. It also seems natural that Muḥammad's followers would have preserved reports of his activities in what would eventually become known as hadith. What may seem so "obvious" and "natural," however, turns out to be far more complex and contentious.

The Quran scholar Angelika Neuwirth has pointed out that one must distinguish between the redaction of the text culminating with an authoritative, *ne varietur* Quran, and the canonization of the text, that is, the endorsement of the Quranic legal and societal ordinances (2003: 2). The traditional account of the origin of Islam and Sharia would suggest that the process of canonization began with Muḥammad's first revelation and culminated with his death, when the Quran was complete and recognized by the generation of Muslims who had known him personally, the Companions. The redaction was more or less complete some 15 years later when the third caliph, ʿUthmān, published an official version of the text. The process of the canonization of the Sunna began as soon as Muḥammad made his first converts and they began to emulate their Prophet. The redaction and canonization of the Sunna of the Prophet, particularly as hadith in the six Sunni collections (*al-kutub al-sitta*) of al-Bukhārī, Muslim, al-Nasāʾī, Abū Dāwūd, al-Tirmidhī, and Ibn Māja, were far more protracted and contested. Modern scholarship has called into question the dates and order of the redaction and canonization of the Quran and the authenticity of the hadith in these collections. This modern scholarship strikes at the heart of the Sharia for it undercuts the "divine" aspect of its two main sources, and it is therefore occasionally viewed as motivated by confessionalism or orientalism. Muslim scholars, however, have a long history of asking surprisingly similar questions about the Quran and the Sunna.

Synopsis of Divine Sources in Islamic Scholarship

Traditionally the Quran is believed to be of divine origin—a claim that the Quran itself advances. It was brought from a heavenly archetype (Q 43:3) to Muḥammad via the angel Gabriel (Q 2:91), and

---

Herbert Berg, Professor in the Department of Philosophy and Religion at the University of North Carolina, Wilmington, is the author most recently of two separate monographs on Elijah Muhammad: *Elijah Muhammad* (Makers of the Muslim World Series, Oxford: Oneworld, 2013) and *Elijah Muhammad and Islam* (New York: New York University Press, 2009).

the Prophet recited only that which God willed (Q 8:76–7) in the clear language of Arabic so that all might understand it. In Islamic theology it came to be seen as the eternal Speech of God. Even the order of the suras was divinely determined. Muḥammad is reported to have said that Gabriel came to review the Quran with him once a year, but in the last year of his life Gabriel did so twice. As such, its contents and authority in religious and legal matters are beyond question. The accounts by Muslims are, of course, more complicated, for the Quran was revealed serially over two decades, certain parts abrogate earlier revelations, and even a brief survey of the exegetical literature (*tafsīr*) makes it clear that it was not universally understood even by the earliest Muslims.

Be that as it may, the Quran was, therefore, a canon in Muḥammad's lifetime, and his Muslim followers preserved it and committed it to writing after his death. Again, on closer inspection, the process is much more complicated. Various traditional accounts claim that the succeeding caliphs, Abū Bakr and later ʿUthmān, initiated the process of its collation and canonization. Abū Bakr (r. 632–34) commissioned one of Muḥammad's scribes, Zayd b. Thābit, to collect the Quran from all available sources, which included the memories of the Companions and written sources on papyrus, leather, bones, and palm leaves. This collection passed to the second caliph, ʿUmar, and at the latter's death, to his daughter Ḥafṣa. Later, when Muslims from Syria and Iraq quarreled over the correct reading of the Quran, the third caliph ʿUthmān (r. 644–56) commissioned Zayd b. Thābit and others to collect an official copy, opting for the Qurashī dialect[1] when differences were found. At this point, the number and order of the suras were fixed as was the consonantal text. ʿUthmān then sent copies of his recension of the Quran to other major Muslim centers with instructions to burn other versions. Thus, with ʿUthmān the *ne varietur* consonantal text is established. By no later than 656 the Quran as we have it today, more or less, had its definitive form and authority. Vowel markings would take a little longer. Al-Ḥajjāj b. Yūsuf al-Thaqafī (d. 95/714), the governor of Iraq under the Umayyads and credited by some as having introduced diacritics into the Arabic script, is also recorded as destroying any collections that deviated from the official one.

A modern Muslim scholar, Muḥammad al-Azami names approximately 65 scribes who at one time or another recorded Muḥammad's dictation of the revelations. "Based on the total number of scribes, and the Prophet's custom of summoning them to record all new verses, we can safely assume that in his own lifetime the entire Quran was available in written form" (2003: 69). Al-Azami is of the opinion that Muḥammad himself even fixed the arrangement of the suras. He recapitulates the traditional accounts of the Quran's compilation under Abū Bakr and then again under ʿUthmān. Thus, the Quran, the *textus receptus*, embodies the will of God—His instructions for His creatures. Ritual, civil, commercial, penal, or social regulations within the Quran are held to be universal and eternal, and the extant legal schools (sg. *madhhab*) of both Sunni and Shiʿi Islam view the Quran as the primary source of law.

Embodied in the form of hadith, the Sunna stands second only to the Quran. The hadith of the Sunna in the six collections are generally considered authentic, particularly if they are found in both al-Bukhārī's and Muslim's collections. Shiʿi Islam has different collections of hadith and a somewhat broader concept of the Sunna which includes the Imams. This literature began with the death of Muḥammad, as an attempt to maintain his guidance. The Companions were a natural source for these reports, which soon branched out into written collections such as the ad hoc *ṣaḥīfa*, the more topic-specific *muṣannaf*, and the source-based *musnad*. Finally, the topically arranged collections of hadith with a full chain of transmitters (*isnād*), called *sunan* or *ṣaḥīḥ* books, appeared. But with the early rivalries within the Muslim community and the incorporation of a multitude of peoples within the rapidly expanding Arab-Islamic empire, reports attributed to Muḥammad—some fabricated, some tendentially altered—had been circulating widely in the earliest decades of Islam. This led to the insistence that the report (*matn*, the body of the hadith) be provided with a list of people who had transmitted it. Since these, too, could be invented or adapted, biographical literature (*rijāl*) developed

1 The dialect of the Quraysh, the Prophet's tribe.

to evaluate the reliability of transmitters and to determine whether a transmitter had met the person from whom it was claimed he had received the report. Traditionists, or *ahl al-ḥadīth*, also sought out corroborating reports. The collectors of the *sunan* or *ṣaḥīḥ* books, such as the compilers of the six collections, painstakingly amassed and selected hadith to ensure their authenticity. It would take much heated debate and several centuries before a handful of books from this vast collection of hadith literature emerged as authoritative, that is, were canonized. Al-Bukhārī's *Ṣaḥīḥ* and Muslim's *Ṣaḥīḥ* in particular were deemed to be the most authoritative and authentic representation of Muḥammad's legacy by Sunni Muslims (Brown 2007). The four major Shiʿi collections of hadith are unique in that the *isnād* traces the origin of the reports to Muḥammad via the Imams, to Imams via later Imams, and to Muḥammad or Imams via followers of the Imams (that is, Shiʿis). The Sunna may be the second divine source for the Sharia, but the contents of the Sunna have always been contested.

Modern Scholarship on the Sunna

Most modern scholarship on the Sunna has focused less on the content of the Sunna and more on its authenticity. The resulting debate is complex, and even the classification of the participants is in dispute; in an earlier work (Berg 2000: 6–64) I classified these scholars based on their conclusions about the authenticity of hadith: early Western skepticism (Ignaz Goldziher and Joseph Schacht), the more sanguine reaction against this skepticism (Nabia Abbott, Fuat Sezgin, and Muhammad Mustafa al-Azami), those who search for a middle ground (G.H.A. Juynboll, Fazlur Rahman, Gregor Schoeler, Harald Motzki, and others), and renewed skepticism (Michael Cook and Norman Calder). Jonathan Brown (2009: 197–236) classifies Western scholarship on the authenticity question into four categories that are based instead on scholarly outlook: the orientalists (Goldziher, Schacht, and Juynboll), the philo-Islamic apologetic (Abbott and al-Azami), the revisionists (Patricia Crone and Cook), and the Western re-evaluation (primarily Motzki). Motzki himself (2005: 204–53) classifies scholars based on their methodologies even if they reach opposite conclusions: dating on the basis of the *matn* alone (Goldziher, Schacht, and R. Marston Speight), dating on the basis of occurrence in collections (Schacht, but primarily Juynboll), dating or reconstruction on the basis of the *isnād* alone (Schacht, Juynboll, and Sezgin), and dating using both *isnād* and *matn* (Motzki).

Ignaz Goldziher was not the first modern scholar to express doubts about the authenticity of the hadith in the Sunna. The Dutch scholar Reinhart Dozy (d. 1883) had remarked that he was surprised not by all of the false materials, but that so much of it, including at least half of al-Bukhārī's collection, was authentic (1879: 124–5); the Scot William Muir (d. 1905) also felt that as much as half of the material was spurious and doubted the value of the information in the *isnād*, although unflattering depictions of Muḥammad suggested that much was genuine (1894). In contrast, Goldziher felt hadith could "not serve as a document for the history of the infancy of Islam, but rather as a reflection of the tendencies which appear in the community during the mature stages of its development" (1971, 2: 19). He urged skeptical caution over optimistic trust. His conclusion was based on the apparent oral transmission of hadith and their proliferation in later collections but absence in earlier collections. He accepted that early Muslims had sought to preserve the Prophet's words, but the tendential interpolations and inventions also began early. It was no surprise, therefore, that the *isnād* of contradictory hadith was equally impressive. Later, he opined, as the hadith scholars began to oppose other sources for Sharia, such as personal view (*raʾy*), the legal schools found it expedient to fabricate hadith to support their particular positions. The widespread fabrication led to efforts to evaluate the authenticity of hadith—based solely on the *isnād*. This effort, however, simply encouraged *isnād* emendation, by repairing gaps or extending Companion and Successor[2]

2 The generation after the Companions, known as *al-tābiʿūn*.

hadith back to Muḥammad. Thus, every opinion, practice, and innovation found expression in the form of a hadith (1971, 2: 126). Only a very small part, if any, of the contents of the collections of al-Bukhārī and Muslim could be confidently assumed to be early. Goldziher's early twentieth-century contemporaries—Leone Caetani, D.S. Margoliouth, and Henri Lammens—expressed similar doubts (Caetani 1905; Margoliouth 1912, 1914; Lammens 1943).

Joseph Schacht refined Goldziher's conclusions by focusing primarily on Sharia and the role of al-Shāfiʿī in its development. Schacht argues that hadith were not originally a source for Islamic law as traditionally assumed. Rather, "The ancient schools of law shared the old concept of *sunna* or 'living tradition' as the ideal practice of the community, expressed in the accepted doctrine of the school" (Schacht 1959: 80). It was al-Shāfiʿī who struggled to narrow the understanding of *sunna* so that it referred exclusively to the example of the Prophet in the form of hadith; the result, according to Schacht, was that the "living tradition" was attributed to Successors and Companions and toward the middle of the second century extended to Muḥammad, the authority of whose hadith becoming supreme only with al-Shāfiʿī. Although he suggested that the *isnād* was irrelevant for historical analysis, Schacht had two methods for dating of hadith—one focused on the *matn*, one on the *isnād*. By placing the *matn* in its relative position within the debate of a particular legal issue, one could determine when the hadith was likely to have emerged. For example, if a hadith seems to react or respond to another, the former is likely to be a later invention. Schacht also argued that a *matn* consisting of short legal maxims was earlier than a more elaborate one, particularly if it was anonymous.[3] Some information, however, could still be gleaned from the *isnād* because of its backward growth from Successors to Companions to Muḥammad: "The more perfect the *isnād*, the later the tradition" (Schacht 1949: 147). A widely attested (*mutawātir*) hadith had no better claim to authenticity, for the *isnād* was fabricated specifically to counter the charge of being isolated. In addition to this "spread of *isnād*s," Schacht also observed that many hadith with the same or a similar *matn* often had a common transmitter ("common link") in the middle of the *isnād*. This indicated to him that the common-link transmitter—or someone using his name—put the *matn* into circulation; common links, therefore, should allow one to determine the *terminus a quo* for the appearance of the hadith. The more recent names in the *isnād* might reflect the actual transmission history, but the earlier names, those below the common link, were fabricated. Based on this argument and methods, Schacht concluded that there was no regular use of the *isnād* prior to AH 100.

Reaction to Goldziher's general skepticism and to Schacht's more specific claims provoked significant counter-reactions. Nabia Abbott argued for an early and continuous transmission of hadith in written form. Initially, she claimed (1967: 29), there had been a fear of a development of a body of literature that could compete with the Quran, but with the death of the second caliph in 644, these hadith were promulgated in the major centers of Islam. The use of terminology that reflects oral transmission (for example, *ḥaddatha* "to relate," and *akhbara* "to tell") belied the use of written transmission. The apparent explosion in the number of hadith a century later resulted from early manuscripts (with a single *isnād*) being broken up into their constituent parts and each given the same *isnād*—thus giving the impression of a sudden huge increase in the number of hadith. Fuat Sezgin is even more adamant than Abbott that oral transmission was supplemented with written materials and is willing to posit the existence of books on the basis of the *isnād*: "In order to establish the first sources of Islamic literature, one must first of all discard the old presupposition that the *isnād* was first introduced in the second and third centuries A.H. and that the transmitters' names were invented" (1967: 83). Al-Azami also argues for a continuous early written tradition, using the evidence supplied in the *isnād* and *rijāl* literature, and he lists hundreds of Companions, Successors, and other early scholars who must have had written sources (1992: 1–211). After systematically critiquing Schacht's claims of the *isnād* being late, arbitrary, and gradually improved over time and of "so-called" common links being used to date hadith, al-Azami concludes that while there may have been mistakes, there is

3 A similar assumption is made by R. Marston Speight as part of his form analysis, though he argues that reported speech is earlier than direct speech (1973).

no reason to question the *isnād* system or the authenticity of hadith literature (1992: 247; 1985: 182). Hence, for Abbott, Sezgin, and al-Azami, there is an implicit or explicit assumption that written sources suggest authenticity.

The Authenticity Debate

Several scholars delved into that assumption in greater detail. Gregor Schoeler argues that, despite protests to the contrary, though early scholars of hadith may not have employed written materials during their public lectures, privately they and their students did rely on written materials as mnemonic aids even in the first century. The variation in hadith as preserved is not surprising—a teacher may have presented materials differently over the years and students may have recorded them differently (1985: 201–30; 1992: 1–43). Not only does Schoeler blur the distinction between written and oral transmission, but also between variation and authenticity. Although different, he avers, all the recensions can be considered authentic. Norman Calder also emphasized the use of private notebooks by students, whose contents in the process of copying and transmission were changeable. But to Calder this did not imply authenticity; the materials therein were not transmitted as books, but as segments, and not verbatim, but acquired, selected, and preserved based on the needs of the "author" (1993: 162–3).

A creative contribution to the authenticity debate came from Fazlur Rahman, who accepted the skepticism of Goldziher and Schacht, proffering only a few critiques, but claimed (1979) that it was irrelevant for the normativity of the Sunna. Rahman argued for the early attempt to preserve the words and deeds of Muḥammad—but without the use of the *isnād*, which was for him a late first-century development. Some hadith may have existed in some form from the time of Muḥammad, but, more importantly, early Muslims organized their lives according to Muḥammad's words and deeds without recourse to hadith. This he called the "silent living Sunna" of Muḥammad. Later, when the need to justify certain practices or beliefs via hadith arose, they naturally referred back to the Companions who embodied this silent Sunna. Reacting to Schacht, Rahman believed al-Shāfiʿī's demand for hadith with a proper *isnād* led not to fabrication but to a reformulation of this Sunna and to the backward growth of the newly formalized *isnād*. The net result, however, was to transform the living Sunna into the structure of Prophetic Sunna. The Sunna as incorporated in hadith may not be literally authentic, but it remains largely normative for Muslims since it authentically reflects the silent living Sunna that is rooted in the words and deeds of Muḥammad.

Rahman's compromise, however, did not put the authenticity issue to rest. Schacht's two approaches were taken up by John Wansbrough and G.H.A. Juynboll. Wansbrough represented the continuation of Schacht's claim that the *isnād* is of no historical value. "The supplying of *isnād*s, whether traced to the prophet, to his companions, or their successors, can be understood as an exclusively formal innovation and cannot be dated much before 200/815" (1977: 179). Wansbrough merely extended Schacht's general principle to all hadith: legal, historical, and exegetical. Juynboll, on the other hand, represented the continuation of Schacht's claim that the *isnād* has at least some historical value. He greatly refined many of Schacht's views about both the vast scale of *isnād* and *matn* fabrication, thus opposing Sezgin, al-Azami, and Abbott (1983: 4), though he did accept that Muḥammad's followers likely preserved his teaching during his lifetime. But Juynboll put himself in neither the Wansbroughian nor the Schachtian camp. "I think that a generous lacing of open-mindedness, which dour skeptics might describe as naïveté, is an asset in the historian of early Islamic society rather than a shortcoming to be overcome and suppressed at all costs" (1983: 6–7). He argued that the systematic use of hadith (that is, with *isnād*) began in the 70s or 80s of the first century, but only fully emerged half a century later, while the narrowly focused Sunna of the Prophet emerged out of the more general *sunna* of the Companions and Muḥammad only toward the end of the first century. In this he agreed with Schacht, but he dated its emergence significantly earlier. Within this framework, it was likely that Successors, or the Successors to the Successors (that is, the third generation of Muslims), were the first to circulate hadith, with later Muslims responsible for the backward growth of the *isnād*. In a view reminiscent of that of Rahman, Juynboll nevertheless concluded,

> [I]t seems likely that at least part of the prophetic tradition listed in one or more canonical—or even non-canonical—collections deserves to be considered as a fair representation of what the prophet of Islam did or said, or might have done or said, but surely it is unlikely that we will ever find even a moderately successful method of proving with incontrovertible certainty the historicity of the ascription of such to the prophet but in a few isolated instances (1983: 71).

Juynboll was, however, far more optimistic about dating a tradition based on its *isnād*, especially when it displayed the common link. He described the common link as the oldest "transmitter who hears something from (seldom more than) one authority and passes it on to a number of pupils, most of whom pass it on in their turn to two or more of their pupils" (1989: 351–2). The older authorities are usually fictitious, whereas the fanning-out links often authentically represent the transmission. Unfortunately, most legal hadith have what Juynboll termed the "spider pattern," not the common-link pattern, that is, most hadith display a multitude of partial common links and single strands that fan out from various locations. Juynboll believed these represented later transmitters inventing the entire *isnād* to bridge the gap between themselves and a suitably early—fictitious or historical—person. This pattern matters because "in the entire canonical tradition literature, spiders occur in their thousands, whereas the true *isnād* bundles, with a historically tenable cl [common link], are at most a few hundred" (1993: 215). It was therefore well-nigh impossible to determine the chronology and provenance of most hadith.

Wael Hallaq and Harald Motzki have sought to overcome this apparent impasse. For Hallaq, the authenticity debate as outlined above is irrelevant. He argues that "mainstream Muslim scholarship" does not consider the vast hadith literature to be a true representation of the words and deeds of Muḥammad. For legal purposes only *mutawātir* hadith—hadith that are preserved "through textually identical channels of transmission which are sufficiently numerous as to preclude any possibility of collaboration on a forgery" (1999: 78)—are authentic. For all other hadith, "authenticity can be asserted only in probabilistic terms" (1999: 81). The hadith scholars (*muḥaddithūn*) were more interested in pious religious practice than in the epistemological concerns of the jurists. They preferred a sound (*ṣaḥīḥ*), good (*ḥasan*), and weak (*ḍaʿīf*) typology. Moreover, the jurist and hadith scholar al-Nawawī (d. 676/1278) even argued that *ṣaḥīḥ* does not imply certainty unless it is *mutawātir*, while his teacher Ibn al-Ṣalāḥ (d. 643/1245) maintained that the hadith in both al-Bukhārī's *Ṣaḥīḥ* and in Muslim's *Ṣaḥīḥ* were trustworthy because Muslims had agreed that they were—that is, consensus (*ijmāʿ*) generated the certainty. With only a handful of *mutawātir* hadith, Hallaq suggests that the debate over authenticity is "pointless" since both jurists and traditionalists acknowledge "the precarious epistemological status of the literature" (1999: 90).

Motzki, on the other hand, is not willing to forgo the debate. He employs two approaches to date traditions: historical source analysis and the *isnād-cum-matn* method. It is with respect to the former that in the past I have characterized Motzki as too sanguine about the value of the *isnād* (Berg 2000). Motzki examines the *Muṣannaf* of the Yemeni hadith scholar ʿAbd al-Razzāq (d. 211/827), reconstructing the earlier collections that he employed. Since ʿAbd al-Razzāq's immediate informants in the *Muṣannaf* have differing numbers of reports and are unique with respect to the types and sources of their materials, it seems implausible that he fabricated his sources. Moreover, there is external biographical material that supports that these informants were his teachers. Their existence established, these sources can, in turn, be analyzed using the same methodology, pushing our knowledge of the sources, and, in particular, Meccan jurisprudence, to the beginning of the second century AH (2012: 5–6; 2002).

Motzki's *isnād-cum-matn* methodology is really a middle position between the skepticism of Goldziher and Schacht and the wholesale acceptance of Abbott and al-Azami. Motzki also represents the continuation of Schacht's claims about the (albeit limited) historical information contained within an *isnād*, although he challenges Juynboll's assertion—that no method for analyzing hadith exists—by not restricting himself to analysis of only the *isnād* as Juynboll had. Motzki starts with the observation that similarities and variations in the *matn* of related hadith are often reflected in the *isnād*. In other words, there is a correlation between the *matn* and the *isnād*. In so doing, Motzki dismisses Wansbrough's contention (1977: 183) that the *isnād* was merely a literary device and a fairly late innovation ("The presence of *isnād*s as halakhic embellishment is, from the point of view of literary criticism, a superfluity"). The only historical value of the *isnād*, therefore, is as an indicator that the text took its extant form quite late.[4] For Motzki, by contrast, this close correlation between textual variant and *isnād* suggests two key facts: (1) the *isnād* may, at least in part, reflect the actual transmission history of the *matn* to which it is attached; and (2) *matn* variations may, at least in part, be a product of that transmission history. Careful analysis of both the *isnād* and *matn* of all the extant versions of related hadith often allows one to reconstruct earlier versions of the hadith. Even a hadith's origins can be determined, and who and how it was adapted during transmission until recorded in extant sources. Although the method often allows the original disseminator or fabricator of the tradition to be identified, Motzki asserts, it can only be used on traditions for which there exist sufficiently large number of closely related, interconnected hadith in the various sources of the Sunna and Prophetic biographical (*sīra*) or exegetical (*tafsīr*) literatures—they must be, in a sense, *mutawātir*. In the examples published by Motzki, most hadith are argued to be considerably earlier than suggested by Goldziher, Schacht, and Wansbrough and thereby undercut the skeptical and revisionist positions. Motzki's intermediate position is not just with respect to his methodology, but also to his conclusions. First, when using the *isnād-cum-matn* method as opposed to source criticism, Motzki speaks only of individual reports, not of the Sunna or individual works as a whole. Second, this methodology seems to support the authenticity of many hadith but not all. Some hadith are fabrications. To completely dismiss Motzki's method, one would have to take the hyper-skeptical position that each and every person listed in the *isnād* has been fabricated. But if even the first person listed is historically accurate, then Motzki's methodology can be employed.

Modern Scholarship on the Quran

Modern scholarship on the Sunna bleeds into Western scholarship on the Quran. Those who are skeptical about the historicity of hadith naturally bring the same perspective to the Quran, which is hardly surprising given that information about the revelation, collection, canonization, and interpretation of the Quran comes to us via the hadith format. Recently Behnam Sadeghi and Mohsen Goudarzi (2012: 3–4) made a useful four-part classification: scholars who more or less accept the traditional Muslim account of the collection and canonization of the Quran are "traditionalists"; in the revisionist camp stand Wansbrough, Patricia Crone, Alfred-Louis de Prémare, and David Powers (and, I would add, Christoph Luxenberg), who each in different ways tend to see the canonization process as a more drawn-out affair; there is a much larger group of skeptics or agnostics who are deeply suspicious of Muslim traditions about the Quran but who find little convincing evidence in the

4 Andrew Rippin makes this point most forcefully:

"The single most important element here is to recognize that the *isnād*, as a mechanism, came to be required at a certain point in Islamic history as the element that provided authenticity and validity to reports supposedly stemming from earlier authorities. The presence of *isnād*s automatically dates a report to the second century or later, at least in its final recension" (1994: 61).

revisionist positions; and a more recent group of "neo-traditionalists," who do not take the traditional account at face value, but critically evaluate the literary sources and in so doing, support the main features of the traditional account. These include Motzki, Muḥammad Muḥaysin, and Michael Cook, the latter being a former revisionist.

Although there is much valuable and exciting scholarship on the Quran, the focus here is on the modern scholarship that most directly touches on the Quran as a "divine source" for Sharia. Most modern scholars of the Quran recognize that there are conflicting accounts in the sources about the collection of the Quran, and that rival codices may have survived for a very long time (Cook 2000: 119–26; Watt and Bell 1970: 40–56). Western Christian critique or, more accurately, criticism, is as old as Christendom's access to the Quran. Modern scholarship on the Quran—which many consider a continuation of this older polemic—began in 1833 with Abraham Geiger, who argued, using the Quran as his primary source since it was "Muḥammad's Quran," that "Muḥammad really did borrow from Judaism, and that conceptions, matters of creed, views of morality, and of life in general, and more especially matters of history and of traditions, have actually passed over from Judaism into the Qurán" (1970: 156). In 1892 Theodor Nöldeke was more circumspect: "How these revelations actually arose in Muhammad's mind is a question which it is almost idle to discuss as it would be to analyze the workings of the mind of a poet" (1992: 5). Nevertheless, Nöldeke saw the Quran as intimately tied to the life of Muḥammad with the revelations of the Quran often responding to current events as they arose. This is particularly evident in Nöldeke's extensive analysis of the chronology of the revelations of the suras (1909–26: 58–234). The traditional Muslim dating relied primarily on the occasions of revelation (*asbāb al-nuzūl*), whereas Nöldeke (and others, such as Hartwig Hirschfeld and Régis Blachère) examined the internal evidence of the Quran, subjecting it to the scrutiny of historical and literary criticism, that is, using references to known public events and the evolving vocabulary and style. The result of this work has won wide acceptance but surprisingly differs only in minor respects from Muslim chronologies. Although Geiger's and Nöldeke's suggestions clearly undercut the divine status of the Quran, they do accept the basic Islamic history of how the Quran came to be and was subsequently collected.

This acceptance was challenged more by Richard Bell and John Burton. Bell saw the changes in grammatical construction, assonance, and subject matter of a sura as evidence of discontinuity within that sura. He attempted to provide a chronology for these independent passages using some of the same techniques as Nöldeke: certain ideas, style, and vocabulary belonged to a certain period and could be used to roughly date the passages in which they appeared. Not only did this produce a far more complex chronology, but one that more intimately tied the Quran to the culture, mind, and events of Muḥammad. Moreover, he argued, "the Quran was in written form when the redactors [Zayd b. Thābit et al.] started their work, whether actually written by Muḥammad himself, as I personally believe, or by others at his dictation" (1937–39, 1: vi; see also Watt and Bell 1970: 16–19). With his co-author W. Montgomery Watt, Bell also points out, following Friedrich Schwally, that the account of the Quran's compilation is problematic: the death of so many Muslims at the battle of Yamāna, which is said to have motivated the collection under Abū Bakr, did not involve many Muslims who would have memorized much of the Quran; Abū Bakr's collection inexplicably had little authority; and there is mention of rival codices with textual variants, different orders of the suras, and even two additional short suras (1970: 40–47). Then, on the basis of the absence of the "stoning verse" from the Quran, Burton suggested that contradictory hadith about the collection of the Quran under the first three caliphs were meant to obscure Muḥammad's hands-on editing of the Quran: "What we have today in our hands is the *muṣḥaf* of Muḥammad" (1977: 239–40). The underlying assumption of Geiger, Nöldeke, Bell, and Burton was that the Quran is a human production—by Muḥammad—and not a divine one.

Although these efforts have been criticized as "orientalist," they are not revisionist, because they all largely accept the traditional Muslim account of early Islam. In 1977 John Wansbrough took a far more skeptical stance, pointing out that most of what we know about early Islam is the product of literary activity from over a century later. As with Geiger and Bell, Wansbrough's Islam was born within a Judeo-Christian milieu, although he suggested that the milieu may have been outside of Arabia. Whereas orientalist scholarship had suggested a stronger, even authorial connection between Muḥammad and the Quran, Wansbrough seemingly severed the connection between the "Arabian prophet" and the scripture. His examination of Quranic style suggested to him not a single author or editor, but "an organic development from originally independent traditions during a long period of transmission" (1977: 47). Just as disconcerting was his late dating for the canonization of the Quran ("it is of course neither possible, nor necessary, to maintain that the material of the canon did not, in some form, exist prior to that period of intensive literary activity") but the *ne varietur* text only occurred "towards the end of the second century" (1977: 44). In addition, Patricia Crone has argued on the basis of an example of exegetes unanimously misunderstanding a Quranic passage and of an example of a discontinuity between Quranic legislation and Islamic law that the traditional account of the Quran's origins and canonization seems very unlikely (Crone 1994).

That Günter Lüling and the pseudonymous Christoph Luxenberg are also labeled revisionists is an indication that the term is applied only to those scholars who deviate from the traditional account and is not based on shared methodologies or specific conclusions. In 1974 Lüling argued that the shorter, poetic, and sometimes obscure suras (up to one-third of the Quran) were revisions of pre-Islamic, originally Christian hymns. The very incoherence of some Quranic passages suggested to him that later editing and misinterpretation took place, aided greatly by the early unvoweled, unpointed Arabic script. Luxenberg also examined Quranic passages that remain problematic. His methodology is to examine exegetical and lexicographical works in order to glean any hint of an Aramaic reading for problematic terms. If he finds none, Luxenberg then searches for Syro-Aramaic homonyms that might better explain the passages. If again unsuccessful, he seeks to discover Aramaic roots by altering the diacritical points and vocalizations (since neither was present in the first written versions of the Quran). Luxenberg intends to demonstrate that the materials that went into the Arabic Quran were excerpted from a Syriac canonical and/or proto-scriptural Urtext. Having found—contested—examples to support his claim, Luxenberg maintains that Mecca was an Aramean settlement in which an Aramaic-Arabic hybrid was spoken. Later Arabic-speaking exegetes and philologists were unfamiliar with the hybrid language and the written Quran's defective script, which was standardized only in the second half of the eighth century. Consequently, there were numerous misinterpretations and misreadings (Luxenberg 2000). Most scholars of Islam, if they do not ignore Luxenberg, heap scorn upon him, but Claude Gilliot points out that Arabia closely interacted with the nearby Aramaic, Jewish, and Christian cultures, and suggests the Aramaic trail set by Lüling, Luxenberg, and others may yet lead to the pre-Quranic lectionary (Gilliot 2010: 164).

Although not deviating as far as Wansbrough and Luxenberg, others still take issue with the traditional account that has the collection and canonization process end with the ʿUthmānic recension. De Prémare and Stephen Shoemaker argue most forcefully that the Quran was relatively fluid well after ʿUthmān and that it was the Umayyad caliph ʿAbd al-Malik (d. 86/705) together with his governor in Iraq, al-Ḥajjāj, who standardized and canonized the Quran—the Marwānid hypothesis first put forth by Paul Casanova (de Prémare 2002: 278–306; also 2010: 189–221; Shoemaker 2012: 146–58; Casanova 1911: 103–42; for an argument against, Sadeghi and Bergmann 2010: 343–435). The most striking examples of this fluidity are the inscriptions on the Dome of the Rock and variant readings of the rival codices. In his study of ʿAbd al-Malik Chase Robinson examines the state of the Quran during his reign. He cites the absence of manuscripts that would support the traditional view (as both Wansbrough and de Prémare did), and questions how in a single generation, God's word moved "from individual lines scribbled on camel shoulder blades and rocks to complete, single, fixed and authoritative text on papyrus or vellum" and how the rudimentary polity could have the authority to canonize a text (2005: 102). ʿAbd al-Malik, on the other hand, had the motivation and means to impose such standardization, and a few sources imply this late canonization (see also Cook 2000: 119–22; Powers 2009: 155–96, 227–33).

Arguing primarily against the Wansbroughian thesis, Fred Donner suggests, however, that the Quranic text "as we now have it, must be an artifact of the earliest historical phase of the community of Believers, and so can be used with some confidence to understand the values and beliefs of that community" (1998: 61). Had the Quran been compiled later, at roughly the same time as hadith began to circulate, he posits, it would contain the intense sectarianisms of the first two centuries of Islam—the debates about religious and political authority, the mention of Muḥammad's contemporaries in order to bolster or hinder their descendants' political aspirations, and the plethora of anachronisms that abound in hadith.[5] Their absence in the Quran suggests that it was complete before they arose. Another argument for an early Quran (Sadeghi and Bergmann 2010: 365–6, 416) is that the Marwānid thesis requires ʿAbd al-Malik to have imposed an empire-wide false memory about ʿUthmān, to whom Muslims of the late first and early second century in different cities and from clashing communities (including the proto-Shiʿis) all traced the standard Quran back. The empire was divided by sects and tribes and spread over such a large geographical region that such an empire-wide conspiracy or amnesia is not plausible.

Motzki also defends the traditional account of the collection of the Quran using *isnād* analysis and his *isnād-cum-matn* analysis. The former shows that 29 transmission lines of the hadith detailing the initial collection by Abū Bakr all intersect with Ibn Shihāb al-Zuhrī (d. 124/741-2), and the latter confirms this because the *matn* variations are closely correlated with their *isnād*. A similar analysis of the hadith describing the collection by ʿUthmān again converge with al-Zuhrī and display the same correlation. Al-Zuhrī is, therefore, the *terminus post quem*, and so both accounts can be dated to the first quarter of the second century AH, or to the last decades of the first century even, since there is no reason to doubt the *isnād* sources that al-Zuhrī cites (2001: 15–31). Motzki has not pushed these traditions back to the time of Companion eyewitnesses, but if he is correct, he has seriously undermined the claims of Wansbrough and other revisionists.

These issues of redaction and canonization are closely tied to the status of the Quran in Sharia. Evidence for the lateness of the completion of those processes is the apparent absence of the Quran in the earliest texts of Islamic law, although several scholars have taken up this challenge. Yasin Dutton has argued that the Quran and hadith—though the *isnād* is not "sufficiently elaborated" (1999: 3)—are present in Mālik's *Muwaṭṭaʾ*. Hallaq goes further, arguing that the Quran was a source of Islamic law even in the Meccan period.[6] Hallaq suggests that our modern dichotomous distinctions between law and morality have influenced our thinking on the role of the Quran in Islamic law (2009b: 256–7). Since the Quranic terms are pervasively and cosmologically moral, "law" took off where and when morality began, with the revelation of the first suras in Mecca. It was then and there that the intricate moral blueprint was given further "legal" and other elaborations, which became the full-fledged Sharia, one that was morally grounded and supremely Quranic from the very start (2009b: 279; also 2005: 19–25).

To be convinced by Hallaq, of course, one must completely reject the revisionist claims and largely dismiss the skeptical ones.

New Departures

A new departure in the study of these two sources would be simply to leave behind the authenticity debate. As Angelika Neuwirth has pointed out, even if questions of redaction and canonization are

5 For example, see the treatment of Muḥammad's uncle al-ʿAbbās, purportedly a late convert and eponymous ancestor of the Abbasid caliphs (Berg 2010).

6 Hallaq is responding to Schacht's almost single-minded focus on hadith as the primary source for Sharia at the expense of the Quran. Others who have challenged Schacht's claim are Motzki—the origin of Islamic jurisprudence is some 70 years earlier than Schacht had it—though he does not give an early or significant enough role to the Quran (2002: 295–6), and Coulson—who emphasizes the early use of the Quran, but minimizes its legal content to 500 verses or even 80 (1964: 12). Hallaq finds both their conclusions problematic.

not solved, other aspects of the Quran remain open to investigation. She points out that the Quran's own stylistic techniques suggest its own orality. As a result, the attempt to link a *ne varietur* text to canonization or canonization to the *ne varietur* text by revisionists and (neo-)traditionalists misses the point. Other needs, besides legal ones, may have driven the desire for a fixed text (2003: 13). Neuwirth's Corpus Coranicum project seeks to document the historical development of the Quran in both written and oral form. Similarly, Jonathan Brown's exploration of the canonization of the *Ṣaḥīḥ* of al-Bukhārī and of Muslim (2007) looks to depart from the authenticity debate and move on to other important questions in the development of the Sunna.

Ignoring the debate is not the same as resolving it. Perhaps the most promising approach would be to apply Motzki's *isnād-cum-matn* method to the entire corpus of the Sunna in so far as possible. This historical-critical approach has provided intriguing (if not always convincing) results when applied to hadith outside the Sunna. An examination of the hadith from the *sīra* literature (Görke and Schoeler 2008) found most, but not all, of the major events of Muḥammad's life in Mecca and especially Medina to be early (which for the authors means "historical"). A similarly exhaustive study (Scheiner 2010) was made of the historical accounts of the conquest of Damascus but the conclusions were far more negative. Similar approaches were taken for early Muslim *tafsīr* (Muranyi 2003) and grammar (Versteegh 1993). Another interesting variation of this method is employed by Sadeghi (2008), who calls it his "traveling tradition test," which compares the content of the *matn* with the cities represented within the *isnād*. Like Motzki, Sadeghi finds evidence for an early provenance for several hadith. It is this wider applicability of the historical-critical approach outside of just the Sunna that is likely to help it overcome skepticism. Moreover, the observed correlations between the text and the *isnād* require an alternative explanation if the method is to be rejected—either organic growth or a widespread fabrication of the *isnād*, as Juynboll suggests and Wansbrough assumes, should have produced randomness, not correlations. Until revisionists proffer an explanation, even the skeptic must admit that at least some part of the *isnād* reflects actual transmission history, and thus Motzki's *isnād-cum-matn* method can be employed. Unfortunately, as his method can only be used if there are enough related hadith with sufficient variation in order to find correlations, it is not applicable on a wide scale.

Still, questions remain about how far this method can be extended and what can be concluded about the reconstructed original version. For example, Motzki concluded that hadith about the ʿUthmānic redaction of the Quran trace back to al-Zuhrī, which is significant because Motzki maintains that chronological proximity increases the likelihood of historical accuracy:

> It may be possible and sensible to ask whether parts of the events that the sources depict really happened. The reason is the closeness of the source to the reported events. Yet the chance is greater that, to give an extreme example, an eyewitness report of an event transmitted some decades later is less affected by later developments than a description of the same event given two centuries later by someone who, although perhaps basing himself on traditions about the event, tries to make sense of it for his time (2010: 288).

But al-Zuhrī worked in the administration of ʿAbd al-Malik. Might not Motzki's conclusions about Abū Bakr's and ʿUthmān's roles in collecting the Quran therefore be evidence in support of the Marwānid hypothesis? It is on these historical claims that Motzki's *isnād-cum-matn* method remains particularly vulnerable.

Research into the origins of the Quran is benefiting from access to new manuscripts—not just reconstructed ones as is the case for the Sunna. Sadeghi examines the lower text of the Ṣanʿāʾ 1 codex, arguing that it is neither an ʿUthmānic text nor one of the "rival" Companion codices of ʿAbd Allāh b. Masʿūd or Ubayy b. Kaʿb. It must therefore have diverged from the former sometime in the mid-seventh century. On this basis he also argues that the formation of the revelations into suras predates ʿUthmān's standardization of the text (Sadeghi and Bergmann 2010; Sadeghi and Gourdarzi 2012).

Moreover, Sadeghi's conclusion also supports the existence of non-extant but reported Companion codices such as those by Ibn Masʿūd, Ibn Kaʿb, and Abū Mūsā l-Ashʿarī, which Wansbrough and Burton had doubted. Like Motzki, Sadeghi believes that "the earliest manuscripts can be used to work one's way back in time. Our knowledge can extend to a period before the manuscripts" (Sadeghi and Gourdarzi 2012: 16). Sadeghi's conclusions certainly contradict the revisionists' views, but they are as damning of the aforementioned widespread skeptical agnosticism, and the traditional view does not come through unscathed either—the ʿUthmānic text was likely "a hybrid formed on the basis of a number of Companion codices … in which preference was usually given to the majority reading" (Sadeghi and Gourdarzi 2012: 22). Sadeghi posits the existence of a prototype of the Quran to Muḥammad, in which the verses of revelations were already fixed into suras in his time, though the order of the suras relative to each other was not fully fixed. He is clearly in the neo-traditionalist camp, since the standard version of the Quran today is the most "faithful representation, among the known codices, of the Quran as recited by the Prophet" (Sadeghi and Bergmann 2010: 346, 413–4). A faithful representation is not quite the same, of course, as an exact copy of a heavenly archetype.

While the scholarly debate continues about the conclusions reached by neo-traditionalists such as Motzki and Sadeghi, skeptics and revisionists must at least contend with their methodologies and the conclusions they have produced. To deny that they might allow us to peer further into the Islamic past than our extant texts would be to deny the methodologies that have given us the Documentary Hypothesis or allowed for the reconstruction of the Q document. And although it might be comforting to those who embrace the traditional position that some of these neo-traditionalist methodologies seem thus far to be confirming some of their beliefs about the origins of the Quran and the Sunna, these methodologies are also a double-edged sword. They ultimately treat both sources of Islamic law not as divine, as they are traditionally understood to be, but as very ordinary, human texts subject to very profane historical analysis.

References

Abbott, Nabia. 1967. *Studies in Arabic Literary Papyri II: Qurʾanic Commentary and Tradition.* Chicago: The University of Chicago Press.

Azami, Mohammad Mustafa. 1985. *On Schacht's Origins of Muhammadan Jurisprudence*. Riyadh: King Saud University.

———. 1992. *Studies in Early Hadith Literature: With a Critical Edition of Some Early Texts*. 3rd ed. Indianapolis: American Trust Publications.

——— (Al-Aʿẓamī, Muḥammad Muṣṭafā). 2003. *The History of the Qurʾānic Text: From Revelation to Compilation. A Comparative Study with the Old and New Testaments*. Leicester: UK Islamic Academy.

Bell, Richard. 1937–39. *The Qurʾān: Translated, with a Critical Re-arrangement of the Surahs*. 2 vols. Edinburgh: T. & T. Clark.

Berg, Herbert. 2000. *The Development of Exegesis in Early Islam: The Authenticity of Muslim Literature from the Formative Period.* Richmond: Curzon.

———. 2003. Competing Paradigms in the Study of Islamic Origins: Qur'ān 15:89–91 and the Value of *Isnāds*. In idem, ed., *Methods and Theories in the Study of Islamic Origins*, pp. 259–90. Leiden: Brill.

———. 2010. Abbasid Historians' Portrayals of al-ʿAbbās b. ʿAbd al-Muṭṭalib. In *Abbasid Studies II: Occasional Papers of the School of Abbasid Studies*, Leuven, 28 June–1 July 2004, ed. J. Nawas, pp. 13–38. Leuven: Peeters.

Brown, Jonathan A.C. 2007. *The Canonization of al-Bukhārī and Muslim: The Formation and Function of the Sunnī Ḥadīth Canon*. Leiden: Brill.

———. 2009. *Hadith: Muhammad's Legacy in the Medieval and Modern World*. Oxford: Oneworld.
Burton, John. 1977. *The Collection of the Qur'ān*. Cambridge: Cambridge University Press.
Caetani, Leone. 1905. *Annali dell'Islam*. 10 in 12 vols. Milan: Ulrico Hoepli.
Calder, Norman. 1993. *Studies in Early Muslim Jurisprudence*. Oxford: Clarendon Press.
Casanova, Paul. 1911. *Mohammed et la fin du monde: Étude critique sur l'Islam primitif*. Paris: P. Gauthier.
Cook, Michael. 2000. *The Koran: A Very Short Introduction*. Oxford: Oxford University Press.
Coulson, Noel J. 1964. *A History of Islamic Law*. Edinburgh: Edinburgh University Press.
Crone, Patricia. 1994. Two Legal Problems Bearing on the Early History of the Qur'an. *Jerusalem Studies in Arabic and Islam* 18: 1–37.
Donner, Fred M. 1998. *Narratives of Islamic Origins: The Beginnings of Islamic Historical Writing*. Princeton: The Darwin Press.
Dozy, Reinhart. 1897. *Essai sur l'histoire de l'Islamisme*, tr. V. Chauvin. Leiden: E.J. Brill.
Dutton, Yasin. 1999. *The Origins of Islamic Law: The Qur'ān, the* Muwaṭṭa' *and Madinan* 'Amal. Richmond: Curzon.
Geiger, Abraham. 1970. *Judaism and Islam*, tr. F.M. Young. New York: KTAV Publishing House.
Gilliot, Claude. 2010. On the Origins of the Informants of the Prophet. In *The Hidden Origins of Islam*, ed. K.-H. Ohlig and G.-R. Puin, 153–87. Amherst: Prometheus Books.
Goldziher, Ignaz. 1971. *Muslim Studies (Muhammedanische Studien)*, ed. S.M. Stern, tr. C.R. Barber and S.M. Stern. 2 vols. London: George Allen and Unwin.
Görke, Andreas, and Gregor Schoeler. 2008. *Die Ältesten Berichte über Muhammads: Das Korpus 'Urwa ibn az-Zubair*. Princeton: The Darwin Press.
Hallaq, Wael B. 1999. The Authenticity of Prophetic Ḥadîth: A Pseudo-Problem. *Studia Islamica* 89: 75–90.
———. 2005. *The Origin and Evolution of Islamic Law*. Cambridge: Cambridge University Press.
———. 2009. Groundwork of the Moral Law: A New Look at the Qur'ān and the Genesis of Sharī'a. *Islamic Law and Society* 16: 239–79.
Juynboll, G.H.A. 1983. *Muslim Tradition: Studies in Chronology, Provenance and Authorship of Early* Ḥadīth. Cambridge: Cambridge University Press.
———. 1989. Some *Isnād*-Analytical Methods Illustrated on the Basis of Several Woman-Demeaning Sayings from *Ḥadīth* Literature. *Al-Qanṭara* 10: 343–84.
———. 1993. Nāfi', the *mawlā* of Ibn 'Umar, and his Position in Muslim *Ḥadīth* Literature. *Der Islam* 70: 207–44.
Lammens, Henri. 1943. *L'Islam: Croyances et institutions*. 3rd ed. Beirut: Imprimerie Catholique.
Lüling, Günter. 1974. *Über den Ur-Quran: Ansätze z. Rekonstruktion vorislam. christl. Strophenlieder im Quran*. Erlangen: Lüling.
Luxenberg, Christoph. 2000. *Die syro-aramäische Lesart des Koran: Ein Beitrag zur Entschlüsselung des Koransprache*. Berlin: Das Arabische Buch.
Margoliouth, D.S. 1912. On Muslim Tradition. *The Moslem World* 2: 113–21.
———. 1914. *The Early Development of Mohammedanism: Lectures Delivered in the University of London, May and June 1913*. London: William and Norgate.
Motzki, Harald. 2002. *The Origins of Islamic Jurisprudence: Meccan Fiqh before the Classical Schools*, tr. M.H. Katz. Leiden: Brill.
———. 2001. The Collection of the Qur'ān: A Reconsideration of Western Views in Light of Recent Methodological Developments. *Der Islam* 78: 1–34.
———. 2005. Dating Muslim Traditions: A Survey. *Arabica* 52: 204–53.
———. 2010. *Analysing Muslim Tradition: Studies in Legal, Exegetical and Maghāzī Ḥadīth*. Leiden: Brill.
———. 2012. Methods of Dating Early Legal Traditions: Introduction. *Islamic Law and Society* 19: 1–10.

Muir, William. 1894. *Life of Mahomet*. London: Smith, Elder, and Co.

Muranyi, Miklos. 2003. A Unique Manuscript from Kairouan in the British Library: The *Samā'*-work of Ibn al-Qāsim al-'Utaqī and Issues of Methodology. In *Methods and Theories in the Study of Islamic Origins*, ed. H. Berg, pp. 325–68. Leiden: Brill.

Neuwirth, Angelika. 2003. Qur'an and History—A Disputed Relationship: Some Reflections on Qur'anic History and History in the Qur'an. *Journal of Qur'anic Studies* 5: 1–18.

Nöldeke, Theodor. 1992. *The Qur'an: An Introductory Essay by Theodor Nöldeke*, ed. N.A. Newman. Hatfield, PA: Interdisciplinary Biblical Research Institute.

——— et al. 1909–26. *Geschichte des Qorans*. 2nd rev. ed. Leipzig: T. Dieter.

Powers, David S. 2009. *Muhammad is Not the Father of Any of Your Men: The Making of the Last Prophet*. Philadelphia: University of Pennsylvania.

de Prémare, Alfred-Louis. 2002. *Les fondations de l'Islam: Entre écriture et histoire*. Paris: Éditions du Seuil.

———. 2010. 'Abd al-Malik b. Marwān and the Processes of the Qur'ān's Composition. In *The Hidden Origins of Islam*, ed. K.-H. Ohlig and G.-R. Puin, pp. 189–221. Amherst: Prometheus Books.

Rahman, Fazlur. 1979. *Islam*. 2nd ed. Chicago: University of Chicago Press.

Rippin, Andrew. 1994. *Tafsīr* Ibn 'Abbās and Criteria for Dating Early *Tafsīr* Texts. *Jerusalem Studies in Arabic and Islam* 18: 38–83.

Robinson, Chase F. 2005. *'Abd al-Malik*. Oxford: Oneworld.

Sadeghi, Behnam. 2008. The Traveling Tradition Test: A Method for Dating Traditions. *Der Islam* 85: 203–42.

———, and Uwe Bergmann. 2010. The Codex of a Companion of the Prophet and the Qur'ān of the Prophet. *Arabica* 57: 343–436.

———, and Mohsen Goudarzi. 2012. Ṣan'ā' 1 and the Origins of the Qur'ān. *Der Islam* 87: 1–129.

Schacht, Joseph. 1949. A Reevaluation of Islamic Tradition. *Journal of the Royal Asiatic Society of Great Britain and Ireland* n.v.: 143–54.

———. 1959. *The Origins of Muhammadan Jurisprudence*. 3rd rev. ed. Oxford: Clarendon Press.

Scheiner, Jens. 2010. *Die Eroberung von Damaskus: Quellenkritische Untersuchung zur Historiographie in klassisch-islamischer Zeit*. Leiden: Brill.

Schoeler, Gregor. 1985. Die Frage der schriftlichen order mündlichen Überlieferung der Wissenschaften im frühen Islam. *Der Islam* 62: 201–30.

———. 1992. Schreiben und Veröffentlichen: Zu Verendung und Funktion der Schrift in den ersten islamischen Jahrhunderten. *Der Islam* 69: 1–43.

Sezgin, Fuat. 1967. *Geschichte des arabischen Schrifttums*. Vol. 1. Leiden: E.J. Brill.

Shoemaker, Stephen J. 2012. *The Death of a Prophet: The End of Muhammad's Life and the Beginnings of Islam*. Philadelphia: University of Pennsylvania Press.

Speight, R. Marston. 1973. The Will of Sa'd b. a. Waqqās: The Growth of a Tradition. *Der Islam* 50: 249–67.

Versteegh, Kees. 1993. *Arabic Grammar and Qur'ānic Exegesis in Early Islam*. Leiden: E.J. Brill.

Wansbrough, John. 1977. *Quranic Studies: Sources and Methods of Scriptural Interpretation*. Oxford: Oxford University Press.

Watt, W. Montgomery, and Richard Bell. 1970. *Introduction to the Qur'ān*. Edinburgh: Edinburgh University Press.

The Schools of Law

Paul R. Powers

The *madhhab* (pl. *madhāhib*; lit. path one takes, thus "method, school") is one of the more distinctive features of Islamic law. It has been asserted that the development of the madhhab, "by which groups of jurists came to have huge followings of lay, uneducated believers, is a singular Islamic phenomenon," and "a new form of social classification" not anticipated in any direct way in the ancient Middle East (Hurvitz 2002: 11). This purported originality will be considered below, but the madhhab is certainly a crucial element of Islamic societies. For a full understanding of the institution, its social, intellectual, and doctrinal dimensions must all be considered. Although "school" fittingly connotes both a formal institution and a more abstract "school of thought," and is the most common translation employed, we will rely on the untranslated term madhhab as we develop an understanding of its proper range of meaning.

This chapter will survey scholarly[1] understandings of, first, the emergence of the madhhab in the formative period (up to the later ninth century), and, second, the form and activities of the classical madhhab—viz., the four Sunni schools of the Hanafis, Malikis, Shafiʿis, and Hanbalis, the three Shiʿi schools of the Twelvers (the Jaʿfaris), the Ismaʿilis, and the Zaydis, and the lone Ibadiyya.[2] It is the formative period that generates the most questions and controversies. The scholarly landscape here is dominated by a few scholars and a few prominent arguments. In brief, in the mid-twentieth century Joseph Schacht set the scholarly terms with his assertion that the madhhab began in the form of "regional schools" that then transformed into "personal schools"; most subsequent work on the origins of the madhhab strives to refine and extend or to challenge and replace this account. As we explore this basic scholarly framework other specific lines of academic inquiry will come into focus. While the emergence of the madhhab is deeply intertwined with the more general emergence of Islamic law, this chapter will seek to isolate the madhhab analytically.

The Emergence of the Madhhab

As stated, the history of the madhhab rests on a relatively small number of scholars and publications—most importantly, Schacht, in a series of publications mostly from the 1950s and 1960s;

Paul R. Powers, Associate Professor in the Department of Religious Studies at Lewis and Clark College, Portland, Oregon, is the author most recently of "Finding God and Humanity in Language: Islamic Legal Assessments as the Meeting Point of the Divine and Human," in *Islamic Law in Theory*, ed. Reinhart and Gleave (Brill, 2014). The author wishes to thank Hannah Brown for editorial assistance.

1 I use "scholar" for modern academics, "jurist/jurisprudent" for classical Muslim practitioners of law, though not all of my sources do the same.

2 All references in this chapter are to Sunni madhhabs and contexts, although in the formative period this distinction was not as clear as in later eras.

Christopher Melchert (building on the work of his mentor George Makdisi) in publications beginning in the later 1990s; and Wael Hallaq, who turned his attention pointedly to this topic beginning around 2001. Together this corpus comprises a thesis (Schacht), a refinement (Melchert), and an antithesis (Hallaq). Whether synthesis looms on the horizon will be discussed below, along with the contributions of others.

Schacht's Thesis

As with so much about early Islamic law, Schacht's work on the origins of the madhhab set the terms of current scholarly inquiry. Schacht often extended lines of thought initiated by Ignaz Goldziher, starting from their shared general conviction that legal doctrine, and more specifically the hadith that express and justify so much of it, took shape relatively late (in the eighth century) to legitimize prevailing legal doctrines and practices. This conviction shaped Schacht's understanding of the early madhhab, which he presented as generated in part by the emergence of hadith-centered traditionalism.

Schacht characterized the "distinguishing feature" of the madhhabs in the earliest period "as neither the personal allegiance to a master nor [...] any essential difference of doctrine, but simply their geographic distribution" (1967: 7). The doctrines of these regional "ancient schools" of law were, in this view, determined by the prevailing practice of the region, which Schacht elsewhere calls "the living tradition of a city" (1955: 63); doctrinal differences were minimal. The major regional groupings were the Hijaz (divided between Mecca and Medina), Syria, and Iraq (divided between Kufa and Basra) (1967: 8). For Schacht, the political needs of the Umayyad state, rather than the Quran or the Prophetic traditions, dictated most actual law (1955: 58–60, 62). Schacht did not provide much detail about the doctrinal positions of the schools, but he was more precise in dating their transformation from regional to personal ones: "Soon after the time of Shāfiʿī [d. 204/820] the geographical character of the ancient schools of law disappeared more and more, and the personal allegiance to a master became predominant" (1967: 10).

Schacht's account of the transition from regional to personal schools is multifaceted but not especially systematic; its coherence, we will see, is much debated. Here is perhaps his most sustained treatment of the matter:

> In the early ʿAbbāsid period [...] the ancient schools of law, which had been based mainly on the teachings in one geographic center, transformed themselves into the later type of school, based on allegiance to an individual master. The religious specialists of each geographical unit in the central parts of the Islamic world began by developing a certain minimum agreement on their doctrines, and by the middle of the second century of the hijra many individuals, instead of working out independent doctrines of their own, started to follow the teaching of a recognized authority in its broad outlines, while reserving to themselves the right to differ from their master on any point of detail. This led in the first place to the forming of groups or circles within the ancient schools of law. ... [T]he extensive literary activity of the followers of Abū Ḥanīfa, particularly of Shaybānī, in ʿIraq, and of the followers of Mālik in North Africa, together with other factors, some of them accidental, brought it about that the ancient school of Kūfa survived only in the followers of Abū Ḥanīfa (or Ḥanafīs) and the ancient school of Medina only in the followers of Mālik (or Mālikīs). This transformation of the ancient schools of law into "personal" schools, which perpetuated not the living tradition of a city but the doctrine of a master and of his disciples, was completed about the middle of the third century of the hijra. It was the logical outcome of a process which had started within the ancient schools themselves, but was precipitated by the activity of Shāfiʿī (1955: 63).

This implies, first, that following a recognized authority came to appear preferable to individual effort, though Schacht did not specify why this is. Second, Schacht suggested that "extensive literary activity" elevated some jurists over others, making them more attractive as masters to be followed. Further, Schacht presented the efforts of al-Shāfiʿī as accelerating the transformation, apparently because al-Shāfiʿī's work helped bridge the gap between rationalists, or those who relied on personal opinion (*raʾy*), and traditionalists, those who relied on hadith, and thus made doctrinal convergence easier.[3] Elsewhere Schacht highlighted the "Islamicizing trend" that had emerged in the later Umayyad period and was exploited by the early Abbasids to legitimize and differentiate themselves. This trend, he suggested, led the early Abbasids to make "a point of consulting specialists in religious law on problems that might come within their competence" and to cement "the permanent connection of the office of qāḍī with the sharīʿa," theoretically independent of the state (1955: 57–8). In actual fact, however, the qadi—the judge of the Sharia court—and the wider group of religious specialists soon found themselves either ignored or bent to the will of the centralizing state, and the religious vigor of the early Abbasids was exposed as "but a polite formula to cover their own absolute despotism" (1955: 57). Apparently, however, this initial Islamicizing push helped precipitate the emergent "personal schools" because such condensation of structure and doctrine facilitated the jurists' pursuit of coveted influence on the state (see 1955: 57–63).

The regional groupings thus went through two stages, first basing shared doctrine on prevailing practice, second using hadith (largely fabricated and back-projected, according to Schacht) to justify this doctrine. These "regional" schools became "personal" when jurists attached their doctrine to an eponymous founding figure (as opposed to attaching it to a place or group or taking credit themselves). Schacht relied heavily on al-Shāfiʿī's account of earlier developments, and he treated al-Shāfiʿī as the "founder of the first school of law on an exclusively personal basis—certainly with a common doctrine, but a doctrine which had once and for all been formulated by the founder" (1955: 64).[4] The outcome was that by the middle of the third Islamic century the Kufan and Basran regional schools merged as Hanafis and the Medinan and Meccan schools merged as Malikis, while the Shafiʿi and Hanbali schools took shape as personal from the start (1964: 57–8).

Melchert's Refinement

Christopher Melchert largely accepts Schacht's basic framework but seeks to more fully explain the causal dynamics of the purported transition from regional to personal schools. Melchert works from the premise that early regional schools developed into personal schools, though he sees the transition occurring some 25–50 years later than Schacht did, viz., stretching from the later ninth into the early tenth centuries, and he takes from George Makdisi the idea of further development into guilds (discussed below). At least once Melchert describes the regional schools as "vague," implying that the shift to personal schools was a step up in doctrinal clarity (1997b: 38; see Hallaq 2001b: 2). In explaining the shift Melchert takes up where Schacht leaves off, suggesting that following a single master-jurist was a simpler and thus more attractive alternative to mastering increasingly complex legal thinking (1997b: 38), and also endorsing Schacht's assertion that greater literary output set apart the leading contenders in the emergent personal schools (1997b: 33, 38). This is especially true for the Hanafis, according to Melchert, as Abū Yūsuf (d. 182/798), Muḥammad al-Shaybānī (d. 189/804), and others were apparently collecting the doctrines of Abū Ḥanīfa in the late eighth century. The early

3 Here we see a potential problem in that Schacht depicted the ancient schools as lacking much doctrinal difference, and then implied that efforts to overcome doctrinal difference partly drove the transformation into personal schools. More on this below.

4 Melchert (1997b: xvii–xviii) notes that in this, and in other ways, Schacht echoes the account of the origins of the madhhabs offered by Ibn Khaldūn (d. 806/1408) in his *Muqaddima*.

works of these followers of Abū Ḥanīfa serve the end of carving out a distinct Hanafi school because they "collect the doctrine (*madhhab*) of one jurisprudent (and a few close to him) and [...] suggest that his doctrine (and theirs) is all one need know" (1997b: 33). Here we see crystallizing the idea of loyalty to a fully sufficient madhhab. Melchert finds confirmation of this general narrative in the biographical literature which, for example, depicts Zufar ibn al-Hudhayl (d. 158/774-5) as preceding Abū Yūsuf and al-Shaybānī at the head of the line of Abū Ḥanīfa's students *cum* teachers-in-their-own-right. Such a "continuously existing group of students with a regular succession of teachers is a mark of a functioning [personal] school" (1997b: 34). Melchert's research modifies several details in the Schacht-based narrative, such as relocating the roots of the Hanafi madhhab from Kufa to Baghdad (1999, 2004b: 13). But on the whole Melchert extends and refines, but does not fundamentally challenge Schacht.

Underlying the various explanations mentioned above, and also echoing Schacht, Melchert's account of the shift from regional to personal is given in terms of the rise of traditionalism as an irresistible challenge to previous rationalistic tendencies. Melchert asserts that "the ideological challenge of traditionalism is what unhinged the old regional system, provoked the formation of personal schools, and eventually forced virtually all jurisprudents to adopt the combination of inspired texts and rational manipulation of them" that came to characterize the theory/method of the mature madhhabs (2004b: 10; cf. 13). In describing the intellectual atmosphere of the formative period, Melchert holds that "the greatest division of Muslim jurisprudents before the tenth century was not among adherents of different schools, whether regional or personal, but between *aṣḥāb al-ra'y*, the rationalistic jurisprudents, and *aṣḥāb al-ḥadīth*, their adversaries the traditionalists" (2004b: 11). Against the claims of later traditionalist Muslim sources, Melchert finds that virtually all early jurisprudence was done in terms of *ra'y*, and the two camps were not distinct and opposed much before the late eighth century—the staunch traditionalist Aḥmad b. Ḥanbal, for example, apparently studied with the rationalist Abū Yūsuf before the latter's death (2004b: 11). For Melchert, the decisive break was triggered in the last decades of the eighth century, apparently by the Hanafi articulation of a thesis of a created Quran (2004b: 11). This theological wedge led to increasing separation on basic issues and a hardening of positions—especially the growing condemnation of rationalism as hopelessly subjective—until we see concerted efforts in the ninth century (especially among the followers of al-Shāfiʿī) to "bridge the gap between rationalism and traditionalism" (2004b: 12). In short, traditionalism gained such momentum that no jurist could reject it outright, but its triumph was significantly tempered by compromise—limited rationalism in the form of analogical reasoning and an appeal to consensus mitigated against the potentially crippling methodological inflexibility and limited doctrinal scope of traditionalism.

Melchert defines the stages of development as regional school, personal school, and, finally, guild-school. The ability to meld rationalism and traditionalism was a necessary (if not sufficient) cause of the success of those madhhabs that survived long enough to mature into guilds, at which point the self-reproducing mechanisms of teacher-student relationships and social and political relevance created reinforcing feedback loops. Melchert's view is clarified further by his account of two prominent early groupings—the Zahiris and the Jariris—that failed to reach guild status. Melchert ascribes their demise to a combination of failure to attract sufficient adherents (the Jariris had "altogether too élite and literary a character to survive in the long term") and political vagaries (the Zahiris associated closely with the Buyids and collapsed when that dynasty did) (2004b: 9, and see 1997b: chap. 9).

Hallaq's Antithesis

In challenging both Schacht and Melchert, Wael Hallaq first highlights what he sees as the troubling vagueness of Schacht's phrasing. As quoted above, Schacht had said that the regional schools "transformed themselves" into personal schools by aligning themselves around the distinctive "theses" of the founders. What were the specific modalities of this transformation? Hallaq finds incoherent the suggestion that schools that Schacht says lacked "any essential difference of doctrine" could nonetheless generate personal allegiance to a master jurist—especially in the earlier cases of Abū Ḥanīfa and Mālik (2001b: 3). Hallaq seeks to show that the sources evince no regional doctrinal groupings, but reveal a plethora of doctrines, many of which were anything but vague. Cutting to the chase, Hallaq asserts that "there were, strictly speaking, no schools during the second/eighth century. All that existed were individual jurists each of whom espoused a legal doctrine that had no binding authority over those who chose to adhere to, or apply, them" (2001b: 21). Hallaq holds that multiple references to, for example, the Iraqi school (*madhhab al-ʿirāqiyyīn* or *madhhab ahl al-ʿirāq*) in relevant sources from the eighth through tenth centuries should emphatically not be confused with "direct reference to the region itself but rather to 'the people of,' or 'the jurists of' Iraq," indicating that "the locus of doctrine here is personal, not regional" (2001b: 13–14). For Hallaq, the doctrines of individual jurists were derived not from the prevailing "anonymous legal practice" in a given area but from the intellectual formulation of other scholars, tracing back to *raʾy* and revealed sources in varying measure (2001b: 12). Thus, no shift from regional schools to personal ones took place, nor did a shift from vague to clear doctrines. Religious law in the formative period, says Hallaq, was "highly individualistic," as legal scholarship "rested on personal-*ijtihādic* effort" (2001b: 26). Hallaq's picture of the pre-classical situation presents a flat field of scholars lacking hierarchies or doctrinal groupings.

Over time groupings of jurists did emerge, according to Hallaq, and these developed internal hierarchies. Hallaq uses the terms "networks" (2001b: 26) and "circles" (2005: 153ff.) for the pre-classical relationship among jurists and suggests that what unity these had was more methodological and doctrinal than geographic (that is, reliant on the prevailing practice of a place): "The embryonic formation of the schools started sometime during the eighth decade after the Hijra [...] taking the form of scholarly circles in which pious scholars debated religious issues and taught interested students. The knowledge and production of legal doctrine began in these circles—nowhere else" (2005: 165). This debating and teaching not only gave shape to emergent doctrine, it also launched the unrivaled epistemic authority of these scholars—their command of "the religious and legal values of the new religion"—and this superior knowledge translated into growing social respect. Hallaq emphasizes the importance of epistemic authority (later dubbed *ijtihād*) in shaping not just the madhhab but the broader emergent patterns of distinctly Islamic legal thought and practice: "masterly knowledge of the law was the determinant of where legal authority resided; and it resided with the scholars, not with the political rulers or any other source" (2005: 165). The jurists thus developed simultaneously as a source of and rival to the authority of the state, generating various tensions and symbioses that are dealt with in Chapter 7, below.

For Hallaq, the combination of sharpening doctrine and epistemic *cum* social authority gave momentum to the scholarly circles that would eventually result in the classical madhhabs. The next phase of development was from debating circles to "personal schools," which formed around the most effective of the major scholars during the eighth century (see 2005: 166). While this reduced some of the volume and variety of legal doctrine, there were still too many such schools (Hallaq names 15 and calls his list partial) to serve as a functional "axis of legal authority" for the Islamic state. The continuing development of the schools in his view was driven by political patronage in the middle and later Umayyad period. The jurists, again, had free-standing authority that was "personal and private" (2005: 165), but to put the law in effect they relied on the enforcement powers of the state. In turn, the scholars served "as the ruler's link to the masses, aiding him in his bid to legitimacy" (2005: 166). This symbiotic relationship included financial support of jurists, access to political power, and social prestige—especially via appointment to government posts including judgeships (see 2005: 167).[5] While jurists singled out for such attention no doubt gained competitive advantage, Hallaq focuses more on

5 Here we should note a similarity to Nimrod Hurvitz's holistic vision of the later madhhab (2002), as noted above.

the need they faced to reduce the variety and thus impracticality of legal thinking: "Rallying around a single juristic doctrine was probably the only means for a personal school to acquire loyal followers and thus attract political/financial support." This rallying impulse would simultaneously make a school more efficiently useful to the ruler and inflate the authority of the central jurist and thus contribute to the "construction of the figure of the absolute *mujtahid*," ultimately the eponymous imam (2005: 167).

Hallaq's progression of stages moves from free-floating individual jurists, to largely informal "circles," to personal schools, and, finally, to doctrinal madhhabs. Hallaq, then, replaces the prevailing Schachtian view of doctrinally uniform yet vague "regional" schools with a view of individual scholars formulating sophisticated doctrines and gradually congregating in networks revolving around emergent masters. The madhhab was driven in part by "the need to control [the] thoroughly individualistic character of Islamic law" (2001b: 26). That is, rather than being a regrouping of scholars from regional to personal affiliation, the madhhab actually functioned to reign in the atomistic tendencies of the previous era. Concomitant with this winnowing tendency, the madhhabs developed further into clearly defined doctrinal schools as they competed for the benefits of political patronage. Hallaq's account of madhhab failure rests on this same doctrine/political patronage foundation: schools failed because doctrinally they did not adapt to the "Great Synthesis" of rationalism and traditionalism, hewing too strongly to one or the other; and they failed because they did not attract political patronage, whether because of their doctrines or their lack of a critical mass of followers (2005: 169–70, and see 122ff.).

Hallaq's depiction of largely independent scholars gradually coalescing around masters is decidedly more precise than the notion of regional schools. It rests on his general conviction that legal doctrine, based not on prevailing practice but on the Quran and hadith, took shape earlier than Schacht believed. In this regard he is supported by Ze'ev Maghen (2003), who has also challenged Schacht's general assertion that the "regional schools" based their legal doctrine on the "living tradition" and "popular practice" of the earlier Umayyad era. Maghen asserts that Schacht's position is both incoherent and at odds with mounting evidence that Muslims of this era did indeed seek to formulate legal rules based on both the Quran and Prophetic example. Thus, Hallaq's account not only adds precision but also appears to enjoy confirmation.

Still, the exact nature of legal reasoning and doctrine in the first 150–200 years of Islamic history must be considered unsettled. The prospects for settling our understanding of these matters has been dealt a blow by scholarship that compellingly argues that prior to the mid-ninth century the very legal texts that we rely on as evidence were themselves variable things. Gregor Schoeler portrays texts of this era as, in the words of Melchert, "more in the nature of lectures, expected to vary from one occasion to another and from one student's notebooks to another's" (Melchert 2004b: 15; see Schoeler 1997). Norman Calder has similarly depicted early jurisprudential writing as fluid while arguing for later final dating of many important early sources (Calder 1993). Calder's work in particular has prompted many efforts to re-establish an earlier dating for some specific texts, but Calder's broader point that our confidence in the dates of early sources must be limited seems to be irreversible (on the responses to Calder, see Melchert 2004b: 15–16). In short, while Hallaq has advanced our understanding of the early madhhabs, the matter is not yet decided.

Synthesis?

Hallaq pointedly repudiates Schacht's treatment of the ancient "regional schools," and calls Melchert's efforts to explain more fully the transition from regional to personal schools "an attempt to solve a non-existing problem and in a less than satisfactory manner" (2001b: 4). It would thus seem that we have a fundamental disagreement, a thesis and antithesis. But can we find common ground that these three at least partly share? I believe so. Melchert responded to Hallaq's critique by saying, "Although Hallaq has left me unconvinced, I would say that he has shifted the burden of proof onto anyone who would still refer to regional schools, which need sharper definition and more documentation than what Schacht offered (naturally enough, 50 years on)" (2004b: 14).[6] Melchert's concession here helps us see that the division between him and Hallaq rests heavily on Melchert's use of Schacht's term "regional."

Let us say for the sake of argument (and because I think it is true) that Schacht's notion of "regional schools" is obscure and out of tune with newer sources and scholarly analyses. Perhaps Melchert is right to shrug at such a prospect. In my reading, Melchert's work suffers surprisingly little if we cut from it the elements inextricably committed to a "regional schools" model. Most of Melchert's work on the madhhab is not devoted to shoring up the "regional" quality of the proto-madhhabs, but rather to addressing the emergence of the classical madhhabs and their shift toward guild-schools. His book is largely devoted to specifying when and by whom the classical madhhabs were formed, and little of this seems at risk if we recast the previous era in the form Hallaq gives us. For example, Melchert shows that the Shafiʿi madhhab coalesced not around al-Shāfiʿī himself but around Ibn Surayj (d. 306/918), and I see no contradiction of this by Hallaq (see Melchert 1997b: chaps. 4, 5; 2004b: 4–5).[7] Melchert appears convinced that the Malikis did indeed generate a regional school, based not on individual authorities but on "anonymous local tradition" (2004b: 14; and see 1999: 319–20). Still, he asserts against Schacht that the Hanafi madhhab of the early ninth century emerged in Baghdad and that the identification of it with Kufa was later Hanafi retrojection (1999, 2004b: 13). This may still reflect an abiding commitment to regionalism, but it is hardly simple fideism to Schacht; Melchert also allows that the Hanafis may simply not fit a regional-to-personal paradigm (1999: 13–14).

Hallaq explicitly repudiates Melchert's emphasis on "education and transmission of legal knowledge" as explanation of the formation of the madhhabs; Hallaq's emphasis on doctrine leads him to insist that "there must first have been a [doctrinal] *madhhab* for it to be taught or promoted" (2005: 164). But Hallaq clearly shares Melchert's view that the ability to meld rationalism and traditionalism was a necessary (if not sufficient) cause of madhhab success, a position staked out earlier by Schacht. And all agree that the eponymous imams are almost entirely fictional in terms of deliberately founding the madhhabs (Hallaq 2005: 158ff.; Melchert 1997b: passim). Hallaq's own explanatory offering is that the madhhab emerged to corral doctrinal individualism, in significant part because doing so served the jurists' political patronage aspirations. The first element rests on Hallaq's original characterization with which he replaces regionalism, but the second echoes both Schacht and Melchert. Hallaq asserts that this occurred under the Umayyads—as the juristic circles personalized in the late seventh and early eighth centuries—while Schacht and Melchert focus on the Abbasid era, but a complete understanding of the emergence of the madhhabs would seem to include both Hallaq's doctrinal/political developments and Melchert's education/transmission of knowledge components, and I see no major contradictions here.

Beyond the Central Scholarly Debate

With the most prominent and influential scholarly debate in mind, we can turn to other important contributions to scholarship on the early madhhab. Hallaq's views are generally supported by the work of Nimrod Hurvitz, though the latter shifts focus from doctrine to social context as he, too, challenges the very notion of early regional schools. Hurvitz asserts that by the eighth century, jurists were aggregating in loose, informal "circles of masters and disciples," a transitional stage between

6 Here (2004b: 14 n. 48) Melchert notes with approval Patricia Crone's efforts (1987: 23) to discern doctrinal blocs in Kufa and Medina.

7 Melchert here is confirming Calder's (1993) redating of the completed version of al-Shāfiʿī's major works to ca. 300/912-3.

earlier, even less well-defined arrangements (his picture resembles Hallaq's portrayal of a flat, fluid, individualistic situation) and the increasing attachment to the most revered masters—and eventually toward the networks of professional and political patronage that marked the mature madhhabs. The defining dynamic of the emergence of the madhhab is to Hurwitz "not the shift from 'geographical' to 'personal schools' but rather, the other way around" (2000: 45). That is, "personal schools" emerged out of the fluid interaction of jurists and only then developed association with geographical locales. This dramatic reversal of Schacht squares well with the established fact that classical and later madhhabs became dominant in distinct geographical regions. Hurvitz insists that the geographic approach and indeed the very use of the terms school and madhhab—following Schacht—have hindered investigation into the real nature of juristic interactions, formation of doctrine, development of group loyalty, and so forth. Here and elsewhere, Hurvitz focuses on the Hanbalis as both a representative case and an opportunity to explore the idiosyncratic aspects of this particular group.

Hurvitz accepts the widespread scholarly chronology that dates the origins of the Hanbali madhhab to the lifetime of Aḥmad b. Ḥanbal, with significant development of his ideas taking place in the decades just after his death (2002: 15). But what it means to be a madhhab, especially in the Hanbali case, looks rather different through Hurvitz's eyes. In de-emphasizing legal doctrine, Hurvitz finds distinct aspects of Hanbali piety and morality to be instrumental in shaping the particular history of this group. Prone to thoroughgoing yet mild asceticism (that is, eschewing extreme self-abnegation), Hanbalis perceived themselves as a moral elite and went to lengths, including violence, to get other Muslims to adhere to their standards of behavior. Their constituency apparently included "relatively ignorant disciples" who "despite their lack of legal knowledge" joined the cause of "zealous imposition of the Hanbali interpretation of moral conduct" (2000: 63)—that is, development of and loyalty to legal doctrine and theory/method were, in these lights, not the driving force behind the Hanbali madhhab or movement. Rather, legal doctrine was only one aspect of this broad movement of piety, theology, and political resistance, which in this case was forged in the crucible of the *miḥna* ("inquisition," from 218–34/833–48).

This approach sheds welcome light on the appeal madhhab affiliation had for the uneducated majority of Muslims, a matter little addressed by other scholars. We should note that Hallaq appreciates this attention to piety, but insists on his own account of madhhab formation: "While a construction of piety and morality was an ingredient in the authoritative image of the supposed founders of the four *madhhab*s, it was peripheral to the process of the *madhhab*'s legal formation, even in the case of Ḥanbalism" (2004: 346). For Hallaq the development of authoritative doctrine is the final stage in madhhab development (again, after "scholarly circle" and "personal school"), and Hurvitz does not account for this definitive aspect of the madhhab, despite contributing to a social history of Hanbalism. One might again downplay the scholarly differences, as Hurvitz's account seems to complement Hallaq's in the project of reaching a more holistic understanding of early Islamic law and its place in Islamic societies.

Hurvitz's nearly singular attention to the Hanbalis is indicative of a trend in scholarship on the formative and classical periods, namely, the forgoing of sweeping accounts of the madhhab as a general phenomenon in favor of isolating individual madhhabs for analysis. Examples of such a trend include Melchert's own attention to the Hanbalis (1997a, 2004a, 2006), Nurit Tsafrir's work on the early Hanafis (2004), Jonathan Brockopp (2000, 2005a) and Maribel Fierro (2005) on early Malikis, and Joseph Lowry (2007) and Ahmed El Shamsy (2007, 2008) on the early Shafiʿis. Perhaps such focused work is needed before a more synthetic understanding can be advanced. Indeed, we should be open to the possibility that no one explanation of all madhhabs will do, and that instead we will have to accept a variety of at least semi-independent histories that resist final integration. Of the works mentioned here, Tsafrir's study of early Hanafism deserves special attention. Tsafrir emphasizes the importance of competition and struggle among madhhabs for political and social influence as a factor sharpening the definition and boundaries of the madhhabs in the ninth to tenth centuries (2005, esp. chaps. 6, 7).

The study of doctrines and circles that failed to survive as mature madhhabs also sheds light on the dynamics of madhhab emergence. One such study, by Steven Judd, is a significant contribution to scholarship on the formative-era madhhab. Taking Hallaq's critique of the notion of "regional schools" as his starting point, Judd sees the Umayyad period as marked by informal "groups of like-minded legal scholars" with only "tentative hierarchies of authority among their 'members'" (2005: 11). Judd pushes beyond even Hallaq's critique of Schacht's regional paradigm in showing how the sheer number, diversity, and especially the frequent travel of jurists challenge any effort at classification (2005: 13, 18–19), illuminating the dynamics of juristic association under the Umayyads by focusing on the groups that formed around Sufyān al-Thawrī (d. 161/778) in Iraq and ʿAbd al-Raḥmān b. ʿAmr al-Awzāʿī (d. 157/774) in Syria—two figures who seemingly could have, but did not, become eponymous imams of mature madhhabs. Judd finds that "the existence of a core group of students who studied with Sufyān and al-Awzāʿī but not with other prominent sheikhs suggests a degree of cohesion" within what amounts to a nascent "Umayyad madhhab" (2005: 20). This (proto-)madhhab leaned toward *raʾy* in method and "emphasized the past practice of the community" (2005: 17); only limited Prophetic hadith and rudimentary analogy appeared in their work. The failure of this madhhab to survive can be attributed to the perils of its Umayyad loyalism, which cost it dearly after the Abbasid revolution, and to the effects of affiliating around not one but two masters. That is, "the emerging eponymous paradigm demanded that [followers] [...] distinguish between Sufyān and al-Awzāʿī," which proved difficult and forced some polemical condemnations of one or the other, thus fatally weakening both (2005: 23–4). Judd's deceptively modest piece confirms the dual role of doctrinal coherence and political patronage, adding to our understanding of pre-classical madhhabs.

Directions for Future Inquiry into the Formation of the Madhhab(s)

A few unresolved questions emerge in the scholarship reviewed here, which might be the topics of further inquiry. For one, several scholars assert, but do not systematically prove, the originality of the madhhab. We saw above that Hurvitz calls the madhhab "a singular Islamic phenomenon" unprecedented in the history of the region (2002: 11). Hallaq likewise claims that "Islam certainly did not borrow the concept of schools from any cultural predecessor, since none is to be found in earlier civilizations. Thus, we can argue with confidence that the *madhhab*s were indigenous Islamic phenomena, having been produced out of the soil of Islamic civilization itself" (2005: 164–5). For Hallaq, both the purported absence of any predecessor and the slow evolution of the institution preclude any roots in extra-Islamic contexts. George Makdisi also treats the madhhab as original to Muslim societies and furthermore suggests that the medieval European "Inn of Court" may have had had its roots in impressions taken home by the Crusaders (Makdisi 1984); that is, the madhhab is *sui generis* and influenced European institutions. Most of these efforts, however, are more assertion than argument and leave the case unproven, and the suggestion that this form of legal, educational, and professional organization is entirely *ex nihilo* seems suspect. Surely a case can yet be made that Muslims were familiar with some specific forms of institutional organization that likely influenced the evolution of the madhhab.

Whether for the formative, classical, or later eras, questions remain regarding the exact nature of doctrinal difference among the madhhabs. Of the scholarship reviewed here, Hallaq remarks in passing that, against the prevailing tone of much current scholarship, doctrinal differences among the madhhabs were far from trivial (2005: 151, 171). One notes the careless tendency of scholars to imply that Hanafis are "liberal" and Hanbalis are "conservative" (the latter claim is often loosely based on the observation that Wahhabis espouse a version of Hanbalism). A great deal of scholarship exists that explores specific aspects of positive law and the differing positions of schools and individual jurists, and a great number of Muslim sources address this aspect of Islamic law, too. The former, however, has not yet led to a systematic historical study of such differences, while the latter tends to serve pious rather than scholarly purposes. At least until someone undertakes a more systematic effort to describe and explain patterns of doctrinal difference, no sweeping characterizations of the doctrinal tone of individual madhhabs are warranted.

On a different note, the study of the madhhab(s), like much specialist scholarship on Islamic law, tends toward insularity. As the specialist understanding of the formation of Islamic law grows, it will need to be incorporated into a broader understanding of early Islamic history and integrated with the work of specialists in other sub-fields of Islamic studies. Of the scholars surveyed here, Hallaq's work does the most in this regard, but this effort is still partial. Gone may be the days of a masterful integrative study the likes of Marshall Hodgson's *Venture of Islam*—our growing body of knowledge makes such synthesis increasingly difficult. Yet, to take just one example, Fred Donner's recent, accessible study of the early period, *Muhammad and the Believers* (2010), reframes earliest Islam as a "Believers' movement" of broad monotheistic reform appealing to many Jews and Christians. He locates the major transformation into a more distinct and self-conscious Islam in the late seventh century, during tumultuous times of the mid-Umayyad period. If this approach is confirmed by further research—including testing it against data of Islamic legal studies—it may reframe our understanding of the formation of Islamic law, including the emergence of the madhhab.

Donner's work also highlights another prospect, namely, the greater use of sociological theory in the study of early Islam. Donner borrows from the Weberian tradition in positing a shift from "charismatic" to "institutional" phases in social, political, and religious patterns (2005, 2010). The lifetime of the Prophet and the succeeding generation or two, he suggests, displays a typical charismatic understanding of authority, with relatively little systematic production of formal knowledge; authority was vested in individuals and groups not because of their command of formal knowledge but because of their sheer embodiment of authority. Only in later generations—Donner sees the shift as part of the establishment of the Umayyad state—did this charismatic authority undergo routinization and bureaucratization. Perhaps the dynamic tensions between rationalism (a more charismatic form of authority) and traditionalism (a routinization of this charisma—perhaps ironically)[8] that specialists agree shaped the formation of the madhhabs would appear more clearly when viewed through this Weberian lens. Would appeals to *ra'y* perhaps appear as a transitional phase between pure charismatic authority and later, more routinized forms? Can the construction of eponymous imams be seen as an effort to domesticate the charisma of earlier generations of jurists in a routinizing moment? Were any failed madhhabs too dependent on charismatic authority to survive routinization? Brockopp (2005b) presents a rare example of explicitly applying this Weberian framework to Islamic legal history, highlighting the potential value of such efforts. Hallaq's portrayal of madhhab formation as a corralling of doctrinal individualism, and Melchert's suggestion that a madhhab might fail due to its perceived elitism are examples of their consideration of social dynamics, while Hurvitz pushes further in this direction, but the theoretically informed social history of early Islamic law seems underdeveloped.

The Scholarly Consensus on the Classical Madhhab

Having surveyed the scholarly controversies about the formation of the madhhab, we now turn to its form and function, a subject of considerably greater scholarly confidence and consensus. By the late ninth and early tenth centuries the Sunni madhhab had taken shape as a distinctive feature of Islamic civilization—mostly stable, broadly uniform, and sophisticated in both structure and theory/method, widespread throughout Islamic societies, large in scale, and with complex relations to other

8 Ironically, that is, as this would be a case of explicit appeal to earlier charismatic authority as a means of establishing a new, post-charismatic and institutionalized order.

institutions. Within roughly the next two centuries their number, already much reduced by the later tenth century, had settled at four, and doctrinally they had reached a mostly comfortable, agree-to-disagree relationship among themselves. Various scholars emphasize different aspects of the nature and function of the mature madhhab, but these views largely harmonize. Hurvitz provides one of the more sweeping characterizations: "The *madhāhib* operated in a variety of ways: patronage systems that furnished their members with work in their religious and educational institutions; political interest groups that acted upon political and ideological views of their members; and an axis around which communities were formed" (2002: 11). Hurvitz's picture of madhhabs as holistic affinity groups signals how pervasive and influential they became, and helps us understand how being, say, a Hanafi as opposed to a Shafiʿi could impact one's social, professional, and political fortunes.

For his part Hallaq again emphasizes legal doctrine, defining the classical madhhab in terms of "a common doctrine accepted by a group or association of scholars" (2001b: 21). For Hallaq, central to the madhhab was loyalty to "a distinct, integral and, most importantly, *collective* legal doctrine attributed [often misleadingly] to an eponym, a master-jurist" (2005: 152, italics in original). As we have seen, Hallaq holds that this loyalty to collective doctrine grew increasingly firm and definitive over time, and should not be confused with personal loyalty to any single "jurist-*mujtahid*" (2005: 152, and see 157ff.). Hallaq further characterizes the mature madhhab as "a body of authoritative legal doctrine existing alongside individual jurists who participated in the elaboration of, or adhered to, that doctrine in accordance with an established methodology attributed exclusively to the eponym" (2005: 163). The imprecise phrase "existing alongside" conveys the fact that "madhhab" referred simultaneously to a body of doctrine on the one hand and a group of scholars on the other, but that the latter did not amount to a madhhab without the former.

The methodology of law was contentious in the formative period, but as the mature madhhabs took shape, the theory/method of all enduring schools largely coalesced into a common form. Hallaq refers to the convergence in theory/method as "the Great Synthesis, namely, the synthesis between rationalism and traditionalism" (2005: 170). This view has its roots in Schacht, and Melchert mostly concurs that the classical madhhabs exhibited significant methodological uniformity as the tension between rationalism and traditionalism largely gave way to compromise and commonality by the end of the ninth century (Melchert 2004b:12). The method so widely shared was produced mostly, if less than directly, along routes laid out most famously by al-Shāfiʿī—this method is commonly summed up as relying on four sources: Quran, sunna, analogy, and consensus, as will be discussed in Chapter 5, below.

For Makdisi and his student Melchert, the madhhab of the early tenth century and beyond was defined by a "regular course of study" in both theory/method and doctrine, "with clearly identified teachers and students, in law (*fiqh*) as distinct from *ḥadīth*" (Melchert 2004b: 4). This course of study served to qualify a jurisprudent as an authority within a given madhhab. Makdisi characterizes the mature madhhab as a "guild," an institution of professionalized teaching, learning, and legal practice, with multiple formalized levels of membership (akin to the apprentice, journeyman, and master levels of craft and trade guilds); these guilds practiced a system of licensing (*ijāza*) to accredit jurists to teach and to issue fatwas, or non-binding legal opinions (Makdisi 1984: 239–42). The guild-madhhab emerged in the physical context of the mosque-school and later the madrasa; the former often included adjacent inns for housing students and faculty, while the latter integrated this housing element directly into the madrasa building itself (1984: 244). In short, from very early the mosque often included a legal-educational function, while from the classical period onward the madrasa developed as a stand-alone college of law (often with its own small mosque within).

Never corporate bodies in the sense of being fictitious legal persons (Makdisi 1984: 251), the madhhabs were supported financially by *waqf* (pl. *awqāf*), a formal system of private "pious endowments" (Makdisi 1984: 241–2; 1981: 35–74). This arrangement kept the madhhabs and jurists independent of the state as "representatives of the umma-community [...] free and autonomous [from the] central power." Makdisi portrays the guild-madhhab as the chief mediator between the individual and the community of Muslims in that it was the institution and social entity that guided the behavior of individuals so that they could coalesce into a community: "the stable grouping of the madhhab, legitimate and permanent [...] was the legitimizing agency under whose umbrella all else became legitimate, or were otherwise declared, by the consensus of the jurisconsults, to be outside the pale of orthodoxy." With its financial autonomy rooted in *waqf*, and its partial monopoly on establishing religio-legal norms (however various its actual doctrines), the madhhab "was in fact more permanent and more legitimate than the state itself" (1984: 251). The madhhabs endured for roughly a millennium, outlasting countless dynasties.[9]

Melchert's portrait of the mature madhhab reflects Makdisi's other prominent term, "college," emphasizing the dynamics of teaching and learning over professional affiliation and socio-political power. Melchert identifies a crucial aspect of the shift toward proper law schools as a shift from jurists seeking out a wide number of teachers to gather the largest possible array of hadith, toward jurists working with a few or just one teacher with a goal of mastering the fiqh (jurisprudence) of that teacher and madhhab (2004b: 5). Alongside this he sees a shift from assembling hadith without producing any "particular literary production" to producing a *taʿlīqa*, "virtually a doctoral dissertation, defending the juridical opinions chosen by [a given] school" (2004b: 5; and see Makdisi 1981: 111–27). The classical school had a local "chief" (*raʾīs*) at the top of the local hierarchy of teachers (see Makdisi 1981: 129–32). Students were distinguished as "graduate students (*aṣḥāb*), seeking a licence from their master to teach, and undergraduates (*talāmīdh*), seeking a licence to give opinions" (Melchert 2004b: 5). The course of study revolved around the "Islamic Sciences," including Quran memorization, exegesis, and recitation; hadith studies; jurisprudence (*fiqh*), including legal theory/method (*uṣūl al-fiqh*); and religious principles (*uṣūl al-dīn*). The "literary arts" and historical studies were mostly reined into the service of the Islamic sciences (Makdisi 1981: 75, 79). The natural and philosophical sciences, deemed to be "foreign" (esp. Greek), were pursued in private study or sometimes included under the umbrella of hadith studies in madrasas (Makdisi 1981: 78). An important mode of training in madrasas was disputation (*munāẓara*), sessions of oral debate of fine points of law; established scholars could draw large crowds to sessions lasting late into the night (Makdisi 1981: 128–52, esp. 133–4; 1984: 240; and Melchert 2004c). The mature madhhab also produced biographical dictionaries (*ṭabaqāt*) of its adherents, combining aspects of a register of membership and an institutional history—these have been an important source of information for historians.

A study of the madhhab in the literature of mature Islamic legal theory (*uṣūl al-fiqh*) has been made by Bernard Weiss. How closely actual practices conformed to theory is an open question, but this source material helps reveal the self-understanding of jurists regarding the nature and role of the classical madhhab. We find that a school—as a grouping of people—was commonly referred to using expressions such as *aṣḥāb* (companions) (Weiss 2005: 2); the term madhhab normally referred to the "legal doctrine that binds members of a school together." This doctrine was that of a *mujtahid*, one of the relatively few individual scholars deemed authoritative due to his masterly skill in deriving specific rules from the textual sources of the law (Quran and hadith). The recognized, inherent ambiguity of these two sources, however, guaranteed that the mujtahids' efforts would produce varied results (2005: 3–5). The majority of Muslims, even many scholars, are not mujtahids, therefore "if they wish to live according to the law, [they have] no recourse but to seek guidance from those who are" (2005: 3). Following a mujtahid (rather than seeking guidance independently and directly from scriptural texts, *ijtihād*) is called *taqlīd*, literally the "adorning" of a mujtahid with authority (2005: 4–5), and adherence to a madhhab is called *iltizām* (2005: 6, "more or less equivalent to the term *taqlīd*"), normally expressed via self-declarations such as "I follow so-and-so's madhhab" (*anā ʿalā madhhab fulān*) which "amounts to making a covenant (*ʿahd*) with oneself." Weiss here highlights the extent to which a madhhab was a conceptual entity.

9 In the post-classical era the Sufi *ṭarīqa* (order, lodge) often had similar—overlapping or competing—legitimacy and influence, a matter beyond the scope of the present chapter.

Weiss's research shows that jurists wrestled with questions of doctrinal variety and with the nature of a mujtahid's authority. In cases of disagreement, mujtahids were either considered all correct or, alternatively, only one was correct—which one only being revealed on Judgment Day. Either view led to accepting doctrinal plurality as an irreducible fact (2005: 5). Jurists debated the leeway of choice afforded to non-mujtahids, and these debates produced a range of positions—from requiring non-transferrable, wholesale loyalty, at one extreme, to the apparently more rare opinion that allowed near total freedom, at the other. A middle position held that once having followed a mujtahid on a particular legal issue one was bound to continue doing so, but for new legal issues one could adopt the doctrine of a different mujtahid (2005: 5–8). One who belonged to a given madhhab might still "propound doctrines not found within the body of doctrine of the eponymic founder," but divergent positions were "viewed as falling within the doctrinal space framed by the madhhab" (2005: 2). That is, the doctrine of a madhhab was less constraining than we might expect, and members of a given madhhab theoretically enjoyed considerable doctrinal freedom.

Taqlīd is today frequently regarded as a non-mujtahid's "blind imitation" of the doctrine established by a mujtahid. For the classical period such a characterization is highly misleading. *Taqlīd* was understood as abiding by the doctrine of a madhhab, a crucial element of loyalty to or "membership" in a madhhab, and laypersons might well unquestioningly take direction from jurists regarding Sharia-sanctioned behavior, but for the many levels of jurists within a madhhab, *taqlīd* "ranged from simple reproduction of doctrine to full reenactment of legal reasoning and textual evidence" (Hallaq 2001a: 113). For trained jurists, *taqlīd* had less to do with meekly getting in line behind an authority and more to do with "defense of the school as a methodological and interpretive entity" (Hallaq 2001b: 21). As the madhhabs matured, *taqlīd* increasingly involved deriving from earlier generations' casuistry a set of systematic and abstract general principles governing the various areas of law, the principles that came to embody madhhab identity (see Hallaq 2001a: 114).

If we now better understand the nature of madhhab affiliation for the elite scholarly class, a few words are in order on the affiliation of the general population. As noted above, Hurvitz attributes the wide appeal of early Hanbalism to the madhhab's emphasis on pious moral conduct and mild asceticism, an appeal enhanced by the success of Hanbalis in resisting perceived government oppression during the *miḥna*. If amenable to generalization (another topic worthy of further inquiry), this would suggest that specific doctrines, so crucial to jurists, were of marginal importance to less educated Muslims. Once established in the classical period, madhhabs came to prevail in geographical regions, and in this situation affiliation was largely inherited—that is, one was born into a Hanafi context, for example, and likely knew little of the prospect or implications of changing affiliations. Madhhab affiliation for many implicitly shaped their daily life: details of ritual practice and of marriage, divorce, and inheritance law. Larger cities might have produced situations in which laypeople would notice details of madhhab doctrinal difference—for example, economic law could differ significantly among the madhhabs and relative advantage in this arena could be pertinent.[10] Still, Hurvitz's descriptions of the madhhab as having "huge followings of lay, uneducated believers," and as combinations of patronage systems, political interest groups, and community axes, however accurate, should not tempt us to see ordinary Muslims as having extensive knowledge of madhhab doctrines or experience of madhhab differences. Perhaps if our understanding of non-elite social history grows, we will revise these impressions.

10 Hanafi jurists in particular produced legal literature outlining ways to meet the letter of the law while maximizing financial or other advantage (see Horii 2002).

References

Brockopp, Jonathan E. 2000. *Early Mālikī Law: Ibn ʿAbd al-Ḥakam and His Major Compendium of Jurisprudence*. Leiden: Brill.

———. 2005a. The Minor Compendium of Ibn ʿAbd al-Ḥakam (d. 214/829) and Its Reception in the Early Mālikī School. *Islamic Law and Society* 12(2): 149–81.

———. 2005b. Theorizing Charismatic Authority in Early Islamic Law. *Comparative Islamic Studies* 1(2): 129–58.

Calder, Norman. 1993. *Studies in Early Muslim Jurisprudence*. Oxford: Clarendon Press.

Crone, Patricia. 1987. *Roman, Provincial and Islamic Law: The Origins of the Islamic Patronate*. Cambridge: Cambridge University Press.

Donner, Fred M. 2005. The Islamic Conquests. In *A Companion to the History of the Middle East*, ed. Y.M. Choueiri, pp. 28–51. Malden, MA: Oxford: Blackwell.

———. 2010. *Muhammad and the Believers: At the Origins of Islam*. Cambridge, MA: The Belknap Press of Harvard University Press.

El Shamsy, Ahmed. 2007. The First Shāfiʿī: The Traditionalist Legal Thought of Abū Yaʿqūb al-Buwayṭī (d. 231/846). *Islamic Law and Society* 14(3): 301–41.

———. 2008. Rethinking *Taqlīd* in the Early Shāfiʿī School. *Journal of the American Oriental Society* 128(1): 1–23.

Fierro, Maribel. 2005. Proto-Malikis, Malikis, and Reformed Malikis in al-Andalus. In *The Islamic School of Law: Evolution, Devolution, and Progress*, ed. P. Bearman et al., pp. 57–76. Cambridge, MA: Islamic Legal Studies Program, Harvard Law School.

Hallaq, Wael B. 2001a. *Authority, Continuity, and Change in Islamic Law*. Cambridge: Cambridge University Press.

———. 2001b. From Regional to Personal Schools of Law? A Reevaluation. *Islamic Law and Society* 8(1): 1–26.

———. 2004. Review of *The Formation of Ḥanbalism: Piety into Power* by Nimrod Hurvitz. *Journal of Islamic Studies* 15(3): 345–7.

———. 2005. *The Origins and Evolution of Islamic Law*. Cambridge: Cambridge University Press.

Horii, Satoe. 2002. Reconsideration of Legal Devices (*Ḥiyal*) in Islamic Jurisprudence: The Ḥanafīs and Their "Exits" (*Makhārij*). *Islamic Law and Society* 9(3): 312–57.

Hurvitz, Nimrod. 2000. Schools of Law and Historical Context: Re-examining the Formation of the Ḥanbalī *Madhhab*. *Islamic Law and Society* 7(1): 37–64.

———. 2002. *The Formation of Ḥanbalism: Piety into Power*. London: RoutledgeCurzon.

Judd, Steven C. 2005. Al-Awzāʿī and Sufyān al-Thawrī: The Umayyad Madhhab? In *The Islamic School of Law: Evolution, Devolution, and Progress*, ed. P. Bearman et al., pp. 10–25. Cambridge, MA: Islamic Legal Studies Program, Harvard Law School.

Lowry, Joseph E. 2007. *Early Islamic Legal Theory: The Risāla of Muḥammad ibn Idrīs al-Shāfiʿī*. Leiden: Brill.

Maghen, Ze'ev. 2003. Dead Tradition: Joseph Schacht and the Origins of "Popular Practice". *Islamic Law and Society* 10(3): 276–347.

Makdisi, George. 1981. *The Rise of Colleges: Institutions of Learning in Islam and the West*. Edinburgh: Edinburgh University Press.

———. 1984. The Guilds of Law in Medieval Legal History: An Inquiry into the Origins of the Inns of Court. *Zeitschrift für Geschichte der arabisch-islamischen Wissenschaften* 1: 233–52. Reprinted in idem, *Religion, Law, and Learning in Classical Islam*. Hampshire, UK: Variorum, 1991.

Melchert, Christopher. 1997a. The Adversaries of Aḥmad ibn Ḥanbal. *Arabica* 44(2): 234–53.

———. 1997b. *The Formation of the Sunni Schools of Law, 9th–10th Centuries C.E.* Leiden: Brill.

———. 1999. How Ḥanafism Came to Originate in Kufa and Traditionalism in Medina. *Islamic Law and Society* 6(3): 318–47.

———. 2004a. Aḥmad Ibn Ḥanbal and the Qur'an. *Journal of Qur'anic Studies* 6(2): 22–34.

———. 2004b. The Formation of the Sunnī Schools of Law. In *The Formation of Islamic Law*, ed. W.B Hallaq, pp. 351–66. Burlington, VT: Ashgate/Variorum.

———. 2004c. The Etiquette of Learning in the Early Islamic Study Circle. In *Law and Education in Medieval Islam: Studies in Memory of Professor George Makdisi*, ed. J.E. Lowry et al., pp. 33–44. Warminster: E.J.W. Gibb Memorial Trust.

———. 2006. *Ahmad ibn Hanbal*. Oxford: Oneworld.

Joseph Schacht. 1955. The Schools of Law and Later Developments of Jurisprudence. In *Law in the Middle East*, ed. M. Khadduri and H.J. Liebesny, pp. 57–84. Washington: Middle East Institute.

———. 1964. *An Introduction to Islamic Law*. Oxford: Clarendon Press.

———. 1967. *The Origins of Muhammadan Jurisprudence*. Corr. ed. Oxford: Clarendon Press.

Schoeler, Gregor. 1997. Writing and Publishing on the Use and Function of Writing in the First Centuries of Islam. *Arabica* 44(3): 423–35.

Tsafrir, Nurit. 2004. *The History of an Islamic School of Law: The Early Spread of Hanafism*. Cambridge, MA: Islamic Legal Studies Program, Harvard Law School.

Weiss, Bernard. 2005. The Madhhab in Islamic Legal Theory. In *The Islamic School of Law: Evolution, Devolution, and Progress*, ed. P. Bearman et al., pp. 1–9. Cambridge, MA: Islamic Legal Studies Program, Harvard Law School.

Deriving Rules of Law

Robert Gleave

In the ninth century Muslim jurists began to conceive of the law as a coherent body of legal norms rather than as a collection of disconnected rules. This understanding of a unified legal framework undoubtedly precipitated many of the legal disputes that contributed to the rise of schools of law. Criticism of an opponent's position in the eighth century was increasingly expressed by appeal to principles that underpinned the legal system and to which one was committed and to which one's opponents had, one argued, failed to adhere. Coherence of the law was expressed in the formulation of these principles, which achieved three objectives: they determined the sources from which the law was derived; they described the mechanism whereby rules might be deduced from these sources; and they delineated the parameters of who could carry out this deduction.

The drive to bring laws into a single, consistent framework of understanding led to the emergence of a distinct genre of literature called *uṣūl al-fiqh*—literally, "the roots of understanding," but more conveniently glossed as legal theory.[1] Consistency was not proposed merely for intellectual satisfaction. It was crucial for the law's continued authority that contradictions between rules were kept to a minimum. Illogical and unexplained incongruities between two rules would not only make the law difficult to enforce; they would also undermine its authority, and the authority of those who were promulgating it. But consistency of the law was important for another reason as well: the body of rules that came together to form the law was increasingly seen as divine in origin. That is, the Sharia, the term that came to be used to refer to the law of Islam, was the expression of God's will for humankind, and consistency, at least at some minimal level, needed to be demonstrated—internal consistency was evidence of a single divine guide who was the author of the law and who had laid down rules for its derivation and implementation. It was the jurists' understanding of these rules that were, by the early eleventh century, set out in works of *uṣūl al-fiqh* in which the sources of law and their authoritative interpretation were described, and it is the prevailing discussions of Western scholarship on *uṣūl al-fiqh* that form the focus of this chapter.

It should be said at the outset that there are a number of general surveys that have helped define the academic field of Islamic legal theory and introduce it to a wider audience. Three that have proven particularly influential are:

Robert Gleave is Professor of Arabic Studies at the University of Exeter and Director of its Institute of Arab and Islamic Studies. He is the author of *Islam and Literalism: Literal Meaning and Interpretation in Islamic Legal Theory* (2012), *Scripturalist Islam: The History and Doctrines of the Akhbārī Shīʿī School* (2007), and *Inevitable Doubt: Two Theories of Shīʿī Jurisprudence* (2000), the (co-)editor of three volumes, and the principal or co-investigator of four large, funded research projects.

1 When it is clear that one is speaking of the law, the phrase is often shortened to *uṣūl*, as it will be here; it is then not to be mistaken for *uṣūl al-dīn* "the fundamentals of the religion." One who engages in *uṣūl al-fiqh* is termed an *uṣūlī*.

Mohammad Hashim Kamali's *Principles of Islamic Jurisprudence* (1991), which gives a detailed and at times quite technical account of the debates and discussions within a work of *uṣūl al-fiqh*, though with little historical analysis;

Wael Hallaq's *A History of Islamic Legal Theories* (1997), which combines a historical and content analysis with a particularly useful section on *uṣūl al-fiqh* in the modern period;

Bernard Weiss's *The Spirit of Islamic Law* (1998), in which a thematic approach is taken to the issues that dominate works of *uṣūl al-fiqh*.

There remains, however, the need for a detailed historical account of the development of the genre. The 1984 doctoral dissertation by Aron Zysow, since 2013 on the market in corrected and slightly updated form, is a fourth work in which the content of works of *uṣūl al-fiqh* are summarized. Unlike the above three works, however, it cannot really be thought of as a general survey; it is, in fact, a piece of fundamental research on the relationship between *uṣūl al-fiqh* and *kalām* (theology) in the Hanafi school, with additional comments on other expressions of *uṣūl al-fiqh*.

Early Scholarship on the Literary Genre

The genre of *uṣūl al-fiqh* has received serious Western scholarly attention only since the mid-1970s, and it remains a minority, though growing, interest. The first proper academic account of *uṣūl al-fiqh* in a European language is given by the pioneering Hungarian Islamicist Ignaz Goldziher in *Die Ẓâhiriten* (1884). The work was limited necessarily by his focus on the Zahiri school, yet it gave a detailed description of many of the commonly accepted underlying principles of *uṣūl al-fiqh*. Joseph Schacht then expounded on the development of theoretical thinking of the law (1950), giving to Muḥammad b. Idrīs al-Shāfiʿī (d. 204/820), eponym of the Shafiʿi school, a founding role. Much of the scholarship following Schacht was taken up by Francophone scholars. Robert Brunschvig published a number of articles (collected in Brunschvig 1976) dealing with the development of major themes in Islamic legal theory, making more explicit the link between theological doctrine and *uṣūl al-fiqh*. George Makdisi wrote a study of the theological and legal theory of Ibn ʿAqīl (1963), a thinker whose *uṣūl al-fiqh* Makdisi was to work on extensively subsequently (1996–2002). One of Brunschvig's students, Abdelmagid Turki (ʿAbd al-Majīd al-Turkī), continued this work in the 1970s and 1980s, producing studies of the early development of *uṣūl* (for example, Turki 1973). Several French scholars along with Turki—Marie Bernand, Daniel Gimaret, Éric Chaumont—have done the field a great service by painstakingly editing a series of *uṣūl* works that were previously in manuscript (Turki 1986, 1995; Bernand and Chaumont 2003; Chaumont 1993–94). Chaumont's translation (1999) of Abū Isḥāq al-Shīrāzī's (d. 476/1083) *Kitāb al-Lumaʿ* remains the most usable translation of an *uṣūl* text in a Western language, and is accompanied by an introduction on the history of the development of *uṣūl al-fiqh*. In the English-speaking world, study of *uṣūl* was largely ignored after Schacht, and only in the 1970s did it reappear with short studies by Bernard Weiss (1974, 1986, with a focus on legal language) and Nabil Shehaby (1975, 1982, with a focus on logical and analogical reasoning). In 1984 two important doctoral theses were completed. The above-mentioned one by Aron Zysow provided for the first time in English an account of the main disputes within the genre of *uṣūl al-fiqh*, outlining the sources of Islamic law according to *uṣūl* works, and how they might be interpreted. The other, that of Wael Hallaq, was a detailed account of the institution of *ijtihād* (the personal reasoning of the individual jurist), as described in works of *uṣūl al-fiqh*. With the contemporaneous studies of Weiss and Norman Calder (1983), the field of *uṣūl al-fiqh* was firmly established within the burgeoning discipline of Islamic legal studies. As scholarly publications on Islamic law increased in the 1990s, studies in *uṣūl*-related matters expanded also and there emerged a number of intra-disciplinary disputes that have animated the field ever since.

The principal areas that have generated academic dispute and discussion, which form the focus of the subsequent sections of this chapter, include (1) the emergence of *uṣūl al-fiqh* as a distinct discipline of study and as a genre of legal literature; (2) the role of *uṣūl al-fiqh* in the process of law derivation; (3) the development of the component parts of Islamic legal theory and their inter-relationship; and (4) the extent to which theological concerns, rather than purely legal matters, determine the character of individual jurists' account of legal theory.

The Emergence and Genre of Legal Theory

Theoretical reflection on law as a system by jurists before al-Shāfiʿī was not entirely absent (see, for example, Brockopp 2001), but it remained at a rudimentary level. By theoretical reflection I mean debates about the content of a particular legal rule (insofar as they expressed general positions concerning the law) as well as more systematic discussions over the right way to derive rules, and, more broadly, the nature of the law itself. Schacht and others identified two opposing groups prior to al-Shāfiʿī, *ahl al-raʾy* and *ahl al-ḥadīth* (see further, Chapter 3, above). The two camps were not only concerned with jurisprudence proper, but represented as well two distinct ways of carrying out religious (including legal) investigation. To determine the most appropriate rule in legal terms, the *ahl al-raʾy* argued for a certain amount of liberty on the part of the individual jurist to reason (that is, use his own opinion or *raʾy*), while the *ahl al-ḥadīth*, as their name implies, required stricter adherence to the behavior and sayings of the Prophet, his Companions, and other notables of early Islam. This was, in a sense, a debate over legal theory, albeit in a less comprehensive manner than the later debates within works of *uṣūl al-fiqh*. Within the Muslim tradition, the schools of law emerged from these two groups, the former based in Kufa and Iraq, the latter in Medina and the Hijaz. These historical, geographical, and ideological associations have been subjected to some questioning in recent scholarship (Melchert 1999; Hallaq 2001; Tsafrir 2004; and see further, Chapter 4, above), but wherever they actually developed, their differences were over matters of legal theory and later became central elements of the discipline.

Another example of a pre-Shāfiʿī dispute of legal theoretical importance is around the term *sunna*. This has already been discussed in Chapter 3, above, although the concept's centrality for understanding the formation of *uṣūl al-fiqh* is important. As has been noted, the term did not have a consistent application, nor was there a unanimously accepted notion of the Prophet's example being legally authoritative. Similarly, the Quran as a source of law may have been generally recognized in the eighth century, but what this meant for the actual derivation of the law does not, as far as we can tell from the sources, seem to have consumed the attention of leading legal thinkers of the period before al-Shāfiʿī such as Mālik and Abū Ḥanīfa. Thus, Western scholarship has generally followed Schacht in giving a decisive role to al-Shāfiʿī in the introduction of theoretical justification for the law as a system. This was brought into question in 1993 by two separate studies. Hallaq proposed that al-Shāfiʿī was not, in fact, particularly influential during his life or immediately after it, evidencing the shortage of references to him, his ideas, or his works until well into the tenth century; Calder went further, arguing that both the terminology and the interpretive mechanisms described in al-Shāfiʿī's *al-Risāla* appear more congruent with intellectual developments after him and therefore the hermeneutic system attributed to him is better dated a generation or so later.

These theories have themselves been subjected to serious criticism since their publication (for example, Lowry 2004; El Shamsy 2007), but they did open up a debate in Western scholarship concerning the origins of *uṣūl al-fiqh*. While al-Shāfiʿī's *al-Risāla* is not on the whole seen as a work of *uṣūl al-fiqh* proper, it is generally recognized as the first surviving attempt to provide a relatively comprehensive set of rules for understanding the sources of law, particularly the idea of Prophetic Sunna, and how, thereby, the law might be derived. The definitive, comprehensive study of al-Shāfiʿī's *al-Risāla* was produced by Joseph Lowry (2007; see also Tillschneider 2006: 31–71; Yahia 2009), but for the history of *uṣūl al-fiqh* it does not solve the puzzle, as was noted by Hallaq, of the next extant works in which are the same theoretical concerns postdating al-Shāfiʿī by over a century and a half—in the development of an intellectual science this is a mystifyingly lengthy pause in literary production. Thus, *al-Muqaddima fī uṣūl al-fiqh* of Ibn al-Qaṣṣār (d. 398/1008) and *al-Fuṣūl fī ʿilm al-uṣūl* of Abū Bakr al-Jaṣṣāṣ (d. 370/980) appear almost as fully formed works of *uṣūl al-fiqh* ex nihilo, with only al-Shāfiʿī's *al-Risāla* some 150 years previous as a credible precursor. The gap in *uṣūl* sources has closed somewhat in recent years by tracing the titles of lost works in the extant literature (Stewart 2002, 2004), by manuscript research that shows continued interest in legal-theoretical matters immediately after al-Shāfiʿī (El Shamsy and Zysow 2012), and by following the continued importance of issues shared by *uṣūl* and other disciplines of the Islamic sciences, particularly theology (Tillschneider 2006; Vishanoff 2011). According to most current scholars, therefore, the absence of extant *uṣūl* works after al-Shāfiʿī is not the result of a lack of theoretical interest within the juristic tradition but simply an accident of history.

The unstructured, almost raw nature of *al-Risāla*'s presentation of legal theory is certainly quite different from the organized, honed discourse of the later extant *uṣūl* works; this can be seen as evidence that there must have been some intervening but now lost material in which the discipline was further developed. It is clear, for example, that al-Shāfiʿī's attempts to conjoin the excesses of the *ahl al-raʾy* with the textualism of the *ahl al-ḥadīth* did not end the dispute between the two trends in his lifetime, and that this dispute eventually gave the particular schools of jurisprudence some of their distinctive intellectual character. What is also clear is that by the late tenth century the basic structure of a work of *uṣūl* was established, the primary topics of concern (the recurrent *masāʾil* or questions) were delineated, and the principal groups of juristic opinion (the Muʿtazila argue this position, the Hanafis argue that one, etc.) were relatively stable. This is not to say that there was no subsequent development. Hallaq (1992) has argued vehemently against the view (attributed by him to Christiaan Snouck Hurgronje, Schacht, Brunschvig, and more recently Patricia Crone) that Islamic law generally and *uṣūl* in particular was fixed and unchanging after the eleventh century. This, Hallaq asserts, is an unacceptable (perhaps deliberately distorted) account of the discipline's development. Nevertheless, after the first wave of extant works in the late tenth century, the works of *uṣūl* from the eleventh century and beyond do fall into a relatively predictable pattern, with issues discussed and elaborated in a steady structure. New discussions were added and new positions evinced, but the tradition of both presentation and thought is recognizable.

The Component Parts of "Classical" Legal Theory

The standard account of the purpose of *uṣūl al-fiqh* works is that they provide a handbook for the jurisprudent in his derivation of legal rules from the sources of law. They provide the jurist with a set of proofs whereby the sources are known to be reliable and authoritative, and they provide a set of hermeneutic mechanisms that the jurist can employ when reading the texts and searching for evidence for this or that legal rule. Thus, for example, the first two sources given for the Sharia are—as is widely described—the Quran and Sunna, and so it is, theoretically, to them that the jurist first turns when searching for a rule to answer a question of law. These truths appear axiomatic, and in a landmark article (1984) Weiss has demonstrated how writers of *uṣūl al-fiqh* generally, and the great Sayf al-Dīn al-Āmidī (d. 631/1233) in particular, established the "primacy of revelation." But this apparently simple principle of legal exegetical procedure is discussed in works of *uṣūl al-fiqh* as problematic in two respects. First, there is the question of why one should follow the Quran and Sunna as sources of knowledge of God's will for mankind. This is answered through recourse to theological principles concerning how to demonstrate the truthfulness of a prophet and therefore follow the message he brings, and why his actions are likely to be accurate reflections of God's will since he is an obedient servant of God. An analysis of these theological questions is often, though not always, present in a work of *uṣūl*; when present it shows the influence of similar discussions in works of strict theology (*kalām*). Once that question is settled, a second, related question is invariably discussed in *uṣūl al-fiqh* works—how does one know that the texts of the Quran and Sunna are accurate reflections of the message brought by the Prophet Muḥammad? For this, one needs a theory of the transmission of texts and it is in works of *uṣūl* that this theory is most extensively explored. In the secondary literature, this theory of the transmission of texts was outlined by A.S. Tritton (1952), and then more fully by Weiss (1985), and revolves around the technical term of *tawātur*. The term is difficult to translate, but in the context of *uṣūl al-fiqh*, it can be glossed "recurrent transmission." Weiss (1985: 86) presents it nicely when he states:

> As a technical term of traditional Muslim scholarship [*tawātur*] has reference to the recurrence of statements about past events. According to the theory which Ghazâlî and other *uṣûlîs* (writers on *uṣûl al-fiqh*) propound, the recurrence of such reports produces in the mind of the hearers a knowledge that such statements are true. The theory is expressed succinctly in the phrase *al-tawâtur yufîd al-ʿilm* ("recurrence impacts knowledge") which appears repeatedly in works of *uṣûl al-fiqh*.

In summary then, a report is *mutawātir* (that is, recurrently transmitted) when it has been transmitted independently by a sufficient number of people such that collusion between them is impossible.[2] When it reaches this stage, the certainty of the sound transmission of the report impresses itself upon the individual in an irrepressible way. This fundamental building block of the theory of textual transmission was not really present in al-Shāfiʿī, though it does form the background of al-Jaṣṣāṣ's thinking in his *Fuṣūl*, and is elaborated upon further by subsequent writers—including al-Ghazālī (d. 505/1111), the subject of Weiss's 1985 article. Anything that falls short of this *tawātur* standard is termed an "isolated report" (*khabar wāḥid*). The Quran, for example, has been transmitted by so many people over such a long period of time that its text is "of certain transmission" (*qaṭʿī l-ṣuḍūr* or *qaṭʿī l-wurūd*). Nearly all the reports (*aḥādīth, akhbār*) that indicate what the Prophet did or said on particular occasions (that is, the Sunna) are "isolated." Contrariwise, Hallaq has argued that the debate over the authenticity or otherwise of hadith, which has troubled both Muslim and non-Muslim commentators since Goldziher and Schacht, is a "pseudo-problem" since Muslim jurists do not, in truth, expect this level of certainty for the derivation of legal opinions (Hallaq 1999). Isolated reports of the Sunna can still be used in legal argumentation; they are merely of less strength in the argumentation than reports that are recurrently transmitted (*mutawātir*). And, of course, within the category of isolated reports there are variable levels of strength, some with more chains of transmission (sg. *isnād*), others with more reliable ones.

Turning to the so-called third source of Islamic law, namely, *ijmāʿ* or consensus, less work has been done on the origins of this doctrine than on its central role in classical legal theory. George Hourani's study was based on his particular reading of Ibn Ḥazm's (d. 456/1064) *al-Iḥkām* and al-Ghazālī's *al-Mustaṣfā*, and strikes the reader today as rather polemical; he argued that since the doctrine of consensus was based on a hadith of the Prophet in which he says "my community shall not agree upon an error," and since the authenticity of this hadith is, itself, based upon a consensus, then the conclusion one necessarily draws is that *ijmāʿ* is a doctrine without foundation and classical Islamic legal theory has been based on a mistake (Hourani 1964). A corrective can be found in Hallaq's contribution (1986) summarizing the manner in which *ijmāʿ* was shown to be a valid source of law in medieval *uṣūl al-fiqh*. Hallaq's method synthesizes his close reading of classical *uṣūl* sources, and the article has been taken as the point of departure for subsequent references to consensus in

2 For explanation of the term *mutawātir* in hadith study, see Chapter 3, above.

Western scholarship (see, for example, Kuran 1989; Fadel 1996). Specific studies on individual doctrines of *ijmāʿ* include Marie Bernand's examination (1969) of two Muʿtazilī thinkers, Ibrāhīm al-Naẓẓām (d. 231/845) and ʿAbd al-Jabbār (d. 415/1025), in which she discusses the early proponents and opponents of *ijmāʿ*—al-Naẓẓām, for example, is said to have rejected *ijmāʿ* because he did not consider the fact of mere agreement of people to be any proof of truthfulness—and Calder's study of *ijmāʿ* within the theory of al-Shāfiʿī (1983), in which he showed how it was tied to a theory of juristic authority about who had the right to interpret the texts. Outside of these, studies of *ijmāʿ* have focused on the theory as found in individual works of *uṣūl al-fiqh*, and the field can still be said to be at the point of description rather than the production of grand theories.

Sunni jurists conceive of a fourth source of Islamic law, namely, *qiyās* (sometimes glossed as "analogical reasoning"). The history of *uṣūlī* discussions of *qiyās* appears as a concerted effort to prevent the accusation of arbitrariness taking hold, which can be seen as a continuation of the pre-Shāfiʿī disputes around *raʾy* vs. hadith. For the critics of *qiyās*, the process consisted of a series of speculations, viz., (1) the "reason" (*ʿilla*) behind a rule is guessed at, (2) the identification of its presence is made in a new context, and (3) the ruling in the known case is subsequently transferred to the unknown case—thus, (1) grape wine is forbidden because it is (thought to be) intoxicating, (2) date wine is also intoxicating, and (3) date wine is forbidden along with grape wine. The engaging way in which the critics condemned the process of *qiyās*, and the clarity of their thought, led to the early studies of *qiyās* being dominated by studies of the rejection rather than elaboration of *qiyās*. Goldziher's exposition of the Zahiri rejection of *qiyās* (specifically that outlined by Ibn Ḥazm in his writings) enables him to describe not only the doctrine but also some of its weaknesses. Ibn Ḥazm's rejection of *qiyās* was due to the uncertainty one has about why in revelation this or that action was prohibited or made obligatory. Unless an indication for one or another ruling was explicitly declared, for Ibn Ḥazm to make a guess was tantamount to claiming access to the mind of God. This was continued in Roger Arnaldez's classic study of Ibn Ḥazm's theories of language and law (1956). Schacht's comments on *qiyās* were brief and hardly scratched the surface of this highly sophisticated theory of when and how legal rules could be applied to novel circumstances. Notwithstanding the subsequent work of Chafik Chehata (1966) and Shehaby (1975), it is the writings of Hallaq (1989) and later Weiss (2010: 542–646) that lay the groundwork for the ensuing detailed study of the doctrine of *qiyās*.

Finally, and perhaps most controversially, there is the debate around *ijtihād*—or personal juristic reasoning. In the 1960s and 1970s Schacht, Noel Coulson, and others had propagated a notion in Western scholarship that the ability of the individual Muslim jurist to interpret the sources and produce new rulings had died out in the eleventh century, and that subsequent jurists resigned themselves to following or imitating the jurisprudence of the great legal minds of the past. This "following" or "imitation" was termed *taqlīd*, and it was viewed by Muslim reformers and many Western scholars in resoundingly negative terms. Schacht in particular (1967) linked this development with the establishment of the four "orthodox" schools of Islamic law in Sunni Islam. It is perhaps not surprising that this notion of the "closing of the gate (*bāb*) of *ijtihād*" had taken hold, since classical Muslim legal scholars had introduced it and a number of Muslim reformers of the day had argued that a new *ijtihād* was necessary in order to revivify the supposedly moribund discipline of traditional Islamic legal studies. The ossification of Islamic legal thought was blamed both by the orientalists and by some Muslim reformers for the "backwardness" of Islamic legal thought. In articles developed out of his Ph.D. thesis, Hallaq challenged this notion in the 1980s. He attempted to show that *ijtihād* did not die out and, in a theme that has been a recurrent feature of his scholarship, Islamic law continued to develop, with new and novel opinions being devised and incorporated into the body of the law (Hallaq 1984). The "closing of the gate of *ijtihād*" was, for Hallaq, primarily a debate around the existence or non-existence of those who performed *ijtihād* (a supposed portent of the end of time) and not, in the main, a debate around the (im)possibility of legal development. As elaborated in Hallaq's later writings, the portrayal of Islamic law as sclerotic was part of an orientalist narrative (even when enunciated by Muslim reformers) that ignores the evidence of medieval jurisprudence. The theories of *ijtihād*, together with related issues of the definition of the madhhab, juristic authority, and epistemological development form the central themes in work by Éric Chaumont with particular focus on the early development of al-Shāfiʿī's *uṣūl* (for example, Chaumont 1992).

An early engagement with *ijtihād* and originality in relation to premodern Muslim jurisprudence was made by Rudolph Peters (1980). Both he and Frank Vogel (1993) recognized the continuous claim to exercise *ijtihād* by different Muslim thinkers in different legal systems since the eighteenth century, but Hallaq's early work on the subject (1984) was an instructive lesson in how a term much used in the secondary literature had not been subject to close scrutiny and its theoretical foundations had not been analyzed. Whether the gate of *ijtihād* is best understood as closed or open, though, depended on what one meant by *ijtihād*. In a carefully worded article (1996) Calder argued that Hallaq had, effectively, conflated the various levels of *ijtihād* into a single entity that was then judged to be present or absent. The discussion of *ijtihād* has to be more nuanced than this, he argued, in recognition of the fact that certain types of *ijtihād* were viewed as unavailable by the medieval jurists (one could not, for example, institute a new madhhab—that type of *ijtihād*, attributed to the schools' founders, was at an end). In this sense, the gate of *ijtihād* was closed. However, other levels of *ijtihād* (performed by jurists of lesser stature than the founders) may have been common: the debate in medieval *uṣūl* was on the other types of *ijtihād* that were available theoretically or in practice. That is, how much *ijtihād* was possible and how much *taqlīd*.

The varying assessments of Hallaq and Calder as to the jurisprudential thinking about *ijtihād* opened the way for a more nuanced assessment of *taqlīd*. Instead of being viewed as the mindless adherence to the conclusions of past scholarship, it was seen as, potentially at least, a constructive engagement with tradition. A special issue of the journal *Islamic Law and Society* devoted to this theme appeared in 1996 (and included Calder's article). It provoked much debate within the field, and with Hallaq's guest-editorial comments (and disagreements) in an introductory section, it demonstrated the vibrancy of the field of *uṣūl al-fiqh* (see also Jackson 1996; Fadel 1996). What was at stake was the extent to which originality in Islamic legal thinking had been circumscribed by the edifice of fiqh, and whether legal theory (*uṣūl al-fiqh*) could provide a way out of these debates.

The jurist qualified to carry out *ijtihād* (the *mujtahid*) was in works of *uṣūl al-fiqh* provided with an arsenal of interpretive techniques. Apart from *qiyās* already mentioned, a categorization scheme of binary opposites was devised. Among these were the general and the particular (*ʿāmm/khāṣṣ*), the unrestricted and the restricted (*muṭlaq/muqayyad*), the literal and the tropical (*ḥaqīqa/majāz*), the clear and the ambiguous (*ẓāhir/mujmal*), the explicit and the implicit (*naṣṣ/mafhūm*), and the abrogating and the abrogated (*nāsikh/mansūkh*). Every statement in revelation could be subjected to analysis using these categorizations, and classification as one or the other had an impact on the understanding of the intended meaning of the speaker. So, for example, the command "Cut off the hands of the thief, male or female ..." (Q 5:38) would seem to apply to all thieves, regardless of how much might have been stolen and under what circumstances the theft was carried out. In this sense the Quranic command appears "general" (*ʿāmm*). However, elsewhere in revelation there are statements that make it clear that the speaker (in this case, God speaking in the Quran) actually meant only certain types of theft (for example, that which was freely carried out, that which concerned something known to belong to another person, that which had a value above a specified amount, etc.). These restrictions "particularize" (*takhṣīṣ*) the general statement, making the intended meaning not *ʿāmm* but *khāṣṣ*. Such particularization obviously affects how a verse acts as an indicator (*dalīl*) of the law. Similarly, the theory of abrogation (*naskh*) requires contradictory and irreconcilable rules in revelation to be situated at different points in the Prophet's life; the rule delivered last was said to be the abrogator (*nāsikh*) of the earlier, abrogated one (*mansūkh*).

Mechanisms such as these occupy much space in works of *uṣūl al-fiqh* texts and are clearly conceived of as central to the *mujtahid's* task (on the development of these hermeneutic mechanisms, and thoughts on language generally, see Schöck 2005; Tillschneider 2006; Vishanoff 2011). Given their prominence it is a little surprising that they have not received attention from Western scholarship until relatively recently. As with *qiyās*, the avid Zahiri opponents of many of these hermeneutic mechanisms were the subject of the most extensive study in early studies of *uṣūl* texts (Goldziher 1884; Arnaldez 1956). The question of whether an imperative expressed by the speaker made the ensuing act obligatory (*wājib*) or whether it fell into another assessment category was discussed by Jeanette Wakin (Wakin 1990). The theory of abrogation was the subject of a sustained analysis not only of *uṣūl al-fiqh*, but also of Quranic commentary, hadith, and other genres, by John Burton (1990); while a dating for its emergence within Islamic legal theory was put forward by Christopher Melchert (2002). The first influential account of the hermeneutic system in *uṣūl al-fiqh*, however, was presented by Zysow in his doctoral thesis (1984), and this was further elaborated by Weiss in his study of the *uṣūl* of the thirteenth-century Shafiʿi jurist Sayf al-Dīn al-Āmidī (2010, to be discussed in more detail below). As with other areas of *uṣūl al-fiqh*, Western scholarship has concentrated on understanding and presenting the theory as found there, although a few theses have been proposed that deviate from the analytical focus. For one, Hallaq (1989) sought to redirect the study of *uṣūl al-fiqh* by making the often overlooked point that *qiyās* was used not only for strict analogical reasoning, but also for many hermeneutic techniques, such as the notion of inference (*mafhūm*). Gideon Libson (2003) widened the field by speculating about the cross-fertilization of (and possible hermeneutic influence between) Jewish and Islamic legal theory in the area of custom, and custom's role in legal derivation.[3] And Calder's controversial dating of *al-Risāla* to after the lifetime of al-Shāfiʿī by using al-Shāfiʿī's *ʿāmm/khāṣṣ* distinction has already been noted. The link between these hermeneutic concerns and theological doctrine will be examined below, but a work that will without doubt define the future study of Islamic legal hermeneutics is David Vishanoff's *The Formation of Islamic Hermeneutics*, in which Vishanoff proposes a number of theories: that al-Shāfiʿī's hermeneutics was a continuation rather than a break with previous theoretical concerns; that his main preoccupation was with the inevitable ambiguity of language, and therefore the ambiguity of the language used in revelatory sources; and that subsequent Islamic legal hermeneutics can be seen as a reaction to al-Shāfiʿī's attempt to incorporate ambiguity into the Sunni system of legal hermeneutics (Vishanoff 2011).

Within the many above-mentioned contributions to the field, non-Sunni jurists have largely been ignored. Generally speaking, Shiʿi and Ibadi jurists are seen as coming late to the genre of *uṣūl al-fiqh* and adapting it for their own purposes (for a heightened difference between Sunni and non-Sunni discourses around legal theory, see Hallaq 1997). However, there is some evidence that legal-theoretical concerns did occupy Shiʿi writers from an early period, if only to reject much of Sunni *uṣūl al-fiqh* as irrelevant. Al-Qāḍī Nuʿmān (d. 363/975), for example, wrote *Ikhtilāf uṣūl al-madhāhib* in order to establish, in part, why the Shiʿa (in particular the Ismaʿili Fatimids) did not need to employ the tool of *uṣūl al-fiqh* since the Imams guaranteed the validity of the law. Similarly, the Imamis and the Zaydis, in different ways, were concerned with legal-theoretical issues. For the Imamis this can be seen in the recorded discussions between Imam Jaʿfar al-Ṣādiq (d. 148/765) and Abū Ḥanīfa, in which the latter's failure to understand the workings of the law are exposed. Work on Imami *uṣūl al-fiqh* was first explored in detail by Brunschvig (1970) and Martin McDermott (1978; on al-Shaykh al-Mufīd [d. 413/1022]), and then by Calder (1989). A major contribution was Devin Stewart's monograph in 1998, *Islamic Legal Orthodoxy*, which examined not only the history of Sunni and Shiʿi *uṣūl al-fiqh* but, importantly, the relationship between them. Stewart's analysis was based on the transfer of Sunni law in general and of *uṣūl al-fiqh* in particular (primarily of the Shafiʿi school) into a Shiʿi milieu. Regarding the structure and content of Shiʿi *uṣūl* works, I have published on the debate in Shiʿi legal theory between Usulis and Akhbaris (Gleave 2000, 2007), on the Shiʿi refutation of *qiyās* (Gleave 2002b), and on ideas of language and legal hermeneutics in Shiʿism and the notion of literal meaning in *uṣūl al-fiqh* more generally (Gleave 2012).

3 This source can be usefully paired with Gregor Schwarb's later study (2007) of the inter-relationship of Muslim and Jewish legal and exegetical theory.

Uṣūl al-fiqh and Its Role in the Process of Law Derivation

Bernard Weiss's monumental *The Search for God's Law: Islamic Jurisprudence in the Writings of Sayf al-Dīn al-Āmidī*, published in 1992 and revised in 2010, is arguably the most important monographic publication in English in the study of classical *uṣūl al-fiqh*. By exploring the interconnected nature of the juristic thought of one scholar, Weiss reproduces the intellectual world of medieval *uṣūl al-fiqh* for the reader with disarming ease. However, with his account, Weiss also raises the fundamental question of why works of *uṣūl al-fiqh* were composed in the first place. Contrary to the *uṣūlī*'s purpose being that of a handbook for the *mutjahid* in the derivation of law, Weiss sees in the writings of al-Āmidī, and possibly in the medieval genre of *uṣūl al-fiqh* more generally, a practical legal theory that informs, or aims to inform, how jurists, judges, and other legal functionaries derive the law from the sources. This, implicitly, corrected the notion found in Schacht's work that *uṣūl al-fiqh*, in its mature phase, had lost its connection with the law in operation. The suggestion that works of *uṣūl al-fiqh* had a practical emphasis was also argued by Hallaq (1991), who indicated that to view *uṣūl* as a theoretical discipline was, ultimately, to continue to propagate the orientalist myth of the dysfunctional nature of Islamic legal thought. *Uṣūl* authors themselves often portray their efforts as an attempt to provide a resource for the jurist in their jurisprudential endeavors. All of this indicates a very close, almost causative, relationship between *uṣūl al-fiqh* and fiqh. The two spheres of Islamic law—the "branches" (*furū*ʿ), viz., substantive law, and the "roots" (*uṣūl*)—stand in an organic relationship to each other.[4]

The causative relationship between *uṣūl* and *furū*ʿ was questioned by Calder in his review of Weiss's *The Search for God's Law* (Calder 1996b). There, and elsewhere in his writings (2010), Calder argued that works of *uṣūl al-fiqh* are best seen as products of a literary tradition and intellectual development in which the concerns were almost artistic and aesthetic rather than practical. Other characterizations have also been proposed. Sherman Jackson argued (2002) on the basis of Maliki texts that the *uṣūl* justified existing rules rather than produced new norms. Zysow makes the point that *uṣūl* often reflect theological concerns rather than the production of law per se, emphasizing (2002, 2008) the inter-relationship of theology and legal theory, which Weiss well understood as at least one of the functions of *uṣūl al-fiqh*. Thus, it could be argued that the primary aim of works of *uṣūl al-fiqh* is not to provide a guidebook for jurists in their quest to discover new rulings, but rather to demonstrate that obedience to the law is theologically important because the individual elements of the law (the *furū*ʿ) are rooted in a system of legal thought sanctioned by the revelatory texts. *Uṣūl al-fiqh* can be seen as the literary expression of the theological doctrine of the unity of God and His authorship of the Sharia for all humankind: to reflect this basic theological premise, a coherent theory (the *uṣūl*) was developed.

Consensus in the field on the purpose and role of *uṣūl* was still elusive when a second conference dedicated to Islamic legal theory was convened to honor Bernard Weiss in 2009; there the relationship between *uṣūl* and *furū*ʿ and between fiqh and the application of law in history continued to be a matter of some dispute (Reinhart and Gleave 2014). This particular question was given greater focus with Ahmed Atif Ahmed's examination (2006) of *uṣūl* works devoted to *takhrīj al-furū*ʿ *min al-uṣūl* ("extracting the branches from the roots"), which was the first to try and develop a common thesis concerning the *uṣūl-furū*ʿ relationship. In the study Ahmed shows how there is no simple universal *uṣūl–furū*ʿ relationship—in fact, the relationship was differently conceived and differently activated by different authors. The tension between theory and practice (by practice, Ahmed means not actual legal practice but the areas of substantive law found in the fiqh) was, he felt, a creative one, which spurred intellectual advances in the legal sciences and prevented ossification, a conclusion that is, at the same time, plausible and difficult to demonstrate.

4 This relationship formed the basis for a conference convened by Bernard Weiss in 1999, the collected papers of which were published as *Studies in Islamic Legal Theory* (Weiss 2002).

The Theological Nature of Legal Theory

The work of Zysow and Weiss in emphasizing the theological nature of the *uṣūl* project has already been mentioned. This theological emphasis can be easily exemplified by a number of features of the *uṣūl* hermeneutic system. The ethical theories of the vying Ashʿaris and Muʿtazilis had an inevitable impact on how the Sharia, as a moral and legal code, was viewed as being justified. In simple terms, the Muʿtazilis viewed the moral qualities of actions to be external, existent properties that could be identified by the human intellect. The followers of Abū l-Ḥasan al-Ashʿarī (d. 324/935), on the other hand, considered the moral qualities of actions to be given by God and only really available through revelation. The interplay of these theological doctrines and the justification of the law (in works of *uṣūl al-fiqh*) has proved to be one of the more productive areas of academic investigation. It was explored first by Zysow and later by Kevin Reinhart (1995), who examined the greater implications of ethical and legal theory of one area of *uṣūl* discussions, namely, the moral ontology of laws given before the coming of the Sharia. More recently, Anver Emon has explored Islamic natural law theories (2010), which at first glance would seem un-Islamic given that most writers of *uṣūl al-fiqh* were Ashʿaris and therefore committed to the notion that moral and legal values were assigned to actions by divine decree and revelation rather than any natural process. However, Emon has identified a number of mechanisms whereby the notions akin to the European idea of "natural law" have crept into *uṣūl al-fiqh*. Muʿtazili theorists (such as al-Jaṣṣāṣ) obviously have a strong notion of a moral code distinct from the Sharia, to which the Sharia adheres and which judges over the Sharia (this Emon terms "hard natural law" theories). What is perhaps surprising is that elements of natural law can be seen in Ashʿari writers of *uṣūl al-fiqh*. That is, they allowed reason to dictate legal rules in certain areas of the Sharia despite their simultaneous commitment to the primacy of scripture as the primary source of legal rules. As with the work of Zysow and Weiss, the hard lines between the various theological groups are reflected in *uṣūl al-fiqh*, but also somewhat softened by the flowing and mingling of ideas from one camp to the other, not least of all in the polemic between the groups.

Worthy of note here are the notions of law that trace their source outside of the usual textual focus of *uṣūl al-fiqh*. For example, Hanafi jurists controversially argued for the validity of a hermeneutic mechanism known as *istiḥsān* (lit., deeming something good). In *istiḥsān*, the results of a piece of strict analogical reasoning (*qiyās*) can be set to one side when it is deemed contrary to grander Sharia principles. The Hanafis approved of this mechanism though many opponents (particularly the Shafiʿis) did not. The appeal to a more general notion of justice or fairness in order to overrule an unpalatable legal rule has led some to see in *istiḥsān* something akin to Western legal notions of equity or natural law. Western research in this area began in earnest in the 1960s and 70s (for example, Makdisi 1965; Chehata 1966), and continued in works that demonstrate how *istiḥsān* provides a theoretical basis for the development of Islamic law when it is threatened with stagnation (J. Makdisi 1985; Johansen 1999). Within the context of *uṣūl al-fiqh*, both the rejection of *istiḥsān* by Shafiʿis (Weiss 2010: 663–8) and the promotion of it by Hanafis (Bedir 2003) have been analyzed.

An understanding of *istiḥsān* acquired an academic imperative as, along with *istiṣlāḥ* (lit., deeming something beneficial [in the public interest]), it was employed by reformers such as Rashīd Riḍā (d. 1935) and Muḥammad ʿAbduh (d. 1905) in the late nineteenth and early twentieth centuries to justify departures from classical fiqh doctrine. *Istiṣlāḥ* is linked to the much employed notion of *maṣlaḥa* (public interest) by which the idea was developed that since the overall aim of the law is to produce benefit for humanity, laws that can be shown to be harmful should be suspended. These are controversial doctrines, which since the publications of Malcolm Kerr in the 1960s have been studied by Felicitas Opwis in both the classical and modern periods (2005, 2010). Of linked interest is the growing emphasis on the "aims of the law" (*maqāṣid al-sharīʿa*), which are seen as a major vehicle for reform, insofar as adherence to the overall aims of the Sharia (once they have been identified) can enable outdated laws to be discarded in order to fulfill these higher aims. The understanding of the higher purposes of the law, though not always explored in works of *uṣūl al-fiqh*, has a long history in Islamic legal thought. It has been most intimately associated with al-Shāṭibī (d. 790/1388), and his approach has received much commentary in the secondary literature, comprehensively by Muhammad Khalid Masud (1977) and later by Hallaq (1999: 162–75). Also associated with *maqāṣid* discourse from the medieval period was Najm al-Dīn al-Ṭūfī (d. 716/1316), whose theories are examined by Reinhart and Opwis, and are likely to continue to be influential in the ongoing "reform" of Islamic law.

Avenues for Future Study and Legal Theory in the Modern Period

Notwithstanding the progress made in the study of *uṣūl al-fiqh* in the last 30 years, there remains much fundamental research to be carried out. In nearly every area of *uṣūl* studies outlined above, there remain many texts unstudied, manuscripts to be edited, and hypotheses to be tested and debated. The relationship between theology and *uṣūl al-fiqh* continues to be complicated and not fully understood. The challenge to produce an adequate account of legal hermeneutics posed by the work of El Shamsy, Lowry, and Vishanoff will undoubtedly spawn further work in support or in criticism of their positions. It is clear that the mechanism whereby laws were derived from the texts in the premodern period remains largely under-researched, and in need of a more nuanced understanding.

The fate of *uṣūl al-fiqh* in the modern period has been the subject of numerous studies, but here, too, there are many avenues for future research. One of the immediate issues in the study of modern Muslim legal theory is its relation to the classical doctrine and the influence of ideas from non-Muslim legal theory (primarily that of Western Europe and North America). There is, it should be said, still much work to be done on modern Islamic legal theory, though the works of Kerr, Opwis, Kamali, and Hallaq provide the field with an initial base on which to grow. It is, I think, fair to say that *uṣūl al-fiqh* has not retained the intellectual prestige it had during the medieval period in the transition to modernity. Indeed, the arcane discussions in *uṣūl al-fiqh* were seen by some reformers as one of the elements of the classical legal structure that was problematic and in need of change. What Chaumont calls "l'inadéquation du *fiqh* avec le monde contemporain" (1997: 7) is based on the inability of *uṣūl al-fiqh* to provide a workable mechanism for adapting to societal and scientific advances. Scholars who have worked on classical *uṣūl* rarely get intellectually excited about what is described as Islamic legal theory in the modern period, and hence there is a paucity of studies in this area. The theories of *maqāṣid al-sharīʿa*, as espoused (for example) by ʿAllal al-Fāsī (d. 1974) or Ibn ʿĀshūr (d. 1973), have not as yet been subjected to sustained analysis in the secondary literature. The penchant for the use of *qawāʿid fiqhiyya* (general legal principles) as a replacement for *uṣūl al-fiqh* in modern reforms of Islamic law is also under-researched. This trend toward *qawāʿid* relies on the notion that fiqh is based on a series of general principles that are universally applicable (or at least when not, the exceptions are easily recognized and justified). Once this is achieved, the formulation of legal rules then flows from these *qawāʿid* rather than *uṣūl al-fiqh*. Wolfhart Heinrichs prepared the basis for future study and understanding of the role of *qawāʿid* in the formulation of classical Islamic legal theory (2000, 2001), but their use in modern Islamic legal theory and its relationship (or otherwise) with the classical model has not, yet, been analyzed. The production of works on *qawāʿid* from within the Muslim world (see Rabb 2009) would indicate that this approach may become more popular. It sells itself as less arbitrary than the appeal to *maqāṣid* (as the *qawāʿid* emerge out of fiqh itself rather than any postulated set of "aims" of the Sharia). *Qawāʿid*-based approaches can take into account societal and scientific changes since they are principles rather than rules, with a sufficient gap between the principle and its application to allow for adjustment and human interpretation. Just as vibrant, though more in the classical mode, is the discussion around *uṣūl al-fiqh* in the Twelver Shiʿi world. Particularly in the Iranian context, there exist exciting possibilities for further research following on from the work of Dahlén (2003), Gleave (2002, 2003), and Roy Mottahedeh's translation of Muḥammad Bāqir al-Ṣadr (2003), the latter providing evidence of the continued importance and sophistication of modern Shiʿi *uṣūl al-fiqh*. Perhaps the greatest challenge is to integrate the many individual studies produced in recent scholarship into a more coherent general account of *uṣūl* and its role in the derivation of laws. *Uṣūl al-fiqh*, which had for so long occupied the principal position as the theory whereby laws were derived from texts, has been seriously challenged by alternative literary forms (*qawāʿid*, *maqāṣid*, and the theories of how law can be codified and promulgated). It is therefore, perhaps, the relationship between *uṣūl* and these challenges that forms the most pressing item for future research.

References

Ahmed, Ahmed Atif. 2006. *Structural Interrelations of Theory and Practice in Islamic Law: A Study of Six Works of Islamic Jurisprudence*. Leiden: Brill.

Arnaldez, Roger. 1956. *Grammaire et théologie chez Ibn Ḥazm de Cordoue: Essai sur la structure et les conditions de la pensée musulmane*. Paris: J. Vrin.

Bedir, Murteza. 2003. The Power of Interpretation: Is *Istiḥsān Qiyās*? *Islamic Studies* 42(1): 7–20.

Bernand, Marie. 1969. L'Iğmāʿ chez ʿAbd Al-Ğabbār et l'objection d'An-Naẓẓām. *Studia Islamica* 30: 27–38.

———, and Éric Chaumont. 2003. *Kitāb fīhi maʿrifat al-ḥujaj al-sharʿiyya taṣnīf Sayf al-Sunna Abī l-Yusr Muḥammad b. Muḥammad al-Bazdawī*. Cairo: al-Maʿhad al-ʿIlmī al-Faransī li-l-Āthār al-Sharqiyya.

Brockopp, Jonathan. 2001. Competing Theories of Authority in Early Mālikī Texts. In *Studies in Islamic Legal Theory*, ed. B.G. Weiss, pp. 3–22. Leiden: Brill.

Brunschvig, Robert. 1970. Les *uṣûl al-fiqh* imâmites à leur stade ancien (Xe et XIe siècles). In *Le Shîʿisme imâmite: Colloque de Strasbourg (6–9 mai 1968)*, pp. 201–14. Paris: Presses Universitaires de France.

———. 1976. *Études d'islamologie / Robert Brunschvig: Avant-propos et bibliographie de l'auteur par Abdel Magid Turki*. Paris: G.-P. Maisonneuve et Larose.

Burton, John. 1990. *The Sources of Islamic Law: Islamic Theories of Abrogation*. Edinburgh: Edinburgh University Press.

Calder, Norman. 1983. Ikhtilâf and Ijmâʿ in Shâfiʿî's Risâla. *Studia Islamica* 58: 55–81.

———. 1989. Doubt and Prerogative: The Emergence of an Imāmī Shīʿī Theory of *Ijtihād*. *Studia Islamica* 70: 57–78.

———. 1993. *Studies in Early Muslim Jurisprudence*. Oxford: Clarendon Press.

———. 1996a. Al-Nawawī's Typology of *Muftīs* and Its Significance for a General Theory of Islamic Law. *Islamic Law and Society* 3(2): 137–64.

———. 1996b. Review of Bernard G. Weiss, *The Search for God's Law. Bulletin of the School of Oriental and African Studies* 59: 556–7.

———. 2010. *Islamic Jurisprudence in the Classical Era*, ed. C. Imber. New York: Cambridge University Press.

Chaumont, Éric. 1992. La problématique classique de l'*ijtihâd* et la question de l'*ijtihâd* du Prophète: *ijtihâd*, *waḥy* et *ʿiṣma*. *Studia Islamica* 75: 105–39.

———. 1993–94. *Kitāb al-Lumaʿ fī uṣūl al-fiqh* de Abū Isḥāq al-Šīrāzī. *Melanges de l'Université Saint-Joseph* 53: 1–249.

———. 1997. Ijtihâd et histoire en islam sunnite classique selon quelques juristes et quelques théologiens. In *Islamic Law: Theory and Practice*, ed. R. Gleave and E. Kermeli. London: I.B. Tauris.

———. 1999. *Kitāb al-Lumaʿ fī uṣūl al-fiqh (Le Livre des Rais illuminant les fondements de la compréhension de la Loi): Traité de théorie légale musulmane*. Berkeley, CA: Robbins Collection.

Chehata, Chafik. 1966. L'«équité» en tant que source du droit hanafite. *Studia Islamica* 25: 123–38.

Dahlén, Ashk. 2003. *Islamic Law, Epistemology and Modernity: Legal Philosophy in Contemporary* Iran. London: Routledge.

El Shamsy, Ahmed. 2007. The First Shāfiʿī: The Traditionalist Legal Thought of Abū Yaʿqūb al-Buwayṭī (d. 231/846). *Islamic Law and Society* 14(3): 301–41.

———, and Aron Zysow. 2012. Al-Buwaytī's Abridgment of al-Shāfiʿī's *Risāla*: Edition and Translation. *Islamic Law and Society* 19(4): 327–55.

Emon, Anver. 2010. *Islamic Natural Law Theories*. Oxford: Oxford University Press.

Fadel, Mohammad. 1996. The Social Logic of *Taqlīd* and the Rise of the *Mukhtaṣar*. *Islamic Law and Society* 3(2): 193–233.

Gleave, Robert. 2000. *Inevitable Doubt: Two Theories of Shīʿī Jurisprudence*. Leiden: Brill.

———. 2002a. Modern Šīʿī Discussions of *ḫabar al-wāḥid*: Ṣādr, Ḫuymaynī and Ḫūʾī. *Oriente Moderno* n.s. 21(1): 179–94.

———. 2002b. Imāmī Shīʿī Refutations of *Qiyās*. In *Studies in Islamic Legal Theory*, ed. B.G. Weiss, pp. 267–92. Leiden: Brill.

———. 2007. *Scripturalist Islam: The History and Doctrines of the Akhbārī Shīʿī School*. Leiden: Brill.

———. 2012. *Islam and Literalism: Literal Meaning and Interpretation in Islamic Legal Theory*. Edinburgh: Edinburgh University Press.

Goldziher, Ignaz. 1884. *Die Ẓâhiriten, ihr Lehrsystem und ihre Geschichte: Beitrag zur Geschichte der muhammedanischen Theologie*. Leipzig: O. Schulze; Eng. trans., W. Behn, *The Ẓāhirīs, Their Doctrine and Their History: A Contribution to the History of Islamic Theology*. Leiden: Brill, 1971, 2008.

Hallaq, Wael B. 1984. Was the Gate of Ijtihad Closed? *International Journal of Middle East Studies*, 16(1): 3–41.

———. 1986. On the Authoritativeness of Sunni Consensus. *International Journal of Middle East Studies* 18(4): 427–54.

———. 1989. Non-Analogical Arguments in Sunni Juridical *Qiyās*. *Arabica* 36(3): 286–306.

———. 1991. The Primacy of the Qurʾān in Shāṭibī's Legal Theory. In *Islamic Studies Presented to Charles J. Adams*, ed. W.B. Hallaq and D.P. Little, pp. 65–86. Leiden: E.J. Brill.

———. 1992. *Uṣūl al-Fiqh*: Beyond Tradition. *Journal of Islamic Studies* 3(2): 172–202.

———. 1993. Was al-Shafiʻi the Master Architect of Islamic Jurisprudence? *International Journal of Middle East Studies* 25(4): 587–605.

———. 1997. *A History of Islamic Legal Theories: An Introduction to Sunnī* uṣūl al-fiqh. Cambridge: Cambridge University Press.

———. 1999. The Authenticity of Prophetic Ḥadîth: A Pseudo-Problem. *Studia Islamica* 89: 75–90.

———. 2001. *Authority, Continuity, and Change in Islamic Law*. Cambridge: Cambridge University Press.

Heinrichs, Wolfhart. 2000. Structuring the Law: Remarks on the *Furuq* Literature. In *Studies in Honour of Clifford Edmund Bosworth*. Vol. 1: *Hunter of the East: Arabic and Semitic Studies*, ed. I.R. Netton, pp. 332–44. Leiden: Brill.

———. 2001. *Qawāʿid* as a Genre of Legal Literature. In *Studies in Islamic Legal Theory*, ed. B.G. Weiss, pp. 365–76. Leiden: Brill.

Hourani, George. 1964. The Basis of Authority and Consensus in Sunnite Islam. *Studia Islamica* 21: 13–60.

Jackson, Sherman. 1996. *Taqlīd*, Legal Scaffolding and the Scope of Legal Injunctions in Post-Formative Theory: *Muṭlaq* and *ʿĀmm* in the Jurisprudence of Shihāb al-Dīn al-Qarāfī. *Islamic Law and Society* 3(2): 165–92.

———. 2002. Fiction and Formalism: Toward a Functional Analysis of *Uṣūl al-fiqh*. In *Studies in Islamic Legal Theory*, ed. B.G. Weiss, pp. 177–201. Leiden: Brill.

Johansen, Baber. 1999. *Contingency in a Sacred Law: Legal and Ethical Norms in the Muslim* Fiqh. Leiden: Brill.

Kamali, Mohammad Hashim. 1991. *Principles of Islamic Jurisprudence*. Cambridge: Islamic Texts Society.

Kerr, Malcolm. 1963. *Islamic Reform: The Political and Legal Theories of Muḥammad ʿAbduh and Rashīd Riḍā*. Berkeley: University of California Press.

Kuran, Timur. On the Notion of Economic Justice in Contemporary Islamic Thought. *International Journal of Middle East Studies* 21(2): 171–91.

Libson, Gideon. 2003. *Jewish and Islamic Law: A Comparative Study of Custom during the Geonic Period*. Cambridge, MA: Islamic Legal Studies Program, Harvard Law School.

Lowry, Joseph. 2004. The Legal Hermeneutics of al-Shāfiʿī and Ibn Qutayba: A Reconsideration. *Islamic Law and Society* 11(1): 1–41.

———. 2007. *Early Islamic Legal Theory: The* Risāla *of Muḥammad ibn Idrīs al-Shāfiʿī*. Leiden: Brill.

McDermott, Martin. 1978. *The Theology of al-Shaikh al-Mufīd (d. 413/1022)*. Beirut: Librairie Orientale.

Makdisi, George. 1963. *Ibn ʿAqīl et la résurgence de l'islam traditionaliste au XIe siècle (Ve siècle de l'Hégire)*. Damascus: Institut Français de Damas.

———. 1965. Ibn Taimīya's Autograph Manuscript on *Istiḥsān*: Materials for the Study of Islamic Legal Thought. In *Arabic and Islamic Studies in Honor of Hamilton A.R. Gibb*, ed. G. Makdisi, pp 446–79. Cambridge, MA: Harvard University Press.

———. 1996–2002. *Al-Wāḍiḥ fī uṣūl al-fiqh*. 4 vols. in 5. Stuttgart: Klaus Schwarz.

Makdisi, John. 1985. Legal Logic and Equity in Islamic Law. *The American Journal of Comparative Law* 33(1): 63–92.

Masud, Muhammad Khalid. 1977. *Islamic Legal Philosophy: A Study of Abu Ishaq al-Shatibi's Life and Thought*. Islamabad: Islamic Research Institute; rev. ed. Kuala Lumpur 2000.

Melchert, Christopher. 1999. How Hanafism Came to Originate in Kufa and Traditionalism in Medina. *Islamic Law and Society* 6(3): 318–47.

———. 2002. Quranic Abrogation Across the Ninth Century. In *Studies in Islamic Legal Theory*, ed. B.G. Weiss, pp. 75–98. Leiden: Brill.

Opwis, Felicitas. 2005. *Maṣlaḥa* in Contemporary Islamic Legal Theory. *Islamic Law and Society*.12(2): 182–223.

———. 2010. Maṣlaḥa *and the Purpose of the Law: Islamic Discourse on Legal Change from the 4th/10th to 8th/14th Century*. Leiden: Brill.

Peters, Rudolph. *Idjtihād* and *Taqlīd* in 18th and 19th Century Islam. *Die Welt des Islams* 20: 131–45.

Rabb, Intisar. 2009. Islamic Legal Maxims as Substantive Canons of Construction: *Ḥudūd*-Avoidance in Cases of Doubt. *Islamic Law and Society* 17: 63–125.

Reinhart, A. Kevin. 1995. *Before Revelation: The Boundaries of Muslim Moral Thought*. Albany: SUNY Press.

———, and Robert Gleave, eds. 2014. *Islamic Law in Theory: Studies on Jurisprudence in Honor of Bernard Weiss*. Leiden: Brill.

al-Ṣadr, Muḥammad Bāqir. 2003. *Lessons in Islamic Jurisprudence*, tr. R.P. Mottahedeh. Oxford: Oneworld.

Schacht, Joseph. 1950. *The Origins of Muhammadan Jurisprudence*. Oxford: Clarendon Press; rev. ed. 1967.

Schöck, Cornelia. 2005. *Koranexegese, Grammatik und Logik*. Leiden: Brill.

Schwarb, Gregor. 2007. Capturing the Meanings of God's Speech: The Relevance of Usul al-fiqh to an Understanding of Usul al-Tafsir in Jewish and Muslim Kalam. In *In a Word Fitly Spoken: Studies in Mediaeval Exegesis of the Hebrew Bible and the Qurʾān Presented to Haggai Ben-Shammai*, ed. M.M. Bar-Asher et al., pp. 111–56. Jerusalem: Ben-Zvi Institute.

Shehaby, Nabil. 1975. The Influence of Stoic Logic on al-Jassas's Legal Theory. In *The Cultural Context of Medieval Learning*, ed. J.E. Murdoch, pp. 61–86. Boston: Springer.

———. 1982. *ʿIlla* and *Qiyās* in Early Islamic Legal Theory. *Journal of the American Oriental Society* 102(1): 27–46.
Stewart, Devin J. 1998. *Islamic Legal Orthodoxy: Twelver Shiite Responses to the Sunni Legal System*. Salt Lake City: University of Utah Press.
———. 2002. Muḥammad b. Dāwūd al-Ẓāhirī's Manual of Jurisprudence: *Al-Wuṣūl ilā maʿrifat al-uṣūl*. In *Studies in Islamic Legal Theory*, ed. B.G. Weiss, pp. 99–158. Leiden: Brill.
———. 2004. Muḥammad b. Jarīr al-Ṭabarī's *al-Bayān ʿan Uṣūl al-Aḥkām* and the Genre of *Uṣūl al-Fiqh* in Ninth-Century Baghdad. In *ʿAbbasid Studies: Occasional Papers of the School of ʿAbbasid Studies, Cambridge, 6–10 July 2002*, ed. J.E. Montgomery, pp. 321–49. Leuven: Peeters.
Tillschneider, Hans-Thomas. 2006. *Die Entstehung der juristischen Hermeneutik im frühen Islam*. Würzburg: Ergon.
Tritton, A. S. 1952. Some Muʿtazilī Ideas about Religion, in Particular about Knowledge Based on General Report. *Bulletin of the School of Oriental and African Studies* 14(3): 612–22.
Tsafrir, Nurit. 2004. *The History of an Islamic School of Law: The Early Spread of Hanafism*. Cambridge, MA: Islamic Legal Studies Program, Harvard Law School.
Turki, Abdel-Magid (al-Turkī, ʿAbd al-Majīd). 1973. *Polémiques entre Ibn Ḥazm et Bāǧī sur les principes de la loi musulmane: Essai sur le littéralisme zahirite et la finalité malikite*. Algers: Études et Documents.
———. 1986. *Iḥkām al-fuṣūl fī aḥkām al-uṣūl [li-] Abū l-Walīd al-Bājī*. Beirut: Dār al-Gharb al-Islāmī.
———. 1995. *Kitāb fī uṣūl al-fiqh [li-] Abū l-Thanāʾ Maḥmūd b. Zayd al-Lāmishī l-Ḥanafī al-Māturīdī*. Beirut: Dār al-Gharb al-Islāmī.
Vishanoff, David. 2011. *The Formation of Islamic Hermeneutics: How Sunni Legal Theorists Imagined a Revealed Law*. New Haven, CT: American Oriental Society.
Vogel, Frank E. 1993. The Closing of the Door of Ijtihad and the Application of the Law. *American Journal of Islamic Social Sciences* 10: 396–401.
Weiss, Bernard G. 1974. Medieval Muslim Discussions of the Origins of Language. *Zeitschrift der Deutschen Morgenländischen Gesellschaft* 124(1): 33–41.
———. 1984. The Primacy of Revelation in Classical Islamic Legal Theory as Expounded by Sayf al-Dīn al-Āmidī. *Studia Islamica* 59: 79–109.
———. 1985. Knowledge of the Past: The Theory of *tawâtur* according to Ghazâlî. *Studia Islamica* 61: 81–105.
———. 1986. Language and Law: The Linguistic Premises of Islamic Legal Science. In *In Quest of an Islamic Humanism: Arabic and Islamic Studies in Memory of Mohamed al-Nowaihi*, ed. A.H. Green, pp. 15–21. Cairo: The American University in Cairo Press.
———. 1998. *The Spirit of Islamic Law*. Athens, GA: University of Georgia Press.
———, ed. 2002. *Studies in Islamic Legal Theory*. Leiden: Brill.
———. 2010. *The Search for God's Law: Islamic Jurisprudence in the Writings of Sayf al-Dīn al-Āmidī: New Edition*. Salt Lake City: University of Utah Press; 1st ed., 1992.
Yahia, Mohyddin. 2009. *Šāfiʿī et les deux sources de la loi islamique*. Turnhout: Brepols.
Zysow, Aron. 1984. *The Economy of Certainty: A Typology of Islamic Legal Theories*. Unpubl. Ph.D. diss., Harvard University; corr. and updated ed. *The Economy of Certainty: A Typology of Islamic Legal Theories*. Atlanta: Lockwood, 2013.
———. 2008. Two Theories of the Obligation to Obey God's Commands. In *The Law Applied: Contextualizing the Islamic Shariʿa*, ed. P. Bearman et al., pp. 397–421. London: I.B. Tauris.

The Judge and the Mufti

Brinkley Messick

The variety of officials and official bodies responsible for the settling of conflicts and the keeping of law and order in the premodern Muslim world differed from state to state and from period to period. Both arbitration and social pressure played a large extrajudicial role, but the most prominent officials in conflict resolution, professional jurists both, were the Sharia court judge (*qāḍī*) and the mufti, who are the focus of this chapter. For other state legal actors, such as the police (*shurṭa*), the market inspector and censor of morals (*muḥtasib*), and the state grievance tribunals (*maẓālim*), see Chapters 7 and 12, below.

By institutional design, the qadi[1] and mufti were in direct contact with the practical affairs of their societies, but their modes of intervention were distinct. In terms of principal roles, the qadi presided over two-party court cases while the mufti responded to questions posed by single parties. Litigation before the qadi entailed the presentation and interpretation of evidence, while the mufti's consideration of the issue at hand was limited to the terms in which the question was posed. Both of these key legal actors were Sharia interpreters, but their efforts may be thought of as proceeding in opposite directions. The thrust of a qadi's interpretive activity was to evaluate the contested facts of a case, with the law taken as available for application or readily ascertainable. The task of the mufti was approximately the reverse: to find the applicable law on the basis of a fact scenario taken as given.

A judgment by a qadi was binding and enforceable, whereas the fatwa given by a mufti had the status of a non-binding opinion. Where a qadi's judgment also was final, the recipient of an adverse fatwa could seek out the opinion of another mufti. Records generally were kept of court decisions, although they were not reported or otherwise cited. Authoritative fatwas were compiled in books or official registers, but ephemeral routine fatwas left no archival trace. Only Muslim males could serve as qadis, and they usually did so under the terms of official appointments in state forums. In contrast, it was possible (although not common) for a woman to act as a mufti, and while the muftiship eventually took official form in a number of historical settings, its basic and widespread form was private.

With respect to the "law on the books," that is, in relation to the corpus of the doctrinal fiqh, there also was an important distinction of purview. A qadi could hear cases concerning all chapters of the doctrine, except for topics treated in the sections on the ritual matters (the *ʿibādāt*). The justiciable thus had limits. A mufti, in contrast, was competent to address questions pertaining to the entire corpus of the law, including the ritual matters. Although the qadi and the mufti represent separate interpretive institutions, the two also could function in tandem, notably when qadis consulted muftis for guidance as to points of law.

Brinkley Messick is Professor of Anthropology at Columbia University, New York City. He has published widely on the authority of Islamic legal writings, especially in *The Calligraphic State: Textual Domination and History in a Muslim Society* (1993) and in articles that include "Textual Properties: Writing and Wealth in a Yemeni Shariʿa Case" (1997), "Genealogies of Reading and the Scholarly Cultures of Islam" (1997), and "Indexing the Self: Expression and Intent in Islamic Legal Acts" (2001).

1 Also transcribed in the secondary literature as cadi and kadi.

Western Historiography

The distinctive division of interpretive labor between qadi and mufti prevailed in Muslim societies until the rise of modernity. A useful starting point for research on these and related historical institutions of application is the comprehensive account by Émile Tyan (1960). Tyan's coverage of "judicial organization" in Islam centers on the judgeship, which is treated both in terms of a primary role in court processes and with respect to the qadi's several supervisory responsibilities in domains such as legacies, endowments, legal instruction, etc. (cf. Schacht 1964: 188). He criticizes the authenticity of early sources on the judgeship, such as the letters of the caliph ʿUmar on the conduct of the qadi, although later scholars such as R.B. Serjeant (1984) would argue for their significance. Tyan additionally covers the alternative, or at times superior jurisdiction of the state *maẓālim* court and also the police function, the institution of the *shurṭa*.

In this all-inclusive account, the mufti figures only briefly (1960: 219–30), essentially as a member of the qadi's entourage, in which role he offered legal guidance for the qadi's decision. After pointing out an institutional analogy with the Roman *jus publice respondendi*, Tyan provides details on both the qualifying conditions for entrance into the muftiship and the rules that pertain to issuing fatwas. However, he places this treatment of the mufti between two sections on the "consilium" (*mashwara*, *shūrā*), a wider mechanism of advice-giving that, according to Tyan (1960: 214), had been neglected in prior Western understandings of the judgeship. He states that research had focused only on the "unitary" dimension of the singly presiding qadi and had ignored this magistrate's interpretive dependence upon accompanying jurists, including the specialized role of the mufti. While the procedural sections in the standard law books recommend that the qadi consult other jurists before rendering his decision, Tyan refers to the formally institutionalized version of such consultations that obtained in the Muslim West, specifically in al-Andalus (see Marín 1985). As a consequence, he understands the muftiship relatively narrowly, as a particular manifestation of advice-giving attached to the qadi-centered judicial system.

Prior to Tyan, a strand of orientalist research on the judgeship had focused on the Islamic genre of the biographical history (*ṭabaqāt*). Produced across the Muslim world, such literary works commonly contain entries on jurists who served in the judiciary. Some specialized entirely on qadis, as, for example, that by al-Kindī (d. 350/961) on the early Muslim judiciary of Egypt. In his edition of this text Richard Gottheil (1908a: iii–xx; cf. 1908b) also provided a concise introduction to the history and structure of the Muslim judgeship.[2] A theme raised in this scholarship concerned the ambivalence among many Muslim jurists toward assuming the judgeship. This was expressed in what Western observers referred to as "ominous" hadiths (Amedroz 1910; Wensinck 1922; Coulson 1956; for an evaluation of such hadiths, see Juynboll 1983: 77–95). This ambivalence also left distinct traces in entries in biographical histories—in mentions of reluctance or refusal to serve or in stereotyped approvals of upright character in office.

Orientalist research by historians and other specialists using philological methods would be complemented by the research of social scientists. In the same period in the early twentieth century, the foundational sociologist Max Weber (d. 1920) drew on existing specialist scholarship for his famous conception of "kadi justice" (Weber 1978: 795, 976–8; for an extended critical assessment, Johansen 1999: 42–72). Rather than representing an informed and specific reference to the Sharia court judge, about whose circumstances and practices relatively little was known at the time, "kadi justice" instead functioned as a term of art in Weber's analytic classification of different systems of justice. Instead of disparaging Islamic justice as meted out by the qadi, the term served to label an ideal type of decision-making. Thus, when Weber states (1978: 976) that "Kadi-justice knows no rational 'rules of decision' (*Urteilsgründe*) whatever" it is important to realize that he also places certain institutions of English common law under the same heading as the Muslim qadi. One contrast Weber makes is with the particular historical forms of abstract legal rationalism associated with Roman law

2 A second such work, by al-Wakīʿ (d. 306/918), was published 1947–50. See also Masud 2006b; Schneider 1990; al-Zuḥaylī 1995; Johansen 1997.

and with continental European legal systems. Weber's general aim has been glossed as follows: "Kadi justice (*kadijustiz*) [...] describe[s] the administration of justice which is oriented not at fixed rules of a formally rational law but at the ethical, religious, political, or otherwise expediential postulates of a substantively rational law" (Weber 1978: 806 n. 40).[3]

The sociologist Bryan Turner (1974: 107–21) provides a chapter-length reassessment not only of kadi justice and the related concept of "substantive rationality" but also of Weber's equally famous designation of the Sharia as a "jurist's law" (Schacht 1964: 5, 209, 284). Turner locates these views concerning the Sharia with respect to Weber's understanding of the history of Muslim states, notably patterns of patrimonial rule, and also to his wider comparative project on the relationship between rational forms of law and capitalism.

The "law and society" perspective of anthropologists also has raised important questions for the historical study of Sharia applications. Anthropologist Lawrence Rosen, for example, bases himself on ethnographic research on a Sharia court in Sefrou, Morocco, which he describes as "a typical Islamic court" (1989: 6). In his analyses, Rosen takes up the Weberian concept of kadi justice (1989: 59–60, 65; 2000: 3, 20–21), centering attention on the issue of the qadi's "discretion."[4] He argues that the principle aim of these modern Moroccan Sharia judges is not to decide cases within the court forum but rather to encourage out-of-court settlements, to "put people back in the position of being able to negotiate their own permissible relationships without predetermining just what the outcome of those negotiations ought to be" (1989: 17, cf. 65). Rosen further asserts that his qadis do not practice "doctrinal consistency." In Islamic law, he maintains, we should think of consistency as pertaining not so much to formal doctrinal issues but rather to wider "cultural assumptions about negotiated social ties" (1989: 61, 66). "Moroccan juridical thought," he states, "eschewed the elaboration of abstract concepts of right action in favor of more pragmatic evaluations of human relationships and the common weal" (2000: 21).

Discussions of Rosen's findings among students of the historical Sharia have been numerous. Critical responses (for example, Mundy 1991) focus mainly on the explicit implication in Rosen's work that his findings from modern Morocco—where the Sharia court is a small jurisdiction appended to a larger, Western-style, civil and criminal court system; where the law had been codified under the postcolonial auspices of a nation state; and where modern lawyers and prosecutors operate—are relevant for understanding the premodern Sharia. Positive responses center on the recognition of the significance of modes of settlement, which Rosen's ethnography foregrounds, as, for example, Leslie Peirce (2003: 5) and Wael Hallaq (2009: 165), who both invoke Rosen's line that the basic aim of the qadi is to "put people back in the position of being able to negotiate their own permissible relationships," etc.

In an article devoted to the connection between muftis and court practices in fourteenth-century Morocco (1994), the historian David Powers carefully documents the "emphasis on reasoned justification." He argues that this "belies the Weberian notion of *kadijustiz* and the stereotype of the Muslim qadi as an unprincipled agent who, unconstrained by any rules, dispenses justice according to considerations of individual expediency rather than doctrinal consistency" (1994: 366; see also Schneider 1993). Muftis providing qadis with doctrinal opinions in this manner also feature in a series of related North African case studies for the 1300–1500 period (Powers 2002). In passing, it may be noted that Weber (1978: 797–99, 821) had considered the muftiship but that it did not figure in Rosen's modern setting.

A critical appraisal of the Weberian legacy, including the treatment by Turner, while also drawing extensively on the work of legal anthropologists, notably Rosen, is given by Haim Gerber, who also contributes to the disciplinary dialogue then emergent between history and anthropology, going so far

3 Twentieth-century common law jurists were not beneath propagating a related simplistic image of the qadi: "The court [...] is really put very much in the position of a Cadi under a palm tree," wrote Lord Justice Goddard; "We do not sit like a kadi under a tree dispensing justice according to considerations of individual expediency," stated Justice Felix Frankfurter.

4 It is important to note the larger reliance of cultural anthropologists such as Clifford Geertz (1973) on Weber's notion of an interpretive social science.

as to characterize legal anthropology as providing his book's "analytical framework" (1994: 3). Yet in contrast to the supposed unfettered judicial discretion and the preference for settlements that involve bargaining and negotiation, Gerber found that his seventeenth- and eighteenth-century Ottoman qadis engaged in the application of regular rules. The "argument that a lack of strict logical structure permeating the entire code of laws necessarily resulted in unprincipled adjudication based on nothing more than intuition was found to be completely off the mark in the area under study" (1994: 18). In addition, where Rosen highlights judicial sensitivity to issues of social context, Gerber saw no evidence of this. Rather than the similarity to common law procedure that is asserted by Rosen (2000: 38–68), Gerber sees the profile of Ottoman qadi as closer to the continental European model of the civil law judge (1994: 37).[5]

Gerber concurs with Rosen's critics that it is not possible to properly test the Weberian thesis in the twentieth century, where the law is "totally mutilated in comparison to its former self" (1994: 26). An important further aspect of this transformed modern reality is that—in Rosen's research setting as in most other modern Sharia courts—the jurisdiction is limited to family law, or personal status. With respect to his premodern Ottoman context, Gerber is at pains to demonstrate the lack of a "gap" between the theory and practice of the Sharia that Weber and, following him, Joseph Schacht (1964), had seen, but also that the prevailing assumptions about the non-applicability of the Sharia in such spheres as criminal and commercial law (see below) were unfounded.

The Sharia court records of Gerber's period were "replete" with fatwas (1994: 23), confirming the earlier findings of Uriel Heyd (1969: 51–2, 54) and Ronald Jennings (1978: 134). For comparative contrast, Gerber cites scholarship on local-level fatwa-issuing found in highland Yemen (Messick 1986). However, at the pinnacle of the Ottoman Sharia system stood the şeyhülislam (Ar. *shaykh al-islām*), the official heading the state fatwa-giving bureaucracy based in Istanbul (for which, see Gerber 1999; Imber 1997).

The Mufti

In the first comprehensive scholarly treatment of the muftiship in a Western language (Masud et al. 1996), the editors locate the origins of the institution in patterns of questioning and authoritative response established during the lifetime of the Prophet Muḥammad. These included both the query addressed to the Prophet that led to the revelation of verses of the Quran and also the query that led to a direct reply from the Prophet himself, this last forming the basis for his Sunna, or authoritative practice. The connections between these early patterns and the eventually elaborated muftiship are built into the specific language used in these early interactions, notably the IVth and Xth verbal forms of the root *f-t-y*—"to give a ruling" and "to seek a ruling," respectively[6]—the linguistic templates for the institution's later established technical terminology—*iftā'* and *futyā* (fatwa-issuing), *istiftā'* (question), and *mustaftī* (questioner).

Weber and Schacht noted that the muftiship began as a private activity of qualified scholars and individuals known for their piety and only later added official and bureaucratized forms, such as the previously mentioned position of the Ottoman şeyhülislam. But in the model of response established by the Prophet, a link with public authority was also established. Other forms of response central to different lines of authority in Muslim states and societies were the *mas'ūl* (lit. the one who is asked), and a parallel official pattern of query and response occurring through the institution of the petition or complaint (Ar. *shakwa*; T. *şekaya*, *'arzuhal*) (on which, see Ursinus 2005). Such petitions presented to a head of state or a governor sometimes initiated action in a *maẓālim* type of venue (Messick 1993: 170–6; Gerber 1994: 154–73).

5 An intermediate view is that the Sharia represents a "codified common law" (Fadel 1996: 198).

6 The first appears five times in the Quran (4:127, 176; 12:43, 46; 27:32) and the latter six times (4:127, 176; 12:41; 18:22; 37:11, 149).

The basic institutional formula of the muftiship generated a spectrum of historical manifestations, although there were also certain consistent features. Our knowledge of this institutional diversity remains spotty (Masud et al. 1996: 9, 11, 13). Compared with research on Sunni muftis our understanding of the related Shiʿi institution remains severely undeveloped, as does knowledge of the similarities and the differences between Sunni and Shiʿi muftis with respect to private and public forms, conceptions of interpretive authority, and discursive genres. The same sort of gap in our knowledge can be observed at the level of the schools of jurisprudence (sg. *madhhab*), both Sunni and Shiʿi. We do not as yet have specific studies of fatwa-issuing within the framework of a particular school, nor do we have comparative studies of the muftiship across schools (but see Wiederhold 1996 in connection with school "boundaries").

Historical muftis are known to the extent that their fatwas were preserved in written form. These sources include those containing the fatwas of various muftis, an example of which is the 13-volume work by al-Wansharīsī (d. 914/1508) for the premodern Islamic West; those containing the fatwas of a single mufti, which are very common; and those that take a more administrative form, such as the records of official fatwas delivered by the Ottoman şeyhülislams. Explorations of genre differences concerning both the standards and the techniques of the various types of fatwa compilations remain in their infancy, however. One example of the sort of distinctive features that structure the textual identities of particular sources is the case of fatwa collections from the Indian subcontinent. These premodern materials typically bear the name of a particular ruler, and the conception of a fatwa in this context actually is closer to "an authoritative and accepted opinion of the Hanafi school, not necessarily an opinion issued in response to a question" (Masud et al. 1996: 14–15; cf. Schacht 1971). The story of the celebrated *al-Fatāwā l-ʿAlamgiriyya* is singular in this respect. Representing the work of a committee charged by the Mughal emperor Awrangzeb (r. 1658–1707) with assembling Hanafi doctrine, this authoritative work held a status closely related to the authoritative doctrinal (*fiqh*) law book of the school, the well-known *al-Hidāya*.

Three further categories of source texts pertain to the study of the institutionalized muftiship. They provide specialized conceptual views of the muftiship and its practices together with legitimizing justifications. In these theoretical genres Muslim jurists sought to regulate the standards and the methods of this crucial institution of Sharia interpretation.

First among these is the literature of *uṣūl al-fiqh*, sometimes referred to as the "roots" doctrine of Islamic jurisprudence (see Chapter 5, above). In these works, interpretation (*ijtihād*) and the role of the mufti are standard topics. In an examination of *uṣūl* writers' treatments of the standards for fatwa-issuing with an emphasis on how this thought developed over time, Wael Hallaq (1996) identifies four positions. The basic issue concerned the qualification of the interpreter, specifically whether the mufti had to be an individual capable of independent interpretation (*mujtahid*) or whether he could instead be a doctrinal "follower" (*muqallid*). Hallaq summarizes his "diachronic" findings as follows:

> The first position to dominate legal discourse lasted from the eighth to the eleventh century, when jurisconsults, in order to qualify for the office of futya, were required to be mujtahids. The second, advocated by al-Amidi, among others, reflected the concession made by a group of theoreticians to a reality in which, it was thought, mujtahids of the highest caliber no longer existed, and what was to be found were only mujtahids whose legal creativity was confined to the application of an already established methodology to new cases of law. The third accepted a muqallid in the role of a mufti, but only where a mujtahid was not available. The fourth approved of a mufti-muqallid, whether or not a mujtahid was to be found (1996: 41).

Muhammad Khalid Masud (1984) brought the second genre, the *adab al-muftī* treatises, to the attention of Western scholarship. Few in number and slight in pages, these works on the comportment and culture of the mufti are the poor cousins to the better known, more numerous, and lengthier treatises focused on the judgeship (see below). This specialized genre receives intensive treatment in Masud et al. 1996 (pp. 15–26). Among the key sources in this analysis is a prominent *adab* text that is found in the introductory section of a work of fiqh commentary by the leading Shafiʿi jurist al-Nawawī (d. 676/1277). Norman Calder (1996) translated part of this text in an important article on the "typologies" of muftis. David Powers (1993) also presented a related three-tiered typology, but this was set forth within a fatwa issued by Ibn Rushd.

The third genre is the literature of positive law, or "branches" (*furūʿ*) of the fiqh. Schacht observed that significant opinions by post-formative-period muftis were "incorporated" into law books (1964: 74–75); 30 years later, Hallaq advanced a stronger claim, namely, that this incorporation of fatwas into law books was "chiefly responsible for the growth and change of legal doctrine" (1994: 65). While some law books explicitly mention the fact that they comprise fatwa material, most do not. Concerning the latter, Hallaq hypothesizes that these incorporated fatwas implicitly, without identifying the source. This occurred by means of a "transmutation," a shift in genre from fatwa to law book entry, through an editing process that he calls textual "stripping" (1994: 39, 44). The stripping of a fatwa removed the identifying markers of the genre so as to render its essential legal substance—a fact configuration and a rule—suitable for incorporation in the law book. The result assumed the new form of a law book sub-genre, such as a *masʾala* (lit. question; "topic," "case"), material thought to represent the jurists' casuistic elaborations, but were in fact the stripped versions of former fatwas.

Norman Calder took issue with this, arguing that the "dominant creative agent" in this system was not the mufti but the author-jurist, and that "the reality of influence was mostly in the opposite direction, that is, from *furūʿ* to *fatwā*s" (1996: 137, 164; cf. Calder 2010), whereupon Hallaq responded that if the movement of ideas from the doctrinal works to fatwas must be acknowledged as the "dominant activity," it nevertheless involved "a lower form of juridical creativity"—the "main locus of creativity," specifically that involving "change, evolution and modification," especially where the law was "ambiguous or silent" (1996: 129), centered on the interpretive acts of the major muftis. Miriam Hoexter raised a third possibility, namely, that the key creative agent was neither the mufti nor the jurist-author but rather the unappreciated figure of the qadi. Departing from the technical definition of the qadi's acts as performative or creative (*inshāʾī*), Hoexter argues that it was the qadi who in fact "initiated many of the developments in Islamic law" (2007: 85). Her perspective recognizes that while judgments were specific to given cases and were not reported or utilized as precedents to decide other cases, qadis worked at the cutting edge of change; the process of change started with them. It is perhaps also conceivable, although Hoexter does not make the argument, that another form of textual "stripping" might have occurred in this connection. An editing of the fact situations and rule applications found in significant judgments could have resulted in versions of these materials as well being incorporated in the law books.

Interest in the distinctions of *mujtahid* and *muqallid* was associated with the assumption advanced by earlier scholars such as Weber and Schacht that independent reasoning (*ijtihād*) had for the most part ceased by the end of what Schacht referred to as the "formative period" of Islamic law (for the formative period, see Chapter 4; and for *ijtihād*, see Chapter 5, above). Muslim jurists elaborated grades of muftis that went beyond the simple binary and identified sub-types of muftis who functioned within a given school. These muftis were considered *muqallid*s and were spoken of as "affiliated" (*muntasib*), with whom other figures were contrasted—those of the teacher-jurist and author-jurist, the denizens of the madrasa, a topic on which revisionist research also began.[7]

As noted, a mufti took a presented question as given, as the starting point for determining the relevant indication in the law. Unlike the qadi, the mufti did not conduct an evidential process and did

7 See, for example, Makdisi 1981; Berkey 1992; Chamberlain 1994; and now Hefner and Zaman 2007. As was the case in research on the judge and the mufti, anthropological studies of the madrasa by scholars such as Eickelman (1978, 1985); Fischer (1980); Messick (1993: chaps. 4, 5); Starrett 1998; and, more recently, Mahmood (2005) and Manoukian (2012) raised new questions for historians.

not decide upon the plausibility or accuracy of assertion and facts. Messick (1986, 1993: 142, 146) develops the idea of the institutional division by citing both the general social thought of Ibn Khaldūn (d. 808/1406), who delineates the two "religious" (*dīnī*) positions, and the focused treatment by the Maliki jurist al-Qarāfī (d. 684/1285) on the "differentiation of fatwas from judgments." As part of his analysis of the dichotomous roles, al-Qarāfī states that whereas the mufti's purpose is to identify "indications" (*adilla*) in the source texts of the law, the qadi is oriented to evidential materials (sg. *ḥujja*). Kevin Reinhart (1993) treats these paired categories of legal actors and their textual products using *adab al-muftī* treatises and related sources, while Frank Vogel (1996) considers their "complementary functions" in contemporary Saudi Arabia. In a posthumous chapter dedicated to scholars, muftis, and judges Calder (2010) argues that we need further "distinctions."

In terms of the locus of interpretation, emphasis conventionally (and rightfully) is placed on the mufti's response to the question, the fatwa. But the *adab* treatises (cf. Masud et al. 1996: 20–26) devote analytic attention to the question posed to the mufti. Rather than providing a simple window on a real-world circumstance, a question embedded either a naïve or tutored framing of the legal issue and also restricted the mufti's view of the relevant facts. A mufti thus was constrained by the question in a manner analogous to how, in the different institutional realm of litigation, a qadi was constrained by the formulation of the claim (*daʿwā*). In addition, the characteristic discourse of the fatwa, involving the use of abstraction and generalization, and the reliance on generic instead of actual names actually began in the formulation of the question.

Some questions posed to muftis probably were hypothetical, although this was frowned upon. Questions posed to muftis by court qadis either conveyed the essentials of difficult cases or presented judgments requiring confirmation. Questions posed to state muftis were reworked administratively to make possible a simple "yes" or "no" response, as in the practice of the Ottoman şeyhülislam. Colin Imber (1996, 1997: 57) has illustrated the analytic technique, especially as systematized by the great şeyhülislam Ebu's-Suʿud (d. 982/1574), of breaking down a complex topic into a series of discrete questions to be treated in a series of closely related fatwas (see also Gerber 1999). In the collections of fatwas as books, differing genre-standards were applied to the inclusion, exclusion, or restatement of the question. Finally, taken together, the interpretive dialogue of question and answer also enacted a specific relation of power. This involved potential hierarchies not only of status and wealth but also of knowledge versus ignorance, which was especially salient in historical societies characterized by what Jack Goody (1968) referred to as "restricted literacy."

The *adab* works established a series of formal "conditions" for entrance into the muftiship (for example, al-Nawawī, discussed in Masud et al. 1996: 18). These also contributed to differentiating the mufti from the qadi. That a woman could serve as a mufti but not as a qadi (except in a minority view) was connected, in part, to the potentially private versus the necessarily public natures of the two offices. It also affirmed the possible intellectual and academic parity between the genders while indexing well-documented patterns of social segregation along gender lines. (Something related may be said for the acceptability of a slave acting as a mufti.) Concerning women in the two positions, the Yemeni jurist al-Shawkānī (d. 1834) explained that where the mufti's interpretive act pertained only to a finding with respect to the law, the Sharia court qadi had to make a practical determination of justness. This last feature necessitated circumstantial knowledge and an associated ability, as he put it, for "clear-sightedness in human affairs (*umūr*), and [for] the comprehension of their realities" (al-Shawkānī 1985, 4: 273). The requirement for the judgeship discriminated therefore not against a woman's intelligence or her potential for scholarly achievements, but rather against her different range of experience and resulting practical knowledge, which were the consequence of gender segregation.[8]

While the debate concerning the continuing vitality of interpretation primarily references the higher grades of muftis and *mujtahid*s, the lower or more popular end of this worldly activity

8 The women who were the most likely to remain secluded and to avoid everyday contacts in the marketplace and other public places were elite women, those most apt to be educated.

also has received some attention (Heyd 1969: 54). Insight into activity at this humble level of the institution has notably been provided by ethnographic research, as in the work on local muftis in Yemen (Messick 1986, 1993, 1996). These very basic and routine fatwas made no enduring impact on existing doctrine and left no archival trace other than the slip of paper carried away by the questioner. Recent work on the heavily modified institution of al-Azhar Fatwa Council provides a related picture (Agrama 2010). The lower typologies of muftis comprised individuals who engaged in simple forms of rule transmission based on the "same" facts, that is, not interpretation per se. Whether such acts can be called fatwas has been questioned by Hallaq (1994: 50, 54) and called the acts of "deficient" muftis by Calder (1996: 143, 148, 159), belonging to a category of the mere "transmitter and informant" (Wiederhold 1996: 242, 272, 291). Yet it should be noted that even the most exalted *mujtahid*-muftis had occasion to issue ordinary and inconsequential fatwas. Al-Shawkānī refers to his numerous "shorter" fatwas, which "could never be counted" and which were neither recorded nor otherwise preserved (cited in Messick 1993: 150), as opposed to his major fatwas, which were collected in book form.

Court Procedure and Literature

The advent of research on Sharia courts was closely associated with the rise in the latter half of the twentieth century of the specialized sub-discipline of social history. By introducing a range of previously unexamined archival and documentary sources to complement the existing reliance upon doctrinal and literary texts, social historical inquiries greatly expanded the field of Sharia studies and also enabled new thinking about the key relationship between theory and practice in the law. They also initiated a range of interests in the lives of ordinary people and their routine undertakings to complement the great men and great events of standard history.

Research on Ottoman Sharia courts represents the lion's share of such social historical studies. Jon Mandaville (1966, 1975) provided an incisive early overview of studies utilizing court records as a historical source, such as Ronald Jennings' pioneering studies of Ottoman court practice (1975, 1978, 1979). With the court register (Ar. *sijill*; T. *sicill*) as the principal source, the available documentary materials included not only the records of court proceedings but also estate inventories, property title registries, marriage contracts, leases, etc. The topics of this voluminous research have ranged from aspects of economic history to family structure, gender relations, and minority access. Beshara Doumani has detailed *sijill* holdings in the Sharia courts of Palestine, beginning with Jerusalem where there are 626 such registers, of which 416 date from the Ottoman period. For this key jurisdiction, "except for a twenty-eight month gap from April 1574 to August 1576, the records are complete for the last 454 years (1985: 161). Abdul Rahman (1991) studied the records of Egyptian Sharia courts under Ottoman rule, 1517–1798, as sources for provincial and village administration. Ottoman registers have been published in facsimile and in modern Turkish translation, while selected Egyptian court records associated with the resident "Maghrebi" population also have been published (Abdul Rahman 1992–2004).[9]

Reviewing this burgeoning field, Dror Ze'evi (1998) reflected in general terms on the status of Ottoman Sharia court records "as a source for Middle Eastern social history." Across modalities of inquiry that vary from the statistical and database approaches of quantitative research to the narrative and micro-history approaches of interpretive history, researchers have struggled with the problematic nature of their principal source. Although the sheer quantity of the records kept by Ottoman jurisdictions is astounding, the individual entries in the court registers, including those produced in connection with litigation, tend to be sparse in nature. Taking the form of summaries, these premodern

9 See also the discussion of the Ottoman sources in Egypt in El-Nahal 1979.

case records omit procedures and legal reasoning, and thus provide only a limited view of the court as a legal institution. It also is rare to find sustained attention to the specifically textual features of court judgments, transcripts, and legal instruments. Ze'evi identifies the "*sijill* as a text" as one of the "areas in which little work has been done" (1998: 53).

Citing documentary caches from the Mamluk era as well as discussions about the keeping of court records by pre-Ottoman writers, Hallaq (1998) demonstrates that the keeping of such records predated the Ottomans. He also criticizes the use of *sijill* to refer to the court "archive," stating that the proper term is diwan—the *sijill* refers to one of two specific types of record associated with litigation, the other being *maḥḍar*. In this two-register model (cf. Little 1997: 539), the *maḥḍar* contained case entries pertaining to litigant claims and responses and also any presented evidence, while the *sijill* recapitulated these materials and added the qadi's final ruling. Many cases initiated in the *maḥḍar* registers were dropped or discontinued; only a subset went on to form the basis for the formal decisions entered in the *sijill*. In addition to these records specific to trials, Hallaq also details the further textual elements in the standard inventory of the Sharia court archive. These included records of legal instruments of different genres, such as deeds, contracts, and endowment documents, as well as records that contained names and related information concerning witnesses, prisoners, trustees, bequests, qadi-to-qadi letters,[10] guarantors, and agents. Ahmet Akgündüz (2009) has comprehensively examined the textual nomenclature that pertained specifically to the Ottoman Sharia court, including the usages adopted during the period of nineteenth-century reforms (Tanzimat); he also discusses the elaborate written guidelines for such record-keeping.

Specifically regarding legal instruments—contracts and other types of routine documents prepared by notarial writers—Western scholarship focused on their "ambiguous" status (Wakin 1972: 4). The starting point for this topic is Q 2:282, which requires the writing of witnessed documents in connection with debt transactions. Ambiguity entered when Muslim exegetes later reduced this divine order to the status of a "recommendation." Gregor Schoeler (2006) places the issues involved in the larger context of the early tensions between oral and written texts in Islam. In terms of historical legal applications, the drafting of and reliance on written documents had predated Islam, and these activities then continued unabated in the Islamic era. In Ottoman times, excerpts of written documents routinely appear in Sharia court records, and the same was true of the traditional court records kept in early twentieth-century Yemen (Messick 1993). Document archives held privately include early Egyptian papyri, the medieval Geniza documents, the above-mentioned Mamluk cache in Jerusalem, and personal archives of more recent times such as those held by families in a rural Egyptian setting (Peters 2011).

Noting this persistent practical reliance on written documents, Schacht maintained that the juridical doctrine "ignored" them. He seized upon what he understood to be the problematic technical status of legal documents as a prime illustration of the "perpetual problem" of Islamic law, namely, the contrast between theory and practice (1964: 193, 209). Johansen (1997) refuted this perspective by demonstrating the jurists' consistent attention to this topic. One of the doctrinal views admitting written documents as evidence places an emphasis on memory, stating that the qadi must remember the indicated legal circumstance before relying upon a document held in his archive. A method for confirming a written text presented as court evidence envisages summoning the document witnesses for supporting testimony. In an early study Tyan (1959) examined how the later Maliki school jurists of the Islamic West "solved" the problem of the written document through the institution of the court-approved notary. For their part, anthropologists of twentieth-century Morocco have emphasized the related role of the "normative witness" (Rosen 1989; Geertz 1973), a theme also taken up by historians (for example, Gerber 1994: 38).

A technical juridical literature devoted to model instruments also emerged. These treatises of stipulations (*shurūṭ*; in the Muslim West, *wathāʾiq* "documents") were designed to buttress the integrity

10 On the issues surrounding qadi-to-qadi communications, see Hallaq 1999.

of written notarial documents. The pioneering Western studies are by Jeanette Wakin (1972), who also provides the Arabic text of al-Ṭahāwī (d. 321/933), and Monika Gronke (1984). Hallaq (1995) examined *shurūṭ* works as a way in to the larger "dialectic of doctrine and practice," and hypothesized that the models of contracts and other legal instruments that appear in the *shurūṭ* treatises are the "stripped"[11] versions of actual documents, their particulars removed and their essential structure laid bare. If this movement from actual transactional usage (historical documents) to doctrinal text (the *shurūṭ* treatises) represents one side of the "dialectic," the other results from notarial writers consulting the models presented in such treatises as guides for drafting new instruments.

Court processes per se have been studied in terms of the relevant doctrine. Schacht (1964: chap. 25) treats "procedure" on the basis of a single later work, *Multaqā al-abhūr* of al-Ḥalabī (d. 956/1549), the authoritative Hanafi law book under the Ottomans. In this treatment, Schacht joins together several discrete chapters from the doctrine, notably those on the judgeship, testimonies (or evidence), and claims. More recently Hallaq (2009: chap. 12) follows the same method of joining the topics of these three doctrinal chapters, but expands his readings to include the other Sunni schools and the major Shiʿi school of jurisprudence. A different approach to the relevant doctrinal texts involves close readings of a single chapter in a single work (Ghazzal 2007: chap. 2, on judgeship in Ibn ʿĀbidīn; Messick 2002, on testimony in Zaydi doctrine). Zouhair Ghazzall, who studies early nineteenth-century Greater Syria, takes the significant further step of integrating his readings of doctrine with parallel readings of archival texts such as court litigation records and contract instruments.

As has been noted, muftis provided some historical jurisdictions with interpretive services; extensive evidence exists in court registers for the role of fatwas in Ottoman Sharia practice. For other settings we know about the incidence of qadis' queries to muftis from questions and answers collected in book form. To Calder, this "judicial fatwa" is a distinct type (2010: 169). Some of these fatwas came into play in courts primarily in the handling of the unusual, significant, political sensitive, or otherwise "hard" case (Ghazzal 2007: 15, 657; cf. Hallaq 2009: 362). Jennings (1978) observed, however, that disputants and litigants themselves also obtained fatwas and that these usually concerned routine matters.

The Qadi

Peirce (2003: 93) found her sixteenth-century judges to be "textually silent"—a silence that is possibly merely an artifact of the sharply summarized form of the court records. Indeed, we are still in the dark as to how judges, for example, conducted themselves in court; what judicial style is presupposed in the procedural doctrine and what styles obtained in specific historical settings; how, beyond generally presiding over the proceedings, judges intervened; whether qadis posed questions in any systematic sense, either to litigants or to witnesses; and whether it should be assumed that judges pronounced their decisions in court and that these also took written form. A comprehensive volume (Masud et al. 2006a) provides an impetus to the study of the qadi. The introduction sets forth an updated account of the state of the field and the status of its sources and comprises an extended discussion of *adab al-qāḍī* works, the literature concerned with the culture or "etiquette" of the judgeship. Irene Schneider (1990) published the basic comparative study of such works up to the thirteenth century. She surveys the key issues, which include the judge's qualifications, relations with the appointing ruler, and procedure. In addition, we have studies of individual *adab* treatises by A.A.A. Fyzee (1964) and Farhat Ziadeh (al-Khaṣṣāf 1978).

Rather than accounts of actual practice, this specialized *adab* genre (like that on the muftiship) offers conceptualizations of practice. Among the many basic issues treated is the perhaps surprisingly controversial question of whether the judge must be capable of formal *ijtihād*, or independent

11 See the above discussion of the "stripping" hypothesis used in his 1994 study.

interpretation. Also raised is the reluctance of many qualified individuals to serve as judge. Al-Khaṣṣāf, in fact, advises avoidance of the position. At the same time, the office was a "collective duty" such that it was incumbent upon the Muslim community to see that it was filled.

While relatively well known in concept, the distinctive features of this system of court justice remain little investigated in terms of applications. Among these features is the judge's allocation of the roles of plaintiff and defendant prior to the start of litigation. This determination was based on the judge's assessment of the apparent status quo, which would be defended. The litigant challenging this presumed state of affairs became the plaintiff, and assumed the initial burden of proof. Such determination of the litigation roles remains obscure, however, since it occurred before the beginning of the official court record, which opened with the plaintiff's claim. The doctrinally normative type of litigation was "simple," or one-sided, in evidential terms. This accorded with the famous maxim that, following the claim by the plaintiff and the denial of the claim by the defendant, the plaintiff alone presented evidence.[12] What do we know of the incidence of this sort of single-sided normative trial? What, on the other hand, was the incidence of "compound" cases, those in which both parties made claims and both presented evidence (Messick 2002)?

While we now have a fairly detailed sense of the variety of interpretive acts carried out by muftis in their fatwas, we know little about those of judges in their rulings. We do not know whether Sharia court judges provided reasoned judgments, or what, beyond the theoretical arguments associated with the judge's qualification for *ijtihād*, "interpretation" amounted to at the level of the Sharia court. In terms of the substantive focus of interpretation, one may (again) note that the specifics of the initiating court claim constrained the judge's decision. The doctrine envisions the qadi establishing a factual basis for his decision through evidence, acknowledgement, oath, and, at least in some schools and with certain restrictions, his own knowledge, but judgments rendered by judges were not reported or otherwise cited.[13]

In general, the legal process was meant to operate on the level of the apparent or manifest (*ẓāhir*) rather than that of the concealed (Johansen 1990). How did the judge's analysis of intent (or consent, or mutual consent, etc.) figure in substantive cases that ranged from contracts to homicide (Arabi 1997; Messick 2001; Paul Powers 2006; cf. Rosen 1995)? Only in North Africa, it seems, did a type of "case law" emerge, which was known as *'amal*.[14] Unlike the possibility of general applicability associated with the authoritative fatwa, the relevance of a judgment was confined to the specific case. Historically, there was no institution of appeal.[15]

12 "The burden of proof (by testimony) lies upon the one who makes the allegation and the oath belongs to him who denies (*al-bayyina 'alā l-mudda'ī wa-l-yamīn 'alā man ankar*)" (Brunschvig 1960: 1151a).

13 In a note that accompanies two of his articles, Jennings states (1975, 1978), "a verdict is not part of the formal registration of cases in the *sicils*." But in the latter article he refers to the "*hüküm* (sentence) given by the kadi." The formal judgment (Ar. *ḥukm*) of a Sharia court judge was known in the later Ottoman empire—and in Egypt—as *i'lam*. Engin Akarli (2006: 263) translates the term as "decision"; Işık Tamdoğan (2008: 59–60) as "court ruling." Ahmet Akgündüz (2009: 216–23), who carefully analyzes its constituent discursive elements, renders it as a "judicial decree" that contains a judge's judgment. For the equivalent usage in nineteenth-century Egypt, see Peters 1990 (p. 101) and Fahmy 1999 (p. 236). Tamdoğan (2008: 59–60) and Akgündüz (2009: 224–6) differentiate the *i'lam* from the other important type of text recorded by the Sharia court in Ottoman times, the *ma'ruz*.

For a much earlier period, Christian Müller (2006) identifies a type of non-litigated outcome, the "judicial certification" (*thubūt*). Akgündüz (2009: 212) also discusses how the issuance of a *ḥujja*, a legal instrument such as a sale contract, might figure in an Ottoman situation of possible litigation. Jennings (1979) refers to procedures for uncontested matters, which typically involve acknowledgements. In court records from early nineteenth-century Syria and Lebanon, Ghazzal (2007: 137–41, and passim) identifies what he terms "procedural fictions," carried out in "fictitious litigations."

14 Jacques Berque (1960) attributes the "discovery" of these texts of judicial practice to L. Milliot, who argued that they were "tending to the creation of a positive law."

15 David Powers examined the practice, referring to it as "successor review" (1992; cf. Masud et al. 2006a: 30–2).

The Witness and Other Forms of Evidence

The evidential scheme per se depended on the testimony of just witnesses (*shuhūd ʿudūl*; sg. *shāhid ʿadl*). According to theory, the testimonies from the normative two witnesses presented by the plaintiff must not differ. Ghazzal (2007: 134) remarks that the Sharia courts "wanted their witnesses to deliver *identical* testimonies" (emphasis original). But Sharia courts did not depend on witness interrogation of any form, whether by the judge, by the litigants, or by attorneys.[16] Not well understood, in terms of practice, are the Sharia judge's method of private consultations to determine witness integrity and the public techniques of witness verification (*tazkiya, taʿdīl*), a version of which could be mounted by the litigants. Witness integrity and veracity could be impugned, of course, but little is known about the implementation of the important countervailing litigation technique known to the evidence doctrine as *jarḥ*, or witness "disparaging" (Messick 2002: 254–61).

Following Tyan, the main emphasis of study has been the role of pre-certified witnesses, which in some quarters (notably in the Muslim West) developed into the institution of the court-controlled witnesses. A much less formalized institution was the Ottoman *shuhūd al-ḥāl*, which involved respected members of the community (Jennings 1978, 1979). Ron Shaham (2010) has examined the reliance upon expert witnesses, who play a role mainly in cases of medical or anatomical matters, building standards, and issues specifically regarding women. Despite the existing conceptual reservations, we also know that written documents were routinely presented as evidence in trials, but not exactly how courts handled them.

According to theory, a litigant's acknowledgment or oath could be decisive in a case. Oaths in the court context are of several distinct conceptual types, but the role of these devices in the conduct of cases—whether such statements figured in actual trials, and, if so, how (Jennings 1996; Bechor 2012; Messick 2006: 216–8)—is unclear. A distinctive feature accepted by some schools of law is the role of the circumstantial "knowledge of the judge" (*ʿilm al-qāḍī*), which could be decisive in certain types of cases. Could applications of this knowledge in specific cases be misread, through a Western lens, as acts of judicial discretion?

We do not know whether the basic rule requiring equal treatment of litigants squared with the range of actual social difference in Muslim communities. This rule also had to be adapted to accommodate the Jews and Christians who appeared in the Sharia court. Their use of these courts is well documented (Al-Qattan 1999; Gradeva 1997; Simonsohn 2011). The integral presence in court of women and their legal problems has also been a major theme of substantive research, starting with the early work of Jennings (1975) on the seventeenth century in the Ottoman empire. Judith Tucker (1998) utilizes both fatwas and court judgments in her study of marriage, divorce, parenting, and sexuality in the seventeenth and eighteenth centuries in the Arab provinces of the empire, while Peirce (2003) focuses on gender issues in a local Anatolian court of the sixteenth century. General studies of women and gender issues in the courts have also appeared (Sonbol 1996; Tucker 2008).

Alternative Forums

The division of courts into civil and criminal jurisdictions is a modern phenomenon. An individual Sharia judge was likely to hear cases that ranged well beyond what would later become thought of as "family law" or "personal status" to include diverse property, contract, or unilateral disposition cases, including commercial and other market-related litigation, as well as cases that fell under the doctrinal categories of either "injuries," which culminated in loss of life, or *ḥudūd*, the five (or six) acts for

16 Our understanding of the limited role of the advocate or litigation agent (*wakīl*) has not advanced much since Ronald Jennings' groundbreaking article of 1975.

which punishments are stipulated in the Quran. The distinctive features of murder and related cases included the determinative role of private initiative by the injured party or the relevant kin and, again, the absence of an institution of public prosecution. Both injuries and *ḥudūd* cases also entailed stricter rules of evidence (see Chapter 12, below).

The prevailing assumption in earlier scholarship was that the doctrinal theory of penal law had little "hold" upon actual practice and that "the political authorities took over the administration of criminal justice at an early period" (Schacht 1964: 76; Heyd 1973: 1). Recent work, however, has noted five murder cases that came before the qadi in the year 1540–41 (Peirce 2003: 336–43), the incidence of criminal cases in court registers in Palestine (Doumani 1985: 157), and the prevalence of criminal law in the Sharia court (Gerber 1994: 17). In the Islamic West of the eleventh and twelfth centuries judges also handled a range of types of penal cases, from slander and blasphemy to wine drinking, theft, and homicide (Serrano 2006; cf. Hallaq 1994).[17]

In fact, it has been demonstrated (Peters 1990, 1997) that up to the reception of French law codes in 1883, homicide trials were quite common in nineteenth-century Egyptian Sharia courts. In this Egyptian setting, however, the Sharia courts, where the cases usually originated, were paired institutionally with "secular" jurisdictions with different evidence rules, and by 1850, as Khaled Fahmy (1999) has shown, non-Sharia types of evidence were being used in homicide investigations. These supplementary investigations relied upon the new forensic expertise of the Egyptian medical establishment, including autopsy reports and certain types of laboratory work.

Known as "councils" (*majālis*, sg. *majlis*), these supplementing jurisdictions were an important institutional feature of mid-nineteenth-century justice both in Egypt and in the central Arab provinces of the Ottoman empire (see Ghazzal 2007). However, the existence of some type of parallel or superior state forum for "secular justice" dates back to the classical institution of the *maẓālim* jurisdiction, the ruler's court where grievances could be heard. In the single historical study, Nielsen (1985) examines an instance from the Mamluk era.[18] State officials also were apt to take action in connection with cases and disputes under the rubric of *siyāsa* (T. *siyaset*), which indicated a modality of secular or "political" intervention. The rights of the Ottoman sultan in this regard have been discussed by historians such as Haim Gerber (1994), who refers to a type of "administrative justice." Peirce (2003: chap. 8) gives examples of agents empowered by a local governor to manage cases in Sharia court trials and also of the implementation of official punishments.

Another Ottoman institution was the imperial divan (Ar. *dīwān*), which Engin Akarli (2006) examines in terms of its functioning as a type of high court, based on the role of the specialized high-level judge known as the *kazasker* (< Ar. *qāḍī ʿaskar* "military judge"). See also Akgündüz (2009: 203) on the composition of this "Imperial Council." The divan holds great promise for our eventual understanding of Ottoman Sharia court processes. Whereas the records of the regular Sharia court jurisdictions tend to be summarized and abrupt, "the judicial files of the divan normally include detailed information about the history of each case and documents indicating the evidence on which the judges based their decision" (Akarli 2006: 248). For the law (*kanun*) of the Ottoman sultans, see Chapter 8, below.

Studies on the Sharia punishments and penalties, known generally as the *ʿuqūbāt*, have been surveyed (Johansen 1997; Lange 2007, 2008; and see Chapter 12, below). Although they did not apply only to criminal matters, imprisonment options also were available to the judge (Schneider 1995), as were lesser types of restraint, such as ankle chaining, for example for the debtor. A summary of the penalty and punishment repertory, which ranges from verbal admonitions and fines to several forms of execution, can be found in Peters 2005 (pp. 30–38). Muslim jurists also produced a specialized literature on wound (and death) evaluation (the *arsh* and *diya* works), based on premodern conceptions of what now would be termed "victim compensation."

17 For a revised general understanding of "crime and punishment" in Sharia jurisdictions, see Peters 2005.
18 See also Amedroz 1911.

Finally, it may be useful to return to Lawrence Rosen's argument that Islamic justice generally preferred settlements to zero-sum decisions by the judge. Prior to Rosen, Jacques Berque had asked whether the judge decided ("le cadi tranche-t-il?"), and had argued, also with reference to North African materials, that the main task of the judge was to arrange settlements (Berque 1973; for a critical appraisal, Hentati 2007). The "moral logic of social equity rather than a logic of winner-takes-all resolutions" (Hallaq 2009: 166, cf. 545) was supported by well-known maxims such as "amicable settlement is the best verdict" (*al-ṣulḥ sayyid al-aḥkām*) (2009: 162). Arbitration and mediation therefore "stand paramount over court litigation, which was usually seen as the last resort" (2009: 163). According to this "social harmony" hypothesis,[19] a preference for informal resolution was tied to an underlying concern of this system of justice, which was to avoid disrupting the social order.

What is the historical evidence of out-of-court settlements and related activity? Relying only on historical court records, it would be difficult, with the notable exception of marriage conflicts, to document whether judges had simply turned disputants away for resolution elsewhere. Marriage disputes (the principal type of case that fell within the limited jurisdiction of Rosen's modern Moroccan courts) represented the single type of case for which the judge was required, by Quranic injunction, to first attempt to refer the disputants to their family members.[20] In some historical jurisdictions there were court-recognized experts in mediation and settlement (*ṣulḥ*) (Jennings 1978, Peirce 2003: 120; for Ottoman Egypt, El-Nahal 1979: 19–20; see also Abdul Rahman 1991: 89 on "conciliation committees"). To the extent that parties who had settled or arbitrated their disputes outside the court subsequently had the terms ratified by the judge and the related documentation entered in his register, court records also provide sources for other types of resolutions. However, a further Sharia maxim that does not condone "making the licit illicit, or the illicit licit" may have barred the ratification of some customary arrangements.

Out-of-court resolution was not the only possibility since settlements also could be arranged in-court under the auspices of the judge. Rather than a sharp distinction between "formal" and "informal" processes, Işık Tamdoğan (2008: 56) argues in light of Ottoman records that the various types of resolution "represent different points on a single continuum that links the court with external sociolegal arenas." At the same time, as both she and Aida Othman (2007) note, a conception of *ṣulḥ* was "integral" to the doctrinal fiqh conception of the court process itself, as judges were required to urge the parties to settle rather than pursue or continue litigation. This new research additionally points out that *ṣulḥ* was a doctrinal topic in its own right and that it also received separate chapter treatment in fiqh works.

Whatever the incidence of the several forms of alternative dispute resolution, whether in or out of court, we should not turn away from efforts to understand the processes of litigation that resulted in a decision by a judge. Social harmony was not always attainable and, as numerous historians have affirmed, these were very litigious societies. Research on court activity leading to formal rulings is vital to the analysis of social conflict. Where personal problems and societal contradictions tended to be obscured in outcomes based on compromise or arbitration, in contentious court cases they were explicitly aired and argued, and also formally decided by a presiding judge. In the doctrinal scheme, *ṣulḥ* had a valued and significant place, no doubt. But the jurists' larger design for justice, their main institutional emphasis, centered on a carefully articulated set of procedural steps intended to mesh with an equally well-elaborated regime of evidential truth finding. These procedures and conceptions of justice and truth provided the institutional bases for litigation that culminated in formal decision-making, in the applied interpretations of the Sharia by court judges.

19 Cf. Hallaq 2009: 163, 166, 366, 386.

20 Quran (4:35, cf. 4:128): "If you fear a breach between them, appoint one arbiter from the people of the man and one from the people of the woman. If they wish to make a settlement then God will reconcile them."

References

Abdul Rahman, Abdul Rahim. 1991. The Documents of the Egyptian Religious Courts (al-Maḥākim al-Shar'iyyah) as a Source for the Study of Ottoman Provincial Administration in Egypt (923/1517–1213/1798). *Journal of the Economic and Social History of the Orient* 34: 88–97.

———. 1992–2004. *Wathā'iq al-maḥākim al-shar'iyya al-Miṣriyya 'an al-jāliyya al-Maghāribiyya ibbāna l-'aṣr al-'uthmānī*. 4 vols. Zaghwan, Tunisia: Markaz al-Dirāsāt wa-l-Buḥūth.

Agrama, Hussein Ali. 2010. Ethics, Tradition, Authority: Toward an Anthropology of the Fatwa. *American Ethnologist* 37: 2–18.

Akarli, Engin. 2006. Law in the Marketplace: Istanbul, 1730–1840. In *Dispensing Justice in Islam: Qadis and Their Judgments*, ed. M.K. Masud et al., pp. 245–70. Leiden: Brill.

Akgündüz, Ahmet. 2009. Shari'ah Courts and Shari'ah Records: The Application of Islamic Law in the Ottoman State. *Islamic Law and Society* 16: 202–30.

Al-Qattan, Najwa. 1999. Dhimmīs in the Muslim Court: Legal Autonomy and Religious Discrimination. *International Journal of Middle East Studies* 31: 429–44.

Amedroz, H. F. 1910. The Office of Kadi in the Ahkam Sultaniyya of Mawardi. *Journal of the Royal Asiatic Society*: 761–96.

———. 1911. The Mazalim Jurisdiction in the Ahkam Sultaniyya of Mawardi. *Journal of the Royal Asiatic Society*: 635–74.

Arabi, Oussama. 1997. Intention and Method in Sanhūrī's Fiqh: Cause as Ulterior Motive. *Islamic Law and Society* 4: 200–23.

Bechor, Guy. 2012. *God in the Courtroom: The Transformation of Courtroom Oath and Perjury between Islamic and Franco-Egyptian Law*. Leiden: Brill.

Berkey, Jonathan. 1992. *The Transmission of Knowledge in Medieval Cairo: A Social History of Islamic Education*. Princeton: Princeton University Press.

Berque, Jacques. 1960. 'Amal. In *Encyclopaedia of Islam*, 2nd ed. Vol. 1: 427–8. Leiden: E.J. Brill.

———. 1973. Cadis de Kairouan d'après un manuscrit tunisien. *Revue de l'Occident musulman et de la Méditerranée* 13: 97–108.

Brunschwig, Robert. 1960. Bayyina. In *Encyclopaedia of Islam*, 2nd ed. Vol. 1: 1150–1. Leiden: E.J. Brill.

Calder, Norman. 1996. Al-Nawawī's Typology of Muftīs and Its Significance for a General Theory of Islamic Law. *Islamic Law and Society* 3: 137–64.

———. 2010. Scholars, Muftis, Judges, and Secular Power: The Need for Distinctions. In *Islamic Jurisprudence in the Classical Era*, ed. C. Imber, pp. 116–66. New York: Cambridge University Press.

Chamberlain, Michael. 1994. *Knowledge and Social Practice in Medieval Damascus, 1190–1350*. Cambridge: Cambridge University Press.

Coulson, Noel J. 1956. Doctrine and Practice in Islamic Law: One Aspect of the Problem. *Bulletin of the School of Oriental and African Studies* 18: 211–26.

Doumani, Beshara. 1985. Palestinian Islamic Court Records: A Source for Socioeconomic History. *MESA Bulletin* 19(2): 155–72.

Eickelman, Dale. 1978. The Art of Memory: Islamic Education and Its Social Reproduction. *Comparative Studies in Society and History* 20: 485–516.

———. 1985. *Knowledge and Power in Morocco: The Education of a Twentieth-Century Notable*. Princeton: Princeton University Press.

El-Nahal, Galal H. 1979. *The Judicial Administration of Ottoman Egypt in the Seventeenth Century*. Minneapolis: Bibliotheca Islamica.

Fadel, Mohammad. 1996. The Social Logic of *Taqlīd* and the Rise of the *Mukhtaṣar*. *Islamic Law and Society* 3: 193–233.

Fahmy, Khaled. 1999. The Anatomy of Justice: Forensic Medicine and Criminal Law in Nineteenth-Century Egypt. *Islamic Law and Society* 6: 224–71.

Fischer, Michael M. J. 1980. *Iran: From Religious Dispute to Resolution*. Cambridge, MA: Harvard University Press.

Fyzee, Asaf Ali Asghar. 1964. The *Adab al-Qadi* in Muslim Law. *Malaya Law Review* 6: 406–16.

Geertz, Clifford. 1973. *The Interpretation of Cultures: Selected Essays*. New York: Basic Books.

Gerber, Haim. 1994. *State, Society, and Law in Islam: Ottoman Law in Comparative Perspective*. Albany: State University of New York Press.

———. 1999. *Islamic Law and Culture, 1600–1840*. Leiden: Brill.

Ghazzal, Zouhair. 2007. *The Grammars of Adjudication: The Economics of Judicial Decision-Making in Fin-de-siècle Ottoman Beirut and Damascus*. Beirut: IFPO.

Goody, Jack, ed. 1968. *Literacy in Traditional Societies*. New York: Cambridge University Press.

Gottheil, Richard J.H., ed. 1908a. *Al-Kindī, The History of the Egyptian Cadis*. Paris: P. Geuthner.

———. 1908b. The Cadi, the History of this Institution. *Revue des Etudes Ethnographiques et Sociologiques* 1: 385–93.

Gradeva, Rossitsa. 1997. Orthodox Christians in the Kadi Courts: The Practice of the Sofia Sheriat Court, Seventeenth Century. *Islamic Law and Society* 4: 37–69.

Gronke, Monika. 1984. La rédaction des actes privés dans le monde musulman médiéval: Théorie et pratique. *Studia Islamica* 59: 159–74.

Hallaq, Wael B. 1994. From Fatwās to *Furū'*: Growth and Change in Islamic Substantive Law. *Islamic Law and Society* 1: 29–65.

———. 1995. Model *Shurūṭ* Works and the Dialectic of Doctrine and Practice. *Islamic Law and Society* 2(2): 109–34.

———. 1996. Ifta' and Ijtihad in Sunni Legal Theory: A Developmental Account. In *Islamic Legal Interpretation: Muftis and Their Fatwas*, ed. M.K. Masud et al., pp. 33–43. Cambridge, MA: Harvard University Press.

———. 1998. The *qāḍī's dīwān* (*sijill*) before the Ottomans. *Bulletin of the School of Oriental and African Studies* 61: 415–36.

———. 1999. *Qāḍīs* Communicating: Legal Change and the Law of Documentary Evidence. *Al-Qanṭara* 20: 437–66.

———. 2009. *Sharī'a: Theory, Practice, Transformations*. Cambridge: Cambridge University Press.

Hefner, Robert W., and Muhammad Qasim Zaman, eds. 2007. *Schooling Islam: The Culture and Politics of Modern Muslim Education*. Princeton: Princeton University Press.

Hentati, Nejmeddine. 2007. Mais le cadi tranche-t-il? *Islamic Law and Society* 14: 180–203.

Heyd, Uriel. 1969. Some Aspects of the Ottoman Fetvā. *Bulletin of the School of Oriental and African Studies* 32: 35–56.

———. 1973. *Studies in Old Ottoman Criminal Law*. Oxford: Clarendon Press.

Hoexter, Miriam. 2007. Qāḍī, Mufti and Ruler: Their Roles in the Development of Islamic Law. In *Law, Custom, and Statute in The Muslim World*, ed. R. Shaham, pp. 67–85. Leiden: Brill.

Imber, Colin. 1996. Eleven Fetvas of the Ottoman Sheikh al-Islam 'Abdurrahim. In *Islamic Legal Interpretation: Muftis and Their Fatwas*, ed. M.K. Masud et al., pp. 141–9. Cambridge, MA: Harvard University Press.

———. 1997. *Ebu's-su'ud: The Islamic Legal Tradition*. Stanford: Stanford University Press.

Jennings, Ronald C. 1975. Women in Early 17th Century Ottoman Judicial Records: The Sharia Court of Anatolian Kayseri. *Journal of the Economic and Social History of the Orient* 18: 53–114.

———. 1978. Kadi, Court, and Legal Procedure in 17th C. Ottoman Kayseri: The Kadi and the Legal System. *Studia Islamica* 48: 133–72.

———. 1979. Limitations of the Judicial Powers of the Kadi in 17th C. Ottoman Kayseri. *Studia Islamica* 50: 151–84.

———. 1996. The Use of Oaths of Denial at an Ottoman Sharia Court Lefkoşa (Nicosia), 1580–1640. *Journal of Turkish Studies* 20: 13–23.

Johansen, Baber. 1990. Le jugement comme preuve: Preuve juridique et vérité religieuse dans le Droit Islamique hanéfite. *Studia Islamica* 72: 5–17. Reprinted in idem, *Contingency in a Sacred Law: Legal and Ethical Norms in the Muslim* Fiqh. Leiden: Brill, 1999.

———. 1997. Wahrheit und Geltungsanspruch: Zur Begründung und Begrenzung der Autorität des Qāḍī-Urteils im Islamischen Recht. In *La Giustizia nell'alto medioevo, secoli IX–XI: 11–17 aprile 1996*. 2 vols, pp. 975–1074. Spoleto: Centro Italiano di Studi sull'alto Medioevo.

———. 1999. *Contingency in a Sacred Law: Legal and Ethical Norms in the Muslim* Fiqh. Leiden: Brill.

Juynboll. G.H.A. 1983. *Muslim Tradition: Studies in Chronology, Provenance and Authorship of Early* Ḥadīth. Cambridge: Cambridge University Press.

al-Khaṣṣāf, Aḥmad b. ʿUmar. 1978. *Kitāb Adab al-qāḍī*, ed. F. Ziadeh. Cairo: American University Press.

Lange, Christian. 2007. Legal and Cultural Aspects of Ignominious Parading (*Tashhīr*) in Islam. *Islamic Law and Society* 14: 81–108.

———. 2008. *Justice, Punishment and the Medieval Muslim Imagination*. Cambridge: Cambridge University Press.

Little, Donald. 1997. Sidjill.2. In *Encyclopaedia of Islam*, 2nd ed. Vol. 9: 538–9. Leiden: Brill.

Mahmood, Saba. 2005. *Politics of Piety: The Islamic Revival and the Feminist Subject*. Princeton: Princeton University Press.

Makdisi, George. 1981. *The Rise of Colleges: Institutions of Learning in Islam and the West*. Edinburgh: Edinburgh University Press.

Mandaville, Jon E. 1966. The Ottoman Court Records of Syria and Jordan. *Journal of the American Oriental Society* 86: 311–9.

———. 1975. The Jerusalem Sharīʿa Court Records: A Supplement and Complement to the Central Archives. In *Studies on Palestine during the Ottoman Period*, ed. M. Maʿoz, pp. 517–24. Jerusalem: Magnes Press.

Manoukian, Setrag. 2012. *City of Knowledge in Twentieth Century Iran: Shiraz, History and Poetry*. London: Routledge.

Marín, Manuela. 1985. Šūrà et ahl al-šūrà dans al-Andalus. *Studia Islamica* 62: 25–51.

Masud, M. Khalid. 1984. Ādāb al-Muftī: The Muslim Understanding of Values, Characteristics, and Role of a Muftī. In *Moral Conduct and Authority: The Place of Adab in South Asian Islam*, ed. B.D. Metcalf, pp. 124–51. Berkeley and Los Angeles: University of California Press.

———, Brinkley Messick, and David S. Powers, eds. 1996. *Islamic Legal Interpretation: Muftis and Their Fatwas*. Cambridge, MA: Harvard University Press.

——— at al., eds. 2006a. *Dispensing Justice in Islam: Qadis and Their Judgments*. Leiden: Brill.

———. 2006b. The Award of Matāʿ in the Early Muslim Courts. In *Dispensing Justice in Islam: Qadis and Their Judgments*, ed. M.K. Masud et al., pp. 349–81. Leiden: Brill.

Messick, Brinkley. 1986. The Mufti, the Text and the World: Legal Interpretation in Yemen. *Man* n.s. 21: 102–19.

———. 1993. *The Calligraphic State: Textual Domination and History in a Muslim Society*. Berkeley and Los Angeles: University of California Press.

———. 1996. Media Muftis: Radio fatwas in Yemen. In *Islamic Legal Interpretation: Muftis and Their Fatwas*, ed. M.K. Masud et al., pp. 310–20. Cambridge, MA: Harvard University Press.

———. 2001. Indexing the Self: Expression and Intent in Islamic Legal Acts. *Islamic Law and Society* 8: 151–78.

———. 2002. Evidence: From Memory to Archive. *Islamic Law and Society* 9: 231–70.

———. 2006. Commercial Litigation in a Sharīʿa Court. In *Dispensing Justice in Islam: Qadis and Their Judgments*, ed. M.K. Masud et al., pp. 195–218. Leiden: Brill.

Müller, Christian. 2006. Settling Litigation without Judgment: The Importance of a *Ḥukm* in *Qāḍī* cases of Mamlūk Jerusalem. In *Dispensing Justice in Islam: Qadis and Their Judgments*, ed. M.K. Masud et al., pp. 47–69. Leiden: Brill.
Mundy, Martha. 1991. Between the Oral and the Written (review of Lawrence Rosen, *The Anthropology of Justice*). *History Workshop* 32: 184–92.
Nielsen, Jørgen S. 1985. *Secular Justice in an Islamic State: Maẓālim under the Baḥrī Mamlūks, 662/1264–789/1387*. Leiden: Nederlands Historisch-Archaeologisch Instituut te Istanbul.
Othman, Aida. 2007. "And Amicable Settlement is Best": *Ṣulḥ* and Dispute Resolution in Islamic Law. *Arab Law Quarterly* 21: 64–90.
Peirce, Leslie P. 2003. *Morality Tales: Law and Gender in the Ottoman Court of Aintab*. Berkeley and Los Angeles: University of California Press.
Peters, Rudolph. 1990. Murder on the Nile: Homicide Trials in 19th Century Egyptian Shariʿa Courts. *Die Welt des Islams* 30: 98–116.
———. 1997. Islamic and Secular Criminal Law in Nineteenth Century Egypt: The Role and Function of the Qadi. *Islamic Law and Society* 4: 70–90.
———. 2005. *Crime and Punishment in Islamic Law: Theory and Practice from the Sixteenth to the Twenty-First Century*. Cambridge: Cambridge University Press.
———. 2011. *Wathāʾiq madīnat al-Qaṣr bi-l-wāḥāt al-Dākhila maṣdarān li-tārīkh Miṣr fī l-ʿaṣr al-ʿuthmānī*. Cairo: Maṭbaʿat al-ʿĀmma li-Dār al-Kutub wa-l-Wathāʾiq al-Qawmiyya.
Powers, David S. 1992. On Judicial Review in Islamic Law. *Law and Society Review* 26: 315–42.
———. 1993. Legal Consultation (*Futyā*) in Medieval Spain and North Africa. In *Islam and Public Law*, ed. C. Mallat, pp. 85–106. London: Graham and Trotman.
———. 1994. *Kadijustiz* or *Qāḍī*-Justice? A Paternity Dispute from Fourteenth-Century Morocco. *Islamic Law and Society* 1: 332–66.
———. 2002. *Law, Society, and Culture in the Maghrib*, 1300–1500. Cambridge: Cambridge University Press.
Powers, Paul. 2006. *Intent in Islamic Law: Motive and Meaning in Sunnī* Fiqh. Leiden: Brill.
Reinhart, A. Kevin. 1993. Transcendence and Social Practice: Muftīs and Qāḍīs as Religious Interpreters. *Annales Islamologiques* 27: 5–28.
Rosen, Lawrence. 1989. *The Anthropology of Justice: Law as Culture in Islamic Society*. New York: Cambridge University Press.
———, ed. 1995. *Other Intentions: Cultural Contexts and the Attribution of Inner States*. Santa Fe, NM: School of American Research Press.
———. 2000. *The Justice of Islam: Comparative Perspectives on Islamic Law and Society*. New York: Oxford University Press.
Schacht, Joseph. 1964. *An Introduction to Islamic Law*. Oxford: Clarendon Press.
———. 1971. Theology and Law in Islam. In *Theology and Law in Islam*, ed. G.E. von Grunebaum, pp. 3–23. Wiesbaden: Harrassowitz.
Schneider, Irene. 1990. *Das Bild des richters in der "Adab al-Qāḍī" Literatur*. Frankfurt: Peter Lang.
———. 1993. Die Merkmale der idealtypischen "qadi"-Justiz: Kritische Anmerkungen zu Max Webers Kategorisierung der islamischen Rechtsprechung. *Der Islam* 70: 145–59.
———. 1995. Imprisonment in Pre-Classical and Classical Islamic Law. *Islamic Law and Society* 2: 157–73.
Schoeler, Gregor. 2006. *The Oral and the Written in Early Islam*, tr. J.E. Montgomery. London: Routledge.
Serjeant, R. B. 1984. The Caliph ʿUmar's Letters to Abū Mūsā al-Ashʿarī and Muʿāwiya. *Journal of Semitic Studies* 29: 65–79. Reprinted in *Customary and Shariʿah Law in Arabian Society*, Hampshire, UK: Variorum, 1991.

Serrano, Delfina. 2006. Twelve Court Cases on the Application of Penal Law under the Almoravids. In *Dispensing Justice in Islam: Qadis and Their Judgments*, ed. M.K. Masud et al., pp. 473–93. Leiden: Brill.

Shaham, Ron. 2010. *The Expert Witness in Islamic Courts: Medicine and Crafts in the Service of Law*. Chicago: University of Chicago Press.

al-Shawkānī, Muḥammad. 1985. *Sayl al-jarrār al-mutadaffiq ʿalā ḥadāʾiq al-Azhār*. 4 vols. Beirut: Dār al-Kutub al-ʿIlmiyya.

Simonsohn, Uriel I. 2011. *A Common Justice: The Legal Allegiances of Christians and Jews Under Early Islam*. Philadelphia: University of Pennsylvania Press.

Sonbol, Amira El Azhary, ed. 1996. *Women, the Family, and Divorce Laws in Islamic History*. Syracuse: Syracuse University Press.

Starrett, Gregory. 1998. *Putting Islam to Work: Education, Politics, and Religious Transformation in Egypt*. Berkeley and Los Angeles: University of California Press.

Tamdoğan, Işık. 2008. *Sulh* and the 18th Century Islamic Courts of Üsküdar and Adana. *Islamic Law and Society* 15: 55–83.

Tucker, Judith E. 1998. *In the House of the Law: Gender and Islamic Law in Ottoman Syria and Palestine*. Berkeley and Los Angeles: University of California Press.

———. 2008. *Women, Family, and Gender in Islamic Law*. New York: Cambridge University Press.

Turner, Bryan S. 1974. *Weber and Islam: A Critical Study*. London: Routledge and Kegan Paul.

Tyan, Émile. 1959. *Le notariat et le régime de la preuve par écrit dans la pratique du droit musulman*. Beirut: Saint Paul; 1st ed., publ. 1945.

———. 1960. *Histoire de l'organisation judiciaire en pays d'islam*. Leiden: E.J. Brill. Revision of 1938 edition, publ. Paris: Librairie du Recueil Sirey.

Ursinus, Michael. 2005. *Grievance Administration (Sikayet) in an Ottoman Province: The Kaymakam of Rumelia's "Record Book of Complaints" of 1781–1783*. Abingdon, UK: RoutledgeCurzon.

Vogel, Frank E. 1996. The Complementarity of Iftāʾ and Qaḍāʾ: Three Saudi Fatwas on Divorce. In *Islamic Legal Interpretation: Muftis and Their Fatwas*, ed. M.K. Masud et al., pp. 262–9. Cambridge, MA: Harvard University Press.

al-Wakīʿ, Muḥammad b. Khalaf. 1947–50. *Akhbār al-quḍāt*, ed. ʿA.M. al-Marāghī. 3 vols. Cairo: Maṭbaʿat al-Istiqāma.

Wakin, Jeanette A. 1972. *The Function of Documents in Islamic Law: The Chapters on Sales from Ṭaḥāwī's* Kitāb al-Shurūṭ al-Kabīr. Albany: State University of New York Press.

al-Wansharīsī, Aḥmad b. Yaḥyā. 1981–83. *Al-Miʿyār al-muʿrib wa-l-jāmiʿ al-mughrib*. 13 vols. Rabat: Ministry of Culture and Religious Affairs.

Weber, Max. 1978. *Economy and Society: An Outline of Interpretative Sociology*. Berkeley and Los Angeles: University of California Press.

Wensinck, A. J. 1922. *The Refused Dignity. In A Volume of Oriental Studies Presented to Edward G. Browne on His 60th Birthday*, ed. T.W. Arnold and R.A. Nicholson, pp. 491–99. Cambridge: Cambridge University Press.

Wiederhold, Lutz. 1996. Legal Doctrines in Conflict: The Relevance of *Madhhab* Boundaries to Legal Reasoning in the Light of an Unpublished Treatise on *Taqlīd* and *Ijtihād*. *Islamic Law and Society* 3: 234–304.

Ze'evi, Dror. 1998. The Use of Ottoman Sharīʿa Court Records as a Source for Middle Eastern Social History: A Reappraisal. *Islamic Law and Society* 5: 35–56.

al-Zuḥaylī, Muḥammad. 1995. *Taʾrīkh al-qaḍāʾ fī l-islām*. Damascus: Dār al-Fikr.

State and Sharia

Mohammad Fadel

One of the most contentious issues in the academic study of Islamic law has been the relationship between the Sharia and the historical polities that Muslims established in diverse times and places. Making this body of inquiry especially difficult to navigate is the fact that scholars' conclusions often depend on unstated and uncritical theories of the "proper" relationship of the state to the law, which may well be disputed among political scientists and legal and political philosophers. Furthermore, because of the heterogeneity of Muslim views on the nature of the Sharia and the nature of the state, as well as on the relationship between the two, a careful scholar must take care to qualify observations in light of the specific sectarian commitments of the work or works being analyzed. Broadly speaking, then, one can speak of different Muslim traditions that articulate competing versions of the normative relationship between the Sharia and the state. The most important sectarian traditions are those of the *ahl al-sunna wa-l-jamāʿa*, the Sunnis; the *shīʿat ʿAlī*, the Shiʿa; and the *shurāt*, known to their detractors as the Kharijis, the secessionists. Within each of these three normative traditions, of course, there are sub-traditions, marking internal disagreements arising out of different interpretations of each community's particular sectarian commitments. The Sunni tradition will be the principal focus of this chapter, something that is justified by the fact that it was the historically dominant tradition among Muslims and has received the bulk of scholarly attention. The chapter will conclude with a brief discussion of future research into this topic.

No account of Muslim thinking on this subject, however, would be complete without due attention to the contributions of the Muslim philosophical tradition (*falsafa*) and, for lack of a better term, the belle-lettrists who often expressed a conception of the law and its relationship to the state from the perspective of the practical statesman rather than the philosopher, theologian, or jurist. Space constraints, however, have made it impossible to devote even cursory attention to their views of the Sharia and the state.

Orientalist Theories of the Sharia and Sunni Constitutional Law

Western scholarship of Islamic law began in earnest with the rise of European colonialism, first in British India and then throughout much of the Islamic world. Hand in hand with European traders and conquering European armies and navies, orientalists worked to produce translations of Islamic law, largely to assist colonial administrators to better govern their Muslim subjects (Hallaq 2009: 376; and

Mohammad Fadel is Associate Professor and Canada Research Chair for the Law and Economics of Islamic Law at the University of Toronto. In addition to an unpublished but widely read doctoral dissertation on Maliki legal process, Fadel has published on a broad range of comparative and Islamic legal subjects, including "Back to the Future: The Paradoxical Revival of Aspirations for an Islamic State" (2009), "Muslim Reformists, Female Citizenship, and the Public Accommodation of Islam in Liberal Democracy" (2012), and "Judicial Institutions, the Legitimacy of Islamic State Law and Democratic Transition in Egypt" (2013).

Chapter 15, below). It was inevitable, given the context in which European studies of Islamic law took place, that parochial conceptions of law, based on these scholars' own experience of the emerging legal systems of an industrializing Europe, would color their impressions of Islamic law. Because the primary motive for studying Islamic law was the instrumental goal of furthering the success of the colonial enterprise, one should not be surprised that unpacking the internal coherence of substantive Islamic law (*fiqh*) was not the most important priority for this generation of scholars.

Parallel with the European expansion into Islamic lands, Max Weber developed his sociological typologies of law, which made links between the formal rationality of legal systems and their capacity to engender the kinds of social changes that had led to capitalist modernity in Europe. Relying on the conclusions of the emerging orientalist studies in Islamic law, particularly that of the Dutch scholar Christiaan Snouck Hurgronje, Weber unsurprisingly concluded that Islamic law was deficient insofar as it lacked, among other things, a sufficient commitment to the formal rationality that Weber believed was a prerequisite for capitalist transformation. This deficiency was in large part a consequence of its status as a religious law that was concerned exclusively with substantive rationality, that is, just outcomes, without regard to abstracting from individual outcomes formally rational rules that were internally consistent and generally applicable. Another consequence of Islamic law being a religious law, according to Weber, was that it was unwilling or unable to adapt in light of changing social circumstances, particularly after "the door of independent legal reasoning" (*ijtihād*) was closed. One particularly pernicious consequence of this failure was the fact that Islamic law became increasingly inapplicable to more and more areas of social life, and, as a result, instead of general rules regulating social life in a reasonably reliable and predictable fashion, Muslim societies were governed by a bewildering array of particular ethical, customary, or practical considerations that were embedded in a system of ad hoc decision-making, thus making capitalist development impossible (Turner 1974: 109, 110, 115, 119). Weber concluded that the Sharia was less a tool of practical governance than an unattainable ideal that had become irrelevant to governance, with the result that Muslim societies, as a practical matter, had become lawless (Turner 1974: 115).

Weber's typology of law and notion of where Islamic law fits into that typology anticipated many of the themes that Western orientalists would subsequently adopt in their study of Islamic law. Thus, Weberian themes such as the difference between religious law and secular law, the tension between legal ideals and reality, legal change versus stagnation, and formally rational law versus substantively rational law represented some of the most important themes guiding Islamic law scholarship from the last quarter of the nineteenth century and much of the twentieth. Indeed, Snouck Hurgronje himself (1957: 261) wrote that,

> *Fiqh* is distinguished from modern and Roman law in that it is a doctrine of duties [*une déontologie*] in the broadest sense of the word, and cannot be divided into religion, morality, and law. It deals only with "external" duties—i.e., those that are susceptible to control by a human authority instituted by God. However, these duties are without exception duties toward God, and are based on the unfathomable will of God Himself. All duties that men can perceive being carried out are dealt with—all the duties of man in whatever circumstances and in their connections with anyone whatsoever.

More than half a century later scholarly opinion had hardly changed. Writing in the middle of the twentieth century, the British scholar of Islamic law Noel Coulson (1956: 223) expressed much of the same sentiment, saying,

> They (i.e., the jurists) produced a comprehensive system of rules governing every aspect of life which expressed the religious ideal. Their fundamental concern was the study and development of "law" for its own sake. Practical considerations were only employed where this could be done without infringement on any theoretical principle.

Joseph Schacht also echoed Weber's criticism of Islamic law as being insufficiently developed, writing in his influential *Introduction to Islamic Law* that although Islamic law is not entirely irrational, "its formal juridical character is little developed; it aims at providing concrete and material norms, and not at imposing formal rules on the play of contending interests" (Schacht 1964: 4). Schacht also asserted, consistent with Weber, that the Sharia "had to resign an ever-increasing sphere to practice and custom," something that was the inevitable outcome of a legal theory that was "from the early 'Abbāsid period onwards unable to keep pace with the ever-changing demands of society and commerce" (1964: 77). Coulson, too, contrasted Islamic law—which as a divine law "is a rigid and immutable system" and to whose dictates all must succumb regardless of their circumstances—with a legal system grounded in human reasoning "based upon the local circumstances and the particular needs of a given community" (Coulson 1964: 5). Thus, the religious character of Islamic law produced its rigidity, which in turn made it impractical for the governance of a dynamic society, thus producing the "gap" between theory and practice that would culminate, ironically, in the substitution of arbitrary and secular law-making for the ideal system of religious law envisioned by the Muslim jurists.

It is here that we see the intersection between legal theory and the state: because Islamic legal theory created an unattainable ideal, according to these scholars, the historical institutions that actually governed Muslim societies were bereft of a legal system that could be used to further the practical interests of their societies. This institutional failure was deemed to be the result of Islamic legal theory's failure to provide an adequate role for the state in governance, and was therefore understood by these scholars to be largely the failure of Muslim jurists to produce a workable system of constitutional law—the law governing the state itself (Schacht 1964: 27, 54–5). Schacht, for example, wrote that of all the topics discussed by Muslim jurists, the least relevant to social practice was constitutional law, if it existed at all (1964: 36). He attributed the failure to develop a practical system of law to the fact that "the religious law of Islam" developed not in connection with the practices of the emerging Muslim state, but rather in direct "opposition to it" (1964: 27).

Ann Lambton succinctly restates this line of scholarship in her introduction to *State and Government in Medieval Islam*. She writes that because the Sharia is pre-existing and eternal, and because it represents the absolute good, it precedes the community and the state, and thus dispenses with any need for political philosophy, even to "ask[] the question why the state exists." The all-encompassing nature of the Sharia, its divine character, and its claim to govern the state, in turn, preclude the possibility of conceiving the person as a rights-bearing individual. The failure to recognize a separation of religion and state "contributed to, if it was not actually responsible for, the creation of a situation in which power was arbitrary and exercised by the last despot who had usurped it" (1981: xiv–xvi).

Western scholars writing specialized works on Islamic constitutional law came to the conclusion that over the course of time Sunni jurists abandoned any attempt to establish a legitimate constitutional order and simply surrendered to the notion that "might equals right" (Gibb 1955: 19; Kerr 1966: 51). This depressing conclusion is almost exclusively the result of Western focus on Sunni discussions about the selection of the caliph. Sunni doctrine asserts that suitably qualified electors (*ahl al-ḥall wa-l-ʿaqd*) should select the caliph from among a pool of candidates who meet certain minimal criteria of eligibility, or in the alternative, the incumbent caliph is to select a suitable candidate during his lifetime. Abbasid-era jurists, however, such as the Shafiʿi al-Māwardī, had made substantial concessions to the warlords who were exercising effective power in the Abbasid state through the conditional validation of the governorship by seizure (*imārat al-istīlāʾ*); Mamluk-era jurists such as Ibn Jamāʿa went even further, effectively legitimating government by usurpation. Sir Hamilton Gibb characterized Ibn Jamāʿa's views on government as "a complete divorce of the imāmate from the Sharīʿa and the abandonment of the Law in favor of a secular absolutism" (1955: 23).

Kerr, too, focused on the failure of Muslim jurists to articulate an objective set of rules governing the process by which the caliph should be selected, noting (1966: 31) that,

> In the election of the caliph by the *ahl al-ḥall wa-l-ʿaqd* (leaders of the Community), not only do we never have a precise account of who these electors are or how they are to be chosen and on what basis, but there is no means described of authoritatively determining whether or not the election has been correctly carried out.

Islamic constitutional law was also seen to be a failure insofar as it failed to provide meaningful independence for judges (Tyan 1955: 236–9; Tyan 1960: 11–12; Coulson 1966: 131). As a result, orientalist scholars asserted that enforcement of judicial decisions "was entirely at the whim of the *de facto* ruler" (Coulson 1964: 83). Émile Tyan argued that the subordination of the judiciary was the direct result of a normative juridical theory that lodged all powers in an autocratic ruler and conceived of all lesser officials as the personal delegate and representative of the ruler (Tyan 1955: 236). The autocratic powers of the ruler, in combination with the idealistic and thoroughly impractical norms of the Sharia, led to the creation of alternative tribunals, known as *maẓālim*, which could dispense an effective form of rough and practical secular justice. For these scholars the *maẓālim* courts represented secular law in contrast to the religious law that the qadis administered (Tyan 1960: 445–6; Tyan 1955: 243; Coulson 1964: 129; Schacht 1964: 54–5). Despite their recognition that Muslim jurists themselves discussed *maẓālim* tribunals and deemed them to be legitimate, this acceptance of the *maẓālim* fora amounted to no more than the further entrenchment and "tolerat[ion] of secular absolutism" (Coulson 1966: 131).

Sunni constitutional law was also deficient insofar as it failed to provide for legitimate legislation, all law having come from God via revelation. It being impossible to govern based solely on revealed sources whose texts were frozen in time, Muslim jurists came to recognize the right of the ruler to "make rules and regulations, to clarify and apply the law," but not in a way that would change it or amend it. This power was known as *siyāsa sharʿiyya* (Lewis 1988: 31). This form of rule-making, however, was not sufficient to remedy the defective nature of Islamic constitutional law. Schacht argued (1964: 53–4) that this doctrine obfuscated the distinction between legislation and administration, and thereby prevented Muslim jurists from addressing the problem legislation posed to their constitutional law squarely. Coulson, on the other hand, believed (1966: 133) that the doctrine gave too much arbitrary power to the ruler, and the jurists, in their typically idealistic stance, legitimated the doctrine in their naïve belief that rulers would be just and only use it for good. In short, Islamic constitutional law was both a cause and an effect of the idealistic, even utopian, nature of the Sharia.

Having concluded that the Sharia dispensed with any need for political theory and that it was essentially utopian, it is not surprising that orientalist scholars writing on Islamic constitutional law, for example Erwin I.J. Rosenthal, W. Montgomery Watt, and Ann Lambton, prioritize "context," that is, empirical historical reality (or what is claimed to be historical reality), over "text" in their analysis of Muslim political writings. Rosenthal, for example, asserts that the purpose of Sunni constitutional theory was to reconcile the doctrinal demand that spiritual and secular powers be united in the caliph and the empirical reality that others—the sultan or the amir—actually wield temporal power. For Rosenthal, this was accomplished by a reciprocal exchange of recognition between the caliphs and the military elites who held effective power: in exchange for the caliph delegating temporal authority to these de facto rulers, the de facto rulers in turn would recognize the spiritual authority of the caliph (1958: 22–3). Indeed, Watt was so convinced of the priority of the empirical to the theoretical that he informed the reader in the introduction to his *Islamic Political Thought* that "the concepts implicit in men's practice are more important than the writings of political theorists," thus justifying the book's focus on "practice more than theory" (1968: x). Consistent with that view, he devoted only four pages to Sunni constitutional law; these four pages were essentially a recapitulation of the eleventh-century al-Māwardī's *al-Aḥkām al-sulṭāniyya*, as interpreted by Gibb (Watt 1968: 101–4). Lambton's approach is in essence the same (1981: 87).

Among the newer generation of contributors to Western scholarship on the theory of the caliphate, Patricia Crone has been one of the most creative. She generally agrees with previous scholars regarding the Sharia's deleterious effect on the political life of the Muslim community (Crone and

Hinds 1986: 109–10), but revitalizes the field by claiming that the Sunni theory, which subordinated the state to the Sharia of the jurists, was a development of classical Islam that represented a radical departure from the views of the early Muslim community, for whom "it was the caliph who was charged with the definition of Islamic law [...]. In short [....] the early caliphate was conceived along the lines familiar from Shīʿite Islam" (Crone and Hinds 1986: 1). The classical view described by orientalists was therefore a post-Abbasid development.

Crone's overview of Sunni political thought and of its relationship to the Sharia is at this moment the best and most comprehensive overview of the subject available in English (Crone 2004: chaps. 16, 18). Her reading of the sources is much more nuanced than prior scholarship and pays greater attention to the details of various scholars' positions, and she usefully draws on the comparative experience of other civilizations in an effort to make sense of some Sunni positions that others have roundly castigated. She makes a persuasive case that al-Ghazālī's insistence on the importance of the caliphate, as set out in his work *Faḍāʾiḥ al-bāṭiniyya* (alternatively, *al-Mustaẓhirī*), is, in contrast to the position taken by his teacher al-Juwaynī in *Ghiyāth al-umam*, best explained by his determination to counter the challenge of Ismaʿili Shiʿism (2004: 238–41). She also roundly criticizes Gibb's outrage at al-Māwardī's attempt to legitimize "governorship by usurpation," saying that "[h]is reaction is peculiar, for what could be more common in history than the recognition of usurpers? It was by casting the barbarian polities of Europe as subordinate kingdoms (*regna*) within the empire (*imperium*) that Christians such as Isidore of Seville (d. 636) maintained the theoretical unity of the Roman Empire" (2004: 233). Nevertheless, because she hews to the general argument of her predecessors that Sunni religious idealism substantially undermined the possibility of a workable political order, her work should be viewed as the most sophisticated presentation of the classical orientalist view, rather than representing a new approach to the subject.

Revisionist Theories of the Sharia and Sunni Constitutional Law

In the 1980s scholars began to question the validity of certain elements of the orientalist account of the relationship between the Sharia and the actual operation of legal systems in premodern Muslim polities. Its assertion that the idealist nature of the Sharia rendered its use as a tool of governance impracticable was questioned through a series of studies that challenged, inter alia, the assumption that formal legal rules were irrelevant to the historical legal systems in existence in Muslim polities; that Islamic substantive law was, for all essential purposes, immutable; and that a sharp ideological division existed between the qadi courts—which applied the formal rules of Islamic law—and *maẓālim* and other tribunals that the orientalist account had taken to be secular jurisdictions that existed outside the normative framework of Islamic law.

Social historians and anthropologists began undertaking studies that tested how irrelevant formal Islamic law was to organizing social life in Muslim societies. One traditional obstacle to challenging the "irrelevancy" hypothesis was that court records had not been systematically preserved until the Ottoman empire, and as a result there was very little documentary evidence that could shed light on the practices of courts in the Muslim world. Legal anthropologists circumvented this problem through a combination of direct observation of the practices of contemporary courts as well as the practices of other members of the legal class, for example muftis and document writers, combined with close readings of relevant legal texts. Rather than demonstrating a binary opposition between the formal legal system and the cultural system, these studies demonstrated how formal legal norms interacted with cultural norms in order to produce a legal system that was both Islamic and customary (Messick 1986, 1989, 1990, 1993; Rosen 1981, 1989).

Social historians also began to make use of fatwas—after successfully challenging the notion that these represented purely theoretical or academic exercises—to demonstrate the relevance of formal Islamic law as a tool for the effective governance of pre-Ottoman Islamic societies (Powers 1998, 2002, 2003, 2006a, 2006b; Masud et al. 2006; Shatzmiller 1995, 2001, 2007). Meanwhile, since the 1990s there has been an explosion in studies exploiting Ottoman court records for the economic and social history of the Ottoman empire, in addition to numerous monographs on its legal culture (Gerber 1994, 1999; Imber 1997). Timur Kuran has to date published a ten-volume collection of judicial records from seventeenth-century Istanbul, with summaries of the decisions in modern Turkish and English (2010–). Numerous historical studies of endowments (*awqāf*) over the same period have also undermined the orientalist position that Islamic law had little relevance to social practice (Ghazaleh 2011). The cumulative weight of these studies has significantly weakened the case that Islamic law was largely a theoretical enterprise that had little relevance to social practice or the practice of courts.

Legal anthropologists and social and economic historians were not the only scholars compromising the orientalist conception of the relationship of the Sharia to society; scholars in legal theory were also challenging the stereotyped notion that Islamic legal theory was too idealistic and rigid to permit principled adaptation to changing circumstances (see Chapter 5, above). They were crucial in paving the way for a more nuanced appreciation of *uṣūl al-fiqh* and its commitment to rational and logical coherence, with the result that our appreciation of Sunni *uṣūl* has now far transcended the "four-source" theory (Quran, Sunna, *ijmāʿ*, and *qiyās*) commonly attributed to al-Shāfiʿī.

The renewed interest in Sunni *uṣūl al-fiqh* was accompanied by the same in post-formative (that is, post-fourth-century AH) developments in Sunni substantive law (*furūʿ al-fiqh*). Once it was demonstrated that Islamic law was not impermeable to legal change, scholars began documenting the actual history of Sunni substantive law. Several specializing in post-formative fiqh demonstrated that substantial diachronic changes took place in Islamic substantive law, and that fiqh became more systematic and abstract—in contrast to the claims of Weber and orientalism—throughout the post-formative period. To offer only a few examples: through a close analysis of Hanafi legal categories, John Makdisi showed (1985–86) that post-formative Hanafi law displayed many of the features of formal rationality and systematization that Weber believed were lacking in Islamic law. With respect to diachronic change, Baber Johansen demonstrated (1988) that Hanafi jurists from the Mamluk and Ottoman periods knowingly and openly adopted positions in matters of taxation contrary to those of the early Hanafi masters, demonstrating that even within the parameters of *taqlīd* there were important venues for substantial and legitimate doctrinal change. Others were able to show that *taqlīd* did not represent a lesser form of Islamic law, but rather a shift from individual to corporate authority (Jackson 1996a: xxx–xxxii), indeed, it placed the law on firmer social footing by making the law more predictable, even code-like, as evidenced by the authoritative accounts of the various madhhab doctrines that Mamluk-era jurists produced, such as *Mukhtaṣar Khalīl* (Fadel 1996). Finally, it was demonstrated how substantive law evolved through the interaction of legal doctrine, social practice, and the practice of *iftāʾ* (giving legal opinions) (Hallaq 1994; Hallaq 2001: 195–208; Fadel 1997: 57–61, 66–7, 69–71).

By demonstrating that Sunni Islamic legal theory and substantive law were neither as rigid nor as idealistic as had been claimed, this line of scholarship effectively challenged some of the most basic tenets of orientalism regarding the relationship of the Sharia, Muslim society, and the state. Sunni constitutional law, however, has yet to receive the same degree of attention from revisionist scholars. Indeed, even a scholar with the stature of Wael Hallaq has failed to revisit orientalist assumptions regarding Sunni constitutional law, omitting the topic entirely from his *Sharīʿa: Theory, Practice and Transformations* (Fadel 2011: 115). Nevertheless, scholarship has begun to make strides in proposing new ways to understand Islamic constitutional law and the legitimacy of the state from the perspective of Islamic law.

The first scholar to provide a new account of Islamic constitutional law was Sherman Jackson in his study of the Maliki Shihāb al-Dīn al-Qarāfī (d. 684/1285). Relying on al-Qarāfī's treatise on constitutional law, *al-Iḥkām fī tamyīz al-fatāwā ʿan al-aḥkām wa-taṣarrufāt al-qāḍī wa-l-imām*, Jackson identified al-Qarāfī's functionalist analysis of Prophetic precedents as laying the foundation for a constitutional approach to the interpretation of Islamic law (Jackson 1993). According to

Jackson, al-Qarāfī states that proper understanding of Prophetic precedent first requires determination of the capacity in which the Prophet Muḥammad was acting at the time: either as the Apostle of God, as mufti, as judge, or as head of state. When the Prophet acted as an apostle, he was conveying God's revelation to humanity. When he was acting as a mufti, he was communicating the meaning of revelation to humanity in the form of rules that were applicable to the end of time—the legal effect of such rules was either to create immutable duties or obligations, or to authorize certain kinds of human actions, in each case on condition that the relevant legal conditions had been satisfied. When the Prophet was acting in the manner of a judge, the effect was that individuals could not exercise the right in question unless and until a judge authorized them to exercise that right. Finally, when he acted in his capacity of head of state, that meant that the legal norm in question did not represent a general rule of law, but rather the decision of the community's temporal ruler, with the consequence that successive rulers of the Muslim community were free to follow the Prophetic precedent, modify it, or ignore it altogether, in each case based on their contemporaneous assessment of the community's welfare.

According to Jackson, the political relevance of al-Qarāfī's taxonomy lies in his assertion that each of Muḥammad's four functions was inherited by various members of the Muslim community. Thus, Quran reciters and hadith transmitters inherited the apostolic function of communicating revelation. Muftis inherited the Prophet's function as authorized interpreter of the textual proofs (*adilla*) contained in God's revelation, but with the crucial difference that, unlike the Prophet, they were not infallible, and so their interpretations of God's revelation bound only those who followed them but not those who followed the views of different muftis. Judges inherited his function of resolving conclusively disputes among people in accord with judicial evidence (*ḥijāj*), such as eyewitness testimony, oaths, denials, etc. And caliphs inherited from the Prophet his role as temporal head of the community with the authority to make binding decisions for the good of the community (*al-siyāsa al-ʿāmma*).

In this way, various public offices in the state were given different roles within the constitutional order of a caliphate: judges' decisions were final so long as they followed legitimate rules of law as articulated by muftis; because of the regime of *taqlīd*, the four madhhabs enjoyed quasi-constitutional status and existed side by side, supplying the rules by which courts would resolve disputes; and rulers, whether called caliphs, amirs, sultans, or kings, enjoyed the power to direct the community's public affairs, engage in giving legal opinions (that is, act as a mufti), and resolve legal disputes (that is, act as a judge), without, however, interfering in the autonomy of the law-making process, or the integrity of the law's application. The result of al-Qarāfī's theory, paradoxically perhaps, was simultaneously to elevate the theoretical powers of the caliph (and by extension other rulers) by recognizing him as a member of the legal class and the judiciary, while effectively neutralizing those powers by subjecting his exercise of those powers to the same standards that applied to ordinary members of the legal class and the judiciary.

As a practical matter, then, this meant that if rulers chose to exercise either the power of interpreting the law or of resolving disputes, they would have to rely on the established opinions of the legal schools. According to Jackson, the upshot of all this was to place substantial limits on the power of the government through the tool of the law. Another important feature of al-Qarāfī's argument was that it placed limits on the reach of the law itself, and, accordingly, helped to check the risk that any one particular school of law could dominate the state and impose its norms on society, including on Muslims holding contrary views—something that particularly concerned al-Qarāfī due to the Shafiʿi school's close relationship to the Ayyubid and Mamluk rulers of his day (Jackson 1996a).

Other scholars of the Mamluk era have also challenged one aspect of the orientalist narrative that asserts that Muslim rulers effectively created their own, essentially arbitrary system of positive law to govern medieval Muslim societies. This alternative system of law, known as *siyāsa*, was said to exist outside the formal normative constraints of the Sharia, and was administered largely through the "secular" tribunals of, for example, *maẓālim* or *jarāʾim*, in contrast to the "religious" tribunals of the qadis. I myself have challenged this account of *siyāsa*, relying on the medieval Hanbali scholars Ibn Taymiyya and Ibn Qayyim al-Jawziyya, as well as on Ibn Farḥūn (d. 799/1396), the Maliki author of *Tabṣirat al-ḥukkām*, and al-Ṭarābulusī (d. 844/1440), the Hanafi author of *Muʿīn al-ḥukkām* (Fadel 1995: 61–75, 79–105, 185–98). Both Ibn Farḥūn and al-Ṭarābulusī incorporated *siyāsa* directly into the ordinary law that judges were expected (or could be expected) to administer; moreover, roughly one-third of each of these works was dedicated to the question of *siyāsa*. Given the normalization of *siyāsa* at the hands of jurists in the Mamluk period, I argued that it was impossible to dismiss *siyāsa* as an Islamically illegitimate mode of law.

Yossef Rapoport has also criticized the continuing prevalence of the orientalist description of Islamic law and the (Mamluk) state, which he describes as "depressing narratives of decay and corruption" (2012: 71), despite the fact that Islamic law scholarship since the 1980s has refined much of the Schachtian (and ultimately Weberian) model of Islamic legal history (2012: 73). According to Rapoport, instead of a growing gulf between the jurisdictions of the qadi courts and the *maẓālim* and other tribunals established by the rulers, the Mamluk period witnessed an ever-greater integration between the two systems. This began when al-Ẓāhir Baybars (r. 1260–77) introduced the system of the four chief judges—one from each of the different schools of law—with the specific goal of taking advantage of particular elements of each school's doctrine in order to promote greater flexibility, predictability, and practicality in the legal system (2012: 77–9). Historical evidence from the period, Rapoport notes, contradicts the notion that *maẓālim* courts were arbitrary or were indifferent to Sharia norms (2012: 80–1). And while *maẓālim* courts originally specialized in remedying administrative abuses, in the later Mamluk period their jurisdiction expanded into both family law disputes and commercial disputes, largely to close what the rulers deemed were loopholes in the formalistic system of fiqh (2012: 84). Indeed, by the end of the Mamluk sultanate, the rulers had become so involved in the administration of justice—justice rendered in the name of the Sharia in contrast to the formal rules of fiqh—that they began to claim the right to interpret the substantive rules of the Sharia themselves, without regard to the views of the jurists (2012: 97). Instead of seeing this conflict, then, as a conflict between "religious" and "secular" authority, it is better viewed as competing conceptions of Islamic authority and Islamic justice writ large, between the formalistic champions of fiqh on the one hand and a more common-sense oriented conception of Islamic justice on the other (2012: 86–92).

Kristen Stilt's work (2012) on the *muḥtasib* of Mamluk Cairo casts further light on the practical relationship that existed in the Mamluk state between formal legal doctrine and the institutions of the state. In Stilt's analysis of this official—often described as the market inspector—he was simultaneously a bearer of the legal tradition, insofar as he oriented his policies in reliance on formal doctrinal manuals reflecting the values of the fiqh tradition, and a representative of the state's institutional power, insofar as he also carried out the ruler's policies and directives, particularly in the economic realm. Her study of the *muḥtasib*'s activities from this period, as reflected in historical chronicles and legal sources, repudiate the notion that rulers were divorced from the generally religious culture in which the Sharia was elaborated; a good portion of the rulers' directives to *muḥtasib*s was directly related to religious policies that the ruler himself took a direct interest in, whether with respect to the proper conduct of ritual prayers or regulation of sexual propriety among the general populace. Through an analysis of 35 case studies across a range of topics, Stilt at minimum raises substantial questions regarding the notion that normative fiqh, along with its conception of public offices such as that of the *muḥtasib*, was irrelevant to the functioning of the medieval legal system.

Shīʿat ʿAlī (the ʿAlids)

In contrast to the Sunnis, the partisans of ʿAlī b. Abī Ṭālib, the Prophet's first cousin and son-in-law, who are popularly known as the Shiʿa, were united—despite their divisions into numerous sub-sects—in the conception that God had designated Imams who were responsible for the spiritual and political guidance of the Muslim community following the Prophet's death. These Imams, moreover, were generally understood to be descendants of Muḥammad through the union of ʿAlī and Fāṭima, the

Prophet's daughter. The three most important branches of the Shiʿa are the Zaydis, the Imamis (also known as the Ithna ʿAsharis or Twelvers), and the Ismaʿilis.

As a general matter, the Shiʿa did not produce a body of cognizable constitutional law, at least not in the sense developed by Sunni jurists such as al-Māwardī. A brief historical review of Shiʿi views on the state is given below; for Western scholarship on Shiʿi classical thought on the state, see further Sachedina 1988; Madelung 1980; Gleave 2009; Calder 1987; Eliash 1969.

The Zaydis take their name from Zayd b. ʿAlī (d. 122/740), a great-grandson of ʿAlī b. Abī Ṭālib, who led an unsuccessful revolt against the Umayyad caliphate in Kufa. In contradistinction to the two other large Shiʿi groups, the Zaydis did not restrict the Imamate to a particular line of the Prophet's descendants, but instead held that any male member of the Prophet's descendants was a legitimate candidate, provided he satisfied its conditions, which were learning and political power. The legitimate Imam must, they believed, be more than a scholar; he must also manifest his learning through capturing (or founding) a state. While it was an obligation upon Muslims to attach themselves to the legitimate Imam when he appeared and claimed his rightful position, there was no requirement that an Imam exist at all times. Accordingly, while the Imamate was obligatory as a moral ideal, the empirical absence of a legitimate Imam did not imperil the spiritual state of the community; the community could endure in the absence of an Imam through its adherence to the Sharia. Zaydis were able to establish small states on the margins of the Islamic world, one along the shores of the Caspian Sea that existed from 864–1120, and the other in Yemen, which lasted more than a millennium, from 897–1962, albeit with the qualification that distinctive Zaydi ideas gradually receded in favor of Sunni theories of legitimacy as the Zaydi state in the Yemen became more firmly institutionalized and subject to principles of dynastic succession (Crone 2004: 99–109).

The Imamiyya, or the Twelvers, is the most numerous of the Shiʿi communities, representing approximately ten percent of Muslims worldwide. The Twelvers are distinguished from the Zaydis by several doctrines, beginning with who was eligible to be the Imam, but more significantly, regarding the role of the Imam in the life of the community. To sum up the differences, first, the Imams descended only from a particular line within the Prophet Muḥammad's family, and instead of earning their position by virtue of learning, political sagacity, courage on the battlefield, and calling men to the establishment of a legitimate political order, they were known by an express designation (*wiṣāya* or *naṣṣ*) from father to son, the sole exceptions being the first Imam, ʿAlī b. Abī Ṭālib, whom the Prophet Muḥammad himself had designated as Imam, and the third Imam, al-Ḥusayn b. ʿAlī b. Abī Ṭālib, whom his brother, the second Imam, al-Ḥasan b. ʿAlī b. Abī Ṭālib, designated as his successor. Thereafter, all Imams had to be a son of the living Imam, until the period known as the occultation (*ghayba*) began, with the disappearance of the twelfth Imam. Second, the Imams not only enjoyed a special line of descent, they also had access to knowledge that was otherwise inaccessible to ordinary human beings, and with respect to their religious instruction, they were infallible (*maʿṣūm*). As a result, recognition of the true Imam was crucial to a person's salvation, even if he was otherwise a Muslim. For this reason—unlike many of the Zaydis—the Imamis uniformly rejected the legitimacy of not only the Umayyad and Abbasid caliphates, but also the early caliphates of Abū Bakr, ʿUmar, and ʿUthmān, recognizing only the caliphate of ʿAlī as having been legitimate, a stance that earned them the designation of *rawāfiḍ*, "the rejecters." Third, because of the essentially apolitical role of the Imam in Twelver thought, the disappearance of the Imam was resolved by empowering religious scholars to speak on his behalf through the medium of their legal expertise; but because Twelver theology maintained the belief that the only legitimate government was the government of the Imam, non-Imami government could never have any legitimacy—the most that could be achieved was to live justly as a faithful community in accordance with the Imam's teachings as elaborated by the jurists (Crone 2004: 110–24).

Unlike the Zaydiyya, located away from the center of the Islamic world, the Imamiyya was largely an urban religious movement, concentrated first in the holy cities of the Hijaz, the garrison towns of Iraq, Baghdad, and Qum in Iran. With the exception of the Twelver Buyid interregnum, 945–1045, in

Iraq and western Iran, the Twelvers had always been subjects of Sunni rulers. Even during the period when the Buyids were in effective control of the Abbasid caliphate, there was no attempt to overthrow it in favor of a state founded on Twelver Shiʿi principles. The reasons for this are clear: Twelver doctrine had evolved to adopt a position of absolute political quietism that was the distinct opposite of the Zaydis. Only government by the Imam could be legitimate, and the possibility of legitimate rule had come to an end, at least until the twelfth Imam returned from his occultation to restore justice by reuniting the political and spiritual (Crone 2004: 120–2).

The quietist stance of the Twelvers remained undisturbed until the Safavids conquered Iran at the beginning of the sixteenth century and imposed Twelver doctrines on its populace. Instead of recognizing the legitimacy of the Safavid state, however, even in a qualified sense, Twelver scholars themselves claimed to be representatives of the Hidden Imam, and as a result, worldly rulers—to the extent they could gain any legitimacy at all—could do so only by agreeing to act as instruments of the Twelver religious class (Lambton 1981: 276–7). Twelver doctrine, then, has never come to recognize a legitimate political space outside the scope of the Imam's authority, or in his absence, the authority of the religious scholars who speak on his behalf, a position that laid the foundation for Ayatollah Khomeini's twentieth-century doctrine of "the rule of the [most eminent] jurist" (*wilāyat al-faqīh*) and the establishment of the Islamic Republic of Iran (Crone 2004: 122).

This conventional apolitical account of Twelver Shiʿism has been challenged by Said Arjomand, who argues that the concept of the *ghayba* actually functioned as a catalyst for the political activism of Twelver theologians with secular political authorities. The fact that the twelfth Imam was in hiding meant that, in practical terms, no living person could claim his authority (Arjomand 1988: 45) and as a result, political legitimacy came to depend on traditional, pre-Islamic norms of patrimonial monarchy, encapsulated in the slogan that the ruler was the shadow of God on earth (1988: 95–9). The non-Imamic ruler, who is otherwise deemed to be a usurper, could become a just ruler by using his powers to further the goals of the Hidden Imam, *ṣāḥib al-amr* (1988: 63–4). To accomplish the Hidden Imam's ends, scholars had to become more world-affirming and actively involved in the affairs of secular government, a process that began with the rise of rationalist Twelver theology at the hands of theologians like al-Sharīf al-Murtaḍā, who were even willing to serve the Abbasid caliphate in Baghdad (1988: 59–63).

From Arjomand's perspective, the Safavid takeover of Iran was not therefore the point at which Twelver Shiʿism became politically active; instead, it introduced a rejuvenated form of messianic Shiʿism that represented an important challenge to orthodox Twelver Shiʿism (1988: 102). Safavid religious policy walked a fine line between its commitment to rationalist Twelver orthodoxy, as evidenced, for example, by Shah Ṭahmāsp's (r. 1524–76) designation of ʿAlī al-Karakī al-ʿĀmilī (d. 940/1534) as *nāʾib al-imām* (1988: 133–4), and its inability to extricate itself fully from its roots as a messianic Shiʿi movement (1988: 179–80). Indeed, orthodox Twelver Shiʿism, with its rationalist commitment to political activism, does not eventually triumph until the nineteenth century, when it finally defeats both Shiʿi millenarianism and the Akhbari school of thought (1988: 14).

The Ismaʿiliyya broke away from the Twelvers/Imamiyya largely as a reaction to the latter's quietist politics. Unlike the Twelvers, who deferred the messianic age to an indefinite future and prohibited any attempts to hasten its advent, Ismaʿilism was largely a millenarian movement that consciously sought to hasten its advent. In addition to its millenarianism, Ismaʿili doctrine always included an important antinomian element that understood the messianic age to coincide with the abrogation of religious law. One branch of the Ismaʿili movement successfully established its own powerful, universal state, the Fatimid caliphate. The Fatimid state originated in 909 in North Africa, but after they successfully conquered Egypt, their newly built capital of Cairo became the center of the movement. The Fatimids, however, were never able to replace the Abbasids, and the messianic origins of the state were quickly replaced by the same bureaucratic logic that governed the Abbasid caliphate and those of its Sunni Turkic and Iranian allies. As a result, the religious movement again separated from the political, and eventually, the Sunni Ṣalāḥ al-Dīn al-Ayyūbī put an end to the Fatimid caliphate in 1171 (Crone 2004: 197–218). The religious movement continued to survive, however, and pockets of Isma'ili communities still exist in Syria, Yemen, Iran, on the Indian subcontinent, and among the Indian diaspora in East Africa and North America.

The *Shurāt* or the Kharijis (the "Secessionists")

The *shurāt*, those who "sold themselves to God," was the appellation preferred by Muslims whose answer to the problem of just governance was to insist on the immutability of the form of government that prevailed in the early Muslim community in Medina, as it existed until the waning days of the third caliph, 'Uthmān b. 'Affān. To their detractors, they were simply *khawārij*, secessionists, who obstinately refused obedience to any realistic form of government in favor of small, anarchic groups prone to periodic fits of violence. The origins of this group lies in the first civil war, when the fourth of the so-called rightly guided caliphs, 'Alī b. Abī Ṭālib, fought against Mu'āwiya b. Abī Sufyān. Each commanded a large body of the early Muslim community; the point of contention was the murder of the caliph 'Uthmān. 'Alī had been declared the next caliph, but Mu'āwiya, a long-serving governor of Syria, refused to recognize 'Alī's legitimacy on the grounds that the very people who had killed 'Uthmān were the ones who then selected 'Alī for the caliphate, and that, in any event, 'Alī refused to hand over the killers to Mu'āwiya, 'Uthmān's cousin and legal next of kin, for justice. The two parties met in battle at Siffin, and instead of finishing off Mu'āwiya's army, 'Alī agreed to submit the dispute to arbitration.

In protest of his decision to cease hostilities, a group of 'Alī's supporters departed from his camp, thereby earning the name of the "secessionists." Their opposition was based on their slogan "God is the only judge!" (*lā ḥukm illā li-llāh*), and they accused 'Alī of impiety by abandoning God's command to fight Mu'āwiya and his followers and submitting the dispute to an arbitrator for resolution. The insistence on the right, and in some early versions, the obligation, of Muslims to act to depose an unjust ruler, became the hallmark of their doctrine. The fact that they would rebel against unjust rulers even when they had no hope of prevailing was the motive behind their self-appellation of *shurāt*: they "sold" themselves to God through their ready willingness to lay down their lives in sacrifice against ungodly authority.

Like other Muslims, they largely agreed in principle on the obligation to have an Imam (although one group of the *shurāt*, the Najdiyya, are reported to have rejected the obligatory character of the Imamate [Crone 1998]); however, their doctrine of the Imamate was so radically egalitarian that it all but obliterated any difference between the Imam and the ordinary Muslim. From this perspective they can be viewed as the radical opposite of the Imamis and the Isma'ilis, whose conception of the Imamate posited radical difference between the Imam and the rest of humanity. For the *shurāt* the Imam could be any free Muslim, without regard to ethnicity or tribal descent. The only qualification was that he must be the most meritorious of the community, and that after he was elevated to the Imamate he continued in office only for so long as his conduct was consistent with the law and he remained virtuous. Once he fell short of this standard, the community was to ask him to repent, and if he did not, he was to be replaced. For the most radical of the early *shurāt* there was no possibility of living in a moral community unless that community was led by its most virtuous man.

Accordingly, Muslims who had not repudiated the Umayyads (and later the Abbasids) were necessarily apostates, and could be legitimately fought. Later *shurāt*, however, modified this doctrine, and came to accept the permissibility of living under an unjust ruler as long as one accepted, as a doctrinal matter, the moral obligation to establish a just Imamate. Under this more moderate platform, a stable doctrinal sect, known as the Ibadiyya, was able to establish itself, and they were able to set up relatively long-lived polities in Oman and North Africa (Crone 2004: 54–64). Muslims who follow *shurāt* teachings today represent less than one percent of the global Muslim community (Crone 2004: 20).

Future Research

Much progress has been made in studying the relationship of Islamic substantive law, as a set of formal doctrines, with the historical practices of various premodern Muslim polities. Given the richness of the archival sources, the most progress has been made in the Ottoman period, but knowledge of the pre-Ottoman Muslim states has also benefited. More progress, however, remains to be done. Islamic law scholarship focusing on the post-formative era, roughly the fifth to the tenth century AH, must make greater use of the formal doctrinal sources produced by that era. Long dismissed as an era of stagnation, we now know that much of the intellectual labor in formulating and adapting the law was taking place in commentaries, specialized treatises, and fatwas. While the work is labor intensive, it is likely to shed light on numerous questions that are of interest equally to legal historians as well as social historians. In this regard, it is crucial that legal scholars work closely with historians of the periods in question. It may be the case that many legal texts that seem unintelligible, or perhaps insignificant, become more intelligible, or gain in significance, when read in the proper historical context. At the same time, historians without a proper understanding of legal doctrines run the risk of misinterpreting their sources if they lack a solid understanding of legal terminology. It is not an exaggeration to say that the future progress of the field will depend on the ability of scholars from different disciplines—law, political history, social history and, ideally, economic history—to work together through legal and historical records in order to fashion a richer history of the legal world that predominated in the post-formative era.

For the classical and early periods, however, our sources are necessarily more limited. Our doctrinal resources are fewer, and so too the historical resources. Nevertheless, we have not exhausted our reading of even the early doctrinal sources. I will speak with regard to one important question that arises out of Sunni constitutional law: the notion that the ruler is a representative (*nāʾib*) or agent (*wakīl*) of the community. While Crone obviously recognizes that this view exists (Crone 2004: 240, 277, 298), she laments the failure of Sunni Muslims to take the "short step [...] [of] forming independent councils authorized to signal when the rules had been breached, to strike out illegal decisions, and to block their execution" (Crone 2004: 277). It may be, however, that we have failed to notice the existence of some forms of institutionalized means of supervising the legality of the government, even if they were rudimentary from the perspective of a modern state. Take the *maẓālim* tribunal, for example. Although the orientalist view was that it existed to make up for the inefficacy of the qadi's court, one of its most basic functions was *radd al-ghuṣūb*, the restoration of property that a government official had misappropriated. Far from being an extra-legal procedure, the efficacy of this remedy depended on recognition of the complainant's property rights as set forth in the fiqh literature, and of the fact that the actions of a government agent, no matter how powerful, could not alter the law's view of who held the legal entitlement.

The notion that the ruler is an agent of the community or its representative stands in sharp contrast to the notion of the ruler as a divine agent, and one would expect to see traces of this doctrine in the fiqh literature, particularly with respect to how jurists evaluate the conduct of the ruler and other public officials. While general works such as al-Māwardī's *al-Aḥkām al-sulṭāniyya* might not delve into these details, ordinary works of positive law routinely discuss issues involving the potential liability of the ruler and his agents when they violate the law; tracing the history of doctrines regulating the ruler's personal liability for wrongdoing, or those of his agents, might be a fruitful line of inquiry for determining the origin and the history of the concept of the imam as the community's representative. Finally, works of positive law, in particular in the post-formative and Ottoman eras, are replete with discussions regarding on what conditions a ruler's command is to be obeyed, and the nature of deference such commands ought to receive, but usually these discussions arise in connection with particular cases, rather than in the form of an abstract, philosophical discussion of the limits of the ruler's authority to legislate. Careful reading of these rules will certainly cast important light on the normative relationship between the authority of the ruler and his agents, and that of the law as interpreted and administered by the scholars.

References

Arjomand, Said. 1988. *Authority and Political Culture in Shiʿism*. Albany: State University of New York Press.

Calder, Norman. 1987. Legitimacy and Accommodation in Safavid Iran: The Juristic Theory of Muḥammad Bâqir al-Sabzavârî (d. 1090/1679). *Iran* 25: 91–105.

Coulson, Noel. 1956. Doctrine and Practice in Islamic Law. *Bulletin of the School of Oriental and African Studies*. 18(2): 211–26.

———. 1964. *A History of Islamic Law*. Edinburgh: Edinburgh University Press.

———. 1966. The State and the Individual in Islamic Law. In *The Traditional Near East*, ed. J. Stewart-Robinson. Englewood Cliffs, NJ: Prentice-Hall.

Crone, Patricia. 1998. A Statement by the Najdiyya Khārijites on the Dispensability of the Imamate. *Studia Islamica* 88: 55–76.

———. 2004. *God's Rule: Government and Islam*. New York: Columbia University Press.

Crone, Patricia, and Martin Hinds. 1986. *God's Caliph: Religious Authority in the First Centuries of Islam*. Cambridge: Cambridge University Press.

Eliash, Joseph. 1969. The Ithnāʿasharī-Shiʿi Juristic Theory of Political and Legal Authority. *Studia Islamica* 29: 17–30.

Fadel, Mohammad. 1995. Adjudication in the Mālikī Madhhab: A Study of Legal Process in Medieval Islamic Law. Ph.D. diss., University of Chicago.

———. 1996. The Social Logic of *Taqlīd* and the Rise of the *Mukhtaṣar*. *Islamic Law and Society* 3(2): 193–233.

———. 1997. Rules, Judicial Discretion, and the Rule of Law in Naṣrid Granada. In *Islamic Law: Theory and Practice*, ed. R. Gleave and E. Kermeli, pp. 49–86. London: I.B. Tauris.

———. 2011. A Tragedy of Politics or an Apolitical Tragedy? *Journal of the American Oriental Society* 131(1): 109–27.

Gerber, Haim. 1994. *State, Society and Law in Islam: Ottoman Law in Comparative Perspective*. Albany: State University of New York Press.

———. 1999. *Islamic Law and Culture*, 1600–1840. Leiden: Brill.

Ghazaleh, Pascale, ed. 2011. *Held in Trust: Waqf in the Islamic World*. Cairo: American University in Cairo Press.

Gibb, H.A.R. 1955. Constitutional Organization. In *Law in the Middle East*, ed. M. Khadduri and H. Liebesny. Washington, DC: The Middle East Institute.

Gleave, Robert. 2009. Public Violence, State Legitimacy: The *Iqāmat al-Ḥudūd* and the Sacred State. In *Public Violence in Islamic Societies*, ed. C. Lange and M. Fierro, pp. 256–75. Edinburgh: Edinburgh University Press.

Hallaq, Wael B. 1994. From *Fatwās* to *Furūʿ*: Growth and Change in Islamic Substantive Law. *Islamic Law and Society* 1(1): 29–65.

———. 2001. *Authority, Continuity and Change in Islamic Law*. Cambridge: Cambridge University Press.

———. 2009. *Sharīʿa: Theory, Practice, Transformations*. New York: Cambridge University Press.

Imber, Colin. 1997. *Ebu's-suʿud: The Islamic Legal Tradition*. Edinburgh: Edinburgh University Press.

Jackson, Sherman. 1993. From Prophetic Actions to Constitutional Theory: A Novel Chapter in Medieval Muslim Jurisprudence. *International Journal of Middle East Studies* 25(1): 71–90.

———. 1996a. *Islamic Law and the State: The Constitutional Jurisprudence of Shihāb al-Dīn al-Qarāfī*. Leiden: E.J. Brill.

Johansen, Baber. 1988. *The Islamic Law on Land Tax and Rent: The Peasants' Loss of Property Rights as Interpreted in the Ḥanafite Legal Literature of the Mamlūk and Ottoman Periods*. New York: Croom Helm.

Kerr, Malcolm. 1966. *Islamic Reform: The Political and Legal Theories of Muḥammad 'Abduh and Rashīd Riḍā*. Berkeley and Los Angeles: University of California Press.

Kuran, Timur. 2010–. *Social and Economic Life in Seventeenth-Century Istanbul: Glimpses from Court Records*. Istanbul: Türkiye İş Bankası.

Lambton, Ann K.S. 1981. *State and Government in Medieval Islam: An Introduction to the Study of Islamic Political Theory. The Jurists*. Oxford: Oxford University Press.

Lewis, Bernard. 1988. *The Political Language of Islam*. Chicago: The University of Chicago Press.

Madelung, Wilferd. 1980. A Treatise of the Sharîf al-Murtaḍâ on the Legality of Working for the Government (*Mas'ala fî 'l-'amal ma'a 'l-sulṭân*). *Bulletin of the School of Oriental and African Studies* 43(1): 18–31.

Makdisi, John. 1985–86. Formal Rationality in Islamic Law and the Common Law. *Cleveland State Law Review* 34: 106.

Masud, M. Khalid, Rudolph Peters, and David S. Powers. 2006. Qadis and Their Courts: An Historical Survey. In *Dispensing Justice in Islam: Qadis and Their Judgments*, ed. M.K. Masud et al., pp. 1–44. Leiden: Brill.

Messick, Brinkley. 1986. The Mufti, the Text, and the World: Legal Interpretation in Yemen. *Man* 21: 102–19.

———. 1989. Just Writing: Paradox and Political Economy in Yemeni Legal Documents. *Cultural Anthropology* 4(1): 26–50.

———. 1990. Literacy and the Law: Documents and Document Specialists in Yemen. In *Law and Islam in the Middle East*, ed. D. Hilse Dwyer, pp. 61–76. New York: Bergin and Garvey.

———. 1993. *The Calligraphic State: Textual Domination and History in a Muslim Society*. Berkeley and Los Angeles: University of California Press.

Powers, David S. 1998. The Art of the Judicial Opinion: On *Tawlīj* in Fifteenth-Century Tunis. *Islamic Law and Society* 5(3): 359–81.

———. 2002. *Law, Society, and Culture in the Maghrib, 1300–1500*. Cambridge: Cambridge University Press.

———. 2003. Women and Divorce in the Islamic West: Three Cases. *Hawwa* 1(1): 29–45.

———. 2006a. Law and Custom in the Maghrib, 1475–1500: On the Disinheritance of Women. In *Law, Custom, and Statute in the Muslim World: Studies in Honor of Aharon Layish*, ed. R. Shaham, pp. 17–39. Leiden: Brill.

———. 2006b. Four Cases Relating to Women and Divorce in al-Andalus and the Maghrib, 1100–1500. In *Dispensing Justice in Islam: Qadis and Their Judgments*, ed. M.K. Masud et al., pp. 383–409. Leiden: Brill.

Rapoport, Yossef. 2012. Royal Justice and Religious Law: *Siyāsah* and Shariʿah under the Mamluks. *Mamluk Studies Review* 16: 71–102.

Rosen, Lawrence. 1981. Equity and Discretion in a Modern Islamic Legal System. *Law and Society Review* 15(2): 272–45.

———. 1989. *The Anthropology of Justice: Law as Culture in Islamic Society*. Cambridge: Cambridge University Press.

Rosenthal, Erwin I.J. 1958. *Political Thought in Medieval Islam*. London: Cambridge University Press.

Sachedina, Abdulaziz A. 1988. *The Just Ruler* (al-sultān al-ʿādil) *in Shīʿite Islam: The Comprehensive Authority of the Jurist in Imamite Jurisprudence*. New York: Oxford University Press.

Schacht, Joseph. 1964. *An Introduction to Islamic Law*. Oxford: Clarendon Press.

Shatzmiller, Maya. 1995. Women and Property Rights in al-Andalus and the Maghrib: Social Patterns and Legal Discourse. *Islamic Law and Society* 2(3): 219–57.

———. 2001. Islamic Institutions and Property Rights: The Case of the 'Public Good' Waqf. *Journal of the Economic and Social History of the Orient* 44(1): 44–74.

———. 2007. *Her Day in Court: Women's Property Rights and Islamic Law in Fifteenth-Century Granada*. Cambridge, MA: Islamic Legal Studies Program, Harvard Law School.

Snouck Hurgronje, Christiaan. 1957. *Selected Works*, ed. J. Schacht and G.H. Bousqet. Leiden: E.J. Brill.

Stilt, Kristen. 2012. *Islamic Law in Action: Authority, Discretion, and Everyday Experiences in Mamluk Egypt*. New York: Oxford University Press.

Turner, Bryan S. 1974. *Weber and Islam*. London: Routledge and Kegan Paul.

Tyan, Émile. 1955. Judicial Organization. In *Law in the Middle East*, ed. M. Khadduri and H. Liebesny. Washington: DC: The Middle East Institute.

———. 1960. *Histoire de l'organisation judiciaire en pays d'islam*. 2nd ed. Leiden: E.J. Brill.

Watt, W. Montgomery. 1968. *Islamic Political Thought*. Edinburgh: Edinburgh University Press.

Qanun and Sharia

Boğaç A. Ergene

The word *qānūn*, for a state decree or directive, is derived from the Greek κανών, which in Byzantine usage referred to fiscal levies and codified legislation (İnalcık 1978a; Howard 1995/96: 80). Used as a collective noun for a body of fiscal regulations and rules regarding land use, the term is found as early as the Abbasid period and possibly before (İnalcık 1978a). Under the Ilkhanids (r. 1256–1335) it took on the meaning of cadastre, "referring both to the dues and to the principles of assessment and collection of dues" (Howard 1995/96: 80). In later periods, penal, administrative, and land laws also entered into the realm of qanun legislation.

According to Islamic jurisprudence, canonical standards (which some scholars call Sharia; see below) regulate the entirety of public and private life. Thus, technically, political leaders do not possess any legislative authority but are responsible solely for enforcing the divine will as reflected in jurisprudential principles. In reality, however, Muslim rulers and their representatives often played important roles in shaping fiscal, administrative, and penal regulations. It is these legislative activities that constitute the basis of qanun legislation. The factors that led to the development of qanun legislation as state law and the nature of its relationship with religious law constitute the focal points of this chapter.

Qanun as state law has been explored most exhaustively in the context of the Ottoman empire, which explains this chapter's focus on the scholarship of and debates entered into by historians of the Ottoman period.[1] The Ottoman *qānūnnāme*, which is a compilation of qanuns, can be defined as a legal code that contained state directives on criminal penalties, urban and rural taxation, land use, market organization, manufacturing and artisanal production, and military matters. These codes were intended to provide legal and administrative authorities with what Leslie Peirce (2003: 117) calls "a blueprint for organizing and administering the vast agrarian and commercially based domain that was the Ottoman empire." Qanunnames could be general, applicable to all imperial domains, as was the case with Mehmed II's (r. ca. 1470–81) *re ʿāyā qānūnnāme* (qanunname for the tax-payers), or limited, enforced only in specific locations, as in district (*sanjaq*) qanunnames. There were also qanunnames for specific groups, usually tax-paying subjects who served the state, and for state institutions (such

---

Boğaç A. Ergene, Associate Professor of History at the University of Vermont, is the author of publications in Turkish and English, among which *Local Court, Provincial Society and Justice in the Ottoman Empire: Legal Practice and Dispute Resolution in Cankiri and Kastamonu (1652–1744)* (Leiden: Brill, 2003). He is grateful to Peri Bearman, Alix Heintzman, Judith Marshall, Rudolph Peters, and Charlotte Weber for their assistance with this chapter.

1 The prominence of the state in the Ottoman legal system has led to particular attention being given to the qanun, in which many scholars have located the unique characteristics of Ottoman bureaucratic and governmental genius, viz., Douglas Howard (1995/96: 79): "The matter of Ottoman *ḳānūn* was central to Ottoman society as it faced its European neighbors: there existed virtually no aspect of Ottoman society the study of which would fail to be enlightened by a thorough understanding of the Ottoman *ḳānūnnāme*s and the legal culture that produced them."

as the janissary core, timars, and customs), court protocol, and ceremonies (İnalcık 1978b: 562; Barkan 1943: xxi–xxxiv).

Pre-Islamic Middle Eastern, especially Persian, administrative practice recognized the ruler's prerogative to issue laws. Some scholars, in particular Halil İnalcık (1978a: 559; 1978b, 1987, 1998, 1999) and Ömer Lütfi Barkan (1943, 1952), point to Turco-Mongol imperial custom as the primary influential source for Ottoman qanun legislation. The strong relationship between political sovereignty and the enforcement of "independent state law" in Inner Asian traditions, İnalcık suggests, shaped the political cultures of all Turkic and Mongolian dynasties in the Middle East, and primarily the Ottoman empire (1978b: 562; 1978a: 558–9; also Heyd 1967: 6).[2] These traditions required the absolute independence of the ruler's authority in legal matters.[3]

Even if there is a historical connection between Ottoman qanun and Turco-Mongolian legislative practice (Heyd 1967: 3),[4] the contents of the qanun codes appear to have been contextually determined and not brought from Central Asia. Colin Imber (1997: chap. 1; 2008) suggests that they were shaped by local, "feudal" customs and practices in tax collection, land use, and administrative matters that the Ottomans encountered in conquered territories.[5] Because these customs and practices differed from one location to another, codes for specific locations and communities could vary significantly (Imber 1997: 44; Peirce 2003: 117; Heyd 1973: 38–40); and since local practices were shaped by previous legal systems, such as Byzantine law in the Balkans and Western Anatolia, qanun law was also influenced by them (Imber 1997: 116; Barkan 1952: 94; Barkan 1943: lxix).

The Ottomans produced the first qanunnames in the late fifteenth century during the reign of Bayezid II (1481–1512), with the district qanunname promulgated for Bursa in 1486 being one of the first (Imber 1997: 41). According to Imber (1997: 46), the earliest attempt to produce a general qanunname appears in a manuscript composed probably in the early 1490s. This compilation likely appeared under Bayezid II, although some of its sections are from Mehmed II's time or even earlier. In general, qanunnames are collections of material from different periods, developed in an organic and cumulative fashion (Barkan 1943: xxxiii, liv, lv, lxiv; Peirce 2003: 117).[6] While, technically, Ottoman sultans had the right to issue their own qanuns when they came to power, in most cases they affirmed the applicability of those of their ancestors, sometimes with modifications (Barkan 1943: 172). Barkan (1952: 192) suggests that the system simultaneously acknowledged the ruler's right to legislate and ensured legal continuity in governance.

The impact of qanun legislation has been best explored in the context of Ottoman criminal law. Historians have demonstrated that many important aspects of Ottoman criminal practices, such as fines, torture, and imprisonment, were prescribed by qanun (Heyd 1973). Rudolph Peters (2005: 93) has suggested that qanun-based provisions constituted as much as one-quarter of the regulations pertaining to procedure, investigation, and jurisdiction in the body of Ottoman criminal law. Qanuns also defined how legal and executive officials were supposed to participate in criminal proceedings and what their responsibilities were. Moreover, they reveal what offences the state wanted to be punished and how. In the latter regard, they functioned, among other ways, to turn many acts of crime into revenue sources (Peters 2005: 71–5, 92–3).

2 According to İnalcık (1978: 560), the notion of "independent state law" became prominent in the region following the Mongol invasions. However, "codified *ḳānūnnāmes* appeared only in Iran, Anatolia, ʿIrāḳ, and India—places with firmly established Turco-Mongol traditions and dynasties—, and in the regions of the Ottoman Empire."

3 For a critical discussion of the literature on Inner Asian traditions pertaining to the enforcement of independent state law, see Morgan 1986.

4 Peirce (2003: 116) has argued that law-making might also be attributed to the Ottomans' Byzantine heritage: "The model of Constantine and Justinian was not so far from the model of Genghis Khan."

5 However, see Barkan (1952: 185–6, 194; 1943: xii, xvi, lxxi), who suggests that ancient Turkish state customs and practices equally influenced the contents of qanunnames.

6 For an illuminating example of the disagreement among historians concerning when different qanunnames were compiled, see Heyd 1973: chap. 1.

Prevalent Approaches to Qanun and Interpretations of Its Relationship to Sharia

There exists significant disagreement among historians with regard to defining the relationship between qanun legislation and Islamic law. This is largely due to the fact that they diverge on how religious law as an ontological entity, its contents, and its ability to adapt to changing circumstances should be characterized. This chapter's discussion begins with an assessment of the ways in which traditional scholarship on qanun approached these questions, after which the focus turns to more recent interpretations that challenge some of the critical claims made in this scholarship. In the context of this discussion, more detail is provided on the functions of qanun legislation in the Ottoman context.

Many scholars have referred to qanun as "secular law" and suggested that its main function was to complement religious law (Imber 1997: 40; İnalcık 1978a: 559–61; Barkan 1952: 185–6; Barkan 1943: xx; Heyd 1967: 2; Heyd 1973: 167, 188; Repp 1988: 124). This position is related to the assertion that the sultanic law developed independently of religious law. Uriel Heyd (1967: 9–10) defines the qanun as a "law of human origin" to explain why it had a lower status in the eyes of religious scholars and the wider public compared to the divine law, while Imber (1997: 40–2) describes Sharia as the law of the religious community and qanun as the law of the empire.

Pertinent to this characterization are two related assumptions about Islamic law. One is that it is largely an unchanging system that has limited ability to adjust to new circumstances. Barkan (1952: 186) suggests that Islamic law was "frozen" (*donmuş kalmış*) in the time of Muḥammad and the first caliphs. Imber emphasizes the "citational" nature of religious law as a reason for its inherent conservatism: because jurists felt obligated to cite the works of earlier scholars to justify their own interpretations, the possibility of formulating novel legal interpretations remained limited. As a divine law, Imber claims (1997: 37), the Sharia had to remain "self-contained" and "self-legitimating." Consequently, "legal concepts as they had developed by the eleventh century remained unchanged in the nineteenth."[7]

The second common assumption about Islamic law is that it does not provide much guidance or easily implemented prescriptions on many aspects of government. For example, İnalcık suggests that "after al-Shāfiʿī, the boundaries of the *uṣūl al-fiḳh* [legal epistemology] were drawn so narrowly that new administrative regulations were left outside them and became the province of a new 'state law' or 'ruler's law'" (İnalcık 1978a: 559). Heyd (1967: 1) argues that "the criminal law of the *sharīʿa* [...] never had much practical importance in the lands of Islam. Its substantive law is rather deficient: fixed penalties are prescribed for a limited number of crimes only, many are not dealt with at all. Moreover, its rules of evidence are so strict that a number of offences cannot be punished adequately." In fact, according to Imber (1997: 38), the jurists "never intended large areas of the *shariʿa* to function as a practical system of law" and most religious and legal experts in the past saw the science of jurisprudence as mainly an intellectual endeavor and studied it in order to hone their skills in logic and rhetoric. Barkan (1943: xiv) has called religious law "dead-on-arrival" (*ölü doğmuş*), implying that it did not have much practical use from the very beginning.

7 One interesting aspect of the discussions found in the works of these historians pertains to the ways in which the term Sharia is used. These authors tend to use Sharia regularly even though what they often mean is fiqh, or jurisprudential interpretation. Although it may not be deliberate, when one defines the religious law as "divine will"—which the term Sharia implies—it becomes easier to attribute to this entity a static and unchanging character. In fact, recent research on Islamic legal history has demonstrated that the science of jurisprudence was not unresponsive to social needs or expectations in post-classical times. See Johansen 1999; Hallaq 1984: 3–41; and Chapter 7, above. For a similar insistence on terminological clarity pertaining to the word Sharia, see Buzov (2005: 13), who rightly suggests that the "distinction between shariʿa and fiqh has been ignored in the studies on Ottoman law." On the confusion between Sharia and fiqh, see Chapter 1, above.

Given these supposed inadequacies of religious law, the prevalent wisdom on the topic suggests that the Ottomans had to adopt a separate, non-religious system of law in order to effectively govern their territories. Heyd (1967: 7; 1973: 169, 188) identifies qanun as *ʿörfi* law, that is, the law of the sovereign and his representatives (*ehl-i ʿörf*). It originates from and represents the sultan's will. The sultan's authority legitimized a qanun, which, technically, did not require the approval of religious authorities (Barkan 1952: 192; 1943: xliii; Heyd 1973: 171). Scholars also emphasize the fact that qanunnames were prepared not by experts on religious law but by bureaucratic and administrative functionaries of the government—in particular, the *nishanci* ("chancellor" or "secretary of state")—who were responsible for formulating laws in accordance with Ottoman bureaucratic traditions and issuing imperial orders in written form (Babinger 1995: 62; İnalcık 1978a: 561).[8] The fact that the earliest qanunnames did not contain any reference to religious law suggests to many that qanuns were free of major fiqh-based concerns. Barkan (1952: 186; 1943: xiv) proposes that Ottoman qanuns were "national" (*milli*) laws in "Turkey." Some researchers, such as Dora Glidewell Nadolski (1977: 520), have even argued that the secular legal system of the modern Turkish Republic emerged from a tradition of legislation that historically remained independent of religious law.[9]

Here we should note that the works of Barkan and İnalcık, the two Turkish scholars whose ideas have shaped modern perceptions of qanun and its relationship to religious law, are influenced by very specific academic and political motivations. Academically, both researchers have taken upon themselves the task of explaining historical change in Islamic legal history with specific reference to Ottoman legal history. However, they attempt to accomplish this task not by acknowledging that fiqh-based interpretations could vary from period to period, but by attributing the potential for change to the influence of supposedly non-Islamic sources on Ottoman law. Barkan (1943: xviii–xx), for example, insists that the "madrasa-minded" commentators, who claimed that Ottoman law was essentially Islamic, did not understand how laws in the Middle East evolved over time. İnalcık (1987: 3; 1998: 136–7), on the other hand, suggests that historians interested in Ottoman legal history should pursue an "empirical historical approach" in their research, instead of trying to locate the roots of Ottoman institutions in the "immutable, eternal precepts of Islam as embodied in the Qur'an and [custom]." In political terms this tendency to ascribe the capacity for legal and institutional change to non-Islamic sources of law and governance is consistent with the attempts by the early generation of nationalist Turkish historians to attribute the legal and political dynamism of the early Ottoman state to its Turkic legacy (rather than its Islamic character) (Berktay 1991).

In the sixteenth century the renowned Ottoman jurist Ebu's-Suʿud Efendi (d. 982/1574) applied concepts, principles, and terminology from Hanafi law to the areas of landholding, taxation, criminal punishment, and charitable endowments in order to recast practices that were part of the Ottoman legal and administrative repertoire in the language of Islamic jurisprudence. His attempts have been seen less as an effort to reform the Ottoman legal system and practices in accordance with fiqh-based legal principles than as an attempt to endow them with religious and legal justification. According to Imber (1997: 271),

> [i]n his approach to the details of the law, Ebu's-suʿud's concern was with the practical task of finding more or less equitable solutions to everyday problems, within the

8 According to İnalcık, the "final and official promulgation" of the qanunnames was the purview of the *nishanci*, "for he possessed the responsibility of affixing to them the *ṭughra* by which they were authenticated. It was he who determined whether a *ḳānūn* remained in force, and whether new [rulings] issuing [*sic*] from the various departments of the administration were in conformity with the existing corpus of *ḳānūns*."

9 Max Weber (1968b: 822; Miller 2003: 178) also emphasizes the different qualities of the "Sharia" and the qanun: "We actually find in all the great Islamic empires of the present time a dualism of religious and secular administration of justice: the temporal official stands beside the khadi, and the secular law beside the *sharî'ah* [...] this secular law (*qânûn*) began to expand from the very beginning [...] and to assume increasing importance in relation to the sacred law, the more the latter became stereotyped."

> constraints of a highly conservative legal tradition. When Hanafi law was unworkable, as it was, for example, in dealing with theft, he made it clear, while supporting his view with canonical authority, that the case fell wholly within the sphere of the secular law. When Hanafi law goes part of the way towards providing a solution, he adopts it with modifications, as, for example, when he demands a penalty in addition to restitution or compensation, in cases of malicious damage to property. When Hanafi law is practical and, in his view equitable, Ebu's-su'ud follows it to the letter.

Barkan went so far as to suggest that Ebu's-Su'ud relied on "legal tricks" (*şer'i hile*), "[unjustified] legal assumptions" (*hukuki faraziye*), and "legal fiction" (*hukuki fiksion*) to make the law of the sovereign (*'örf-i hukuk*) appear jurisprudence-based (1952: 191; 1943: xli). According to Barkan (1943: xxxiv–xxxvi), Ebu's-Su'ud's rendering of the content of the qanuns in fiqh-based language functioned to help the *madrasa*-educated Ottoman judges, who had difficulty comprehending and interpreting these alien practices, understand them in a terminology with which they were familiar.

Unlike Barkan, who has suggested that the qanuns that regulated landholding contradicted jurisprudence-based principles of landholding and inheritance (1952: 190–1; 1943: xxxiv–xxxvi), few today hold that qanun prescriptions contained elements that explicitly contradicted Islamic law. Also rare is the claim that qanun-sanctioned practices came to completely replace jurisprudence-based ones. Pace Nadolski (1977: 520), who avers that qanunnames went "beyond supplementing the Shari'a" by, for example, replacing *ḥadd* punishments with qanun-based *ta'zīr*, most scholars now insist that qanun-based *ta'zīr* punishments were implemented in those instances when there were no established fiqh-based prescriptions applicable to the cases at hand, or when, as in most *ḥadd* allegations, it was difficult to satisfy the stringent evidentiary standards prescribed by Islamic law (Peters 2005: 70–4).

Nevertheless, many continue to maintain that qanun- and fiqh-based legal directives exhibit different orientations toward, in particular, crime and punishment. For example, it has been pointed out that the criminal prescriptions in qanunnames made distinctions among individuals that did not exist in the fiqh literature, such as prescriptions of different punishments for identical crimes depending on whether they were committed by Muslims or non-Muslims, free individuals or slaves, the wealthy or poor, or veiled women or non-veiled women. Dror Ze'evi (2006: chap. 2) has argued that the ways in which qanunnames treated sexual crimes and transgressions were considerably more lenient than the punishments recommended in fiqh literature for such offences (see also Semerdjian 2008: chap. 2). Heyd (1967: 11), on the other hand, claims that, except for Quranic offences with fixed punishments, qanunnames "inflict penalties more readily, for many more offences and, in numerous instances, with much greater severity than the *sharī'a*."

Furthermore, it has been pointed out that many criminal provisions of qanun had no counterparts in religious law. For example, while for the Hanafis murder and injury generated private claims, in the qanun they also gave rise to public claims (Imber 1997: 246). And, while intent is only secondary in fiqh in determining compensation for injury, it is quite important in qanun (Imber 1997: chap. 9). Thus, for Imber (1997: 221), "the development of the Ottoman criminal code [...] owed very little to Hanafi jurisprudence"; any lip-service paid to fiqh-based prescriptions constituted nothing more than "a form of words" and "any resemblance between the criminal code and the *shari'a* in the area of property offences is entirely superficial."[10]

According to İnalcık (1978a: 560), the "conflict of the *sharī'a* and the ruler's law" was an enduring element of the Ottoman administration until the eighteenth century. Mehmed II and Selim I (ca. 1470–81; 1512–20) established centralized and absolutist governments through qanun-based

10 Sami Zubaida agrees: "A whole range of punishments and fines were specified in the *qanun-name* which were classified as *siyaset*, administration, as distinct from *shari'a*. In this regard, the *shari'a*, often mentioned with reverence in the *qanun-name*, was nevertheless subordinated and marginalized in the actual substance of the law" (2003: 113).

legislative efforts, successfully blocking interference from proponents of religious law, although the "upholders of the *sharīʿa*" were more successful in resisting the legislative authority of Bayezid II (also Repp 1988: 129). The tension between qanun- and fiqh-based orientations remained palpable during and after Süleyman's reign (1520–66), despite the best efforts of Ebu's-Suʿud ("Although Süleymān I was inclined to assert the *sharīʿa*'s control over state law, the latter preserved its independence as being the province of the *nishāndjī*"). One aspect of the Kadızadeli puritanical criticism directed against the Ottoman socio-political order in the late sixteenth and seventeenth centuries, İnalcık claims, was the prevalence of laws and practices that were not sanctioned by Islamic jurisprudence.

Others also assert that qanun-based legislation began to lose ground from the seventeenth century onward and possibly earlier (Heyd 1967: 15), perhaps as a consequence of the increasing popularity of Kadızadeli puritanism during this period (Repp 1988: 131–2). For İnalcık, the fatwas of "the *muftīs* progressively restricted the law-making powers of the *nishāndjis*, and the influence of the Shaykh al-Islām in state affairs progressively increased—to such a degree that in 1107/1696 the use of the word *ḳānūn* side by side with the word *sharīʿa* was forbidden by a firman of the Sultan" (1978a: 560). Heyd suggests that fines, "the backbone of the penalty system" of the sultanic decrees, were abolished in many Ottoman provinces in the second half of the seventeenth century. In the newly conquered territories, such as the islands of Crete and Mytilene, non-religious taxes such as *rüsum-u divaniye* or *tekalif-i ʿörfiye* were never imposed (Heyd 1967: 15; 1973: 153; Barkan 1952: 191; 1943: xli–xlii). According to Barkan (1943: xvii, xix) increasing religious conservatism, the disappearance of qanuns, and the gradual decline of the Ottoman socio-political order went hand in hand after the seventeenth century.[11]

Challenges to the Traditional Scholarship

Objections have been raised recently about defining qanun as "secular law" and "sultan's law." Although still not widely accepted, these objections reflect alternative approaches to Islamic law and political attitudes among those who proposed them. Below I will elaborate on how these scholars have challenged the established scholarship on qanun.

Objections to Qanun Depicted as "Secular Law"

The main challenge to this characterization came from the Turkish historian Ahmet Akgündüz, who in 1990, in his massive compilation of Ottoman qanunnames, took issue with the claim that qanun and religious law were separate legal systems (1990: 106, and passim).[12]

Akgündüz (1990: 67) points out that qanunnames contained prescriptions that can be found in fiqh treatises. In fact, he argues, one of the functions of qanunnames was to implement, if selectively, relevant fiqh-based prescriptions in particular circumstances, and therefore these documents reflect Ottoman efforts to apply fiqh-based principles in their own context. More specifically, he suggests that qanunnames (1) exemplified judicial attempts to interpret and reformulate Islamic legal principles

11 Başak Tuğ (2011: chap. 1) has recently cast doubt on the claim of the decline of qanuns after the seventeenth century by adducing frequent references to qanun in eighteenth-century petitions addressed to the central government and in imperial decrees.

12 The debate presented here had appeared before in Ottoman legal historiography. In 1952 Barkan (1952: 190) regarded his interpretations of qanun and its relationship to religious law as correcting the claims of earlier scholars, such as the Ottoman legal scholar Halis Eşref Efendi, that qanuns had been formulated according to Islamic jurisprudence traditions.

for practical purposes and easier enforcement, and (2) contained selective endorsements of specific judicial interpretations and of their enforcement for public benefit (1990: 64).

While Akgündüz acknowledges that political authorities also became directly involved in legislative processes, these efforts, he insists, were sanctioned and strongly influenced by Islamic jurisprudence. Relevant to his discussion is the fact that fiqh-based practice explicitly recognizes the legislative privileges of political authorities, especially in administrative, financial, and military areas (1990: 53). Moreover, the common sources for such legislative actions on the part of political authorities—viz., custom, practices associated with other legal systems, and the notions of *istiḥsān* and *istiṣlāḥ*[13]—are also legitimate, if secondary, sources of Islamic jurisprudence. If they did not conflict with clear Quranic and hadith-based injunctions (*naṣṣ*), prescriptions based on them had long been included in the compendia of Islamic legal interpretations (1990: 45, 53). Finally, Akgündüz points out that qanuns issued by the Ottoman sultan or his representatives were often checked by legal authorities to confirm that they did not conflict with Islamic legal principles (1990: 51, and passim).

Most researchers, including Barkan, İnalcık, and Imber, acknowledge that fiqh-based tradition recognizes the right of political authorities to legislate in various circumstances. They also cite secondary sources of Islamic jurisprudence, including *istiḥsān* and *istiṣlāḥ*, as bases for qanun legislation. Nevertheless, they insist on treating "Sharia" as independent of legislative activities based on these factors. Although the term Sharia is never clearly defined, it is often used to refer exclusively to Quranic and hadith-based commands as well as the jurisprudential interpretations that originate from the first two centuries of Islamic history. Their discussions give the impression that the Ottoman tendency to cite the ruler's right to legislate and Ottoman references to jurisprudential concepts such as *istiḥsān* and *istiṣlāḥ* were merely attempts to justify their efforts to manipulate religious law (for example, Barkan 1943: xix, xlvi–xlviii; İnalcık 1978a: 558; İnalcık 1999: 6; Imber 1997: chaps. 2, 4; Heyd 1973: 182–6).[14]

Akgündüz's characterization of the relationship between the traditions of fiqh and qanun is in line with contemporary scholarship on Islamic law in that it does not consider Islamic law as an inflexible system that required independent, legal intervention on the part of the political authority. Instead, Akgündüz interprets qanun legislation as a means to arrive at novel legal interpretations in Islamic law. Consistent with this interpretation, Akgündüz does not refer in his account to Inner Asian imperial traditions of government that recognized law-making as a basis of sovereignty. This is likely because he considers Islamic legal traditions as capable of producing new legislation without any outside help.

There are also methodological reasons to be skeptical about the claim that qanun and religious law represent mutually inconsistent approaches to law. As Reem Meshal states,

> [t]he only orthodoxy one may speak of in Islamic law is methodological. A consensus on the methods by which the law is derived (*uṣūl al-fiqh*) exists, but not necessarily on the legal opinions derived therefrom (2010: 188).

From this perspective it does not make sense to separate qanun and other forms of legislative action because their contents, interpretations, and foci of interest diverge. As a matter of fact, fiqh itself does not constitute a uniform system of legal thinking, but comprises a multitude of, often inconsistent, interpretive positions on specific issues and themes. Islamic jurisprudence by its very nature is expected to be polyvocal and even inherently conflicted, because human interpretations of the divine will are subject

13 *Istiḥsān* is abandoning a rule based on an obvious analogy from a text in favor of a rule based on another, more subtle analogy that is deemed preferable; *istiṣlāḥ* is the term for more or less the same notion, used by the Malikis.

14 The inclination to consider legislation by the political authority founded on policy-based considerations (*siyāsa*) as a legitimate source of legal practice has been also gaining traction among scholars who specialize in non-Ottoman contexts. See Stilt 2011 for Mamluk Egypt.

to misunderstanding and error and are influenced by contextual variables. Since it is the methodology of law-making rather than the content of the law that determines the legitimacy of legislative efforts, the fact that some qanun legislations may have not been consistent with other legal interpretations considered to be part of classical Islamic jurisprudence does not necessarily make them non-religious.

Haim Gerber is also suspicious of the claim that qanun and religious law remained separate. According to Gerber (1994), claims that through qanun legislation the Ottomans (1) "continued and even exacerbated the trend of keeping the *shari'a* on the sidelines" and (2) "created a sovereign whose very word became an arbitrary and whimsical source of law," are exaggerated.[15] The Ottomans were not simply seeking to fill in the gaps left by fiqh but were critically engaging and reinterpreting them in order to establish a legal system that satisfied their own needs. At the same time Gerber questions the claim that qanunnames declined after the late seventeenth century. He argues that qanun-based principles were too enmeshed in the system to allow such a development (1994: 61).

Dror Ze'evi also questions the characterization of the Ottoman legal system as dual in nature:

> Our new understanding of the dynamic nature of lawmaking in the Muslim world, coupled with a better comprehension of the *şeriat* as a set of premises rather than a legal code, have supplied us with sufficient contradictory evidence to doubt the veracity of the old "dual-system" view.[16]

Ze'evi suggests instead that the qanun "was interwoven with the *şeriat* with painstaking care within the sphere that legal experts of the time could have accepted as Islamic, inside the boundaries of *örf* and *siyaset*" (2006: 69). The perceived differences between qanun and fiqh-based legal interpretation, Ze'evi insists, should not be interpreted as

> two conceptions of law, but rather as evolution within the same legal and cultural sphere. Thus we may assume that those loci where the *kanun* insists on parting with the *şeriat* and promulgating a different set of laws are not accidental, but rather replicate the cultural and political dynamics of the period (2006: 69).

As such, Ebu's-Su'ud's work cannot simply be considered an effort to translate the sultan's secular will into religious language but rather one that was plainly jurisprudential in nature (Buzov 2005: chap. 4).

The ideas presented in this subsection have the merit of treating Islamic law as a dynamic entity capable of responding to ever-changing historical circumstances. At the same time they carry the risk of perpetuating a different sort of ahistoricity in regard to the nature of religious law, unless we recognize the contextual character of any legislative action. This risk is explicit in Akgündüz's deliberations, which depict Islamic law as a semi-perfect, almost divine legal system that is inherently capable of adapting to new circumstances. What is missing in this depiction is an acknowledgement of the gradual, often inconsistent, and usually conflict-ridden nature of the ways in which Islamic legal interpretations came to accommodate some non-Islamic practices and traditions while rejecting others for not necessarily legal reasons. In other words, Akgündüz disregards the contingent and historically situated nature of legislative and jurisprudential actions. In his attempts to demonstrate how flexible Islamic law is, Akgündüz ignores the questions of how and why new formulations emerged and old ones became unpopular. For example, in order to demonstrate that qanuns were consistent with Islamic jurisprudence principles he proclaims that

15 Gerber (1994: 62) has suggested that the "penal code of the *shari'a* finds its way into the *kanun*. The *kanun* merely goes a little further by adding the option (no more than that) of prescribing fines as punishments." Wael Hallaq (2009: 78) argues that religious law and qanun "had far more in common than they differed upon."

16 Barkan (1952: xii, xlix) is the scholar who uses the phrase "legal duality," alongside "the duality of books" (*hukuk ikiliği* and *kitap ikiliği*), when describing Ottoman law, referring to the qanun- and jurisprudence-based nature of this system.

> the *miri* [state-owned] land [in qanun terminology] is *kharāj* [land acquired through conquest in the fiqh terminology] [...] The taxes collected from these types of lands, which were called *rüsum-ı şer'iyye* in Ottoman law, were assigned and collected according to the prescription in Islamic books of fiqh. The tax that is called *öşür* [in the Ottoman context] is [fiqh-based] *kharāj al-muqāsama* and [the tax called] *çift akçesi* is really *kharāj al-muwazzaf* [...]. All directives in Ottoman qanunnames pertaining to *öşür* and *çift akçesi* are consistent with what we find in the [fiqh] texts (1990: 67; cf. Barkan 1943: xli).

Yet Akgündüz does not explain why the Ottomans waited until Ebu's-Su'ud's time to express these correspondences, nor the motivations behind Ebu's-Su'ud's interpretive efforts, nor the social, political, and religious circumstances in which these interpretive efforts took place. More generally, Akgündüz also does not discuss, as any historian tackling the topic should be expected to do, why the Ottomans themselves changed their thinking about qanun and its relationship to religious law over time, as is demonstrated by the fact that while the earliest qanunnames did not contain any references to the religious law, any reference to qanun in legal prescriptions was prohibited after the seventeenth century (cf. Tuğ 2011: chap. 1).

Objections to Qanun Depicted as "the Sultan's Law"

A different objection to the predominant representations of qanun is related to recent criticisms directed at the state-centric nature of Ottoman studies as a field. As Snjezana Buzov (2005: 1–2) has pointed out, the representation of qanun "as the sultan's law" or "the legislation of the ruler's will" creates the impression that the central government was the primary agent in defining the content of the law. It may be true that, in order to be valid, qanunnames required the sultan's approval. But if Ottomans did indeed use qanuns to accommodate local customs and practices, as many researchers have suggested, then qanuns should also be regarded as local law, representing communal expectations and definitions of justice and legitimacy. In other words, qanun has been represented in the literature as both a tool for state centralization and the mechanism through which the government accommodated provincial particularities.

This tension between alternative functions of qanun has not been explored. Although Heyd (1973: 168–9) briefly notes two meanings of the term *'örf* ("customs" and "royal authority"), he does not delve into the issue. It has been suggested that in certain contexts, such as in post-conquest Egypt, the Ottomans appear to have imposed laws that might have been at variance with local practices and that were contested by the Egyptian judiciary (Meshal 2010); however, two authoritative historians of Ottoman Egypt, Michael Winter (1998: 27) and Nelly Hanna (1995: 47), do not agree. According to both, Ottoman attempts at legal reform in Egypt involved mostly a restructuring of the pre-conquest administration of law without any significant legal codification. Also in conflict, for example, is the attempt in the 1530s by Süleyman's grand vizier Ibrahim Pasha to enforce new qanuns that disregarded local customs and practices in Rumelia, including the long-established exemption of many Christian groups from the *jizya*, and the imperial government faced a pushback from local people. In a short time (in or around 1540, according to Buzov) these qanuns were replaced with ones that were in line with local expectations (Buzov 2005: chap. 2). Dina Rizk Khoury (2001: 311–3) has also suggested that the Ottoman state was not only capable of but also willing to modify its qanuns in concession to local interests in Mosul and Basra.[17]

In the last decade or so, scholars have begun to pay more attention to the processes in which legal practices were shaped in different milieus under the influence of a variety of factors. This orientation, particularly noticeable in scholarship on the Ottoman court records (sg. *sijill*), has demonstrated that

17 See also Heyd (1973: 14–15) for a discussion of the legal negotiations that took place between the Christian community of Montenegro and the imperial center in the early sixteenth century.

legal processes were often locally shaped. Results generated by this research have led students of Ottoman court records to hypothesize that local law was often constructed in a process of negotiation among multiple parties that took into consideration a multiplicity of factors, including fiqh-based principles, the imperial center's interests and objectives, and provincial expectations of fairness and equity (Peirce 2003; Agmon 2006; Ergene 2003). Although there has as yet been no specific call for a reinterpretation of state-centric definitions of qanun, insights into Ottoman legal practice gained to date carry important implications for future research on this topic.

Of particular importance are the questions of how qanuns (general or district-based) were understood in specific locales and how they were regularly challenged and forced to be modified by local communities. Other than the studies already cited above, there has been little research into these issues, which are essential for an understanding of the ways in which qanun was construed in both the center and on the margins of the empire in conflictive as well as collaborative fashions (cf. Buzov 2005: 13–14). Admittedly, a research orientation that focuses on these types of questions is difficult because it requires significant language skills and access to archives and libraries in many countries. However, an approach that represents qanun as a common legacy of all those components making up the empire, including the peripheral agents, has the potential to make significant contributions to our knowledge of the subject.

Conclusion

This chapter has explored how scholars have characterized the functions and development of qanun or state legislation. In doing so, it has demonstrated that the literature on qanun is extensive and that there exists significant disagreement among them on the nature of the relationship between qanun and Islamic law. I have suggested that the earlier, but still widely accepted inclination to treat qanun and religious law as separate but complementary legal systems has recently been challenged by approaches that emphasize the synthetic connections between the two, ones that point out the overlaps between qanun legislation and Islamic jurisprudential interpretation, or fiqh. The chapter has also highlighted the tension between the tendency to define qanun legislation as a top-down operation (qanun as "sultan's law"), as is still common in the scholarship, and the more recent and increasingly popular inclination to define legal developments as negotiated processes that involved all segments of the society.

The discussion makes it clear that scholarly interpretations of the topic have been sensitive to wider trends in the literature on Islamic law and legal practice. Indeed, it is the recent recognition that Islamic law is not a historically static or inflexible phenomenon that has generated doubts about some of the foundational assumptions made by many Ottoman historians with regard to qanun legislation. We should expect more such revisions in our collective understanding of qanun, its functions, and its relationship to religious law, since future research on Islamic law and practice is likely to challenge more of our preconceived notions on the topic.

References

Agmon, Iris. 2006. *Family and Court: Legal Culture and Modernity in Late Ottoman Palestine*. Syracuse: Syracuse University Press.

Akgündüz, Ahmet. 1990. *Osmanlı kanunnameleri ve hukuki tahlileri*. Vol. 1. Istanbul: FEY Vakfı Yayınları.

Babinger, Franz. 1995. Nishāndji. In *Encyclopaedia of Islam*, 2nd ed. Vol. 8: 62. Leiden: E.J. Brill.

Barkan, Ömer Lütfi. 1943. *XV ve XVIıncı Asırlarda Osmanlı imparatorluğunda zirai ekonominin hukuki ve mali esasları: Kanunlar*. Istanbul: Burhaneddin Matbaası.
———. 1952. Kanunnameler. In *Islam Ansiklopedisi*. Vol. 6: 185–95. Ankara: Milli Eğitim Bakanlığı Yayınevi.
Berktay, Halil. 1991. Dört tarihçinin sosyal portresi. *Toplum ve Bilim* 54/55 (1991): 19–45.
Buzov, Snjezana. 2005. The Lawgiver and His Lawmakers: The Role of Legal Discourse in the Change of Ottoman Imperial Culture. Ph.D. diss., University of Chicago.
Ergene, Boğaç A. 2003. *Local Court, Provincial Society and Justice in the Ottoman Empire: Legal Practice and Dispute Resolution in Çankırı and Kastamonu (1652–1744)*. Leiden: Brill.
Gerber, Haim. 1994. *State, Society, and Law in Islam: Ottoman Law in Comparative Perspective*. Albany: State University of New York Press.
Hallaq, Wael B. 2009. *An Introduction to Islamic Law*. Cambridge: Cambridge University Press.
Hanna, Nelly. 1995. Administration of Courts in Ottoman Cairo. In *The State and Its Servants*, ed. N. Hanna, pp. 44–59. Cairo: American University of Cairo Press.
Heyd, Uriel. 1967. Ḳānūn and Sharīʿa in Old Ottoman Criminal Justice. *Proceedings of the Israel Academy of Sciences and Humanities* 3(1): 1–18.
———. 1973. *Studies in Old Ottoman Criminal Law*. Oxford: Oxford University Press.
Howard, Douglas. 1995/96. Historical Scholarship and the Classical Ottoman Ḳānūnnāmes. *Archivum Ottomanicum* 14: 79–107.
Imber, Colin. 1997. *Ebu's-su'ud: The Islamic Legal Tradition*. Stanford: Stanford University Press.
———. 2008. The Cultivation of Wasteland in Hanafī and Ottoman Law. *Acta Orientalia Academiae Scientiarum Hungaricae* 61: 101–12.
İnalcık, Halil. 1978a. Ḳānūn.iii. In *Encyclopaedia of Islam*, 2nd ed. Vol. 4: 558–62. Leiden: E.J. Brill.
———. 1978b. Ḳānūnnāme. In *Encyclopaedia of Islam*, 2nd ed. Vol. 4: 562–66. Leiden: E.J. Brill.
———. 1987. Ḳānūn and the Sharīʿah. In *Sharīʿah, Ummah and Khilāfah*, ed. Y.A. Hashmi, pp. 1–13. Karachi: University of Karachi Press.
———. 1998. Şeriat ve Kanun, Din ve Devlet. *İslamiyat* 1: 135–42.
———. 1999. Türk Devletlerinde Sivil Kanun Geleneği. *Türkiye Günlüğü* 58: 5–11.
Johansen, Baber. 1999. Legal Literature and the Problem of Change: The Case of Land Tenure. In idem, *Contingency in a Sacred Law: Legal and Ethical Norms in the Muslim* Fiqh, pp. 444–64. Leiden: Brill.
Khoury, Dina Rizk. 2001. Administrative Practice between Religious Law (Shariʿa) and State Law (Kanun) on the Eastern Frontiers of the Ottoman Empire. *Journal of Early Modern History* 5: 305–30.
Meshal, Reem. 2010. Antagonistic Sharīʿas and the Construction of Orthodoxy in Sixteenth-Century Ottoman Cairo. *Journal of Islamic Studies* 21: 183–212.
Miller, Ruth. 2003. Apostates and Bandits: Religious and Secular Interaction in the Administration of Late Ottoman Criminal Law. *Studia Islamica* 97: 155–78.
Morgan, D.O. 1986. The "Great Yāsā of Chingiz Khān" and Mongol Law in the Īlkhānate. *Bulletin of the School of Oriental and African Studies* 49: 163–76.
Nadolski, Dora Glidewell. 1977. Ottoman and Secular Civil Law. *International Journal of Middle East Studies* 8: 517–43.
Peirce, Leslie. 2003. *Morality Tales: Law and Gender in the Ottoman Court of Aintab*. Berkeley: University of California Press.
Peters, Rudolph. 2005. *Crime and Punishment in Islamic Law: Theory and Practice from the Sixteenth to the Twenty-First Century*. Cambridge: Cambridge University Press.
Repp, Richard. 1988. Qanun and Shariʿa in the Ottoman Context. In *Islamic Law: Social and Historical Contexts*, ed. A. Al-Azmeh, pp. 124–45. London: Routledge.
Semerdjian, Elyse. 2008. *Off the Straight Path: Illicit Law, Sex, and Community in Ottoman Aleppo*. Syracuse: Syracuse University Press.

Stilt, Kristen. 2011. *Islamic Law in Action: Authority, Discretion, and Everyday Experiences in Mamluk Egypt*. New York: Oxford University Press.

Tuğ, Başak. 2011. Politics of Honor: The Institutional and Social Frontiers of "Illicit" Sex in Mid-Eighteenth-Century Ottoman Anatolia. Ph.D. diss., New York University.

Weber, Max. 1968. *On Charisma and Institution Building: Selected Papers*, ed. S.N. Eisenstadt. Chicago: University of Chicago Press.

———. 1968b. *Economy and Society: An Outline of Interpretive Sociology*, ed. G. Roth and C. Wittich. Vol. 2. New York: Bedminster Press.

Winter, Michael. 1998. The Ottoman Occupation. In *The Cambridge History of Egypt*, vol. 1, ed. C.F. Petry and W.M. Daly, pp. 490–516. Cambridge: Cambridge University Press.

Ze'evi, Dror. 2006. *Producing Desire: Changing Sexual Discourse in the Ottoman Middle East, 1500–1900*. Berkeley: University of California Press.

Zubaida, Sami. 2003. *Law and Power in the Islamic World*. London: I.B. Tauris.

Part II

Substantive Islamic Law

Equality before the Law

Gianluca P. Parolin

Equality before the law is a tremendous, impenetrable field and few would venture to accompany a guide through its brambles. By limiting myself in this chapter to jurisprudence (*fiqh*) and avoiding the crucial test of practice, I hope to come through unscathed. What you will find below is therefore equality before the law as premodern Muslim jurists treated it, regardless of whether that was a wishful construction confined to their works or reality. Due to the space allotted to the topic, elements of gender affecting legal capacity are necessarily covered separately (Chapter 10, below).

This chapter ends in the nineteenth century, when the interest in alternative conceptions of law and legal status began. In his chronicle of Napoleon's Egyptian expedition, al-Jabartī (d. 1825) records the strange French practice of addressing each other as *citoyen*. Lacking a comparable category in Arabic, al-Jabartī simply arabicized the French word. The idea of a common law (the code) regulating the affairs of all citizens—regardless of their different affiliations and status—attracted the attention of rulers in Istanbul and elsewhere who sent missions to France and supported an emerging literature on the French legal system. The most prominent example of this trend in Arabic is Rifāʿa al-Ṭahṭāwī's (d. 1873) memoirs of his mission to Paris and his translations of French laws. The interest in the "modern" conception of law (and legal status) was later reciprocated by a European interest in the "traditional" conception of law (and legal status) precipitated by the colonial encounter. Two early representatives of the colonial enterprise were Christiaan Snouck Hurgronje, Dutch scholar and advisor to the colonial office of the Netherland's Indies who wrote seminal works on Islam, including a collection of lectures given in the United States in 1914 (Snouck Hurgronje 1916), and Marcel Morand, dean of the Faculty of Law of the University of Algiers who prepared a draft code of Algerian Muslim law known as *Code Morand* (1916). The ensuing vast Western literature on the status of non-Muslims, slaves, and women can be considered a development of this earlier interest.

Classical fiqh does not address all the issues related to equality under a single heading. Early scholars, such as David Santillana and Joseph Schacht, who wanted to describe the differentiated nuances of legal capacity employed in classical fiqh had to sort through the individual rules under various headings and compile them in a general narrative. Schacht (1964) borrowed the scheme of the German civil code to rearrange the content of a Hanafi fiqh treatise. Later scholarship adopts a more faithful approach to the traditional outline of classical fiqh treatises, avoiding coercing materials related to legal capacity under a single heading, as, for example, Wael Hallaq, who follows this orientation in his recent study (2009: 229–354) by discussing legal capacity at the beginning of chapters dealing, for instance, with contracts and family law.

Considering the legal context and cultural heritage in which fiqh addressed the issue of legal status—both the Byzantine and Sasanid legal systems largely employed legal categories—it is surprising to see to what lengths Muslim legal scholars went to avoid using them, at least in the

Gianluca Parolin is Assistant Professor of Law at the American University in Cairo. Among his publications is *Citizenship in the Arab World* (2009).

general theory of law. They hereby signaled a clear intention to disengage from the previous model and offer a theologically conscious statement of Islam's universalism. This chapter will first look at equality before the law as laid out in the classical works on the general theory of law (*uṣūl al-fiqh*), and will then sift the works on substantive law (*furūʿ al-fiqh*), identifying the main subject matters in which issues of legal capacity arise.

General Theory of Law (*uṣūl al-fiqh*)

In their *uṣūl al-fiqh* jurists restrict to a bare minimum the recourse to legal status. What jumps out at one is the very limited number of cases on legal capacity, and these are clearly precipitated by theological and jurisprudential debates. The fundamental motive animating such debates is to whom the divine message (*khiṭāb*) is addressed, followed by two further questions: first, the ability of the addressee to understand the message, and, second, the ability to comply with it. As in many other areas of fiqh, the sharp doctrinal distinctions along theological lines between the Muʿtazilis and Ashʿaris or along jurisprudential lines between Sunni madhhabs tend to be overplayed, but the operational rules tend to converge.

Questions of capacity are unpacked as matters of responsibility for the acts whose legal qualifications (sg. *ḥukm*) are premised on God's message. An instance of apparent divergence based on different theological assumptions is responsibility for the impossible act (*muḥāl*, or *taklīf mā lā yuṭāq*). Muʿtazili scholars consider that responsibility is waived for the impossible act, whereas Ashʿari scholars refute this position in order to safeguard God's absolute liberty but are then forced to broaden the categories of exemption of responsibility for those who cannot comply with the legal obligation (*kulfa*), often qualifying such liability exemptions as limitations to capacity. Modern scholarship in Arabic captures the jurisprudential implications of the theological debate, whereas that in other languages tends to focus on the theological debate per se (Gimaret 2000).

In fiqh works, Shafiʿi, Hanbali, and Maliki legal theorists treat issues of capacity under the heading of *taklīf* (duty) and its conditions, Hanafis under the heading of *ahliyya* (legal capacity). Hanafis further distinguish between *ahliyyat al-wujūb* (legal personality) and *ahliyyat al-adāʾ* (capacity to act). Non-Hanafis also employ a cognate concept to that of legal personality, which they refer to as *dhimma* (al-Qarāfī 2001, 3: 226), defined by most jurists as an attribute by virtue of which a person is capable of having rights and obligations (*ahl li-l-ījāb lahu wa-ʿalayhi*). According to all jurists, all humans are born with *dhimma*, in contrast to animals (al-Jurjānī 1321/[1938]: 74).

Regardless of their different jurisprudential orientations, *dhimma* and *ahliyyat al-wujūb* feature as preconditions for full responsibility or capacity. Legal theorists of all schools discuss issues of legal capacity when considering the subject upon whom a certain divine command applies, identifying the subject either as *mukallaf bihi* ("obligated with [upholding the divine command]") or *maḥkūm ʿalayhi* ("charged with [upholding the divine command]").

Legal Personality

Dhimma or *ahliyyat al-wujūb* is generally acquired at birth and lost at death. The fetus in the mother's womb is accorded a limited legal personality—giving it the right to inherit, for example—but being born alive is required to confirm the rights acquired before birth. Significant traces of the theological debate can be found in the fiqh discussions on legal personality, as in the early fourteenth century concerning the jinn (al-Minyāwī 2011b: 222, citing al-Ṭūfī, d. 716/1316). The Hanbali jurist Ibn Taymiyya (d. 728/1328) issued a legal opinion to the effect that the jinn is *mukallaf* but in a different way than for humans (al-Minyāwī 2011a: 90).

As a direct consequence of the theological premise that in order to be responsible for one's actions one needs to understand God's message, the guiding principle in matters of capacity to act is the possession of the mental faculty of *ʿaql* ("intellect") (Kamali 2003: 450). Age generally operates as a presumption of lack or presence of *ʿaql*. Full capacity to act is attained at puberty (*bulūgh*), which is either signaled by nocturnal emission or menstruation, or by reaching a certain age (jurists disagree on the relevance of the age, on the actual number of years, and on a difference of age between boys and girls; most set the coming of age of a girl between nine and 15 lunar years, and between 12 and 15 for a boy). Even when puberty is attained, full capacity to act may be impeded by insanity (*junūn*) and sleep (*nawm*). An oft-quoted hadith observes that there is no responsibility for three: the sleeping person until he wakes, the child until he has a nocturnal emission, and the insane until he reasons.[1] The hadith is strongly gendered in its reference to the child, but the jurists did not seem to have given any weight to this element in their elaboration of female legal capacity. The jurists identified further impediments—ignorance (*jahl*), forgetfulness (*nisyān*), unconsciousness (*ighmāʾ*), and intoxication (*sukr*)—but conditions and effects vary. Duress (*ikrāh*) was counted among the impediments affecting capacity to act by Muʿtazilis, but Ashʿaris limit it to the threat of death (al-Suyūṭī 1990: 203–6). Cases of extreme duress are considered under the heading of unavoidability (*iljāʾ*); the person incapable of avoiding the consequence (*muljaʾ*) is not deemed responsible for the act—here jurists usually refer to the case of a person thrown from a tower who kills a person below without being able to avoid hitting her (al-Sīnāwanī 1928: 9).

In line with the centrality of the divine command (either as *kulfa* or *ḥukm*), Maliki jurists emphasize that responsibility is waived for the minor (*ṣabī*) only insofar as obligations and prohibitions (*al-wājib wa-l-muḥarram*) are concerned; they insist that minors and their guardians are responsible for the acts that are qualified as recommended (*mandūb*), reprehensible (*makrūh*), or indifferent (*mubāḥ*) (al-Sīnāwanī 1928: 7).

Legal theorists do not treat questions of limitations to the capacity to act, which are articulated and regulated in compendia of substantive law (*furūʿ al-fiqh*) under the heading of *ḥajr*. I will nonetheless briefly refer to them in what follows. Limitations are usually classified as such in the interest of the person whose capacity is limited (*ḥajr li-maṣlaḥat al-maḥjūr*), in the interest of the public good (*ḥajr li-l-maṣlaḥa al-ʿāmma*), and in the interest of third parties (*ḥajr li-maṣlaḥat al-ghayr*).

An intermediate status between full capacity to act and the complete lack thereof is identified for the discerning minor (*al-ṣabī al-mumayyiz*) and the person with defective intellect (*maʿtūh*), but only if in their interest (al-Sarakhsī 1973, 2: 340). A distinction between the minor and the discerning minor affects the enforceability of the act for Hanafis and Malikis; for Shafiʿis and Hanbalis it affects the validity of the act itself. Ritual acts (*ʿibādāt*) can be performed by the person with limited capacity to act but are not mandatory; transactions (*muʿāmalāt*) are judged according to the effects. If the effects are beneficial—as in the case of a received gift, whether the result of a charitable donation or a simple act of generosity—they are allowed; if the effects are detrimental—as in the case of divorce, manumission, generosity, or liability—they are not allowed and will not be considered valid even if performed by the minor's guardian (*walī*); and if the effects are partly beneficial and partly detrimental—as in the case of sale, lease, and marriage—their validity depends on the authorization (*ijāza*) of the guardian.

Capacity can also be limited through interdiction (*ḥajr*), the judicial constraint on disposing of one's wealth freely, but the schools of jurisprudence differ on when this is allowed. Moreover, the term *ḥajr* can refer to an automatic limitation of capacity as well as judicial interdiction. In the first sense, *ḥajr* denotes both the total absence of capacity of the minor and of the insane and the limited capacity of the discerning minor and the person with defective intellect (for Hanafis and Malikis); in the second sense, *ḥajr* is qualified by the intervention of a judicial decision according to an extensive

1 *Rufiʿa al-qalam ʿan thalātha: ʿan al-nāʾim ḥattā yastayqiẓ, ʿan al-ṣabī ḥattā yaḥtalim, ʿan al-majnūn ḥattā yaʿqil.*

taxonomy. In the case of the spendthrift (*safīh*, lit. fool), Abū Ḥanīfa rejected the possibility of limiting capacity, but on the authority of Abū Yūsuf and al-Shaybānī, the later Hanafis—just as the Shafiʿis and Hanbalis—allow judicial interdiction; Malikis allow interdiction by the father within a year of the minor's coming of age but later require the intervention of the qadi. In the case of the forgetful (*mughaffal* or *dhū l-ghafla*), all the schools require judicial intervention in order to determine the level of *ghafla* and consequently limit capacity; only Abū Ḥanīfa again considers interdiction a harsher outcome than the ensuing squandering of the patrimony. In the case of the grave sinner (*fāsiq*), all schools agree with the Shafiʿis that if the grave sins (*kabāʾir*) are not coupled with dissipation to the degree of spendthrift squandering (*safāha*), there is no limitation of capacity. In the public interest, scholars agree on the judicial interdiction of three categories: the ignorant physician (*al-ṭabīb al-jāhil*), the impudent mufti (*al-muftī al-mājin*), and the insolvent donkey- (or other beasts of burden) driver (*al-mukārī al-muflis*). Exceptionally Abū Ḥanīfa recognized the validity of interdiction for these last three categories as a form of prevention for their causing bodily, religious, and commercial harm. In the interest of third parties, capacity can be partially limited, as in the case of disbursements beyond the bequeathable one-third for those affected by mortal illness (*maraḍ al-mawt*),[2] extended by analogy to the available one-third for wives, and to the existing debts for the insolvent.

Legal theorists seem to agree that the legal obligation (*kulfa*) needs to fall on the widest possible category. The way in which this is constructed, however, varies significantly while generally allowing for different degrees of configuration, as exemplified by opinions regarding the responsibility of infidels (*kuffār*). According to the Shafiʿi jurist al-Juwaynī (d. 478/1085) (1997: 107, 110), Hanafis do not include infidels among those to whom the obligation is directed, but Shafiʿis do, distinguishing, however, between commands (*maʾmūrāt*) and prohibitions (*manhiyyāt*); infidels would be punished for not respecting the latter, but not for not following the former. Al-Juwaynī further defers the punishment to the afterlife. But among Hanafis are also jurists like al-Jaṣṣāṣ (d. 370/981) who claim that infidels need to be counted among those who are obligated (*mukallafūn*) on the authority of Abū Bakr. Al-Jaṣṣāṣ's argument (2000, 2: 158–60) is based on the existence of a punishment for acts against God's commands, but conversion to Islam is a precondition for the performance of legal obligations since embracing faith (*īmān*) is a precondition to the fulfillment of the law (*sharīʿa*). Other scholars recognize a general responsibility (*taklīf*) on the non-Muslim, which does not extend, however, to substantive law.

Substantive Law (*furūʿ al-fiqh*)

The absence of an extensive set of statuses in the general theory of law does not mean that distinctions among individuals are not employed in substantive law. In substantive law, however, these are not treated as statuses or general limitations of capacity, but rather as conditions (*shurūṭ*)—or lack thereof—for the legal qualification (*ḥukm*) of an individual act. When compiled under a single heading, a series of conditions may be perceived as constituting a status, but it is an optical effect. Besides creating the optical effect of statuses, compilations have strong normative and performative implications—implications that become all the more problematic when considering two main elements of inaccuracy of the compilations. On the one hand, the selection and extraction of the individual condition (*sharṭ*) from its context hinders locating the condition within the wider jurisprudential discourse of the original author, with serious ramifications. If we just think of the divergence in definitions—the qualification of *kāfir* (infidel) can be loosely or strictly constructed, for instance, even by the same author within the same work. On the other hand, compilations not only fail to account for the high degree of variation in the treatment of legal issues in fiqh works across generations and centers of legal productions, but also sketch a monolithic, all-inclusive, uni-dimensional image where

2 On the development by Medinan and Iraqian scholars of the concept of *maraḍ al-mawt*, see Yanagihashi 1998.

space and time ebb. In compilations, a condition set on a ritual act by an eighth-century Kufan scholar can be followed by one set on a transaction by a thirteenth-century Maghribi scholar.

This second section will indicate the areas of substantive law where particular conditions reflecting certain fault lines in the equality spectrum can be found. A first group of conditions, based on religious affiliation (*islām*), will be followed by one based on freedom (*ḥurriyya*), a third one based on lineage (*nasab*), a fourth on justice (*ʿadl*), and a last one on the variable and puzzling concept of *iḥṣān*. These fault lines have attracted very different levels of attention across the ages, with the regulations on non-Muslims and slaves featuring as the most explored.

Religious Affiliation

Non-Muslims

Jurists conventionally consider someone to be Muslim on the basis of three separate circumstances. The first is by explicit pronouncement (*bi-l-naṣṣ*), that is, by uttering the Islamic statement of faith (*shahāda*) (belief in the oneness of God and the prophethood of Muḥammad) in the presence of witnesses. Scholars disagree whether purification (*ghusl*) is in order after conversion. Malikis and Hanbalis prescribe it as obligatory on the authority of a Prophetic tradition; Hanafis and Shafiʿis consider it only recommended if the non-Muslim was not impure (*junub*).

The second is as a result of someone else's actions (*bi-l-tabaʿiyya*) by the fact of (1) being born of a Muslim parent—either one for Hanafis, Shafiʿis, and Hanbalis on the basis of the Prophetic tradition: "Islam is superior and is not surpassed" (*al-islām yaʿlū wa-lā yuʿlā ʿalayhi*); only the father for Malikis; but even if only the grandfather converts, according to Shafiʿis on the basis of Q 52:21); (2) a minor slave without parents in Islamic territory; (3) a foundling in a Muslim area of the Islamic territory; and (4) an orphan raised through *kafāla* (guardianship) by Muslims in Islamic territory (Ibn Qayyim al-Jawziyya 1995a: 298).

Finally, according to Hanafis and Hanbalis, one is Muslim implicitly (*bi-l-dalāla*) by performing ritual acts specific of Islam (Ibn Nujaym 1999; Ibn Qudāma 1996).

Non-Muslims are identified as those who are not considered Muslims on any of the above-mentioned grounds. Because of the scattered nature of sources and regulations, Muslim jurists from a very early period engaged in collecting and systematizating all the provisions affecting non-Muslims in compendia, of which the most renowned is Ibn Qayyim al-Jawziyya's *Aḥkām ahl al-dhimma*. Consequently, writings on the status of non-Muslims in what is broadly defined as Islamic law is vast, in Arabic as well as other languages, with—from the nineteenth century on—literature in Arabic on the status of non-Muslims focusing on the needs of modern state regulations. Western scholarship on Islamic law, embracing historical as well as legal perspectives, has also devoted significant coverage to the status of non-Muslims, going as far back as A.S. Tritton (1930) and Antoine Fattal (1958).

The variety of sources on which specific regulations affecting non-Muslims are based is large. Besides Quranic texts and Prophetic hadith, provisions can be found in agreements entered into by the Prophet and non-Muslim communities, as well as in the practice of the first caliphs. These latter sources are historiographically problematic in that they are mentioned only in late accounts (Fattal 1958: 58; Tritton 1930) and should therefore be treated with care. In the formative stages of Islam, the regulation of non-Muslim status shows a lack of uniformity that can be attributed partly to the differences in the contents of the above-mentioned agreements and to the subjects to which they applied, and partly to the use of multiple, overlapping references to "non-Muslims" in the various categories of textual sources. The Christian tribe of Banū Taghlib, for instance, paid the alms tax levied on Muslims (*zakāt*) instead of the poll tax levied on non-Muslims (*jizya*), and Samaritans were exempted from the land tax levied on non-Muslim-owned land (*kharāj*) (Fattal 1958: 59).

The term "condition of Islam" (*sharṭ al-islām*) is largely preferred by jurists to refer to non-Muslim status, but a variety of other terms are also used, in particular *dhimma* ("protection"). The origin of this term seems to be associated with the agreements or pacts made with non-Muslim communities (sg. *'ahd al-dhimma*). Following a sort of metonymical process, the understanding of *dhimma* became so ingrained with that of *'ahd* that when jurists explained the concept of legal capacity within *uṣūl al-fiqh*, they often referred to the *dhimma* of non-Muslims as the pact (rather than *'ahd*) on which their status was based.

Dhimma is organized under the headings of *jihād*, *jizya*, or *kharāj* in the fiqh books. The term for the protected non-Muslim, who is a permanent resident of Muslim-ruled territory (*dār al-islām*), is *dhimmī*; the non-Muslim temporary resident of Muslim-ruled territory is referred to as *musta'min* (beneficiary of a temporary safeconduct, or *amān*); and the non-Muslim who is neither a permanent nor a temporary resident is called *ḥarbī* (with reference to the individual's main residence in non-Muslim-ruled territory, called in classical law the abode of war, *dār al-ḥarb*).

In other areas of fiqh, however, we can find Quranic terms such as *ahl al-kitāb* (lit. people of the Book), *kāfir* ("infidel"), or *mushrik* ("associator"), which are, however, not univocally interpreted and seldom applied to the same categories of subject in different areas of substantive law. Within the category of people of the Book are usually included Jews and Christians, but on the basis of a hadith attributed to Muḥammad the category was extended to Zoroastrians (for the application of the regime of *dhimma* based on Q 9:29) and by later jurists also to followers of other religions. For the categories of infidel and associator the boundaries are more porous and subject to even more divergent scholarly interpretation. The status of apostates (sg. *murtadd*) will be treated separately below.

In marriage, there is wide agreement that a Muslim woman may not marry a non-Muslim man. This is for a presumed lack of equality (*kafā'a*), predicated on a Quranic verse, the "verse of interdiction" (Q 2:221), and on a hadith stipulating the preeminence of Islam over other religions. A Muslim man is allowed to marry a non-Muslim woman as long as she belongs to the people of the Book and is *muḥṣana*, in this case generally understood as "free" (Abū Ḥanīfa, who interprets the term differently, allows the marriage of a Muslim male with a slave woman who belongs to the people of the Book). This is based on the so-called verse of permission that allows such unions (Q 5:5), but jurists differ in their rulings on marriage to a non-Muslim woman, especially if she is not a permanent resident of a Muslim-ruled territory. Unlike the inclusion of Zoroastrians in the regime of *dhimma*, in this case the category of people of the Book does not extend to them, on the authority of the same hadith.

In inheritance, the schools agree that a non-Muslim cannot inherit from a Muslim, and vice versa. This rule is based on a hadith that in a different transmission is interpreted to allow non-Muslims to inherit from non-Muslims providing they both belong to the same "category" (Jews, Christians, Zoroastrians, and pagans for Hanbalis; Jews, Christians, and pagans for Malikis). The ability of a non-Muslim to dispose of his or her assets freely is fully recognized by Abū Ḥanīfa but rejected by Abū Yūsuf and al-Shaybānī, as well as by Mālik and al-Shāfi'ī (bequeathing them for the construction of a non-Muslim place of worship, for instance, because of its intrinsic violation of the law). Testamentary dispositions of a non-Muslim in favor of a Muslim are allowed, but the reverse is not, except for Abū Ḥanīfa.

Rules affecting the establishment of religious endowments (sg. *waqf*) follow the same logic of testamentary dispositions. The non-Muslim and the Muslim can endow property in favor of each other or for their own coreligionists, with the exception of the construction of a non-Muslim place of worship.

Equality in property rights is almost complete; the exceptions are wine and pork, which can be validly owned, bought, and sold only by non-Muslims, and copies of the Quran, a Muslim slave, and taller houses, which can be validly owned, bought, and sold only by Muslims. Even if jurists at times frowned upon joint ventures with non-Muslims or upon the use of non-Muslim slaves in commerce for fear of the slave engaging in non-interest-free activities, only rarely did they prohibit them. Higher fees apply to the *ḥarbī*, and to the *dhimmī* when commercing with foreign lands. Beyond a minimum value, a customs tax (*'ushr*) applies to the Muslim to the sum of 2.5 percent of the overall value, five to the *dhimmī*, and ten to the *ḥarbī*.

Service in the army and public service follow considerations of loyalty to Islam that jurists do not feel comfortable trusting non-Muslims with. They generally agree that non-Muslims cannot regularly serve in the Muslim army but can be employed in warfare operations. Based on Quranic verses and hadith referring to authority (*wilāya*), non-Muslims are also generally excluded from positions of authority, but by distinguishing between a ministry with delegated authority (*wizārat al-tafwīḍ*) and one with a mere executive scope (*wizārat al-tanfīdh*), the Shafiʿi al-Māwardī (Wahba 1996: 23ff.) allows the latter to be assumed by a non-Muslim.

Whereas all ritual duties (including paying *zakāt*) fall on Muslims alone, there are two fiscal obligations that fall only on non-Muslims: *jizya* (poll tax) and *kharāj* (later, land tax). Explicitly mentioned in Q 9:29, *jizya* is a personal tax levied on non-Muslim residents in exchange for the protection (*dhimma*) afforded them. A few categories are exempted, generally including women, minors, elderly, monks, and nuns—the extension of exempted categories depending on the consideration of the function of *jizya*, which surprisingly varies quite significantly. With the exception of the Malikis, all other schools apply three tax brackets (rich, medium, and poor), even though *jizya* is not calculated on the amount of wealth of the person but paid per capita.

Kharāj, which used to indicate the tax levied on non-Muslims, synonymous with the *jizya* tax, began to be employed in classical law to refer mainly to the general land tax (originally levied only on non-Muslim-owned land). The fiscal regime of land ownership is extremely complicated and varies geographically. According to al-Māwardī's classical categorization, lands that remain the property of or can be disposed by non-Muslims after *dhimma* is attained, are levied *kharāj*, whereas the *ʿushr* tax is levied on most of the land owned by Muslims. The kind of taxation applicable to land, however, increasingly became independent of the religious affiliation of the owner or possessor, attaching only to the land.

A clear distinction between Muslims and non-Muslims is drawn in matters of retaliation (*qiṣāṣ*) for killing and its regulation. A killing is lawful when there is no obligation of protection over the person (*muhdar al-dam*), as is the case with the *ḥarbī* or the apostate. The distinction of religious status appears also in the amounts of blood money (*diya*) for the different legal categories of persons. The Hanafis and Hanbalis rule that there is no difference between that of a *dhimmī* and a free Muslim; according to the Malikis, *diya* for the non-Muslim is one-half that of a Muslim; while for the Shafiʿis it is one-third.

The differentiation in blood money extends also to gender and slavery: the *diya* for a woman is half that for a man; that for a murdered slave is the victim's market value. See also Chapter 12, below.

A few elements of differential treatment of non-Muslims can be found in procedural law as well. The qadi, who will hear the case when one party to the action is Muslim, has a duty of impartiality, but there are considerations of unequal status. While Muslims can act as witnesses against non-Muslims, non-Muslims can only act as witnesses against other non-Muslims.

Muslim Apostates

Like the non-Muslim, the apostate fails to fulfill the condition of Islam, but the definition of what constitutes apostasy (*ridda* or *irtidād*) has fluctuated across generations and territories. A broad, preliminary definition is that apostasy entails the abandoning of Islam, either by embracing another religion or simply by rejecting Islam (or one of its tenets). Substantive law regulates the acts of and punishment for the apostate; variations among the jurists concerning the gravity of consequences stem from different versions of the definition of apostasy, but it is clear that abandoning Islam needs to be coupled with evidence of a threat to the Islamic community.

Scholarly interest in the legal consequences of apostasy has been considerable, but has primarily focused on the punishment. The most comprehensive study on both the penal and civil consequences of apostasy in classical law is that of Peters and de Vries (1976–77). More recently, Frank Griffel

(2001) has written on the invitation to repent (*istitāba*) before declaring a Muslim an apostate, an essential analysis that lays the foundations for reconsidering the modern understanding of the classical rules. Even more recently, another important contribution offering a full appreciation of the different rationales and complexities of the classical rules on apostasy appeared (Saeed 2004).

Marriage with an apostate is void (*bāṭil*), regardless of the apostate's gender. Apostasy also annuls an existing marriage. Repentance during the woman's waiting period (*ʿidda*) reactivates the marriage which was held in abeyance (*mawqūf*) only for Shafiʿis, whereas for other schools repentance has only the effect of making possible a new marriage, which can be contracted immediately since the previous dissolution was not premised on *ṭalāq*, the husband's unilateral repudiation. Malikis and Hanafis regulate the case of a woman who resorts to apostasy in order to free herself from her husband (apostasy followed by repentance).

In inheritance, the capacity of the apostate to inherit is limited beyond the usual bar of difference of religious affiliation (*ikhtilāf al-dīn*); the apostate cannot inherit from Muslims or, after conversion to another religion, from new coreligionists. Upon the death of the apostate, apostasy is retrospectively treated by most Hanafis and Shafiʿis as a legal death—the apostate's assets that were accumulated before apostasy are divided among the Muslim heirs, and the *mudabbar* slave (a slave whose emancipation becomes effective after death) and *umm walad* (the slave who has borne a child to her master) are set free. Al-Shāfiʿī and Malikis consider the property of the apostate as booty (*fayʾ*) that returns to the treasury upon the apostate's death, while Hanafis apply this rule only to the property acquired after apostasy. Later Shafiʿis extend to the issue of inheritance the principle of holding in abeyance the apostate's assets, as with property rights.

Property rights are generally retained by the apostate, but the capacity to dispose of them is considered to be held in abeyance (*mawqūf*) until repentance. Capacity to act after apostasy therefore depends retrospectively on repentance—if the apostate does not repent, all acts concluded after apostasy are void. Shafiʿis consider acts that cannot be held in abeyance (sales, gifts, guarantees) irredeemably void, whereas Hanafis tend to expand the number of valid acts. Hanafis, moreover, consider the female apostate to be fully capable to act and dispose of her property, and some of them, on the authority of Abū Yūsuf and al-Shaybānī, also extend the rule to male apostates—the latter doing so by invoking an analogy with mortal illness. A stricter approach can be found with some Malikis and Hanbalis, who refuse to recognize the existence of any property right after apostasy.

Freedom

The general theory of law does not define a particular status for the slave, and the regulations in substantive law treat the slave alternatively as chattel or as a person; as chattel the slave is subject to a number of rights of ownership (with a series of remarkable exceptions to the general rules), but as a person the slave enjoys a number of rights (with a series of remarkable exceptions to the general rules). This section will look at the main areas where the latter exceptions can be found. The hybrid nature of the slave is the basic consideration underpinning the principle according to which the slave needs to be treated as a half person for any numerical account in the law.

According to legal scholars, slavery (*riqq*) can originate only by capture in war or by birth. A Muslim cannot be enslaved, but can be born as a slave. Non-Muslim war captives can be enslaved (*istirqāq*), on the basis of the Quran (for example, 8:69–70) and a Prophetic tradition attributed to ʿĀʾisha on the enslavement of women and children of the Banū Qurayẓa. All the children of a slave mother are also slaves, whether the father is a free man or a slave, with the single exception of her master's children—they are born free providing he acknowledges them as his own (which, according to the Malikis, may be implicit if no express denial of fatherhood is forthcoming). Analogy between the fruits of chattel and the children of a female slave (considered as fruits or increase, *namāʾ*) is at the origin of the rule that the children of the female slave belong to her master (with the already mentioned exception of his own, who are born free). Change of ownership over the slave follows the ordinary rules of change of ownership over chattel (by sale, gift, will, inheritance, etc.), with some minor exceptions (Brunschvig 1960).

In ritual acts (*ʿibādāt*) the exceptions to the general rules applying to Muslim free men are less pervasive than in other fields, and are premised on the slave's limited freedom of movement and financial responsibility. As a consequence of the first, the Muslim slave is not obliged to attend the Friday congregational prayer, perform the pilgrimage, or take part in the lesser holy war (*jihād*); and as a consequence of the second, responsibility for the Muslim slave's annual *zakāt* tax falls on the master.

In transactions (*muʿāmalāt*), the lack of capacity to act is the general rule, often articulated by the imposition of interdiction (*ḥajr*). However, the slave is recognized to have a limited capacity to act in marriage and in patrimonial transactions. Any form of authority (*wilāya*) over free persons is denied, whether for matrimonial purposes or in public affairs, including the custody of children.

In marriage, the Muslim male slave can contract a marriage, but the master's consent is either required immediately for the validity of the contract (in his capacity as guardian, *walī*) or can be exercised later to void or terminate the contract, on account of the master's liability for the patrimonial obligations related to the slave's marriage (dower and maintenance). In imposed marriages (*jabr*), the father's authority is extended to the master also beyond the male slave's attainment of puberty. On the principle of being half a person, the male slave can marry up to two wives instead of four (this does not apply for Malikis), and repudiation by the husband (*ṭalāq*) becomes a bar to remarry the same woman after the second pronouncement instead of the third. For Hanafis the half-treatment in repudiation applies only when the wife is a slave. A male slave is not considered an adequate spouse (*ghayr kufʾ*) to a free woman, but if neither the woman nor her guardian (*walī*) object, the marriage can still be contracted and stand. The waiting period after termination of marriage is reduced by a half for the female slave, and sexual intercourse with her is also prohibited before the lapsing of the shorter, initial waiting period (*istibrāʾ*) after any change of ownership or status (emancipation or marriage).

In patrimonial transactions, the slave is usually considered to be acting on behalf of the master, who has full capacity to act. Only Malikis allow the slave limited ownership rights, but the latter's capacity to act needs to be complemented by the master's. The master can also affect the slave's capacity to act in patrimonial matters by authorization (*idhn*), which raises a number of questions in terms of liability for the authorized slave's (*maʾdhūn*) transactions. For Shafiʿis and Hanafis, the slave cannot act as executor of a will (*waṣī*).

In *ḥadd* punishments (*ʿuqūbāt*, see further Chapter 12, below), a more lenient treatment is afforded to the slave in sexual offences, as slaves do not qualify as *muḥṣan*. For unlawful sexual intercourse, the punishment is half that of the non-*muḥṣan* free person (in this case *muḥṣan* is generally constructed as the person who has concluded and consummated a valid marriage with a free person): 50 lashes instead of 100 (Schacht 1964: 125). For false accusation of unlawful sexual intercourse, the punishment is half that of the free person (here the quality of *muḥṣan* does not apply, as the slave cannot be a victim of a false accusation in fiqh): 40 lashes instead of 80.

Retaliation (*qiṣāṣ*) for the intentional killing of a slave is recognized only by Hanafis, who nonetheless do not hold the master responsible for killing his own slave or his slave's son. They are also the only school not to permit retaliation for bodily harm; the other schools allow for retaliation only among equals. Blood money is not a set value as for the free person, but based on the market value of the victim (which for Hanafis cannot be higher than the free person's set value).

The slave's testimony is not accepted in court, except by Hanbalis, who, however, do not accept it in major offenses. Acknowledgement (*iqrār*) is accepted only in matters affecting the slave's person, not in property issues.

Most changes in a slave's status bring about their full effects only in the future, but jurists register a partial change even if they often allow change of ownership or inheritance considerations to prevent the operation of prospective emancipations. The only emancipation with immediate effects is manumission (*ʿitq*), which stems from the master's will alone. Prospective emancipation can occur in three ways: (1) the master's will (*tadbīr*), which will produce effects upon the master's death; as such, emancipation is conditional upon the bequeathable one-third and the payment of the master's extant debts; (2) a contract of emancipation (*kitāba* or *mukātaba*), which will produce effects when the slave's payments have reached the amount set in the contract. In this case, jurists limit the possibility of frustrating the contract by not allowing or by conditionally allowing the transfer of ownership over the slave by the master; and (3) bearing the master's child (that is, becoming *umm walad*), which will produce effects upon the master's death.

After manumission, substantive law continues to regulate in a partially differentiated way the freed slave's relationships. Between the manumitter and the freed slave (*mu'taq*), the relationship is usually referred to as patronage (*walā'*) and is premised on an unequal bond that imposes uneven obligations on the parties. Manumission also leaves a limited yet meaningful number of traces on the freed slave's relationship with a third party. Some of these traces are based on the status of being a former slave, some on the status of the manumitter, in line with the principle that manumission projects the freed slave into the manumitter's kin group (*ta'ṣīb*)—the slave freed by a manumitter of lesser lineage is, for example, not an adequate husband for a slave freed by a manumitter of higher lineage. As pointed out above, the freed slave himself is not an adequate husband for a free born woman. This extends into generational divides, viz., the son of a freed slave is not an adequate husband for the granddaughter of a free man.

Lineage

Lineage (*nasab*) is an element that Islamic legal theory clearly recognizes without ever defining a clear role for it. Preservation of lineage prominently features in al-Ghazālī's (1997) listing of the five essential objectives (*maqāṣid*) of Sharia, but the expression may encompass such a variety of legal provisions that it is almost impossible to properly identify its meaning. Considerations of lineage can be found in substantive law under a variety of headings, and below I will treat two in the area of family law, wedding adequacy and fair nuptial dower (*mahr al-mithl*), and one in the area of public law, the caliphate (*imāma*).

The principle of equality in marriage, or wedding adequacy, also requires the groom to be of equal or higher standing than the bride in terms of lineage, in the classical Hanafi taxonomy. The lack of it allows the bride's guardian to ask the judge to void the marriage before the appearance of signs of pregnancy.

The origins and reasoning behind wedding adequacy have been explored in all the major studies of Islamic law, but the main reference on *kafā'a* is certainly Farhat Ziadeh's article from 1957. A recent study by Louise Marlow (1997) further underlines how the projection of social stratification in the law was the product of jurists who selected their textual sources, deliberately ignoring abundant egalitarian materials. Wedding adequacy is given more thorough coverage in Hanafi (and Shafi'i) law, which is explained either by the Kufan milieu or by the possibility in Hanafi law for the adult woman to marry without her guardian's consent (*riḍā al-walī*).

Wedding equality based on lineage is often traced to the hadith "Arabs are equal [spouses] (*akfā'*) to one another, tribe by tribe and man by man; and *mawlās*[3] are equal [spouses] to one another, tribe by tribe and man by man, except for the weaver and the cupper" (al-Bayhaqī 2003: 13769–70–71). Thus, for (Hanafi) jurists, the general rule applied that non-Arabs were not adequate grooms for Arab brides. The lineage of non-Arabs was not a factor, their only source of pride being Islam (*mufākharat al-'ajam bi-l-islām lā bi-l-nasab*, in al-Kāsānī 1986, 2: 319).

The non-Arab lineage distinction, combined with the condition of wedding adequacy based on seniority in Islam, operated until the third generation—the newly converted was not a marriage equal

3 Usually translated as "client," *mawlā* often refers in early Islam to a non-Arab who was allied with an Arab patron (confusingly, also *mawlā*) to facilitate entrance into society. For an extended discussion, see Crone 1987: chap. 3.

to a bride whose father was Muslim, and the son of the newly converted was not for a bride whose grandfather was Muslim.

When the amount of the dower (*mahr*) is not stipulated in the marriage contract, substantive law gives the qadi the parameters according to which to fix a fair dower (*mahr al-mithl*), and lineage re-emerges as one of the focal elements. Hanafis are the only madhhab to compare only the female members of the woman's father's kin group in the appreciation of the due dower; further considerations usually include wealth, beauty, youth, intelligence, and piety. Hanbalis compare both the father's and the mother's kin groups, while Malikis and Shafiʿis compare other women on the father's side (although they also introduce the groom into the equation) (al-Zuḥaylī 1984, 9: 6775ff.).

Considerations of lineage are also central in public law, especially when it comes to the requirements for the caliphate. See Chapter 13, below.

Justice

The quality of being just (*ʿadl*) is a requirement for public office, but it is also a key requirement in the selection of witnesses in Sharia court cases. In light of the centrality of oral testimony in the law of evidence, the concept of *ʿadl* deserves thorough examination. To use the definition given by Emile Tyan (1938), a person of good morals is *ʿadl*. It is not sufficient to be a sane, adult, male Muslim to bear witness in court. A person's good morals must be ascertained before acting as a witness.

The procedure through which the quality of *ʿadl* is established makes the condition of having good morals not simply a generic, blanket requirement. The procedure is referred to as *tazkiya* or *taʿdīl* (moral examination or probation) and includes two stages. In the first (*al-tazkiya al-sirriyya*), the judge investigates secretly by inquiring about the potential witness with persons of trust by letter, while in the second (*al-tazkiya al-ʿalāniyya*), these persons of trust can be summoned to court to publicly confirm their assessment of the potential witness. The preemptive recognition of the quality of *ʿadl* to certain persons generated the phenomenon of the *ʿudūl*, individuals who assumed some of the functions of notaries public due to their ability to bear witness in court without fear of disqualification.

The definition of *ʿadl* heavily depends on the interpretation of the individual judge and on the questions that he addresses to the persons of trust. This can in turn explain the considerable interest in regulating the process of *takziya* in the works on rules of conduct for qadis (*adab al-qāḍī*). The elements to be considered for the *ʿadl* label fell into three main categories: not having committed unexpiated major sins, not persevering in minor sins, and not displaying unbecoming behavior (Peters 1997).

Iḥṣān

A problematic, yet understudied category is that of *iḥṣān*, the quality of being *muḥṣan*. It applies in penal law in two *ḥadd* crimes, the one unlawful sexual intercourse (*zinā*) and the other the false accusation of such (*qadhf*). In the case of the first, the *muḥṣan*—defined as the "free person who has concluded and consummated a valid marriage with a free spouse"—is punished by death, whereas in the case of the second, the *muḥṣan*, who is protected against the accusation of *zinā*, is defined as the "free person who has never committed unlawful intercourse" (Schacht 1964: 125), possibly referencing Q 5:5. Most classical Quran commentators of this verse and jurists emphasize the "free" aspect, but some translators of the Quran in English, such as Marmaduke (Muḥammad) Pickthall and Yūsuf ʿAlī, interpret *muḥṣan(āt)* in Q 5:5 as "virtuous" or "chaste" women,[4] raising interpretative

4 "[Lawful unto you in marriage] are [not only] chaste women who are believers, but chaste women among the People of the Book, revealed before your time—when ye give them their due dowers, and desire chastity, not lewdness, nor secret intrigues" (ʿAlī 1996).

problems. Such a translation would prevent non-*muḥṣan* Muslim women from ever getting married, and fails to account for non-*muḥṣan* Muslim men, leaving the door open to four apparently only loosely related uses of the concept of *iḥṣān*.

An attempt to give a coherent reading of *iḥṣān* was advanced by W. Montgomery Watt (1956: 389–92). Considering the centrality of Islam's concern for "observing the purity of paternity," Watt suggested that *iḥṣān* refers to men and women in monandric relations. This reading takes into account the different Quranic verses in which the root *ḥ-ṣ-n* appears and the relation in these verses of *iḥṣān* to *sāfaḥa* (unlimited polyandry) and *fatayāt* (women in matrilineal households with polyandric relations), but has to discard *mā malakat aymānukum* ("those whom your right hands possess," referring to slaves) in Q 4:24, 25 as a later addition. Classical Muslim scholars, however, do not follow this line, and offer an interpretation that considers *mā malakat aymānukum* as an integral part of the verse.

Concluding Remarks

Muslim legal theory (*uṣūl al-fiqh*) and substantive law (*furūʿ al-fiqh*) show a striking contrast in their treatment of the issue of equality before the law. While theory displays a universalist tendency that tries to avoid any categorization not based on the ability to receive and understand God's commands, the substantive law finds itself in need of resorting to categories (some of which are employed by the textual sources themselves), but tries to de-emphasize them. Yet jurists also subtly introduce categories in substantive law that are not strictly necessitated by the textual sources.

The outcome is an intricate, fluctuating system of statuses in substantial law that allows jurists to exploit the loose definitions and pursue (almost) any desired solution. These statuses, in the form of conditions (*shurūṭ*), populate the *furūʿ* works in their various sections, eluding general definitions. Attempts to compile these conditions in single compendia have tended to produce either oversimplified or overdetailed works, and are almost inevitably bound for failure—detaching individual regulations from the overall architecture of a legal corpus has the unavoidable effect of absolutizing the abridged solution, and at the same time depriving the user of any possible contextual consideration, not to mention the legal reasoning employed to reach such a solution.

References

ʿAlī, ʿA. Yūsuf. 1996. *The Meaning of the Holy Qurʾān*. Bethesda, MD: Amana.

al-Bayhaqī, Abū Bakr. 2003. *Al-Sunan al-kubrā*. Beirut: Dār al-Kutub al-ʿIlmiyya.

Brunschvig, Robert. 1960. ʿAbd. In *Encyclopaedia of Islam*, 2nd ed. Vol. 1: 24–40. Leiden: E.J. Brill.

Crone, Patricia. 1987. *Roman, Provincial and Islamic Law: The Origins of the Islamic Patronate*. Cambridge: Cambridge University Press.

al-Dasūqī, Muḥammad ʿArafa. 2003. *Ḥāshiyat al-Dasūqī ʿalā l-Sharḥ al-kabīr*. Beirut: Dār al-Kutub al-ʿIlmiyya.

Fattal, Antoine. 1958. *Le statut légal des non-musulmans en pays d'Islam*. Beirut: Impr. Catholique.

al-Ghazālī, Abū Ḥāmid. 1997. *Al-Mustaṣfā min ʿilm al-uṣūl*. Beirut: Muʾassassat al-Risāla.

Gimaret, Daniel. 2000. Taklīf. In *Encyclopaedia of Islam*, 2nd ed. Vol. 10: 138–9. Leiden: Brill.

Griffel, Frank. 2001. Toleration and Exclusion: Al-Shāfiʿī and al-Ghazālī on the Treatment of Apostates. *Bulletin of the School of Oriental and African Studies* 64: 339–54.

Hallaq, Wael B. 2009. *Sharīʿa: Theory, Practice, Transformations*. Cambridge: Cambridge University Press.

Ibn Nujaym, Zayn al-Dīn. 1999. *Al-Ashbāh wa-l-naẓāʾir*. Beirut: Dār al-Kutub al-ʿIlmiyya.

Ibn Qayyim al-Jawziyya, Muḥammad b. Abī Bakr. 1995a. *Shifāʾ al-ʿalīl fī masāʾil al-qaḍāʾ wa-l-qadar wa-l-ḥikma wa-l-taʿwīl*. Beirut: Dār al-Kitāb al-ʿArabī.
———. 1995b. *Aḥkām ahl al-dhimma*. 2 vols. in 1. Beirut: Dār al-Kutub al-ʿIlmiyya.
Ibn Qudāma, ʿAbd Allāh b. Aḥmad. 1996. *Al-Mughnī*. 16 vols. Cairo: Dār al-Ḥadīth.
al-Jaṣṣāṣ, Aḥmad b. ʿAlī. 2000. *Fuṣūl fī l-uṣūl*. 2 vols. Beirut: Dār al-Kutub al-ʿIlmiyya.
al-Jurjānī, ʿAlī b. Muḥammad. 1321/[1938]. *Al-Taʿrīfāt*. Miṣr: al-Bābī al-Ḥalabī.
al-Juwaynī, ʿAbd al-Malik. 1997. *Al-Burhān fī uṣūl al-fiqh*. Beirut: Dār al-Kutub al-ʿIlmiyya.
Kamali, Mohammad Hashim. 2003. *Principles of Islamic Jurisprudence*. Cambridge: Islamic Texts Society.
al-Kāsānī, Abū Bakr. 1986. *Badāʾiʿ al-ṣanāʾiʿ fi tartīb al-sharāʾiʿ*. 7 vols. Beirut: Dār al-Kutub al-ʿIlmiyya.
Marlow, Louise. 1997. *Hierarchy and Egalitarianism in Islamic Thought*. Cambridge: Cambridge University Press.
al-Minyāwī, Maḥmūd. 2011a. *Al-Muʿtaṣar min sharḥ mukhtaṣar al-Uṣūl min ʿilm al-uṣūl*. Cairo: al-Maktaba al-Shāmila.
———. 2011b. *Al-Sharḥ al-kabīr li-mukhtaṣar al-Uṣūl min ʿilm al-uṣūl*. Cairo: al-Maktaba al-Shāmila.
Morand, Marcel. 1916. *Avant-projet de code présenté à la Commission de codification du droit musulman algérien*. Algiers: A. Jourdan.
Peters, Rudolph. 1997. Shāhid. In *Encyclopaedia of Islam*, 2nd ed. Vol. 9: 207–8. Leiden: Brill.
Peters, Rudolph, and Gert J.J. de Vries. 1976–77. Apostasy in Islam. *Die Welt des Islams* 17: 1–25.
al-Qarāfī, Aḥmad b. Idrīs. 2001. *Al-Furūq, aw anwār al-burūq fī anwāʾ al-furūq*, ed. M. Sirāj. 4 vols. Cairo: Dār al-Salām.
Saeed, Abdullah, and Hassan Saeed. 2004. *Freedom of Religion, Apostasy and Islam*. Aldershot, UK: Ashgate.
al-Sarakhsī, Muḥammad. 1973. *Uṣūl al-Sarakhsī*. 2 vols. Beirut: Dār al-Maʿrifa.
Schacht, Joseph. 1964. *Introduction to Islamic Law*. Oxford: Clarendon Press.
al-Sīnāwānī, Ḥasan b ʿUmar. 1928. *Al-Aṣl al-jāmiʿ li-īḍāḥ al-durar al-manẓūma fī silk jamʿ al-jawāmiʿ*. Tunis: Maṭbaʿat al-Nahḍa.
Snouck Hurgronje, Christiaan. 1916. *Mohammedanism: Lectures on Its Origin, Its Religious and Political Growth and Its Present State*. New York and London: G.P. Putnam's Sons.
al-Subkī, Tāqī al-Dīn. 1984. *Ibhāj fī sharḥ al-Minhāj*. 3 vols. Beirut: Dār al-Kutub al-ʿIlmiyya.
al-Suyūṭī, ʿAbd al-Raḥmān. 1990. *Al-Ashbāh wa-l-naẓāʾir fī qawāʿid wa-furūʿ fiqh al-shāfiʿiyya*. 2 vols. Beirut: Dār al-Kutub al-ʿIlmiyya.
Tritton, A.S. 1930. *The Caliphs and Their Non-Muslim Subjects: A Critical Study of the Convenant of ʿUmar*. Bombay: Oxford University Press.
Tyan, Émile. 1938. *Histoire de l'organisation judiciaire en pays d'Islam*. Paris: Librairie du Recueil Sirey.
Wahba, Wafaa H. 1996. *The Ordinances of Government*. Reading: Garnet (Eng. trans. of al-Māwardī, *al-Aḥkām al-sulṭāniyya*).
Watt, W. Montgomery. 1956. *Muhammad at Medina*. Oxford: Clarendon Press.
Weiss, Bernard G. 1992. *The Search for God's Law: Islamic Jurisprudence in the Writings of Sayf al-Dīn al-Āmidī*. Salt Lake City: University of Utah Press; rev. ed. 2010.
Yanagihashi, Hiroyuki. 1998. *Islamic Law and the State*. Tokyo: Islamic Area Studies Project.
Ziadeh, Farhat J. 1957. Equality (*Kafāʾa*) in the Muslim Law of Marriage. *American Journal of Comparative Law* 6: 503–17.
al-Zuḥaylī, Wahba. 1984. *Al-Fiqh al-islāmī wa-adillatuhu*. 10 vols. Damascus: Dār al-Fikr.

Gender Relations

Christina Jones-Pauly

The usual approach to understanding Islamic law is to start with the sources, namely, the Quran and the Sunna as found in the hadith literature. However, this may not be the best way to study gender in Islam: these texts are not unequivocal and this is certainly the case with regard to issues related to gender (or, for that matter, any other subject). Scholars disagree on whether or not the Quran's message is one of gender equality. There are textual arguments for this position, but they exist also for the notion of inequality. The Quran itself was revealed over a period of time representing changing historical circumstances in the consolidation of Muslim power, while the Prophetic traditions and the exegetical commentaries are even more reflective of wide-ranging geographical and socio-economic variations throughout the Islamic lands. Despite the source texts that can be read as supporting gender equality and the minority opinions of even some key jurists to this effect, the majority of jurists became increasingly more conservative in their interpretations, undesirous of going against the tide. Most jurists from the premodern period interpreted texts in such a way as to create legal doctrine in some domains of the law that assigned women a role under the protection of men and subordinate to them, for instance in the law of evidence, where the commonly given justification for a woman's credibility being half that of a man—a sociological, not religious justification—was that women were more emotional than rational and that, being mainly confined to their homes, they were not familiar with society. For the same reason, most jurists held that women could not hold public functions such as head of state or judge. In criminal law doctrine, the blood money for killing a woman was therefore half that for a man. In other fields of the law, such as family relations and inheritance, the legal position of woman was dominated by the notion of complementarity of the distinct social functions of men and women.

In the following discussion of gender relations in the Sharia, the focus will be on family law, with a subsequent presentation of the classical law of succession and a few related topics such as women in litigation and the dress code. This will be followed by a presentation of the reform of family law during the last 100 years, ending with an example of how the sources can be understood and reinterpreted from the viewpoint of gender equality.

Christina Jones-Pauly is a consultant on issues of rule of law on location in East Africa, and the author of *Women Under Islam: Gender, Justice and the Politics of Islamic Law* (2011) and (with E. Niesner) *Frauenhandel in Europa: Strafverfolgung und Opferschutz im europäischen Vergleich* (2001), as well as articles and an edited volume, *Access to Justice: The Role of Court Administrators and Lay Adjudicators in the African and Islamic Contexts* (2002, with Stefanie Elbern).

A Historical Dimension

Western views of Islamic gender relations in the law have vacillated between positively appreciating Islamic law for the fact that it was even more advanced in women's rights than, for example, English common law—long before 1885, when English women were first permitted to own property separate from their husbands, the Quran had conferred on women the right to inherit and to own property in their own names[1]—and rejecting it as a model for gender equality.

The message of Islam was revealed in pluralistic societies where there already existed coherent legal systems such as Mosaic law, canonical Christian law, and customary or desert law as it is sometimes called (Hamzeh 1994). Islam acknowledged a variety of customs, but set out to correct and reform them. It is hardly surprising then that the two principal sources of Islamic law reflect continuous, sometimes tumultuous, historical debate over many social and political issues. As in any other faith-based law, the sources can be used to support a variety of social and political positions, even contradictory ones.

It is acknowledged that the Quran and hadith texts from the first 100 years portray a plurality of gender relations law, both open and restricted. The nascent Islamic religion was faced with the task of reconciling not only customs that restricted women (Coulson 1964: 14–15) but also customs that permitted more liberties to women.[2] Some of the novel principles that the Sharia introduced while having to accommodate pre-existing attitudes are manifest in the stories of women who were prominent in the life of the Prophet.[3]

The story of the first wife of the Prophet, Khadīja, with whom he remained monogamously married until her death, is in itself evidence of women owning properties in their own right. She was a wealthy merchant with far-flung trading agents outside the Arabian peninsula, and a widow who had no concerns about marrying someone younger than herself. The Prophet's daughter, Fāṭima, was a public leader without any fear of leading troops into battle because she believed she had a right to succession and leadership after her father's death. Since the Quranic revelations permitted daughters to share in inheritance along with sons, although their share was half that of a male, why should not the rules of political succession equally allow women to assume public office? (Mernissi 1990).

The hadith narratives relate the dilemmas that faced ʿĀʾisha, the youngest wife of the Prophet, who entered into the (polygamous) marriage when only a child, unable to give informed consent. As a mature woman ʿĀʾisha is on record as favoring monogamous marriages,[4] and as granting the wife the right to divorce her husband if she disagreed with his taking a second wife. This was contrary to the opinion attributed to the fourth caliph ʿAlī, who was married to ʿĀʾisha's stepdaughter Fāṭima, when he sought approval for taking a second wife (Spellberg 1994). ʿĀʾisha reportedly also stood against those who argued that the Quran allows men to have a total of nine wives (two plus three plus four, adding up to nine), not just four. Regarding obedience, ʿĀʾisha reminded men that the husband as well as the wife is to avoid disobedience. She regarded his taking a second wife as a form of disobedience.[5]

ʿĀʾisha set examples of how Islamic law could be used for gender inequality as well as for gender equality. She is said to have been nine years old when she married the Prophet and her age was used for recommending child marriages for females. At the same time, ʿĀʾisha was known for setting an example

1 Cf. Q 4:11, "[…] for the male, [a portion] equal to that of two females; if only daughters, two or more, their share is two thirds of what he leaves behind; if only one, for her is half […]"; and Q 4:32, "And do not wish for that by which God has made some of you exceed others; for men is a share of what they have earned, and for women is a share of what they have earned […]."

2 Cf. the hadith wherein ʿUmar recounts that the women of Quraysh were imitating the forward ways of the Anṣārī women ("the Anṣārī women had the upper hand over their men") (al-Bukhārī, *kitāb al-nikāḥ, bāb mawʿiẓat al-rajul ibnatahu li-ḥāl zawjihā*; and Ahmed 1992: 41–3).

3 Because the sources take a very historical perspective, it becomes necessary to add a historical dimension in interpreting the law. This is not novel—another legal system that similarly relies on a historical lineage is the English common law, which places a high value on precedent. The case law of the 1500s can be as valuable as more recent decisions (Denning 1959).

4 For example, Muslim, *kitāb al-birr wa-l-ṣila wa-l-ādāb, bāb faḍl al-iḥsān ilā l-banāt.*

5 Al-Bukhārī, *kitāb al-nikāḥ, bāb wa-in imraʾatun khāfat min baʿlihā nushūzan ….*

of sparing married women from death by jealous husbands. The legend is that she lagged behind in the desert in the company of a young man. While this might have been cause for death because of the hint of an affair, the occasion gave rise to protection of women against suspicion (Q 24:8). It is common in any society for husbands to suspect their wives and become murderously jealous. Islamic law provided a way out for women. A husband acting on his own emotions was not allowed to kill his wife. He could not be judge in his own cause but had to undergo a procedure before the court. He was to give an oath swearing that his suspicions were true and the final oath entitled God to strike him dead if his accusations were false. The wife could in response take the same set of oaths to counter her husband. She could swear that she did nothing wrong, and with the last oath ask that God strike her dead if she swore falsely. With the wife being able to counter her husband, this procedure balanced the gender relationships insofar as the woman's life was spared. If neither husband nor wife was struck dead, the husband always had the right to divorce his wife if he could not still his suspicions. Such procedural proofs constitute a key protective feature in Islamic law. Other hadith texts have been used, however, to allow a male to kill a wife or female relative if he considers his patriarchal honor compromised by her (allegedly) having an affair.[6]

Quranic rules and hadith relating to the acts of adultery or fornication also offer to a certain extent the protection of women. Both men and women can be accused of an extra-marital sexual act (*zinā*) (for example, Q 4:15, 16; 17:32; 24:2–3). If the parties are not legally married to each other, further proof is required as to whether they in fact engaged in penetrative sexual intercourse. If the act was non-consensual on the part of the woman, that is, rape, a hadith has the Prophet only applying punishment on the man. Proof consists of confession at four different times by the parties or testimony of four upright Muslim men (arguably eight upright Muslim women) who witnessed the actual penetration. This level of proof rendered a conviction extremely difficult. Circumstantial evidence was not allowed in principle. If by perchance against all odds there were witnesses, and the offence clearly proven, punishment was disbursed for both the man and the woman equally. On the basis of Quran 49:12, spying on one another is prohibited, so that men and women not married to each other but in each other's company without chaperones cannot be victimized by society.

In this area of the law, the sources generally took a rational and balanced approach to gender relations. Certain basic principles of gender equality could be extracted from historical accounts of the most important women in the life of the Prophet as well as from the Quran and hadith. But certain basic principles of gender inequality could also be extracted, and, as we will see below, in fiqh the latter overshadowed the former.

Classical Islamic Law

In many areas of the law, especially in the law of property and contracts, women and men enjoyed the same legal position, while historical sources show that women had agency in asserting their rights in court. Below I will examine those fields of the law in which gender is an issue and women and men do not have equal rights.

Marriage

The basic principle in Islamic law is that marriage is a contract, not a sacrament.[7] A marriage is contracted, or entered into, upon an offer being made by a groom that is correspondingly accepted by

6 Ghulam Yaseen vs The State PLD 1994 Lahore 392.
7 For overviews of classical fiqh on marriage and gender, see Ali 2006, 2010; Linant de Bellefonds 1965; Peirce 2003; Rapoport 2005; Spectorsky 2010; Tucker 1998, 2008.

the bride (or a person acting on her behalf). According to most schools of law (sg. *madhhab*), a woman cannot conclude a marriage contract by herself, but must be represented by a matrimonial guardian (*walī*), usually her father or a close agnatic male relative. This is rooted in the fact that in the early Islamic community—indeed, in many societies—the family was the woman's paramount source of economic welfare and support; thus the jurists required some form of family control over whom the woman married. Considering the family wishes in all social decisions became the norm, although the jurists developed variations on how far the individual right of the woman to consent could be withheld.

The guardian could not act without the bride's consent, but he could withhold his own. If the matrimonial guardian was not the bride's father and she had the stamina to resist her family, she could ask the court to agree to her sole consent as sufficient, which would be granted if the groom-to-be was of equal or higher social status and offered a proper marriage settlement (*mahr*). Only in two situations could a guardian marry a woman without her consent: if she was a minor and if she was marrying for the first time. In the first case, minors (both girls and boys) could legally marry since Islamic law did not provide for a minimum legal marrying age, but given that they were, as minors, not legally capable, the marriage must be arranged by their guardians. Such a marriage, however, could entail no cohabitation until the bride reached puberty. In the second case—that of a woman marrying for the first time (she is thus a virgin, *bikr*)—her matrimonial guardian must be her father (or, for some schools, her grandfather). The jurists' assumption was that a father could be trusted to give his daughter to the best spouse. The Hanafis were the only school to allow women to conclude their marriages by themselves, arguing that if a legally capable woman could lawfully enter into a contract of sale or hire, she should also be able to conclude a marriage contract. However, they gave the family some control: if the bride chose a groom whose social status was inferior to hers, male agnatic relatives could have the marriage rescinded in court.

The parties could negotiate various stipulations in the contract. The Hanbalis were known for permitting the parties to stipulate as many conditions as they could agree upon as long as the essentials of marriage were not waived. The marriage contract became a means by which women could enforce restrictions on their husbands, an example being his entering into a second marriage, although it was disputed whether polygyny was a right and hence could not be waived or a privilege and thus could be renounced. Or she could stipulate that her husband could not require her to move to another place or home. The other Sunni schools were less generous, permitting conditions that curtailed the husband's rights only if he agreed in the marriage contract to transfer his right to divorce to the wife, either conditionally or unconditionally.

Sunni jurists regarded consent to marriage to be consent to a permanent marriage, that is, the marriage was expected to last until divorce or death. The Shiʿis to the contrary permitted a marriage contract to set a time limit, allowing for what is called a *mutʿa* marriage (Haeri 1989). The parties could agree to as long or as short a duration as they wished. Regardless of what the parties might otherwise wish or contract, certain conditions were imposed, to wit, the marriage partners could not inherit from each other if either died during the duration of the contract; if any children were born, they would be deemed the father's children, who would be then responsible for their maintenance; and the children born from the union could inherit from either parent.

Quranic restrictions on the freedom to marry were upheld: for instance, relatives within certain degrees could not conclude a valid marriage. For most jurists, difference of religion was also a bar for marrying. Thus, although men were free to marry Jewish or Christian women, the prevailing opinion was that women could marry only Muslim men. Another prohibition limited the woman to one husband while the man could marry up to four wives simultaneously. Finally, there was a temporary impediment placed on the woman: upon the termination of her marriage, she had to wait before remarrying to determine whether she was pregnant. If the marriage was dissolved by divorce, she had to wait three menstrual periods (or three months after menopause, or, if pregnant, until delivery). If she was widowed, she had to wait four months and ten days (until delivery if pregnant), viz., the ordinary waiting period of three menstrual cycles to which was added a 40-day period of mourning.

The legal effects of the marriage contract differed for the spouses. The husband was obliged to pay his wife a marriage settlement (*mahr*, *ṣadāq*)[8] at the time of the conclusion of the marriage and to maintain her during the marriage; the wife was obligated to be sexually available to the husband, to obey him, and to reside in his home. As a rule the amount and nature of the *mahr* was agreed upon with the marriage contract. However, if the parties failed to do so, the wife was entitled to a proper *mahr* (*mahr al-mithl*), that is, one that a woman of her status and age normally would receive. The payment of the *mahr* was deemed to be an essential part of the contract;[9] if the contract stipulated that it not be paid, the jurists held that either the clause or the marriage itself was null and void. Over time, the husband was allowed to pay a portion of the marriage settlement (*muʿajjal*, prompt *mahr*) before concluding the marriage and complete the payment upon termination of the marriage (*muʾajjal*, deferred *mahr*). This placed an extra burden on the divorced wife who often had to sue for her remaining *mahr* portion; however, owing the remaining portion was often a financial disincentive for the husband to repudiate his wife. If she was widowed, the portion was owed to her out of the husband's estate.

A husband's maintenance consisted of providing the wife with food, clothing, and housing (including furniture and kitchen utensils), and, under certain circumstances, a domestic servant. Medical costs were excluded on the basis of the rather awkward analogical argument that the person who rents a house is not liable for repairs necessary for the upkeep of the house. The wife could demand that she be housed alone or at some distance from her co-wives, and not be forced to share accommodation with her husband's relatives. Over time, the husband's maintenance was coupled with the notion of the wife's obedience to the husband (Meron 1971). If a wife left her husband without good reason, returning to live with her parents, she forfeited her right to maintenance. Even a woman's leaving the house, intermingling with the public, or earning her living came to be subject to the consent of her husband. This last right—a relatively clear Quranic prescription allowing the woman to keep her own earnings (Q 4:32)[10]—became so circumscribed by the rules of obedience that it became useless. The jurists' conferring on the husband control over a woman's access to alternatives to his maintenance, such as earnings from her own labor, cut off her access to economic security that would have allowed her to be financially able to challenge her husband. One area apart from maintenance where a wife could demand payment from her husband was breastfeeding. The husband owed the wife payment either for her work in this regard or for a woman whom she could hire as a substitute.

Marriage did not change the status of ownership. Each spouse retained control over his or her own properties brought into or acquired during the marriage. If the marital home belonged to the wife, she could choose to charge her husband rent for living there (Hanna 1996: 147–8).

Sexual intercourse was only lawful between spouses or between an owner and his female slave. Sexual intercourse could be demanded from the wife at any time (except in the daytime during Ramadan); her refusing it without a valid excuse, such as impairment of her health or prevention of her performance of religious obligations, was regarded as a sin on the wife's part. Some jurists classified it as disobedience, which would forfeit her right to maintenance. Wives did not have the right to demand sex from their husbands, but the latter had a moral obligation to comply. Sexual intercourse was not only lawful for procreation, but valued also for the pleasure derived from it. Birth control was allowed through coitus interruptus (*ʿazl*), but, according to the majority of jurists, the man had to ask his wife for permission (Ali 2006: 6–13).

8 The marriage settlement could be either of substantive value, such as money, land, a house, etc., or of symbolic value, such as a sweet cake or a Quran. I choose to use the Arabic term *mahr* henceforward, rather than the usual translation of "bride price" or "dower," to avoid an otherwise slightly incorrect rendering in English.

9 Q 2:229, 236.

10 Cf. n. 1, above.

Divorce

Since marriage is a contract, its termination—divorce—was never a problem in Islamic law. Both husband and wife were given rights to divorce, though on different terms, reflecting the way many jurists conceived marriage. Some likened the husband's paying of the *mahr* to the right of ownership—like the owner, the husband could unilaterally renounce his right (Ali 2010: 136–7). Women could dissolve the marriage by an agreement with her husband or through a judicial divorce by proving certain grounds. The Quran (4:35) enjoins arbitration or mediation before a divorce; if the spouses could not agree and were incompatible such that resolution was fruitless, they were to call upon relatives from both sides to mediate or arbitrate between them.

A single repudiation by the husband was followed by a waiting period (*'idda*) of three menstrual periods by the wife—or until delivery if she was pregnant—during which time she could not marry and the husband could take her back unilaterally. Once the waiting period was completed, the marriage was dissolved. If the husband took her back during the waiting period or they remarried later, he could repudiate her again, but no more than twice. The third repudiation between the same man and woman created an impediment for marriage between them that could only be removed by an intermediary-dissolved marriage of the woman to another man. This procedure is elaborately laid down in Quran and Sunna, but over time the jurists accepted that the triple repudiation could also be brought about during one session, by the husband repeating the repudiation three times or by coupling it to the number three (for example, saying "you are repudiated thrice").

Repudiation entailed financial obligations for the husband. If he had paid only a portion of the agreed upon *mahr* at the time of marriage, which was the custom in most regions, he had to fulfill the outstanding debt. After pronouncing the repudiation, he had to maintain his wife until the expiry of the waiting period. The Quran instructs men to pay a gift to the wives they had divorced (Q 2:241); most jurists, however, understood this as a moral prescription and not an enforceable obligation.

Divorce for the wife was a less simple and more negotiated process, subject to many more uncertainties for her. Her options were either to persuade her husband to agree to a *khul'* divorce by offering a financial consideration, such as waiving the deferred part of the *mahr* or returning the portion she had received, or to go to court and demand a divorce on certain specified grounds. In that case she had to produce evidence to support her case. The Malikis, who restricted the right of the bride to choose a husband on her own initiative, provided the most grounds on which a woman could petition for divorce—desertion, cruelty, lack of maintenance, insanity, impotency—while the Hanafis, who gave women the most freedom to choose their partners, provided the most restrictive: the only ground was that the marriage was never consummated due to his impotency. If he became impotent after consummation, she could not get a divorce from the court. Apostasy on the part of one of the spouses (see Chapter 9, above) was grounds for annulment and dissolution of the marriage in all schools.

Thus, while the right to divorce was extended equally to both genders, the exercise of this right differed procedurally for men and women. Beyond the divorce, Islamic jurists did not extend the tie between former spouses; upon dissolution of the marriage, neither spouse had a claim upon the other. Once lawful sexual relations ceased, all other ties, including financial ones, were also ended.

Unlawful Sexual Intercourse

As discussed in Chapter 12, below, extra-marital sexual intercourse (*zinā*) is a punishable offence subject to capital punishment (if the parties are married) or lashing (if the parties are single). All but the Maliki school of jurisprudence consider circumstantial evidence of extra-marital relations unacceptable; the act is only proven by the testimonies of four Muslim eyewitnesses of good reputation or by four voluntarily given confessions of the accused. The Maliki school, however, regarded pregnancy of an unwed woman as proof of unlawful sexual intercourse. The Malikis introduced some safeguards, for instance, the woman could protect herself by alleging rape, but had to provide evidence. Another protection offered to the woman was what was called the dormant fetus. The Malikis opined that an embryo could survive in the womb up to seven years before delivery. If the woman became pregnant within seven years of being divorced or widowed, the child would be considered the child of the marriage bed and the mother would be exonerated from the presumption of *zinā*.

Custody of Children

Children born between six months after the beginning of marital cohabitation and the end of the wife's waiting period were recognized as the offspring of both husband and wife and were regarded as the husband's children. The relation between parents and children was created by birth (for the mother) and birth and marriage (for the father). As for children of a female slave, by acknowledging paternity the slave's owner could become the legal father. The legal father was the child's guardian and obliged to support him (for more on the slave's status, see Chapter 9, above). Adoption, which was prevalent before the appearance of Islam, was prohibited by Q 33:5, and is not a legal option in Islamic law. A child born out of wedlock belonged to the mother, who alone bore all the consequences of having a child and could not claim any maintenance payments from the father. She and her family were responsible for sustaining the child, and the child could inherit only from the mother and her family.

The basic principle of custody in Islamic law was the interest of the child. Since the children of the marriage bed constituted the only tie between ex-spouses, there being no financial ties, and ex-spouses could make trouble for each other when it came to jointly taking care of the children, the decision as to which parent would gain custody (*ḥaḍāna*) was reached by using legal presumptions. Taken into account was the fact that the full responsibility to maintain the children had been the father's during the marriage. It was presumed therefore that it was in the best interest of the child to live with the father rather than the mother; but it was also presumed that as long as the mother had not remarried, she would provide better care up to a certain age. As for that age, the Sunni jurists set the bar high. The mother was presumed to be the better guardian of a daughter up to the age of nine (or 11 or puberty, when she could marry), and a son until he reached the age of seven, the age of reason. The Shiʿi jurists set the bar lower, presuming it to be in the better interests of a son to stay with the mother until two years of age (the start of the weaning period) and a daughter until the age of seven, the age of reason.

Inheritance

The system of intestate inheritance, introduced by the Quran and elaborated by the jurists, improved the legal position of women, although it did not give them the same rights as men.[11] The rules of succession in pre-Islamic tribal Arabia are not known in detail, but as there were some pre-Islamic religious rules denying daughters with no male siblings the right to inheritance,[12] it can be assumed that women could not own property or inherit, or at least very restrictedly, from their relatives. One's heirs were essentially close male agnatic relatives, such as sons, father, germane and consanguine brothers, paternal uncles, etc. This system was amended by the Quranic prescriptions of inheritance (Q 4:11, 12, 176), which assigned portions in the deceased's estate (consisting of all types of properties) to women, some close relatives, and spouses, who were excluded in the pre-Islamic systems. Thus daughters, sisters, mothers, and spouses were heirs, with shares whose size depended on the presence

11 For overviews of Islamic inheritance, see Coulson 1971; Powers 1986; Zaid 1986.
12 See Num 27:1–8.

of other heirs. If the total of the Quranic shares was less than 100 percent, the remainder would be assigned to the closest agnatic relatives. Daughters and sisters, who inherited with their brothers, were regarded as agnatic heirs.

The Quranic succession system has a female inheriting half of the share of a male in the same degree, for example, sons and daughters, brothers and sisters (Q 4:11). The exception applies to parents of the deceased, who inherit equal shares. Widows (even when multiple) inherit one-eighth of the husband's estate if there are children; he is assigned one-fourth of hers, in case she leaves issue. These shares are doubled if there are no offspring (Q 4:12). There was limited intestate division allowed—no more than one-third of the value of an estate could be bequeathed, unless the heirs agreed, and the beneficiary could not be one of the heirs lest the divine division be disrupted.

Since a daughter is assigned half of the share of a son, in the case of one daughter and one son inheriting, the daughter receives one-third and the son two-thirds. If the heirs were only daughters, the Sunni and Shiʿi jurists differed. The Shiʿis assigned the entire estate to the daughters. This reflected the Shiʿi doctrine according to which Fāṭima, the sole surviving daughter of the Prophet, was regarded as having the right to transmit the entire Prophet's legacy, financial as well as political, to her sons al-Ḥasan and al-Ḥusayn. The Sunni doctrine adhered to the wording of Q 4:11, laying down that one daughter without brothers is given one-half of the estate and two or more would receive together two-thirds, leaving the remainder to the closest agnatic heirs. In the absence of the deceased's children and brothers, sisters likewise received similar shares (Q 4:176).

The gender differential in Islamic inheritance law posed a dilemma for parents who wanted to equalize the shares of their children. The most obvious instrument for that purpose was a gift, which had to be given during the lifetime of the parent. Other legal devices evolved to exempt the distribution of an estate from the Islamic inheritance rules, such as making the property a religious trust (*waqf*), which must also have been created during the lifetime of the parent but could never be alienated; the distribution of its proceeds could then be shared equally among both genders. There were no gender restrictions for the administrator of the trust.

Litigation and Witnessing

As mentioned above, women and men enjoyed the same legal status in the law of property and contracts. Women could, and often would, practice a trade and run a business. They acted as court-appointed guardians for their minor children and as administrators of *waqf*s. As a consequence they would also engage in litigation. Since there was a general feeling that women—especially those in the upper class—should not be seen too often in public, many women, but by no means all, used male agents as their representatives in commercial and legal affairs.

Women could take cases to the courts and be party to lawsuits. They were at a disadvantage in one aspect of the procedure, however, that of witnessing. Women could act as a witness in court, but their testimony was deemed to have less probative force than that of men. In trials wherein capital punishment or corporal punishments (*ḥudūd*) were at stake, the testimony of women was not accepted. In most types of litigation, however, a woman's testimony was valued at one-half that of a man; hence two female witnesses equaled one man. For full proof, four female witnesses were required or one man and two women. The jurists made exceptions in cases that involved only women, such as disputes surrounding childbirth.

Dress

The Quran instructs both men and women to dress modestly, as a sign of humility and lack of extravagance (Q 24:30, 31). Women are urged to avoid displaying their finery except for the benefit of their husbands in their private spaces. In elaborating more precise rules of decent dress the jurists developed the notion of *ʿawra*, that part of the human body that must not be seen in public. For men, the *ʿawra* was defined as the part of the body between the knees and the navel, for women, the whole body except her face and hands. When Islam spread to Persia and the Christian Byzantine territories, it was found that women of the upper class were veiling their faces while enslaved women did not. The cloak (Q 33:59) and the reluctance to display feminine ornaments were then transformed into covering the female body and face. One exception was made for women no longer of marriageable age, who were exempted from covering their faces.

Modernist Islamic Law

Since the early twentieth century Muslim states have enacted legislation in the fields of family law and the law of succession, generally to the benefit of women.[13] This began with the Ottoman Family Code of 1917 (which was abolished in the Republic of Turkey in 1926, but continued to be applied in Syria, Palestine, and Lebanon until the 1950s) and Egyptian legislation of 1920 on maintenance and divorce. Under the impact of English law, the states in the Indian subcontinent introduced substantial reform through case law, apart from legislation. Several motivations were the impetus for such reforms: (1) it was easier for the state to obtain information about the civil status of their subjects—and thus to control them—by creating legal rules; (2) greater legal security was ensured by removing ambiguities in the legal doctrine, thus facilitating the application of the Sharia by the courts, and by creating greater clarity about the civil status of persons (marriage, divorce, filiation) through obligatory registration; and (3) the rights of women would be strengthened or, generally, certain social problems would be remedied by introducing reforms of the substantive law, such as, for example, a minimum age for marriage, abolition of forced marriages, restriction of polygyny and of the husband's unilateral right of repudiation, and the introduction of more grounds for obtaining divorce by women.

In order to confer greater legitimacy on the reforms in the substantive law, the legislators took care to remain within the orbit of the Sharia, modern Turkey being the exception. This was achieved by way of the following means:

(1) Using procedural or penal law to realize a certain objective, without changing the substantive majoritarian Sharia view—for example, making child marriages punishable offences for the parents of the minor spouse or, if adult, for the spouse himself; forbidding marriage registrars to register marriages in the event one of the couple is a minor and at the same time introducing the rule that marriages can only be proven by marriage documents issued by an official registrar; allowing polygynous marriages to be registered only after the court is satisfied that the husband has a lawful reason for such a marriage and is financially able to support all wives.

(2) Selecting opinions from the various schools of jurisprudence, or from any one scholar within a school, that are most conducive to the objectives of the legislator, as used, for example, by countries that applied Hanafi law when they introduced Maliki grounds for divorce with the aim of extending the possibilities for women to end their marriages, and by countries that applied Maliki law when they introduced the Hanafi rule that legally capable women must give their consent to a marriage and cannot be forced into a marriage by their fathers or grandfathers.

And, finally, (3) using *ijtihād* to reinterpret the relevant texts of the Quran and Sunna. This was the case, for example, when the Tunisian government abolished polygyny in 1956. The legislators argued that Q 4:3 in combination with 4:129 actually implied a ban on polygyny.[14] A fresh reading

13 For reform of family law in the Muslim world, see Anderson 1976; Jones-Pauly 1995; An-Naʿim 2002; Mir-Hosseini 1993; Nasir 2009; Pearl and Menski 1998; Welchman 2004, 2007.

14 Respectively (4:3) "If you fear that you will not be able to deal fairly by the orphans, marry women of your choice, two or three or four; but if you fear that you cannot do justice [to so many] then [marry] one

of the verses offers the understanding that instead of being just a moral admonition, polygyny is only permitted under strict conditions. The additional wives must be orphans who are not being treated fairly. If a man decides to marry one of the orphans, he must be certain that he can treat his existing and new wives justly. But, as the Quran asserts in 4:129, that is not possible. This implies a prohibition of polygyny and this argument was raised and accepted in Tunisia for its abolition.

Most Muslim countries today have codified their family law and the law of succession, or at least have introduced legislation on points where reform was deemed necessary (see Chapter 16, below). Saudi Arabia and Northern Nigeria are among the very few countries or regions where uncodified Sharia law is applied. The main reforms found in most codes are: the mandatory registration of marriages and divorces; the introduction of a minimum age for marriage; measures to restrict polygyny; the introduction of legal possibilities for brides to add clauses to the marriage contract that strengthen their legal position vis-à-vis their husband; the banning of forced marriages and the limiting of the powers of matrimonial guardians; and the increase of grounds for divorce for women. In some countries, far-reaching reforms have been introduced. In Egypt and Pakistan a woman may obtain a divorce without her husband's consent and without having to prove certain grounds. The only condition is that she is willing to pay a consideration (usually the waiver of the remaining part of the *mahr*). This is based on a reconsideration of the meaning of the Quranic verse on *khulʿ* divorce (Q 2:229). Another unique reform is the Tunisian prohibition of polygyny (see above).

The state reforms in the law of succession are fewer. The most prominent one is to create a share in the inheritance for orphaned grandchildren, who did not inherit under the classical Sharia interpretation. No reforms have been enacted to remedy the unequal treatment of women in the law of succession. The usual justification for her reduced portion compared to that of a male in the same relationship is the advantageous financial position that women have in marriage, as they are entitled to receive both the *mahr* and maintenance from the husband. For modern-day *ijtihād* that equalizes the portions between females and males, see Shaḥrūr 2000; Jones-Pauly 2011.

The reform of family law was partly the result of debates on the legal position of women and, more generally, on the modernization of Sharia opinion from premodern times. These debates began around the end of the nineteenth century; by the end of the twentieth century a full-fledged Muslim feminism had developed. One of the central modernist questions relevant to the understanding of the classical Sharia is whether the Quran embraces gender equality, a challenge to the majority of Sharia views informed by gender inequality and by the notion of complementary rights of wife and husband.[15] Some scholars interpret Q 4:1—which proclaims that God created man and woman from the same soul—to aver that the Quran's message is one of gender equality. They assert that verses that seem to have a different purport can and must be interpreted from a standpoint of equality. These assertions have a precedent in late-nineteenth-century Muslim reformists, such as Sayyid Aḥmad Khān in India and Muḥammad ʿAbduh in Egypt, who claimed that the message of Islam is rational and that verses that seem to be irrational must be reinterpreted. Some modernists argue that the original meanings of the Quran (rationality, gender equality) were replaced by obscure and patriarchal readings by the religious scholars.

The following verse in particular is the focus of the debate that the Quranic message is essentially gender equal and that the Sharia must be read accordingly:

> Q 4:34: Men are in charge of women, because God has made the one excel more than the other, and because they support them from their wealth. Therefore righteous

or [a slave] whom your right hands possess. That is more suitable, to prevent you from doing injustice" and (4:129) "You are never able to be fair and just as between women, even if it is your ardent desire: but turn not away [from a woman] altogether, so as to leave her [as it were] hanging. If you come to a friendly understanding, and practice self-restraint, God is ever-forgiving, most merciful."

15 On reformist readings of the Quran and the law, see Ali 2006; Barlas 2002; Jones-Pauly 2011; Larsen et al. 2013; Wadud 1999.

> women are obedient (*qānitāt*), and guard in [the husband's] absence what God would have them guard. As to those from whom you fear rebellion (*nushūz*), admonish them, banish them to their beds, and strike them (*iḍrabūhunna*); but if they return to obedience, seek not against them means [of annoyance]: For God is exalted, great.

Traditionally, this is regarded as the main textual proof to justify male dominance over women and to link it with the obligation for husbands to provide maintenance for their wives. According to the traditional reading, God has made men excel in strength, or even in perfection, over weak or deficient women. However, a gender equality reading understands the opening of this verse as obliging husbands to support their wives because God has allowed them to excel financially. This does not point to an ontological male strength justifying male dominance, but to a common situation in which men have more possessions than women and therefore are enjoined to support them. In the second sentence, the Arabic word *qānitāt* is usually understood as "obedient [to husbands]." However, this word is often used in the Quran as "obedient to God" or complying with His commands. So the sentence can be read differently and not only in the sense that good women are obedient to their husbands. In the third sentence, "rebellion" (*nushūz*) is generally read as disobedience, that is, that of the wife vis-à-vis her husband. However, *nushūz* is also used elsewhere in the Quran with regard to men, where it is understood as "ill treatment" (Q 4:128, "If a woman fears ill treatment from her husband ..."). Therefore, the term may be understood as marital disorder, regardless of its cause. Finally, the verse advises on how to solve conflicts between husband and wife: admonishment, separation at night, and striking, in that order. Most advocates of a gender equal message in the Quran argue that the last recourse (*iḍrabūhunna*) cannot mean "to strike, to beat." The verb *ḍaraba* has many different connotations—it is used in the Quran in 17 different ways, for one (Barlas 2007: 32)—or must be understood in the cultural context of seventh-century Arabia, where violence was controversial but more common, but is today unacceptable (for example, Barlas 2002: 184–9; Ali 2006: 117–26; Jones-Pauly 2011: 31–3).

Conclusions

When Islam was revealed it was confronted with the pluralistic legal systems of the different tribes, religions, and nationalities living in the Arabian peninsula. Islam offered a chance to unite and find ways by which the different groups could live compatibly. These differences included gender relations, some more liberal than others, some more restrictive. The pluralism was reflected in the variety of opinion among the hadith narrators and jurists, even within the same school of thought. A premium seems to have been placed on living together within a larger framework that allowed flexibility as Islam sought acceptance in different societies and as needs changed over time. The same dialectic continues during modern times but with different players. The state has become the mechanism for offering a unitary umbrella and the states form larger international bodies to reach a degree of consensus about commonalities all humans share, whether female or male, for example, in the area of human rights, as well as about the extent to which deviation can or cannot be tolerated. Islamic law is once again faced with how to deal with a new order of pluralism and unity and how to put its best efforts forward. For example, most Muslim countries have ratified the United Nations Convention for the Elimination of Discrimination against Women, but some have reserved on certain aspects such as equal rights of men and women to divorce (though international law requires that reserving countries show on a regular basis what they are doing to meet the spirit of the treaty).

Islamic law can draw on its long history to adapt and to take into account social necessities in various societies. At the same time it has a history of alternating forces that on the one hand encourage freedom of debate and on the other try to impose a monolithic point of view by use of force. To do justice to that part of its history of openness, Islamic law needs to find means to preserve a healthy non-polarized scientific-based debate. In the modern age the debate ought to be accompanied by clear explanations about the social policy, necessity, or personal preferences that will be furthered by a particular interpretation. To encourage this, more research is needed into, for example, how the abolition of slavery in Islamic law as the first step toward equality among human beings influenced notions of gender equality and discrimination in other areas of the law. Also needed is a re-examination of pre-Islamic history in the Arabian peninsula and other lands colonized by Muslims as to the extent of tribal differences regarding women's emancipation (Purohit 1995). Clues can be found in current customary law, for example of the Arab Bedouin and of the mountainous regions of Pakistan and Afghanistan (Stewart 1988; Mehdi 1994; Jones-Pauly 2005). This would help in a better understanding of how Islamic law expanded some preexisting freedoms and gender equality while also perpetuating some preexisting restrictions.

References

Ahmed, Leila. 1992. *Women and Gender in Islam: Historical Roots of a Modern Debate*. New Haven: Yale University Press.

Ali, Kecia. 2006. *Sexual Ethics and Islam: Feminist Reflections on Qur'an, Hadith, and Jurisprudence*. Oxford: Oneworld.

———. 2010. *Marriage and Slavery in Early Islam*. Cambridge, MA: Harvard University Press.

An-Na'im, Abdullahi A., ed. 2002. *Islamic Family Law in a Changing World: A Global Resource Book*. London: Zed Books.

Anderson, J.N.D. 1976. *Law Reform in the Muslim World*. London: Athlone.

Barlas, Asma. 2002. "Believing Woman." In *Islam: Unreading Patriarchal Interpretations of the Qur'ān*. Austin: University of Texas Press.

———. 2007. "Still Quarrelling over the Quran: Five Interventions." *ISIM Review* 20: 32–3; available at https://openaccess.leidenuniv.nl/bitstream/handle/1887/17203/ISIM_20_Still_Quarrelling_over_the_Quran_Five_Interventions.pdf?sequence=1.

Coulson, Noel J. 1964. *A History of Islamic Law*. Edinburgh: Edinburgh University Press.

———. 1971. *Succession in the Muslim Family*. Cambridge: Cambridge University Press.

Denning, Alfred Thompson, Lord. 1959. *From Precedent to Precedent*. Oxford: Oxford University Press.

Haeri, Shahla. 1989. *Law of Desire: Temporary Marriage in Shi'i Iran*. Syracuse: Syracuse University Press.

Hanna, Nelly. 1996. Marriage among Merchant Families in Seventeenth-Century Cairo. In *Women, the Family, and Divorce Laws in Islamic History*, ed. A. Sonbol, pp. 143–54. Syracuse: Syracuse University Press.

Hamzeh, Nizar A. 1994. Qatar: The Duality of the Legal System. *Middle Eastern Studies* 30(1): 79–90.

Jones-Pauly, Christina. 1995. Reforms in the Islamic Legal Judicial System and the Sharia Inheritance and Family Law in Tunisia. *Yearbook of African Law* 7: 3–23.

———. 2005. Between Society and State: Legal Steps toward National Reconciliation and Reconstruction in Afghanistan. *American Journal of Comparative and International Law* 52: 825–56.

———. 2011. *Women Under Islam: Gender, Justice and the Politics of Islamic Law*. London: I.B. Tauris.

Larsen, Lena et al., eds. 2013. *Gender and Equality in Muslim Family Law: Justice and Ethics in the Islamic Legal Process*. London: I.B. Tauris.

Linant de Bellefonds, Yvon. 1965. *Traité de droit musulman comparé*. Vol. 2. The Hague: Mouton.

Mehdi, Rubya. 1994. *The Islamization of the Law in Pakistan*. Richmond: Curzon Press.
Meron, Ya'akov. 1971. *L'obligation alimentaire entre époux en droit musulman hanéfite*. Paris: Librairie générale de droit et de jurisprudence.
Mernissi, Fatima. 1990. *Sultanes oubliées: Femmes chefs d'état en Islam*. Paris: Albin Michel; Eng. trans. *The Forgotten Queens of Islam*, tr. M.J. Lakeland. Minneapolis: University of Minnesota Press, 1993.
Mir-Hosseini, Ziba. 1993. *Marriage on Trial: A Study of Islamic Family Law. Iran and Morocco Compared*. London: I.B. Tauris.
Nasir, Jamal J. 2009. *The Status of Women under Islamic Law and Modern Islamic Legislation*. 3rd ed. Leiden: Brill.
Pearl, David, and Werner Menski. 1998. *Muslim Family Law*. 3rd ed. London: Sweet & Maxwell.
Peirce, Leslie P. 2003. *Morality Tales: Law and Gender in the Ottoman Court of Aintab*. Berkeley and Los Angeles: University of California Press.
Powers, David S. 1996. *Studies in Qur'an and Ḥadīth: The Formation of the Islamic Law of Inheritance*. Berkeley and Los Angeles: University of California Press.
Purohit, Nishi. 1995. *The Principles of Mohammedan Law*. Pune, India: C.T.J. Publications.
Rapoport, Yossef. 2005. *Marriage, Money and Divorce in Medieval Islamic Society*. New York: Cambridge University Press.
Shaḥrūr, Muḥammad. 2000. *Naḥwat uṣūl jadīda li-l-fiqh al-islāmī: Fiqh al-mar'a, al-waṣiya, al-irth, al-qiwāma, al-ta'addudiyya, al-libās*. Damascus: al-Ahālī li-l-Ṭibā'a wa-l-Nashr wa-l-Tawzī'.
Spectorsky, Susan A. 2010. *Women in Classical Islamic Law: A Survey of the Sources*. Leiden: Brill.
Spellberg, Denise A. 1994. *Politics, Gender, and the Islamic Past: The Legacy of 'A'isha bint Abi Bakr*. New York: Columbia University Press.
Stewart, Frank Henderson. 1988. *Texts in Sinai Bedouin Law*. Wiesbaden: Harrassowitz.
Tucker, Judith E. 1998. *In the House of the Law: Gender and Islamic Law in Ottoman Syria and Palestine*. Berkeley and Los Angeles: University of California Press.
———. 2008. *Women, Family and Gender in Islamic Law*. New York: Cambridge University Press.
Wadud, Amina. 1999. *Qur'an and Woman: Rereading the Sacred Text from a Woman's Perspective*. New York: Oxford University Press.
Welchman, Lynn, ed. 2004. *Women's Rights and Islamic Family Law: Perspectives on Reform*. London: Zed Books.
———. 2007. *Women and Muslim Family Laws in Arab States: A Comparative Overview of Textual Development and Advocacy*. Amsterdam: Amsterdam University Press.
Zaid, Abdulaziz M. 1986. *The Islamic Law of Bequest*. London: Scorpion.

Socio-Economic Justice

Hiroyuki Yanagihashi

At issue in a chapter on socio-economic justice are the basic legal rules of trade—property, its protection, and contracts—and the fiscal rules underlying a welfare system. In the below I will present general rules in Islamic law concerning ownership, contract, civil liability, and *zakāt*, the tax to be spent, among other purposes, for the poor.

In the discussion of ownership and contracts, I will examine whether the two pillars of Western private law—sacrosanctity of ownership and freedom of contract—exist also in Islamic law, first by investigating the extent to which owners of an object are exclusively and without restrictions entitled to use and enjoy their property and can alienate their goods by virtue of mutual agreement without interference from a third party; and second, by asking whether persons, within the limits of the law, are free to conclude enforceable agreements.

I will then discuss in the context of Islamic law a third principle recognized in most legal systems in order to guarantee the functioning of the economy—the liability for damage caused by a person's activities. Finally, the issue of how a moral society such as the Islamic one deals with the collective responsibility toward the poor and needy will be taken up, leading to a discussion of the alms tax, *zakāt*.

Rules Governing Ownership

The Shafiʿi jurist Ibn al-Subkī (d. 756/1355) defines ownership (*milk*) as "a legal effect ordained with regard to the substance or the usufruct of an object (*ʿayn*) that authorizes in itself the person to whom it belongs to use it and to be paid in consideration of it." In other words, ownership of an object confers to the owner the right to use the object and to alienate it, for example, by selling or donating it. In his comment on this definition, the later Shafiʿi polymath al-Suyūṭī (d. 911/1505) states that the term "in itself" implies that the owner of a thing can only be prevented from disposing of it due to "an accidental obstacle" or "an external cause"—for example, when he is put under interdiction (al-Suyūṭī 1403/1983: 316). The earlier Shafiʿi and Hanafi views, later abandoned as we shall see, authorize the owner of a thing to use and dispose of it in an absolute manner. Abū Ḥanīfa is said to have stated that exercise of property is subject to no restraint even if one of the owner's neighbors suffers damage from it. According to the Hanafi jurist al-Kāsānī (d. 587/1189):

Hiroyuki Yanagihashi is Professor in the Graduate School of Humanities and Sociology, University of Tokyo. He is the author of *A History of the Early Islamic Law of Property: Reconstructing the Legal Development, 7th–9th Centuries* (2004) and editor of *The Concept of Territory in Islamic Law and Thought* (2000). He has published widely in Japanese, English, and French, inter alia in *Islamic Law and Society*.

> The legal effect of property is to authorize the owner to treat his thing at will. No one has the right to enforce him to do something [against his will] except in case of necessity, nor has anyone the right to prevent him from doing something [in his thing] even if the former suffers a loss from the latter's act, unless the right of another person is attached to that object (1402/1982, 6: 263–4).

Not all objects can be legally owned. There are, for instance, objects from which one cannot benefit, either in fact, such as an insect or blood in a living body, or legally, such as wine, pigs,[1] and musical instruments, charitable trusts (*awqāf*), and free persons. Property is classified into immovables (*ʿaqār*), that is, land, trees, and buildings, and movables (*manqūl*). Objects that are not immovables are movables.

Ownership of land is subclassified in various ways. There is land owned privately (*milk*), and land owned by the state (*khāṣṣ*, *mīrī*), the usufruct of which can be granted by the state to farmers. In later periods this usufruct could be alienated by the users with the permission of the state. A third category is endowed land (as a *waqf*) which is therefore not alienable. Finally, land that is devoid of any private or public right is termed dead (*mawāt*) but it can be transformed into privately owned land by reclamation.

Privately owned land is divided into two types depending on how it is taxed. The distinction is explained by historical circumstances during the period of the Islamic conquests. Land in Arabia that was already owned by Muslims and non-Muslim lands that were taken by Muslims forcibly (*ʿanwatan*) as booty were subject to the *ʿushr* tax, whereas the lands on which non-Muslims were allowed by treaty to stay as owners were subject to a higher tax called *kharāj*. The encumbrance of the *kharāj* tax adhered to the land itself and the owner's conversion to Islam or the acquisition of the land by a Muslim did not change the fiscal obligation. From the point of view of private law *milk* and *kharāj* lands are identical. But with respect to movable objects such a distinction is not made and they are always *milk*.

A privately owned object may be removed from legal traffic if its owner has made it into a *waqf*, an endowment or trust, usually consisting of land and buildings. *Waqf* property is inalienable, that is, it cannot be sold, donated, or inherited, and its proceeds must be distributed to its beneficiaries as stipulated by the founder upon its establishment. The functions of a *waqf* are diverse; it can be established for charitable purposes, to provide alms for the poor, as a soup kitchen, mosque, hostel, and school, or for more mundane, financial ones: it can be used to prevent the fragmentation of one's estate through inheritance or to favor some heirs—such as one's children—over others. The management of the *waqf* and the distribution of the proceeds are the duty of the administrator, who is appointed by the founder or in accordance with the stipulations of the *waqf*'s establishment. The classical jurists debated who was to be regarded as the owner of the *waqf*, with some asserting that *waqf* land belonged to God and others that it belonged to the beneficiaries or the founder.

The Islamic and Western legal systems have a very similar approach to ownership. In the latter it is an absolute right—the French Declaration of the Rights of Man and the Citizen (1789) calls ownership an inviolable and sacrosanct right. Fiqh also formulates the power of owners as absolute and lays down that they may use their owned objects as they wish. The extent of an owner's freedom is illustrated by the Hanafi rules concerning hoarding. If a person hoards foodstuffs or fodder and the inhabitants of the city or region have complained about it three times to the caliph, the latter may castigate and imprison the hoarder. However, the caliph is only entitled to confiscate the goods in the event the inhabitants are starving (in which case theft is also lawful). He may then distribute them, but he must return them in the same quantity and quality once they are again available on the market (al-Kāsānī 1402/1982, 5: 129).

1 Items such as wine and pork can be owned by a non-Muslim; their ownership is protected inasmuch as a person who destroys property belonging to a non-Muslim must compensate him for its value.

However, both Western and Islamic legal systems gradually abandoned the view that ownership entitled unrestricted use and began to recognize that the use of the owner's rights may be prevented if it causes damage to others. The later Hanafis required that the damage be excessive (*ḍarar fāḥish*). As per Article 1197 of the Mecelle, the Ottoman civil code, summarizing the later Hanafi doctrine: "No person may be prevented to use his property unless this causes excessive damage, in which case it may be prevented." Excessive damage applies, for instance, when the owner uses his property in such a way as to weaken or destroy another building or make it impossible for the building to be used for the purpose for which it is meant, such as living in it (Mecelle Article 1199; Qadrī 1909, Article 59). Other schools use broader definitions of damage, including stench and noise caused by industrial activities or inserting a window into a wall and thereby making available a view of a neighboring private garden or rooftop where women can be seen. In such cases the neighbor has the right to prevent this use (Kahera and Benmira 1998). This is justified by the hadith "there should be no harm and no reciprocated harm (*lā ḍarar wa-lā ḍirār*)."[2] Moreover, the use of the owner's land or building may be restricted by the rights of neighbors attached to this property and serving the use of the neighboring property (*ḥaqq al-irtifāq*). The most common rights are the right to access to publicly owned water (*ḥaqq al-shirb*), the right of way for persons, cattle, and carts (*ḥaqq al-murūr*), and the right of drainage (*ḥaqq al-majrā, ḥaqq al-masīl*) to discharge unused or dirty water over neighboring land (Mecelle, Articles 1224–33; Qadrī 1909, Articles 37–56). A final restriction of an owner's rights is the institution of *shufʿa* (preemption) which gives certain persons the right to supplant the buyer of land for the same price, even against the will of the seller. This right belongs to the co-owner of real estate, and, according to the Hanafis, also to the owner of adjacent property. Thus, if a person wants to sell his land or a share in commonly owned land, the neighbor (according to the Hanafis) or the co-owner is entitled to acquire the land or the remaining share in the land for the same price and to oust the original buyer.

Rules Governing Contracts

In his *Mukhtaṣar* the Shafiʿi jurist al-Muzanī (d. 264/878) quotes al-Shāfiʿī as having said:

> God said: O ye who believe! Eat not up your property among yourselves in vanities: But let there be amongst you traffic and trade by mutual good will [Q 4:29]. And as the Messenger of God (God's blessing and peace be upon him) prohibited some sales upon which the contracting parties agreed, we can conclude that God has legalized sales except those that He prohibited through His Messenger or that are assimilated to them. If the contracting parties conclude a permitted sale and parted after they reached agreement, neither of them can cancel it unless there is a defect in the object or an option was stipulated (1393/1973, 8: 75).

Can we infer from this statement that Islamic law sanctions contractual liberty, that is to say, that contracting parties are free to determine the terms and conditions of a contract by mutual agreement insofar as it does not violate the law? This question will be addressed at the end of this section, preceded by an explanation of the rules concerning the formation and validity of contracts (*ʿuqūd*, sg. *ʿaqd*), primarily according to the Hanafi doctrine.

A contract is the joining of two corresponding phrases, that is, legal acts (*taṣarrufāt qawliyya*) containing a formal offer and acceptance (*ījāb wa-qabūl*), uttered during the same session (*majlis*). In legal treatises the principles common to various contracts are usually treated in the chapter on sales (*buyūʿ*).

2 There are several interpretations of this hadith.

Therefore they apply best to the onerous contracts such as sales and lease, but also partially to voluntary acts such as donation. In the following I will discuss the formation and validity of contracts, the issue as to whether or not the Islamic law of contracts recognizes contractual liberty, and the rules of default.

In order to understand the Sharia rules of contract, a useful approach is to examine defects in its conclusion. The majority of Hanafis classify sales into four categories according to their legal effects.

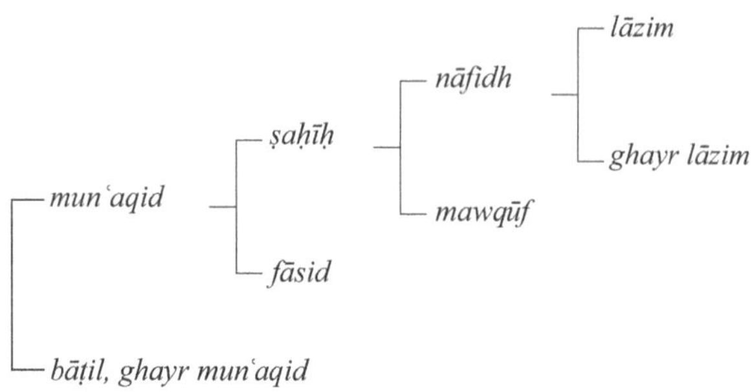

Figure 11.1 The four categories of sales in Hanafi law

Invalid

A contract is invalid (*bāṭil*) or not concluded (*ghayr mun'aqid*) when an essential element (*rukn*) of the contract is lacking, meaning that there is no contract. In general, this implies the absence of an agreement, occurring, for instance, in cases when one of the parties is not competent or when no agreement has been reached on the object of the contract. The former is the case if one of the contracting parties is a minor who does not have the faculty of discernment (*tamyīz*) or is insane (see Chapter 9, above) or if the acceptance was not made in the same contractual session (*majlis al-'aqd*) as the offer. Lack of agreement on the object of the contract is the case if the object cannot be legally owned, if there is risk (*gharar*) for either of the parties since their performances are not well defined, or in the case of an error (*ghalaṭ*) due to the fact that the object of the contract differs from what has been agreed upon.

Risk exists if either or both of the contracting parties are uncertain whether their obligations can be met. For example, the sale of an embryo, which may or may not be in an animal, is invalid due to risk, since it is uncertain that the seller can deliver the embryo, if any, on the date on which it will be born. The same rule applies to the sale of the harvest of a particular field or a tree. A case of an error invalidating a contract applies if someone said, for instance, "I will sell this sapphire to you for so many dirhams," and the buyer accepted the offer, whereas the object was actually glass; the sale is invalid because the object of the sale, that is, the sapphire, did not exist. In other words, the sale is invalid because the seller made a mistake as to the identity of the object and there was thus no agreement on the object. An error concerning the value of the object does not nullify the contract, but it can be invoked to rescind the contract as will be mentioned below.

Defective

Most schools of law do not distinguish between *bāṭil* "invalid" and *fāsid* "defective." The Hanafis do, however, and according to them a contract is defective if it violates the law on a minor point. Ibn Nujaym (d. 970/1563) asserts that a sale is defective "if it is lawful in its essence (*aṣl*), but unlawful in its quality (*waṣf*)" (1400/1980: 337). A defective contract is different from an invalid contract in its effects in some respects, but the most remarkable difference is that once it has been executed and it is no longer possible to restore the original state, a defective contract—unlike the contract that is invalid—creates to some extent the legal effect that the contracting parties intended to produce. For example, if a buyer resold an object that he had taken possession of based on a defective sale, ownership of the object is considered to have been transferred to the buyer by virtue of the defective sale at the moment of delivery and subsequently ownership is transferred to the second buyer. But since the contract was invalid—which also invalidates agreement on the price—the first buyer is not required to pay the agreed price; however, in order to prevent unjustified enrichment, the value of the object is calculated as of the date on which he took possession of the object (*qīma, thaman al-mithl*).

The most prominent ground for a contract to be defective has to do with the prohibition of *ribā* (lit. excess; "interest"), stemming from a Prophetic hadith. In one version of the report the Prophet said:

> If gold is paid for gold, silver for silver, wheat for wheat, barley for barley, dates for dates, salt for salt, payment should be made like for like (*sawā' bi-sawā'*), equal for equal (*mithl bi-mithl*), and hand to hand; if these species differ, [you may] sell them as you please if payment is made from hand to hand (Ibn Ḥajar al-ʿAsqalānī n.d.: no. 69).

On the force of this hadith, the jurists specified that the prohibited *ribā* applies only to transactions that exchange the same types of goods as mentioned in the hadith. An exchange between two different quantities of dates for gold would be unlawful unless delivered on the spot. The schools interpret the hadith differently as to the definition of *ribā* goods. The Hanafis classify *ribā* goods into two classes: goods defined by weight, represented by gold and silver, and goods defined by volume, represented by wheat, barley, dates, and salt. For example, in an exchange of gold for silver, both gold and silver should be delivered on the spot, otherwise the contract becomes defective. The Malikis on the other hand distinguish the two groups of goods as precious metals and foodstuffs.

On the basis of this hadith also, jurists distinguish two kinds of *ribā*: the *ribā* of excess (*ribā al-faḍl*)—the excess in measure (weight or volume)—and the *ribā* of delay (*ribā al-nasīʾa, ribā al-nasā*—when the goods are not exchanged at the same moment. As for the first, if *ribā* goods of the same species are exchanged but in different quantities or qualities, the exchange is defective; and as for the second, a delay of delivery in an exchange of *ribā* goods for *ribā* goods of a different species but belonging to the same class makes the exchange defective. But according to most schools of law, a contract stipulating *ribā* is valid, to the exclusion of the *ribā* of the contract. Thus, a contract for the loan of 100 dinars with the condition that the repayment after one year is 110 dinars would be valid to the repayment of only 100 dinars.

If a contract is not defective, that is, it is lawful in both its essence and its quality, to employ the expression of Ibn Nujaym, it is valid (*ṣaḥīḥ*). But this does not necessarily mean that the contract takes effect. It may be either effective or suspended. Let us consider the following two cases: (1) a minor able to understand what it means to sell or buy (cf. Article 943 of the Mecelle) sells his object; (2) a person sells a specified object belonging to another person. In both cases the sale contract is *ṣaḥīḥ* but it is not effective—the buyer does not have the right to demand that the seller deliver the object to him, unless the guardian in the first case or the owner in the second case ratifies the contract. Some jurists justify this solution on the ground that the seller does not have the authority (*wilāya*) to make the contract effective.

Suspended

Such a contract is suspended (*mawqūf*) until it is ratified or rescinded by a person who has the right to ratify it. If ratified, a suspended contract is considered to have been effective (*nāfidh*) from the date on which it was concluded; if rescinded, it is considered to have been invalid from the outset. A contract is suspended to protect either the right of the contracting party, as in the first case, or the right of a third party, as in the second case.

Not Binding

Many contracts are not binding (*ghayr lāzim*) by nature for one or both of the contracting parties. For example, either party to a partnership (*sharika*) or agency (*wakāla*) can unilaterally cancel the contract. According to all but the Malikis, both the donor and the donee can unilaterally cancel a donation before the donee takes possession of the object. Once the pledgee has taken possession of the pledge, the pledgee has the right to unilaterally cancel the pledge, but not the pledger.

Onerous contracts are binding unless an option is conferred upon one or both of the contracting parties by law or by agreement. Such an option confers on the party to whom it is given the right to cancel the contract. There are two options that can be stipulated with the main contract—the conditional option (*khiyār al-sharṭ*), by virtue of which either or both parties reserve the right to confirm or cancel the contract before a certain point of time, and that of designation (*khiyār al-ta ʿyīn*), which gives one party the right to choose between two obligations and determine which objects shall be delivered. There are many more legal options whose number has grown over the years. There are also differences of opinion among the schools of law on which options are acceptable. The chapter of sale in fiqh books mention inter alia the following five important ones:

(1) The option of defect (*khiyār al- ʿayb*), which allows the buyer to cancel the sale if he finds a defect in the purchased object (recognized by all the schools); (2) the option of contractual session (*khiyār al-majlis*), which allows either party in a sale to cancel the contract that has been made by the offer and the acceptance until the contractual session is concluded (recognized by the Shafiʿis and the Hanbalis); (3) the option of description (*khiyār al-waṣf*), also called the option of the lack of the desired description (*khiyār fawāt al-waṣf al-marghūb fīhi*) or the option of discrepancy (*khiyār al-khulf*), which allows the buyer to annul the sale if the object that was sold is missing a description stipulated in the contract. For example, someone who has bought a male slave on the condition that he can read and write may annul the sale if the slave proves to be illiterate (recognized by all the schools); (4) the option of inspection (*khiyār al-ru ʾya*), which can be exercised if the sold object was not present during the contractual session. In this case the buyer may annul the sale after inspecting the goods (recognized by the Hanafis); and (5) the option of grave lesion, or deception (*khiyār al-ghabn al-fāḥish*). This option is only recognized by later Hanafi jurists. It can be used by either party in the event the stipulated price of an object is much higher or much lower than current market prices.

Islamic law does not recognize the total freedom of contracts. In principle it only admits a limited number of contracts and prohibits clauses to be added to these contracts. The legal system was not entirely rigid, however, and in time certain contracts that were originally deemed illegal came to be legalized. This was the case with, for instance, the long-term lease of a *waqf* property, the cash *waqf* (allowed by the Hanafis and some Shafiʿis), the *khammāsa* (a kind of sharecropping contract in which the tenant typically retains one-fifth of the produce of the land) (allowed by the Malikis), and the recurring agency (*wakāla dawriyya*), an agency by virtue of which the agent is automatically commissioned every time the principal terminates his commission) (allowed by some Shafiʿis). Such contracts were ultimately accepted as lawful because they were deeply ingrained in custom and thus standard in practice.

The closed system of the law of contract was mitigated, at least by some schools of law, by the freedom to stipulate a clause altering the terms and conditions of the contract. The Hanbalis and Malikis were the most lenient in this respect, the Hanafis and Shafiʿis more strict. The Hanafi jurist al-Sarakhsī (d. ca. 490/1096-7) cites the Prophetic saying "Any clause not found in the Quran is invalid" to explain the Hanafi principle about the effect of a (modifying) clause (1993, 13: 13). However, a closer examination of the positive law reveals that in some instances the Hanafis take a more liberal position than either the Hanbali or Maliki school. For example, the Hanafis are divided over the validity of a redemption sale (*bayʿ al-wafāʾ*, *bayʿ bi-l-wafāʾ*), that is, a sale whereby the seller has the right to repurchase the object by paying the same price as he received. This is de facto a contract providing security to a loan. The borrower sells property to the lender with a clause in the contract entitling him to buy it back for the same price. The lender earns interest by exploiting the purchased goods—if land, for instance, by leasing it. Most Hanafis regard this contract as legal on the ground of customary practice, while the other schools of law reject it as it violates the prohibition regarding inclusion of clauses that modify the contract. Hanafis are also more lenient as regards the use of legal expedients (*ḥiyal*, sg. *ḥīla*), as in the combining of two or more contracts in order to get around a legal prohibition. For instance, a loan on interest, forbidden by the doctrine of *ribā*, could be circumvented by concluding two contracts of sale: in one, the debtor sells property to the creditor for price P; in the other, the creditor resells it immediately for price P+I, to be paid after a stipulated period. Moreover, the possibility of concluding certain contracts with added stipulations could also be enhanced by having the contracts notarized by judges affiliated with different schools of law, thus profiting from doctrinal diversity.

The rules regulating default of contract are elaborated in detail in the works of fiqh. In the following I will explain first the (Hanafi) rules regarding a default in repaying a financial obligation, and subsequently those with regard to the case of a person hired to perform something who did not fulfill his contractual obligation.

If the debtor does not repay a debt, the Quranic verse (2:280) "If someone is in difficulty, grant time till it is easy" applies. All schools but the Hanafi interpret this to mean that if the debtor is penniless (*mu'sir*) a creditor must wait until the debtor is able to easily repay the debt in full. The Hanafis allow the creditor to follow the debtor so that the debt can be paid off every time the debtor acquires assets.

If the value of the debtor's assets is equal to or greater than the debt, a creditor can bring the case before a qadi to collect the debt, either by confiscating money in the debtor's possession, by selling the debtor's property, or by imprisonment until the debtor satisfies the creditor, depending on the type of property owned. If the debt exceeds the value of the debtor's assets, a creditor has recourse to the measures mentioned above as well as another option—creditors whose claims are greater than the value of the debtor's assets can jointly bring the case before a qadi, who at their demand declares the debtor to be insolvent (*muflis*). Such a declaration (*taflīs* or *iflās*) puts the debtor under interdiction (*ḥajr*), whereupon he cannot gratuitously alienate his assets. His assets will then be sold and the earnings distributed among the creditors in proportion to the amount of their claims. The debtor at this stage is penniless and thus subject to the schools' interpretation of Q 2:280, as explained above; debts that are not repaid are not extinguished. The merit of *taflīs* seems to lie in the fact that creditors can prevent a debtor from reducing his assets, for the debtor could otherwise dispose of property that is not known to the creditors. From a procedural point of view the question arises as to how creditors can know the debtor's financial condition. There are differences of opinion among Hanafis, but one opinion holds that if the presumption exists that the debtor is hiding assets, the qadi should imprison the debtor until such time that the qadi is convinced that if the debtor had actually hidden assets he would have admitted it.

Regarding the second case, of someone who did not provide the stipulated service, the Hanafis rule that wages cannot be claimed—in the same way as a seller cannot request payment if the sold object perished while in his possession—but, according to some, the hirer can force the worker to provide the service. The Shafi'is and the Hanbalis are more willing to give relief to the hirer. Let us take the example of a *musāqāt*. This denotes a contract concluded between the owner of a plantation and a cultivator, by virtue of which the latter is contracted to take care of the plantation's trees for one season, at the end of which the harvested fruit is divided according to predetermined portions. If the cultivator refuses to work, the owner can sue in order that the qadi force the cultivator to work. If the cultivator is unable to work due to illness or another reason, the owner can charge the cultivator with the expenses incurred to employ someone else to perform the plantation work, either by taking the cultivator's money if he has sufficient means, or by repossessing the portion—or part of it—that was to be distributed to the cultivator once the fruit was harvested. If the fruit is not ready to be harvested, the plantation owner can demand that the cultivator borrow money from a third party or from the public treasury (*bayt al-māl*) and repay it from his portion when the fruit is harvested. If the plantation owner is unable to advance the expenses to employ someone by either of the above-mentioned means, he can cancel the *musāqāt* contract under certain circumstances.

Finally, it is not clear how the jurists in general understood the liability for loss arising from default of a contractual obligation, but some considered it as part of the issue regarding the attribution of civil liability, which will be examined in the next section.

Rules Governing Civil Liability

Islamic jurists treat the liability (*ḍamān*) for damage or loss of objects belonging to another person irrespective of whether it is based on contract or on tort. Under the same heading can be found a discussion of the liability of a depositary holding goods for another or of a seller who has not yet delivered the sold object on the one hand, and of a person who caused damage to an object belonging to another person or of a person who has unlawfully taken possession of it on the other hand.

In most contractual relations the person who holds property belonging to another party is liable for damage caused by a breach of the terms of the contract. This is based on the fiduciary relationship (*amāna*) and possession is called fiduciary possession (*yad amāna*). Thus, a depositary who has been given a horse to take care of for another person is not liable if the horse dies, unless this is the result of something the depositary has done or failed to do, for example, not feeding it properly or riding it (the depositary is not allowed to use or benefit from the object).

Breach of contract does not have to be the cause of the damage; a violation of the terms of the contract transfers strict liability (that is, liability irrespective of culpability). If, for instance, the depositary deposits the object with a third party without due cause (that is, to save it from fire, flood, or an enemy raid), and without the owner's permission, he will be liable for damages regardless of their cause. The schools of law differ as to what constitutes the contents of the terms of the contracts. The Hanafis regard the prevention of theft as an obligation of the depositary, with the consequence that the depositary is liable for the stolen object if the theft could have been averted, whereas the other schools do not.

Strict liability exists in the law of sale. Under Islamic law the sale contract transfers ownership to the buyer. If a specific good has not yet been delivered to the buyer, the seller, holding the buyer's property, is obligated to deliver it. If he cannot do so, even if the cause is due to an act of God (unless, of course, it can be attributed to the buyer), he is liable and cannot demand payment. As such it is similar to a guaranty in which a person warrants that certain obligations will be met whether or not they are under his control. A similar strict liability exists for the artisan. If a tailor receives some cloth from a client in order to make a piece of clothing from it, he is liable for damage or loss of the cloth for any reason. In these cases possession by the seller or the artisan is called *yad ḍamān*, possession for which one is fully liable.

The Sharia does not recognize a general liability for tort and restricts it to two types of action in tort—a liability for misappropriation or usurpation of property (*ghaṣb*) and a liability for damage to objects (*itlāf*) and persons (*jināya*). Regarding usurpation, the owner can sue the usurpator to demand that the object is returned to him in the same state as it was when taken away. However, if for whatever reason the usurpator is unable to do so, he must compensate it (in the case of movable objects) by providing a similar object or, if this is not possible, with its value. With regard to land, according to most schools the usurpator must pay damages caused to buildings and plants. This is a strict liability: the usurpator must compensate any damage regardless of its cause. The Shafiʿis and Malikis hold the usurpator also liable for the missed rent of land and buildings.

The other action in tort arises from unlawfully causing damage to the property of another person. This action is very similar to that for blood money (*diya*) for killing or wounding a person (see

Chapter 12, below). The owner of the damaged object can demand compensation from the person who has caused the damage, regardless of whether this was done by acting or by failing to act. Moreover, in contrast to Western legal systems, fault is not required for liability: causation and an unlawful act are sufficient. And since fault is not required, liability extends to persons who are legally incompetent, such as minors and the insane. The act, however, must have been unlawful, that is, no right was conferred on the individual to commit the act in this way.

Causes of destruction are divided into two categories: direct causes (*mubāshara*) and indirect causes (*tasabbub*). A direct cause is if a person damages an object, with or without an instrument; indirect causation means that the chain of causation originating from the act is extended. Jurists discuss to what extent the liability continues, especially when the acts of other living beings are part of the chain. Take, for instance, the person who opens the door of a bird cage. If the bird flies away and becomes lost, is the person who opened the door liable for its loss? Some jurists answer in the affirmative, but others deny liability because the chain of causation was disturbed by the bird's having flown away—it could also just have stayed in the cage. However, if the person opening the cage had scared the bird by making noise, then he would be liable. The rules of causation are the same as those applying to the responsibility of killing (that is, the liability for *diya*). A famous case of indirect causation is that of a hole one has dug into which a person falls and dies. Here also the jurists' opinions vary; according to some the victim's falling into the hole disturbed the continuity of the chain of causation. The Hanafis restrict causation a great deal. They deny the liability of a person who gives poisoned food to another whereupon the latter dies from eating it. Here, too, they argue that the victim's act (of eating) interrupted the causation—by eating, the victim is responsible for his own death.

Compensation for the object can be effected in different ways. Most jurists prefer that the obligation is met by returning a similar object or goods to the victim. The creditor may appropriate whatever is left of the damaged goods. However, if the object or the goods are not available on the market or if they are so common that they can be found in any household, then the obligation may be settled by giving the value in money.

Rules Governing *Zakāt*

A man had not only to support his wife and children in early Muslim society, but also his parents and other relatives. In addition, from the earliest beginnings, there was a collective responsibility for the poor and the weak; over time moral obligations became legal ones and institutions were developed to strengthen the solidarity of the Muslims. One of these originally moral duties—one of the five pillars of Islam—was that of alms-giving (*zakāt*), for which an elaborate fiscal system was created, built on productive wealth (Aghnides 1961: 203–347). As the Quran testifies, the affluent members of society were exhorted to purify their wealth by spending part of it on the poor—the term *zakāt* ("growth," "increase") is related to the words of purification and cleansing. *Zakāt* is annually levied on assets and wealth that grow, that is, provide their owner with profit and benefit. These are divided into several classes: livestock (cf. Q 16:5 and 36:71), gold and silver (cf. Q 9:34), merchandise (cf. Q 9:267), and agricultural products (cf. Q 6:141), including, according to some jurists, honey, and minerals and buried treasure (cf. Q 2:267). Below is an explanation, in above order, of how the *zakāt* tax is calculated and levied and who is entitled to benefit from it.

The category of livestock, such as camels, cows, sheep, and goats, must meet several conditions to be subject to *zakāt* payments. First, their number should reach the minimum taxable number (*niṣāb*), which is five for camels, 30 for cows, and 40 for sheep and goats. If a person owns fewer than the *niṣāb* no *zakāt* need be paid. Second, one year must have passed since the date on which the number of a person's livestock reached the *niṣāb*. This rule applies to any livestock subject to *zakāt*. Third, livestock must graze on natural and cost-free pasture, since *zakāt* is levied only on what is a surplus over one's needs. If it costs too much to breed livestock, *zakāt* is not levied. Finally, livestock used for work, such as for cultivation and transport, is exempt from *zakāt* payment. After meeting these conditions, the rate of taxation then differs depending on the kind of livestock and the number owned. For example, a one-year-old cow is due as *zakāt* for ownership of 30 to 39 cows, a two-year-old cow for 40 to 59 cows, two one-year-old cows for 60 to 79 cows, etc.

As for the category of gold and silver, the jurists cite Q 9:34 ("There are those who hoard gold and silver, and spend it not in the way of God. Announce unto them a most grievous penalty") as the rationale for the imposition of *zakāt* on gold and silver, namely, *zakāt* is due on these two items to induce their owner to put them into circulation in order to enhance economic activity. Several conditions must be met for gold and silver to be subject to *zakāt*. First, the amount should reach the *niṣāb*, which is 200 dirhams for silver and 20 dinars for gold. Second, the passage of one year is required, as noted above. Third, if the amount of debt that one owes is so great that its payment would reduce the value of his gold and silver to an amount smaller than the *niṣāb*, *zakāt* is not due. After meeting these conditions, the ratio of *zakāt* is 2.5 percent for gold and silver respectively.

Unlike the taxation on the other categories, which is a taxation in kind, *zakāt* on merchandise is a monetary tax. The obligation is calculated by assessing the goods for trading and deducting any debts. The *niṣāb* and the rate of taxation are the same as those for gold and silver: no taxation under 200 dirhams of silver or 20 dinars of gold and then 2.5 percent.

There is much difference of opinion among the schools of law on which crops should be taxed. Most jurists hold that crops that can be stored are taxed but they differ as to the details. The Hanafis tax nearly all crops and do not take a *niṣāb* into account. Others fix the *niṣāb* on certain quantities measured by capacity. The rate of taxation is 10 percent for the produce of crops watered by natural sources (rain, surface water) without any need for human or animal labor (wheels, buckets, sprinklers) and 5 percent for the produce of crops requiring such labor.

The tax on precious minerals from mines and on buried treasures is the same as for gold and silver.

Although Muslims must pay *zakāt*, only tax on property that is "apparent" (*ẓāhir*) is collected by the state. These are goods that are visible, such as livestock and crops. *Zakāt* of goods, precious metals, and merchandise that are not visible (*bāṭin*) to the public is not collected by state officials but left to the individual to pay. They may pay it to the state or directly to the beneficiaries of *zakāt* (see below). The reason for this distinction seems to have been the prevention of the intrusion of state officials into the private sphere of believers and of official abuse.

Most or all jurists hold that only free Muslims are obliged to pay *zakāt*. They disagree as to whether an insane person or a minor is taxable. Hanafis exempt them from payment of *zakāt* on all but agricultural products, on the ground that payment of *zakāt* is like worship which requires intention (*niyya*), which is absent in an insane person or a minor. The other schools of law, which consider *zakāt* to be a right of the poor over the assets of the rich, make it obligatory to pay *zakāt* on all free Muslims, whether legally competent or not.

Distribution of *zakāt* is laid down in Q 9:60, which reads "Alms (*ṣadaqāt*) are for the poor, the needy, those employed to administer them, those whose hearts are being reconciled (to truth), those in bondage, in debt, and in the cause of God, for the traveler." In accordance with this verse, the eight beneficiaries of *zakāt*, as enumerated by the jurists, are:

(1) and (2) the needy and the poor. Most jurists differentiate the poor from the needy, but they are divided over the definition of each; (3) those who collect and distribute *zakāt*; (4) "those whose hearts are being reconciled (to truth)," meaning, among others, unbelievers who incline to Islam and would convert to it upon receiving *zakāt*, and a convert who might revert to his former belief without receiving *zakāt*; (5) slaves who want to pay the price of manumission or Muslims who are willing to manumit a slave; (6) debtors whose debts are immediately due and who are in need of financial aid; (7) those who want to participate in jihad and need financial support, for example, for their equipment; (8) travelers in need while away from home. With the exception of (3) and (4), they are all classes of persons who in general or for specific (religious) purposes are in need of financial assistance.

Conclusions

This chapter has outlined the legal framework of the economic life. It first dealt with private wealth as seen through the eyes of the law, that is, the concept of ownership. The basic concept of ownership in Islamic law is very close to that prevailing in most Western legal systems, where ownership is also an almost absolute right, only restricted if exercising it would disproportionally harm the interests or rights of others. Whereas this section dealt with wealth, the last section focused on the lack of it, viz., poverty. It discussed the Islamic social and fiscal systems that protect the destitute vis-à-vis the propertied classes—by means of both a fiscal institution in which the state works as a clearing-house and a religious doctrine consisting of a set of religious obligations for the well-to-do to distribute part of their wealth to the indigent.

An important aspect of economic life consists of the transfer of ownership and of its use. Here we enter the domain of contracts: the agreements of individuals to sell or to hire property as well as other legal institutions (for example, agency, pledge, partnership, etc.) that support trade. Although there are many characteristics that Islamic and Western legal systems have in common in the law of contracts, there is one essential difference: Islamic law does not recognize the principle of freedom of contract. Enforceable contracts are only those mentioned in the law and agreements not covered in the law books have no legal effect. In practice, however, the system was sufficiently flexible to meet the requirements of economic practice.

Finally, a section on the protection of property was included. This section set forth, first, the protection of property within a contractual relationship, dealing with questions of who is liable for loss or damage if the property is held by a depositary, a renter, or an artisan who uses a client's property that is destroyed before delivery. And, second, this section discussed the law of tort, or rather the two separate actions of tort recognized in the Sharia: the one dealing with the misappropriation or usurpation of property and the other with loss and damage. These actions protect property against the actions of third parties and spell out the rules regarding the returning of the usurped goods and the making good of eventual damage to such goods.

References

Aghnides, Nicolas P. 1961. *Mohammedan Theories of Finance: With an Introduction to Mohammedan Law and a Bibliography*. Lahore: Premier Book House.

Ibn Ḥajar al-ʿAsqalānī, Aḥmad b. ʿAlī. n.d. *Fatḥ al-bārī bi-sharḥ Ṣaḥīḥ al-Bukhārī*. [Cairo]: Dār al-Kitāb al-Jadīd.

Ibn Nujaym, Zayn al-ʿĀbidīn b. Ibrāhīm. 1400/1980. *Al-Ashbāh wa-l-naẓāʾir ʿalā madhhab Abī Ḥanīfa al-Nuʿmān*. Beirut: Dār al-Kutub al-ʿIlmiyya.

Kahera, Akel and Omar Benmira. 1998. Damages in Islamic Law: Maghribī Muftis and the Built Environment (9th to 15th Century C.E). *Islamic Law and Society* 5: 131–64.

al-Kāsānī, ʿAlāʾ al-Dīn Abū Bakr b. Masʿūd. 1402/1982. *Badāʾiʿ al-ṣanāʾiʿ fī tartīb al-sharāʾiʿ*. 7 vols. Beirut: Dār al-Kitāb al-ʿArabī.

Mecelle. 1305. = *Majallat al-aḥkām al-ʿadliyya*. Istanbul: Qusṭanṭīniyya.

al-Muzanī, Ismāʿīl b. Yaḥyā. 1393/1973. *Mukhtaṣar*. = Vol. 8 of al-Shāfiʿī 1393/1973.

Qadrī, Muḥammad. 1909. *Kitāb Murshid al-ḥayrān ilā maʿrifat aḥwāl al-insān*. Cairo: al-Maṭbaʿa al-Amīriyya.

al-Sarakhsī, Muḥammad b. Aḥmad. 1993. *Al-Mabsūṭ*. 30 vols. in 15. Beirut: Dār al-Maʿrifa.

al-Shāfiʿī, Muḥammad b. Idrīs. 1393/1973. *Al-Umm*, ed. M.Z. al-Najjār. 8 vols. Beirut: Dār al-Maʿrifa.

al-Suyūṭī, Jalāl al-Dīn. 1403/1983. *Al-Ashbāh wa-l-naẓāʾir fī qawāʿid wa-furūʿ fiqh al-Shāfiʿiyya*. Beirut: Dār al-Kutub al-ʿIlmiyya.

For Further Study

Property Law in General

El-Gamal, Mahmood A. 2007. *Financial Transactions in Islamic Jurisprudence*. Damascus: Dār al-Fikr (Eng. trans. of al-Zuḥaylī, *al-Fiqh al-islāmī wa-adillatuh*, vol. 5, 4th ed., Damascus: Dār al-Fikr, 1997). The most detailed manual of the Islamic law of property in general.

Makdisi, John. 2005. *Islamic Property Law: Cases and Materials for Comparative Analysis with the Common Law*. Durham: North Carolina Academic Press.

Property

Chehata, Chafik. 1973. *Etudes de droit musulman*. Vol. 2: *La notion de responsabilité contractuelle: Le concept de propriété*. Paris: Presses Universitaires de France.

Hakim, Besim Selim. 1986. *Arabic-Islamic Cities: Building and Planning Principles*. London: Kegan Paul International. Includes a detailed analysis of the rules governing urban organizations primarily according to the Maliki doctrine.

Johansen, Baber. 1988. *The Islamic Law on Land Tax and Rent*. London: Croom Helm. Traces the development of the theory of land regime in the Hanafi school.

Contract

Chehata, Chafik. 1969. *Théorie générale de l'obligation en droit musulman hanéfite*. Paris: Sirey.

Dib, Pedro. 1952. *Essai sur une théorie des mobiles en droit civil ḥanafite*. Beirut: Imprimerie Catholique. A treatise on the theory of intent in contract.

Linant de Bellefonds, Yvon. 1965. *Traité de droit musulman comparé, théorie générale de l'acte juridique*. Vol. 1. Paris and The Hague: Mouton & Co.

Rayner, Susan E. 1991. *The Theory of Contracts in Islamic Law: A Comparative Analysis with Particular Reference to the Modern Legislation in Kuwait, Bahrain and the United Arab Emirates*. London: Graham and Trotman.

Yanagihashi, Hiroyuki. 2004. *A History of the Early Islamic Law of Property: Reconstructing the Legal Development, 7th–9th Centuries*. Leiden: Brill. Chapter three is dedicated to the origins of the prohibition of *ribā*.

Civil Liability

Chehata, Chafik. 1969 (see above).

el-Hakim, Jacques. 1964. *Le dommage de source délictuelle en droit musulman*. Paris: Librairie Générale de Droit et de Jurisprudence.

Yanagihashi, Hiroyuki. 2004 (see above). Chapter one is an analysis of doctrinal development of the theory of *ḍamān*.

Zakāt

al-Qardawi, Yusuf. 1999. *Fiqh az-Zakat. A Comparative Study. The Rules, Regulations and Philosophy of Zakat in the Light of the Qur'an and Sunna*. London: Dar Al Taqwa.

Public Order

Christian R. Lange

Public order prevails when criminal and political violence—riots, civil unrest, murder, kidnapping, arson, and threats or physical assaults against groups or individuals—is absent, when property and accepted moral standards are duly protected, and when trespassers against the public order are prosecuted, detained, and punished. Western scholars of Islamic law have often asserted that governmental maintenance of public order in traditional Islamic societies was largely independent of—or at times willfully ignored—the substantive public law formulated by Muslim jurists. It has also been asserted that because of Islamic law's "idealism," seen as both the precondition and the result of the oppressive nature of the political organization of premodern Islamic societies, Muslim jurists chose to abandon public law, or at least showed no real interest in regulating the rights and duties of the state vis-à-vis the individual (and vice versa). According to this view, the jurists did not develop a public law of note; they were content to leave the control and ideological justification of public order to the powers-that-be, instead focusing their lofty discourse on areas such as ritual, family, and commercial law (Coulson 1964: 120–34; Schacht 1964: 76).

This perception has resulted in two enduring and interconnected challenges for the study of Islamic legal doctrines of public order. On the one hand, the areas of Islamic jurisprudence that do treat issues of public order are, to this day, less well researched by Western legal historians than other areas of the law.[1] On the other hand, because Muslim jurisprudence on public order is perceived to have been insubstantial, the procedural and executive institutions to which it relates have fallen off the radar of Western Islamic Studies. Notwithstanding a number of specialized studies, we currently lack a proper understanding of how government agents and institutions of public order—the police (*shurṭa*), the market inspector and censor of morals (*muḥtasib*), the prisons, and the state tribunals of justice (*maẓālim*)—interacted with the experts of Islamic law, that is, the Muslim jurists, muftis, and qadis. As a recent critic has noted (Reinhart 2009: 220), Western scholars of Islamic law have often been content to mimic emic accounts of legal doctrines. This has obstructed a broader vision of how legal doctrine confirmed or challenged, explicitly or *e silentio*, the existing state apparatus for the maintenance of public order.

The problem is especially acute with regard to pre-Ottoman times. It is a scholarly truism that in the absence of court records, a situation that applies with very few exceptions[2] to all but the

---

Christian Lange is Professor of Arabic and Islamic studies at Utrecht University, the Netherlands. In addition to articles and a monograph, *Justice, Punishment, and the Medieval Muslim Imagination* (2008), he has co-edited, with Maribel Fierro, *Public Violence in Islamic Societies* (2009) and, with Songül Mecit, *The Seljuqs* (2011).

1 Bambale 2003 is concise and reliable, though not always easy to obtain. Peters 2005 is noteworthy in that it is fully steeped in the conceptual apparatus of Western criminal law. El-Awa 1982 provides more details, but takes a somewhat more traditional approach. Surveys in other languages than English include Arévalo 1939; El-Baradie 1983; Johansen 1979.

2 See, in particular, the Mamluk-era collection of court records kept at the Ḥaram al-Sharīf in Jerusalem (Little 1984). To the best of my knowledge, this collection has not been studied with an eye to issues of public order.

Ottoman and modern periods, students of Islamic law must largely forgo the vital task of historical contextualization of legal doctrine. It could be contended, however, that historians of Islamic law ought to study Muslim legal texts in conjunction with non-legal genres of Islamicate literature, such as political theory, historiography, the biographical literature, and *belles lettres* (including folk literature and even poetry). Whatever one may think of such interdisciplinary approaches to Islamic law, the point stressed here is that the history of public order in premodern Islam is not found in juristic discourse alone; rather, it is the history of competing interests between those who theorized about the measures designed to protect the public order, those who implemented them, and those who suffered them. In consequence, more attention deserves to be given to the social actors involved in this history, whether they be the institutions of the judiciary or the state apparatus, the different types of legal experts, or the victims, that is, those who were punished as criminals.[3]

Below I review the Islamic substantive law of public order and describe how scholars of Islamic law of the last century have approached and evaluated this literature. I further restrict this scope to a survey of Islamic criminal law, arguably the central, though by no means the only legal mechanism to maintain public order. Toward the end I shall raise the question how Muslim jurists viewed some of the law-enforcement methods for maintaining public order, in particular the shaming punishments and imprisonment.

Basic Principles and Divisions of Islamic Criminal Law

Western scholars of Islamic criminal law have traditionally emphasized the dearth of general principles in the classical textbooks of Islamic jurisprudence (Schacht 1964: 187; Peters 2005: 19). However, such principles do exist, whether they be general formulations of the aims of punishment or specific rules determining criminal responsibility, duress, complicity and plurality of perpetrators, etc.; they are imbedded within the separate chapters of criminal law and can be deduced from the system as a whole (Johansen 1977). By contrast, modern textbooks of Islamic criminal law usually preface their chapters on crimes and on punishments with a number of generalities. For example, in ʿAbd al-Qādir ʿAwda's (d. 1954) influential textbook *al-Tashrīʿ al-jināʾī al-islāmī* (Islamic Criminal Legislation), used widely in faculties of Islamic law to this day, the aims of punishment are defined as "reforming the people, protecting people from acts leading to corruption, making them abstain from foolish behavior, guiding them away from error, deterring them from transgressions, and encouraging them to obey [the law]" (ʿAwda 1248/2005, 1: 493).

Arguably, this formulation emphasizes only some of the rationales for punishment that are provided in the premodern literature, while underrating or dismissing others. One of the paramount principles of Islamic criminal law is general deterrence (*zajr*), as one sees in the jurists' oft-voiced insistence that punishments must be carried out in public. In addition, the idea of compensation (*jabr*) plays an important role, most conspicuously in the area of the talionic punishments.[4] There is also a "vertical" dimension to the Sharia punishments, in the sense that most schools of jurisprudence (with the notable exception of the Hanafis) opine that punishment serves to atone for the sin of the crime, thereby preempting punishment in the hereafter.[5] The idea of individual deterrence or reformation is particularly pronounced in the area of discretionary punishment (*taʿzīr*), as will be discussed below.

3 Elsewhere, I have attempted to sketch out such an actor-centered approach to the history of crime and punishment in Islamic societies (Lange 2010).

4 Johansen 1979: 5. ʿAwda (1248/2005, 1: 494) passes over this aspect, arguing that "revenge" (*intiqām*) has no place in Islamic criminal law.

5 Expiatory acts (*kaffārāt*, sg. *kaffāra*) for (usually) minor offenses, such as breaking some of the ritual rules of Islam, are therefore also regarded as "punishments" (*ʿuqūbāt*) of Islamic law. The legal concept of *kaffāra* has been dealt with by only a few scholars. Cf. Lange 2012b with further references.

In classical Islamic jurisprudence, the idea that punishment serves to protect the public good (*maṣāliḥ al-ʿibād*) is also given as a rationale, although it entered the discourse of Muslim jurists quite late. Paralleling a development in European canon law, one finds traces of this notion from roughly the eleventh century onward, but the jurists of later centuries at times resisted all-too-broad definitions of the "common good" (*al-maṣlaḥa al-ʿāmma*) as a principle invoked to derive legal rules, fearing that considerations of political expediency would undermine the jurists' authority as keepers and protectors of the law (Opwis 2005, 2010).

The most basic distinction made by the jurists (the one that structures the chapters in legal handbooks) is between offenses that are punished with a fixed punishment (*ḥadd*, pl. *ḥudūd*); offenses that call for talionic punishment (*qiṣāṣ*) or alternatively the payment of blood money (*diya*); and offenses that receive discretionary punishment (*taʿzīr*) by the qadi or the temporal ruler. Alongside this classification by penalties, Islamic criminal law is divided according to the rights that were violated by the perpetrator of the crime. Jurists distinguish between the rights of God (*ḥuqūq Allāh*), that is, sacred claims vis-à-vis the subjects of Sharia, and the (private) rights of humans (*ḥuqūq al-ʿibād*). The rights of God overlap in important ways with public well-being: punishments of violations against the rights of God, as the phrase has it, "rid the world of evil" (*ikhlāʾ al-ʿālam ʿan al-fasād*) (Emon 2006).

The schools of jurisprudence generally agree on a core group of five offenses that are to be punished by a fixed punishment, primarily in order to protect the rights of God: theft (*sariqa*), brigandage (*ḥirāba*), unlawful sexual intercourse (*zinā*), unfounded accusation of unlawful sexual intercourse (*qadhf*), and consumption of alcoholic drinks (*shurb al-khamr*). Apostasy (*irtidād*) is a borderline case: the Hanafi and Shiʿi schools do not regard this as a *ḥadd* offense, while all schools agree that the apostate should be given an opportunity to repent (Peters 2005: 64–5; Vikør 2005: 291–6; Johansen 2003). The talionic punishments are aimed at those who commit physical assaults on persons, that is, homicide and wounding, and are generally conceived as protecting the rights of humans. The discretionary punishments are meted out in reaction to a heterogeneous and wide range of offenses, and include those that cannot be judged as *ḥadd* crimes for procedural reasons, for example lack of evidence. The discretionary punishments combine elements of both the rights of God and the rights of humans.

In the following sections I shall discuss in more detail the crimes and penalties of *ḥadd*, *qiṣāṣ*, and *taʿzīr*. Because of their salient importance for actual criminal prosecution in the history of Islamic law, I shall highlight the *ḥadd* provisions against brigandage as well as the much understudied category of *taʿzīr*. Along the way I shall point out some differences between the schools of jurisprudence and the various scholarly interpretations of diverse aspects of Islamic criminal law, but due to space constraints I cannot do so in every instance. The picture that will emerge, therefore, cannot do justice to the full complexity of the Muslim legal doctrine of crime and punishment; in fact, almost every rule mentioned in the following sections might have been called into question by a particular Muslim jurist from a particular school of jurisprudence.

Fixed Punishments

The *ḥadd* penalties are typically characterized as "divinely ordained punishments" (*ʿuqūbāt muqaddara*) by the Muslim jurists (al-Jazīrī 1422/2002, 5: 9). The adjective *muqaddar* indicates that the punishment is fixed or mandatory and related to God's *qadr*, the sovereign imposition of His will on the created world. In this sense *ḥadd* norms are divine givens whose logical structure and purpose, unless made explicit in revelation, remain fundamentally inaccessible to human understanding, a point of view that was particularly stressed by Hanafi jurists (see al-Pazdawī n.d., 4: 1643; Ibn ʿĀbidīn 1421/2000, 3: 210, 6: 407). Accordingly, the fixed punishments are anchored in an explicit provision (*naṣṣ*) of the Quran or Sunna:

1. Thievery, punished by amputation of the hand, is based on Quran 5:38. One should note that the jurists also insist that the thief must make reparation to the victim, that is, theft violates both a right of God and a right of humans;
2. Brigandage, also called "the great theft" (*al-sariqa al-kubrā*) by the jurists, can be punished with execution, crucifixion, amputation of hands and feet, and exile or imprisonment, on the basis of Quran 5:33–4;
3. Unlawful sexual intercourse is punished by 100 lashes, according to Quran 24:2. The jurists also based their doctrine on a hadith in which the Prophet sentenced a married fornicator to stoning (al-Bukhārī 1407/1987, 2: 971, and passim [*shurūṭ* 6]). There is also a tradition according to which ʿUmar b. al-Khaṭṭāb (second caliph, r. 634–44) asserted that the Quran had originally included a verse stipulating stoning for those who fulfill the requirements of *iḥṣān* (being Muslim, adult, free, and having previously been in a lawful consummated relationship), but that this "stoning verse" (*āyat al-rajm*) had been forgotten when the final redaction of the Quranic text was produced (Muslim n.d., 3: 1317 [*ḥudūd* 15]);[6]
4. An unfounded accusation of unlawful sexual intercourse is punished, according to Quran 24:4–5, by 80 lashes and the loss of the right of testimony. As in the case of theft and brigandage, *qadhf* is interpreted as a violation of both the rights of God and the rights of humans; for some schools of jurisprudence, notably the Shafiʿis and the Hanbalis, the latter claims have priority, so that the insulted person can pardon the offender and thus avert punishment;
5. While the consumption of alcoholic drinks is condemned strongly in the Quran (5:90), its legal punishment, consisting of 80 lashes (40, according to the Shafiʿis), is derived from a hadith (Muslim n.d., 3: 1330 [*ḥudūd* 35]);
6. Apostasy in the Quran is only threatened with punishment in the hereafter. The schools of jurisprudence that consider apostasy a *ḥadd* crime, to be punished by the earthly authorities, base this view on a Prophetic hadith that commands Muslims to kill (usually by beheading) "those who change their religion" (al-Bukhārī 1407/1987, 3: 1098, and passim [*jihād* 149]).

Ḥadd offenses tend to be defined narrowly by the jurists, which greatly restricts the opportunities to implement *ḥadd* punishments. The *ḥadd* crime of theft, for example, must contain all of the following elements in order to be punishable by a fixed punishment: the stolen object must have a certain minimum value (*niṣāb*); it must have been taken from a safe place (*ḥirz*) in a surreptitious fashion; and it must not be partially owned by the perpetrator nor have been entrusted to him by the owner. Other *ḥadd* crimes are defined in similarly restrictive fashion. This also greatly complicates analogical extension (*qiyās*) from a *ḥadd* case to another *ḥadd*-like case. In fact, the Hanafis reject the validity of *qiyās* reasoning in *ḥadd* altogether (Lange 2008: 179–214).

Rules of Evidence and Criminal Responsibility

Conviction is further made difficult by the rules of evidence that apply to *ḥadd*. The standards for proof in *ḥadd* are stricter than in the general rules for evidence in civil law cases. (The same applies to the requirements for evidence in cases of retaliation for murder or wounding, see below.) Barring confession by the perpetrator, only eyewitness testimony is regarded as acceptable evidence; circumstantial evidence is generally not accepted. Both confessions and testimonies must be worded

6 As John Burton (1978) has suggested, this tradition was put in circulation by Shafiʿi jurists who believed that a hadith could never abrogate a Quranic verse. Other jurists, preferring to strike a more conciliatory tone, spoke of a "specification" (*takhṣīṣ*) of the Quranic verse through the hadith.

in an unequivocal fashion, explicitly naming the *ḥadd* crime (that is, mere insinuation, use of euphemisms, etc. do not count). The confessor or the witnesses can retract their testimony at any given time until the moment of the execution of the sentence. In cases of unlawful sexual intercourse, instead of the usual two, the testimony of four male witnesses is required, all of them describing in intimate detail the act of penetration. In practice, such testimony must have been especially difficult to obtain, given the threat of punishment for unfounded accusation of unlawful sexual intercourse to which witnesses exposed themselves (Peters 2005: 12–16).

Another important mechanism that was apt to circumscribe the applicability of fixed punishments is legal doubt, or uncertainty (*shubha*). This notion was conceived generously by the jurists and covered cases of doubt with regard to the facts, including uncertainty about the adequateness of evidence, and uncertainty about the law on the part of the perpetrator. The jurists based this view on a hadith of the Prophet Muḥammad according to which fixed punishments ought to be averted on the strength of doubt (Fierro 2007; Rabb 2010). Criminal responsibility is also limited by considerations of age, mental capacity, duress (*ikrāh*), and self defense (cf. Peters 2005: 20–27).

The narrow definition of crimes and the strict rules of procedure and evidence in *ḥadd* give the impression of a "paradoxical reluctance of the jurists to implement the serious *ḥadd* penalties" (Peters 2005: 55). The secondary literature proffers various explanations to account for this phenomenon. For example, Ruud Peters (2005) suggests that theological sensibilities revolving around the notion of "God's rights" played a role—jurists held the view that God is without needs and "so sublime that it is not necessary that all of His claims be satisfied." It has also been argued that the doctrine of *ḥadd*, especially for the Shiʿi jurists, was "an intellectual puzzle through which issues of state legitimacy might be explored." In other words, fixed punishments played only a tangential role in day-to-day legal practice but in theory buttressed the "sacerdotal role" of the state or political leader (Gleave 2009: 272). Others have stressed that the doctrine of *ḥadd* was symbolic and designed to educate the broad populace, serving moral and didactic rather than legal purposes. In this view fixed punishments would have functioned as rhetorical devices that served to remind the community of the seriousness of the offense (Peirce 2003: 333).

The jurists may also have had other reasons to oppose the staging of public spectacles of punishment, as *ḥadd* penalties usually implied. Violent punishment had been from early Islamic times the province of the government and its agents of public order. The chronicles from Umayyad to Ottoman times provide many cases in which the authorities made an example of offenders against the public order by publicly shaming, torturing, and executing them.[7] Thus, the jurists' careful limitation of *ḥadd* crimes and punishments may have been an attempt to protect the law against abuse and to rein in state violence. From the start, the legal experts of Islam were famously suspicious of state involvement in the sacred law and of those among their peers who accepted posts in the judiciary, appointments made by local governors in the Umayyad and Abbasid caliphates and, later, by the caliph (Hallaq 2005: 57, 60). This may explain why they decided to seal off from practice some areas of the legal doctrine, in particular the law of *ḥadd*. Actual historical cases of the implementation of fixed punishments are exceedingly rare before the twentieth century (Katz 2012).

The Case of Brigandage

A conspicuous example of how the penal provisions contained within Islamic revelation could be co-opted and misused by the authorities is the case of brigandage (*ḥirāba*), which therefore deserves

7 An incomplete list of recent studies of historical examples of public punishment includes Marsham 2011 (Umayyads); Lange 2008: 61–98 (late-Abbasids/Seljuqs); Petry 2013 (Mamluks); Martel-Thoumian 2012 (Mamluks); Zarinebaf 2010 (early modern Turkey). See also Lange 2012a.

a separate discussion. The "brigandage verse" (*āyat al-muḥāraba*) of the Quran (5:33–4) states that "the reward of those who make war (*yuḥāribūn*) upon God and His Messenger and strive after corruption (*fasād*) in the land is that they be killed or crucified, or have their hands and feet cut off on alternate sides, or that they be banished from the land [...] but this will not be the case with those who repent before you have power over them." As Muslim historians and Quran commentators tell us, the context for this verse was the Prophet's struggle with unruly elements among his Bedouin followers in Medina. Some mendicant tribesmen from the clans of ʿUkl and ʿUrayna who had sought the Prophet's protection are said to have killed a Medinan shepherd and made off with a number of camels. The Prophet apprehended them, cut off their hands and feet, gouged out their eyes, and left them to die in the desert. Some commentators suggest that the verse was revealed immediately after this event in order to restrict the scope of punishment for "those who make war" (*muḥāribūn*), since the gouging of eyes is not mentioned in the verse. Accordingly, this was the first and last time that Muḥammad punished by way of mutilation (*muthla*) (al-Ṭabarī 1373/1954: nos. 11808–17; Abou El Fadl 2001: 49–50). Whether of humans or of animals, mutilation is strongly condemned in hadith and the legal literature (al-Sarakhsī 1993, 16: 145).

The Quranic phrase "causing corruption on earth" lends itself to expansive interpretation. The ʿUrayna and ʿUkl explanation also leaves open the question whether the Bedouin were punished on account of their challenging political leadership or as retribution for their combined crimes of murder and theft. The Umayyad (and also early Abbasid) caliphs invoked the incident to justify the execution of political rebels as "those who wage war upon God," and it has been suggested that the story is in fact not historical but an invented precedent that the Umayyads eagerly co-opted and imitated in practice (Abou El Fadl 2001: 52–3).

Khaled Abou El Fadl's landmark study *Rebellion and Violence in Islamic Law*, which traces the gradual development of the legal doctrine of *ḥirāba*, represents a powerful challenge to the traditional notion that the Muslim jurists by and large accepted the occasional violence and cruelty of rulers as long as these rulers ensured public order (cf. Gibb 1937). Abou El Fadl contends that the vast majority of Muslim jurists came to argue that *ḥirāba* refers exclusively to brigandage and not to other forms of disturbances of the public order, in particular rebellion (*baghy*). The legal discourse about rebellion (*baghy*) served the jurists to militate against the cruelty that rulers usually reserved for rebels. In fact, the doctrine of rebellion, while outlawing certain unacceptable behavior such as rape, murder, and the poisoning of water sources, provided a rationale for legitimate insurrection against unjust governments.

Abou El Fadl also shows that the jurists' treatment of brigandage argued for a more restricted application of the Quranic punishment. The basic principle of *ḥirāba* is that there must be a direct correspondence (*tartīb*) between the crime and the penalty: if a bandit kills, he must be killed; if he kills and usurps property, he must be killed and crucified; if he usurps property alone, his limbs are to be severed from opposite ends; and if he terrorizes but does not kill or usurp property, he is to be exiled or banished. If he repents before being captured, he must be pardoned. This principle of *tartīb*, according to Abou El Fadl, arose among the early Kufan jurists and is prominent in the work of al-Shāfiʿī, while there is evidence that the Umayyads and early Abbasids followed free choice (*takhyīr*) in punishing banditry, that is, the ruler claimed the power to inflict a combination of *ḥirāba* penalties as he saw fit.[8]

The jurists' careful distinction between brigands and rebels was not always followed by the political authorities. Not only the Umayyads and early Abbasids but also the Ottomans in many instances did not distinguish between brigands and rebels (Barkey 1994: 152–6, 240). But, as Abou El Fadl points out (2001: 327), "[w]hether the state would give effect to or implement the injunctions of the jurists or not, it could not deny the jurists the power to embarrass, shame, and castigate." This

8 On the differences between the schools of jurisprudence with regard to the issue of *tartīb* and *takhyīr* in *ḥirāba* cases, see also Peters 2005: 57–8.

is an important reminder of how the doctrine of *ḥadd* can be viewed and analyzed as a discourse that is not just idealized and as such divorced from reality, but instead seeks to engage, challenge, and undermine government practice.

Talionic Punishments

The Quran regulates murder and corporal injuries only insofar as the victim's immediate relatives are given a right to seek retaliation (*qiṣāṣ*) or monetary recompense (*diya*) (Q 2:178–9, 4:92, 5:45). The jurists conceive of *qiṣāṣ* and *diya* as rights of men. Therefore prosecution is strictly private; even though the judge's presence during the proceedings is required, he only acts as an arbiter who supervises the trial and, if applicable, the execution of the sentence, which remains conditional on the will of the plaintiff. While an element of private vendetta thus remains, the law of *qiṣāṣ* and *diya*, in historical perspective, "must also be seen as an attempt to draw such conflicts away from the private circle of revenge and make it a public responsibility" (Vikør 2005: 287). If a sentence cannot be obtained under the rules of personal retribution, the legal authorities can still sentence the offender to discretionary punishment (see below). Because the rules that govern issues such as evidence, causation, degrees of intentionality, the rights of inheritance of the offender, and the value of the financial compensation are nuanced and complex, they can be described only in summary fashion.

Retaliation consists either of the execution of the murderer (in cases of homicide) or of the infliction of bodily wounds similar to those suffered by the victim, and it is only permitted if the offense was intentional. Most schools of jurisprudence define intentionality not in terms of the offender's state of mind but in light of external indicators, in particular the weapons that were used. Degrees of intentionality are *ʿamd* (intentional, where weapons were used that can be expected to produce death); *shibh ʿamd* (semi-intentional, where other weapons were used, such as sticks or other blunt instruments); and *khaṭaʾ* (accidental). Other taxonomies and further distinctions exist, regulating, for example, cases in which death or bodily harm were caused indirectly (*qatl al-sabab*, *jarḥ al-sabab*), or cases of self-defense, which is exempted from prosecution as long as the act of self-defense was proportional to the level of violence of the attack.

In cases of homicide the prosecutors are the victim's next of kin (*walī l-dam*, pl. *awliyāʾ al-dam*). A fundamental difference of opinion among the schools of jurisprudence concerns the question whether prosecutors have a right to financial compensation for murder in lieu of retaliation or pardon. As Peters has highlighted (2005: 45–6), this has consequences for cases in which the murderer dies before punishment can be meted out. According to Hanafi and Maliki doctrine, in such a scenario the next of kin lose all their rights. The Shafiʿis, Hanbalis, and Shiʿis, on the other hand, argue that the next of kin can still demand financial compensation from the killer's heirs. Another set of rules determines the equivalence of blood price between the killer and the victim. According to all schools except the Hanafis, a Muslim free man is not executed in retaliation for the killing of a slave, nor can a Muslim be put to death in retaliation for the killing of a non-Muslim resident (*dhimmī*).

In cases of homicide or wounding in which retaliation is not applicable, the solidarity group (*ʿāqila*) of the perpetrator is liable to pay financial compensation to the victim's estate. The *ʿāqila* is defined differently by the schools of jurisprudence, but it usually includes all male agnatic relatives of the offender. If the latter has no *ʿāqila*, liability falls to the state treasury. Differences in sex, religion, and legal status further determine the blood price: the *diya* to be paid for a woman is half that of a man, while that of slaves is their market value; the amount to be paid in compensation for killing a *dhimmī* is fixed differently by the schools, the Hanafis and Hanbalis holding that it is the same as that for a Muslim.

An exception to the strict rules of evidence that apply in murder cases is the legal doctrine of *qasāma*, whereby if no confession or eyewitness testimony is available, but there is strong suspicion as to the identity of the murderer, the next of kin may swear 50 oaths in order to substantiate the suspicion and bring the murderer to justice. This concerns cases, for example, in which a body is found in a hostile settlement or in which there is incomplete evidence, such as the testimony of a single witness instead of the required two. As is the case with the rules governing financial liability of the *ʿāqila*, the *qasāma* procedure is most likely a survival from pre-Islamic tribal law (Brunschvig 1955: 69–70; cf. Crone 1984). Against an earlier view (Pedersen 1978), fatwas from twelfth-century Muslim Spain, the Ottoman period, and nineteenth-century Egypt have shown that the *qasāma* procedure had some purchase on judicial practice (see Peters 2002: 132 n. 2; 2005: 17–19).

Discretionary Punishment

The range of offenses not directly addressed in either the Quran or the Sunna fall under a third category of Islamic criminal law, that of discretionary punishment (*taʿzīr*). Although *taʿzīr* in this sense constitutes a residual category of punishments, it represents, as is often affirmed, "ordinary criminal law in the premodern Islamic context" (Fadel 2009, 5: 20; cf. Hallaq 2009: 323). The legal doctrine of discretionary punishment is more inchoate and less formalized than that of *ḥadd* and *qiṣāṣ*. For example, a comprehensive taxonomy of *taʿzīr* crimes and punishments is not found in the legal literature, even though lists of offenses punishable by *taʿzīr* have been a characteristic element of attempts in modern times to codify Islamic criminal law. As has been observed, "[t]he fact that *ḥadd* [and *qiṣāṣ*, CL] crimes are so easily studied and examined in *fiqh* books makes them, circularly, the subject of voluminous study and examination, whereas discretion requires investigation largely from historical sources rather than doctrinal ones" (Stilt 2011: 29 n. 64). Given space limitations, I will introduce *taʿzīr* only as discussed by the Muslim jurists, with no more than occasional nods to historical practice.

Taʿzīr is generally defined in the negative, as the punishment for every crime or sinful act for which no concrete penalty is specified in the revealed law (al-Kāsānī 1982, 7: 63). It can also be applied if the evidence for *ḥadd* or *qiṣāṣ* is not conclusive, or if other procedural reasons (such as the presence of doubt or a pardon by the victim or his nearest kin) prevent sentencing. Attempts by some jurists of the pre-Mongol period to impose procedural limits on *taʿzīr* (for example, by forbidding evidence based on indirect testimony, as in *ḥadd*) were not successful, as it was generally agreed that procedural standards were on a level with those in civil law cases (Johansen 1979: 55).

According to most jurists, *taʿzīr* punishment must be less than the mildest fixed punishment, that is, 39 lashes with the whip (Wahba 1996: 257). Some contemporary scholars tend to take such directives at face value, emphasizing, for example, that "*taʿzīr* appears to have been [...] often entirely lacking in obvious physical violence" (Hallaq 2009: 323). However, other opinions circulated. The Malikis knew no upper limit for *taʿzīr*, as in general such restrictions seem to have played little role in practice. *Taʿzīr* punishments include everything from a stern look from the judge to light slapping and pulling ears, lashing, fining, ignominious parading, and imprisonment. From the twelfth century on there is also a tendency to merge the concept of *taʿzīr* with that of *siyāsa*, or governance (Johansen 1979: 55). Eventually, *taʿzīr* and *siyāsa* became the backdoor entry for the imposing, for policy reasons (*siyāsatan*), of severe punishments by the authorities, from torture and imprisonment to capital punishment. While some jurists continued to uphold the notion that *taʿzīr* was to be implemented only at the discretion of the qadi, others openly declared *taʿzīr* to be the province of the government authorities (al-Shīrāzī n.d., 2: 288; Ibn Nujaym n.d., 5: 18).

One important aim of *taʿzīr* is deterrence (*radʿ*) or reformation (*taʾdīb*) of the offender. Jurists therefore reasoned that punishment should differ according to social rank. The Syrian Hanafi jurist al-Kāsānī (d. 587/1189) proposed an influential fourfold classification of discretionary punishment—the more honorable the offender, the less harsh (and the less public) the punishment. According to al-

Kāsānī (1982, 7: 64), descendants of the Prophet and the jurists (the "noblest of the noble," *ashrāf al-ashrāf*) must only suffer a reprimand from the judge in private. Noblemen—land owners (*dahāqīn*) and military leaders (*quwwād*)—were to receive a reprimand from the judge in the public setting of the court. The middle classes (*awsāṭ*), that is, the market people (*sūqa*), were to be punished with a reprimand in the judge's court and with imprisonment. Finally, the vulgar (*akhissā'*, the nether classes, *sifla*), should suffer public reprimand, imprisonment, and beating. Al-Kāsānī's model reverberates in many of the chronicles of premodern Islam.[9] The Mughal emperor Akbar (r. 1564–1605), for example, is said to have averred that "punishment of everyone should be befitting his status [...] a severe glance at a man of lofty nature is equivalent to killing him, while a kick is of no avail to a man of low nature" (Singha 1998: 11). Despite the fact that the principle of punishment according to social status has long been known (cf. Heffening 1927; Heyd 1973: 179; Johansen 1979: 50–51), it has not received much critical attention and deserves closer study, especially since it so obviously clashes with the notion of equality before the law.

The conflict between the jurists' efforts to safeguard the law and the state's claims to *siyāsa*-based penal authority looms large in the background of the legal discourse on *ta'zīr*. A case in point is the Hanafi handbook known as *al-Fatāwā al-'ālamgīriyya*, compiled for the Mughal emperor Awrangzeb (r. 1658–1707) by a committee of jurists under the leadership of Shaykh Niẓām of Burhānpur (d. 1679), the result of a strategic collaboration between the ruler and the jurists. The handbook is a vast compilation of the opinions found in the writings of earlier Hanafi authorities (in the relatively short chapter on *ta'zīr*, no less than 43 different works are quoted) and was intended, it appears, to standardize Islamic law, and thus to allow and to empower the state authorities to implement Sharia while also defining the limits of *siyāsa* authority. The following description is taken from Shaykh Niẓām (1421/2000); the work's criminal provisions in general have been studied by Robert Gleave (2007).

Ta'zīr punishments serve both the rights of God and the rights of men (cf. Johansen 1979). The former are violated in cases of gross misdeeds and threats to the public order—as in the case of violent robbery—even when committed by state agents such as tax collectors or police, including the torture of family members of a criminal on the run (2: 187.31–188.3). Execution of such offenders is allowable or is even a duty of the ruler (2: 185.1). Other crimes that fall into this category include forgery of contracts and written deeds, taking interest (*ribā*), extortion, selling wine, sexual misbehavior that does not amount to unlawful sexual intercourse (such as masturbation and bestiality), marrying off one's underage daughter, pimping, physical abuse of slaves, fisticuffs, and violent assaults on fellow Muslims (such as striking them with the hand, or pulling off their headgear in the marketplace) (2: 187.5–11, 22–31, 188.4–8). No attempt is made in the handbook to develop a systematic taxonomy of such misdeeds or to match them with specific types of *ta'zīr* punishment. The principle of punishment according to class, or perhaps the sheer heterogeneity of possible cases to be covered, may have impeded this.

The bigger part of the chapter on *ta'zīr* is in fact an inventory of insults, culled from some 900 years of legal writing about the issue, for most of which *ta'zīr* is not necessitated (2: 186.17–20, 28–9). In cases of *qadhf* "and the like" (2: 185.10) *ta'zīr* is meted out in order to satisfy the rights of humans.[10] Accusing someone of being a "sodomite" or "catamite" is not punished in the Hanafi school with the fixed punishment for *qadhf*, since sodomy (*liwāṭ*) is not considered a case of *zinā* but is punishable by *ta'zīr* (2: 186.14, 26).[11] Voicing public disapproval with the legal opinions expressed by the jurists is likewise subject to *ta'zīr* (2: 186.30–2).

9 Modern-day Muslim jurists also openly embrace the idea. According to 'Awda (2005, 1: 494) the punishment of honorable people must be lighter than that of insolent riffraff (*ahl al-badhā' wa-l-safāha*).

10 It is noteworthy that the *'Ālamgīriyya* handbook deals with the *ḥadd* crime of *qadhf* in one chapter together with *ta'zīr* (*Bāb fī ḥadd al-qadhf wa-l-ta'zīr*) (2: 177–88).

11 For recent scholarship on sodomy, see Schmitt 2001–2; El-Rouayheb 2005; Lange 2008: 179–218; Mezziane 2008.

Shaming Punishments

The prominent attention given to slander and calumny in the *ʿĀlamgīriyya* and in other Muslim writings about *taʿzīr* is indicative of an ethos to protect personal honor and to not expose sins. This is a well-known feature of traditional Muslim ethics. For example, the theologian al-Ghazālī (d. 505/1111) defines mercy as "the willingness to cover for a person" (1910: 36). Conversely, the jurist al-Sarakhsī (1993, 9: 85; 16: 126) speaks of violence as "the tearing of the veil of integrity that lies over Muslims." It is not surprising, then, that one of the worst punishments that jurists could conceive of was the systematic destruction of honor by exposing one's sins and transgressions in the public arena and by giving the offender over to public scorn. In Islamic societies, this often took the form of the punitive ritual of *tashhīr*, or ignominious parading. To judge by the chronicles, this punishment was a common sight until at least the nineteenth century; it is also one of the most frequently mentioned punishments in the *Arabian Nights* (Rescher 1919: 69–70). Offenders were led through the city sitting backwards on donkeys, camels, or oxen, their faces blackened with smut or embers, their crimes called out to the public, while the mob pelted them with stones and abused them verbally. The sixteenth-century Egyptian jurist Ibn Nujaym was of the opinion that to suffer *tashhīr* was more painful than lashing, the usual *taʿzīr* punishment (n.d., 7: 127). Many later authorities echo this sentiment.

The jurists discuss *tashhīr* as the punishment for false testimony or perjury (*shahādat al-zūr*), but in passing, which may explain why it has only recently come to the attention of scholars of Islamic criminal law (see Lange 2007; Rowson 2009), even though in practice it was meted out to all kinds of offenders, not just false witnesses. *Tashhīr* is an old penal practice in Islam, as is attested by a number of reports in the earliest hadith collections that connect it to the second caliph ʿUmar b. al-Khaṭṭāb and to Shurayḥ b. al-Ḥārith, a judge in Kufa around the second half of the seventh century (al-Ṣanʿānī 1970–72: 325–7). Ignominious parading came to be considered an instance of discretionary punishment only gradually; the process seems to have been finalized when *taʿzīr* was established as a penal category in its own right around the eleventh century (al-Samarqandī 1405/1984, 3: 137). Before then, jurists such as Abū Ḥanīfa (d. 150/767) categorically differentiated between *tashhīr* and *taʿzīr* (al-Sarakhsī 1993, 16: 145). Later Mamluk and Ottoman authors flatly assumed that *tashhīr* was a type of discretionary punishment (Ibn ʿĀbidīn 1421/2000, 7: 238).

It is characteristic that the jurists at times also sought to impose limits on *tashhīr*, holding that the offenders must not be stripped of their clothes to the point of revealing what should remain covered (*ʿawra*), discouraging additional beating of the offender, and polemicizing against the practice of face-blackening or other acts directed against the face, such as shaving the hair or the beard, which they declared to be a form of mutilation and therefore illicit (al-Kāsānī 1982, 2: 141; al-Sarakhsī 1993, 4: 33; Wahba 1996: 259). At stake in such discussions was the question of who had control over the public ritual—who decided upon its legitimacy, who sentenced offenders, and who was entrusted with carrying it out. In the chronicles of early and medieval Islam, one usually sees the urban police (*shurṭa*) and the market inspector and censor of morals (*muḥtasib*) parade offenders (Stilt 2011: 51). The jurists generally accepted that the *muḥtasib* could implement discretionary punishment on the authority of the ruler, without prior consultation of the legal authorities, although they were at pains to stress that the jurisdiction of the *muḥtasib* only extended to offenses committed in the public arena, thereby exempting the private sphere from the *muḥtasib*'s power to investigate and punish (Lange 2009).

Prisons

Little is known about what prisons looked like in the premodern period, since the chronicles are largely silent on the issue. Under the early Abbasids, the infamous Muṭbaq prison in Baghdad is described by the chroniclers as an imposing structure with high walls and almost unspeakable inside conditions. Likewise, conditions in the great prison in the Cairo citadel during the Mamluk period appear to have been miserable, with prisoners starving to death if unaided by family.[12]

The legal literature in Islam focuses on imprisonment for debt and, sometimes, on pretrial detention, but gives little attention to punitive incarceration (Schneider 1995). A certain amount of legal reasoning about punitive imprisonment, however, can be found in commentaries on the "brigandage verse." Commentators understood the passage "or they shall be banished from the land" (*aw an yunfaw min al-arḍ*) to refer to imprisonment rather than banishment (al-Qurṭubī 1387/1967, 4: 153; al-Jaṣṣāṣ [1965], 3: 59). This invites reconsideration of the notion that *ḥadd* punishments are by definition corporal and that imprisonment is not a punishment in Islamic law except as *taʿzīr* (Schacht 1964: 175–6). Particularly the Maliki doctrine that embraced the principle of *takhyīr* in applying the "brigandage verse" (see above) makes room for punitive detention as a fixed punishment (al-Qurṭubī 1387/1967, 4: 152). One might also add that the jurists stipulated imprisonment as a punishment for repeatedly committing *ḥadd* offenses, as well as in certain cases of *qiṣāṣ*.

In practice, imprisonment was probably a rather common *taʿzīr* punishment. It has been suggested (Vikør 2005: 297–8) that in the course of the middle period, imprisonment and shaming punishments gradually replaced *ḥadd* and *qiṣāṣ*, while toward the end of the premodern period fines and financial penalties grew in prominence, a development that would parallel the situation in Europe. As is the case with other forms of *taʿzīr* punishments, the reticence of jurists to address the issue of punitive detention may have to do with the fact that prisons were usually under the direct authority of the ruler and his local governors (*wālī, shiḥna*), not the judges. The dual jurisdiction of *siyāsa* and Sharia also extended to the carceral system: the judge supervised a civil prison for pre-trial detention and detention for debts, while the chief of police (*ṣāḥib al-shurṭa*) was in charge of the "prison of crimes" (*ḥabs al-jarāʾim*) (Khaṣṣāf 1978: 264). A certain functional overlap and collaboration between these two institutions does not appear to have been uncommon (Tillier 2008: 394), although there could also be "a rather sharp rivalry between the judge and the governor with regard to the administration of prisons" (Hentati 2007: 177).

Conclusion

Legal doctrines in areas outside of penal law also aim to uphold and protect the public order. These include the rules for the organization of public space—for example, how property ought be properly fenced off and protected against intrusion (whether by ordinary Muslims or by the political authorities); how the physical movement and interaction of individuals and of groups in public is to be delimited and thus brought under control (gender relations in public fall under this heading); what physical shape the urban landscape, the city's buildings, streets, and venues of public gathering ought to take so as to prevent threats to the public order. Despite a number of pioneering studies, the legal construction of public order in Islamic societies is a field ripe for research.

The outstanding feature of the Islamic law of public order in the premodern period would appear to be the dual system of jurisdictions, that of Sharia and *siyāsa*. However, researchers of Islamic criminal law of the premodern period increasingly argue that the notion of a dichotomy tends to obfuscate rather than elucidate a more complex and dynamic reality. The division of labor between Islamic judges and state agents was not clear-cut. Historians of Islamic law are increasingly attentive to the symbiotic relationship and the functional overlap between the various jurisdictions of Sharia and *siyāsa*, the exact configuration of which differed from place to place and from period to period (for example, Rapoport 2012). In addition, the extent of the jurists' influence in criminal law practice—again, likely to have differed under different political regimes—is open to debate. Arguably,

12 For studies on the history of prisons in the Islamic world, see Ḥusayn 2002; Peters 2002; de la Puente 2004; Hentati 2007; Tillier 2008; Anthony 2009.

the contribution of the jurists, who often operated in opposition to state-imposed application of the law, was significant because it circumscribed definitions of crimes and punishments and defended the inviolability (*ḥurma*) of the human body as well as that of the privacy of Muslim households. As Knut Vikør puts it, "the letter of the law has generally been known and had a normative force even when the actual court practice has deviated from the precise rules and procedures" (2005: 282).

References

Abou El Fadl, Khaled. 2001. *Rebellion and Violence in Islamic Law*. Cambridge: Cambridge University Press.

Anthony, Sean. 2009. The Domestic Origins of Imprisonment: An Inquiry into an Early Islamic Institution. *Journal of the American Oriental Society* 129(4): 571–96.

Arévalo, Rafael. 1939. *Derecho penal islámico: Escuela malekita*. Tanger: F. Erola.

ʿAwda, ʿAbd al-Qādir. 1248/2005. *Al-Tashrīʿ al-jināʾī al-islāmī muqāranan bi-l-qānūn al-waḍʿī*. 2 vols. Beirut: Dār al-Kutub al-ʿIlmiyya; Eng. trans. *Criminal Law of Islam*. 3 vols. Karachi: International Islamic Publishers, 1987–<1990>.

Bambale, Yahaya Yunusa. 2003. *Crimes and Punishments under Islamic Law*. 2nd ed. Ibadan, Nigeria: Malthouse Press.

Barkey, Karen. 1994. *Bandits and Bureaucrats: The Ottoman Route to State Centralization*. Ithaca: Cornell University Press.

al-Bukhārī, Muḥammad b. Ismāʿīl. 1407/1987. *Al-Ṣaḥīḥ*, ed. M.D. al-Bughā. 6 vols. Beirut: Dār Ibn al-Kathīr.

Burton, John. 1978. The Origin of the Islamic Penalty for Adultery. *Transactions of the Glasgow University Oriental Society* 26: 16–26.

Brunschvig, Robert. 1955. Considérations sociologiques sur le droit musulman ancien. *Studia Islamica* 3: 61–73.

Coulson, Noel J. 1964. *A History of Islamic Law*. Edinburgh: Edinburgh University Press.

Crone, Patricia. 1984. Jāhilī and Jewish Law: The *Qasāma*. *Jerusalem Studies in Arabic and Islam* 4: 153–201.

El-Awa, Mohamed S. 1982. *Punishment in Islamic Law: A Comparative Study*. Indianapolis: American Trust Publication.

El-Baradie, Adel. 1983. *Gottes-Recht und Menschen-Recht: Grundlagenprobleme der islamischen Strafrechtslehre*. Baden-Baden: Nomos Verlag.

El-Rouayheb, Khaled. 2005. *Before Homosexuality in the Arab-Islamic World: 1500–1800*. Chicago: Chicago University Press.

Emon, Anver M. 2006. *Ḥuqūq Allāh* and *Ḥuqūq al-ʿIbād*: A Legal Heuristic for a Natural Rights Regime. *Islamic Law and Society* 13(3): 325–91.

Fadel, Mohammad. 2009. Public and Private in Islamic Law. In *Oxford International Encyclopedia of Legal History*, ed. S.N. Katz et al. Vol. 5: 19–20. New York: Oxford University Press.

Fierro, Maribel. 2007. "*Idraʾū l-ḥudūd ʿinda l-shubuhāt*": When Lawful Violence Meets Doubt. *Hawwa* 5(2–3): 208–38.

al-Ghazālī, Abū Ḥāmid Muḥammad. [1910]. *Al-Maqṣad al-asnā sharḥ asmāʾ Allāh al-ḥusnā*. Cairo: al-Maktaba al-ʿAlāmiyya.

Gibb, Hamilton A.R. 1937. Al-Māwardī's Theory of the Caliphate. *Islamic Culture* 11: 291–302. Reprinted in idem, *Studies on the Civilization of Islam*. Princeton: Princeton University Press, 1962.

Gleave, Robert. 2007. Crimes against God and Violent Punishment in *al-Fatāwā al-ʿĀlamgīriyya*. In *Religion and Violence in South Asia: Theory and Practice*, ed. J.R. Hinnells and R. King, pp. 83–106. London: Routledge.

———. 2009. The *Iqāmat al-Ḥudūd* and the Sacred State. In *Public Violence in Islamic Societies: Power, Discipline, and the Construction of the Public Sphere, 7th–19th Centuries*, ed. C. Lange and M. Fierro, pp. 256–75. Edinburgh: Edinburgh University Press.
Hallaq, Wael B. 2005. *The Origins and Evolution of Islamic Law*. Cambridge: Cambridge University Press.
———. 2009. *Sharīʿa: Theory, Practice, Transformations*. Cambridge: Cambridge University Press.
Heffening, W. 1927. Taʿzīr. In *Encyclopaedia of Islam*, 1st ed. Vol. 4: 710–1. Leiden: E.J. Brill; repr. 1987.
Hentati, Nejmeddine. 2007. La prison en Occident musulman médiéval. *Arabica* 54: 149–88.
Heyd, Uriel. 1973. *Studies in Old Ottoman Criminal Law*. Oxford: Oxford University Press.
Ḥusayn, ʿAlāʾ Ṭāhā Rizq. 2002. *Al-Sujūn wa-l-ʿuqūbāt fī Miṣr: ʿAṣr salāṭīn al-mamālik*. [Giza]: ʿAyn li-l-Dirāsāt wa-l-Buḥūth al-Insāniyya wa-l-Ijtimāʿiyya.
Ibn ʿĀbidīn, Muḥammad Amīn. 1421/2000. *Al-Ḥāshiya = Radd al-muḥtār ʿalā l-Durr al-mukhtār*. 8 vols. Beirut: Dār al-Fikr.
Ibn Nujaym, Zayn al-Dīn Ibrāhīm. n.d. *Al-Baḥr al-rāʾiq = sharḥ Kanz al-daqāʾiq*. Beirut: Dār al-Maʿrifa.
al-Jaṣṣāṣ, Aḥmad b. ʿAlī. [1965]. *Aḥkām al-Qurʾān*, ed. M. al-Ṣ. Qamhāwī. 5 vols. Cairo: Dār al-Muṣḥaf.
al-Jazīrī, ʿAbd al-Raḥmān. 1422/2002. *K. al-Fiqh ʿalā l-madhāhib al-arbaʿa*. 5 vols. Beirut: Dār al-Fikr.
Johansen, Baber. 1977. Zum Prozeßrecht der *ʿuqūbāt*. *Zeitschrift der Deutschen Morgenländischen Gesellschaft*, Supplement 3,1: 477–86. Reprinted in idem, *Contingency in a Sacred Law: Legal and Ethical Norms in the Muslim* Fiqh, pp. 421–33. Leiden: Brill, 1999.
———. 1979. Eigentum, Familie und Obrigkeit im hanafitischen Strafrecht: Das Verhältnis der privaten Rechte zu den Forderungen der Allgemeinheit in hanafitischen Rechtskommentaren. *Die Welt des Islams* 19: 1–73. Reprinted in idem, *Contingency in a Sacred Law: Legal and Ethical Norms in the Muslim* Fiqh, pp. 349–420. Leiden: Brill, 1999.
———. 2003. Apostasy as Objective and Depersonalized Fact: Two Recent Egyptian Court Judgments. *Social Research* 70(3): 687–710.
al-Kāsānī, ʿAlāʾ al-Dīn Abū Bakr. 1982. *Badāʾiʿ al-ṣanāʾiʿ fī tartīb al-sharāʾiʿ*. 7 vols. Beirut: Dār al-Kitāb al-ʿArabī. Reprint of Cairo: al-Maṭbaʿa al-Jamāliyya, [1910].
Katz, Marion Holmes. 2012. The *Ḥadd* Penalty for *Zinā*: Symbol or Deterrent? Texts from the Early Sixteenth Century. In *The Lineaments of Islam: Studies in Honor of Fred McGraw Donner*, ed. P.M. Cobb, pp. 251–76. Brill: Leiden.
al-Khaṣṣāf, Aḥmad b. ʿUmar. 1978. *K. Adab al-qāḍī*, ed. F. Ziadeh. Cairo: The American University in Cairo Press.
Lange, Christian. 2007. Legal and Cultural Aspects of Ignominious Parading (*Tashhīr*) in Islam. *Islamic Law and Society* 14: 81–108.
———. 2008. *Justice, Punishment and the Medieval Muslim Imagination*. Cambridge: Cambridge University Press.
———. 2009. Changes in the Office of *Ḥisba* under the Seljuqs. In *The Seljuqs: Politics, Society, and Culture*, ed. C. Lange and S. Mecit, pp. 157–81. Edinburgh: Edinburgh University Press.
———. 2010. Crime and Punishment in Islamic History (Early to Middle Period): A Framework for Analysis. *Religion Compass* 4(11): 694–706.
———. 2012a. Capital Punishment. In *The Encyclopaedia of Islam*, 3rd ed. Online. Leiden: Brill.
———. 2012b. Expiation. In *The Encyclopaedia of Islam*, 3rd ed. Online. Leiden: Brill.
Little, Donald P. 1984. *A Catalogue of the Islamic Documents from al-Ḥaram al-Šarīf in Jerusalem*. Wiesbaden: F. Steiner.
Marsham, Andrew. 2011. Public Execution in the Umayyad Period: Early Islamic Punitive Practice and Its Late Antique Context. *Journal of Arabic and Islamic Studies* 11: 101–36.

Martel-Thoumian, Bernadette. 2012. *Délinquance et ordre social: L'État mamlouk syro-égyptien face au crime à la fin du IXe–XVe siècle*. Pessac: Ausonius.

Mezziane, Mohammad. 2008. Sodomie et masculinité chez les juristes musulmans du IXe au XIe siècle. *Arabica* 55: 276–306.

Muslim, Abū l-Ḥusayn. n.d. *Al-Ṣaḥīḥ*, ed. M.F. ʿAbd al-Bāqī. 5 vols. Beirut: Dār Iḥyāʾ al-Turāth al-ʿArabī.

Opwis, Felicitas. 2005. *Maṣlaḥa* in Contemporary Islamic Legal Theory. *Islamic Law and Society* 12(2): 182–223.

———. 2010. *Maṣlaḥa and the Purpose of the Law: Islamic Discourse on Legal Change from the 4th/10th to the 8th/14th Century*. Leiden: Brill.

al-Pazdawī, Abū l-ʿUsr ʿAlī. n.d. *Uṣūl al-fiqh*. Karachi: Maṭbaʿat Jāwīd Barīs.

Pedersen, J. [and Y. Linant de Bellefonds]. 1978. Ḳasam. In *Encyclopaedia of Islam*, 2nd ed. Vol. 4: 687–90. Leiden: E.J. Brill.

Peirce, Leslie. 2003. *Morality Tales: Law and Gender in the Ottoman Court of Aintab*. Berkeley: University of California Press.

Peters, Rudolph. 2002. Murder in Khaybar. *Islamic Law and Society* 9(2): 132–67.

———. 2005. *Crime and Punishment in Islamic Law: Theory and Practice from the Sixteenth to the Twenty-First Century*. Cambridge: Cambridge University Press.

Petry, Carl F. 2013. *The Criminal Underworld in a Medieval Islamic Society: Narratives from Cairo and Damascus under the Mamluks*. Chicago: Middle East Documentation Center, University of Chicago.

Puente, Cristina de la. 2004. En las cárceles del poder: Prisión en al-Andalus bajo los Omeyas (ss. II/VIII–IV/X). In *De muerte violenta: Política, religion y violencia en al-Andalus*, ed. M. Fierro, pp. 103–33. Madrid: Consejo Superior de Investigaciones Científicas.

al-Qurṭubī, Abū ʿAbdallāh Muḥammad. 1387/1967. *Al-Jāmiʿ li-aḥkām al-Qurʾān*. 20 vols. Cairo: Dār al-Kutub al-ʿArabiyya.

Rabb, Intisar. 2010. Islamic Legal Maxims as Substantive Canons of Construction: *Ḥudūd*-Avoidance in Cases of Doubt. *Islamic Law and Society* 17: 63–125.

Rapoport, Yossef. 2012. Royal Justice and Religious Law: *Siyāsa* and Shariʿah under the Mamluks. *Mamluk Studies Review* 16: 71–102.

Reinhart, A. Kevin. 2009. Law. In *Key Themes for the Study of Islam*, ed. J. Elias, pp. 220–44. Oxford: Oneworld.

Rescher, Otto. 1919. Studien über den Inhalt von 1001 Nacht. *Der Islam* 9: 1–94.

Rowson, Everett. 2009. Reveal or Conceal: Public Humiliation and Banishment as Punishments in Early Islamic times. In *Public Violence in Islamic Societies: Power, Discipline, and the Construction of the Public Sphere, 7th–19th Centuries*, ed. C. Lange and M. Fierro, pp. 119–29. Edinburgh: Edinburgh University Press.

al-Samarqandī, ʿAlāʾ al-Dīn Muḥammad. 1405/1984. *Tuḥfat al-fuqahāʾ*. Beirut: Dār al-Kutub al-ʿIlmiyya.

al-Ṣanʿānī, ʿAbd al-Razzāq. 1970–72. *K. al-Muṣannaf*, ed. Ḥ. al-R. al-Aʿẓamī. 11 vols. Beirut: al-Maktab al-Islāmī.

al-Sarakhsī, Muḥammad b. Aḥmad. 1993. *K. al-Mabsūṭ*. Beirut: Dār al-Maʿrifa. Reprint of Cairo 1324–31/[1906–13].

Schacht, Joseph. 1964. *An Introduction to Islamic Law*. Oxford: Clarendon Press.

Schmitt, Arno. 2001–2. *Liwāṭ* im *Fiqh*: Männliche Homosexualität?" *Journal of Arabic and Islamic Studies* 4: 49–110.

Schneider, Irene. 1995. Imprisonment in Pre-Classical and Classical Islamic Law. *Islamic Law and Society* 2: 157–73.

al-Shīrāzī, Abū Isḥāq Ibrāhīm. n.d. *Al-Muhadhdhab fī fiqh al-imām al-Shāfiʿī*. 2 vols. Beirut: Dār al-Fikr.

Singha, Radhika. 1998. *A Despotism of Law: Crime and Justice in Early Colonial India*. Delhi: Oxford University Press.

Stilt, Kristen. 2011. *Islamic Law in Action: Authority, Discretion, and Everyday Experiences in Mamluk Egypt*. New York: Oxford University Press.

Shaykh Niẓām, 1421/2000. *Al-Fatāwā al-ʿĀlamgīriyya*. 6 vols. Beirut: Dār al-Kutub al-ʿIlmiyya.

al-Ṭabarī, Abū Jaʿfar Muḥammad. 1373/1954. *Jāmiʿ al-bayān ʿan taʾwīl āy al-Qurʾān*, ed. M. and A. Shākir. 16 vols. Cairo: Dār al-Maʿārif.

Tillier, Mathieu. 2008. Prisons et autorités urbaines sous les Abbassides. *Arabica* 55: 387–408

Vikor, Knut. 2005. *Between God and the Sultan: A History of Islamic Law*. London: Hurst & Co.

Wahba, Wafaa H. 1996. *The Ordinances of Government*. Reading: Garnet (Eng. trans. of al-Māwardī, *al-Aḥkām al-sulṭāniyya*).

Zarinebaf, Fariba. 2010. *Crime and Punishment in Istanbul: 1700–1800*. Berkeley: University of California Press.

Constitutional Authority

Andrew F. March

While "constitutional authority" is an anachronistic expression that we should not expect to find translated literally in premodern works of law and theology, there is a range of endogenously developed concepts in Islamic legal, theological, and political writing and practice that reflect the core ideas behind constitutionalism: legal and moral limitations on executive powers, standards of legitimacy for assuming offices of authority, an idea of an ultimate source of authority external to the rulers' own claims, and some separation of powers and authorities. The term "constitutional" will be used below to refer to the family of concepts pertaining to political legitimacy and the limitations on executive political power.

For all early Muslims, the discussion of political legitimacy began with the office of the caliphate (or imamate). Disagreement over the succession to Muḥammad was eventually to develop into a doctrinal disagreement over what exactly the caliph or imam[1] was, a disagreement that gradually produced the main sectarian schism in Islam between Sunnis and Shiʿis.

The core Islamic doctrines that compose premodern thinking on constitutional authority are that: God is the source of all normative authority; the caliphate is the supreme unifying institution of the Muslim community (*umma*); that office is elective and contractual, not a hereditary or divine right; it is a "trust" (*amāna*) that imposes obligations of guardianship, requires certain eligibility requirements, and imposes strict duties; the divine law (*sharīʿa*) is the ultimate standard of moral judgment and politico-legal legitimacy; and there is a separation of authorities between the executive and judicial functions and a limitation of discretionary executive authority to specific realms and to immediate spatial and temporal validity.

The Prophet and the First Caliphs

Like all prophets, the Prophet Muḥammad was an archetypical "charismatic" ruler. He preached his message, acquired followers, and demanded obedience on the basis of his claim to have received an uncorrupted revelation from God. Like all radical moral conversions, the choice of Muḥammad's earliest followers to follow and obey him rested on nothing other than this choice itself. Max Weber's (d. 1920) notion of charismatic authority has, if anything, been too well received, but certainly the following captures much of what the earliest followers of Muḥammad must have experienced:

Andrew F. March, Associate Professor of Political Science, Yale University, is the author of *Islam and Political Citizenship: The Search for an Overlapping Consensus* (Oxford: Oxford University Press, 2009) as well as numerous articles.

1 Although imam and imamate are as appropriate in a constitutional context, I will consistently use caliph and caliphate herein for the ruler of the polity, unless I am referring to an Imam (Imamate) in Shiʿi theological terms.

> The holder of charisma demands obedience by virtue of his mission. His charismatic claim breaks down if his mission is not recognized by those to whom he feels he has been sent. If they recognize him, he is their master—so long as he knows how to maintain recognition through 'proving' himself. But he does not derive his 'right' from their will [...]. Rather, the reverse holds: it is the duty of those to whom he addresses his mission to recognize him as their charismatically qualified leader (Weber 1968: 20).

If something like that notion applies for those early Muslims who accepted the veracity of Muḥammad's prophecy, Muḥammad's long career as statesman, judge, and general also records non-charismatic foundations for his political authority. The Prophet often took a formal oath of loyalty (*bayʿa*) from his followers. After the migration (*hijra*) to Medina in 622, the basis for Muḥammad's authority in that city also appears to have been above all contractual. Tradition records the *Wathīqat al-Madīna*, often translated as the "Constitution of Medina." As Muḥammad was invited to that city by feuding local tribes who did not immediately accept Islam, it is natural that the terms of his assumption of power there should have been negotiated and recorded. That document both prescribed specific standards of conduct between tribes, which included Jews, Christians, pagans, and Muslims, and announced as a general principle of authority that disagreements "should be referred to God and Muḥammad."

Sunni tradition records that Muḥammad did not appoint a successor intentionally so that the people might choose the leader who would best serve their interests. This precedent was established by the election of the first successor, or caliph, Abū Bakr (r. 632–34). The succession to the second caliph, ʿUmar b. al-Khaṭṭāb (r. 634–44, assassinated by a disgruntled slave), occurred through a mixture of election and designation: ʿUmar reportedly appointed an electoral college of the (most likely) six main contenders for the succession and instructed them to elect from among themselves a caliph on the basis of consultation (*shūrā*). ʿUmar was followed by ʿUthmān (r. 644–56), whose compromise election marked the last time the Muslim community would be united around a leader whose legitimacy all recognized.

ʿUthmān's assassination by delegates from territories conquered under ʿUmar not only created bitterly opposed political factions, with a basis in pre-Islamic kin relations, but also competing political theologies and theories of legitimacy. By what right did the subjects of a legitimate ruler kill him and appoint his successor? A "loyalist" camp held that even a ruler who erred or acted egregiously maintained his right to obedience; thus, ʿUthmān's murder was akin to treason and his successor should be chosen on the basis of wide consultation. The contrary position held, at least after the fact, that ʿUthmān had become a tyrant and forfeited entirely his right to hold the office. It is not clear that at this point there was an actual doctrine of rebellion that provided guidance on who may depose a ruler and under what conditions, but this party clearly held that the emergency election of ʿAlī b. Abī Ṭālib (r. 656–61) was legitimate and that all should now obey him.

ʿAlī's caliphate was occupied entirely by the fallout from the events surrounding ʿUthmān's assassination and his own election, and these short years became known as the first civil war, or *fitna*. The key events are widely known: ʿAlī won the "Battle of the Camel" against one set of ʿUthmān loyalists (including the Prophet's wife ʿĀʾisha) but was then fought to a standstill the following year (657) at Ṣiffīn in northern Mesopotamia. The ʿUthmānī loyalist leader Muʿāwiya b. Abī Sufyān (r. 661–80) proposed an arbitration and ʿAlī accepted. A large group of his followers, however, regarded this concession as a sin and impiety, on the grounds that "judgment belongs to God alone" (*lā ḥukm illā li-llāh*). These dissenters, the Kharijis ("those who go out"), were to assassinate him three years later; ʿAlī was in effect swallowed by the same doctrine of rebellion that brought him to power.

It is hardly surprising to any student of state-formation, revolution, and empire-building that control over the early Muslim community-cum-empire was fiercely contested to the point of civil war, especially with the existing tribal and clan divisions that Muḥammad's authority had submerged.

However, why did the early civil wars in Islam generate sectarian divisions down the line, with the fullness of theological, credal, legal, and eschatological differences eventually to emerge? The wars of succession to Julius Caesar did not reverberate through Roman history in the form of sectarian divisions within Roman civil religion.

It has been argued that the answer lies in the meanings that were attributed to the office of the caliphate in early Islam. Clearly, the combination of charismatic and contractual foundations of political authority that characterized the life of the Prophet did not immediately disappear with his death. Modern scholars have therefore speculated that early Muslims must have regarded the caliph as crucial to salvation because he gave the community legal status and guided it through this world (Crone 2004). The Muslim community was thus regarded as a vehicle of salvation and its arrival there depended on a "leader of guidance" (*imām al-hudā*). The ideas of following a law (*shar'*) and of the closure of direct revelation upon the death of the Prophet were present, but as the full richness of Islamic legal doctrine was lacking in the first decades after the Prophet, rightful application of that law and the inspired rule over the faithful were thought to be heavily dependent on the personal rule of the rightful leader of guidance. The difference between following the right ruler and the false one was literally the difference between (eternal) life and death, and thus disagreements over the rightfulness and implications of the assassinations of 'Uthmān and 'Alī went far deeper than partisan rivalries between the clients of great men who stood to lose position and power should the other camp prevail. "The *imām* ['Uthmān] has been killed and the Muslim cause has been lost. The paths of guidance have become dispersed," lamented a poetess, and Muslims not affiliated with either 'Uthmān or 'Alī were remembered as asking, "Which party shall I deem infidel and which believing?" (Crone 2004: 23).

With the assassinations of 'Uthmān and 'Alī, the seeds of Islam's primary sectarian division were sown. However, these divisions did not spring forth fully developed from those events but emerged gradually, largely in response to subsequent political developments. The meanings of the caliphate were heavily and actively contested in the first centuries of Islam before the Sunni and (Twelver) Shi'i doctrines were to settle.

Early Islamic Sectarian Doctrines of the Caliphate

The most irreconcilable disagreement over the meaning and status of the caliphate was between those who held that the office belonged by right to certain persons on grounds of descent or designation (what we might call a doctrine of inheritance or legitimism) and those who held that the office was earned on grounds of merit and attained through legal election or appointment. Blending these two doctrinal ideal-types (Shi'i and Sunni, respectively) was one that restricted the election of the most meritorious to either the Prophet's tribe (the Quraysh) at large or his family (*ahl al-bayt*).

Umayyads (r. 661–750)

Like all governing regimes the Umayyads exploited multiple sources of legitimacy. Initially they invoked the legitimacy of 'Uthmān's caliphate and their right to avenge their kin's death; but once in power they also claimed to be restoring the practice of electing through tribal council (*shūrā*) the best man from among the Quraysh. From the standpoint of "constitutional" doctrine the real trouble came with their adoption of dynastic succession, which rested on two grounds. The first was the legal fiction that each dynastic ruler was in fact "elected" on the basis of his being the best man of his age (*al-afḍal, khayr al-nās*). As long as the caliphate was not declared hereditary in the sense of a personal quality transmitted by descent, dynastic succession and designation could proceed in fact. The caliphate became in theory an office bestowed by the community (which is no less compatible with absolutism than Hobbes's social contract). The second was that without relying on a familial right to the office because of genealogical continuity or continuous designation, the Umayyads could claim that their regnal success suggested both their merit and God's will, the latter being a well-known politicization of deterministic theology. Beyond these explicit arguments, the Umayyads are known to have often enunciated their power in messianic and charismatic terms, often drawing on pre-Islamic kingship symbols and myths from the wider eastern Mediterranean region (Crone and Hinds 1986; Al-Azmeh 1997; Crone 2004)

Shiʿis (ʿAlids)

Opposition to the Umayyads was widespread and an amorphous group of Muslims invoked as more meritorious and more legitimate candidates for the caliphate men closer in lineage to the Prophet. This group narrowed the claim to rightful rulership to the family of the Prophet through the line of ʿAlī (married to the Prophet's daughter, Fāṭima), thus becoming known as ʿAlids. Since many Muslims could not accept that ʿAlī's descendants were owed the office by right, some ʿAlids began to defend the claim that ʿAlī had been appointed caliph by the Prophet and that Abū Bakr, ʿUmar, and ʿUthmān had been usurpers. This doctrine, called *rafḍ* ("rejection"), represents the full crystallization of a distinct ʿAlid Shiʿi creed in opposition to the later Abbasid attempt to create a broad account of their own status. Mature Shiʿi doctrine was to hold that the Imamate is an office passed down through designation (*naṣṣ*) from one true Imam to the next. For Twelver Shiʿism, their line ended at 12 Imams after the Abbasids successfully excluded them politically.

Kharijis

Despite their being behind the assassination of ʿAlī for submitting to arbitration, the Kharijis combined in one the most democratic, meritocratic, and theocratic strands of early Islam, as far from the doctrines of inheritance or designation that characterized later Shiʿism as possible. For the Kharijis, any pious Muslim man could be the caliph on the sole basis of merit and they insisted on strict electoral conditions, some (the so-called Najdiyya Kharijis) holding that he must be elected unanimously by all Muslims. A final crucial difference with the Umayyads and later Sunnis was the Khariji sanctioning of rebellion against and assassination of the caliph for the slightest departure from piety or justice. While such puritanism prevented Kharijism from functioning as the ruling ideology of a large and diverse empire, it does represent important enduring Islamic ideals of strict divine sovereignty and radical egalitarianism.

Abbasids (r. 750–1258)

The Umayyads were overthrown in 750 by a political movement originating in the eastern lands of Islam that also invoked legitimate government through—in this case, their—right lineage, via the Prophet's uncle ʿAbbās. Their doctrine, which early in their reign intimated a donation from ʿAlī to the Abbasids or alternatively the bequeathal of the caliphate from the Prophet to ʿAbbas, also implied *rafḍ*. They gradually moderated their more "Shiʿi" claims to authority and came to acknowledge limitations on the caliph's authority to pronounce on creed and law; as part of their own "Sunnification" and the crystallization of Sunni identity more broadly, they helped to reformulate a doctrine that recognized the legitimacy of Abū Bakr and ʿUmar, and then ʿUthmān and ʿAlī, resulting in the commonly-known "four rightly-guided (*rāshidūn*) caliphs" thesis. The Abbasids continued to stress that they were members of the Prophet's family who had justly seized the caliphate, but rather than repair the wounds of the early civil wars, their success only served to solidify Twelver Shiʿi identity.

"Sunni" Scholars (ulema)

As noted above, many early Muslims regarded the caliphate as an office of supreme religious significance. Getting its occupancy right was not a religiously indifferent matter. However, there were also many who were reluctant to contribute to the fragmentation of the Muslim community and who lamented the toll caused by the civil wars. They became known much later as Sunnis (from their appellation as *ahl al-sunna wa-l-jamāʿa*, "people of the Prophetic example and communal unity"). They held that the caliphate was elective—not one of hereditary succession—but only for candidates from the Quraysh; in this way both the Umayyad and the Abbasid caliphates were legitimate. Like the Kharijis they asserted that the community was formed by acceptance of the guidance left by the Prophet (through hadith) and not by any single ruler. Unlike the Kharijis (and some Shiʿis), however, Muslim unity and well-being were more important than following a perfectly legitimate and impeccably just caliph. Thus, while rulers were obliged morally and religiously to be just and pious, Muslims were advised to tolerate and passively resist, not openly rebel against, those who were sinful and tyrannical. Nonetheless, this view fell short of an absolute obligation to obey. It was still held that rulers were only due obedience in what was also obedience to God, and there was a residual sense that rulers could be lawfully deposed if they crossed some ill-defined line of entering into "clear disbelief."

Sunni Constitutional Theories

Despite the early communal preoccupation with the office of the caliphate, the idea that the legitimacy of a ruler depended on the extent of his fidelity to God's law, and that this law was separate from and prior to the office of caliph, was present from the beginning of Islam, and often encapsulated in two dicta: "There is no [duty of] obedience in sin" and "Do not obey a creature in defiance of the Creator" (al-Bukhārī 1997, 9: 163). As the caliphate in general, and the identity of specific holders of it, came to be less important for the religion of the majority of Muslims, this basic legalistic conception of political legitimacy was to be formalized in Sunni jurisprudence.

Just as the final contours of Twelver Shiʿism were only to develop in response to the Abbasid revolution, so was Sunni thought and political identity to crystallize in response to both the successes and the failures of the Abbasids. The direction of the Abbasid polity was far from overdetermined at the time of its victory in 750. Many Muslims viewed this as the restoration of the Prophet's family, and thus the caliphate became meaningful again. This expectation of meaning was above all a problem and not just a political resource. Who was the caliph, now that a scion of *ahl al-bayt* once again occupied the office? Was he to be the all-purpose leader of guidance? Presuming the Abbasid "turn" (*dawla*, the original meaning of the term for "state") did not usher in the end times, what were the limits of the caliph's authority? Did he pronounce law authoritatively? What about creed?

The eighth to tenth centuries were among the most intellectually vibrant and unsettled in Islamic history. This was the period of the rise and fall of Muʿtazilism, the emergence of scholastic theology, the translation of Greek philosophy into Arabic, the formation of the Islamic legal schools, and the elaboration of Islamic legal theory and positive law. In politics, the firm autocratic grip of the Abbasids over their empire, including their core lands, was over almost as quickly as it began, with the low point coming during the Buyid occupation (945–1055). When the caliphs did execute power, their theories and policies toward the various competing religious camps were unpredictable and variable, even after the landmark end of the *miḥna*. There was no single Abbasid doctrine in this period of the caliphate's origins, foundations, characteristics, rights, duties, and limitations.

The historical details of the caliphal policies during this period are beyond the scope of this chapter, except to note that we should avoid identifying any single moment or event as the point when "religion" and "politics" definitively parted ways and the caliph was reduced to the execution of secular functions, his symbolic participation in the community's self-understanding as a salvific vehicle notwithstanding. Rather, over the course of the first two centuries of the Abbasid dynasty, whatever messianic or charismatic associations attached to the office of caliph were moderated and routinized, even as caliphs continued to favor sects and legal schools with their appointments and patronage. The caliph's charisma, and in this sense participation in divine sovereignty, was shared with the community-at-large, represented by the ulema who during this time developed increasingly technical standards for knowledge of revelation, the Prophet's example, the rulings of positive law, legal theory, and creed. Even the religious scholars themselves "did not proceed to draw up a clear line of demarcation between their own and the caliph's jurisdiction" (Crone 2004: 132).

So successful was the scholars' assumption of this role—to the point that the last referent in the Quranic verse enjoining "obedience to God, Muḥammad, and those in authority [*ūlū l-amr*]" (4:59) came to refer to the scholars rather than the rulers—that the increasingly frequent changes in actual power at the top (from 861 on, when the Abbasid caliph al-Mutawakkil was assassinated by freed slave soldiers) meant increasingly less for the purposes of religious continuity and cohesion. Indeed, by the time we see the emergence of explicitly constitutional legal writing around the end of the tenth century, the purpose seems to be more about building the caliph up—creating legal fictions of caliphal authority when real power on the ground was held by sultans of one dynasty or another—than cutting him down to size.

Abbasid Constitutional Theories

During the tenth and eleventh centuries, Sunni jurists in effect constitutionalized the caliphate in the form of comprehensive legal treatises that elaborated rules pertaining to the caliph's situation, even as there persisted important debates about the nature and extent of his authority. The most important questions discussed in this tradition were the necessity of the caliphate, the procedures for choosing a caliph, the necessary qualifications of eligible candidates, the caliphal functions and duties, the limits of obligation, and the rights of rebellion. Important figures in this tradition, which has a certain Minervan (or even wistful) rather than critical or regulative quality to it, include Abū Bakr b. al-Ṭayyib al-Bāqillānī (d. 403/1013), Abū Manṣūr ʿAbd al-Qāhir Ṭāhir al-Baghdādī (d. 429/1037), Abū l-Ḥasan al-Māwardī (d. 450/1058), Abū Yaʿlā Ibn al-Farrāʾ (d. 458/1065), ʿAbd al-Mālik b. ʿAbd Allāh al-Juwaynī (d. 478/1085), and Abū Ḥāmid al-Ghazālī (d. 505/1111).

The first question addressed by the jurists was the necessity of the office. A few Kharijis and Muʿtazilis had questioned it—importantly, on "Sunni"-esque grounds: if religious knowledge is located in revelation and in the memory and knowledge of the community of Muslims, sufficiently pious and just believers could regulate their own affairs without a ruler. This was a minority view, to be sure, but in response the Sunni jurists gave both revelatory and rational proofs for the necessity of the office (Wahba 1996: 3). Ideally there could only be one at a time, but perhaps if they coordinated with each other, or were separated by a sea, multiple rulers could co-exist.

This tradition affirmed that the office was elective—although only open to members of the Quraysh—and not passed down by inheritance and designation through a single line of Ḥusaynids (Ḥusayn being ʿAlī's youngest son, killed at the battle of Karbala in 680). Examining the practices of the first four caliphs, these Sunni jurists argued that the caliph may be chosen by election, nomination, or testamentary designation. The contract (*ʿaqd*) was in effect whenever the electoral pool (even if it consisted only of the sitting caliph) had chosen a successor and the new caliph had received the oath of loyalty, which served as his formal investiture. However, as with the composition of the council to elect the ruler, there was disagreement on such issues as what to do in the event of failure to choose between multiple equally qualified candidates and on how many Muslims, and which ones, had to give the oath for an election to be formal and official. Because the actual person of the caliph ceased to be of profound religious significance for Sunnis, the important factors were that there be a set of procedures that recognized a caliph as the legitimate political head of the *umma* and that he fulfill the duties articulated for the office by the jurists.

Al-Māwardī lists three qualifications for electors—probity; knowledge relevant for selecting the most qualified leader; and the prudence and wisdom needed to choose the best candidate—and seven conditions of eligibility for the caliphal candidate: justice or probity (*ʿadāla*); knowledge conducive to good judgment in statecraft; soundness of hearing, speech, and vision; physical fitness and freedom from handicaps; prudence in moral and practical judgment; courage in defense of the *umma* against its enemies; and descent from any Quraysh branch. A caliph should possess significant religious legal knowledge, ideally at the *ijtihād* level so as to be able to adjudicate between senior scholars. Broadly speaking, he should be the most meritorious man of his time, but his talents were emphatically human rather than supernatural. He was not infallible (*maʿṣūm*), and the presence of a superior candidate did not justify deposing a sitting caliph who was sufficiently meritorious (*mafḍūl*).

More than in who the caliph was, the jurists were interested in what he and the offices he validated did. In broad terms, he was an agent (*wakīl*) of the community, tasked with executing the Sharia. For the jurists there were certain public aspects of the divine law that required the caliph in order to be executed lawfully. Al-Māwardī lists ten such *sharʿī* duties: (1) guarding the faith (by inter alia upholding the community's established sources and consensus, suppressing heretics and dissenters, and promoting the true faith); (2) enforcing law and settling disputes; (3) protecting the country and the household; (4) dispensing *ḥadd* punishments; (5) strengthening border posts to deter enemies, thereby protecting the lives of Muslims and protected non-Muslims (dhimmis); (6) waging expansionary jihad against those who reject the call to Islam; (7) collecting the legal taxes and alms "on the basis of text and the exercise of judgment, intrepidly but without tyranny"; (8) making the appropriate payments from the public treasury; (9) appointing reliable and competent men to perform state functions; and (10) personally overseeing affairs of state and looking into the conditions and well-being of the community (Wahba 1996: 16). The caliph was also responsible for validating the public prayers, appointing ministers, judges and governors, marrying off orphan girls, and commanding right and forbidding wrong, particularly in appointing market inspectors (sg. *muḥtasib*) and other guardians of public morality. The jurists also spoke of non-*sharʿī* duties, which were recommended or beneficial for public welfare but not mandatory, viz., providing internal security; building roads, bridges, inns, walls, mosques, and other infrastructure; charity and social welfare; medical services; and providing for education and culture.

Once a new caliph was elected and invested, "the whole *umma* must entrust public business to him without violence or opposition so that he can carry out his duties in protecting their interests and managing their affairs" (Wahba 1996: 15). What, if anything, justified suspending obedience to a caliph or deposing him? The caliphate could be forfeited if there was loss of probity by reason of heresy, injustice, or sin (*fisq*); physical or mental infirmities, such as deafness, muteness, madness, loss of facilities, and old age; and loss of liberty through captivity. If the caliph was taken captive, the *umma* could elect a new one; a caliph imposed by a heretical sect was not to be obeyed. Islamic law never developed a fully satisfactory and authoritative account of who was to determine whether the caliph had slipped into the kind of heresy, sin, or injustice that would justify deposing him, and still less of the appropriate procedures for doing so. In the case of both moral as well as physical and mental infirmities, al-Māwardī simply calls on the caliph to step down.

The quintessential Sunni approach was to avoid armed rebellion and further splintering of the community, which was made easier by the diminished role and status of the caliph. He was not personally significant enough to risk the disruption, disorder, bloodshed, and corruption caused by civil war. In principle, if the caliph's heresy or sin was blatant and manifest enough that it could not be ignored, especially if it could be said to reach the level of apostasy, then the leaders of the *umma* (read, the scholars themselves) could call for his deposition. But who could execute this decision effectively and efficiently?

For this reason, the flip-side of the Sunni doctrine of obedience and patience was a deep pragmatism about the morality of rebellion. One should not rebel and the caliph has the right to put down rebellions and kill the rebels. Yet rebels who took up arms on the basis of a plausible religious rationale (a *ta'wīl*) and with sufficient strength and numbers (*shawka*) that their rebellion was not reckless and whimsical were to be treated leniently and not held responsible for destroyed lives and property. Rebels who won would be accepted and obeyed.

The position articulated in Sunni legalism is, thus, not strictly absolutist or cynically ideological. The Sunni scholars valued unity, peace, and legal order above all else, but not without limits. The caliphate, or the state, was not the highest object of loyalty, and public officials had no monopoly on religious or moral interpretation (contrast this with Shi'i views of their Imam and Catholic views of the Church as an institution). Both loyalty and religious interpretation reposed in the community and its true representatives, the scholars. The Sunni prohibition on rebellion but acceptance of successful rebels does not reflect a contradiction so much as pragmatism and realism. Sunni thought stressed obedience, order, and stability, while holding up piety, justice, and "commanding right and forbidding wrong" as political ideals. This basic dialectic is still present today (Abou El Fadl 2001).

As noted, this Sunni legalism was a fiction, as was the authority of the nominal caliph itself. Various solutions to the conflict between the authority of the caliph and the power on the ground held by local rulers were proposed. Al-Juwaynī (d. 478/1085), the Ash'ari theologian who lived under the first few Seljuq sultans and the powerful vizier Niẓām al-Mulk, raised the possibility of fully secularizing the caliphate by proposing to call "caliph" whichever sultan or vizier succeeded in enforcing obedience. More common (and reflected in historical reality) was the attempt to create various legal and theological fictions. Al-Māwardī dealt legally with the fact of local rulers who had usurped caliphal power in the provinces by theorizing the concept of "seized rulership" (*imārat al-istīlā'*). If the caliph recognized the regional sultans, the latter would consent to the caliph, acknowledging them as governors under his sovereignty, much like the relationship between the pope and medieval kings in pre-reformation Europe. In this way, both the fictional unity of the *umma* and the continuity of legal order could be preserved.

Al-Ghazālī also preferred to keep the office of a "legitimate" caliph, although this was achieved by a combination of recognizing the right of local rulers to acknowledge the caliph to whom they would offer their allegiance and a redefining downward of the qualifications required of him. Both caliph and local ruler benefited, the former from being formally acknowledged through coinage and mention in the Friday prayer sermon, and the latter from the legitimacy bestowed upon him by the caliph. Al-Ghazālī's hope seemed to be twofold—the caliph's office would exemplify the (veneer of) legality and legitimacy the community needed (especially at a time when Isma'ilis were trumpeting their own living infallible Imam) and the promise of recognition and prestige would tempt local rulers into honoring the caliph and, above all, lending their might to the defense of right religion. Thus, al-Ghazālī's constitutional scheme was a kind of tripartite division of authority: caliph-ruler-scholars.

Siyāsa shar'iyya

After the decisive end of the Abbasid dynasty at the hands of the Mongols in 1258, Sunni jurists theorized the conditions of just, legal governance without the assumption of even a figurehead caliph. Important thinkers in this tradition include Shihāb al-Dīn al-Qarāfī (d. 684/1285), Taqī al-Dīn Ibn Taymiyya (d. 728/1328), Badr al-Dīn Muḥammad Ibn Jamā'a (d. 733/1333), and Ibn Qayyim al-Jawziyya (d. 751/1350). These jurists still yearned for a strong figure that would provide for security, stability, and public welfare, but were not in a position to uphold what were by this point somewhat precious legalist concerns about the necessity of and conditions for electing a caliph. In *I'lām al-muwaqqi'īn*, Ibn Qayyim declares,

> God sent his message and his books to lead people with justice [...]. Therefore, if a just leadership is established, through any means, then therein is the way of God. [...] In fact, the purpose of God's Way is the establishment of righteousness and justice [...] so any road that establishes what is right and just is the road Muslims should follow. (As quoted in Abou El Fadl 2012: 42)

Thus, a dominant view emerged that the mere seizure of government gives a local sultan the presumption of legitimacy and that obedience to even a vicious one is superior to anarchy. Jurists during this period often tried to extend a veneer of legitimacy to this reality by referring to commanders (*umarā'*) and other local notables as comprising the traditional electorate of a new caliph, the "people who loose and bind" (*ahl al-ḥall wa-l-'aqd*).

However, in the long run, post-Abbasid constitutional thought involves an increased emphasis on the authority of the scholars. Since all legitimate authority is derived from the Sharia and the scholars are the guardians of that law, they are the ones who provide the community with its continuity and legality. Ibn Qayyim again:

> Properly speaking the rulers are obeyed [only to the extent] that their commands are consistent with the religious sciences. Hence, the duty to obey them derives from the duty to obey the jurists. Obedience is due only in what is good *[ma'rūf]*, and what is required by the religious sciences. Since the duty to obey the jurists is derived from the duty to obey the Prophet, then the duty to obey the rulers is derived from the duty to obey the jurists. Furthermore, since Islam is protected and upheld by the rulers and the jurists alike, this means that the laity must follow these two. (As quoted in Abou El Fadl 2012: 49)

Therefore, the symbolic figure of the caliph in classical Sunni constitutional theory is folded into the figure of the sultan, leaving a condominium of authority between sultans and scholars.

In this vein post-Abbasid scholars tried to formulate doctrines of both the rights and duties of rulers who come to power through force. Ibn Jamā'a's list of the former is instructive: (1) obedience within the law; (2) advice in public and in secret; (3) help; (4) making the greatness of his office known and acting in a way to magnify his dignity and respect for him; (5) admonishment when he is neglectful, guidance when he goes astray, and help to preserve his religion and his honor; (6) being warned against enemies; (7) being informed of the conduct of his subordinates and those he is occupied in protecting; (8) help in his efforts in the public welfare; (9) help to win hearts and minds; and (10) diversion of all harm and evil from him through any means necessary. In return, the sultan was obligated to protect the lands under his control, disseminate the religious sciences, protect and consult the scholars, appoint officials to carry out prescribed religious duties, decide cases, restrain tyrants, impose Sharia punishments, collect the ordained taxes, and oversee the administration of religious endowments.

Al-Qarāfī formulated one of the most famous theoretical elaborations of the constitutional distribution of authority on the basis of a creative reading of the Prophetic Sunna. Rulers were entitled to act as scholars, judges, and heads of state, but precisely for this reason their ability to define and potentially corrupt the meaning of God's law was limited. If a ruler issued a fatwa, it was just one voice among many. If he acted in his discretionary capacity as head of state, it must be within the limits of public welfare (*maṣlaḥa 'āmma*) as defined by the legal scholars in broad outlines, if not precise detail, and such discretionary acts were valid only for their own time and place as discretionary acts of public policy, not timeless law (Jackson 1996; and see Chapter 7, above).

This somewhat paradoxical legalization of governance by authorizing discretionary judgments beyond the limits of fiqh within the broader umbrella of the Sharia is also associated with the writings of Ibn Taymiyya, whose *al-Siyāsa al-shar'iyya fī iṣlāḥ al-rā'ī wa-l-ra'iyya* is organized as a commentary on two important Quranic verses (4:58–9): "Surely God commands you to make over trusts (*amānāt*) to those worthy of them, and then when you judge among people you judge with justice. Surely God admonishes you with what is excellent. [...] obey God and obey the Messenger and those in authority from among you ... ." The vision is a familiar shepherd-and-flock model of rulership. Ibn Taymiyya does not even bother at this point to imply that a sultan can acquire the de facto status of the caliph. He argues instead that the caliphate was never truly obligatory and never truly elective.

The text is largely a summary and reassertion of the Islamic legal rules related to public law (criminal punishments, public order and security, jihad) and private law (retaliation or compensation for homicide, injuries, or insults, marriage, sales), and also includes some discussion on the nature and necessity of governance in human society. However, within these more general discussions Ibn Taymiyya engages in some intriguing reflections on morality and public life. His *siyāsa shar'iyya* doctrine seeks not only to legitimate some discretionary authority on the part of rulers and their deputies, but also to validate certain measures of seemingly immoral action. It is a deeply pragmatic, realistic vision of politics that does not decide between means and ends, but insists that means and ends are always implied by one another and that men of politics are never free from judgments in real time about how the goods of justice, virtue, piety, and communal welfare are best balanced. Politics and justice is about the "middle path" (*wasaṭ*) between expediency and morality, but acting on this wisdom is less about rules than about a certain kind of disposition and capacity for judgment, much like Aristotelian *phronesis*.

Ibn Taymiyya astutely notes that the virtues do not always go together, and that part of the ruler's job is knowing which virtues and vices are acceptable for which offices. It is thus more acceptable for a military commander to be sinful and strong than pious but weak, whereas the guardian of the treasury must be loyal and pious. This realistic, unsentimental vision of politics is based on the judgment that the highest good of preserving religion often depends on minor acts of impiety and corruption. There is something of Weber's ethics of responsibility here: God will forgive some dirty hands but not weakness if it imperils the *umma*. "God will strengthen His religion even through the dissolute," recites Ibn Taymiyya, and he excoriates the man of excessive piety who is more concerned with his soul than with the welfare of the *umma*: "He who chooses to hold back [from joining a call for jihad, paying taxes, accepting public office] because in his opinion he might be helping a transgressor, he is the one who has neglected a duty imposed on every individual Muslim or on the community at large, imagining that his non-commitment is piety. But how often are cowardice and weakness confounded with piety since both are timidity and neutrality" (Farrukh 1966: 58).

Ottoman Contributions to Islamic Constitutionalism

The Ottoman state institutionalized and bureaucratized some of the ideas implicit in Mamluk-era *siyāsa shar'iyya* writings justifying a condominium of power between the rulers and the religious scholars. The Ottomans developed elaborate parallel bureaucracies and legal systems that separated certain military, administrative, and feudal hierarchies from the spheres of society governed by the religious scholars according to Islamic law.

First, the ulema were organized by the state into a formal, hierarchical structure to a greater degree than by any preceding Muslim polity. Religious colleges (sg. *madrasa*) were centrally funded and rank-ordered, judges were centrally selected and appointed for all regions and levels of society, the Hanafi school was adopted as the official state legal doctrine, and an official state office of the highest-ranking religious authority (Grand Mufti, T, *şeyhülislam*) was created. By the sixteenth century, this office came to be responsible for issuing official fatwas on the religious status of public policies, supervising the sultan's religious endowments, and appointing and dismissing supreme judges, high-ranking college professors, judges, and heads of Sufi orders. Unlike in classical Islamic law, these fatwas were binding, although not always on the sultan. The Grand Mufti served at the sultan's pleasure and could be dismissed by him, but was otherwise largely autonomous in his sphere of authority; the religious scholars as a class enjoyed a large degree of independence—they were officially immune from confiscation of their property, which they could pass on to their heirs, applied Hanafi fiqh rules in their own civil courts, and were subject only to their own internal discipline.

At the same time, large spheres of administration, the disposal of land, coercive power, criminal punishments, and taxation were outside of the direct control of the religious scholars and their law. In traditional parlance, this was the sphere of *siyāsa*, governed by the sultan's own legal codes (sg. *qānūn*). For a discussion of how Sharia and qanun played out in the Ottoman period, see Chapter 8, above.

The "constitutional" legitimacy of the Ottoman dynasty was primarily derived from the fact of their having established coercive rule and then acting as good Muslim rulers should: protecting right religion, enforcing the laws of Islam, ruling over their subjects with justice, and expanding the territory ruled by Islam by waging jihad successfully against the unbelievers. As they built their empire also by conquering Muslim lands, their court chroniclers circulated stories of the donation or designation of authority to the dynasty from the last Seljuq sultan, with one attempt to trace the family's lineage through the Oghuz Khans all the way back to Noah. Ultimately, in 1517, the Ottomans were to assume the title of caliph when they subjugated the remainder of the Mamluk sultanate and took control of the central Arab lands, including Mecca and Medina. Formally, the Ottoman assumption of the caliphate was based on a donation to Selim I of the office (along with the sword and mantle of the Prophet) from the last living Abbasid "shadow caliph" whom the Mamluks had kept up for symbolic and ritual purposes, al-Mutawakkil III (although they used the title to less official effect at least since 1421). A former Grand Vizier (Lutfi Pasha) authored a treatise around this time attempting to prove, contra classical legal theory, that descent from the Quraysh was not a necessary qualification of the caliph.

The Ottoman sultans and their court scholars enunciated the fullest authority, status, and majesty associated with the early meanings of the caliphate with the great jurist Ebu's-Su'ūd proclaiming that as caliph the Ottoman sultan "performs the command of the Hidden Book" and "expounds the signs of the luminous Shari'a" (Imber 1997: 75–6). By this point the Ottoman claims went beyond both the traditional contractual and realist conceptions of constitutional authority in Islam to full-fledged charismatic and divine-designation enunciations of sovereign power. In some public inscriptions, the Umayyad-era title *khalīfat Allāh* ("caliph of God") is used, and Ebu's-Su'ūd explicitly claimed that the House of Osman had been directly chosen by God to rule and that this status was thus hereditary within that line, in complete contradiction with classical Sunni theory. It was, indeed, a unique development within Islam when the sultans Mehmed II and Süleyman I issued formal legal codes (*kanunname*) on their own legislative and executive authority and claimed the right to command authoritative interpretations of Sharia.

Conclusion

For those who eventually came to call themselves *ahl al-sunna wa-l-jamā'a*, the caliphate was a form of contract with elective components. While election may have been limited to a select group of people who "loose and bind," in principle the caliph was to receive the oath of loyalty from all adult, male Muslims. While in practice the elective and contractual nature of the caliphate was often a legal fiction and in theory it was often treated as a formality that did not impose any ongoing requirements of consent from the governed, for some early Muslims—most famously the Kharijis—consent could be revoked at the merest sinful or impious act on the part of the caliph. While radically anarchic and egalitarian in one sense, this view was based on carrying the basic premise of Islamic political theology—"judgment belongs to God alone"—to its extreme conclusion.

In contrast, for those who eventually came to call themselves Imamis, or Shiʿis, the Imamate was a hereditary status passed down by designation (*naṣṣ*) through the line of ʿAlī until the twelfth Imam went into occultation. The modern world is most familiar with this mainstream Twelver Shiʿism, but similar ideas about political legitimacy residing with the family of the Prophet inspired other sectarian or ideological groupings in early Islam, including the Abbasids, the Zaydis, and the Ismaʿilis and their various offshoots.

For the Sunni majority, the emphasis on election and contract led to a broader set of constitutional ideas. Both the office of caliph itself and its occupancy by a particular person had to be justified. The requirement of having the specific office of caliph, by which was meant a single ruler for all Muslims with both secular and religious duties, was given theoretical justification both through revelation and reason. The power and authority of the caliph, and later mere sultans, was conceived as a form of agency (*wakāla*) or trust (*amāna*). This fiduciary, almost contractual, status of rulership came with the legalistic elaboration of certain qualifications or conditions that a prospective ruler would have to fulfill to be eligible for the office and of the duties that he would have to fulfill in order to remain a legitimate holder of it. Indeed, the mere fact that treatises could be written on the legal rules of governance (*al-aḥkām al-sulṭāniyya*) is an indication of the "constitutional" quality of the Sunni Islamic political imagination. It is impossible to imagine a Shiʿi treatise on the rules of governance under the returned Imam.

Alongside a legal-theoretical justification for the office as such, its duties, and the rules of eligibility, the law functioned (in theory) as a constitutional limitation on the executive in at least two further ways. One, the Sharia was prior to and separate from the office and the person of the caliph. Eventually, the settled Sunni view was that, while the ideal caliph ought to be a learned jurist capable of giving religious opinions, the law resided in the Quran, in the practice of the Prophet, and in the community of interpretation, not in the arbitrary opinion or will of the executive. The ruler may act in various ways according to his own judgment, and those acts may be alternatively validated or rejected, according to the scholars' understanding of Sharia, but the ruler may not pronounce by fiat what the correct, authoritative ruling on a question of law for all times and places is. And two, the ruler's practical authority in the application of the law at the social level is meant to be limited. One of his central tasks, and why later jurist-theologians such as al-Juwaynī and al-Ghazālī tried to preserve the legal fiction of his office, was to create and validate courts and lower offices. But the courts were meant to remain strictly independent of the executive. The law they applied was the law of the religious legal schools and the qualifications for judges were set and elaborated by those schools.

While many modern-day Muslims imagine that the only legitimate "Islamic state" is the one that applies the Sharia to the exclusion of all other law or standards, this is itself a simplification and an anachronism. The ruler had *sharʿī* duties and he was meant to support the scholars in their application of the religious civil law, but his sphere of authority was wider than what could be regulated and enumerated in the law books. The ruler had to take countless actions and decisions that could not be anticipated or prescribed by the law, but such actions were not lawless or outside legal norms.

First, of course, only certain persons or office-holders could act legitimately in specific areas of communal life (war, engineering, finance, administration, market-inspection, morality-enforcement, etc.). Second, all such actions could be evaluated according to broad standards of public, collective welfare, or *maṣlaḥa*. The law could give normative content to the public good, which both politics and the law itself served—famously, the protection of life, religion, property, reason, and progeny—but whether specific actions were conducive to this good was often left to the discretion of rulers, generals, market inspectors, judges, or regional governors.

This gives us a new conceptual frame for understanding classical Islamic constitutionalism, sometimes called the *siyāsa*–fiqh dichotomy. *Siyāsa*, often translated as "politics" or "policy" today, refers to governance, ruling, or direction in premodern Arabic. Fiqh refers to the corpus of positive legal rulings elaborated by the religious scholars as representing the best approximation of the divine law. *Siyāsa* is the world of secular discretionary authority; fiqh is the world of religious legalism. *Siyāsa* is necessary but contingent, and valid only for its immediate context; fiqh is meant to constitute a tradition of norms and practices that bind Muslims across space and time. It has been argued that this distinction should not be understood as marking the limits of the application of "Sharia" in the Islamic polity (Vogel 2000). Rather, Sharia should be seen to demarcate the widest possible sphere of religious legitimacy or normativity. Legitimate and mandatory religious norms can be expressed and upheld through both *siyāsa* and fiqh, which we can now understand as parallel and at times overlapping spheres of public religious life. Both "secular" rulers and "religious" scholars-cum-judges operate within the sphere of God's law, since the tasks of government—securing and advancing the *salus populi*—are requirements of Sharia.

References

Abou El Fadl, Khaled. 2001. *Rebellion and Violence in Islamic Law*. Cambridge: Cambridge University Press.

———. 2012. The Centrality of Shari'ah to Government and Constitutionalism in Islam. In *Constitutionalism in Islamic Countries: Between Upheaval and Continuity*, ed. R. Grote and T.J. Röder, pp. 35–62. Oxford: Oxford University Press.

Afsaruddin, Asma. 2006. The "Islamic State": Genealogy, Facts, and Myths. *Journal of Church and State* 48: 153–74.

———, ed. 2011. *Islam, the State, and Political Authority: Medieval Issues and Modern Concerns*. New York: Palgrave Macmillan.

Al-Azmeh, Aziz. 1997. *Muslim Kingship: Power and the Sacred in Muslim, Christian and Pagan Polities*. London: I.B. Tauris.

Anjum, Ovamir. 2012. *Politics, Law and Community in Islamic Thought: The Taymiyyan Moment*. New York: Cambridge University Press.

Bearman, Peri, Wolfhart Heinrichs, and Bernard G. Weiss, eds. 2008. *The Law Applied: Contextualizing the Islamic Shari'a. A Volume in Honor of Frank E. Vogel*. London: I.B. Tauris.

Berkey, Jonathan P. 2002. *The Formation of Islam: Religion and Society in the Near East, 600–1800*. Cambridge: Cambridge University Press.

Black, Antony. 2001. *The History of Islamic Political Thought: From the Prophet to the Present*. New York: Routledge.

al-Bukhārī, Muḥammad. 1997. *Ṣaḥīḥ al-Bukhārī*, tr. M.M. Khān. 9 vols. Riyadh: Dār al-Salām.

Crone, Patricia. 2004. *God's Rule: Government and Islam: Six Centuries of Medieval Islamic Political Thought*. New York: Columbia University Press.

Crone, Patricia, and Martin Hinds. 1986. *God's Caliph: Religious Authority in the First Centuries of Islam*. Cambridge: Cambridge University Press.

Ess, Josef van. 2001. Political Ideas in Early Islamic Religious Thought. *British Journal of Middle Eastern Studies* 28: 151–64.

Farrukh, Omar A. 1966. *Ibn Taimiyya on Public and Private Law in Islam: Or Public Policy in Islamic Jurisprudence*. Beirut: Khayats (Eng. trans. of Ibn Taymiyya, *al-Siyāsa al-shar'iyya fī iṣlāḥ al-rā'ī wa-l-ra'iyya*).

Grote, Rainer, and Tilmann J. Röder, eds. 2012. *Constitutionalism in Islamic Countries: Between Upheaval and Continuity*. Oxford: Oxford University Press.

Ibn Khaldun. 1967. *The Muqaddima: An Introduction to History*, tr. F. Rosenthal. Princeton: Princeton University Press.

Imber, Colin. 1997. *Ebu's-su'ud: The Islamic Legal Tradition*. Palo Alto: Stanford University Press.

Jackson, Sherman A. 1996. *Islamic Law and the State: The Constitutional Jurisprudence of Shihāb al-Dīn al-Qarāfī*. Leiden: E.J. Brill.

Johansen, Baber. 2008. A Perfect Law in an Imperfect Society: Ibn Taymiyya's Concept of "Governance in the Name of the Sacred Law". In *The Law Applied: Contextualizing the Islamic Shari'a*, ed. P. Bearman et al., pp. 259–94. London: I.B. Tauris.

Kohlberg, Etan. 1976. From Imamiyya to Ithna-'ashariyya. *Bulletin of the School of Oriental and African Studies* 39: 521–34.

Lambton, Ann K.S. 1981. *State and Government in Medieval Islam: An Introduction to the Study of Islamic Political Theory. The Jurists*. Oxford: Oxford University Press.

Malkawi, Banan, and Tamara Sonn. 2011. Ibn Taymiyya on Islamic Governance. In *Islam, the State, and Political Authority: Medieval Issues and Modern Concerns*, ed. A. Afsarrudin, pp. 111–27. New York: Palgrave Macmillan.

Modarressi, Hossein. 1993. *Crisis and Consolidation in the Formative Period of Shi'ite Islam*. Princeton: Darwin Press.

Stilt, Kristen. 2012. *Islamic Law in Action: Authority, Discretion, and Everyday Experiences in Mamluk Egypt*. New York: Oxford University Press.

Vogel, Frank E. 2000. *Islamic Law and Legal System: Studies of Saudi Arabia*. Leiden: Brill.

Wahba, Wafaa H. 1996. *The Ordinances of Government*. Reading: Garnet (Eng. trans. of al-Māwardī, *al-Aḥkām al-sulṭāniyya*).

Walker, Paul E. 2011. The Responsibilities of Political Office in a Shi'i Caliphate and the Delineation of Public Duties under the Fatimids. In *Islam, the State, and Political Authority: Medieval Issues and Modern Concerns*, ed. A. Afsarrudin, pp. 93–110. New York: Palgrave Macmillan.

Watt, W. Montgomery. 1968. *Islamic Political Thought: The Basic Concepts*. Edinburgh: Edinburgh University Press.

Weber, Max. 1968. *On Charisma and Institution Building: Selected Papers*, ed. S.N. Eisenstadt. Chicago: University of Chicago Press.

Yücesoy, Hayrettin. 2011. Justification of Political Authority in Medieval Sunni Thought. In *Islam, the State, and Political Authority: Medieval Issues and Modern Concerns*, ed. A. Afsarrudin, pp. 9–33. New York: Palgrave Macmillan.

Zaman, Muhammad Qasim. 1997. *Religion and Politics under the Early 'Abbāsids: The Emergence of the Proto-Sunnī Elite*. Leiden: Brill.

War and Peace

Sohail H. Hashmi

Classical Islamic jurisprudence is rich in reflection on war and peace. In depth and breadth of the topics covered, Islamic law in this period (roughly the ninth through the fourteenth centuries) dealt more systematically and comprehensively with international relations—including war, peace, and diplomacy—than any contemporary legal system. The legal compendia produced by early Muslim jurists cover the range of issues germane to Muslim rulers, military commanders, and soldiers of that time, such as the conditions under which armed force is justified, who may authorize and direct the use of force, who is the enemy and how are they to be fought, who among enemy populations are to be spared from direct attack, how is captured enemy property to be disposed of, and under what conditions and for how long may truces or peace settlements be contracted.

This chapter outlines the key points of the classical Islamic law of war and peace, as elucidated by scholars of the four principal Sunni schools of law and by the Jaʿfari Shiʿi school. It begins with a brief treatment of the sources and methodology employed by classical jurists. This is followed by a discussion of the theory of world order that framed the more specific rulings relating to war and peace. Then the substance of classical jurisprudence is treated in sections on the grounds for war, the conduct of war, and, finally, the end of hostilities through truces and peace treaties.

I present in this chapter the views of the jurists with a minimum of interpretation. Jihad and the classical legal dicta on war and peace are today perhaps the most controversial, contested, and "explained" of all topics in Islamic law. My aim here is to allow the classical scholars to speak for themselves and thus to present a broad overview of both the agreements and disagreements in juristic discourses.

Sources and Methodology

As in other fields of Islamic law, Muslim jurists grounded their rulings on war and peace in the Quran and example (*sunna*) of the Prophet Muḥammad. The Quran deals with war using primarily three terms: *ḥarb*, *qitāl*, and *jihād*. The suras that are believed to be from the Prophet's Meccan period—the 86 suras revealed from approximately 610–22—are notably devoid of martial content. The verbal root *ḥ-r-b*, from which the specific Arabic word for war (*ḥarb*) is derived, does not occur; the root *q-t-l*, from which comes *qitāl* ("fighting, killing"), is found infrequently, and only in contexts other than war, such as homicide;[1] and similarly, *j-h-d*, from which *jihād* is derived, occurs only a

Sohail H. Hashmi is Professor of International Relations and Alumnae Foundation Chair in the Social Sciences at Mount Holyoke College. His most recent publication is an edited volume titled *Just Wars, Holy Wars, and Jihads: Christian, Jewish, and Muslim Encounters and Exchanges* (2012).

1 As in Q 6:151, which prohibits the killing of one's children for fear of poverty and the general command to "take not life (*lā taqtulū l-nafs*) which God has made sacred, except with just cause."

few times in the Meccan verses, and in each case the reference is limited strictly to spiritual effort or metaphysical struggle.

The Quran's silence on war during the Meccan period is mirrored by the absence of any military activity by the Prophet. There is no recorded instance in Muḥammad's biography during these 12 years where he responded to the mounting persecution directed against him and his followers by advocating or preparing for war. His policy throughout this period seems to have been one of sufferance of abuse and strictly nonviolent resistance. He may have sought a modus vivendi with his polytheist townspeople, as indicated by the closing line of Q 109: "You have your religion, and I have mine." When the abuse of his most vulnerable followers became intolerable, he ordered them to flee Mecca for the safety of Abyssinia, the realm of a Christian ruler.

War enters the Quran and Sunna upon the Prophet's emigration (*hijra*, ca. 622) to Yathrib (renamed Medina). On the eve of his departure, a delegation from the northern town pledges to protect Muḥammad against all enemies and in return the Prophet pledges, "I am of you and you are of me. I will war against them who war against you and be at peace with those at peace with you" (Ibn Hishām 1988, 2: 96; Guillaume 1990: 204).

According to Quranic commentators, the first verses sanctioning war (Q 22:39–40) are revealed soon thereafter ("To those against whom war is made, permission is given [to fight] ..."). In subsequent verses the permission to fight is transformed into a duty: "Fight in the path of God those who fight against you ..." (Q 2:190–3). Then, if any doubts lingered in the minds of the Prophet's followers that war was now incumbent upon them, Q 2:216 was revealed: "Fighting is prescribed (*kutiba*) for you, and you dislike it. But it is possible that you dislike a thing that is good for you, and that you love a thing that is bad for you. But God knows and you know not." This verse does not say anything about when and why Muslims ought to go to war—for those answers scholars turned to other verses—but resolved for the vast majority of Muslim jurists that war is an aspect of human existence sanctioned and even willed by God. As such, its ethical-legal dimensions must be charted as an intrinsic part of Sharia.

In the 28 suras revealed in the Medinan period (from 622–32), the vocabulary of war enters the Quran directly and dramatically. The root *ḥ-r-b* appears five times with the meaning of armed conflict. The root *q-t-l* appears some 80 times with the clear meaning of fighting and killing in battle; and in at least ten instances, the root *j-h-d* is linked to *qitāl*, giving the concept of jihad a martial element that it seems to have lacked in the pre-Islamic period (Landau-Tasseron 2003: 36).

The Quran came to deal with—or at least touch upon—a number of subjects relating to war and peace that have legal import. These include:

1. the problem of war, that is, why war and other forms of violence exist among human beings; and the related theological question, how much is war an act of man or of God?

2. the moral status of war, that is, is war evil or good, and how are humans to discern the answer to this question—on the basis of reason or revelation? The broader concerns under which these issues are subsumed are the sanctity of life, the enormity of taking life wrongfully, and who bears responsibility for wrongs committed. A related topic is the moral status of Muslim martyrs, those who give their lives on the battlefield;

3. the legitimate grounds for war, that is, what are the just causes and proper goals of war, against both non-Muslims and other Muslims? Within this category should be included a number of verses exhorting Muslims to fight and not shirk from the burdens of war;

4. the legitimate means of war, under which are treated subtopics including (a) mobilization for war, (b) restrictions in time and place for fighting, (c) restrictions on damage to persons and property, (d) strategy and tactics, including when and how to advance on the enemy and when to retreat, (e) treatment of prisoners, and (f) grants of quarter to enemy soldiers;

5. the proper end of war, including diplomacy and the conclusion of treaties; and the division of booty.

These topics are often dealt with in the context of actual battles and parlays, including the battles of Badr, Uḥud, Ḥunayn, Tabūk, and the important treaty of Ḥudaybiyya. Muslim jurists read these verses as bearing legal significance beyond their historical context, adducing general directives in the Islamic law of war and peace.

The Medinan period spawned the Quranic verses on war as well as all instances of the Prophet's military activity—a total of 38 expeditions, including nine major battles (Ibn Hishām 1988, 4: 340–85; Guillaume 1990: 659–78). The biographical literature (*sīra*) devotes such a disproportionate amount of space and attention to the Prophet's martial activities during a roughly eight-year span out of the total 23 years of his prophethood that the plural of *sīra*, *siyar*, became virtually synonymous with *maghāzī* (military campaigns).

When looking to the sources to adduce principles of Islamic law, Muslim jurists had to deal with the often vague and sometimes seemingly contradictory directives of the Quranic verses. By and large they embraced the method of abrogation (*naskh*), that is, when two verses appear to give different rulings, the verse revealed earlier in time was held to be abrogated (*mansūkh*) by the verse revealed later (*nāsikh*). The basis of the juristic approach to war was that by the end of the Quranic revelation jihad no longer meant only a spiritual or metaphysical struggle, but also a physical struggle—war, if required—to defend the Muslim community and to spread the Islamic faith (al-Shāfiʿī 2002, 4: 218–22; Ibn Qayyim al-Jawziyya 1992, 3: 5–18, 71–89; Ibn Taymiyya 1992: 71; Peters 2005: 45).

Despite the abundance of material in the Quran and the Sunna dealing with war and peace, neither source is exhaustive. By the time the major legal works were compiled, the Muslim experience with war, diplomacy, and peace treaties was centuries old. Muslims now governed vast territories and complex societies completely removed from the Medinan and broader Hijazi milieu in which the Quran and Sunna developed. Faced with these realities, the classical jurists embraced custom in their jurisprudence—including that of non-Muslim peoples, albeit implicitly and with no formal acknowledgment—and precedents established by the first four caliphs, later rulers, and field commanders. Precedents established by ʿAlī ibn Abī Ṭālib were particularly determinative in Shiʿi jurisprudence, but given the important role he played in combating dissidents, his directives and actions also played a decisive role in Sunni jurisprudence on fighting rebels.

Finally, the jurists demonstrated a willingness to rely on reason or intuition, particularly in the realm of military necessity. The operative principle seems to have been that where no explicit directive could be found in the Quran or Sunna, Muslim rulers and military commanders were to be given wide latitude in achieving the triumph of Islam over its enemies.

Theory of World Order

The Prophet's biographer Ibn Isḥāq (d. 150/767) records that soon after arriving in Medina, the Prophet concluded an agreement among its three principal groups: the newly converted Muslims native to Medina (*anṣār*), the Muslim migrants from Mecca (*muhājirūn*), and some of the Jewish tribes resident in Medina. The covenant sought mainly to achieve three goals: to establish all the Muslims as one community (*umma*) regardless of tribal allegiances; to link the *umma*, the Jewish tribes, and other parties to the covenant into a single community in which Muḥammad would serve as the ultimate arbiter of disputes; and to bind all the parties in a mutual defense pact against all internal and external enemies (Ibn Hishām 1988, 2: 167–72; Guillaume 1990: 231–3). Each of these three goals is promoted in numerous Quranic verses from the Medinan period.

Together the Quran and Sunna establish some foundational principles that are reflected in the later juridical theory of world order, namely, that all Muslims are and ought to be one community, that the Islamic polity comprises both Muslims and non-Muslims, particularly the People of the Book, and that the supreme authority in this polity is and ought to be the Word of God as interpreted by His Prophet, which later came to be known as *sharīʿa*. It is important to emphasize that the covenant in Medina might have inspired the classical theory of world order, but the Muslim theorists might also have borrowed ideas of imperial rule from the Byzantines or Sasanids (see Donner 1991). Claims about the origins of the classical theory of world order remain speculative because no independent treatises on Islamic conceptions of international relations were composed. Instead, the jurists' views were embedded in their discussion of legal questions relating to war, peace, commerce, and other forms of contact between Muslims and non-Muslims.

At the heart of Islamic theory is the division of the world into different realms (lit. abodes; sg. *dār*), as depicted schematically in Figure 14.1, below. The three that received the most attention among jurists were the abode of Islam (*dār al-Islām*), the abode of war (*dār al-ḥarb*), and the abode of treaty (*dār al-ʿahd*). Even these three, however, did not receive detailed or consistent treatment.

The abode of Islam was generally understood by all legal schools as the territory over which Muslims held political sovereignty and where Islamic laws (*aḥkām al-Islām*) were applied (Ibn Qayyim al-Jawziyya 1994: 366). In its ideal form it was conceived as a single, unified abode of the Muslim community of believers, where Muslim faith, lives, property, and honor were safeguarded. It could comprise non-Muslim communities (*ahl al-dhimma*, dhimmis), whose lives, property, and religious autonomy were "protected" by the Islamic state, so long as they did not challenge Muslim sovereignty and paid the poll tax (*jizya*), as mentioned in Q 9:29, or the land tax (*kharāj*).

The abode of war was understood broadly as territories inhabited by infidels where Islamic law did not prevail.[2] According to the majority of jurists, it was the duty of Muslims as a collective and of the Muslim ruler (*imām*) in particular to wage jihad—through peaceful means if possible, through forcible means if necessary—to reduce the abode of war and expand the abode of Islam. An area of the abode of war could be incorporated through capitulation (*ṣulḥ*) or through conquest (*ʿanwa*). According to the Hanafi jurist al-Kāsānī (d. 587/1189), the scholars were all agreed that the establishment of Islamic law makes an abode of war an abode of Islam (1974, 7: 130).

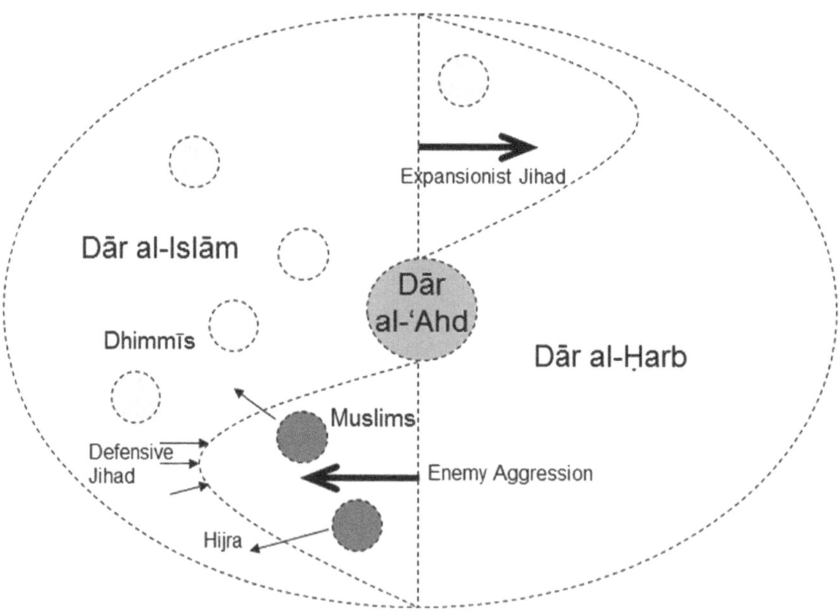

Figure 14.1 A representation of the classical jurists' theory of world order

2 The term *dār al-kufr* (abode of infidelity) was commonly interchanged with *dār al-ḥarb*.

However, the conditions under which a part of the latter becomes the former did cause some controversy among Hanafi jurists. Abū Ḥanīfa (d. 150/767), the eponym of the Hanafi school, held that three conditions had to be fulfilled: (1) enforcement of non-Islamic laws (*aḥkām al-kufr*), (2) contiguity with another territory of the abode of war, and (3) the absence of security for Muslims and dhimmis. His two leading disciples, Abū Yūsuf (d. 182/798) and Muḥammad al-Shaybānī (d. 189/804), argued that the enforcement of non-Islamic laws was sufficient. Al-Sarakhsī (d. ca. 490/1096) elaborates that for Abū Ḥanīfa the defining characteristic of the abode of war was the total domination of non-Muslims and the complete lack of security for Muslims and dhimmis, which he believed required all three conditions that he enumerated (al-Sarakhsi 1989, 10: 114; see also al-Kāsānī 1974, 7: 130–1). In other words, Abū Ḥanīfa was unwilling to surrender any of the abode of Islam so long as even a small possibility existed that the imposition of non-Muslim rule was temporary and reversible.

The abode of treaty (also called abode of peace, *dār al-ṣulḥ*) was a category posited mainly by Shafiʿi jurists, although with even less specificity than is the case with the other two abodes (al-Shāfiʿī 2002: 4: 258). One of the most detailed expositions is given by al-Māwardī (d. 450/1058) (1994: 243–5; Wahba 1996: 152–4), who categorizes territory seized by Muslims through jihad into three types: those acquired forcibly through conquest, their former owners having been killed, captured, or exiled; those acquired incidentally with the flight of their former owners in fear; and those acquired without force and whose owners are allowed to remain on their land through treaty. Al-Māwardī further divides the third category into two possible scenarios: one, that the land becomes the property of the Islamic state and is held as mortmain (*waqf*) within the abode of Islam. The original owners are permitted to remain on the land so long as they pay the land tax and—if they remain non-Muslims—the poll tax. Under such terms these non-Muslims are considered "treaty people" (*ahl ʿahd*); or two, the land remains the property of the original owners who pay the land tax to the Islamic state so long as they remain non-Muslims. They are free to sell or mortgage the land, including to a Muslim, in which case the land tax is no longer assessed. This land is not considered part of the abode of Islam, and the non-Muslims remaining on it pay no poll tax because they do not have dhimmi status. The land is considered part of the abode of treaty. Al-Māwardī notes that Abū Ḥanīfa did not agree—for him, the land had become part of the abode of Islam as a result of the treaty and its non-Muslim inhabitants dhimmis on whom the poll tax should be imposed.

Al-Māwardī also mentions disagreements among the jurists on the status of the abode of treaty should its inhabitants violate the treaty. Al-Shāfiʿī (d. 204/819) argued that if ownership of the land had been transferred to new owners, the land's status did not change; otherwise, the territory would revert to the abode of war. Abū Ḥanīfa held, in keeping with his views on the conditions under which the abode of Islam becomes the abode of war, that as long as a Muslim remained in the territory and Muslim territories separated this land from the abode of war, the territory remained part of the Islamic territory, and its unfaithful inhabitants should be treated as rebels. Abū Yūsuf and al-Shaybānī considered such territory to be the abode of war.

Grounds for War

Classical jurisprudence deals primarily with three types of war: defensive jihad to counter aggression from the abode of war into the abode of Islam; expansionist jihad to enlarge the abode of Islam by incorporating enemy territories into it; and state action to suppress rebels and renegade apostates.

Self-defense as a ground for war is amply supported in the sources. Perhaps because they considered it self-evident, the jurists devoted very little attention explicitly to it. All schools of law considered jihad in defense of Muslim faith, lives, and property to be an individual obligation (*farḍ ʿayn*) on all able-bodied, adult Muslims, removing the requirement that the slave receive the permission of his master, the wife the permission of her husband, and the son the permission of his parents. The obligation fell upon Muslims on the front line of the enemy attack as well as those behind them, who, if they could not participate in the fighting directly, must aid the defenders materially and morally (al-Kāsānī 1974, 7: 98). Defensive jihad included both actively repulsing an assault on Muslim lands as well as preemptively thwarting an impending attack (al-Qurṭubī 2006, 10: 223, commentary on Q 9:41).

Defensive jihad raised the prospect that some Muslims would be left stranded behind enemy lines as the frontiers of enemy territory pushed into the abode of Islam. Whether or not these Muslims could legitimately remain within the abode of war occupied a considerable amount of the jurists' attention. The majority counseled that, like the *hijra* of the Prophet and the earliest Muslims, such Muslims should migrate back to the abode of Islam at the earliest possible occasion (see the summary of debates in Abou El Fadl 1994). But, as we saw above, the jurists never defined with precision the characteristics of the Islamic and enemy abodes and disputed the conditions under which a territory of the first is transformed into the second. Controversies over the status of territory and the fate of Muslims under non-Muslim jurisdiction intensified as large Muslim populations were overrun by the Reconquista, the Crusades, and the Turkish and Mongol invasions.

The fourteenth-century Hanbali jurist Ibn Taymiyya dealt squarely with these concerns in a fatwa on the status of the northern Mesopotamian city of Mardin. Ruled by the Ilkhan Mongols but with its Muslim and Christian population intact, Mardin in Ibn Taymiyya's judgment had neither "the status of the abode of Islam in which are implemented the rules of Islam, such as the presence of a Muslim army, nor does it have the status of the abode of war, whose inhabitants are unbelievers. Instead, it is a third type [of domain]," a hybrid of the abode of Islam and of war. Muslims should not aid the enemy with either their person or property. They must avoid doing so by any means available, including evasion, equivocation, and artifice; if that was not possible, emigration was incumbent on them, as it was if they were unable to comply with their religious requirements. Muslims should not label those remaining in Mardin collectively as hypocrites; instead, "each shall be treated as he deserves and the one who departs from Islamic law (*sharīʿat al-Islām*) shall be fought as he deserves" (Ibn Taymiyya 1988, 4: 278; Michot 2006: 63–5).

Expansionist jihad is the focus of classical jurisprudence on war. The Maliki jurist Ibn Rushd (d. 595/1198) begins his comparative summary of legal rulings on jihad by stating that according to the overwhelming majority of jurists, jihad is a collective obligation (*farḍ kifāya*), not an individual one, based on Q 9:122 and 4:95,[3] and on the Prophet's example of always leaving some of his followers to defend Medina. It is incumbent upon free, adult, financially secure, and able-bodied males, and the performance of this duty by those eligible absolves the rest of the responsibility to perform it (Ibn Rushd 1995, 2: 454–5; Nyazee 1994, 1: 329–30).

Ibn Rushd mentions only one scholar, ʿAbd Allāh ibn al-Ḥasan (d. 144/762), as dissenting from the majority view that this type of jihad is a collective obligation, considering it voluntary (*taṭawwuʿ*) instead. Other writers mention other scholars, most prominently Ibn Shubruma (d. 144/761) and Sufyān al-Thawrī (d. 161/778), who considered jihad other than for defense to be voluntary, that is, a supererogatory (*mandūb*) act. Their arguments have not survived in the original, and even subsequent references to them are merely in passing and offer few details on their legal reasoning (Haykal 1993, 2: 891–903).

In a section titled "Why do we fight?" Ibn Rushd elaborates:

> The Muslim jurists agreed that the purpose of fighting the People of the Book, excluding the People of the Book from Quraysh and the Christian Arabs, is one of two things: it is either for their conversion to Islam or the payment of the poll tax. The

3 "And the believers should not all go out to fight ..." and "... God has preferred those who strive in the way of God with their wealth and their lives over those who sit [at home] by degree, yet to all God has promised good ..." respectively.

> payment of the poll tax is because of the words of the Exalted, "Fight against those who have been given the Scripture but believe not in God or the Last Day, and forbid not that which God and His Messenger have forbidden, and follow not the religion of truth, until they pay the *jizya*, having been subdued" (Q 9:29). They disagreed about the polytheists other than the People of the Book, whether poll tax is to be accepted from them. A group of jurists said that it is to be charged from all polytheists. This is Mālik's opinion. Another group exempted from this the Arab polytheists. Al-Shāfiʿī, Abū Thawr, and a group of jurists said that the poll tax is only to be imposed upon the People of the Book and the Magians (Ibn Rushd 1995, 2: 347–8; Nyazee 1994, 1: 464–5).

In other words, the majority held that jihad against the People of the Book (namely, Jews, Christians, and Sabeans) and the Magians (Zoroastrians) was incumbent on the Muslim community so long as they refused to accept the Islamic faith or to pay the poll tax, which entitled them to residence within the abode of Islam as dhimmis. This ruling was based primarily on Q 9:29, called the "*jizya* verse," believed to be one of the last verses revealed on the subject of jihad and thus considered to have abrogated earlier, more accommodating or tolerant verses.

According to the majority, the Arab polytheists were excluded from the option to become dhimmis upon payment of the poll tax because they were the objects of Q 9:5, the "verse of the sword":

> But when the forbidden months are past, then fight and slay the polytheists wherever you find them. Seize them, besiege them, and lie in wait for them using every stratagem. But if they repent, and establish regular prayers, and pay the alms tax, then open the way for them. For God is most forgiving, most merciful.

This verse also was considered to be among the last revelations received by the Prophet, and thus, according to al-Shāfiʿī and others, it abrogated all previous verses—a total of 124, more than any other Quranic verse (Powers 1988: 130–1)—dealing with the Arab polytheists. Accordingly, the only options available to the Arab polytheists were conversion or war. A second group of jurists, led by Mālik, did not consider Q 9:5 as abrogating earlier verses or the Prophetic tradition of accepting the poll tax from the polytheists. Because the majority held that Q 9:5 applied only to Arab polytheists, the verse's injunction had to all practical purposes lapsed by the time the jurists were commenting on it; no such group of non-Muslims remained in the Arabian peninsula (al-Ṭabarī 2001, 11: 303–46). Some exegetes, such as al-Rāzī, al-Qurṭubī, and Ibn Kathīr, asserted that the polytheists included apostates, and thus the verse continued to apply to any Muslim who recanted the faith until they repented, performed prayer (*ṣalāt*), and paid the alms tax (*zakāt*) (al-Rāzī 1981, 15: 233–4; al-Qurṭubī 2006, 10: 112–4; Ibn Kathīr 2000, 7: 148; see further discussion in Afsaruddin 2013: 276).

Expansionist jihad required a declaration of war, which entailed a formal call to accept Islam. This requirement was based on Q 17:15 ("We never punish until We have sent a Messenger") and on the hadith that whenever the Prophet dispatched an armed force, he would instruct its commander as follows:

> When you come to face your enemy, the polytheists, invite them to opt for three choices, and whichever of these they agree to, accept, and withhold the attack. Invite them to Islam, and if they agree, refrain from attacking them. Call on them, then, to move from their territory to the territory of the emigrants [i.e., Medina], and inform them that if they do this they shall have the rights granted to the emigrants. If they refuse to do this, and choose their own abode, let them know that their status will be that of the Muslim Bedouin. The law of God, which is applicable to the believers, would be applicable to them, and they would have no share in the booty or in the

> spoils, unless they fight along with the Muslims. If they, then, refuse, call on them to pay the *jizya*. If they agree, accept it from them and refrain from [fighting] them, but if they refuse seek support from God and fight them (Ibn Rushd 1995, 2: 342; Nyazee 1994, 1: 462).

Ibn Rushd notes controversy among the jurists on whether this hadith is still binding or whether it has been abrogated by other reports that the Prophet on occasion attacked without warning. Al-Ṭabarī (d. 310/922) presents a detailed commentary on this same controversy, focusing on the views of al-Shāfiʿī, who maintained that fighting a group that had not received the summons was not permissible. War against them could start only after they had been called to accept Islam if they were not People of the Book or, if they were, to accept Islam or pay the poll tax. Al-Shāfiʿī could not imagine that there were still peoples whom the invitation to convert to Islam had not reached unless there was "beyond the realm of the Byzantines, Turks, or Khazars a nation [of polytheists] of which we do not know." If Muslim armies kill persons who have not received the call, he avers, they are liable to pay the blood money (*diya*) due for wrongful deaths (al-Ṭabarī 1933: 3; Ibrahim 2007: 59–60).

The concept of expansionist jihad raised also the question of proper authority: who is authorized to call for such an effort, to mobilize, equip, and train the warriors, to issue the call to Islam or to dhimmi status that precedes hostilities, and, finally, to approve the cessation of hostilities? The Medinan covenant contains a vague clause that "None of them may go out [presumably from Medina] without Muḥammad's permission" (*wa-innahu lā yakhruju minhum aḥad illā bi-idhn Muḥammad*) (Ibn Hishām 1988, 2: 170). Some orientalist scholars, including Ibn Isḥāq's translator Alfred Guillaume (1990: 233), have glossed this passage as prohibiting anyone from going to war without Muḥammad's permission (Lecker 2004: 155–7), but it does not seem to have been understood this way by most Sunni jurists.

Following the Prophet's death, the caliph was naturally invested with primary responsibility for war and peace by Sunni theorists. In the ten caliphal duties listed by al-Māwardī (1994: 52; Wahba 1996: 16), his military functions loom large. The first three have to do with internal conflicts: specifically, he must defend the faith and suppress heretics and rebels, by force if necessary; prevent internal strife by enforcing the laws; and combat all threats within Islamic territory so that people can live and travel securely. The fifth duty relates to defensive jihad: the caliph must fortify the frontier districts in order to deter a potential aggressor. The sixth and seventh relate to expansionist jihad: he must fight those who were invited to Islam but refused, until they convert or become tributaries, having accepted the superiority of Islam over all other religions; and he must faithfully collect and distribute taxes and alms, including, presumably, *jizya* and *kharāj*.

All of the caliphal duties were theoretical rather than practical when al-Māwardī enumerated them—by his time the Abbasid caliph could not act independently of his ministers at court or the warlords who effectively controlled the empire. In view of this reality, al-Māwardī recognizes the authority of the caliph's minister (*wazīr*) and the governor (*amīr*) in military matters (1994: 62, 79–112; Wahba 1996: 23, 38–59). Most importantly, al-Māwardī invests the *amīr* who rules a border province adjacent to enemy territory with the authority to wage jihad "across the border and divide the spoils taken in action" (1994: 72; Wahba 1996: 32).

Al-Māwardī's discussion of authority in war captures the dilemmas that Sunni jurists faced on this topic and the pragmatism that informed their consensus. The majority of Sunni jurists reasoned that as a collective obligation of the Muslim community, expansionist jihad did not require the approval or even the presence of a caliph (Haykal 1993, 2: 871–4). The Shafiʿi jurist al-Nawawī (d. 675/1277) considered waging expansionist jihad without the authorization of the ruler or his deputy reprehensible (*makrūh*), but not forbidden (2005: 519).

In contrast, many of the earliest Twelver Shiʿi jurists required that expansionist jihad be waged only under the authority of the just Imam, namely, ʿAlī or one of his 11 successors, or in their absence, under the authority of their designated representative. Abū Jaʿfar al-Ṭūsī, known as Shaykh al-Ṭāʾifa (d. 460/1067), writes:

> For those of whom it is required, jihad has certain conditions. They are that there be a just (*ʿādil*) Imam who makes fighting permissible with his command. Jihad is not permissible when he is not apparent or when the Imam's representative is not present to govern the Muslims. Then, when he summons them to jihad, it is obligatory for them whenever it is undertaken. When the Imam is not apparent and when the Imam's representative is not present, it is not permissible to fight the enemy. Jihad with false (*jawr*) imams or with no Imam is wrong, and he who does it sins (1970: 290).

According to this view, the obligation of the Shiʿa to perform expansionist jihad had lapsed with the beginning of the Greater Occultation in 941 and will remain in abeyance until the return of the Hidden Imam. Twelver Imami jurists made clear that the individual obligation to fight in self-defense remained in place, even under a false Imam, for, as Muḥaqqiq al-Ḥillī (d. 726/1326) states, this type of war is not (true) jihad (Muḥaqqiq al-Ḥillī 1969, 1: 307).

The third broad category of legitimate war is state action against a host of domestic enemies, including apostates (*ahl al-ridda*), Muslim rebels (*ahl al-baghy*), and highwaymen and pirates (*muḥāribūn*). Sunni jurists generally considered these conflicts as being outside the technical meaning of jihad; al-Māwardī, for example, classifies them under "wars for the public welfare" (*ḥurūb al-maṣāliḥ*) (1994: 114; Wahba 1996: 60). Shiʿi jurists, however, routinely included wars against rebels, namely, all those who break from the just Imam, to be jihad (al-Ṭūsī 1970: 296–7; Muḥaqqiq al-Ḥillī 1969, 1: 310; Kohlberg 1976: 69–70).

The definition of apostasy (*ridda*) is a highly controversial topic in classical Islam (see Chapter 9, above), but jurists who wrote on war were clear that apostates should be fought. As al-Māwardī writes (1994: 115; Wahba 1996: 61), apostates who acquire cohesion and strength in a territory apart from the Muslims should first be admonished to return to Islam, and if they refuse, fought as any unbeliever would be fought. The precedence for this type of war were the so-called Ridda Wars (632–33) authorized by the first caliph, Abū Bakr, against various Arab tribes that broke from Medina by withholding *zakāt*, among other things.

Rebels were understood in both Sunni and Shiʿi jurisprudence as those who had departed from orthodoxy by embracing erroneous understandings of the faith and by refusing obedience to the rightful ruler, but they nevertheless remained Muslim. On the basis of ʿAlī ibn Abī Ṭālib's response to the Khariji insurgency (see Chapter 13, above), both Sunni and Shiʿi jurists held that if dissenters simply withdraw to an isolated area but do not commit an act of open hostility or disloyalty, they may not be fought. If they commit an act of open rebellion—by refusing to obey the ruler or by killing his agents, for example—they must first be admonished to desist according to the terms of Q 49:9 ("If two parties of believers fight, make peace between them"). If they refuse, they must be fought (as per the continuation of Q 49:9: "If one of them transgresses against the other, then fight the one that does until it returns to the command of God") (al-Māwardī 1994: 118–21; Wahba 1996: 64–5; al-Ṭūsī 1970: 297; Muḥaqqiq al-Ḥillī 1969, 1: 336).

Rebellion by dhimmis who break their covenant received attention from some jurists. Abū Ḥanīfa held that if dhimmis rebelled against the Islamic state and gained dominance in a territory, they would remain part of the abode of Islam so long as some Muslims remained in security among them. Once the Islamic state regained control over them, the rebellious dhimmis could not be enslaved. If, however, the rebellion resulted in death or insecurity for Muslims, in the establishment of non-Muslim laws, and the territory abutted the abode of war, the dhimmis should be treated as enemies of the abode of war. If Muslims regained control over them, all of them could be enslaved unless they agreed to resume their former status as *ahl al-dhimma* (Khadduri 1966: 218–9).

The Conduct of War

In one of the earliest verses on war, the Quran commands, "Fight those who fight against you, but do not transgress limits (*lā ta'tadū*), for God loves not the transgressors" (2:190). Although the verse is vague on whether "limits" refers to the grounds for war, its conduct, or both, from an early date jurists took the verse to mean that Muslims must observe restraints in how they fight wars (see, for example, al-Ṭabarī 2001, 3: 290–2; al-Qurṭubī 2006, 3: 237–42). Classical jurists dealt with the conduct of war in great detail, much more than with the grounds for war. We can organize their discussion around three broad questions: What type of harm may be inflicted upon different categories of people among the enemy? What types of weapons and tactics may be used against the enemy? What damage may be done to the enemy's property?

Ibn Rushd begins his discussion of what harm may be inflicted on the enemy by asserting that the jurists are agreed that all disbelievers, "men and women, old and young, the lowly and the elite," are subject to enslavement. The exception is monks, who, according to some jurists, are not to be enslaved or otherwise harmed if they remain isolated in their devotions (1995, 2: 332; Nyazee 1994, 1: 456). The jurists differed on who should not be killed. The majority held that women and children must be spared, based on a number of hadith, including one in which the Prophet, coming upon the body of a slain woman during a campaign, said, "She is not one who would have fought," before ordering his fighters not to kill women and children. As for males who should be spared, most jurists included the very old, peasants, the insane and otherwise infirm, and others who ordinarily do not take part in fighting, again on the basis of Prophetic hadith and instructions from the rightly guided caliphs. If any of these groups does engage in fighting the Muslim forces, however, adult males and females may be killed, according to the majority (Ibn Rushd 1995, 2: 336–7; Nyazee 1994, 1: 458; al-Ṭabarī 1933: 8–12; Ibrahim 2007: 67–72).

Ibn Rushd mentions that a minority of jurists—most notably al-Shāfi'ī, in his "most authentic opinion" (see al-Ṭabarī 1933: 11–12; Ibrahim 2007: 71–2 for varying reports on al-Shāfi'ī's views)—held that all adult unbelievers may be killed. Al-Māwardī is less ambiguous about whom al-Shāfi'ī meant: "If the women belong to a people without a scripture, such as atheists or idolators, and refuse to become Muslims, al-Shāfi'ī thinks they should be killed" (1994: 238; Wahba 1996: 149). The reason for the disagreement is the apparent conflict between the specific instructions given by the Prophet and the more general injunctions in the Quran and Sunna, such as Q 9:5, "Slay the polytheists wherever you find them" and the hadith, "I have been commanded to fight mankind (*nās*) until they say 'There is no god but God.'" Al-Shāfi'ī and others held that Q 9:5 abrogated earlier verses and that the general hadith overruled more specific ones. Therefore, the legal rationale (*'illa*) for sparing the life of an enemy is not capacity to fight but belief or disbelief in Islam (Ibn Rushd 1995, 2: 337–41; Nyazee 1994, 1: 458–60). Ibn Taymiyya asserts, however, that this position is incorrect, noting that even the minority who argue that all enemy persons may be killed nevertheless "make an exception for women and children since they constitute property for Muslims" (1992: 74–5; Peters 2005: 49).

With regard to adult, able-bodied enemy males, Ibn Rushd states that all Muslims agree that in war it is permitted to kill male combatant polytheists who have reached puberty. However, the fate of male prisoners did raise controversy. The reason for the dispute is the apparently contradictory Quranic pronouncements "It is not for a Prophet to have captives until he has made slaughter in the land" (8:67) and "So when you meet the disbelievers [in battle], strike their necks until you have inflicted slaughter on them, then secure their bonds and either [confer] favor afterwards or ransom [them] until war lays down its burdens" (47:4). The first verse seems to prohibit any policy but execution of prisoners, while the second seems to prohibit execution. Adding to the confusion were reports that the Prophet on some occasions ransomed prisoners and on other occasions executed them. The majority opinion of the jurists, according to Ibn Rushd, is that the ruler has the option of pardoning, executing, ransoming, enslaving, or imposing the *jizya* on prisoners. His decision should be governed by the best interests of the Muslims. A second group held that prisoners cannot be executed (Ibn Rushd 1995, 2: 332–4: Nyazee 1994, 1: 456–7).

The jurists unanimously agreed that a belligerent given quarter (*amān*) by Muslims cannot be harmed. Most agreed that any free adult Muslim male could grant quarter to a belligerent (or protection to a nonbelligerent visitor from the abode of war), but disagreed on whether it was valid when granted by a woman or slave without the ruler's approval (Ibn Rushd 1995, 2: 335–6; Nyazee 1994, 1: 457–8; al-Ṭabarī 1933: 25–30; Ibrahim 2007: 97–104).

As for weapons and military tactics, the jurists granted considerable leeway to Muslim forces in order to maximize their chances for victory. Muslim forces could ambush the enemy by night, lay siege to enemy strongholds, breach fortress walls using catapults, cut off the water supply, or flood the enemy, even if women and children were mixed with enemy fighters. Al-Māwardī writes: "If enemy troops shield themselves behind their women and children as they are being killed, killing the women and children should be avoided, unless killing [the fighters] is not possible without killing the women and children." If the enemy uses Muslim captives as human shields, al-Māwardī counsels Muslim soldiers not to fight if it requires killing the hostages (1994: 90–1; Wahba 1996: 45). The Hanafis disagreed; they permit Muslim fighters to continue the battle, aiming at the enemy and avoiding as much as possible the Muslim hostages. If some of the hostages are killed, however, the Muslim fighters are not liable because their death is unintentional. Abū Ḥanīfa appeals to military necessity to justify this position: Muslims could not wage war at all if they were prevented from attacking targets where noncombatants might be killed (Khadduri 1966: 100–2; more views on this controversy, al-Ṭabarī 1933: 4–8; Ibrahim 2007: 61–6).

Fire as a weapon raised particular difficulties for the jurists because the Prophet reportedly ordered: "Do not punish the creatures of God with the punishment of God." Ibn Rushd reports that Mālik did not allow deliberately burning the enemy or even attacking them with fire. The majority, however, permitted the use of incendiary devices to set enemy installations on fire, some unreservedly, others only if the enemy initiated the use of such weapons (Ibn Rushd 1995, 2: 339–40; Nyazee 1994, 1: 460). The Prophet's instruction seems to have been understood as proscribing only the targeted burning of individuals (al-Māwardī 1994: 110–1; Wahba 1996: 58).

With regard to damage to enemy property, there was considerable confusion about prevailing opinions. Ibn Rushd reports that Mālik permitted cutting down trees, picking fruit, and destroying inhabited buildings, but not slaughtering animals and burning date palms. Yet al-Ṭabarī reports that Mālik said: "I do not see any harm in burning palm trees and destroying what has been built in enemy territory." According to Ibn Rushd, al-Shāfiʿī said that "houses and trees may be set on fire if the enemy used them as fortresses, otherwise the destruction of houses and the cutting of trees is disapproved" while al-Ṭabarī records "whatever of the enemy has no soul, there is no harm if Muslims burn and destroy it by any means, because it does not feel pain" (Ibn Rushd 1995, 2: 340; Nyazee 1994, 1: 461; al-Ṭabarī 1933, 102–3, 106–7; Ibrahim 2007: 229, 235). Thus, both Mālik and al-Shāfiʿī distinguished between the enemy's landed property and their livestock. The former may be destroyed, they argued, based on reports that the Prophet on at least two occasions destroyed crops,[4] but there are no recorded instances of the Prophet's slaughter of animals in war, and thus most jurists were reluctant to sanction the killing of livestock.

The Hanafis tended to be the most permissive of large-scale destruction to the enemy's property. Enemy property seized as spoils of war should not be destroyed, they argued, because that would be averse to Muslim interests. However, if Muslim forces could not secure the territory, they had license to "burn their fortresses, cities, and churches, and destroy their palm trees and [other] trees and burn them. And whatever of their animals and cattle they acquire and cannot take out [to the abode of Islam], they should slaughter and burn them" (al-Ṭabarī 1933: 107; Ibrahim 2007: 236; see also Khadduri 1966: 98–9).

4 In 625 when he burned the date palms of the Banū Naḍīr during the siege against their stronghold (referenced in Q 59:5) and in 630 when he uprooted the grape vines of the Banū Thaqīf during the siege of Ṭāʾif.

The conduct of wars against rebels differed significantly from those against all other enemies. The main reason was that in spite of their rebellion against the head of state, the rebels remained Muslim. Therefore, the goal in fighting them was foremost to rehabilitate them speedily into the body politic. Al-Māwardī lists eight ways in which fighting rebels differs from fighting polytheists and renegade apostates, including: the aim is to deter them from further acts of rebellion, not to kill them; they may not be pursued during a rout; their injured and able-bodied prisoners may not be executed; their women and children may not be enslaved; and their homes and property may not be seized as spoils or destroyed (al-Māwardī 1994: 121–2; Wahba 1996: 65–7).

Cessation of Hostilities

A number of Quranic verses point to the cessation of hostilities. Two of the most direct are "Fight them until there is no more strife and religion is for God, but if they cease let there be no hostility except for the oppressors" (2:193) and: "But if they incline to peace, incline you to it as well, and place your trust in God" (8:61, known as the verse of peace). In addition, the Prophet's biography from the Medinan period contains numerous accounts of negotiations and agreements, of which the most significant by far was the treaty of Ḥudaybiyya concluded by the Prophet with his Quraysh opponents in 628.

The basic question for the jurists was whether these sanctions for stopping war short of total Muslim victory were still in force or had been abrogated by later Quranic verses and actions of the Prophet. If the former, a number of derivative questions arose, including what terms were acceptable and what kind of peace was permitted—a truce or something more. Ibn Rushd offers a brief and sketchy treatment of this topic, which he frames under the heading "The permission for truce (*muhādana*)." He divides jurists into two camps. The first permitted truces if the ruler deemed them in the interest (*maṣlaḥa*) of the Muslims. In this camp, he lists Mālik, Abū Ḥanīfa, and al-Shāfiʿī. The second group allowed truces only in case of necessity (*ḍarūra*), to avoid strife and calamity for the Muslims. The difference of opinion stemmed from the first camp's view that Q 8:61 (the verse of peace) restricted the general directives of Q 9:5 (the verse of the sword) and Q 9:29 (the verse of *jizya*), while the second group held that Q 8:61 was abrogated by Q 9:5 and Q 9:29 (Ibn Rushd 1995, 2: 345–6; Nyazee 1994, 1: 463–4).

The jurists opined as well on whether Muslims could negotiate a truce on the condition that they pay the enemy a tribute. All permitted some type of concession in cases of dire necessity. Abū Ḥanīfa and his disciples allowed a one-time payment but did not sanction payment by the Muslims of an annual tribute to the enemy, unless they were about to be defeated in their own territory. Al-Shāfiʿī allowed the payment of tribute only when the Muslims fear complete destruction at the hands of an overwhelmingly stronger foe.

As for the permissible duration of peace agreements, the clear presumption in the juristic literature is that they are permitted only for specified periods. Al-Ṭabarī states flatly: "They [Muslim jurists] agreed unanimously that concluding an agreement with polytheist idolators or peace with the People of the Book in which the laws of Muslims are not applicable to them forever is invalid if the Muslims have the power to war against them." Based on varying reports of the intended duration of the treaty of Ḥudaybiyya, the jurists gave maximum limits for truces ranging from three to ten years, frequently adding the advice that the ruler may and should nullify the truce before its term if he deems the Muslims able to resume the war. If he chooses to do so, he must give clear notice to the enemy that the truce has ended before launching an attack. Al-Shāfiʿī considered ten years the limit, but allowed the ruler to renew the treaty up to the time limit in the original agreement if the Muslims did not have the ability to resume hostilities. He also allowed agreements with no specified expiration, so long as the right of the ruler to nullify them was included, basing this ruling on the Prophet's open-ended agreement with the Jews of Khaybar in 629.

As a group, the Hanafis were perhaps the most receptive to the idea of an indefinite peace treaty. Abū Ḥanīfa left open the possibility that truces could be negotiated for periods longer than ten years. His disciple al-Kāsānī went furthest in approving treaties of no specified limit. Two things can nullify a treaty unlimited in its term, he writes: an explicit declaration to that effect by either party, or an implicit repudiation through some action by the non-Muslims, for example a group leaving its territory, entering the abode of Islam, and committing offenses there, all with the approval of its leader. If the agreement is violated without the leader's approval, the treaty remains in force for all but those who violated it (for all the above, al-Ṭabarī 1933: 14–20; Ibrahim 2007: 77–86; Ibn Rushd 1995, 2: 345–6; Nyazee 1994, 1: 463–4; al-Kāsānī 1974, 7: 109–10).

Conclusion

As noted at the beginning of this chapter, the Islamic laws of war and peace are today perhaps the most contested aspect of classical jurisprudence. Only personal status and family law, especially as they relate to women, elicit as much controversy.

Underlying the theory of world order outlined by classical jurists is the notion of the superiority of Islamic civilization, the abode of Islam (*dār al-Islām*), compared to all contemporaneous civilizations. Al-Kāsānī draws a simile between *dār al-Islām* and heaven and the abode of infidelity (*dār al-kufr*) and hell (1974, 7: 130–1). God has placed on Muslims collectively the duty to enlarge the earthly heaven by reducing the earthly hell through their utmost efforts. The expansionist jihad, by far the focus of the classical jurists' attention, emerges as a vehicle for imperialist enlargement of the Islamic state, a civilizing mission to disseminate the blessings of Islamic law and ultimately, it was hoped, Islamic faith. Muslim armies had to observe limits in the conduct of this civilizing mission, but as the jurists made clear, they also had to be given leeway to ensure their success.

Over the past two centuries Muslims have responded, broadly speaking, in three ways to the classical juridical rulings. One response has been to dismiss the jurists' views as either false to the Quran and Sunna or limited in scope to the jurists' historical time and place. For these Muslims, the classical legacy is, to put it bluntly, an embarrassment and has no relevance to modern Muslims. A second response is to pay homage to the work of these great scholars of Islamic law and to engage their work seriously, but in the end to limit severely its application in the modern age. A third response is to take the output of the classical jurists as still authoritative, requiring study, interpretation for modern needs, and implementation. A casual browsing of the Internet threads on jihad, many of them Salafist in orientation, reveals just how engrossed some Muslims are with the classical jurisprudence on war. In short, modern Muslims reject, marginalize, or reify the work of the early scholars, but none can afford to ignore it.

References

Abou El Fadl, Khaled. 1994. Islamic Law and Muslim Minorities: The Juristic Discourse on Muslim Minorities from the Second/Eighth to the Eleventh/Seventeenth Centuries. *Islamic Law and Society* 1(2): 141–87.

Afsaruddin, Asma. 2013. *Striving in the Path of God*: Jihād *and Martyrdom in Islamic Thought*. New York: Oxford University Press.

Donner, Fred M. 1991. The Sources of Islamic Conceptions of War. In *Just War and Jihad: Historical and Theoretical Perspectives on War and Peace in Western and Islamic Traditions*, ed. J. Kelsay and J.T. Johnson, pp. 31–70. New York: Greenwood.

Guillaume, Alfred, tr. 1990. *The Life of Muhammad: A Translation of* Sīrat rasūl Allāh. Karachi: Oxford University Press.

Haykal, Muḥammad Khayr. 1993. *Al-Jihād wa-l-qitāl fī l-siyāsa al-sharʿiyya*. Beirut: Dār al-Bayāriq.

Ibn Hishām, Abū Muḥammad ʿAbd al-Mālik. 1988. *Al-Sīra al-nabawiyya*. Al-Zarqāʾ, Jordan: Maktabat al-Manār.

Ibn Kathīr, Abū l-Fidāʾ Ismāʿīl. 2000. *Tafsīr al-Qurʾān al-ʿaẓīm*. Cairo: Muʾassasat Qurṭuba.

Ibn Qayyim al-Jawziyya, Muḥammad ibn Abī l-Bakr. 1992. *Zād al-maʿād*. Beirut: Dār al-Kutub al-ʿIlmiyya.

———. 1994. *Aḥkām ahl al-dhimma*. Beirut: Dār al-ʿIlm al-Malāyīn.

Ibn Rushd, Abū l-Walīd Muḥammad ibn Aḥmad. 1995. *Bidāyat al-mujtahid wa-nihāyat al-muqtaṣid*. Cairo: Maktabat Ibn Taymiyya.

Ibn Taymiyya, Aḥmad ibn ʿAbd al-Ḥalīm. 1988. *Al-Fatāwā al-kubrā*. Cairo: Dār al-Maʿrifa.

———. 1992. *Fiqh al-jihād*. Beirut: Dār al-Fikr al-ʿArabī.

Ibrahim, Yasir S. 2007. *Al-Ṭabarī's* Book of Jihād: *A Translation from the Original Arabic*. Lewiston, NY: Edwin Mellen Press.

al-Kāsānī, Abū Bakr ibn Masʿūd. 1974. *Badāʾiʿ al-ṣanāʾiʿ fī tartīb al-sharāʾiʿ*. 7 vols. Beirut: Dār al-Kitāb al-ʿArabī.

Khadduri, Majid, tr. 1966. *The Islamic Law of Nations: Shaybānī's Siyar*. Baltimore: Johns Hopkins University Press (Eng. trans. of al-Shaybānī, *Kitāb al-Aṣl, abwāb al-siyar fī arḍ al-ḥarb*).

Kohlberg, Etan. 1976. The Development of the Imami Shiʿi Doctrine of Jihad. *Zeitschrift der Deutschen Morgenländischen Gesellschaft* 126: 64–86.

Landau-Tasseron, Ella. 2003. Jihād. In *Encyclopaedia of the Qurʾān*, ed. J.D. McAuliffe. Vol. 3, pp. 35–43. Leiden: Brill.

Lecker, Michael. 2004. *The "Constitution of Medina": Muḥammad's First Legal Document*. Princeton: Darwin Press.

al-Māwardī, Abū l-Ḥasan. 1994. *Al-Aḥkām al-sulṭāniyya wa-l-wilāyāt al-dīniyya*. Beirut: Dār al-Kitāb al-ʿArabī.

Michot, Yahya. 2006. *Ibn Taymiyya: Muslims under Non-Muslim Rule*. Oxford: Interface.

Muḥaqqiq al-Ḥillī, Jaʿfar ibn al-Ḥasan. 1969. *Sharāʾiʿ al-islām fī masāʾil al-ḥalāl wa-l-ḥarām*. Najaf: Maṭbaʿat al-Ādāb.

al-Nawawī, Abū Zakariyyā Yaḥyā ibn Sharaf. 2005. *Minhāj al-ṭālibīn wa-ʿumdat al-muftīn*. Jidda: Dār al-Minhāj.

Nyazee, Imran Ahsan Khan. 1994. *The Distinguished Jurist's Primer*. Reading: Garnet (Eng. trans. of Ibn Rushd, *Bidāyat al-mujtahid wa-nihāyat al-muqtaṣid*).

Peters, Rudolph. 2005. *Jihad in Classical and Modern Islam*. 2nd ed. Princeton: Markus Wiener.

Powers, David S. 1988. The Exegetical Genre *nāsikh al-Qurʾān wa mansūkhuhu. In Approaches to the History of the Interpretation of the Qurʾan*, ed. A. Rippin, pp. 117–38. Oxford: Clarendon Press.

al-Qurṭubī, Abū ʿAbd Allāh Muḥammad. 2006. *Al-Jāmiʿ li-aḥkām al-Qurʾān*. Beirut: Muʾassasat al-Risāla.

al-Rāzī, Fakhr al-Dīn Muḥammad. 1981. *Tafsīr al-Rāzī*. Beirut: Dār al-Fikr.

al-Sarakhsī, Muḥammad ibn Aḥmad. 1989. *Kitāb al-Mabsūṭ*. Beirut: Dār al-Maʿrifa.

al-Shāfiʿī, Muḥammad ibn Idrīs. 2002. *al-Umm*. Beirut: Dār al-Kutub al-ʿIlmiyya.

al-Ṭabarī, Abū Jaʿfar. 1933. *Kitāb Ikhtilāf al-fuqahāʾ*. Leiden: E.J. Brill.

———. 2001. *Jāmiʿ al-bayān fī taʾwīl āy al-Qurʾān*. Cairo: Markaz al-Buḥūth wa-l-Dirasāt al-ʿArabiyya wa-l-Islāmiyya.

al-Ṭūsī, Abū Jaʿfar Muḥammad ibn al-Ḥasan. 1970. *Al-Nihāya fī mujarrad al-fiqh wa-l-fatāwā*. Beirut: Dār al-Kitāb al-ʿArabī.

Wahba, Wafaa H. 1996. *The Ordinances of Government*. Reading: Garnet (Eng. trans. of al-Māwardī, *al-Aḥkām al-sulṭāniyya*).

Part III
Islamic Law through the Prism of the Modern State

15 ASHGATE RESEARCH COMPANION

Sharia and the Colonial State

Léon Buskens

This chapter deals with the rupture in the Sharia law and order regime that took place in the Muslim colonies, in which local rulers and assistants played an important role as intermediaries in the making of the colonial legal modernity.[1] Although the national legal framework of the "mother countries" was often decisive for the shape Islamic law would take in the colonies, I will focus on a limited number of structural features in which the drastic changes in both the content and conceptualization of the Sharia manifested themselves, and which these different colonial regimes more or less shared.[2] The following issues will be treated: the relationship between the law and the political and economic framework; the ensuing "framing" of Sharia and customs in the overall structure of state law, its resulting legal pluralism, and the conceptualization of Islamic law; the application of Islamic law through transformed or new legal institutions such as a judicial hierarchy; the accompanying forms of writing and textualization on normativity; and the dialectical relationships between European modernity and its representatives and Islamic forms of reform and nationalism. All these developments resulted in a notion of colonial legal modernity and of colonial Sharia. The subsequent understanding of Sharia as "Islamic law" forms the basis of contemporary Islamic legal systems and underlies the focus on the relationship between theory and practice in the academic study of Islamic law.

In overviews of Islamic law the colonial era is primarily understood as the period of the major transformation of Sharia into its present, "modern" form. Works from the second half of the twentieth century suffer from a Weberian understanding of law combined with modernization theory, while more recent studies emphasize Muslim reformism as an active ingredient. In addition to general overviews, historians and anthropologists have published a considerable body of case studies on Islamic law and colonialism during recent years, in which two approaches dominate. On the one hand, legal sources are consulted in order to write social history (for example, Lydon 2007), which can be considered analogous to the use of court records for the social history of the late Ottoman empire, and, on the other hand, there is a preoccupation with issues of orientalism, an agenda set by Edward

---

Léon Buskens, Professor of Law and Culture in Muslim Societies, Leiden University, is the author of numerous chapters, including the recent "Sharia and National Law in Morocco" (in J.M. Otto, ed., *Sharia Incorporated*, Leiden 2010); "L'invention du droit musulman: Genèse et diffusion du positivisme juridique dans le contexte normatif islamique" (with B. Dupret, in F. Pouillon and J.C. Vatin, eds., *Après l'orientalisme*, Paris 2011); and "Le droit de la famille au Maroc" (in N. Bernard-Maugiron and B. Dupret, *Ordre public et droit musulman de la famille*, Brussels 2012), as well as *Islamitisch recht en familiebetrekkingen in Marokko* (1999). The author wishes to thank Arjan Post for assistance in collecting references; the late Mostapha Naji and Robert Rutten who helped in collecting and understanding the cultures of colonialism in Morocco and Indonesia; and Baudouin Dupret for fruitful cooperation.

1 For a general framework for the study of colonial law, see Benton 2002; Mommsen and de Moor 1992; and, specifically in a Muslim context, Asad 2003: 205–56. Schacht 1966 offers extensive references to earlier, often colonial, primary sources and studies.

2 As such this chapter can be read as a sequel to an earlier attempt to identify some structural features of medieval Sharia (Buskens 2007).

Said's seminal work. The literature on both Africa and South Asia is especially rich.[3] The study of the legal order as a social and political phenomenon in itself is more limited. A major exception is that of Brinkley Messick, whose *The Calligraphic State* (1993) examined the transformation of the legal system of Yemen in detail, while at the same time setting a research agenda for the wider study of modern Islamic legal systems. It is to Messick that we owe the felicitous expression "colonial Sharia."

A lacuna is the absence of a truly comparative study of the complex interplay between Sharia, customs, and state law in the different forms of colonial order.[4] Although scholars and policymakers from the colonizing European countries were in contact, or were one and the same, many different forms of colonial Sharia existed. In this chapter I tentatively offer some ideas for a future comparative study of similarities and differences, on the basis of published work and my own research in law in French and Spanish Morocco and Dutch Indonesia.[5]

Historical Context: Colonialism, the Nation State, and Modernity

At the end of the eighteenth and the beginning of the nineteenth centuries the relations between European countries and states in Asia and Africa changed profoundly. Starting with the British in India, Europeans were no longer satisfied with the existing trade relations, represented by the trading posts, and began actively colonizing and creating overseas territorial possessions. This fundamental transformation of the political and legal bonds, creating colonizers, colonized, and colonies, was guided by economic changes in Europe related to the industrial revolution and the search for new markets.

The new economic interests required stringent political control, which led to the introduction of the European nation state overseas as the framework for colonial administration. The model for legal relations between the mother countries and the new states—the colonies, protectorates, mandates—and between the rulers and their subjects, with its apparatus of civil servants, constituted a radical rupture with pre-existing state systems. Colonizers followed various models of governance, either incorporating the already existing rulers and elites in the new framework and having them governed by colonial civil servants (indirect rule), or replacing them and creating a new administrative system (direct rule). The imposition of the nation state and its accompanying colonial administration was justified by an ideology of a *mission civilisatrice* and the taking up of the "white man's burden." Foreign colonial rule would bring justice, progress, and prosperity through modernity, instead of despotism, backwardness, and poverty.

The model of the nation state implied a new conceptualization and practice of normativity. Which rules and norms would lead to prosperity and justice? No modern state was deemed possible without "law," nor was the imposition of modern law possible without a modern state. The law was not only a practical tool for administration, but also a lens to analyze indigenous society, and an ideology to justify colonial rule. The multiple functions raised practical questions: which norms (state law, Sharia, or customs) should be recognized, to whom should they apply and in what textual forms (codifications, compilations), and who (Europeans only or with local scholars and rulers) should be involved in the administration of justice?

The new legal culture was the outcome of political and cultural changes in Europe that we generally indicate with the term "modernity." The development of nation states, especially the actions of the

3 For volumes on colonial and post-colonial forms of Islamic law, see Jeppie et al. 2010; Maussen et al. 2011 (Africa); Sartori 2011; Cohn 1987, 1996 (South Asia); Sartori and Shahar 2012 (Central Asia).

4 Several partial comparative studies exist, viz., Powers 1989 (a study of French and British colonial policies on Muslim family endowments in Algeria and India); Hooker 1975 (compared the various approaches to religious and customary law in the colonial empires); Hussin 2007 (a case study of Malaysia); Yahaya 2012 (the legal position of Arab merchants in British Malaysia and Dutch Indonesia).

5 I owe the underlying method of "experimental comparison" to Blok 1978: 79–91.

French guided by Napoleon, and the rise of the middle class resulted in a new legal system in which codifications of norms were central. At about the same time related changes took place in other fields, such as the rise of orientalist scholarship and a secular approach to religion, which led to a surge of historical-critical Bible studies. The rising middle class, increasingly educated at university, sent civil servants and soldiers to the colonies, who brought with them these new understandings of law and religion as instruments to deal with the new world. Their scholarly background offered advantageous cultural models of knowledge, governance, and behavior to the local elites in the colonies in the guise of civilization and modernity.

The collaboration of Islamic scholars in the formation of colonial Sharia was of vital importance. They assisted the European scholars and administrators as informants, and later acted as judges and clerks in the newly created judiciary. The sons of the indigenous elites were schooled according to the European understanding of their culture, thereby internalizing the orientalist view, and they reproduced the colonial Sharia in their work as lawyers, judges, administrators, and scholars.

Although most of the population accepted colonial rule, if unwillingly, the political, legal, and cultural colonization was met with resistance by some—jihad was resorted to in a number of Muslim societies, for example in Algeria, Aceh, Morocco, and Nigeria (Bennison 2002; Peters 1979). The oppression of colonization led to Islam becoming a marker of political identity, which it had not been before (Hallaq 2009b: 158), and at the end of the nineteenth century the colonizers were greatly concerned about pan-Islamist plots aimed at overthrowing the existing international colonial order (Laffan 2003). Gradually, daily life underwent a profound change through administration, taxation, law, and education. The new culture contributed to ideals of nationalism and reformism; in fact, colonialism created its own opponents by making the colonized imagine new communities founded on new legal orders.

Nevertheless, the dichotomy between Westernization and local reception is misleading. Muslim scholars, civil servants, and politicians were active participants in the nineteenth- and twentieth-century transformation of Sharia into Islamic law (Buskens and Dupret 2011). Colonial modernity and Islamic reformism, in which renewed interest in *ijtihād* and thinking beyond the madhhab played an important role, worked together in the creation of a radical new understanding of Islamic normativity.

Knowledge: The Invention of "Islamic Law"

With the adoption of a colonial policy and the imposition of the modern state the colonizers faced the question of what law to apply. Did previous legal norms exist? Whom should they ask? Where to look for these norms? What to read? Trained in the emerging study of oriental cultures, European scholars were of help in the creation of a new legal system for the recently acquired territories.

In several cases colonizing powers sponsored the study of the pre-colonial state and society as a preparation for colonization, as the example of the *Mission scientifique du Maroc* led by Édouard Michaux-Bellaire (d. 1930) demonstrates. The British in India were the first to undertake a systematic study of Hindu and Islamic law. Scholars-cum-administrators such as William Jones (d. 1794) consulted local Hindu and Muslim scholars about important texts and began editing and translating them (Cohn 1996; Anderson 1999). A famous result of such endeavors is the English translation of what was to become a major reference work in the study of Hanafi law: the *Hedaya* (Hamilton 1791). The help of locals proved to be vital to access the texts, which were in manuscript and sometimes difficult to obtain, and to understand them, not only because the language was foreign, but also because the culture of scholarship in which they were rooted was entirely different from the world of the European grammar schools and the law faculties.

The different professional and social backgrounds of the Europeans in the colonies amassing knowledge of the overseas law—scholars, lawyers, administrators, merchants, and plantation owners—resulted in a mixture of both scholarly and normative perspectives. Questions of what the native law was were conflated with what the law should be. Three important themes were conspicuously present in their work: the image of disorder of the pre-colonial state; a preoccupation with the relationship between Islamic law and custom; and a conceptualization of Sharia.

Early scholars identified Sharia as the law governing the lives of the Muslim colonial subjects. They equated Islamic norms with the texts of the fiqh books rather than with the practices of the courts and other institutions. Soon "practical men" began to criticize this view, arguing that custom was much more important in informing principles in Muslim daily life than the rules of the scholarly treatises. Promoting custom had the additional benefit of being a means to control and subdue Islam as a subversive ideology, which fit with a widespread fear of Islam.

The study and promotion of custom as an alternative to Sharia became an important field of scholarship and action in the course of the nineteenth century (Kemper and Reinkowski 2005; for Russian colonial policy, Kemper 2005; for Italian colonial legal policy in Libya, Gazzini 2012). Two well-known examples are the study and description of customary law in Kabylia (Algeria) by Adolphe Hanoteau and Aristide Letourneux in 1872–73 (for a recent study, Scheele 2008) and the transformation of *adat* into *adatrecht* in Indonesia by C. van Vollenhoven and C. Snouck Hurgronje (Burns 2004). European scholars tended to understand Sharia and customs as mutually exclusive normative systems. The learned opinions of the muftis and the practice of the courts (*ʿamal* in Morocco; cf. Toledano 1981) of the pre-colonial Islamic legal system leaned toward accommodation without forsaking the primacy of the Sharia, but colonial rulers opted for an exclusive approach, privileging either Islamic law or customary law. The British in Northern Nigeria, for example, chose in 1900 to champion Sharia at the expense of custom, thereby imposing an Islamic legal system that had never existed before (Schacht 1966: 86–7; Peters 2009). The French, on the other hand, inspired by the examples of Kabylia and Indonesia, decided that the Berbers in Morocco should live according to their customary law (Lafuente 1999; Hoffman 2010).

The oppositional understanding of the relationship between Sharia and local custom resulted from Europeans viewing the norms existing in Muslim societies through the lens of their own legal tradition, thus equating normativity with law. This European approach to normativity made clarity of norms necessary, whereas the ambiguity of the Islamic legal system allowed for an accommodation of customs and flexibility in judicial practice. What resulted was an equation of Sharia with "Islamic law," an authoritative and unequivocally formulated set of binding rules to be imposed by the state, which did not fit the classical Islamic model of normativity. Snouck Hurgronje (d. 1936) protested strongly against this distortion. He stressed that Islamic legal notions such as Sharia and fiqh should not readily be translated with terms taken from European jurisprudence (*Recht*, *droit*, law), but his critique proved unsuccessful against the lawyers and politicians who invented "Islamic law" to cater to the needs of colonial societies, transforming fiqh into Islamic law and local custom into customary law. The foreign perspective sacrificed the flexibility and openness of the classical Islamic legal system—epitomized by the accumulation of commentaries glossing basic texts, the space left to custom in the name of public interest, the use of fatwas as a means to develop the norms, and the discretionary authority of judges—to the uniformity and predictability of legalism.

In the colonial conceptualizations of Islamic and customary law, a notion of modernity (Rabinow 1989) and a view of governance were implied. Islamic normativity could only be applied in a modern state in the form of Islamic "law." For the colonial administration, the ambiguity and flexibility of the classical tradition was unworkably complex. The functioning of the new polity was based on the codification of law and judicial review under control of a Ministry of Justice (Dresch and Skoda 2012).[6] The burning question of the relationship between theory and practice in Islamic law—or

6 In hindsight, we might side with Snouck Hurgronje and emphasize that pre-colonial Islamic notions of Sharia and European notions of law operated in different educational, interpretive, judicial, political, economic, cultural, and textual settings, and that thus the "positivization" of Sharia into Islamic law was a misunderstanding of how Islamic normativity had functioned.

between law and society—emerged during the colonial period as a direct result of normative debates about which law should apply to Muslim subjects. This phrasing was definitely colonial, with no counterpart in the existing Islamic discourse. When Islamic jurists discussed divergent practices, they did so in terms of *bid'a* ("innovation") or *'urf* ("custom"), neither of which might be in contradiction to Sharia and could therefore be tolerated in the public interest (*maṣlaḥa*).

The transformation of jurisprudence and custom into law created both the notion and the "problem" of the plurality of legal norms, which had not existed before. Decades after decolonization, this colonial doctrine was developed in the 1970s into the critical legal studies paradigm of "legal pluralism" which is still dominant in studies of law and society (cf. Buskens and Kommers 2002). The nineteenth-century issue that animated debates between men training civil servants in Islamic law in Delft and men involved on the ground in the colonizing of Indonesia is still echoed in academic discussions today, viz., the subtitle (*Theory, Practice, Transformations*) of a magisterial overview (Hallaq 2009a).

Thus, the scholarly and political debates led colonial governments to join Islamic and customary law into a system of state law modeled after the national law of the mother country. The mechanisms for this framework were the establishment of legal institutions, the appointment of judges and civil servants to administer justice and to control the administrators, and the creation of authoritative legal texts. Colonial Sharia became part of the national legal traditions of the colonizing states, both conceptually and substantively.

Colonial Legal Practice

Formal Foundations

The actual shape that the colonial legal order took depended partly on whether the colonized state was a colony, protectorate, mandate, or one of the several other political constructions that formalized the ties between it and the mother country. The different national traditions of governance and justice also played a role, with one of the main questions being whether to respect the local rulers and their rules, or to replace them by new structures and laws. Generally Britain preferred indirect rule, France often opted for direct rule, while the Dutch in Indonesia singled out certain areas, such as some of the sultanates in Central Java and later also in southwestern Sulawesi (Bone and Gowa), as self-governing areas (*zelfbesturende landschappen*), in which they left administration and justice to the "traditional" rulers (Bongenaar 2005).[7]

According to the terms of the protectorate treaty that the French concluded with the Moroccan sultan in 1912, his law would be respected, hence the *droit chérifien* became part of the Moroccan legal system in which the sultan promulgated all laws by decree (*dahir* in Moroccan Arabic). In contrast, a new legal system commonly known as *droit musulman algérien* was created in Algeria, in which Islamic judges applied Maliki rules, rooted in a newly created judicial hierarchy in which appeal played an important role. Legal decisions or precedents (*jurisprudence*) and French legal thinking (*doctrine*), developed by legal scholars such as Marcel Morand, became important factors (Collot 1987; Henry and Balique 1979; Christelow 1985).

The British implemented in India a Sharia court system that applied a hybrid law, ultimately leading to a body of law termed "Anglo-Muhammadan." Judges in these courts were trained in English law and applied common law principles of "justice, equity, and good conscience" to cases in which there were no explicit Islamic legal rulings. Only for a few specific domains, notably family law, was

7 This policy also left considerable space for the (re)invention of traditions, as Friedericy 1932, 1933 shows.

legislation inspired by Sharia enacted (Cohn 1987, 1996; Anderson 1999; Kugle 2001; Guinchi 2010). The corpus of case law was developed under supervision of the Privy Council based in London.

Both for Islamic law and for customary law systems, control of legal practice by European administrators was deemed necessary in order to guarantee a proper functioning of the indigenous system. The Europeans then transmitted their knowledge in manuals, for example for the reading and translating of judgments and other legal documents.

Pluralist Legal Orders

In contrast to the uniformity that characterized the post-Napoleonic legal systems of Europe, for the most part the colonial governments created pluralist legal orders, applying different rules for the various populations according to ethnic, racial, or religious criteria (Hooker 1975; Sartori and Shahar 2012). The crucial distinction between Europeans and "natives" were supplemented with further categories for Muslims, Jews, and Hindus, for "foreign orientals," such as Arabs, Chinese, and Japanese, or with distinctions between Arabs and Berbers. A new set of laws to deal with conflict of law (in Dutch *intergentiel recht*) governed the relations between members of these subcategories. These laws dealt with such questions as whether a member of one group could marry a member of another, and which law should apply to their marriage.[8] Further important areas of contact were commerce, property, and procedural rules and legal proof. These rules not only protected the colonists' interests in their possible conflicts with the natives, but also served to maintain social order.[9]

Another division that operated was the jurisdiction of the law. Criminal offences were generally submitted to European law, in accordance with colonial ideas about public order and general legal principles. Two notable exceptions to this were the application of Islamic penal law in India until 1861 and in Northern Nigeria, both part of the British empire (Peters 2009). For the regulation of land law several options existed, given the importance and sensitivity of the issue for both settlers and the local population, such that a mixed system in which titles were registered in accordance with European, Islamic, or customary law resulted. The family was of such little importance to colonial rule, as well as such a sensitive topic, that the authorities exercised little impact on the jurisdiction of Islamic law in this field, except in the above-mentioned case of mixed marriages.

Codification

After a territory had been pacified by the army, law was the tool par excellence to create social order. Several mechanisms existed for imposing rule of law: by decree of the ruler, transplanting laws from the mother country, creating new legislation, codifying Islamic law, and incorporating customs by recognizing these as customary law. Colonial civil servants translated the distinctions of ethnic or religious group and legal jurisdiction into different forms of legal texts, such as codifications, translations of officially recognized Islamic norms, and compilations of local custom as customary law.

Interesting questions arose in these processes, to which orientalists and European legal scholars were supposed to give answers. If new laws needed to be made, who should draft a proposal (often legal scholars in the metropolis), in which language (often in the language of the colonizers, with

8 Dutch law in Indonesia, for example, permitted mixed marriage—Dutch men with Muslim women—which occurred despite the social taboo on these unions, as the life of Snouck Hurgronje shows. On sexuality and the colonial order in Indonesia, see Stoler 2010.

9 In the 1879 De Lestaubière report to the *Conseil général du department d'Alger* on legal issues related to colonization and the transition from a military to a civil system, questions of property and transfer of property rights according to indigenous laws play an important role, as do the creation of a civil register and the levying of taxes on the natives. For land rights in colonial Algeria, see Ruedy 1967.

translations into "local languages" to be made afterwards), which sources should be used, and what should be the place of Islamic norms? European scholars were also asked to make drafts for codifying Islamic law (for example, David Santillana for Tunisia; Marcel Morand for Algeria) to replace the "confusing" and "ambiguous" fiqh treatises. In many cases colonial authorities refrained from actually promulgating these proposed codifications as positive law, for fear of creating too much upheaval.

There is no easy generalizing about colonial Sharia policies on account of the vast differences. Governments also enacted important changes during one and the same administration, as in India where the British replaced Islamic criminal law in 1861 with British law and then abolished rules adhering to customary law by promulgating the Shariat Act in 1937, whereby the Islamic law of personal status—covering marriage, divorce, inheritance, maintenance, custody, trusts, etc.—was applied to Muslims, another new course in the British project of Anglo-Muhammadan law. Often colonial styles that were developed in the main colony radiated to other areas. Algeria was an important model for the French, but in protectorate Morocco they experimented with an indirect approach to Islamic law and custom. In practice we see a mix of both direct and indirect approaches, combining legislation with the promotion of local customs.

Institutions

Alongside the imposition of new law, another important element of practice was the creation and reform of institutions. Ministries of Justice and of Religious Affairs and Endowments—or their precursors, such as Departments for Native Affairs—were responsible for the actual execution of the policy. Their exact formal status and questions as to whether the local ruler might have his own ministers and advisers depended again on the legal form colonization took.

The creation of a new, hierarchically structured judiciary constituted an important institutional reform. Colonial authorities considered the ability to revisit judicial decisions essential for the proper functioning of justice, and therefore the colonial system was constructed in opposition to the "authentic" Islamic system in which appeal did not exist. For British India and its system of Anglo-Muhammadan law, the Privy Council in London became the highest authority. The creation of the judiciary was related to the introduction of case law as source for positive law, an innovation rooted in European legal thinking, both continental and English, albeit with considerable doctrinal differences. Making judicial decisions into a source of law led to new textual resources, such as the publication of judgments in journals and their compilation in volumes and registers, requiring new archival practices—the keeping and storing of records went hand in hand with the acquisition of stationery and furniture. The material environment for Islamic law consisted of new court buildings, and judges and clerks sitting at new desks in new clothes.[10] These innovations and invented traditions were all part of an intellectual and material colonial modernity.

Other institutions were the appointment of Islamic witnesses to establish legal proof, of overseers of the religious endowments, and of inspectors of the markets and corporations. Again, depending on the colonial style, several of these institutions were presented as reformed and controlled versions of "original" Islamic institutions. The management of religious endowments was of considerable importance for the functioning of the colonial economy, which was founded in reliable access to real estate, and received corresponding scholarly and administrative attention (Powers 1989; Kogelmann 2005).

10 If not for space limitations, a rich iconography could accompany this article. Court buildings became important centers in the new colonial cities and were proudly reproduced on postcards to be sent to the metropolises in order to demonstrate civilizational progress. Another example is the official portrait of Louis Milliot dressed as a judge, serving as a frontispiece to his introduction to Islamic law (1953).

Other newly constructed professions in the colonies, such as lawyers, legal counselors, and notaries, were connected to the innovative institution of the law faculty, where the new science of Islamic law, as opposed to the traditional training in Islamic law in the madrasa system, was produced and reproduced. In the beginning young men went to study law in the mother countries, such as the sons of the Javanese elite who came to Leiden to study with Van Vollenhoven and Snouck Hurgronje. Later, the colonial authorities established institutes for legal higher learning in the colonies themselves, where the sons of colonists and of the local elites could be trained to administer the country (Vatin 1984).

Personnel

The new institutions required personnel with knowledge of the new laws and practices and willing to serve the new masters. Colonial Sharia marked the transition from ulema, who lived off the revenue of religious endowments, to civil servants and lawyers, who were either appointed by the government and received a salary from the state, or practiced independently. Part of the judiciary was recruited among Europeans with a law degree and occasionally some knowledge of Arabic and Islamic law. Local scholars were a vital link in the functioning of the legal systems and also served as judges, or they were employed as clerks, witnesses, translators, and assistants to the judges. Some were part of privileged Christian and Jewish minorities, who acted as intermediaries and informants. Through their involvement in the practice of colonial Sharia these local collaborators contributed greatly to the production of the orientalist conception of Islamic law, also by literally embodying it in their new legal worldview.

Whether Islamic scholars acted as independent judges or as assistants to the courts, legal practice was controlled by the colonial administration. The corps of civil servants and military officials who had been trained in the colonial vulgate of Islamic law as constructed by orientalists were present in all the colonies, making up the respective Bureaux Arabes, Affaires Indigènes, Native Affairs, or Binnenlands Bestuur. The precise organization and responsibilities varied according to the specific colonial legal system, but memoirs written by several of these officers offer precious information on their understanding and practice of Islamic law.

Texts

The practice of premodern Sharia was transformed into text, according to European model, by orientalists and lawyers who thus fundamentally altered the main focus of colonial Sharia. With printed manuals playing an important role in producing and reproducing knowledge of colonial Sharia, ultimately the new type of legal specialists with their "modern" consciousness could only exist because of print culture (Robinson 1993; Messick 1993). The primary model of these legal texts was the law code, and an important medium for official publication and for scholarly discussion was the journal. The state communicated its decisions and laws in an official gazette. Scholars published in learned journals and legal practitioners consulted professional periodicals for the latest developments in jurisprudence. Both types of legal journals often became embroiled in debates of proper legal policy, also in matters concerning Islamic and customary law (for Indonesia, see Dekker and van Katwijk 1993), and were thus essential for the creation of a legal public sphere. An example of the role a periodical played is the Egyptian *al-Manār*, published between 1898 and 1936, which was vital in the development of modernist Islamic thinking.

The good philological practice of consulting texts was a first step in the creation of colonial Sharia. Once orientalists had decided that Muslim norms were to be found in the fiqh texts, their task became to collect, edit, and translate these texts. One of the first translations was that of Charles Hamilton (1791), who explained the genesis of the work in his introduction (Preliminary Discourse). In order to dispense justice to the Muslim population in the subcontinent, an authoritative overview of Islamic law according to the ruling Hanafi school was needed. A compendium made by non-Muslims would lack such authority, so *al-Hidāya* by al-Marghīnānī (d. 593/1197) was chosen, whereupon "a number of the principal Mohammedan professors in Bengal" first made a translation of the Arabic original into Persian. This was done because "the Arabic [...] is known only among the learned, and the idiom of the Author is particularly close and obscure" (p. xliv). By having it be translated into Persian, the double advantage would be that "the ambiguities" could be elucidated and the judges would be better served as the language would be more familiar. Although Hamilton understood possible objections to the use of an intermediate version, he based his English translation on this Persian version. He also explained why he considered it necessary to use Arabic terms for technicalities instead of English.

In French colonial practice we see a similar quest for canonical texts. French scholars in the Maghrib identified *al-Mukhtaṣar* of Khalīl (d. 1365) as the main compendium of Maliki fiqh. A succession of French translations and studies followed, including an edition that was especially aimed at native judges and scholars (Bousquet 1956). An abridged English translation of a French version was made by the British military officer Fitz Herbert Ruxton (d. 1954, later lieutenant-general of Southern Nigeria) for use in Nigeria and published in 1916. A French translation by Léon Bercher with a parallel edition of the Arabic original of another canonical Maliki text, *al-Risāla* of al-Qayrawānī, originally published in Algiers in 1945, continues to be reprinted under the aegis of the Algerian government.

In Indonesia the first Dutch handbook of Islamic law for civil servants was an edition of a Malay text of a Shafiʿi handbook, published in 1844 by Albert Meursinge, who taught in Delft. His successor in Delft, Salomon Keijzer, combined his activities as a translator of Islamic legal texts with an outspoken plea for the application of "pure" Islamic law in Indonesia without giving in to custom, a line more or less followed by his successor, L.W.C. van den Berg. Both were lawyers by training (cf. Buskens 2006). Their handbooks were harshly critiqued by Snouck Hurgronje.

Another colonial genre were facsimiles of legal documents that were printed in volumes often accompanied by translations and notes. These collections were used in training administrators in drafting judgments, contracts, and written proof. These books also contained valuable lists of translated terms, which without the help of informants were difficult to understand (Zeys and Ould Sidi Saïd 1886).

Scholars also contributed directly by transforming customs they encountered into a legal framework whereby customary law was created. The most famous example is probably the above-mentioned codification of the customs of Berber-speaking Kabylia "according to the categories of the Napoleonic code" by the French military officer Hanoteau and the lawyer Letourneux in 1872–73. Their work became the model for French policy toward customary and Islamic law in the Maghrib, although later scholars also heavily criticized their views.

Much of all this compilation, translation, and editing was done for the purpose of applying Islamic and customary law in the form of legislation. With the codification of custom and legal norms, the transformation of Sharia into Islamic law became complete (Buskens 1993). Some of this reworking into law codes was made by Muslim scholars, viz., the Ottoman Mecelle (*Majallat al-aḥkām al-ʿadliyya*) of 1877. Snouck Hurgronje considered the codification of Sharia, as undertaken by the Ottoman government and by the French in the Maghrib, to be contrary to the essence of Islamic law (1923–27, 4,2: 259–66), but for his colleagues Santillana and Morand, who prepared these codifications, or the Egyptian Muḥammad Qadrī Pasha, who published a book of codified family law in 1875, this was apparently not so. Nor did the Egyptian jurist al-Sanhūrī (d. 1971) deem codification problematic. The debate whether codified law is Islamic law continues even today (Peters 2002; Layish 2004).

Another important new source of law were the judicial decisions. In contrast to the classical Islamic view that judicial decisions were relevant only to the case at hand, unlike fatwas of respected ulema, which, although non-binding, were generally applicable, the decisions of colonial-era higher courts that reviewed judgments were considered authoritative interpretations of the law, which judges should follow in future cases. Although doctrinally completely different, these collections of court decisions took the place of fatwa collections of the classical Islamic legal culture. A revealing example is Louis Milliot's research in Morocco (1918; cf. Toledano 1981) on the rulings governing Islamic endowments. He discovered a kind of proto-jurisprudence peculiar to the understanding of Maliki law in the Maghrib, especially in Morocco, the so-called *'amal* (judicial practice). He developed this understanding of "case law" further in the introduction to his four-volume compilation of decisions of the Islamic High Court. In this book, facsimiles of handwritten judgments and annotated French translations were printed on facing pages.

Conclusion

During the colonial period European scholars and administrators worked with local scholars and Islamic reformists to transform classical Islamic jurisprudence into a fixed body of Islamic law. This new Islamic law was constructed from various resources and took on many forms: legislation, court decisions, institutional and archival practices, teaching programs, and printed handbooks and studies, which were produced and reproduced by the plethora of personnel involved in the colonial enterprise—scholars, law professors, lawyers, judges in courts of appeal, clerks, translators, interpreters. The newly created colonial state enabled and required this transformation.

This transformation of Sharia into a new legal practice, one both institutional and textual, was rooted in a conceptualization of Sharia as law, on a normative-political as well as a scholarly level. At that time, scholarship in Islamic law was closely linked to policy-making and colonial administration, and was guided by the concerns of the "practical men." Maintaining law and order, dispensing justice to Muslims, and protecting the economic interests of the colonizers all required a correct understanding of indigenous Islamic forms of normativity.

These Western-style conceptualizations and practices of Islamic normativity tallied with important developments in Islamic reformist thinking and (proto-)nationalist political movements. It would be grossly misleading to understand the genesis of Islamic legal modernity as solely the result of external influences. In these processes of exchange and dialectics local collaborators played a considerable role, internalizing legalist-orientalist understandings of Sharia and combining these with Islamic renewal and political aspirations.

The intimate connection between knowledge production and colonial practice and the fusion of orientalist and Islamic perspectives make the critical analysis of colonial Sharia into an ideal test case for the orientalism debate. Knowledge production enabled the exercise of European power, as it in turn was enabled by colonial rule. Local collaborators interiorized the European perspective as a form of auto-orientalism. At the same time there were harsh critics of both the ethnocentric misconceptualization of Islamic normativity and colonial policy.

The critical analysis of the history of the concept of Islamic law leads to a radical epistemological critique of our contemporary scholarly study of Islamic law (Buskens and Dupret 2011). Both our concepts and tools, such as critical editions and textbooks, are deeply rooted in the colonial practice. In fact, the main question structuring the Western academic study of Islamic law—that of the relationship between theory and practice—arose in the middle of the nineteenth century as a direct result of debates among colonialists. But this analysis also leads to a critical understanding of contemporary Islamic thinking and activism. The views of both current legislators and Islamist activists calling for the reintroduction of Sharia and an Islamic state are also rooted in this specific form of Islamic modernity that originated during the colonial era, built on the foundations of Islamic law laid in the colonial era. Since the nineteenth century different sets of rulers have consistently modeled Sharia after law, and not law after Sharia.

Without a critical analysis of colonial Sharia, no understanding of contemporary Islamic law, or of our academic study of Sharia, is possible.

References

Anderson, Michael. 1999. Legal Scholarship and the Politics of Islam in British India. In *Perspectives on Islamic Law, Justice, and Society*, ed. R.S. Khare, pp. 65–91. Lanham, MD: Rowman and Littlefield.

Asad, Talal. 2003. *Formations of the Secular: Christianity, Islam, Modernity*. Stanford: Stanford University Press.

Bennison, Amira K. 2002. *Jihad and Its Interpretations in Pre-Colonial Morocco: State-Society Relations during the French Conquest of Algeria*. London and New York: RoutledgeCurzon.

Benton, Lauren A. 2002. *Law and Colonial Cultures: Legal Regimes in World History, 1400–1900*. Cambridge: Cambridge University Press.

Blok, Anton. 1978. *Antropologische perspectieven*. Muiderberg: Dick Coutinho.

Bongenaar, Karel E.M. 2005. *De ontwikkeling van het zelfbesturend landschap in Nederlandsch-Indië 1855–1942*. Zutphen: Walburg Pers.

Bousquet, Georges-Henri, tr. 1956. *Abrégé de la loi musulmane selon le rite de l'Imâm Mâlek*, vol. 1: *Le rituel*. Alger: Editions Algériennes en-Nahdha.

Burns, Peter. 2004. *The Leiden Legacy: Concepts of Law in Indonesia*. Leiden: KITLV Press.

Buskens, Léon. 1993. Islamic Commentaries and French Codes: The Confrontation and Accommodation of Two Forms of Textualization of Family Law in Morocco. In *The Politics of Ethnographic Reading and Writing: Confrontations of Western and Indigenous Views*, ed. H. Driessen, pp. 65–100. Saarbrücken: Breitenbach.

———, and Jean Kommers. 2002. The Delayed Reception of Colonial Studies about Adat Law and Islamic Law in Dutch Anthropology. In *Tales from Academia: History of Anthropology in the Netherlands*, ed. H. Vermeulen and J. Kommers. Vol. 2: 733–55. Saarbrücken: Verlag für Entwicklungspolitik Saarbrücken.

———. 2006. Twee negentiende eeuwse ontdekkers van het Islamitisch recht te Delft: Een begin van het debat over theorie en praktijk. In *Crossing Borders: Essays in European and Private International Law, Nationality Law and Islamic Law in Honour of Frans van der Velden*, ed. P. van der Grinten and T. Heukels, pp. 153–71. Deventer: Kluwer.

———. 2007. A Medieval Islamic Law? Some Thoughts on the Periodization of the History of Islamic Law. In *O Ye Gentlemen: Arabic Studies on Science and Literary Culture. In Honour of Remke Kruk*, ed. A. Vrolijk and J.P. Hogendijk, pp. 469–84. Leiden: Brill.

———, and Baudouin Dupret. 2011. L'invention du droit musulman: Genèse et diffusion du positivisme juridique dans le contexte normatif islamique. In *Après l'orientalisme: L'Orient créé par l'Orient*, ed. F. Pouillon and J.C. Vatin, pp. 71–92. Paris: Karthala.

Christelow, Allan. 1985. *Muslim Law Courts and the French Colonial State in Algeria*. Princeton: Princeton University Press.

Cohn, Bernard S. 1987. *An Anthropologist among the Historians and Other Essays*. Delhi: Oxford University Press.

———. 1996. *Colonialism and Its Forms of Knowledge: The British in India*. Princeton: Princeton University Press.

Collot, Claude. 1987. *Les institutions de l'Algérie durant la période coloniale (1830–1962)*. Paris: Editions du CNRS, and Alger: Office des Publications Universitaires.

De Lestaubière, F. 1879. *De la colonisation en Algérie*. Alger: Imprimerie Duclaux.

Dekker, Albert, and Hanneke van Katwijk. 1993. *Recht en rechtspraak in Nederlands-Indië*. Leiden: KITLV.

Dresch, Paul, and Hannah Skoda, eds. 2012. *Legalism. Anthropology and History*. Oxford: Oxford University Press.

Friedericy, Herman J. 1932. Ponre: Bijdrage tot de kennis van adat en adatrecht van Zuid-Celebes. *Bijdragen tot de Taal-, Land- en Volkenkunde* 89(1): 2–34.

———. 1933. De standen bij de Boegineezen en Makassaren. ’s-Gravenhage: n.p.

Gazzini, Claudia. 2012. When Jurisprudence Becomes Law: How Italian Colonial Judges in Libya Turned Islamic Law and Customary Practice into Binding Legal Precedent. *Journal of the Economic and Social History of the Orient* 55: 746–70.

Guinchi, Elisa. 2010. The Reinvention of Shari‘a under the British Raj: In Search of Authenticity and Certainty. *Journal of Asian Studies* 69(4): 1119 –42.

Hallaq, Wael B. 2009a. *Sharīʿa: Theory, Practice, Transformations*. Cambridge: Cambridge University Press.

———. 2009b. *An Introduction to Islamic Law*. Cambridge: Cambridge University Press.

Hamilton, Charles, tr. 1791. *The Hedaya, or Guide: A Commentary on the Mussulman Laws*. London: T. Bensley. 4 vols; abridged ed. in 1 vol. London: W.H Allen, 1870.

Hanoteau, Adolphe, and Aristide Letourneux. 1976. *La Kabylie et les coutumes kabyles*. 2 vols. Paris: Imprimerie Nationale.

Henry, Jean-Robert, and François Balique. 1979. *La doctrine coloniale du droit musulman algérien: Bibliographie systématique et introduction critique*. Paris: Editions du CNRS.

Hoffman, Katherine E. 2010. Berber Law by French Means: Customary Courts in the Moroccan Hinterlands, 1930–1956. *Comparative Studies in Society and History* 52(4): 851–80.

Hooker, M.B. 1975. *Legal Pluralism: An Introduction to Colonial and Neo-Colonial Laws*. Oxford: Clarendon Press.

Hussin, Iza. 2007. The Pursuit of the Perak Regalia: Islam, Law, and the Politics of Authority in the Colonial State. *Law and Social Inquiry* 32(3): 759–88.

Jeppie, Shamil, Ebrahim Moosa, and Richard Roberts, eds. 2010. *Muslim Family Law in Sub-Saharan Africa: Colonial Legacies and Post-Colonial Challenges*. Amsterdam: Amsterdam University Press.

Kemper, Michael. 2005. ‘Adat against Shari‘a: Russian Approaches toward Daghestani “Customary Law” in the 19th Century. *Ab Imperio* 3: 147–174. Repr. in *Religion et politique dans le Caucase post-soviétique: Les traditions réinventées à l’épreuve des influences extérieures*, ed. B. Balci and R. Motika, pp. 97–119. Paris: Maisonneuve Larose, 2007.

———, and Maurus Reinkowski, eds. 2005. *Rechtspluralismus in der Islamischen Welt: Gewohnheitsrecht zwischen Staat und Gesellschaft*. Berlin: Walter de Gruyter.

Kogelmann, Franz. 2005. Legal Regulation of Moroccan Habous under French Rule: Local Legal Practice vs. Islamic Law. In *Shattering Tradition: Custom, Law and the Individual in the Muslim Mediterranean*, ed. W. Dostal and W. Kraus, pp. 208–32. London: I.B. Tauris.

Kugle, Scott A. 2001. Framed, Blamed and Renamed: The Recasting of Islamic Jurisprudence in Colonial South Asia. *Modern Asian Studies* 35(2): 257–313.

Laffan, Michael F. 2003. *Islamic Nationhood and Colonial Indonesia: The Umma below the Winds*. London: RoutledgeCurzon.

Lafuente, Gilles. 1999. *La politique berbère de la France et le nationalisme marocain*. Paris: L’Harmattan.

Layish, Aharon. 2004. The Transformation of the Sharīʿa from Jurists’ Law to Statutory Law in the Contemporary Muslim World. *Die Welt des Islams* 44(1): 85–113.

Lydon, Ghislaine. 2007. Droit islamique et droits de la femme d’après les registres du Tribunal Musulman de Ndar (Saint-Louis du Sénégal). *Canadian Journal of African Studies/Revue Canadienne des Etudes Africaines* 41(2): 289–307.

Maussen, Marcel, Veit Bader, and Annelies Moors, eds. 2011. *Colonial and Post-Colonial Governance of Islam: Continuities and Ruptures*. Amsterdam: Amsterdam University Press.

Messick, Brinkley. 1993. *The Calligraphic State: Textual Domination and History in a Muslim Society*. Berkeley and Los Angeles: University of California Press.

Milliot, Louis. 1918. *Démembrements du habous: Menfaʿâ, gzâ, guelsâ, zînâ, istighrâq*. Paris: E. Leroux.

———. 1953. *Introduction à l'étude du droit musulman*. Paris: Recueil Sirey.
Mommsen, W.J., and J.A. de Moor, eds. 1992. *European Expansion and the Law: The Encounter of European and Indigenous Law in 19th- and 20th-Century Africa and Asia*. Oxford: Berg.
Peters, Rudolph. 1979. *Islam and Colonialism: The Doctrine of Jihad in Modern History*. The Hague: Mouton.
———. 2002. From Jurists' Law to Statute Law or What Happens when the Shariʿa is Codified. *Mediterranean Politics* 7(4): 82–95.
———. 2009. Sharīʿa and "Natural Justice": The Implementation of Islamic Criminal Law in British India and Colonial Nigeria. In *Islamica: Studies in Memory of Holger Preissler (1943–2006)*, ed. A. Christmann and J.-P. Hartung, pp. 127–49. Oxford: Oxford University Press.
Powers, David S. 1989. Orientalism, Colonialism, and Legal History: The Attack on Muslim Family Endowments in Algeria and India. *Comparative Studies in Society and History* 31(3): 535–71.
Rabinow, Paul. 1989. *French Modern: Norms and Forms of the Social Environment*. Cambridge, MA: MIT Press.
Robinson, Francis. 1993. Technology and Religious Change: Islam and the Impact of Print. *Modern Asian Studies* 27(1): 229–51.
Ruedy, John. 1967. *Land Policy in Colonial Algeria: The Origins of the Rural Public Domain*. Berkeley and Los Angeles: University of California Press.
Sartori, Paolo. 2011. The Birth of a Custom: Nomads, Sharīʿa Courts and Established Practices in the Tashkent Province, ca. 1868–1919. *Islamic Law and Society* 18(3–4): 293–326.
———, and Ido Shahar. 2012. Legal Pluralism in Muslim-Majority Colonies: Mapping the Terrain. *Journal of the Economic and Social History of the Orient* 55: 637–63.
Schacht, Joseph. 1966. *An Introduction to Islamic Law*. 2nd printing. Oxford: Clarendon.
Scheele, Judith. 2008. A Taste for Law: Rule-Making in Kabylia (Algeria). *Comparative Studies in Society and History* 50(4): 895–919.
Snouck Hurgronje, Christiaan. 1923–27. *Verspreide geschriften*. 6 vols. Bonn and Leipzig: K. Schroeder.
Stoler, Ann. 2010. *Carnal Knowledge and Imperial Power: Race and the Intimate in Colonial Rule*. Rev. ed. Berkeley: University of California Press.
Toledano, Henry. 1981. *Judicial Practice and Family Law in Morocco: The Chapter on Marriage from Sijilmāsī's* al-ʿAmal al-mutlaq. Boulder: Social Science Monographs.
Vatin, Jean-Claude. 1984. Exotisme et rationalité: A l'origine de l'enseignement du droit en Algérie (1879–1909). In *Connaissances du Maghreb: Sciences sociales et colonisation*, ed. J.-C. Vatin, pp. 161–83. Paris: Editions du CNRS.
Yahaya, Nurfadzilah. 2012. Courting Jurisdictions: Colonial Administration of Islamic Law Pertaining to Arabs in the British Straits Settlements and the Netherlands East Indies, 1860–1941. Unpubl. Ph.D. diss., Princeton University.
Zeys, E., and Mohammed Ould Sidi Saïd. 1886. *Recueil d'actes judiciaires arabes avec la traduction française et des notes juridiques*. Alger: Adolphe Jourdan; rev. ed. 1946.

Sharia and the Nation State

Maurits S. Berger

This chapter will discuss the effects of emerging Muslim nation states on the interpretations and practices of Sharia, and vice versa. It will show that since the late nineteenth century, legislative and judicial authority over Sharia has shifted from the religious scholars to the state, but from the late 1970s it was reclaimed by a third party, lay Muslims. In connection with these developments it will also be described how the authority of Sharia itself has evolved from a source of normativity in the private domain into a source of codification, and then into a driving force of morality in the public domain. Consequently, the rising status of Sharia within the framework of the nation state opened up a Pandora's box of interpretations, ranging from conservative to liberal. Generally speaking, these developments took place in three stages: codification as a modernization project, codification as an Islamization project, and Sharia as a source of public morality.

First Stage: Codification of Sharia as a Modernization Project

Modernization of Legal Systems

As described in Chapter 15, above, by the late nineteenth century, almost all Muslim-majority countries were colonized by European powers.[1] Their development into states with legislative, judicial, and governmental authority is therefore of relative recent date. The unification of the legal system took central stage in these endeavors (see seminal studies by Botiveau 1993; Brown 1997; Otto 2010). Until then, many Muslim nations had sets of parallel laws and legal systems that were specifically aimed at ethnic or religious communities, or at foreigners only. This long tradition of legal pluriformity was ruptured by the modern notion of one state for a single nation. All citizens of the new nation state were from then on to be subject to a single legal system that applied to all.

The overhaul of existing legal practices required simultaneous reforms in different segments of the legal system: the parallel court systems had to be unified in a single system of national courts; the parallel legal regulations and traditions had to be unified in a single system of national law; the new legal system had to be codified in laws; and a new profession of legal practitioners with knowledge of this new national legal system had to be developed (Peters 2002).

Maurits Berger is Professor of Islam in the Contemporary West and Sultan of Oman Chair for Oriental Studies at the University of Leiden. In addition to many encyclopedia and journal articles, book chapters, op-ed columns, and policy papers, he has published *Sharia and Public Policy in Islamic Law* (2005) and co-edited *Legal Pluralism in the Arab World* (1999).

1 The main exceptions were Iran and the Ottoman empire (later Turkey), the tribal areas of Afghanistan and several Gulf emirates.

To understand the impact of these reforms on Sharia, we must distinguish between the legal structure on the one hand, and the legal contents on the other, as implemented by the legal modernization projects in Muslim countries. The legal structure was almost entirely based on the—for the Muslim world—novel concept of *trias politica*, or division of powers, whereby laws were promulgated by the legislature, executed by the government, and used as the sole basis for adjudication by the courts. The extent to which this new system was compliant with Sharia or with the existing systems of governance and adjudication in Muslim-majority countries can be discussed and even disputed, but for the purpose of this chapter it suffices to say that these structures have been seldom disputed for lacking Islamic validity. Parliaments, elections, legislation, codification, constitutions, and courts—all of these modern novelties have been adopted by Muslim-majority countries, even by those countries that claim to be explicitly Islamic.

It is important to realize that the discussions on Sharia and on the nature of the Islamic state were—and still are—not about legal structures, but about legal content. When it came to the role of Sharia in the legal modernization projects, the question was therefore reduced to that of codification: what fields of national law will be governed by Sharia and, when it comes to the codification of that field, what elements of Sharia will be selected to make up the law?

Codifying Islamic Family Law

In the first stages of codification, that is, in the late nineteenth century, most Muslim-majority countries restricted the Sharia to the domain of family law. Exceptions are the Ottoman empire, which also codified a civil law based on Sharia (the Mecelle), and most of the Gulf emirates and kingdoms which did not participate in the modernization project until much later and retained their legal system based on Sharia and customary law. Within the domain of family law, however, Muslim countries showed a great variety in their selection of rules that were to be codified. The following two practices can be discerned.

In some countries—such as British India (officially under British rule in 1858) and French North Africa, in particular Algeria (annexed in 1834)—the colonial powers exerted a considerable degree of influence on the modernization project and claimed these territories to be part of their national judiciary, with English and French judges respectively dominating the local courts. As a result, a hybrid system emerged with an amalgam of local interpretations of Sharia law with English law (Anderson 1993; Fyzee 1963; Hooker 1983; Horowitz 1994), and with French law (Henry and Balique 1979; Weil 2003).

In other countries, however—such as Egypt, Iran, and the realm of the Ottoman empire—indigenous initiatives led to codifications of Islamic family law. Later, in particular after the Second World War when most colonies had gained their independence, similar codifications were also promulgated in other Muslim countries. These national codifications are all based on Sharia, but show a great variety in their selection and interpretations of Sharia rules to be codified. This selection and reinterpretation constituted in itself a new development in the scholarship of Sharia. Before the unification and codification projects, Sharia scholarship was divided among schools of law (sg. *madhhab*; see further Chapter 4, above) that proposed different interpretations of the revelatory sources. The Islamic legal system allowed for difference of opinion among legal scholars and for local customs to be taken into account on a case-by-case basis. With the drafting of national family laws, this legal flexibility had to be abandoned. To compensate for this, the legislators allowed themselves a freedom that was new in Sharia scholarship: arguing that all law schools were equally valid, they freely selected the rules of their choice from among the law schools (a process called *takhayyur*) and even combined the rules of different law schools (a process called *talfiq*) (Coulson 1964: 197–201; Hallaq 2009: 448–9). In some cases the legislature did not restrict itself to the four Sunni law schools, but also made use of the Shiʿi ones (as in Iraqi inheritance law, cf. Coulson 1971). As a result, the legislators had more leverage in composing their ideal Islamic personal status law.

This process became prominent in the case of women's rights under Sharia family law. Most legislators in the early twentieth century, and later in the 1950s and 1960s, were very keen on improving the position of the woman in family law. In the drafting of their national personal status laws they therefore chose rules among the many law schools that served this aim best; for instance, the Maliki school allowed women certain grounds for divorce without the consent of her husband, the Hanafi school allowed a woman to marry without a guardian's consent, the Hanbali school allowed for stipulations and conditions in the marriage contract. Another way they went about to improve the legal position of women in family law was to make changes in the laws of procedure, a field of law that is little covered in the Sharia and therefore provided opportunities for the legislator for change. For instance, although the Quranic right given to the man in the cases of unilateral divorce (*talāq*) and polygamy was not contested, it could be restricted and even modified by procedural requirements.

A Shift in the Monopoly on Sharia

The modernization project was detrimental to the ulema, the body of religious scholars (Faghfoory 1993; Green 1980; Zaman 2002). For centuries they had held a monopoly on the interpretation of Sharia. Their scholarship was of such complexity that few judges or rulers ventured their own interpretations, and a system had come into existence whereby a ruler or judge would consult a religious scholar when confronted with a question that required the Sharia viewpoint. The opinions of these scholars were often issued in writing as a fatwa, and would become part of the court ruling.

The process of legal modernization undermined this monopoly on Sharia in two distinctive ways (cf. Layish 2004). First, the monopoly of interpreting Sharia was transferred to the legislature. Parliament, and not the religious establishment of ulema, decided what was to be codified as Sharia for the country. In doing so they might consult with religious scholars—and they often did—but the ultimate power of selecting and interpreting Sharia rules was exclusively consigned to the legislature. Second, the monopoly on issuing opinions on Sharia was transferred to the judiciary. Since the complexities of Sharia scholarship were replaced by a relatively simple codified set of rules, judges no longer needed to seek counsel from religious scholars. Moreover, applying a codified law in the modern sense required different professional skills than applying the rules of Sharia as was practiced by religious scholarship—skills in which a new professional class of lawyers and judges were trained at newly established faculties of law, where the study of Sharia was limited to family law and an introduction to the basics of Sharia (Botiveau 1993; Cardinal 2005; Oba 2008).

Codified Sharia, therefore, can be considered a revolutionary phase in the history of Sharia. Not only was its interpretation and application transferred to others than those who had traditionally been in charge of it for centuries, the approach to Sharia changed from that of religious legal scholarship to that of modern law. Khaled Abou El Fadl laments this development (2001: 268), arguing that,

> if Islamic jurisprudence is about a methodology for a reflective life that searches for the Divine, and about a process of weighing and balancing the core values of *Shari'ah* in pursuit of a moral life, then I think one would have to concede that it has disintegrated and disappeared in the last three centuries, but particularly in the second half of the twentieth century.

In a similar vein, Wael Hallaq has argued (2004: 24) that the introduction of this new legal system over a century ago heralded "the demise" of Sharia by a strategy of "demolish and replace." I would argue to the contrary, however, that the replacement of traditional institutions for modern ones has created new channels and means for the Sharia to be resuscitated—perhaps not in ways anticipated or hoped for, but Sharia was definitely given a new life, as will be seen in the next section.

Second Stage: Codification as an Islamization Project

When scholars were predicting that the Sharia would be subsumed by secular modern legal systems and ultimately quietly disappear (Anderson 1960; Coulson 1964: 222), the Sharia began an unexpected rebirth. Starting in the 1970s, proponents of a resurgent Islam increased the call for the reinstatement of Sharia to the extent that Muslim governments thought it prudent (or necessary, depending on the political-religious affiliation of the government) to take further legislative initiatives regarding Sharia. Only Turkey (Starr 1992) set aside all Islamic regulations and opted for a legal system that was entirely secular in content; Tunisia was close behind but did not quite go the distance, keeping some Sharia rules—for instance, with regard to inheritance—in its personal status code.

The Sharia initiatives undertaken by many Muslim-majority countries comprised a variety of fields of law, of which constitutional, criminal, and family law were the most important. These legislative initiatives will be set out in brief below.

Open Norms in Constitutional and International Law

Since the 1970s, several Muslim countries have made constitutional amendments so as to introduce Sharia as a source of legislation (see for country studies, Abiad 2008; Otto 2010). As is typical of modern-day lawyers, the exact wording of these amendments becomes very important in this respect. In Syria, the constitution demands that legislation must comply with the fiqh, while the Iranian constitution requires that all legislation be based on "Islamic criteria," and the Pakistani constitution of 1985 refers to "Qur'ān and the Sunnah." Other constitutions refer explicitly to "Islamic Sharia" as source of legislation, whereby a differentiation can be made between constitutions that mention Sharia among other sources of legislation, such as customary law (Sudan), or constitutions that mention Sharia as "a" source of legislation (Bahrain, Iraq, the United Arab Emirates, and Kuwait), or as "the" (only) source of legislation (Egypt, Yemen). Further, there is a distinct difference between the requirement that legislation should have Sharia as either a source or the source on the one hand, and legislation that should "comply with" (Pakistan) or "not contradict" (Afghanistan) Sharia on the other hand. The interpretation of these modalities can differ greatly, as will be seen below in the discussion of the role of the judiciary.

An interesting aspect of these constitutional stipulations is that Sharia is nowhere defined; neither as to scope—what fields of law it encompasses—nor as to the interpretation or school of law that is applicable. The wealth of Islamic legal scholarship allows for many interpretations, and Muslim states had already made their choices from this legacy when drafting their Muslim family laws, as we have seen above. But now Sharia was reintroduced not as a specific law but as an open norm, leaving the possibility for multiple interpretations. This phenomenon is also encountered in the reservations that many Muslim states made to international human rights treaties (Abiad 2008; Otto 2010). Often such reservations refer to "Islam," "Islamic Sharia," or "Islamic law," without any further specification.[2]

Implementation of Islamic Criminal Law

In addition to the constitutional pledge to promulgate all future laws in accordance with Sharia, some Muslim-majority states also introduced new laws that were considered typical of Sharia. The most prominent and notorious example is that of Islamic criminal law (Peters 2005). It must be noted that Islamic criminal law is not a full legal system or law, but pertains to several specific crimes and their punishments (*ḥudūd*; see further Chapter 12, above), with limited rules of procedure or evidence. Countries

2 See for these reservations and their exact wording, the United Nations Treaty Collection, at http://treaties.un.org/Pages/Treaties.aspx?id=4&subid=A&lang=en.

that introduced Islamic criminal law merely added this confined set of rules to the already existing secular criminal code. As a result, for example, a thief could be absolved from punishment under the Islamic regulation (where the rules of evidence are quite strict), but still be found guilty under the criminal code. A country like Iran, on the other hand, drafted an entire criminal code on the basis of Sharia, often stretching the definitions of the *ḥudūd* crimes or developing new "Islamic" crimes (Peters 2005: 232–7; Otto 2010: chap. 8).

Islamic criminal law already existed in several Gulf states where it had never been abrogated. It was reintroduced, albeit in a codified form, first in Libya (1972), followed by Pakistan (1979), Iran (1982, revised in 1996), Sudan (1983, revised in 1991), the Malaysian state of Kelatan (1993), northern Nigeria (2000–1), and Brunei (2014) (see country studies in Otto 2010; Peters 2005; and see Chapter 17, below). The abuses and misuses of these systems have been widely commented upon, so I will limit myself to two observations. First, the implementation of these laws is often subject to political motives as "a symbol for the Islamicity of a regime and its steadfastness against Western pressures" (Peters 2005: 269). Second, most of these criminal laws are criticized by Muslim scholars for not adhering to the conditions set by Islamic legal scholarship and, as will be further discussed below, were often in the hands of a judiciary that was not well trained in these matters.

More Reforms in Family Law

An unexpected development was that Sharia could be put to use in achieving an advantage to women. Throughout the twentieth century Muslim feminist movements had continuously fought for improvement of the position of women in family law, but had done so mostly with a secular legal argumentation. Both their legal reasoning and the resulting legal amendments were considered anathema to what religious forces considered an important bastion of Sharia. The feminist movements then changed their strategy and used Islamic reasoning and rules to reach the same goals—and were much more successful (Künkler 2004; Singerman 2005).[3]

As a result, several personal status laws in Muslim countries have undergone changes—all on the basis of Islamic arguments—that have considerably improved women's rights, in particular her autonomous right of divorce: Morocco has introduced "discord"(*shiqāq*) as a reason for divorce; Egypt allows the wife to divorce without consent by the judge or her husband if she returns the bride-gift, *mahr*; Iran obliges the husband who divorces his wife to pay her "working wages" for the year she spent as a housewife (Otto 2010: chaps. 2, 3, 8).

New and Successful: Financial Law

Islamic finance has gained enormous popularity since the 1970s (see further Chapter 18, below). Its development and practice have been restricted mostly to the private domain, however, with banks and financial institutions deciding for a variety of reasons to strictly adhere to Islamic tenets when conducting business. Few nation states have codified these tenets in their national laws. Pakistan did so in 1979, followed by Iran and Sudan in 1983, but in all three cases the Islamic banking system was introduced half-heartedly, or with enough loopholes to remain functioning within the international financial market (Amuzegar 1993; Kuran 2004; Al-Suwaidi 1994).

An aspect of financial law that has gained much attention is *zakāt*, the alms as a percentage of one's income that every Muslim is obliged to pay as one of the five pillars of Islam (Zysow 2002). Islamic economists believe that it is a very powerful instrument for bringing an economy in line with

3 Diane Singerman speaks of a "broader international movement" within the Muslim world that uses this strategy (Singerman 2005: 165ff.).

the principle of equality (see for a discussion, Kuran 1989). This tax was easier to introduce than an interest-free banking system, and several countries have done so: Saudi Arabia (1951), Libya (1971), Yemen (1975), Pakistan (1980), Sudan (1984), and several states in Malaysia.

The Roles of the Legislature and Judiciary

The striking aspect of the call for Islamization of the national laws is that it was done within the framework of a non-Islamic legislative and judicial system. In other words, the structure of the legal system was never questioned as to its Islamic nature, but all attention focused on its content, the law. Even conservative Islamic activists hardly ever called for an abrogation of the legislative, judiciary, parliamentary, or entire state system; they merely called for Sharia law. How, then, did the two main actors of law, the judiciary and the legislature, respond to this development?

It was mentioned above that the judiciary had taken over the traditional role of the ulema in interpreting the Sharia for codification purposes. The judiciary was entirely modeled after and trained in accordance with modern concepts of law, and it took the codified Sharia—which was mostly limited to family law—in its legal stride. However, with the growing number of codifications of rules, and the increased number of challenges by Islamist lawyers of existing laws as being contrary to Sharia, the role of the judiciary has become crucial in the implementation of codified Sharia.

In Egypt and Pakistan, the constitutional courts have demonstrated a remarkable knowledge of Islamic jurisprudence in connection with an equally remarkable independence and tenacity in upholding an interpretation of Sharia that one might call liberal. In the case of Pakistan, several Islamic criminal laws have been dismissed or muted on the grounds that they were not consistent with "Qur'ān and Sunnah" as required by the constitution (Mehdi 1994; Wasti 2005). In Egypt, the court's jurisprudence holds that the state is free to make its own interpretation (*ijtihād*) of what is to be codified unless it pertains to those rules that are considered immutable (mostly rules of religious ritual) (Lombardi and Brown 2006). An example of such a ruling was the case of the veil (*niqāb*) at universities: Egyptian's Constitutional Court ruled that since there were no "fixed and immutable" rules in the Sharia requiring such a garment, the Egyptian legislature was free to ban it (Bälz 1999). The courts were much less liberal, on the other hand, in the issue of apostasy: the Pakistani Constitutional Court has been heavily criticized for gradually caving in to fundamentalist voices with regard to the issue of apostasy (Mahmud 1995), while the same appears to be the case for the Egyptian Court of Cassation (Berger 2003); I will return to this particular issue below.

Opposed to these few—and mostly higher—courts are the multitude of lower courts with judges whose legal training is often deficient. Examples are the abuse or misinterpretation of Islamic criminal laws by lower courts in Pakistan that indict rape victims on the charge of illicit sex (*zinā*)—since Islamic evidence law demands either four witnesses to the act or a confession, the lodging of a complaint by a rape victim is considered a confession of fornication (Quraishi 1997). Verdicts with similar interpretations have been issued by lower Nigerian courts regarding pregnancy out of wedlock. These cases are often overturned by higher courts, but until that happens—mostly a lengthy process—the woman remains incarcerated. Such practices are not due entirely to the law itself, but also to its faulty application by incompetent judges (Peters 2003). In Egypt the poor quality of the legal education in general is blamed for giving leeway to Islamist tendencies among the judiciary (Moustafa 2010). On the other hand, the need to reintroduce more solid Islamic legal training in the otherwise secular law faculties has been advocated for countries such as Nigeria (Oba 2008), Malaysia (Mahmod and Kamal 2006), and Indonesia (Juwana 2006).

From the preceding paragraphs we may observe that there is no straightforward method of "implementing" Sharia. There does not appear to be a tendency to refer to a madhhab, as took place prior to the 1960s, but rather a preference to go directly to the sources of Quran and Sunna. Moreover, we can discern a variety of ways in which the legislatures of modern Muslim nation states apply Sharia: it can be adopted, adapted, or otherwise considered not violated.

Sharia rules can be adopted in full in the sense that they are transplanted into the national legal system. This has been in particular the case with family law and criminal law. Insofar as changes are made, care is taken by legislators as well as judges to make use of principles and methods developed by Islamic legal scholarship.

Sharia rules can also be adapted, meaning that rules and concepts of Sharia are combined with modern notions. Examples are constitutional law—the Islamic state—and Islamic finance. Both fields of law are underdeveloped in Sharia, but certain principles that are mentioned in the revealed sources are given a new meaning in a modern context. For instance, concepts such as *shūrā* ("consultation") or *ijmāʿ* ("consensus") are combined with modern notions of "republic" and "democracy."[4]

Finally, Sharia rules can be considered not in violation of, or—to use a different phrasing—in conformity with Sharia. Instead of asking whether a law stems from Sharia, the question is whether the law as drafted by the legislature is compliant with Sharia, or otherwise does not infringe it. In other words, when Sharia is silent about a rule or field of law—and that is the case in many instances—the legislature is free to make up its own law albeit within the general parameters of Sharia. This method is the one that is applied in most fields of law; in almost all Muslim countries, their civil law, state law, criminal law, international law, and, in particular, their financial and commercial laws, to mention only a few, make use of modern and international legal standards and concepts that are not considered in violation of Sharia law (for a discussion of Sharia being "secularized" by the legislature, see Bälz 1999).

Third Stage: Expansion of Sharia as a Source of Public Morality

From the 1990s onwards, Sharia gained headway in many Muslim countries as a source of public morality (see further Chapter 1, above). In several countries Islamic norms of decency, piety, and dress were regulated by law: several Muslim-majority countries have full or limited bans on alcohol, in Iran and Saudi Arabia women must wear the headscarf (hijab) by law (in Northern Sudan this only applies to female civil servants), and in Iran and Saudi Arabia special religious police units enforce correct public religious behavior.

Islam-compliant behavior is further enforced by means of blasphemy laws and violations of public order or state security. In the latter case, individuals have been persecuted for behavior that was specifically labeled as un-Islamic, such as publishing books and airing films that are allegedly critical about Islam (Abu Samra 2009), but also in certain cases of homosexuality. Since Islam has become important as a public and political discourse, blasphemy has increasingly become a meaningful tool in upholding public order, especially when the state is identified with Islam. Rules against blasphemy have existed in most criminal codes of Muslim-majority countries (often based on European codes). Iran and Pakistan are the only two countries that have promulgated anti-blasphemy laws for the explicit protection of Islam. Iran prescribes the death penalty on insulting "holy persons" if that equals insulting the Prophet.[5] Pakistan imposes a jail sentence on the desecration or damaging of a Quran, and the death sentence on defiling the Prophet.[6] But even in Muslim-majority countries with a blasphemy law phrased in general terms, the aim of that law is increasingly interpreted as the protection of Islam. In Sudan,[7] for instance, a British teacher was prosecuted, convicted, and imprisoned in 2007 for allowing her pupils to

4 It is interesting in this respect that most modern states that use the adjective "Islamic" in their official name do so in combination with the term "republic."

5 Article 513 of the Iranian Criminal Code.

6 Article 295-B and C of the Pakistani Criminal Code.

7 Article 242 of the Sudan Criminal Code.

call a teddy bear Muḥammad.[8] Other examples are Indonesia and Malaysia, both with overall neutrally phrased blasphemy laws,[9] but ones that are increasingly used against those who allegedly blaspheme against Islam. In 1992, for example, two Indonesian students received sentences of two and a half years because they used phrases from the Quran in a typical Javanese word game while warming up the crowd prior to a rock concert.[10] In Malaysia, a 2007 governmental injunction that the word Allah was to be exclusively used by Muslims was finally overturned in 2010 by a court ruling.

Islamic public morals can also be enforced indirectly. An example is apostasy from Islam, which is considered a capital crime under Islamic law, but is prohibited by law only in a few Muslim-majority countries. In those countries where apostasy from Islam is not legally forbidden, however, other means can be used to reach the same end. One of these is the identity card that in most Muslim countries contains the religion of the card's holder. If a Muslim converts to another religion there could be administrative difficulties: conversion to Islam is usually quickly recorded on the identity card, but conversion from Islam is often not accepted by the officials (for Malaysia, Carroll 2009; for Egypt, Stork and Bahgat 2007). The converted Muslim therefore officially remains a Muslim, with as consequence, if the convert is a woman, she will not be able to marry anybody but a Muslim, since that is prohibited by all national Muslim family laws.

Recourse to the National Courts

For many centuries of Islamic history, parts of the Muslim world featured a state authority in the functionary of the *muḥtasib*, who enforced Islamic morals in the public domain (see Chapter 12, above). With the legal modernization project, the state's enforcement of Islamic public morals largely disappeared. From the 1970s on, however, the enforcement of these morals was gradually taken over by social pressure. This was caused partly by a general resurgence of Islamic piety, but also by a tendency to express such piety in a normative manner, that is, by means of rules that preferably had to apply to all. To be Islamically compliant was therefore not only an ambition for oneself, but also a demand of others. This demand was further facilitated by two developments: the emergence of Muslim laypeople in defining Islam and their use of the justice system.

With Muslim laypeople I mean modern-day intellectuals, also described as "alternative elites" (Hallaq 2004: 23) or "new authorities with inferior credentials" (Bulliet 2002: 12). I prefer the term Muslim laypeople to offset them against those who have received and adhere to the classical training in fiqh. Some of these laypeople are indeed intellectuals and scholars, but many belong to the ever-expanding numbers of young people in the Muslim world[11] who combine their newfound self-esteem through education[12] with an acute awareness of their Muslim identity. Being Muslim has brought these young people to study the religious sources for themselves without intercession of the ulema. Both they and the lay scholars pose a serious challenge for the traditional hegemonic authority of the class of ulema (Ayoob 2005; Bulliet 2002; Abu Zayd 2006: 25), causing the line between them and the ulema to become blurred (Zaman 2002: 147).

So while the religious establishment of ulema may profess a degree of consensus on matters of religion and Sharia, and while the state arguably does the same by promulgating codifications of

8 She was granted a presidential pardon after eight days in prison and released.

9 Article 156A of the Indonesian Criminal Code; Article 298A of the Malaysian Criminal Code.

10 Examples of these word games were "Peace be upon you, heavy metal experts" and "Commit adultery as you wish" (vol. 5, no. 5, Human Rights Watch, March 16, 1993).

11 At the time of writing, an estimated more than half of the population in the Muslim world is younger than 24 years.

12 While these Muslims may have college and university degrees, it should be borne in mind that education in most Muslim countries is considered very poor (see reports from World Bank at www.web.worldbank.org/education).

Sharia (which, as we have seen, means that certain choices had to be made), the Muslim laypeople have become an important third voice in determining what is or is not Sharia. Some make their voices heard by actively engaging in political and legislative processes, some by proselytizing their views or by forming isolated communities where they live in accordance with their interpretation of Sharia, and some by resorting to violence. But the ones who interest us in the context of our discussion of the nation state are those who make use of the national laws and the judiciary system.

Since the 1990s private individuals have filed court cases against other individuals accusing them of un-Islamic behavior or even apostasy. This was a particular use of the modern judicial system, because such accusations usually pertain to the domain of criminal law where not the individual citizen but the state acts as accusing party. Moreover, such criminal proceedings can only take place if the law provides for them, that is, someone can only be charged with apostasy if that is a criminal offense by law. Interestingly, most criminal laws in Muslim-majority countries do not contain such clauses, and if they did, then it was still up to the public prosecutor to undertake action. This was unacceptable to some radical elements among lay Muslims, who took it upon themselves to act against persons with a public profile whom they deemed to be un-Islamic. In doing so, they made clever use of the existing laws and were admittedly dealing with judges of lower courts who were increasingly favorable to Islamic interpretations of the law.

The most infamous case is that against the Egyptian university professor Naṣr Ḥāmid Abū Zayd (d. 2010), which played out in the early 1990s. In order to have him removed from his position, fellow academics leveled against him the accusation of apostasy, claiming his writings on interpreting the Quran were un-Islamic. However, Egyptian law did not provide for such an accusation. The claimants then found the following loophole in the law: the Egyptian Muslim family law, which is based on Sharia, stipulates that a Muslim woman may not be married to a non-Muslim man, and the request was made to dissolve the marriage between Abū Zayd and his (Muslim) wife since he was no longer to be considered a Muslim. After going through lower courts, this argument was finally accepted by the Egyptian Court of Cassation in 1994, which considered Abū Zayd's writings blasphemous for the mere reason that they were not in line with strict Islamic theological doctrine, so that he was to be considered an apostate (Bälz 1997; Berger 2003).

Similar cases took place in other Muslim countries, from Jordan to Bangladesh. In most instances the cases were dismissed by the court because there was no legal basis for the accusation. However, bringing the case to court was itself sufficiently terrifying to subdue the accused and make him or her give in to the claims of the accusers, such as retracting certain statements, withdrawing a book or film, or merely proclaiming one's utter devotion to Islam.

Conclusion

Contrary to the predictions and expectations of many legal scholars in the 1950s and 1960s, the codification projects of emerging Muslim nation states did not lead to a quiet disappearance of Sharia. Although since the late nineteenth century legislative and judicial authority over Sharia have shifted from the religious scholars to the state, the 1970s heralded its rebirth. This Sharia differed from the classical notion of Sharia in various aspects. The complexity and flexibility of classical scholarship was substituted by codified law, which, in turn, was promulgated by a legislature and applied by a professional class of lawyers.

Once tightly tied into this new legal framework (which we have called the first stage of the development of Sharia through codification), the Sharia evolved throughout the twentieth century by way of two more stages. Starting in the 1970s, the legal spheres influenced by Sharia expanded from the traditional fields of religious ritual, family law, and piecemeal criminal law into other fields of law. Then, from the 1990s on, Sharia as law of the nation state acquired the role of public moral authority.

Part of this authority was enforced by means of legislation and the state, but part was also enforced by individuals who made use of both the law and the existing justice system.

Sharia has thus come to combine an ideological discourse with the legal system of a modern nation state. One can argue that in terms of substantive law, Sharia in itself is not unlike much of the "secular" law that is or has been in place in many Muslim-majority states. Indeed, many of its laws are rubberstamped as Sharia by the mere fact that they are not considered in violation of Sharia. Given the fact that the formal legal system—parliament, judiciary, legal professionals—is also not challenged on Islamic grounds, one might well wonder what exactly is the difference between a secular and an Islamic legal system. This is also the example set by the "liberal" interpretations of higher courts in countries such as Pakistan and Egypt.

However, two developments appear to have reversed this situation, reducing "Sharia" to a system that is in several aspects oppressive and restrictive. One is that Islamic public morality has become part of this legal system, whereby especially the rules of Islamic criminal law are extensively interpreted to maintain an illusive state identity and public order. The other development is that the training of legal professionals has eroded in many countries so that Islamic fundamentalist ideas have been able to root in the minds of the judiciary and lawyers.

It is my impression that this latter situation is not welcomed by a majority of Muslims who deem these developments that are otherwise seen as positive to have overshot their goal. It is therefore foreseeable that the next phase of interaction between Sharia and the nation state will be a corrective phase, whereby Muslim-majority nation states emphasize the need for "proper" Islamic law—as opposed to erratic and politically driven law mainly aimed at fighting off opponents—and consequently restructure the training of legal professionals accordingly.

References

Abiad, Nisrine. 2008. *Sharia, Muslim States and International Human Rights Treaty Obligations: A Comparative Study*. London: British Institute of International and Comparative Law.

Abou El Fadl, Khaled. 2001. *Speaking in God's Name: Islamic Law, Authority and Women*. Oxford: Oneworld.

Abu Samra, Muhammad. 2009. Liberal Critics, 'Ulama' and the Debate on Islam in the Contemporary Arab World. In *Guardians of Faith in Modern Times: 'Ulama' in the Middle East*, ed. M. Hatina, pp. 265–90. Leiden: Brill.

Abu Zayd, Nasr. 2006. *Reformation of Islamic Thought: A Critical Historical Analysis*. Amsterdam: Amsterdam University Press.

Al-Suwaidi, Ahmed. 1994. *Finance of International Trade in the Gulf*. London: Graham and Trotman.

Amuzegar, Jahangir. 1993. *Iran's Economy under the Islamic Republic*. London: I.B. Tauris.

Anderson, J.N.D. 1960. The Significance of Islamic Law in the World Today. *The American Journal of Comparative Law* 9: 187–213.

Anderson, Michael R. 1993. Islamic Law and the Colonial Encounter in British India. In *Institutions and Ideologies: A SOAS South Asia Reader*, ed. D. Arnold and P. Robb, pp. 165–85. Richmond, UK: Curzon. Reprinted as WLUML Occasional Series Paper 7, 1996.

Ayoob, Mohammed. 2005. Deciphering Islam's Multiple Voices: Intellectual Luxury or Strategic Necessity? *Middle East Policy* 12(3): 79–90.

Bälz, Kilian. 1997. Submitting Faith to Judicial Scrutiny through the Family Trial: The "Abû Zayd Case". *Die Welt des Islams* 37(2): 135–55.

———. 1999. The Secular Reconstruction of Islamic Law: The Egyptian Supreme Constitutional Court and "Battle over the Veil" in State-Run Schools. In *Legal Pluralism in the Arab World*, ed. B. Dupret et al., pp. 229–43. The Hague: Kluwer Law International.

Berger, Maurits S. 2003. Apostasy and Public Policy in Contemporary Egypt: An Evaluation of Recent Cases of Egypt's Highest Courts. *Human Rights Quarterly* 25(3): 720–40.

Botiveau, Bernard, 1993. *Loi islamique et droit dans les sociétés arabes: Mutations des systèmes juridiques du Moyen-Orient*. Paris: Karthala.

Brown, Nathan J. 1997. *The Rule of Law in the Arab World: Courts in Egypt and the Gulf*. New York: Cambridge University Press.

Bulliet, Richard. 2002. The Crisis within Islam. *The Wilson Quarterly* 26(1): 11–19.

Cardinal, Monique C. 2005. Islamic Legal Theory Curriculum: Are the Classics Taught Today? *Islamic Law and Society* 12(2): 224–72.

Carroll, Bruce A. 2009. A Struggle with Faith: Freedom of Religion in Malaysia. *Religion and Human Rights* 4(2-3). 101–6.

Coulson, Noel J. 1964. *A History of Islamic Law*. Edinburgh: Edinburgh University Press. Repr. Piscataway, NJ: First Transaction Publishers, 2011.

———. 1971. *Succession in the Muslim Family*. Cambridge: Cambridge University Press.

Faghfoory, Mohammad H. 1993. The Impact of Modernization on the Ulama in Iran, 1925–1941. *Iranian Studies* 26(3–4): 277–312.

Fyzee, A.A. 1963. Muhammadan Law in India. *Comparative Studies in Society and History* 5(4): 401–15.

Green, Arnold H. 1980. A Comparative Historical Analysis of the Ulama and the State in Egypt and Tunisia. *Revue de l'Occident musulman et de la Méditerranée* 29(29): 31–54.

Hallaq, Wael B. 2004. Can the Shari'a Be Restored? In *Islamic Law and the Challenges of Modernity*. ed. Y.Y. Haddad and B.F. Stowasser, pp. 21–53. Walnut Creek, CA: AltaMira Press.

———. 2009. *Shari'a: Theory, Practice, Transformations*. Cambridge: Cambridge University Press.

Henry, Jean-Robert, and François Balique. 1979. *La doctrine coloniale du droit musulman algérien: Bibliographie systématique et introduction critique*. Paris: Editions de CNRS.

Hooker, M.B. 1983. Muhammadan Law and Islamic Law. In *Islam in South-East Asia*, ed. M.B. Hooker, pp. 160–82. Leiden: E.J. Brill.

Horowitz, Donald L. 1994. The Qur'an and the Common Law: Islamic Legal Reform and the Theory of Legal Change. *The American Journal of Comparative Law* 42: 233–93.

Juwana, Hikmahanto. 2006. Legal Education Reform in Indonesia. *Asian Journal of Comparative Law* 1(1): [online publication].

Künkler, Mirjam. 2004. In the Language of the Islamic Sacred Texts: The Tripartite Struggle for Advocating Women's Rights in the Iran of the 1990s. *Journal of Muslim Minority Affairs* 2(2): 375–92.

Kuran, Timur. 1989. On the Notion of Economic Justice in Contemporary Islamic Thought. *International Journal of Middle East Studies* 21(2): 171–91.

———. 2004. *Islam and Mammon: The Economic Predicaments of Islamism*. Princeton: Princeton University Press.

Layish, Aharon, 2004. The Transformation of the *Sharī'a* from Jurists' Law to Statutory Law in the Contemporary Muslim World. *Die Welt des Islams* 44(1): 85–113.

Lombardi, Clark B., and Nathan J. Brown. 2006. Do Constitutions Requiring Adherence to *Shari'a* Threaten Human Rights? How Egypt's Constitutional Court Reconciles Islamic Law with the Liberal Rule of Law. *American University International Law Review* 21(3): 379–435.

Mahmod, Nik, and Nik Ahmad Kamal. 2006. The Importance of Understanding and Teaching Islamic Law in Asia. *Asian Journal of Comparative Law* 1(1): [online publication].

Mahmud, Tayyab. 1995. Freedom of Religion and Religious Minorities in Pakistan: A Study of Judicial Practice. *Fordham International Law Journal* 19(1): 40–100.

Mehdi, Rubya. 1994. *The Islamization of the Law in Pakistan*. Richmond, UK: Curzon Press.

Moustafa, Tamir. 2010. The Islamist Trend in Egyptian Law. *Politics and Religion* 3: 610–30.

Oba, Abdulmumini A. 2008. Towards Rethinking Legal Education in Nigeria. *Journal of Commonwealth Law and Legal Education* 6(1): 97–114.

Otto, Jan Michiel, ed. 2010. *Sharia Incorporated: A Comparative Overview of the Legal Systems of Twelve Muslim Countries in Past and Present*. Leiden: Leiden University Press.

Peters, Rudolph. 2002. From Jurists' Law to Statute Law or What Happens When the Shari'a is Codified. *Mediterranean Politics* 7(3): 82–95. Reprinted in *Shaping the Current Islamic Reformation*, ed. B. A. Roberson, pp. 81–94. London: Frank Cass, 2003.

———. 2003. *Islamic Criminal Law in Nigeria*. Ibadan: Spectrum Books.

———. 2005. *Crime and Punishment in Islamic Law: Theory and Practice from the Sixteenth to the Twenty-First Century*. Cambridge: Cambridge University Press.

Quraishi, Asifa. 1997. Her Honor: An Islamic Critique of the Rape Laws of Pakistan from a Woman-Sensitive Perspective. *Michigan Law Review* 18(2): 287–320.

Singerman, Diane. 2005. Rewriting Divorce in Egypt: Reclaiming Islam, Legal Activism, and Coalition Politics. In *Remaking Muslim Politics: Pluralism, Contestation, Democratization*, ed. R.W. Hefner, pp. 161–88. Princeton: Princeton University Press.

Starr, June. 1992. *Law as Metaphor: From Islamic Courts to the Palace of Justice*. Albany: State University of New York Press.

Stork, Joe, and Hossam Bahgat. 2007. *Prohibited Identities: State Interference with Religious Freedom*. Vol. 19, 7(E). New York: Human Rights Watch.

Wasti, Tahir H. 2005. *The Application of Islamic Criminal Law in Pakistan*. Leiden: Brill.

Weil, Patrick. 2003. *Le statut des musulmans en Algérie coloniale: Une nationalité française dénaturée*. San Domenico, Italy: European University Institute.

Zaman, Muhammad Q. 2002. *The Ulama in Contemporary Islam: Custodians of Change*. Princeton: Princeton University Press.

Zysow, Aron. 2002. Zakāt. In *Encyclopaedia of Islam*. 2nd ed. Vol. 11: 406–22. Leiden: Brill.

The Re-Islamization of Legal Systems

Martin Lau

The Arab Spring of 2011 that sought the demise of authoritarian regimes in a number of Middle Eastern countries ushered in not only fresh expectations of democracy but also concerns about the rise to power of political parties intent on introducing Islamic forms of government and laws. Apprehensions about the impact of constitutional provisions providing for the recognition of Islamic law on the human rights of religious minorities and women have been a frequent topic of academic discourse in recent years (Baderin 2005; Hirschl 2008). Most recently, they were raised in the run-up to the framing of the new constitutions of Iraq in 2005 (Lau 2005) and Afghanistan in 2004 (Mahmoudi 2004; Benard and Hachigian 2003; Mattar 2006). While the issue is more usually discussed in relation to Muslim-majority states, there is also a growing body of literature on the recognition of Islamic law in European countries and indeed North America (see Chapter 19, below; Lau and Freeland 2008).

The re-Islamization of legal systems in Muslim-majority countries is a development that began in the last quarter of the twentieth century. Most of these states have hybrid legal systems, in the sense that they consist of laws of both Islamic and Western inspiration (see Chapter 16, above). However, in many the domain of Islamic law has expanded during the last few decades. The process of re-Islamization has been studied from the perspective of various disciplines—religious studies, political science, anthropology, human rights studies, and also law, from which perspective it can be demarcated through a classification of three distinct, but often overlapping, gateways that allow for the introduction of Islamic law into the legal systems of contemporary states: first, as a constitutional standard and aspiration; second, as a source of substantive law, usually by codification; and third, as a result of the operation of rules of international private law. In addition, the literature on legal pluralism has also identified the existence of Islamic law operating outside the confines of the official legal system, being applied by non-judicial forums for community-based systems of dispute resolution, for instance, by so-called Sharia councils operating in Muslim communities in the UK (Bano 2012).

In this chapter the first two gateways will be examined, focusing on four case studies that illuminate the techniques and contexts of re-Islamization. Pakistan has been chosen as an example of the institutionalized and therefore continuous process of Islamization through the judicial review of legislation on the basis of Islam; and re-Islamization by codification in the context of federal constitutions will be examined by reference to Nigeria, Malaysia (Kelantan), and Indonesia (Aceh). A final section is given over to the secular state of India, where a re-Islamization process occurred but with unexpected results. Countries such as Saudi Arabia and Yemen, where the legal system was never Westernized but remained the law of the land, will not be treated.

Martin Lau is a Barrister and Professor of South Asia Law in the Department of Law of the School of Oriental and African Studies. He is co-editor of the *Yearbook of Islamic and Middle Eastern Law*, and author of *The Role of Islam in the Legal System of Pakistan* (2006) and, most recently, "Islam and the Constitutional Foundations of Pakistan," in *Constitutionalism in Islamic Countries*, ed. Rainer Grote et al., pp. 171–200 (2012).

In terms of importance, it can be argued that of all areas of Islamic law, the rules on family law have the widest reach given that it is applied even in countries that describe themselves as secular, for instance, India. By comparison, the reach of Islamic criminal law is more limited. Despite this, however, the most conspicuous characteristic of legal re-Islamization in recent years has been the reintroduction of Islamic criminal law in, for example, Pakistan, Libya, Iran, Sudan, and northern Nigeria (Peters 2005: 153–74; Lau 2006; Mir-Hosseini 2010; Köndgen 2010; Peters 2003).[1] Calling for Islamic criminal law seems to be the hallmark of political Islamization, but other politically tinged laws have been reintroduced as well in some states, such as Islamic fiscal laws regulating mandatory *zakāt* collection (for *zakāt*, see Chapter 11, above) and bans on interest clauses in loans (for Islamic finance, see Chapter 18, below).[2]

Judicial Review on the Basis of Islam

The constitutions of many modern Muslim-majority states contain a provision to the effect that all laws must be in harmony with Islam (Brown and Sherif 2004; Lombardi 2006; Yassari 2005). Such constitutional aspirations can be found in the recent Provisional Constitution of Somalia 2012, which provides in Article 2 (3) that "No law which is not compliant with the general principles of Shari'ah can be enacted," and the Constitution of Afghanistan 2004, which provides in Article 3 that "No law shall contravene the tenets and provisions of the holy religion of Islam in Afghanistan." Equally, the new Constitution of Iraq 2005 provides in Article 2 B that "No law may be enacted that contradicts the established provisions of Islam." All three constitutions also establish Islam as the religion of the state and all three contain constitutionally guaranteed fundamental human rights, such as the right to equality before the law, to life, and to liberty.

The effect of a constitutional stipulation that all laws conform to Islam on the re-Islamization of a legal system will be examined with reference to the Islamic Republic of Pakistan, a country that came into existence in 1947 when the crown colony of British India gained independence while at the same time being partitioned into two states: the secular Republic of India and the Islamic Republic of Pakistan (Talbot 2009). The latter was formed from the provinces of British India in which Muslims formed a majority and from the division of the provinces of Punjab and Bengal along religious lines—the parts with a Muslim majority were allotted to Pakistan and those with a Hindu majority became part of India.

The religious identity of Pakistan as a homeland of British India's Muslims is reflected in all three constitutions of Pakistan: Pakistan's current Constitution of 1973, adopted after the eastern section of Pakistan declared independence and became the state of Bangladesh in 1971, provides in Article 227 (1) that "All existing laws shall be brought in conformity with the Injunctions of Islam as laid down in the Holy Quran and Sunnah, in this Part referred to as the Injunctions of Islam, and no law shall be enacted which is repugnant to such Injunctions." Similarly worded stipulations were also contained in the first Constitution of 1956, which provided in Article 198 (1) "No law shall be enacted which is repugnant to the Injunctions of Islam as laid down in the Holy Quran and Sunnah, hereinafter referred to as Injunctions of Islam, and existing law shall be brought into conformity with such Injunctions," and in the second of 1962, which in Article 6 (1) contained the shortest Islamization provision: "No law should be repugnant to Islam."

1 For northern Nigeria, see also the publications by P. Ostien and G.J. Weimann in the bibliography, below. In 2014, Brunei became the latest Muslim country to introduce Islamic criminal law.

2 For newly introduced laws on *zakāt* collection: Saudi Arabia, Royal Decree no. 17/2/28/8634; Libya, Law 89 of 1971; Pakistan, Ordinance XVIII of 1980 (Zakat and Ushr Ordinance); Sudan, Zakat and Tax Law 1984, replaced by the Zakat Law of 1406h (Law 72 of 1986), replaced by the Zakat Law of 1990, replaced by the Zakat Law of 2001. For the ban on interest: Pakistan, Banking and Financial Services Ordinance and Banking Tribunal Service (1984); Iran, Law of Riba-free Banking 1983. And see Usmani 2001.

All three constitutions had in common the absence of any means to enforce the stipulations to ensure that laws were not repugnant to Islam—a constitutionally mandated body of experts on Islamic law, called the Council of Islamic Ideology, was tasked with advising the parliament on the repugnancy to Islam of any new law, but its recommendations were advisory only. As a result, the Islamic repugnancy clause was in the nature of a constitutional aspiration, since it did not restrict the legislative powers of the law-making bodies nor could courts invalidate laws on the ground of repugnancy to Islam. The purely symbolic nature of the Islamic repugnancy clause was transformed in dramatic fashion in 1980, however, when general Zia ul Haq, who had come to power in a coup d'état, established the Federal Shariat Court (Lau 2006). This court was to act as a court of appeal for cases decided under the so-called Hudood Ordinances[3] but was also given an original jurisdiction, namely, to judicially review laws on the basis of Islam. Article 209 D (1) of the Constitution provides that "The Court may, either of its own motion or on the petition of a citizen of Pakistan or the Federal Government or a Provincial Government, examine and decide the question whether or not any law or provision of law is repugnant to the injunctions of Islam, as laid down in the Holy Quran and Sunnah of the Holy Prophet, hereinafter referred to as the Injunctions of Islam." Unlike the purely advisory decisions of the Council of Islamic Ideology, the judgments of the Federal Shariat Court are enforceable: under Article 209D (2) a law declared to be repugnant to Islam becomes invalid on the day specified by the court itself.

Among the legal systems of the Muslim world, Pakistan's establishment of the Federal Shariat Court (FSC) is unique: there is no other that includes a dedicated court solely concerned with the judicial review of legislation on the basis of Islam. However, there are other examples of more indirect attempts to empower courts to review legislation on its Islamic validity. Article 121 of the Afghan Constitution of 2004 confers on the Supreme Court the jurisdiction to examine the validity of "[...] the laws, legislative decrees, international treaties as well as international covenants for their compliance with the Constitution and their interpretation in accordance with the law." Given that the Constitution provides that no law should be repugnant to Islam, it can be argued that Afghanistan's Supreme Court has the power to invalidate laws on the basis of Islam (Lau 2008). However, there has not been any judgment of the Afghan Supreme Court on this issue. In Egypt, the Supreme Constitutional Court has had the power to review the validity of laws on the basis of Islam since 1980. In contrast to Pakistan's case, this power only applies to new laws and does not allow the Egyptian Supreme Constitutional Court to review any of the laws predating 1980 (Lombardi 2006).

Given that the FSC is the only court in the Muslim world that has the power to review both existing and prospective laws on the basis of Islam and, additionally, is able to exercise this power on its own motion—it can actively review and examine existing laws without any application from either the state or a petitioner being required—its unique and unprecedented powers deserve closer examination. The potentially sweeping jurisdiction of the FSC has, however, been carefully circumscribed in order to reduce the risk of large parts of the legal system, or indeed the Constitution itself, from being invalidated on the basis of Islam. Articles 203 B–C of the Constitution of 1973 exclude several areas of law from the jurisdiction of the FSC, including all procedural laws, laws concerned with taxation, and Muslim family law. Furthermore, as an additional safeguard against judicial overreach, all decisions of the FSC can be appealed to the Supreme Court's Shariat Appellate Bench (SAB). Pending such an appeal, the decision of the FSC remains suspended and the law declared invalid by the FSC continues to be in force. Many of the more controversial decisions of the FSC, such as its decision declaring several provisions of the Muslim Family Law Ordinance 1961 un-Islamic and therefore invalid,[4] have

3 The term describes six ordinances promulgated by General Zia ul Haq in 1979 in order to introduce Islamic criminal law into the legal system. The most controversial of these was the Zina (Enforcement of Hadd) Ordinance 1979, which made any sexual intercourse outside of a valid marriage a criminal offense and also provided for corporal punishments, including stoning to death, for particular offenses if the evidential requirements for such a punishment had been met. See Cheema and Mustafa 2009.

4 Although the Constitution of 1973 provided that the FSC had no jurisdiction over Muslim family law, the SAB held that this meant only those laws that were specific to a school or sect and that the "general"

been appealed to the SAB, where they have remained without any sign that the Supreme Court is keen to decide the appeal.[5] In other cases, the SAB has simply sent the decision of the FSC back to the FSC for a fresh hearing, citing mistakes in the way the FSC had reached its decision.

The most significant and far-reaching impact of the work of the FSC has been in the area of Pakistan's criminal law. In its very first decision, the FSC in the case of Muhammad Riaz v. The Federal Government (PLD1980 FSC 1) declared the provisions on murder and culpable homicide of the Pakistan Penal Code 1860, a colonial statute that had continued to apply in Pakistan since independence, to be un-Islamic and therefore invalid. An appeal against this decision was decided by the Shariat Appellate Bench of the Supreme Court almost ten years later in the case of Federation of Pakistan v. Gul Hassan Khan (PLD 1989 SC 633). The SAB upheld the decision of the FSC and declared sections 299 to 388 of the Pakistan Penal Code to be repugnant to Islam. Whereas the Pakistan Penal Code provided that it is the state that prosecutes a murderer and that it is for the court to apply the sentence stipulated for the offense, the SAB held that under Islamic law the heirs of the murder victim decide the fate of the murderer—they can demand execution, the payment of compensation, or can pardon him. In compliance with the judgment of the SAB, the government of Pakistan promulgated an ordinance that introduced the law of *qiṣāṣ* (talion) and *diya* (blood money). The changes to the Pakistan Penal Code were made permanent in 1997 when the parliament passed the Criminal Law (Amendment) Act, 1997. The promulgation of the Qisas and Diyat Ordinance in 1990 revolutionized the administration of criminal justice in Pakistan with Tahir Wasti (2009: 285–6) observing that in the period of 1990 to 2000 "due to the compromise provision in the new law, an average of 83% of the murderers escaped punishment for their crimes. [...] On average, eight out of ten convicted murderers got away with their crimes."

After a very active role throughout the 1990s, the FSC has since reduced its profile significantly: it is now a rare event for the FSC to strike down a law as un-Islamic and in the few cases in which it has done so, the court has advanced a liberal and human interpretation of Islamic law. This can be illustrated with reference to a recent decision of the FSC on gender equality. In Re: Suo Moto Case No.1/K of 2006 (Gender Equality) PLD 2008 FSC 1 the FSC took *suo moto* notice of a newspaper report according to which men, but not women, were allowed to obtain Pakistani citizenship for their foreign spouses. The relevant rule is contained in section 10 of the Citizenship Act, 1951. The FSC took the matter up and examined whether or not the rule was in accordance with Islam. In its response the government defended the rule on several grounds, mostly concerns of national security and immigration control: allowing women to bring their husbands into the country would lead to an increase of immigration because it would be misused, especially by illegal immigrants "like Afghan refugees, Bengali, Bihari and other South Asian States/Countries," would allow foreign governments to plant spies in Pakistan, and would "provide legal ingress to Indian male citizens into Pakistan" (pp. 4–5). The FSC rejected the arguments of the government. In an enlightened judgment the FSC not only referred (p. 16) to a number of Quranic verses providing for the equality of the sexes—Q 7:189 ("He created you [man and woman] from a single being") and 4:124 ("whosoever does good works, whether male or female and he (or she) is a believer, such will enter paradise")—but also to Pakistan's international commitments to gender equality, including the Convention for the Elimination of All Forms of Discrimination against Women. As a matter of Islamic law, these treaties had to be adhered to. The FSC ordered the President to change the rule within six months of the date of the judgment.

The decision of the FSC demonstrates that the re-Islamization of a legal system by way of judicial review does not invariably lead to conflicts with secular fundamental rights—in this case at least, the application of the Quranic injunctions on gender equality led to a result identical with the application

Muslim family law was within their jurisdiction. Dr. Mahmood-ur-Rehman Faisal v. Federation of Pakistan PLD 1994 SC 607.

5 Allah Rakha v. Federation of Pakistan PLD 2000 FSC 1.

of the right to equality contained in the fundamental rights chapter of Pakistan's constitution—nor with ratified international commitments, which the FSC considered un-Islamic to breach.

The following conclusions can be drawn from Pakistan's experience of the use of the judiciary as an institutional arrangement for the re-Islamization of its legal system. First, it significantly reduces the power of the elected legislative bodies because judges control and determine which laws can be enacted. Second, it significantly increases the power of the judiciary and as a result risks upsetting the constitutionally mandated separation of powers. The result of these two conclusions lead to a third, namely, the composition, backgrounds, and personal attitudes of judges determine the pace and the direction of the Islamization process. In the current political climate of Pakistan, the judges of the FSC and of the Supreme Court seem to have little inclination to advance an active Islamization agenda—the large number of appeals against decisions of the FSC dating from the 1990s and early 2000s that remain pending before the Supreme Court with no indication as to when they might be heard testifies to this (Cheema 2012: 916). Furthermore, the creation of powerful courts equipped with the power of judicial review also makes it tempting to interfere with their independence. As Aziz Huq observes (2003–4: 37): "Pakistan's experience shows how judicial review and democratic failure also can become a vicious circle, as successive non-democratic leaders use courts to legitimate their rule, thereby developing an insalubrious symbiosis between the judiciary and the executive."

Re-Islamization under Federal Constitutions

Nigeria offers a case study for the introduction of Islamic criminal law in a federal system, with the 12 Muslim-majority states using their state legislative bodies to re-Islamize their legal systems. The predominantly Islamic north of Nigeria had lost its Islamic criminal law on the eve of Nigeria's independence in 1960 when the colonial and entirely secular Penal Code and Code of Criminal Procedure were introduced (Peters 2003: 12). Only family law continued to be governed by Islamic law, applied by a hierarchy of Sharia courts, with the Shariat Court of Appeal at the apex. Nigeria's new Constitution of 1999—proclaimed after many years of military rule—is also secular; its only references to Islam are in relation to the establishment of Sharia courts in the northern states of the Federation. However, the Constitution accords legislative power to the elected parliaments of the states,[6] and as a result, all Muslim-majority states have reintroduced Islamic criminal laws (for the codes, Ostien 2007). In addition, the jurisdiction of the Sharia courts has been extended to include criminal law, and laws have been enacted aimed at eliminating "un-Islamic" behavior, such as the consumption of alcohol, gambling, and prostitution. According to Philip Ostien (2010: 576): "Not all the sharia states have done all of these things, and what has been done has been done differently from state to state. Still, taken together, these interlocking measures—in theory at any rate—have restored the application of Islamic law to Muslims, in the states that have enacted them, to a state of completeness and a degree of autonomy from the 'English' legal system, that it has not had for over a century."

The return of Islamic criminal law to the northern states of Nigeria has, however, been accompanied by controversy. Three issues stand out: first, the sentencing of corporal punishments, including the amputation of hands as an Islamic punishment for the offense of theft, has attracted national and international attention and condemnation. In two sentences of stoning to death for unlawful sexual intercourse (*zinā*), which caused an outpouring of international disapprobation, the defendants were acquitted on appeal (Ostien 2007: vol. 5; Peters 2006). Second, while non-Muslim minorities living

6 In this respect the Nigerian Constitution resembles the Constitution of the United States. In conjunction with the Exclusive Legislative List (appended to the Constitution), section 4 confers the power to legislate penal laws to the states.

in the northern states are exempt from the application of Islamic criminal law, they are nevertheless affected by other aspects of the Islamization policies, such as the banning of alcohol. Third, there are concerns that the reintroduction of Islamic criminal law and the extension of the jurisdiction of the Sharia courts to issues of criminal law are in fact unconstitutional. Ostien observes (2010: 592) that despite hundreds of sentences of amputation of hands, only three have actually been carried out, for the simple reason that the consent of the governor required for them to be executed is hardly ever given. The position of non-Muslim minorities and the constitutional validity of introducing Islamic criminal law remain unresolved. The latter is particularly surprising given that several features of the Islamic criminal codes prima facie violate constitutionally guaranteed rights. Thus, the amputation of hands and death by stoning cannot but amount to a breach of the constitutional ban on cruel and inhuman punishments, contained in Article 34 of the Constitution. Moreover, many of the penal codes violate the principle of nulla poena sine lege, since they contain provisions that acts not mentioned in the codes but punishable under the Sharia can be prosecuted (Peters 2003: 37–42; Ostien 2010: 599). To date, however, none convicted has challenged the conviction before Nigerian courts on the ground of alleged violations of the Constitution, and as a result, the Nigerian Supreme Court has not had to decide whether or not the bodies of Islamic criminal law introduced in the Muslim-majority states of Nigeria are unconstitutional.

Localized introductions of Islamic criminal law have also been attempted in other parts of the world. In Malaysia, another federal state consisting of several states with Muslim majorities, the Constitution gives limited legislative powers to the state legislatures and also provides for a dual system of Islamic and secular courts (Harding 2010). The criminal jurisdiction of the Islamic courts is limited to the issuance of fines or awarding a sentence of imprisonment of up to three years for the breach of criminal laws applicable only to Muslims (Hamayotsu 2012). In 1993, the legislature of the Muslim-majority state of Kelantan passed the Sharia Criminal Code (II) Bill 1993 in an attempt to re-Islamize its criminal laws, until then governed by the Malaysian Penal Code. The Sharia Bill comprised the *ḥudūd* offenses of theft, highway robbery, unlawful sexual intercourse, the false accusation of unlawful sexual intercourse, the consumption of alcohol, and apostasy as well as provisions on punishments, including corporal punishments such as amputations and stoning to death, and Islamic rules of evidence (see Chapter 12, above). If implemented, the Sharia Bill would have changed the character of the state's criminal laws profoundly. However, even at the time of its passage, the government of Kelantan admitted to the largely symbolic nature of the law, with the Chief Minister of Kelantan stating a few days after its unanimous passage that it "could not be implemented until the Federal Government of Malaysia makes changes to the Federal Constitution" (Kamali 1998: 204). The Malaysian Constitution limits the legislative power of the state legislatures in such a way as to exclude the power to pass criminal laws except those that are concerned with the "creation and punishment of offences by persons professing the religion of Islam against precepts of that religion, except in regard to matters included in the Federal List." Further, the very same constitutional provision also extends the jurisdiction of the Sharia courts with respect to offenses only over Muslims and only as conferred on them by federal law.[7]

As a result, the Sharia remains unimplemented in Malaysia, albeit it that the Parti Islam Se-Malaysia (PAS), the political party that had introduced the Bill, remains in power in Kelantan today and is committed to its eventual implementation (on PAS, see Harding 2002).

An unsuccessful attempt to introduce Islamic criminal law at the provincial level also occurred in Pakistan where an alliance of Islamic political parties, the Muttahida Majlis-e-Amal (MMA), passed the Hisba Bill 2003. The proposed Hisba Bill provided for the creation of an Islamic "ombudsman" and an Islamic police force tasked with monitoring the population's adherence of Islamic morals in public places (Ali 2003–4).[8] Even before the Hisba Bill was signed into law by the provincial governor,

7 Constitution of Malaysia, Schedule 9, List II (1).

8 Similar organizations for enforcing public morals and the banning of alcohol have been successfully created in Aceh (see below), Sudan, and some states in northern Nigeria. For Sudan, see *Qānūn al-amr bi-l-maʿrūf*

the Supreme Court intervened and held the Bill to be *ultra vires* the Constitution of Pakistan 1973, observing that "private life, personal thoughts and the individual beliefs of citizens cannot be allowed to be interfered with." The Supreme Court ordered the provincial governor not to sign the Bill into law, because of the law "being vague, overbroad, unreasonable, based on excessive delegation of jurisdiction, denying the right of access to justice to the citizens and attempting to set up a parallel judicial system" (Ali 2004–5).[9]

The last example of re-Islamization under a federal constitution is that of Aceh, a Muslim-majority province of Indonesia, where the demand for the establishment of an autonomous Islamic state was accompanied by the implementation of Islamic law. With the fall of the Suharto government in 1998, successive Indonesian governments have used concessions with respect to the application of Islamic law in order to appease insurgents; as a result, Aceh's legal system contains a range of Islamic criminal laws, applied by Sharia courts and local communities. In the rest of Indonesia Muslims are governed by Islamic law only in the area of family law (Otto 2006–7: 78ff.; Setyowati and Toengkagie 2006–7).

Aceh's Islamic criminal laws were introduced in stages as part of ultimately successful attempts to quell the insurgency by granting increased political autonomy to the restive province. Unlike Nigeria and Malaysia, where some state legislatures arrogated the power to introduce Islamic criminal law themselves, in the case of Aceh the provincial parliament was specifically empowered to legislate in this area. In September 1999 Aceh was granted inter alia the power to implement Islamic criminal law under the law on the Special Status of Aceh. This was followed by a law enacted in 2001 on the "Special Autonomy" of Aceh that extended the power of the province "to implement Sharia as a formal legal system, establish a Sharia court system, and articulate rules in the form of local regulations, known in Aceh as qanuns" (Siregar 2008: 12–3).[10] Between 2002 and 2004 the legislature of Aceh passed five such qanuns concerned with: the requirement to wear Islamic attire (Qanun 11/2002), the prohibition of the consumption and sale of alcohol (Qanun 12/2003), the prohibition of gambling (Qanun 13/2003), the prohibition of unmarried couples of the opposite sex to be together without anyone else being present (referred to as seclusion, Qanun 14/2003), and the establishment of a compulsory tax for the purposes of charity, called zakat (Qanun 7/2004). Apart from the prohibition of gambling, none of the other activities amounts to a criminal offense in the rest of Indonesia (Human Rights Watch 2010: 14).

In the wake of the devastating tsunami of December 2004, renewed efforts to quell the insurgency in Aceh led to the passing of the Law on the Governing of Aceh in 2006. This law remains in force today, again granting substantial autonomy to the province of Aceh. Since coming into force, two more Islamic criminal laws have been passed by Aceh's provincial legislature, namely, Qanun on Criminal Procedure and Qanun on Criminal Law. The latter consists of a comprehensive codification of the Islamic criminal laws already introduced in parts between 2002 and 2004, as well as such new offenses as *zinā*, sexual harassment, rape, and homosexual intercourse. The Qanun on Criminal Law also introduces enhanced punishments, for instance, stoning to death for the crime of *zinā*. Its inclusion led the Governor of Aceh to refuse to sign the law into force, however, and therefore both Qanuns remain unimplemented in Aceh today.

Unusually in comparative perspective, the enforcement of Aceh's Islamic criminal laws does not rest on the ordinary police force alone, but is also carried out by a specifically constituted local, Islamic police force called Wilayatul Hisbah,[11] as well as by the communities themselves. Although Human

wa-l-nahy ʿan al-munkar, 1983 (Propagation of Virtue and the Prevention of Vice Act, 1983); for Nigeria, Olaniyi 2011.

9 Reference No. 2 of 2005, Supreme Court of Pakistan, decided on August 4, 2005.

10 For an analysis of the human rights' implications of the Islamization of Aceh's criminal law, see Human Rights Watch 2010; International Crisis Group 2006.

11 According to Human Rights Watch 2010, Wilayatul Hisbah is the principal enforcer of Aceh's Sharia-inspired criminal laws.

Rights Watch (2010: 25) observes that the laws on seclusion and on the wearing of Islamic attire are enforced in a discriminatory manner, affecting predominantly the poor, women, and juveniles, it also reports that since 2006—upon the coming to power of Governor Irwandi—the execution of the corporal punishment of caning, which can be imposed for offenses such as gambling, the consumption of alcohol, and indecency ("seclusion") declined sharply, with only two cases of caning reported for the period from 2007 to 2010. While many are critical of the introduction of Islamic criminal law in Aceh, Hasnil Siregar, professor of law at the University of North Sumatera, takes a more positive view: "The drafters of the qanuns have prepared provisions that are sensible, workable and, most importantly, not violent. The hudud penalty of amputation, for instance, is not mentioned in the qanuns" (2008: 13).

"Re-Islamization" in a Secular Legal System: India

The current focus on the re-Islamization of modern legal systems of Muslim-majority countries obscures the fact that even in some expressly secular states Islamic law continues to play an important role. Such is the case in India. India's system of personal laws, according to which the religion of an individual determines the body of family law that applies to him or her, was not introduced by India's parliament but was included in the legal system as a part of the legacy of colonial laws upon independence in 1947. The principal purpose of the Muslim Personal Law (Shariat) Application Act, 1937 was to exclude the application of "un-Islamic" customary laws in preference to Islamic law and, as a result, all Muslims of British India were governed by Islamic family law.

The country's first, and only, Constitution came into force in January 1950. The future of the legacy of gender discriminatory family laws under the new Constitution was considered by India's Constituent Assembly not in the context of the rights to equality or to freedom of religion but as part of the debates on the Directive Principles of Social Policy. The latter was an innovative feature of the Indian Constitution. They contained a number of policy prescriptions that were fundamental rights but not enforceable in court. Two arguments were advanced against making the introduction of a uniform family law binding on the state: that it would violate the fundamental right to freedom of religion, contained in Article 25, and that doing so would amount to a "tyranny to the minority" (Singh 1990: 241), meaning the Muslim community.

The Constitution also guaranteed the fundamental right to equality, however, and prima facie Muslim family law was in breach, given that in most areas of family law it discriminates against women (see Chapter 10, above). A "solution" to this inconsistency was found by the High Court of Bombay in State of Bombay v. Narasu Appa Mali,[12] where it was held that the system of gender discriminatory family laws was not subject to judicial review on the basis of the fundamental right to equality, thus creating the legal precedent that saved the system of personal laws from being challenged on the ground of gender-based discrimination. The decision has stood the test of time: no other challenge to the constitutionality of the personal law system has been successful.[13] The body of Islamic family law has remained largely unchanged and all significant reforms have taken place by way of judicial reinterpetation.

One of the most recent instances of re-Islamization occurred in the Indian Muslim-majority state of Jammu and Kashmir, which occupies an unusual position within the Union of India, being part of it but retaining its own Constitution. As a result of its status, the Muslim Personal Law (Shariat) Application Act, 1937 did not apply to its Muslim citizens, who continued to be governed after

12 AIR 1952 Bom 84.

13 A summary of the cases that were unsuccessful in challenging the constitutionality of gender discriminatory personal laws can be found in Ahmedabad Women Action Group (AWAG) v. Union of India AIR 1997 SC 3614.

independence by customary law (Mahmood 1981). In 2007 the state's legislative assembly passed the Jammu and Kashmir Muslim Personal Law (Shariat) Application Act, 2007 in order to re-Islamize the state's system of family laws. A court case in the spring of 2012 testifies to the "re-Islamization" being at the mercy of judicial reinterpretation:

Justice Hasnain Masoodi had to decide whether a Muslim marriage had been effectively dissolved through the pronouncement of a so-called triple *ṭalāq* divorce by the husband. Proceeding on the basis of an interpretation of Quranic verses, Justice Masoodi held that in order for a *ṭalāq* divorce to be legally valid a husband had to prove not merely that he had pronounced it but "(i) that effort was made by the representatives of husband and wife to intervene, settle disputes and disagreements between the parties and that such effort for reasons not attributable to the husband did not bear any fruit; (ii) that he had a valid and genuine cause to pronounce divorce on his wife, (iii) that Talaak was pronounced in presence of two witnesses endued with justice; (iv) that Talaak was pronounced during the period of tuhr (between two menstrual cycles) without indulging in sexual intercourse with the divorcee during said tuhr" (at para 27). The case before him, the judge decided, did not have the ingredients of a valid divorce and he ordered the trial court to determine the amount of maintenance payable to the wife.[14]

Conclusion

Contemporary experiences of re-Islamization take place in diverse legal and political contexts but share some common characteristics. First, programs of Islamization are based on the belief that Muslims have the right and the duty to be governed by Islamic law. Second, the demand for the introduction and application of Islamic law has become a central, if not the dominant, programmatic content of political Islam and Islamic political movements. Third, while there are differences of opinion about the exact nature of the content of the new Islamic legal systems, there is nevertheless agreement on the core areas of a legal system that need to be re-Islamized. In the area of criminal law these core areas are concerned with sexual offenses, prohibitions on the consumption of alcohol and on the free mixing of unrelated members of the opposite sex, the introduction of the concepts of talion and monetary compensation controlled by the victim of an assault or the heirs, apostasy, and blasphemy. These new offenses are accompanied by Islamic sentences and Islamic rules of evidence, albeit that there are divergent views on their exact nature and content. The establishment of a system of compulsory charitable taxes, *zakāt*, and a prohibition on the charging of interest, *ribā*, also appear prominently in these programs. It is noticeable that the political movements calling for the re-Islamization of laws and the establishment of Islamic states have been less vociferous on the introduction of Islamic family law, very simply because in many parts of the world, even in secular legal systems such as India, Muslims are already governed by it.

The centrality of law in the Muslim world cannot only be explained by reference to the prominent role that law plays in the religion of Islam, but also in the ideological and programmatic premise of contemporary political Islam. This premise is based on the belief that economic development, justice, and prosperity are dependent on the will of God. If Muslims follow Islamic tenets and rules, economic development and prosperity will follow. Thus, the establishment of an Islamic legal order and social system become the primary objective of political Islam with the re-Islamization of laws forming a central role in realizing this objective. A statement of Sani Abacha, who successfully campaigned to be governor of the northern Nigerian state of Zamfara in 1999, illustrates this:

> In any town I went to, I first started with *kafaral*, which is chanting *Allahu Akbar* thrice. Then I always said, 'I am in the race not to make money, but to improve on

14 Mohammed Naseem Bhat v. Bilquees Akhter, High Court of Jammu and Kashmir at Srinagar, No. 158/2009, decided on April 30, 2012.

our religious way of worship, and introduce religious reforms that will make us get Allah's favour. And then we will have abundant resources for development' (Ostien and Dekker 2010: 575).

The techniques used in attempts to re-Islamize legal systems are dependent on the legal and political contexts and as such there is a high degree of variation. Of all the countries discussed above, Pakistan offers the widest range of Islamization experiences, from the dictatorial promulgation of Islamic criminal laws to the judicial review of legislation on the basis of Islam, as well as the localized introduction of Islamic laws and courts in order to appease radical Islamic insurgencies such as the Taliban.

The resistance encountered by programs of re-Islamization revolve around several issues. In federal states, the legislative competence of provincial parliaments is often expressly or implicitly limited and excludes the competence to enact new criminal laws, as is the case in Malaysia and Pakistan. Furthermore, many of the punishments associated with some of the Islamic criminal offenses are in breach of constitutional bans on cruel and unusual punishments and of the right to equality before the law, protected in the constitutions of all of the countries discussed in this chapter.

The process of re-Islamization is fluid and ongoing. To what extent re-Islamization represents a permanent and sustainable legal paradigm is uncertain. In Pakistan, Islamic parties have seen a steep decline in popularity while in Egypt, as this chapter is being written, the rule of the Muslim Brotherhood has been brought to an abrupt end. Calls for the implementation of harsh Islamic punishments have also become less frequent. The case studies above indicate that the most visibly objectionable feature of the Islamization of criminal law, namely, the amputation of limbs and stoning to death, have either never been executed, as in Pakistan, or are in abeyance, as in Nigeria.

References

Ali, Makhdoom Khan. 2004–5. Pakistan: Legality of a Hisba Bill to Introduce an Islamic Ombudsman in the North-Western-Frontier Province. *Yearbook of Islamic and Middle Eastern Law* 11: 413–62.

Ali, Shaheen Sardar. 2003–4. Sigh of the Oppressed? "Islamisation" of Laws in Pakistan under Muttahida Majlis-e-Amal: The Case of the North West Frontier Province. *Yearbook of Islamic and Middle Eastern Law* 10: 107–24.

Baderin, Mashood A. 2005. *International Human Rights and Islamic Law*. Oxford: Oxford University Press.

Bano, Samia. 2012. *Muslim Women and Shari'ah Councils: Transcending the Boundaries of Community and Law*. London: Palgrave MacMillan.

Benard, Cheryl, and Nina Hachigian, eds. 2003. *Democracy and Islam in the New Constitution of Afghanistan*. Santa Monica: RAND Corporation.

Brown, Nathan, and Adel Omar Sherif. 2004. Inscribing Islamic Shari'a in Arab Constitutional Law. In *Islamic Law and the Challenges of Modernity*, ed. Y.Y. Haddad and B.F. Stowasser, pp. 55–81. Walnut Creek, CA: AltaMira Press.

Cheema, Moeen H. 2012. Beyond Beliefs: Deconstructing the Dominant Narratives of the Islamization of Pakistan's Law. *American Journal of Comparative Law* 60(4): 875–917.

———, and Abdul-Rahman Mustafa. 2009. From the Hudood Ordinances to the Protection of Women Act: Islamic Critiques of the Hudood Laws of Pakistan. *UCLA Journal of Islamic and Near Eastern Law* 8: 1–48.

Hamayotsu, Kikue. 2012. Once a Muslim, Always a Muslim: The Politics of State Enforcement of *Syariah* in Contemporary Malaysia. *South East Asia Research* 20(3): 399–421.

Harding, Andrew. 2002. The *Keris*, The Crescent and the Blind Goddess: The State, Islam and the Constitution in Malaysia. *Singapore Journal of International and Comparative Law* 6: 154–80.

———. 2010. Sharia and National Law in Malaysia. In *Sharia Incorporated: A Comparative Overview of the Legal Systems of Twelve Muslim Countries in Past and Present*, ed. J.M. Otto, pp. 491–528. Leiden: Leiden University Press.
Hirschl, Ran. 2008. The Theocratic Challenge to Constitution Drafting in Post-Conflict States. *William and Mary Law Review* 49(4): 1179–211.
Human Rights Watch. 2010, *Policing Morality: The Abuses in the Application of Sharia in Aceh, Indonesia*. New York: Human Rights Watch.
Huq, Aziz Z. 2003-4. Mechanisms of Political Capture in Pakistan's Superior Courts. *Yearbook of Islamic and Middle Eastern Law* 10: 21–37.
International Crisis Group. 2006. *Islamic Law and Criminal Justice in Aceh*. International Crisis Group Asia Report No. 117. Brussels: International Crisis Group.
Kamali, Mohammad Hashim. 1998. Punishment in Islamic Law: A Critique of the Hudud Bill of Kelantan, Malaysia. *Arab Law Quarterly* 13(3): 203–34.
Köndgen, Olaf. 2010. Sharia and National Law in the Sudan. In *Sharia Incorporated: A Comparative Overview of the Legal Systems of Twelve Muslim Countries in Past and Present*, ed. J.M. Otto, pp. 181–230. Leiden: Leiden University Press.
Lau, Martin. 2005. Islam and Human Rights in Comparative Perspective: The New Constitutions of Iraq and Afghanistan. *Comparative Law Journal (Hikakuho Kenkyu)* 66: 208–22.
———. 2006. *The Role of Islam in the Legal System of Pakistan*. Leiden: Brill.
———. 2008. Legal Reconstruction and Islamic Law in Afghanistan. In *The Law Applied: Contextualizing the Islamic Shari'a. A Volume in Honor of Frank E. Vogel*, ed. P. Bearman et al., pp. 216–34. London: I.B. Tauris.
———, and Richard Freeland. 2008. The Shari'a and English Law: Identity and Justice for British Muslims. In *The Islamic Marriage Contract: Case Studies in Islamic Family Law*, ed. A. Quraishi and F.E. Vogel, pp. 331–48. Cambridge, MA: Islamic Legal Studies Program, Harvard Law School.
Lombardi, Clark B. 2006. *State Law as Islamic Law in Modern Egypt: The Incorporation of the Sharī'a into Egyptian Constitutional Law*. Leiden: Brill.
Mahmood, Tahir. 1981. Application of Muslim Personal Law in the State of Jammu and Kashmir: Perspectives and Prospects. *Islamic and Comparative Law Quarterly* 1(4): 273–81.
Mahmoudi, Said. 2004. The Shari'a in the New Afghan Constitution: Contradiction or Compliment. *Zeitschrift für Ausländisches Öffentliches Recht und Völkerrecht* 64: 867–80.
Mattar, Mohamed Y. 2006. Unresolved Questions in the Bill of Rights of the New Iraqi Constitution: How will the Clash between "Human Rights" and "Islamic Law" Be Reconciled in Future Legislative Enactments and Judicial Interpretations? *Fordham International Law Journal* 30(1): 126–57.
Mir-Hosseini, Ziba. 2010. Sharia and National Law in Iran. In *Sharia Incorporated: A Comparative Overview of the Legal Systems of Twelve Muslim Countries in Past and Present*, ed. J.M. Otto, pp. 318–71. Leiden: Leiden University Press.
Olaniyi, Rasheed O. 2011. Hisbah and Sharia Law Enforcement in Metropolitan Kano. *Africa Today* 57(4): 70–96.
Ostien, Philip. 2007. *Sharia Implementation in Northern Nigeria, 1999–2006: A Sourcebook*. 5 vols. Ibadan: Spectrum Books.
———, and Albert Dekker. 2010. Sharia and National Law in Nigeria. In *Sharia Incorporated: A Comparative Overview of the Legal Systems of Twelve Muslim Countries in Past and Present*, ed. J.M. Otto, pp. 553–612. Leiden: Leiden University Press.
Otto, Jan Michiel. 2006–7. Islam, Family Law and Constitutional Context in Indonesia. *Yearbook of Islamic and Middle Eastern Law*, 13: 73–86.
Peters, Rudolph. 2003. *Islamic Criminal Law in Nigeria*. Ibadan: Spectrum Books.
———. 2005. *Crime and Punishment in Islamic Law: Theory and Practice from the Sixteenth to the Twenty-First Century*. Cambridge: Cambridge University Press.

———. 2006. The Re-Islamization of Criminal Law in Northern Nigeria and the Judiciary: The Safiyyatu Hussaini Case. In *Dispensing Justice in Islam: Qadis and Their Judgments*, ed. M.K. Masud et al., pp. 219–43. Leiden: Brill.

Setyowati, Hesti, and Toengkagie, M. Harris. 2006–7. Introduction to the Indonesian Legal System: Major Developments in the Past Decade. *Yearbook of Islamic and Middle Eastern Law* 13: 57–72.

Singh, Mahendra P. 1990. *V.N. Shukla's Constitution of India*. 8th ed. Lucknow: Eastern Book Company.

Siregar, Hasnil Basri. 2008. Islamic Law in a National Legal System: A Study on the Implementation of Shari'ah in Aceh, Indonesia. *Asian Journal of Comparative Law* 3(1): 1–26.

Talbot, Ian. 2009. *Pakistan: Modern History*. London: Hurst.

Usmani, Muhammad Taqi. 2001. *The Historic Judgement on Interest Delivered in the Supreme Court of Pakistan*. Karachi: Idaratul-Ma'arif.

Wasti, Tahir. 2009. *The Application of Islamic Criminal Law in Pakistan: Sharia in Practice*. Leiden: Brill.

Weimann, Gunnar J. 2007. Judicial Practice in Islamic Criminal Law in Nigeria: A Tentative Overview. *Islamic Law and Society* 14(2): 240–86.

———. 2009. Divine Law and Local Custom in Northern Nigerian *zinā* Trials. *Die Welt des Islams* 49(3–4): 429–65.

———. 2010a. *Islamic Criminal Law in Northern Nigeria: Politics, Religion, Judicial Practice*. Amsterdam: Amsteram University Press.

———. 2010b. Islamic Law and Muslim Governance in Northern Nigeria: Crimes against Life, Limb and Property in *Sharīʿa* Judicial Practice. *Islamic Law and Society* 17(3–4): 375–419.

Yassari, Nadjma. 2005. *The Sharīʿa in the Constitutions of Afghanistan, Iran and Egypt: Implications for Private Law*. Tübingen: Mohr Siebeck.

Part IV

Present-Day Discussions about Sharia

Sharia and Finance

Abdullah Saeed

The extent to which Sharia should be relevant to all aspects of Muslim life is one of the most frequently debated issues in contemporary Islamic thought. In the twentieth century, this debate began to intensify among Muslims particularly after the Second World War. The ideology of Islamization that developed out of these debates had their genesis in the context of colonialism and the influence of colonial powers in the Muslim world. Many Muslims sought to move away from colonial enterprises, projects, and administration, and to formulate ideas about how Muslims should function and live. Two highly influential Islamization movements to arise out of the experience of colonialism were the Muslim Brotherhood, founded in Egypt in 1928 by Hasan al-Banna (d. 1949), and Jamaat-e-Islami of Pakistan, established in 1941 by Abul Ala Mawdudi (d. 1979).

One of the key ideas to arise in the context of Islamization is that Muslims should develop their own systems to govern their lives, and that this should extend to spheres of education, politics, economics, law, and finance. The Islamization movement aims to demonstrate that Muslims made important contributions to learning and civilization in the past 1,400 years that should be utilized to develop an indigenous set of Islamic institutions and practices for contemporary life. It argues in particular that Muslims must develop institutions that are unquestionably Islamic and in opposition to the practices and values being imposed by the West—that Sharia should be brought into the public sphere in a significant way, influencing the political, economic, social, cultural, intellectual, and financial life of Muslims. This chapter focuses on a specific aspect of that argument: the extent to which Sharia has a role in contemporary financial transactions.

There is no aspect of modern life that can escape financial influence. The wide range of financial activities (including the earning, spending, borrowing, saving, and investments of individuals, businesses, organizations, and governments) makes this a very complex topic, one too large for the scope of this chapter. In the following I will therefore concentrate on a few key areas, to wit, the emergence of Sharia-based finance in the twentieth century, the basic principles of Sharia-based finance, and the manifestation of Sharia-based finance in Islamic banking.

The Emergence of Sharia-Based Finance

The interest in reviving Sharia-based ideas in the area of finance developed after a significant number of states with Muslim majorities came into being, soon after the Second World War. Many of these

Abdullah Saeed is Sultan of Oman Professor of Arab and Islamic Studies at the University of Melbourne. He is the author of *Islamic Banking and Interest* (1996), on which some of the arguments in this chapter rely, as well as *Reading the Qur'an in the Twenty-First Century* (2014); *Islam and Human Rights* (edited, 2012); and *The Qur'an: An Introduction* (2008).

states had gained their independence from colonial rule and this new independence set the stage for interest in reviving Sharia norms, with a view to developing Muslim societies in the newly established Muslim states. Virtually all of these newly created states struggled with poverty, lack of infrastructure, and lack of developed institutions. The economies of these countries were often dominated by a small number of wealthy families and feudal lords, and as a result there was widespread imbalance in the distribution of wealth. Ideologies of socialism and communism in the wider world did not fail to influence the Muslim *umma*, particularly during the 1930s to 1960s; thus, ideas such as the fair distribution of wealth and development were incorporated into wider debates about the shape that Muslim nations should take.

At this time, a number of Muslim thinkers—particularly from within the Islamization movement—were concerned with matters of banking and finance, and of how Islam should provide some kind of guidance to deal with the massive challenges that Muslim societies were facing in the areas of finance, economic development, and the redistribution of wealth. However, when they examined their own societies they found not only that the feudal lords were in control of the country's wealth and resources, but also that the financial institutions—and especially the banks—that had come into existence during the colonial period were simply serving the dictates of the privileged, wealthy, and powerful. In many cases, the privileged few in these new states had access to most of the financial capital of the society, to the exclusion of the average citizen. The feeling among scholars from Pakistan, India, and Egypt, such as Muhammad Uzair, Muhammad N. Siddiqi, and Ahmad al-Najjar, was that financial institutions were not assisting the economic development of their societies or helping raise the standard of living for the average citizen: the majority, who were struggling with poverty, had little access to the wealth and resources that were available within the country.

These proponents of Islamization therefore sought to determine the extent to which banks and financial institutions could be changed to deal with the massive economic and financial challenges that Muslim societies were facing. Their aim was to move these societies beyond where they were and to develop some kind of system through which those who were less fortunate could access capital, and perhaps also to achieve a redistribution of wealth in the country. Their analysis and reflection focused on the unfairness of the existing mechanism of interest in the financial and banking systems. From their point of view, this use of interest corresponded with what the Quran prohibited as riba (*ribā*). The pervasiveness of interest in all aspects of society was seen as the pervasiveness of riba, and removing the unfairness required removing riba from society. Toward this end, their focus was on rethinking the way financial institutions were structured, by adopting a framework that was based on a proper Islamic, ethical, and moral basis (in other words, a basis of Sharia). They argued that if financial institutions were reformed along these lines, this would take care of a large number of the financial and economic problems that they saw in much of the Muslim world at the time.

These scholars, however, had no blueprint for an alternative model of finance, or for how to move from existing interest-based models to a riba-free (interest-free) Islamic model. In the absence of this, there was no way the newly independent Muslim states could—even if they had wanted to—become more Sharia-friendly in terms of their economy and in changing borrowing and lending practices to exclude interest. At an ideal level, interest could still be considered riba and prohibited, but in practical terms interest had to be accommodated in the meantime. Banking and other financial institutions throughout the Muslim-majority countries thus continued to function on an interest-based basis.

The focus of the elites in these societies was on the development of the country, or at least successful management of the emerging nation, rather than on the initiation of an Islamization drive. Many of the leaders came from secular backgrounds, and for them the idea of going back to some traditional form of governance in managing economic or financial institutions was unacceptable. They aimed toward modernization, to the greatest extent possible within the—albeit limited—resources that were available to them. Given their heavy dependence on wealthy Western powers, they simply had to follow what those offered in terms of models for development, and financial institutions were at the very core of these Western models.

Basic Principles of Sharia-Based Finance

Given the context outlined above, a number of Muslim scholars focused their energies on exploring the idea of an alternative financial system that was derived from, or based on, Sharia, relying on a range of principles that were sourced from the Quran, the Prophetic Sunna, and traditional Islamic jurisprudence (*fiqh*). These were related to concepts of wealth, permissibility of trade and profit, and prohibition of practices such as riba and gambling. For them, a new financial system had to be based on such principles.

From a Quranic point of view, wealth is considered a trust given by God. Those who are entrusted with wealth must use it in ways that are legitimate (according to Sharia). Spending from this wealth should not just be for the benefit of the individual entrusted with it, but also for the benefit of the overall interests of the community, including the needs of the poor and disadvantaged. This wealth should be kept in circulation and therefore hoarding is strongly discouraged (and often prohibited). Means for distributing it include alms, compulsory (*zakāt*) and voluntary (*ṣadaqa*), and inheritance, based on the idea that from one generation to the next the wealth will be distributed, thereby avoiding the problems of heavy concentration of wealth in the hands of a few. Acquisition of wealth must occur through permissible (*ḥalāl*) ways; prohibited (*ḥarām*) means of acquisition include riba, gambling, and selling products and services that are considered to be haram (such as alcohol and prostitution). One of the most important ideas in the Sharia in relation to finance is the understanding that God made buying and selling (*bayʿ*) permissible while prohibiting the concept of riba.

The concept of money is also important in this context. In Islamic jurisprudence—at least in theory—money is understood in a unique way. Its primary function is considered to be as a medium of exchange, and therefore no price should be charged as rent on money. The basic rule of lending therefore is that an equal amount should be both borrowed and returned. Thus, if a sum of one hundred dollars is borrowed, the borrower must return only the initial amount of one hundred dollars.

The idea that profit arising from trade (the buying and selling of goods) is permissible is also important. Profit, in partnerships and the like, is connected to the notion of risk, and this risk is shared. Thus, where there is a profitable partnership, the gains should be shared based on an agreed-upon ratio; where a partnership results in a loss, it should be shared strictly according to the capital contribution by various parties. Thus, if the percentage of capital contribution from two parties is 40:60, any loss must be shared according to this ratio.

Of all the concepts, the prohibition of riba is perhaps the most important. The Quran states:

> Those who devour riba shall not rise except as he rises whom Satan has confounded by his touch. That is because they said, "Buying and selling is like riba." Yet God has made buying and selling lawful and riba unlawful (Q 2:275).

Although the Quranic verses are clear about the prohibition of riba, there are controversies about the type of financial transactions that come under this injunction (Mashkoor 2010: 59). Among contemporary Muslim jurists there are disagreements as to whether the riba prohibited in the Quran applies to modern bank interest. These differences appear to stem from the issue of whether the emphasis should be on the rationale for the prohibition or on the legal form of riba that was conceptualized in traditional Islamic jurisprudence.

One group of scholars, including Fazlur Rahman (d. 1988), tends to emphasize the moral aspect of the prohibition of riba (Rahman 1964). They argue that the reason for the prohibition is to prevent injustice (as formulated in Q 2:279, "do not commit injustice and no injustice will be committed against you") (Saeed 1996: 41) and the exploitation of the needy. In his translation and commentary of the Quran, Muhammad Asad (d. 1992), for example, argues that the kinds of transactions that fall into the category of riba are closely connected to the socio-economic motivation that underlies the relationship between the borrower and lender (1984: 633). The Indian scholar Abdullah Yusuf Ali (d. 1953) also attempts to define riba from this moral perspective:

> There can be no question about the prohibition [of riba] [...]. The definition I would accept would be: undue profit made, not in the way of legitimate trade, out of loans of gold and silver, and necessary articles of food such as wheat, barley, dates and salt [...]. My definition would include profiteering of all kinds, but exclude economic credit, the creature of modern banking and finance (Ali 1975: 111).

These scholars emphasize the importance of analyzing each transaction in order to understand whether the underlying reason for the prohibition applies to the transaction or not, because, for them, certain transactions that might include the element of interest might not be considered as riba. Other scholars (see Mawdudi 1986) object to this reasoning, and argue that interest is riba and therefore must be prohibited whether its form is simple, compound, nominal, or real.

ʿAbd al-Razzāq al-Sanhūrī (d. 1971), one of the leading Muslim jurists of the twentieth century, suggests that compound interest is prohibited by Q 3:130,[1] but that simple interest (in certain circumstances) may be lawful (1967, 3: 241–2). Al-Sanhūrī distinguishes between various forms of riba: pre-Islamic riba (*ribā l-jāhiliyya*), riba of deferment (*ribā l-nasīʾa*), riba of increase (*ribā l-faḍl*), and the riba of loans (*ribā l-qarḍ*). He maintains that the prohibition of riba in all its forms should be the norm, although the level of prohibition may vary between different kinds. He suggests that in some cases riba can be permitted because of necessity (*ḍarūra*) or need (*ḥāja*). In these instances, simple interest can be charged but the interest rate, method of payment, and total interest to be paid should be specified in advance (1967, 3: 234). He considers pre-Islamic riba, which is similar to compound interest today, to be prohibited without qualification.

Some thinkers distinguish between interest on consumption and production loans, arguing that the prohibition of riba only applies to consumption loans because the Quranic verses about riba occur in the context of protecting the poor and weaker sections of the community, particularly those who cannot easily get out of debt once in it (Abū Zahra 1970: 52–7). For these scholars, production loans are a post-Quranic phenomenon and therefore must be evaluated based on the rationale for the prohibition, namely, injustice (Jafarey 1988); however, others disagree and argue that these loans were prevalent in Mecca and Medina during the Prophetic period (see Saeed 1996: 44).

Further debates in the modern period include whether the prohibition of riba (as interest) applies only to individuals or also includes corporations like banks, companies, or governments; whether an individual can receive interest from corporate bodies since they are less vulnerable to exploitation; and whether interest may be charged in order to take into account the loss to be suffered by a creditor due to inflation (Saeed 1996: 45–6).

Overall, the modernist thinkers who allow some use of interest have failed to have much impact on the debate about riba. Their arguments have been countered strongly by their opponents (in particular traditionalists and proponents of Islamization) who have provided scriptural and economic counterarguments. The inability of modernist thinkers to present a consistent theory of riba and the rise of Sharia-based banking institutions that are based on a traditional understanding of riba have also weakened their position (Saeed 1996: 48–9). The different understandings of riba in the modern period and the discussions on riba and interest have led many to conclude (at least in Islamization and traditionalist circles) that the safest option is to declare all interest as prohibited riba. One of the leading contemporary Sharia-based banking theorists, Muhammad Nejatullah Siddiqi, states of this:

> Efforts of some pseudo-jurists to distinguish between *ribā* and bank interest and to legitimise the latter met with almost universal rejection and contempt. Despite the fact

1 "O, ye who believed, do not devour riba, doubled and re-doubled ... ."

> that circumstances force many people to deal with interest-based financial institutions, the notion of its essential illegitimacy has always remained (1983: 9–10).

However, there have also been fatwas that take a slightly lenient view of interest under certain circumstances, for example in the complete absence of Sharia-compliant financial institutions. In 1999 the European Council for Fatwa and Research (ECFR) issued a fatwa on the permissibility of purchasing a house by means of an interest-bearing mortgage for Muslims in the West (Caeiro 2004: 352). The fatwa emphasizes the majority opinion that interest is prohibited as riba and asks Muslims to seek Islamic alternatives to interest. But recognizing the lack of such alternatives in the West, it gives a limited permission to purchase homes for residential purposes and pay interest. It makes very clear that the permission is based on a principle of fiqh—necessity (*ḍarūra*) or need (*ḥāja*), which makes lawful temporarily what is unlawful (Caeiro 2004: 359):

> The use of mortgages, estimates the ECFR, will further "help the Muslim community, being a minority, to free themselves from the financial pressure that renting accommodation often causes, and focus their attention to the call to Islam and help the host community wherever possible and permissible" (Caeiro 2004: 360, quoting Resolution 2/4).

However, fatwas such as these are constantly under attack by proponents of Sharia-based finance.

Development of Sharia-Based Financial Institutions

From the early 1950s on, a number of Muslim scholars began to explore the practicality of setting up interest-free financial institutions. Initially, short papers on the idea were presented, such as that of the Pakistani Muhammad Uzair, who published a document in which he argued that finance that is free from interest is possible if states are prepared to adopt certain models or contracts and ideas from traditional Islamic jurisprudence that have been modified for contemporary needs (1978). This approach involves bringing together labor and capital without necessarily giving preference to capital in the exercise. Uzair's model relies heavily on the idea of profit and loss sharing (PLS), which is seen as the alternative to interest. Profit and loss sharing-based contracts (such as *muḍāraba* and *mushāraka*, see below) are borrowed from traditional Islamic jurisprudence. These ideas were later developed by scholars in other countries, including Egypt.

Alongside these efforts another development aimed at developing models of interest-free banking took place on the ground. Believing that interest was prohibited riba, some institutions in Muslim-majority countries tried to find ways of getting around it in their finance businesses and economic activities. An example is the Tabung Haji in Malaysia, a fund for would-be pilgrims to Mecca. Given the importance of the pilgrimage as an Islamic institution, any income used to perform the hajj must be free from what is prohibited by Sharia. The heads of this institution argued that, given the discussion about interest and the possibility that interest is riba, the pilgrim fund should invest all of its money only in Sharia-compliant ways and should not use interest to generate more income.

The theoretical developments that were taking place in the 1950s and 1960s, and the practical application of the idea of interest-free financial activities, led to a realization that an alternative to interest was possible, and perhaps even feasible. Although this idea was not taken up by governments in Muslim-majority countries, the developments had a strong impact within the Islamization movement. A significant amount of literature appeared that argued that interest was riba and must be prohibited. Mawdudi himself wrote a book on riba arguing that riba was equivalent to interest and Muslims must move away from riba, as did the influential Iraqi Shiʿi scholar Muḥammad Bāqir al-Ṣadr (d. 1980), who published *al-Bank al-lā-ribawī fī-l-islām* (The Riba-Free Bank in Islam) in 1969.

The theoretical insights of the thinkers and the practical application that was occurring on the ground led to an interesting experiment in Egypt in the early 1960s called the Mit Ghamr Project. This was a small village-based savings project where savings were used to generate more wealth, using concepts such as *muḍāraba* and *mushāraka*. The project showed great promise, and those who implemented it believed that it demonstrated the feasibility of the idea of profit and loss sharing in developing a viable interest-free financial institution.

These developments were boosted by global political circumstances. Oil exploration and the export of oil had been ongoing for many years in the twentieth century (particularly in the Gulf region). The oil companies based there were largely functioning under colonial arrangements and did not inject much capital back into the countries from which the oil was being extracted (despite the endemic poverty of these countries). With their establishment as independent states in the 1960s, these countries were finally able to assert themselves, and they argued that the oil income should be fairly distributed between the oil companies and the countries in which they were based. The tremendous rise in oil prices in the wake of the 1973 Arab-Israeli war was arguably the most important factor for the emergence of Sharia-based finance. An oil embargo was imposed by a number of OPEC countries (led by Saudi Arabia, whose King Faisal argued that it was time to use oil as a weapon) and because of America's strong support for Israel in the war, the embargo was directed against the United States in particular. When the embargo was lifted, oil prices increased fourfold, leading to a significant rise in the money generated by oil wealth. Moreover, by this time many countries involved had renegotiated with the oil companies to obtain a significant share of the oil profit, and were slowly asserting national dominance over the companies in terms of what these companies could and could not do.

The oil revenue in these Muslim states in the mid- to late 1970s was such that there was no absorptive capacity in many of these oil-exporting countries and the excess funds (which amounted to billions of dollars) had to be invested in international markets. A significant movement led by men who were directly or indirectly associated with the Islamization movement was at the forefront of the argument for utilization of at least some of the oil wealth in the project of Sharia-based finance, while on a practical level, various groups (such as Dar al-Mal al-Islami) led by key figures such as Muhammad al-Faisal, one of the sons of the late Saudi king, were set up to promote the idea of Sharia-based finance and financial institutions which attracted capital from wealthy Muslim individuals who were sympathetic to the idea of Islamization and also believed interest to be prohibited as riba.

This Sharia-based finance movement was able to establish research institutions, publish a host of documents and research papers, and design courses in universities, resulting in a remarkable body of literature that supported the growth of Sharia-based financial institutions. Many of the initial challenges, such as applying some of the ideas from Sharia, were met and countered, and the tools and ideas that were being used to keep the prohibition of interest at the center of attention were gradually refined through their use.

A major watershed in this context was the drafting and adopting of a resolution by the Organisation of the Islamic Conference (OIC), an umbrella organization for Muslim-majority countries, with respect to establishing an Islamic bank. At least on a symbolic level, the resolution represented a commitment from the organization to support interest- or riba-free financial institutions. As a result of this resolution the very first international Islamic bank, Islamic Development Bank (IDB), was launched in 1975 in Jeddah with a capital of approximately two billion US dollars, with much of the capital provided by oil-rich countries such as Saudi Arabia, Libya, and Kuwait (Saeed 1996: 13). The purpose of this bank was to foster economic development and social progress in member countries and Muslim communities, individually as well as jointly, in accordance with the principles of Sharia (IDB 1990: 1).

Not only did Muslim nations become members of the newly created IDB, but some of them (for instance, Kuwait, UAE, Sudan, Egypt) also began to promote Islamic banks domestically by promulgating special laws and decrees for their establishment, or by becoming shareholders. A number of other Muslim countries (for instance, Bangladesh, Tunisia, Bahrain, Malaysia) followed suit and became shareholders in the Islamic banks in their countries. Today, there is perhaps no Muslim government that has not dealt in some way with the Islamic banks. Three countries in particular—Pakistan, Iran, and Sudan—have attempted to transform their financial systems from interest-based to Sharia-based with varying degrees of success. Growing confidence in Islamic banking has led to more accommodation of Islamic banks, even by so-called secular governments of Muslim countries. Even many Western interest-based banks have opened Sharia-based branches.

From the mid-1970s Sharia-based financial institutions have embarked on providing a range of consumer and business services, much like traditional financial institutions. Once these mechanisms were refined they moved onto other new areas, such as takaful insurance, based on ideas of partnership and mutuality.

Sharia-Based Contracts

In order to provide a Sharia-based set of financial services, a large number of contracts and products were developed. Many of these are based on concepts and contracts in traditional Islamic jurisprudence (including *muḍāraba, mushāraka, ijāra, istiṣnāʿ*, and *ṣukūk*, described below). These were implemented in order to facilitate the bringing together of people's skills (including management labor) and capital to produce wealth and to offer the kind of services available in conventional interest-based systems, from deposit taking to financing of multi-billion dollar projects, but without interest.

Muḍāraba is a form of partnership where one party provides capital to another for investment in a commercial enterprise. The partner who provides the capital is called *rabb al-māl*, and the party responsible for managing the investment is called *muḍārib*. In some cases, the capital provider may specify a particular business or enterprise for which their investment may be used, in which case it is a restricted *muḍāraba* (*muḍāraba muqayyada*); if not, the *muḍārib* may use the investment unrestrictedly. Both parties agree in advance on the profit sharing ratio (which can be any ratio). Any losses, however, are borne entirely by the *rabb al-māl*. *Muḍāraba* in Islamic banking is often used for equity financing in the form of start-up capital, venture capital, or a mixture of both.

The *muḍāraba* contract also provides the basis for investment deposits (which in turn form the bulk of deposits) in Islamic banking. Other types of deposits (such as saving deposits or current account deposits in which the depositor is not interested in a return) simply exist for safekeeping or similar purposes. The depositor in the case of the *muḍāraba* is the *rabb al-māl* (investor), the bank the *muḍārib*. The bank accepts the funds for specified periods of time and uses them in investment operations. Since the funds are placed on a profit and loss sharing basis, the bank and the client share in the profit, and the profit sharing ratio is agreed upon in advance. If a loss results, the depositors (investors) bear this loss.

Equally important is the *mushāraka* contract, in which two or more parties provide the capital to the partnership and agree on a profit sharing ratio in advance; losses are shared according to the capital contribution ratio. All terms and conditions of the *mushāraka* must be agreed upon in advance. It can be used for a very specific purpose, for example to purchase equipment for which the bank and the partner provide capital and the partner manages the buying and selling of the item and actual business. This short-term *mushāraka* can be liquidated quickly, if need be, thus providing much needed wiggle room for the bank. Used to provide finance in wide-ranging areas and therefore one of the most flexible concepts available, *mushāraka* is conceived in Islamic banking as the most important profit and loss sharing contract.

An important form of *mushāraka* that is widely used in Islamic banking is *mushāraka mutanāqiṣa* (decreasing partnership). This is a partnership in which the bank enables the partner to gain ownership of a project or a business gradually, which is particularly useful for partners who do not want the bank's continued co-participation in their project and who wish to gain full ownership in the shortest possible time (Saeed 1996: 63). Both the bank and the partner agree in advance on capital contribution, shareholding, profit sharing based on the shareholding, and how the bank will sell its shares to the partner in order to gradually decrease its share in the business.

In addition to PLS contracts, there are important contracts such as *murābaḥa*. In this contract there are three parties. A buyer (A) requests that a seller (B) buy a certain item. The seller (B) does not have the item but promises to buy it from a third party (C). The *murābaḥa* contract is settled between the buyer (A) and the first seller (B). The contract is defined as a sale of a commodity at a price that the seller paid for it, plus a profit margin known to the seller and buyer (Saeed 1996: 70). *Murābaḥa* can be used easily in short-term finance to allow clients to purchase goods, and both consumers and businesses can take advantage of it as a deferred payment sale. An example of when a *murābaḥa* contract would be useful is when a client wants to buy a car but does not have the necessary cash to pay for it. The bank buys the car from a third party for the client, sells it to the client at a profit (cost of the purchase plus a certain percentage of the cost of the car as a profit), and the client pays the amount over a period of time.

In the early literature on Islamic banking and finance (in the 1950s and 1960s), *murābaḥa* was not considered a relevant concept. However, it has become one of the most important contracts in Islamic finance today. In fact, it is now one of the most important contracts through which Islamic banks invest their funds. The attractiveness of *murābaḥa* lies in the near certainty of the profit to be generated from the transaction, unlike the PLS contracts of *mushāraka* or *muḍāraba*, where the profit to be realized is—at least in theory—uncertain.

Ijāra is an exchange transaction where the benefit arising from a specific asset is made available in return for a payment, although the ownership of the asset itself is not transferred. This form of contract is similar to that of an installment leasing agreement where an asset is leased to a client and returned at the end of the lease period. In an alternative arrangement, the person who leases the asset can make an arrangement to purchase the asset at the end of the lease period. In this case, the contract operates essentially as a hire-purchase (*ijāra wa-iqtinā'*) arrangement. In *ijāra* contracts, the period of the lease must be specified, along with the conditions of the lease. The lessor takes responsibility for maintaining and insuring the asset throughout the period of the lease.

Another important contract is *istiṣnā'*, which is commonly used by Islamic banks to finance the construction of buildings, aircrafts, ships, and the like. *Istiṣnā'* involves a made-to-order item of which delivery is at a later date. As such it is a contract of sale that is transacted before the asset comes into existence. In such agreements, payment can be made upfront or by installment and the manufacturer agrees on the nature and quality of the item to be delivered. The date of delivery is determined by the manufacturer and is not fixed. In some cases the manufacturer may subcontract the manufacturing of the item to another business.

One of the most recent developments in Sharia-based finance is the large-scale development and use of sukuk (*ṣukūk*, sg. *ṣakk*, "certificate of financial liability"). Representing undivided shares in ownership of tangible assets or an investment activity, sukuk grant the investor a share of an asset, along with the commensurate cash flows and risk. In recent years corporations and public sector entities have experienced a surge in the issuance of sukuk amid growing demand for alternative financial investments. Notably, sukuk are now issued by non-Muslims in addition to Muslim corporations and governments. The German State of Saxony-Anhalt launched the first sovereign sukuk in a non-Islamic jurisdiction and the World Bank has also issued such sukuk (Iqbal and Tsubota 2006).

Sukuk have similar characteristics to conventional bonds, although with the major difference that the sukuk are asset-based. They represent the proportionate beneficial ownership of the sukuk holders in the underlying tangible assets, usufruct, or services. Profits, which depend on the performance of the underlying assets, are periodically paid to the sukuk holders according to their proportionate ownership in them. The primary difference between sukuk and conventional bonds is that the former represent ownership of real assets, whereas conventional bondholders own debt (Hayat 2010).

Sukuk were used extensively by medieval Muslims to represent the financial obligations that originated from trade and other commercial activities. However, their present structure is akin to the conventional concept of securitization: a process in which ownership of the underlying assets is transferred to a large number of investors through certificates representing proportionate value of the relevant assets. Since the influential Pakistani Sharia scholar Muhammad Taqi Usmani critiqued the vast majority of sukuk as not Sharia-compliant (2007), the focus is on ensuring that sukuk remain distinct from conventional bonds and observe Sharia prescriptions.

In order to ensure the Islamicity of their transactions and activities, Sharia-based financial institutions employ a Sharia supervisory board (SSB). The composition of such boards varies; they are generally made up of scholars who are experts in both Sharia and finance. The practices and duties of such boards vary from country to country, depending on the regulatory laws in force in a particular country. In general, an Islamic financial institution is required to establish operating procedures to ensure that no form of investment or business activity is undertaken that has not been approved in advance by the SSB. The management is also required to periodically report and certify to the SSB that the actual investments and business activities undertaken by the institution conform to practices previously approved by the SSB.

Questions have been raised about the independence and potential conflict of interest posed by an SSB being in the employment of the Sharia-based financial institution it governs. In addition, in the absence of many available and expert Sharia scholars, some scholars sit on multiple SSBs, which raises questions of confidentiality (van Greuning and Iqbal 2008: chap. 11). To combat these questions, a number of Islamic regulatory organizations have been set up, such as the Accounting and Auditing Organization for Islamic Financial Institutions (AAOIFI) in 1991 and the International Islamic Rating Agency (IIRA) in 2002, which aim at ensuring independent assessment and more transparency.

The Question about the Islamicity of Sharia-Based Finance

At its theoretical inception, Islamic banking was conceived on the principle of profit and loss sharing, and proposed a two-tier *muḍāraba* contract in place of the deposit/loan system of commercial banking that was perceived as involving riba. As explained above, in the Sharia-based system—based on the *muḍāraba*—providers of funds (depositors) were viewed as partners who extended their funds to an Islamic bank (which was viewed as an investment agent). The Islamic bank would then invest funds on behalf of the providers of funds in exchange for a share in profits. If investments were not profitable, the bank would lose only its effort, and the partners who provided the funds would bear all financial losses.

In practice, Islamic banks found the concept of profit and loss sharing to be too risky; they therefore moved away from the early emphasis on strict profit and loss sharing ideas. The banks had to strip the concepts of *muḍāraba* and *mushāraka* of their basic characteristics in order to make them more appropriate for less risky short-term ventures where the bank could advance capital on the basis of a more or less predetermined return by inserting into *muḍāraba* or *mushāraka* contracts terms that limited the scope available for the clients in the contract under traditional norms (Saeed 1996: 143). The banks also began to minimize their use of these contracts, as experience showed them that relying on them could lead to significant losses for the bank. Gradually, the banks introduced a large number of less risky contracts such as *murābaḥa* and *ijāra*. Some critics argue that *murābaḥa* in particular has come to function as an interest-bearing loan transaction in almost everything but name.

As Islamic banks attempt to provide all the types of products and services that are offered by conventional banks, they often follow the available models but restructure them based on certain Sharia principles, ideas, and contracts. The bulk of Islamic finance operations today involve this type of mark-up credit sales, or more sophisticated hire-purchase transactions with similar built-in mark-ups designated as rent. The mark-up is often based on a market interest rate such as LIBOR, which some jurists defend on the basis that it serves as a benchmark (El-Gamal 2006: 74–6). Such developments have led to significant criticism of Sharia-based finance as being too similar to interest-based finance. Islamic bankers naturally respond to such criticism with their own reasons for this similarity, usually emphasizing legal differences between the contracts and pointing out that under Islamic finance there are always tangible assets and that it does not involve lending money at interest.

Many in the Sharia-based finance movement argue that this similarity is superficial and is not really a serious problem, given that in developing Sharia-based finance they need to benefit from ideas, structures, and mechanisms available in conventional finance. Another argument is that Sharia-based financial institutions are competing with interest-based financial institutions in the modern age and therefore must be pragmatic in applying some of the ideas from Sharia. Critics of this argument counter that the fact that interest comes through various channels into Sharia-based finance products does not seem to bother a large number of Sharia financial practitioners. However, within the Sharia-based financial industry there has always been a movement that has been against the manipulation of traditional Sharia principles and the twisting of them to suit contemporary needs by bringing in elements that they consider to be prohibited. This movement continues to question the Islamicity of Islamic banking; the movement's contributions from this movement are useful for correcting some of the excesses of Sharia-based finance.

Concluding Remarks

Since the 1960s Sharia-based finance has grown considerably: from its humble roots of small-scale experiments and business ventures into a multi-billion dollar, fast-growing business, spanning all continents and Muslim and non-Muslim-majority countries. In both, Sharia-based and conventional financial systems function side by side. The growth of Sharia-based finance and its attractiveness to many customers show that this form of finance is here to stay. Although there are questions as to the extent to which these financial institutions are Sharia-based in practice, a large number of Muslims seem to be comfortable in dealing with them as Islamic institutions and believe that by doing so they are applying the Quranic prohibition of riba in their financial activities. Since the global financial crisis of 2008, major non-Muslim international financial institutions and investors are also looking at the Sharia-based financial system as a viable and stable system of finance, and the future of Sharia-based finance seems to be good. No doubt more refinements of its products and services will be offered, and with a growing confidence, Islamic financial institutions will be well positioned to attempt to make their products more closely aligned with Sharia-based principles than they have been thus far.

References

Abū Zahra, Muḥammad. 1970. *Buḥūth fī l-ribā*. Kuwait: Dār al-Buḥūth al-ʿIlmiyya.

Ali, A. Yusuf. 1975. *An English Interpretation of the Holy Qur'an*. Lahore: Muhammad Ashraf.

Asad, Muhammad. 1984. *The Message of the Qur'ān*. Gibraltar: Dar al-Andalus.

Caeiro, Alexandre. 2004. The Social Construction of *Sharīʿa*: Bank Interest, Home Purchase, and Islamic Norms in the West. *Die Welt des Islams* 44(3): 351–75.

El-Gamal, Mahmoud A. 2006. *Islamic Finance: Law, Economics and Practice*. New York: Cambridge University Press.

van Greuning, Hennie, and Zamir Iqbal. 2008. *Risk Analysis for Islamic Banks*. Washington, DC: The World Bank.

Hayat, Usman. 2010. Islamic Finance's Sukuk Explained. Available at: www.sukuk.me/news/articles/73/Islamic-finances-sukuk-explained.html. Accessed February 16, 2013.

IDB (Islamic Development Bank). 1990.*Technical Cooperation Programme among IDB Member Countries*. Jeddah: IDB.

Iqbal, Zamir, and Hiroshi Tsubota. 2006. Emerging Islamic Capital Markets. *Islamic Finance Review*: 5–11.

Jafarey, N.A. 1988. The Case for Ijtihad in Respect of Interest on Production Loans. *Journal of Islamic Banking and Finance*: 15–20.

Mashkoor, Masood. 2010. The Meaning of Riba and Its Prohibition in Islam. *Research Journal of International Studies* 16: 58–63.

Mawdudi, Abul Ala. 1986. Prohibition of Interest in Islam. *Al-Islam* (June): 6–8.

Rahman, Fazlur. 1964. *Ribā* and Interest. *Islamic Studies* 3(1): 1–43.

Saeed, Abdullah. 1996. *Islamic Banking and Interest: A Study of the Prohibition of Riba and Its Contemporary Interpretation*. Leiden: E.J. Brill.

al-Sanhūrī, ʿAbd al-Razzāq. 1967. *Maṣādir al-ḥaqq fī l-fiqh al-islāmī*. 6 vols. in 2. Beirut: al-Majmaʿ al-ʿIlmī al-ʿArabī al-Islāmī.

Siddiqi, Muhammad Nejatullah. 1983. *Issues in Islamic Banking: Selected Papers*. Leicester: Islamic Foundation.

Usmani, Muhammad Taqi. 2007. Sukuk and Their Contemporary Applications. Available at: www.sukuk.me/library/education/MuftiTaqiSukukpaper.pdf. Accessed February 16, 2013.

Uzair, Muhammad. 1978. *Interest-Free Banking*. Karachi: Royal Book Company.

19 ASHGATE RESEARCH COMPANION

Sharia and the Muslim Diaspora

Mathias Rohe

Sharia in Different Types of Diasporas

Per the extremist view, Sharia in the diaspora is either indispensable—cf., for example, Sharia4Belgium[1] and Sharia4Holland,[2] two Muslim groups explicitly rejecting Belgian and Dutch democratic systems respectively—or the biggest danger for Western values—cf. the slogan *Maria statt Scharia* (Maria instead of Sharia) of the right-wing, populist, and anti-Islamic Swiss People's Party (SVP) in the 2009 electoral campaign.[3] But what do they mean by the use of "Sharia"?

In the narrow understanding as "Islamic law" Sharia is often perceived to be the opposite of secular legal systems, by both Islamists (Laurence 2012: 70–104) and a broad European public. In the broad sense, Sharia means the totality of Islamic normativity, including religious commands and the methods of discerning and interpreting norms. This includes rules for a pious conduct of life falling within the scope of freedom of religion. In the narrow sense—common among non-Muslims, but also to be found among a considerable number of Muslims—Sharia stands only for harsh penal sanctions, for unequal treatment of sexes and religions, and for a non-democratic organization of the state under the rule of Islam. The heated reaction to the archbishop of Canterbury's speech in February 2008 about a possible introduction of some parts of Sharia law into the English legal system is but one example of fierce resistance to Sharia defined in the narrow sense (Williams 2008; cf. Milbank 2010; Gaudreault-DesBiens 2010a). Thus, it is imperative to clarify what exactly is being discussed or demanded when addressing Sharia.

And what do we mean by "diaspora," since the issue of applying Sharia norms there is being addressed? Traditional definitions do not seem to fit here. Given the religious, ethnic, and social diversity of Muslims, there is no collective memory about a common "homeland," no idealization of a real or imagined ancestral home, no return movement, no (generally) troubled relationship with the "host" society (many Muslims are citizens of the countries they are living in), just to mention some typical aspects of diasporic life (Cohen 2008: 17; Ceylan 2012: 11f.). In addition, the Muslim population is particularly heterogeneous in immigration countries (Moghissi et al. 2009: 7ff.).

Mathias Rohe is Professor at the University of Erlangen-Nürnberg, former judge at the Court of Appeals in Nuremberg (2001–7), and author of *Das islamische Recht: Eine Einführung* (2013), *Das islamische Recht: Geschichte und Gegenwart* (2011), and *Muslim Minorities and the Law in Europe: Chances and Challenges* (2007), as well as countless articles on the subject of the legal conditions of Muslims in Europe.

1 This group was officially dissolved on October 7, 2012; its leader was imprisoned in February 2012 for two years for incitement to ethnic hatred.

2 Cf. the report in *Trouw* of February 22, 2010, available at www.trouw.nl/tr/nl/4324/Nieuws/article/detail/1798930/2010/12/22/Shariah4Holland-wil-vechten-voor-de-wetgeving-van-Allah.dhtml. Accessed February 19, 2013.

3 Cf. www.tagesanzeiger.ch/schweiz/standard/SVP-moechte-lieber-Maria-statt-Scharia/story/10749271. Accessed February 19, 2013.

Diaspora in the sense used in this chapter cannot solely be defined by the proportions of religious groups in a particular state. Certainly, states with a Muslim majority applying Sharia law in total or in considerable part would be the opposite of diaspora; but there are states with a Muslim majority, such as Albania or some Central Asian countries, that have introduced Western legal systems and left only limited space to the application of Sharia norms, and, in the past, states with a non-Muslim majority (under the Ottoman empire, for instance) that were ruled by Sharia law. Therefore, the differentiation as to whether the application of Sharia norms is the rule or an integral part of the existing state law, or whether it is an exceptional case that has to be justified under a secular legal order might be helpful as a general rule of thumb. Nevertheless, the proportions of religious groups is not irrelevant either—while the religious part of Sharia would fall under freedom of religion, which is granted to a large extent by many Western countries and is neither "foreign" nor "exceptional" from a legal point of view, the religious life of Muslim minorities is not equally recognized on a social level in many countries with a non-Muslim majority.

In consequence, there is no clear-cut distinction between diasporic and non-diasporic situations. Many contemporary Muslim scholars thus tend to abandon the traditional dichotomic worldview of "abode of Islam" (*dār al-Islām*) and "abode of war" (*dār al-ḥarb*), mitigated by the category of "abode of treaty" (*dār al-ʿahd*) (Rohe 2011a: 147ff.; and see Chapter 14, above), and replace it by the new concept of "a single abode" (*dār wāḥida*) where all human beings live together (Rohe 2011a: 260ff.). Given these shifting borders, it nevertheless makes sense to restrict this chapter to states where Muslims are a minority group and where on the level of legal rules secular orders not rooted in a Sharia tradition prevail.

From a historical point of view, we must also distinguish between new and genuine diasporas, since the possible conflicts and tensions between the existing legal order and Sharia are fundamentally different in certain aspects.

The most prominent example of a new diaspora is India. Large parts of the Indian subcontinent were part of powerful Muslim realms since the thirteenth century. After partition in 1947, Muslims in India suddenly became a diasporic minority under secular rule dominated by a Hindu majority. The preservation of Sharia rules has become an important part of their "political and cultural self-defense" (Rohe 2011a: 279ff.).

Muslims living in those parts of the world that have never been under Islamic rule make up genuine diasporic minorities. Again, regarding the application of Sharia rules we discern two different systems of legal managing of religious diversity. In states like South Africa, where systems of ethnically or religiously defined laws of personal status operate, some Muslims struggle for the establishment of a Sharia-based legal system under the auspices of equal treatment (South African Law Commission 2002; Manjoo 2007). In Nigeria this has been established historically, but here conflicts have emerged even on the level of penal law (Peters 2003: esp. 13ff.). Where such systems are not in force (the West, Australia/Oceania), dealing with Sharia-based norms is predominantly an issue of Muslim self-orientation within the broad scope of secular legal systems.

The Application of Sharia Rules and the Public Debate

The acceptance or rejection of Sharia has become a topic of heated debate in Western public discourse (Cesari 2010: 145). The developments regarding the ultimately failed establishment of officially recognized Sharia boards in the Canadian province of Ontario from 2003 to 2006 (Bakht 2006; Rohe 2011a: 321ff.) demonstrate this impressively.[4] Such debates are not restricted to non-Muslims,

4 For anti-Sharia legislation without any differentiation between religious and legal aspects, brought forward for consideration in several southern states in the US, see Glazer 2012: 5, 16ff.

but are also conducted among large numbers of Western Muslims.[5] Some Muslim activists or "ex-Muslims" such as Ayaan Hirsi Ali,[6] Magdi Allam,[7] or Necla Kelek[8] are among the fiercest critics of Muslim religious presence in the Western public space, while Muslim fringe groups—many of them based in the UK[9]—call for Sharia, including the *ḥadd* punishments according to traditional Islamic penal law, as the only valid normative order for Muslims everywhere. This is also true for the Salafi youth culture. A former German rapper by the name of Deso Dogg, now calling himself Abou Maleeq, wrote a rap song with the title "Awake finally! Allahu akbar" that calls upon Muslims to engage in jihad and in which Sharia is used as a token of extremist self-definition.

Such understandings of Sharia, from both sides of the spectrum, are far from representative of the general Muslim population; nevertheless, they contribute to the blunt rejection of Sharia by the Western public. Furthermore, the debate is often overshadowed by clear (mis-)perceptions and by the exploitation of an abstract fear of Islam in Western societies for political reasons, of which the burqa ban in France and Belgium serves as an example (Silvestri 2012). In addition, problems arising in the context of labor migration or asylum-seeking are often ascribed to the religion of the persons involved. But an insufficient command of a language and thus failure to gain access to the labor market is a question of language training, not of the migrant's religion. The debate on Sharia very often suffers from a remarkable lack of precision.

Legal Sharia Rules in the Diaspora

When it comes to legal Sharia provisions (in the form of modern state law), their application can cause considerable tensions, for while European legal systems guarantee freedom of religion, foreign laws are possible "competitors" of these orders. It is necessary to distinguish legal norms enforceable by official state measures on the one hand, and norms and acts operating in civil society without required validation of the official legal system of enforcement on the other. As regards the latter, normative pluralism is indeed widespread. But in the event of conflict, compulsory state rules will prevail over social or religious ones, according to the principles of secular legal systems. Within this framework, however, the legal system has the flexibility to accommodate pluralism to a considerable extent (Witte 2010: 279ff.).

5 For Germany, see the representative study of the Ministry of the Interior (Brettfeld and Wetzels 2007: 389): 72.9 percent of Muslims rejected the idea of Sharia influence on the existing laws in Germany, and 64.9 percent rejected it regarding the laws of the country of origin. Birgitte Schepelern Johansen and Riem Spielhaus (2012) rightly criticize the study, since the evaluation of the questions related to Sharia follows a generally negative pre-understanding of Sharia, reducing it to its critical legal parts.

6 Of Somali origin, fled to Europe, and living in the US. Active against female genital mutilation, she employs an essentialist approach to her criticism of Islam. While she has received prizes for defending Western ideals of freedom of expression, she is criticized by scholars for excessive generalizations.

7 Of Egyptian origin, an Italian Muslim convert to Christianity who gained public attraction by the public baptism performed by Pope John XVI in 2008.

8 A sociologist living in Germany, who after initially examining Islamic religiosity in daily life of pupils of Turkish origin in Germany, has shifted to strong emotional views against Islam and its culture, generalizing her personal negative experiences to an extent that is untenable from a scholarly perspective (Bahners 2011: 131–74).

9 For example, Sharia4UK, a small group derived from the former extremist group "al-Muhajiroun" led by the extremist solicitor Anjem Choudary; see an interview with him from August 2012, available at www.cbn.com/cbnnews/world/2012/August/UK-Islamist-Leader-Islam-Will-Dominate-America (accessed February 19, 2012); Hizb al-Tahrir, an extremist group acting worldwide, founded in Jerusalem in 1953 by the Muslim scholar Taqi al-Din Nabhani (d. 1977), aiming at restoring the Islamic caliphate and rejecting democracy (Rohe 2006: esp. 120, 135ff.); and Khilavet Devleti (Schiffauer 2000).

In the course of a century-old development, personal law systems implementing a kind of legal pluralism have been replaced in Europe and other parts of the world by territorially unified laws granting internal pluralism but reserving the right of last decision to state law in case of conflicting norms (Gaudreault-DesBiens 2010b). The legal system is not multicultural as far as it concerns the decisive exercise of legal power. This is true despite the fact of normative pluralism within Western societies (Nielsen and Christoffersen 2010, esp. Shah 2010; Zucca 2012: 194–6). On the one hand, the secular state does not and cannot claim to provide spiritual guidance or a coherent system of giving sense to human life. On the other hand, it claims the right of last decision concerning the legally binding regulations of human interaction (Bielefeldt 2003: 32–6). Within this range, legal Sharia norms might be applied to a certain extent under the respective state law. This legal framework is of prime importance for the development of Muslim normativity in the diaspora; as far as state law leads to or enables such application, Muslims who appreciate this application would be satisfied with the existing system. On the other hand, the readiness of state laws to apply Sharia-based norms leads to criticism among other Muslims and many non-Muslims. In the following an outline of the range and limits for the application of legal Sharia norms will be given, followed by some observations on the Muslim debate about it.

Fields of Application

Public law, which regulates the legal relations between the state and its citizens or inhabitants, and penal law are today strictly territorial worldwide. In consequence, no foreign legal rules can apply in these fields. It is different in matters of private law, which mainly regulates legal relations between private parties. In cross-border cases—for example, when foreign citizens are involved—the parties might rely on legal relations created under foreign law. Can a marriage concluded according to Sharia-based family law be recognized? What about the repudiation of a wife (*ṭalāq*) pronounced in an Islamic country or in the diaspora? Is Islamic investment protected under secular laws? In all these fields possibly conflicting interests must be accommodated. The parties deserve protection in their expectations of stable legal relations irrespective of where they happen to reside. The legal order can accept pluralistic arrangements to a certain extent under the principle of private autonomy, but must grant as much of an amount of unity as is necessary to preserve peace in society. Thus, legal differences can be accepted (only) to a certain degree, which has to be evaluated thoroughly.

Private international law (PIL), which regulates conflicting laws pertaining to civil matters, is the most prominent level on which Sharia-based legal rules can be directly applied. With the exception of Saudi Arabia, there is no legal system known today that denies the general application of foreign legal norms. Civil law essentially regulates the legal relations between private individuals, whose welfare is of prime importance. This includes the continuity of existing legal relationships (such as marriage) when crossing "legal borders." Thus, in such primarily private matters of an international dimension it is desirable to apply the substantive law having the most significant relationship to the case at hand. The idea underlying this concept is the principal equality of all legal systems, which is why foreign law can be applied.

Nevertheless, the legal community in a particular country may decide that in certain matters the same substantive law should be applicable to every resident. This would be the case particularly in matters affecting legal and societal common sense like those regulated by family law. When foreign legal norms are applied, the result must comply with the law of the land and public policy. This is the necessary limit drawn by every legal system in order to preserve peace in society by maintaining the most important common standards, human rights standards in particular.

Within Sharia-based law there are many provisions that do not contradict Western laws (in the area of contract law, for example) and therefore may be easily applied. In the UK, contracts including a choice of law provision ("principles of the Glorious Sharia") have been dealt with in courts (Bälz 2005). The main conflicts between Islamic and European laws concern family matters and inheritance. They arise over constitutional (and human) rights such as gender equality and freedom of religion, including the right not to believe, and protection of minors. Provisions reflecting classical Islamic law preserve strict separation between the sexes with respect to their social roles as well as far-reaching segregation of religions under the supremacy of Islam; child marriage is abolished in some Islamic countries, but still practiced in others.[10] The different ways of reasoning within European legal systems shall be demonstrated using the case law examples concerning repudiation (Foblets 2001, 2007; Gärtner 2008; Büchler 2011; Rohe 2011a: 353 ff.; Koch 2012).

According to traditional Islamic law, which is still in force in many Islamic countries despite a number of domestic reforms in favor of women (Mir-Hosseini 2009; Rohe 2011a: 207ff.; Voorhoeve 2012), only the husband is entitled to terminate the marriage without any reason to be given, by way of a unilateral declaration of repudiation. This must be repeated two times, and attempts at reconciliation must be made, but if they fail the marriage is dissolved. Such a procedure is clearly inconsistent with the European legal principle of equality of sexes, since wives have only very limited rights to divorce (Rohe 2011a: 216 ff.).[11] Thus, according to unanimous regulations in European legal systems, *ṭalāq* cannot be validly pronounced on European soil (as opposed to the *khul'* or other forms of divorce for discord).[12] Moreover, European legal systems usually refuse to recognize *ṭalāq* declarations issued abroad when their own citizens or residents are involved.[13] Nevertheless, they had to deal with the question of the *ṭalāq* that was valid abroad. Would European public policy (*ordre public*) prevent its being recognized in all cases or only in those in which the wife was unable to defend her rights and did not agree to the divorce? There is a remarkable shift within European legal systems in the last decade, whereby the traditional private international law approach concerning the application of public policy—which only looked at the outcome of the application of the respective foreign law, not at the foreign norm as such—is increasingly challenged (Alidadi 2005; Foblets 2007).

German,[14] Italian,[15] and Spanish[16] courts still follow the traditional approach broadly. Thus, recognition of *ṭalāq* contradicts public policy in cases where the wife is not able to claim her legitimate interests or is not informed about the divorce. In cases where the prerequisites for divorce are fulfilled in accordance with, or comparable to, the law of the land or where the wife agrees, the legality of *ṭalāq* is accepted. Belgium ruled thus until 2005 when the courts started to handle recognition more strictly after the enactment of the new law on PIL.[17] The same development can

10 See, for example, a recent decision of the Court of Appeals (Kammergericht) of Berlin (*FamRZ* 2012: 1495), in which the marriage between a former Lebanese German Shi'i Muslim and a 14-year-old Lebanese Shi'i girl valid under Lebanese law (according to the still valid Ottoman family code) was not recognized due to a violation of German public order. A 14-year-old is not considered to be able to freely and responsibly decide on a fundamental issue such as marriage (the minimum age in Germany, dependent on the consent of the parents or the competent court, is 16).

11 Courts usually differentiate between Islamic forms of divorce and foreign decisions are recognized if the cases meet the prerequisites of an "equal rights"-divorce; see French Court of Cassation, February 23, 2011, no. 10–14.760.

12 See, for example, Civil Court Brussels, May 26, 1978; House of Lords, R. v. Secretary of State for the Home Department ex p. Fatima Ghulam, [1986] AC 527 (HL). For *khul'*, see French Court of Cassation February 23, 2011, no. 10–14.760, regarding a French-Moroccan case where the spouses had lived apart for three years and the divorce was not qualified as a unilateral divorce by the Moroccan court; Court of Appeals Versailles, March 25, 2010, no. 08/08808; Dutch Supreme Court, July 13, 2001, rechtspraak.nl LJN AB2623 (WPNR 2001 (6470)); Cour d'Appel Antwerpen, June 30, 1982, J.D.I. 1982, 740–741.

13 Article 46 Family Law Act 1986 of England and Wales; Article 57 section 2.2., 2.3. Belgian PIL code 2004.

14 For example, Court of Appeals Düsseldorf, FamRZ 1998, 1113; Court of Appeals Köln, FamRZ 2000, 895; Court of Appeals Zweibrücken, NJW-RR 2002, 581; Court of Appeals Hamm March 7, 2006, BeckRS 2007, 00423; Court of Appeals Frankfurt a.M., May 11, 2009, 5 WF 66/09. See also Rohe 2003: 46, 50.

15 Cf. Court of Appeals Cagliari, May 16, 2008, no. 198.

16 Cf. Supreme Court, ATS April 21, 1998, RJ 3563.

17 Court of Cassation April 29, 2002; after 2005, cf. Court of Appeals Mons, December 20, 2007; Civil Court Liège, June 26, 2009; Labour Court Brussels, May 27, 2010; but also Labor Court Brussels, January 12, 2011. Cf. Foblets 2007; Koch 2012: 175–8.

be found in court decisions in France since 2004,[18] where in the past the differentiation made by German courts equally applied.[19] In Austria, the Supreme Court from the beginning refused to accept any kind of *ṭalāq* whatsoever.[20] Thus, there is an emerging trend in PIL to follow a policy of legal symbolism, which means to abstractly defend principles as such instead of deciding concrete cases according to their particularities only.

The crucial legal question is whether legislative bodies and the courts compare foreign legal norms as categorically as their normative domestic counterparts in the abstract, or whether the results of the application of foreign norms must be controlled in specific cases. Whereas the abstract "human rights approach" leads to clear results—the rejection of *ṭalāq* in all cases—the specific approach lacks such clarity. This might be one of the main reasons for the increasing popularity of the abstract approach in several European legal systems. In addition, it can be used as a political instrument to demonstrate Western "cultural self-defense" against Sharia-based law.

On the other hand, only the specific approach might help the divorced wife when, for instance, she wants to remarry and needs the *ṭalāq* she underwent to be recognized.[21] If not recognized, she is forced to apply for divorce in European courts, which is often equally time-consuming and expensive, in particular if the husband lives in a country that is not easily accessible for judicial correspondence, or if his address is unknown. The abstract "human rights approach" would then turn against the person it intends to protect.[22]

Such "international" legal cases have been the mainstay for the application of Sharia-based foreign laws until the recent past in many Western countries. But increasingly, former "international" cases have turned into "domestic" ones, as Muslims obtain the citizenship of their country of residence or are simply born there. Usually it is the law of the land that applies to their private transactions and family status and relations; in consequence, Sharia rules can only be applied under dispositive substantive law—the part of the private law order that is not governed by mandatory rules. For example, to enable business financing, Islamic law permits types of companies and contracts, such as *muḍāraba* and *murābaḥa*, in which unearned gain (*ribā*; see Chapter 18, above) does not play a role. None of these transactions contradicts European contract laws in general.

In the field of marriage law, the introduction of Islamic norms into marriage contracts has also been addressed within several European legal systems. This field has gained importance in the West, since most PIL systems now make habitual residence the prime connecting factor. Jurisdiction rules usually lead to the courts of habitual residence, and usually the law of the land will apply there. Institutions of Islamic family law will now regularly be scrutinized by the principles of the established family law rules.

Reasonable accommodation (Beaman 2012) in the sense of inclusive evenhandedness has to be sought by clarifying misunderstandings and false conflicts (in cases where legal institutions are not contradictory in fact), and by examining to what extent party autonomy opens up space for private choice, for example, in arranging matrimonial property (Rohe 2011a: 368ff.). Contractual conditions regulating the payment of dower (*mahr* or *ṣadāq*) in Muslim marriages must be particularly scrutinized (Fournier 2010: esp. 35–100;

18 Older decisions by the Court of Cassation from 2001, 2002 were now overruled since a turn of the same court in 2004 (February 17, 2004, nos 01–11.549, and 02–11.618; Court of Cassation, January 3, 2006, no. 04–15.231; Court of Cassation, November 4, 2009, no. 08–20.574). The decisions of 2004 were implicitly approved by the ECHR in its decision of November 8, 2005 (Affaire D.D. c France, no. 3/02, available in the French version at the court's website: http://hudoc.echr.coe.int, with the relevant new French decisions).

19 The last decisions in this sense were Court of Cassation, July 3, 2001 (Rev. crit. int. privé 2002, 704 note Gannagé).

20 OGH decision of August 31, 2006 (6Ob189/06), *Zeitschrift für Rechtsvergleichung* 2007: 35; OGH decision of June 28, 2007 (3Ob130/07z); both decisions available at www.ris.bka.gv.at.

21 This was the case in decisions of the German Supreme Court from 2004 (BGH FamRZ 2004, 1952) and from 2007 (NJW-RR 2007, pp. 145, 148ff.).

22 See Spanish Supreme Court, ATS, April 21, 1998, RJ 3563; Koch 2012: 181.

and Chapter 10, above). Such payments are owed to the bride, not her father or family,[23] as is the case in Yemen, Afghanistan, and Pakistan, whose customary practices are not recognized under European—even Turkish (Rumpf 2004: 118)—law.[24] Payments to the woman's father or family challenge her human dignity as well as her free will to decide whether or not to marry, while *mahr* improves her legal situation and cannot be considered a violation of her rights.[25] In traditional Islamic law, the *mahr* can be an effective instrument for the divorced woman or widow, who can waive her claim for the deferred *mahr* in exchange for the husband's agreement to a favorable custody regulation. In Britain, such an agreement was accepted in 2010,[26] while Dutch,[27] French,[28] and German[29] courts have accepted them in principle. Thus, this could be a future trend toward the "contractualization" of former "foreign" Islamic legal institutions by simply examining them under the domestic rules of dispositive contract law. In sum, Sharia-based regulations among private parties are to be judged according to the common principles of private (dispositive and mandatory) law without any specificities.

In addition, in some diaspora states, Sharia law regulating personal status, family issues, succession, and charities have become a part of state law for mainly historical reasons. This is, for example, the case in India, where the Shariat Application Act 1937 and other legislation concerning Muslims are still in force (Rohe 2011a: 286ff.). Article 44 of the Indian constitution, which mandates the promulgation of a uniform civil code, is still a dead letter, despite demands by courts, Hindu nationalists, and secularly oriented Indians to enforce it. The preservation of traditional personal status law is a highly sensitive political issue that no Indian government has so far dared to touch. Courts have indirectly intervened by interpreting Sharia rules contrary to traditional approaches. Interestingly, the Shah Bano case from 1985 (concerning a maintenance case decided in favor of the divorced wife) triggered heated debate and broad protest from traditionally oriented Muslims, whereas a newer case (Danial Latifi) from 2001 was practically overlooked by the public (Menski 2012: 249). Indeed, the official application of Islamic law in Indian courts relies on judges without specific training. Since colonial times courts have often stuck to very traditional sources, paralyzing an original fluid system of norms and sometimes completely misunderstanding them (Mahmood 1995).

Another example is found in Greece, where Sharia norms based on Ottoman family law apply to Muslims of Turkish and Bulgarian origin in Thrace, in accordance with the 1923 Treaty of Lausanne (Tsitselikis 2004: 417ff.). In recent years, a paper on family law and the full implementation of gender equality was drafted by Greek professors of law and other lawyers on behalf of the Ministry of Justice. It proposes the abolishment of the Sharia regime. In fact, the legal "freeze" by the Lausanne treaty is increasingly in contrast with the family law reforms that took place within Turkey in the course of the "secularization policy" under Mustafa Kemal Atatürk in the 1920s, which culminated with gender-neutral legislation in 2002 (equal rights for males and females in family law issues). Because of its sensitivity, however, the Greek government does not seem to be inclined to present the drafted suggestions to Parliament (Papadopoulou 2010).

---

23 As stressed by the French Court of Cassation, November 22, 2005, no. 03–14.961, whereby *mahr* cannot qualify as a *prix de vente*.

24 For example, Court of Appeals Hamm, January 13, 2011 (I-18 U 88/10). The Turkish Court of Cassation rejected a *başlık* (bride-price) claim due to the "breach of the law and ethical values" of the country: T.C. Yargıtay (19. Civ) no. 2009/6565; decision no. 2010/4421.

25 The *mahr* was misinterpreted in this sense by Regional Court Köln IPRspr. 1980, no. 83; Court of Appeals Lyon, December 2, 2002, reversed by Court of Cassation (1ère civ), November 22, 2005, no. 03–14.961.

26 Radmacher v. Granatino [2010] UKSC 42. The prior decision approving *mahr* (Uddin v. Choudhury [2009] EWCA Civ 1205) concerned a case of informal marriage. Dower agreements seem to have been seen as contractual in earlier decisions under previous legal rules (Shahnaz v. Rizwan [1964] 2 All E.R. 993; Qureshi v. Qureshi [1971] 1 All E.R. 325).

27 Rb Alkmaar, October 16, 2008; Rb Rotterdam, February 22, 2010.

28 Court of Cassation, December 2, 1997, no. 95–20.026 and November 22, 2005, no. 03–14.961.

29 Federal Supreme Court, NJW 1999, p. 574; OLG Celle FamRZ 1998, p. 374; OLG Saarbruecken NJW-RR 2005, p. 1306.

A few other European states have introduced Islamic legal provisions concerning family matters that can be applied to Muslims on a voluntary basis. In Britain Muslims may apply to register marriages under the Marriage Act 1949 (section 46) with civil effects. The British Adoption and Children Act of 2002 amended the Children Act of 1989 by provisions introducing "special guardianship," to legally enable parental relationships other than adoption, which is forbidden by Islamic law.[30] This option is not formulated on the basis of religion and is thus open to all.

In Spain, Islamic legal norms regulating marriage contracts have been applied to Muslims since 1992 (Mantecón Sancho 2004: 130ff.). In contrast, Article 107 of the civil code, which regulates the right to divorce, has been amended. The amendment enables women living in Spain to get a divorce even if matrimonial law in their country of origin or the country in which they married prevents them from doing so. This amendment was expressly intended to provide domestic legal remedies for Muslim women, thus limiting the application of foreign norms.[31] In sum, the formal incorporation of Islamic law in Spain is an exceptional case relating to merely formal legal provisions such as the procedural—not substantive—aspects of marriage contracts.

Such legislation has not been proposed in other European countries. In Germany, most Muslims of Turkish and Bosnian origin would vehemently oppose the introduction of Sharia legal norms, as traditional Islamic family and inheritance law—embracing patriarchal concepts and legal inequality of religions—were abolished in their home countries long ago.

A broader discussion has emerged in the UK among Muslims on the introduction of an (optional) Muslim law of personal status and inheritance. Given the present status of legal developments and evidence from Islamic Sharia councils in Britain, this would lead to forms of legal inequality of sexes and religions (Shah-Kazemi 2001; Bano 2012; Malik 2012). Contrary to the informally working Sharia councils, the British Muslim Arbitration Tribunals (MAT), established since 2007 in London, Birmingham, Bradford, Manchester, and Nuneaton under the Arbitration Act (1996),[32] are entitled to issue formal awards under this act related to commercial disputes, including economic issues arising from family disputes. They have no competence in personal status cases (most notably divorce and custody of children) (Douglas et al. 2011: 17, 22f.), but provide informal aid relating to, for example, an Islamic divorce equal to other Sharia councils.

When asked about gender-biased provisions of traditional Islamic divorce law, the founder of MAT, Faisal Aqtab Siddiqi, has said that there is no significant difference between husband and wife in *ṭalāq*, the husband giving the declaration of divorce and the wife receiving it. The exclusive right of the husband to pronounce the divorce, other gender-biased regulations in favor of the husband, and the dimension of legal-cultural conflicts between traditional Sharia provisions and European family law were a non-issue.[33] This attitude does not necessarily reflect the work of these institutions as a whole. According to Samia Bano (2012: 24), 22 Sharia councils in the UK seek to avoid any conflict with civil law by, for example, requiring the civil divorce of a registered marriage before issuing an Islamic divorce. Nevertheless, such pronouncements as those of Siddiqi are likely to trigger more resistance in the broader public, since they seem to verify the widespread prejudice against Sharia law, as mentioned earlier.

The work of such councils and tribunals thus serves persons seeking religious support, but also those who live at a distance from British legal institutions and seek socially acceptable conflict regulation within the community. It also serves Muslims whose divorces under British law are not fully accepted by the parties or in the community unless an Islamic divorce (*ṭalāq* or *khulʿ*) has taken place as well. The price to be paid is a loss of rights as compared to the standards of the law of the land (Shah-Kazemi 2001; Malik 2006).

30 For adoption in the Islamic world today, see Pearl and Menski 1998.

31 BOE, September 30, 2003, Ley Orgánica 11/2003, de 29 de septiembre, de medidas concretas en materia de seguridad ciudadana, violencia doméstica e integración social de los extranjeros, 4.

32 See also the MAT website, www.matribunal.com.

33 Remarks made at the annual LUCIS conference, June 20–21, 2011; for an overview of the conference, http://hum.leidenuniv.nl/lucis/eerder-bij-lucis/lucis-conference-2011-sharia-in-the-west.html.

Efforts by small numbers of extremist Islamist groups and the Salafi movement aimed at the construction of an exclusive Muslim normative order oppose the governing rules of the land. According to research done in the German state of Bavaria in 2012,[34] there are some cases of culturally or Sharia-inspired "parallel justice" in family matters in which undue pressure was placed on women to refrain from exercising their rights under German law. More research seems to be necessary in this field.

Reasons for the Application of Sharia

A number of reasons are given for applying Sharia-based legal norms in the diaspora. Insofar as PIL law leads to the application of such norms, there are reasons that do not stem from the parties' intentions. Sometimes the parties might even reject such application, as, for instance, Iranian citizens living in Europe who are forced to apply Iranian inheritance law according to the existing legal situation. In addition, in some cases the countries of origin of the parties only recognize decisions under Western laws if their own laws are applied, thereby forcing parties into accepting the application of this law irrespective of their own preferences.

The application of Sharia-based norms might play a role in cultural self-definition and self-defense in a new diasporic situation. This is certainly the case in India, where Urdu, Muslim Personal Law, and the Islamic University of Aligarh represent what is left over from former Muslim rule and pride (Rohe 2011a: 307f., 314).

Finally, religious motives might prevail. Sharia norms, whether religious or legal, are an intrinsic part of Muslim faith. This is unproblematic when these norms accord with the legal system of the country of residence, but it becomes problematic when an unofficial parallel legal system to replace them is implemented by social pressure. Not everyone who applies Islamic norms to arrange his or her personal affairs necessarily rejects the existing legal order (Rohe 2011b). In recent years there are new forms of social arrangements among young Muslim couples who marry (unofficially) in accordance with Islamic provisions so as to placate their families, but also to avoid legal consequences (for example, of maintenance and inheritance claims) under the law of the land.

Religious Sharia Rules in the Diaspora

Formal Application

In applying Sharia norms in the West, the legal systems fundamentally differentiate between religious and legal issues. In Europe, religious issues are regulated by the European and national constitutional provisions including Article 9 of the European Convention on Human Rights (ECHR), which grants freedom of religion, including state neutrality toward religions. The same kind of protection is granted by constitutions in the Americas and in Australia/Oceania. Thus, from a legal (certainly not a socio-cultural) point of view there are no "foreign" religious norms as opposed to "domestic" ones.

Freedom of religion is not limited to private worship, but also grants an adequate (but not an unlimited) protection of religious needs in various aspects of public life regulated by public law (Rohe 2007: 79, 82–8). Nevertheless, Western countries vary in their applications of these provisions due to differing interpretations regarding the desirable degree of distance between the state and

34 A research group of legal practitioners and social organizations, led by the author and initiated and funded by the Bavarian Ministry of Justice, is researching preventive and repressive measures. The results are forthcoming.

religion (Ferrari and Bradney 2000; Aluffi Beck-Peccoz and Zincone 2004; Potz and Wieshaider 2004; Rohe and Elster 2006; European Parliament 2007; Foblets et al. 2010). Muslims are reacting to the situation they find themselves in by broadly accepting the existing legal framework. The debates and demands regarding Islam in the public space largely differ—while in France students, teachers, and civil servants are not allowed to wear the hijab (Bowen 2009), in the UK they may.

Another level where religious norms can have an impact are social relations governed by civil law, specifically (but not exclusively) employment law. In this field, possible conflicting interests of employers and employees have to be weighed with respect for the employee's religious needs on the one hand and the employer's specific needs on the other (Hoevels 2003; Rohe 2011a: 346ff.). Many Muslims do not face legal problems concerning their employment as in most cases acceptable solutions can be found. Although in Britain a bus driver claiming the right to interrupt his work five times a day for prayer lost his case for obvious reasons (Shadid and van Koningsveld 1995: 102), most Muslim employees have found a middle way by praying during regular breaks or concentrating their prayers in the morning and evening. Employers often allow Muslim employees to participate in communal prayer at mosques on Fridays or to finish working earlier in the day. Muslim workers can also generally use vacation days for the two Eids. Nevertheless, in many cases headscarves or other religious garments are not allowed in Western labor markets.[35]

Informal Application

Religious norms can be "applied" at an informal level, merely by practicing them. It is mainly in the sphere of religious rules—concerning the relations between God and human beings (*ʿibādāt*) and the non-legal aspects of relations between human beings (*muʿāmalāt*)—where a European or Western Sharia (in this context: Islamic "theology") is possibly developing (Shadid and van Koningsveld 2002: 149; Waardenburg 2003: 241, 308, 336; Rohe 2004: 161ff.). In such cases, the opinions contained in fatwas do not conflict with the existing law of the land, but regulate Muslim behavior and transactions only according to religious standards, without any worldly legal sanctions. The Dublin-based European Council for Fatwa and Research and the London-based Islamic Sharia Council issue fatwas particularly pertaining to Muslim life in a secular environment among a non-Muslim majority.[36] In the US, the Fiqh Council of North America operates in this field.[37]

Advice asked of these institutions mostly concern women's and family issues (how to deal with inter-religious marriages; how to preserve Muslim family life), but include a range from labor and education issues (should a Muslim accept employment forcing him or her to serve alcohol or pork; is a Muslim entitled to postpone ritual prayers until the evening on account of school or work) to legal and political issues (can a Muslim be punished for adultery in a Western country; how to deal with apostates; is a Muslim allowed to or obliged to accept a secular non-Muslim government; should Muslims participate in elections) (Rohe 2004; Hellyer 2009: 79–99; Albrecht 2010; Caeiro 2011).

The answers show four trends: First, legal Sharia(-based) sanctions that must be implemented by state institutions are declared inapplicable in a non-Islamic state. Thus, there is no room for penal sanctions according to traditional Sharia law. Other legal norms should be considered within the scope of the law of the land, but the legal institutions of the law of the land should be respected and used, as, for example, in the case of marriage.

Second, Islamic religion, ethics, or morals should be upheld as much as possible in the diasporic environment. The traditional patriarchal view on gender and family issues is mostly maintained, but mitigated by appeals not to use violence or exercise pressure to implement the rules; this is also the

35 For an internal Muslim debate on the necessity of wearing headscarves, see Alvi et al. 2003.
36 Their respective websites are www.e-cfr.org/ar/ and www.islamic-sharia.org/.
37 See www.fiqhcouncil.org.

main topic of religious literature offered in mosques and Islamic bookstores. Concretely, there is a trend to apply traditional Sharia norms in the way that is most favorable for women on the basis of new interpretations (*ijtihād*), but still preserving their patriarchal framework. Sometimes very traditional approaches are kept. Concerning the Sharia provisions of evidence, which in some cases exclude women from witnessing or require two female witnesses as the equivalent of one male, the London Sharia Council does not shy away from explanations that were common worldwide until the nineteenth century, viz., women are emotional and men rational; men are able to concentrate on one task, women are multitaskers (for example, in the kitchen) and might therefore be distracted from the relevant observations, etc.[38]

Third, muftis mostly look for viable solutions to reconcile economic and social needs and religious commands, using the principles of necessity (*ḍarūra*) and public interest (*maṣlaḥa*), to take into account the particular circumstances of Muslim minorities. These are the most significant characteristics of the newly adapted jurisprudence for Muslim minorities, *fiqh al-aqalliyyāt*.

Fourth, the religious commands of Islam should be preserved to the largest possible extent, but open and friendly relations with non-Muslims are not only permissible but required. Fatwas such as these might be seen as a response to challenges from Muslim-majority countries such as Saudi Arabia, where influential institutions try to influence Muslims with a more inflexible interpretation of Islam. For example, Saudi fatwas by Bin Bāz (d. 1999) and al-ʿUthaymīn (d. 2000) are distributed for free in mosques and elsewhere, advising Muslims to found their own institutions in opposition to the secular ones within the country, to refrain from congratulating Christians on their religious feasts, etc. In contrast, proponents of minority fiqh are more moderate and open to inter-religious communication, as long as it does not challenge the core of Muslim belief. Their argument is that living in a non-Muslim environment requires being friendly to everyone, this being the only way to convince people of the values of Islam.

Distinguishing between legal and religious aspects of Sharia is not new in Islam, viz., the classical distinction between what is forbidden (*ḥarām*), and what is invalid (*bāṭil*) (Rohe 2011a: 9ff.). It reflects a broader trend among Western Muslims toward a de-territorialization and de-legislation of Sharia, interpreting it anew as a primarily ethical or moral set of norms. This approach is developed by Muslim scholars under the heading of Sharia provisions providing guidance rather than governance (An-Naʿim 2008: esp. 28–44). The scholars range from traditionally oriented (those represented by the European Council for Fatwa and Research; Rohe 2004: esp. 176–9) and other proponents of minority fiqh to innovative thinkers such as Abdulaziz Sachedina (2006), Ahmad Moussalli (2001), Tareq Oubrou (1998, 2003), Khaled Abou El Fadl (2001, 2005: 142ff.), Amina Wadud (2006: 92ff.), Farid Esack (1997, 2000), Abdullah Saeed (2003: esp. 114ff., 198ff.), or Mouhanad Khorchide (2012: 116ff.). Some reject the concept of *fiqh al-aqalliyyāt*, arguing that Muslims should not perceive themselves as a (distinct) minority but as an integral part of the societies they are living in ("entrenchment approach"; Rohe 2011a: 389ff.).

Within the broader Muslim debate on Sharia in the diaspora, four major trends can be discerned: (1) removing the "ethnic-cultural layer" from "true Islam," aiming at reconciling Islam with human rights standards and democracy; (2) its opposite, developing an imagined "original pure Islam" opposed to democracy and human rights, which are denounced to be a Western invention;[39] (3) perhaps the dominant one—preserving moderate Islamic religious and cultural traditions to avoid in equal measure rigidity and leniency in interpreting Sharia norms. Representatives of this trend tend to hold on to the culture of their country of origin. Younger generations are defining themselves increasingly as Muslims rather than in the light of the migration past of their families, thus, (4) adapting

38 See the relevant fatwa at www.islamic-sharia.org/general/on-the-testimony-of-women-2.html.

39 This Salafi-type argument is supported by, for example, the Jamaica-born convert Bilal Philips, who does not shy away from demanding the death penalty for homosexuals. Philips was expelled from Germany in 2011 (see "Islamprediger Philips wird ausgewiesen" from April 21, 2011, available at www.n24.de/news/newsitem_6828865.html).

religious rules to local circumstances and developing a religious basis of self-definition (creating a self-conscious Muslim identity) as part of Western society. Tariq Ramadan, one of the most influential Muslim thinkers in Europe, aims at a culture of entrenchment while preserving Muslim identity:

> we are to feel at home and apply in a positive way the Islamic principle of integrating all that does not contradict the prohibitions and making it our own. [...] As citizens of states that recognize human rights, Muslims are no longer under the law of foreign states or former colonies and they should reject the status of subcitizens [...]. To regain confidence in oneself, one's values, one's role also means in practice, reclaiming one's rights and respect. Through involvement in education reform, social and political participation, economic resistance, interreligious dialogue, and contributions to culture [...] (2009: 224f.).

In India, the Delhi-based Islamic Fiqh Academy (2001, 2007) is one of the institutions of a Muslim advisory culture. While the trends of its fatwas are similar to those mentioned above, in India the issue of Muslim personal law plays an important role as well.

Last but not least, the effects of an increasing globalization should not be overlooked. It has the effect of delimiting the Sharia debate from two sides, since Internet fatwa institutions and websites are bridging the borders between the diasporas and the Muslim "mainland" in both directions, offering new levels of exchange, while at the same time opening fields of new competition (Kutscher 2009). The effects of these new forms of interaction are unclear as of yet, but deserve future research.

References

Abou El Fadl, Khaled. 2001. *Speaking in God's Name: Islamic Law, Authority, and Women*. Oxford: Oneworld.

———. 2005. *The Great Theft: Wrestling Islam from the Extremists*. New York: HarperCollins.

Albrecht, Sarah. 2010. *Islamisches Minderheitenrecht: Yūsuf al-Qaraḍāwīs Konzept des* fiqh al-aqallīyāt. Würzburg: Ergon.

Alidadi, Katayoun. 2005. The Western Judicial Answer to Islamic Talaq: Peeking through the Gate of Conflict of Laws in the U.S. and Belgium. *UCLA Journal of Islamic and Near Eastern Law* 5: 1–80.

Aluffi Beck-Peccoz, Roberta, and Giovanna Zincone, eds. 2004. *The Legal Treatment of Islamic Minorities in Europe*. Leuven: Peeters.

Alvi, Sajida Sultana, Sheila McDonough, and Homa Hoodfar, eds. 2003. *The Muslim Veil in North America: Issues and Debates*. Toronto: Women's Press.

An-Na'im, Abdullah Ahmed. 2008. *Islam and the Secular State: Negotiating the Future of Shari'a*. Cambridge, MA: Harvard University Press.

Bahners, Patrick. 2011. *Die Panikmacher: Die deutsche Angst vor dem Islam. Eine Streitschrift*. München: C.H. Beck.

Bakht, Natasha. 2006. Were Muslim Barbarians Really Knocking On the Gates of Ontario? The Religious Arbitration Controversy – Another Perspective. *Ottawa Law Review* 40th Anniversary Edition: 67–82.

Bälz, Kilian. 2005. Das islamische Recht als Vertragsstatut? Kommentar zur Entscheidung des London High Court v. 1. 8., Shamil Bank of Bahrein vs. Beximco Pharmaceuticals Ltd. and Others. *Praxis des Internationalen Privat- und Verfahrensrechts* 25: 44–7.

Bano, Samia. 2012. *An Exploratory Study of Shariah Councils in England with Respect to Family Law*. Available at www.reading.ac.uk/web/FILES/law/An_exploratory_study_of_Shariah_councils_in_England_with_respect_to_family_law_.pdf.

Beaman, Lori G. 2012. Conclusion: Alternatives to Reasonable Accommodation. In idem, ed., *Reasonable Accommodation: Managing Religious Diversity*, pp. 208–23. Vancouver: UBC Press.

Bielefeldt, Heiner. 2003. *Muslime im säkularen Rechtsstaat: Integrationschancen durch Religionsfreiheit*. Bielefeld: Transcript.

Bowen, John. 2009. *Can Islam Be French? Pluralism and Pragmatism in a Secularist State*. Princeton: Princeton University Press.

Brettfeld, Katrin, and Peter Wetzels. 2007. *Muslime in Deutschland: Integration, Integrationsbarrieren, Religion sowie Einstellungen zu Demokratie, Rechtsstaat und politisch-religiös motivierter Gewalt*. Available at www.bmi.bund.de (search under Brettfeld). Accessed February 19, 2013.

Büchler, Andrea. 2011. *Islamic law in Europe? Legal Pluralism and its Limits in European Family Law*. Farnham, Surrey, UK: Ashgate.

Caeiro, Alexandre. 2011. Transnational "Ulama," European Fatwas and Islamic Authority: A Case Study of the European Council for Fatwa and Research. In *Producing Islamic Knowledge: Transmission and Dissemination in Western Europe*, ed. M. van Bruinessen and S. Allievi, pp. 121–41. Abingdon, UK: Routledge.

Cesari, Jocelyne, ed. 2010. *Muslims in the West after 9/11: Religion, Politics and Law*. London: Routledge.

Ceylan, Rauf. 2012. Muslime und Diaspora – interdisziplinäre Forschungsfragen im Einwanderungskontext. In idem, ed., *Islam und Diaspora: Analysen zum muslimischen Leben in Deutschland aus historischer, rechtlicher sowie migrations- und religionssoziologischer Perspektive*, pp. 9–30. Frankfurt am Main: Lang.

Cohen, Robin. 2008. *Global Diasporas*. An Introduction. London: Routledge.

Douglas, Gillian et al. 2011. Social Cohesion and Civil Law: Marriage, Divorce and Religious Courts. Available at http://papers.ssrn.com/sol3/papers.cfm?abstract_id=1940387.

Esack, Farid. 1997. *Qur'ān, Liberation and Pluralism: An Islamic Perspective on Interreligious Solidarity Against Oppression*. Oxford: Oneworld.

———. 2000. *On Being A Muslim: Finding a Religious Path in the World Today*. Oxford: Oneworld.

European Parliament, Directorate General for Internal Policies of the Union. 2007. *Islam in the European Union: What's at Stake in the Future*? May 2007 (PE 369.031).

Ferrari, Silvio, and Anthony Bradney, eds. 2000. *Islam and European Legal Systems*. Aldershot, UK: Ashgate.

Foblets, Marie-Claire. 2001. Le statut personnel musulman devant les tribunaux en Europe: une reconnaissance conditionnelle. In *L'étranger et le droit de la famille: Pluralité ethnique, pluralisme juridique*, ed. P. Kahn, pp. 33–71. Paris: La Documentation Française, Mission de Recherche Droit et Justice.

———. 2007. The Admissibility of Repudiation: Recent Developments in Dutch, French and Belgian Private International Law. *Hawwa* 5: 10–32.

——— et al., eds. 2010. *Cultural Diversity and the Law*. Brussels: Bruylant.

Fournier, Pascale. 2010. *Muslim Marriage in Western Courts: Lost in Transition*. Farnham, Surrey, UK: Ashgate.

Gärtner, Veronika. 2008. *Die Privatscheidung im deutschen und gemeinschaftlichen Internationalen Privat- und Verfahrensrecht*. Tübingen: Mohr Siebeck.

Gaudreault-DesBiens, Jean-François. 2010a. Religious Courts' Recognition Claims: Two Qualitatively Distinct Narratives. In *Shari'a in the West*, ed. R. Ahdar and N. Aroney, pp. 59–69. New York: Oxford University Press.

———. 2010b. Religious Courts, Personal Federalism, and Legal Transplants. In *Shari'a in the West*, ed. R. Ahdar and N. Aroney, pp. 159–80. New York: Oxford University Press.

Glazer, Sarah. 2012. Sharia Controversy. *CQ Global Researcher* 6: 1–27.

Hellyer, H.A. 2009. *Muslims of Europe: The "Other" Europeans*. Edinburgh: Edinburgh University Press.

Hoevels, Niloufar. 2003. *Islam und Arbeitsrecht*. Cologne: Carl Heymanns.

Islamic Fiqh Academy. 2001. *Important Fiqh Decisions*. New Delhi. IFA.

———. 2007. *Juristic Decisions on Contemporary Issues*. New Delhi: IFA.

Johansen, Birgitte, and Riem Spielhaus. 2012. Counting Deviance: Revisiting a Decade's Production of Surveys among Muslims in Western Europe. *Journal of Muslims in Europe* 1: 81–112.

Khorchide, Mouhanad. 2012. *Islam ist Barmherzigkeit: Grundzüge einer modernen Religion*. Freiburg: Herder.

Koch, Julia. 2012. *Die Anwendung islamischen Scheidungs- und Scheidungsfolgenrechts im Internationalen Privatrecht der EU-Mitgliedstaaten: Eine Rechtsvergleichende Analyse unter besonderer Berücksichtigung des nationalen und europäischen ordre public*. Frankfurt am Main: Peter Lang.

Kutscher, Jens. 2009. The Politics of Virtual Fatwa Counseling in the 21st Century. Available at http://www.digitalislam.eu/article.do?articleId=2349. Accessed March 15, 2014.

Laurence, Jonathan. 2012. *The Emancipation of Europe's Muslims: The State's Role in Minority Integration*. Princeton: Princeton University Press.

Mahmood, Tahir. 1995. *Statute-Law Relating to Muslims in India: A Study in Constitutional and Islamic Perspectives*. New Delhi: Institute of Objective Studies.

Malik, Maleiha. 2006. "The Branch on Which We Sit": Multiculturalism, Minority Women and Family Law. In *Feminist Perspectives on Family Law*, ed. A. Diduck and K. O'Donovan, pp. 211–34. Abingdon, UK: Routledge-Cavendish.

———. 2012. *Minority Legal Orders in the UK*. London: British Academy Policy Centre. Available at www.britac.ac.uk/policy/Minority-legal-orders.cfm.

Manjoo, Rashida. 2007. *The Recognition of Muslim Personal Laws in South Africa: Implications for Women's Human Rights*. Harvard Law School, Human Rights Program, Working Paper Series. Accessible at www.law.harvard.edu/programs/hrp/documents/Manjoo_RashidaWP.pdf. Accessed February 19, 2013.

Mantecón Sancho, Joaquín. 2004. *L'Islam en Espagne. In Islam and the European Union*, ed. R. Potz and W. Wieshaider, pp. 109–42. Leuven: Peeters.

Menski, Werner. 2012. Ancient and Modern Boundary Crossing between Personal Laws and Civil Law in Composite India. In *Marriage and Divorce in a Multicultural Context: Multi-Tiered Marriage and the Boundaries of Civil Law and Religion*, ed. J.A. Nichols, pp. 219–52. New York: Cambridge University Press.

Milbank, John. 2010. The Archbishop of Canterbury: The Man and the Theology Behind the Shari'a lecture. In *Shari'a in the West*, ed. R. Ahdar and N. Aroney, pp. 43–57. New York: Oxford University Press.

Mir-Hosseini, Ziba. 2009. Islamic Family Law and Social Practice: Anthropological Reflections on the Terms of the Debate. In *Family, Law and Religion: Debates in the Muslim World and Europe and Their Implications for Co-operation and Dialogue*, ed. S. Haas, pp. 37–48. Vienna: Austrian Association for the Middle East Hammer-Purgstall.

Moghissi, Haideh, Saeed Rahnema, and Mark J. Goodman. 2009. *Diaspora by Design: Muslim Immigrants in Canada and Beyond*. Toronto: University of Toronto Press.

Moussalli, Ahmad S. 2001. *The Islamic Quest for Democracy, Pluralism, and Human Rights*. Gainesville: University Press of Florida.

Nielsen, Jörgen S., and Lisbet Christoffersen, eds. 2010. *Shari'a as Discourse: Legal Traditions and the Encounter with Europe*. Farnham, Surrey, UK: Ashgate.

Oubrou, Tareq. 1998. Introduction théorétique à la chari'a de minorité. *Islam de France* 2: 27–34.

———. 2003. *La Charia de minorité: Contribution pour une integration légale de l'islam*. Available at www.islamlaicite.org/article24.html. Accessed February 24, 2013.

Papadopoulou, Lina. 2010. *Trapped in History: Greek Muslim Women under the Sacred Islamic Law*. Available at http://papers.ssrn.com/sol3/papers.cfm?abstract_id=1877048. Accessed February 22, 2013.

Pearl, David, and Werner Menski. 1998. *Muslim Family Law*. 3rd ed. London: Sweet & Maxwell.

Peters, Rudolph (Ruud). 2003. *Islamic Criminal Law in Nigeria*. Ibadan: Spectrum Books.

Potz, Richard, and Wolfgang Wieshaider, eds. 2004. *Islam and the European Union*. Leuven: Peeters.

Ramadan, Tariq. 2009. *Radical Reform: Islamic Ethics and Liberation*. Oxford: Oxford University Press.

Rohe, Mathias. 2003. Islamic Law in German Courts. *Hawwa* 3: 46–59.

———. 2004. The Formation of a European Shari'a. In *Muslims in Europe: From the Margin to the Centre*, ed. J. Malik, pp. 161–84. Münster: Lit.

———. 2006. Islamismus und Schari'a. In *Integration und Islam*, ed. M. Fischelmayer et al., pp. 120–56. Nürnberg: Bundesamt für Migration und Flüchtlinge.

———. 2007. *Muslim Minorities and the Law in Europe: Chances and Challenges*. New Delhi: Global Media Publications.

———. 2011a. *Das islamische Recht: Geschichte und Gegenwart*. 3rd ed. München: C.H. Beck (Eng. trans. forthcoming Leiden: Brill).

———. 2011b. *Alternative Dispute Resolution in Europe under the Auspices of Religious Norms*. RELIGARE working paper no. 6. January 2011. Available at www.religareproject.eu/content/alternative-dispute-resolution-europe-under-auspices-religious-norms.

Rohe, Mathias, and Sebastian Elster. 2006. Zur öffentlichrechtlichen Situation von Muslimen in ausgewählten europäischen Ländern. In *Perspektiven und Herausforderungen in der Integration muslimischer Mitbürgerinnen in Österreich*. Vienna: Bundesministerium des Inneren Wien/Sicherheitsakademie.

Rumpf, Christian. 2004. *Einführung in das türkische Recht*. München: C.H. Beck.

Sachedina, Abdulaziz. 2006. The Role of Islam in the Public Square: Guidance or Governance? In *Islamic Democratic Discourse: Theory, Debates, and Philosophical Perspectives*, ed. M. Khan, pp. 173–91. Lanham, MD: Lexington Books.

Saeed, Abdullah, and Shahram Akbarzadeh, eds. 2003. *Islam and Political Legitimacy*. London: RoutledgeCurzon.

Schiffauer, Werner. 2000. *Die Gottesmänner—türkische Islamisten in Deutschland: Eine Studie zur Herstellung religiöser Evidenz*. Frankfurt am Main: Suhrkamp.

Shadid, Wasif, and P.S. van Koningsveld. 1995. *Religious Freedom and the Position of Islam in Western Europe: Opportunities and Obstacles in the Acquisition of Equal Rights*. Kampen: Kok Pharos.

———. 2002. Religious Authorities of Muslims in the West: Their Views on Political Participation. In *Intercultural Relations and Religious Authorities: Muslims in the European Union*, ed. W.A.R. Shadid and P.S. van Koningsveld, pp. 149–68. Leuven: Peeters.

Shah, Prakash. 2010. Between God and the Sultana? Legal Pluralism in the British Muslim Diaspora. In *Shari'a as Discourse: Legal Traditions and the Encounter with Europe*, ed. J. Nielsen and L. Christoffersen, pp. 117–39. Farnham, Surrey, UK: Ashgate.

Shah-Kazemi, Sonia N. 2001. *Untying the Knot: Muslim Women, Divorce and the Shariah*. London: Nuffield Foundation.

Silvestri, Sara. 2012. Comparing Burqa Debates in Europe: Sartorial Styles, Religious Prescriptions and Political Ideologies. In *Religion in Public Spaces: A European Perspective*, ed. S. Ferrari and S. Pastorelli, pp. 275–92. Farnham, Surrey, UK: Ashgate.

South African Law Commission. 2002. *Discussion Paper 101: Islamic Marriages and Related Matters*. Available at www. justice.gov.za/salrc/dpapers/dp101.pdf. Accessed February 19, 2013.

Tsitselikis, Konstantinos. 2004. The Legal Status of Islam in Greece. *Die Welt des Islams* 44: 402–31.

Voorhoeve, Maaike, ed. 2012. *Family Law in Islam: Divorce, Marriage and Women in the Muslim World.* London: I.B. Tauris.

Waardenburg, Jacques. 2003. *Muslims and Others: Relations in Context.* Berlin: De Gruyter.

Wadud, Amina. 2006. *Inside the Gender Jihad: Women's Reform in Islam.* Oxford: Oneworld.

Williams, Rowan. 2008. *Civil and Religious Law in England: A Religious Perspective.* Available at http://rowanwilliams.archbishopofcanterbury.org (speech of February 8, 2008). Accessed February 19, 2013.

Witte, John Jr. 2010. The Future of Muslim Family Law in Western Democracies. In *Shari'a in the West*, ed. R. Ahdar and N. Aroney, pp. 279–92. New York: Oxford University Press.

Zucca, Lorenzo. 2012. *A Secular Europe: Law and Religion in the European Constitutional Landscape.* Oxford: Oxford University Press.

Sharia and Modernity

Kristine Kalanges

A comprehensive treatment of Sharia and modernity, for which there is no single definition or experience, would necessarily engage the rest of the chapters in this volume, for the intersection of Islam with the modern world implicates all of Islamic law, both its historical and contemporary significance. The aim of this chapter, therefore, is limited to introducing some of the relevant lines of discourse, with a particular focus on Sharia and governance—more specifically, democracy, constitutionalism, and human rights.

Islam and Modernity

As the twentieth century drew to a close, the secularization thesis—that modernization leads to a decline in religious values and practices, especially in the public realm—came under increasing scrutiny (Rubin 1994). While modernization has had some secularizing effects (for example, in Europe), elsewhere it has generated counter-secularization movements (Berger 1999) and a greater role for religious institutions in public politics and culture (Casanova 1994; Hefner 1998). This certainly applies to Muslim societies, where the relationship of Islam and modernity is particularly contested and where religious intellectuals are making vital contributions to an emerging public sphere (Eickelman 2000). At stake are such issues as the proper interpretation of Islamic law, the compatibility of Islam with democracy and human rights, the integration of Muslim-majority countries into the modern world on Islamic terms, and the means by which to prevent fundamentalism from dominating Islamic thought and practice (Khalil 2004).

In the Muslim reaction to modernity, various specific and interrelated factors have been said to have played a significant role—for example, the aggravation of a preexisting sense of decline by colonial rule; the arrival during colonialism of Christian missionaries who attacked Muslim beliefs; and the education of Muslim youth in newly created institutions that linked modernization with Westernization and further ridiculed Islam and Muslim practices (Masud 2009). When modernity is defined more broadly to incorporate such phenomena as the formation of states, the organization of capitalist economies, the rise of science and technology, and attendant social and cultural changes, then Islamic revival movements are simultaneously a reaction against and an expression of modernity (Lapidus 1997). This engagement with modernity has emerged differently over time. The modernism of Muḥammad ʿAbduh (d. 1905), which called for "a commitment to the revitalization of Islam in

Kristine Kalanges is Associate Professor of Law at the University of Notre Dame, where she is also a faculty fellow in the Kellogg Institute for International Studies and the Kroc Institute for International Peace Studies. She is the author of *Religious Liberty in Western and Islamic Law: Toward a World Legal Tradition* (2012).

the face of European ascendance, a revival that consisted in part in casting Islam as the 'religion of reason'," contrasts with his compatriot Sayyid Quṭb's (d. 1966) critique that "the vitality of Islamic *umma* (community) and the veiled truths that sustain it require instead a repudiation of Western, rationalist ways of knowing and thus organizing the world" (Euben 1997: 434).

Also helpful in avoiding the oversimplification of a highly complex network of discourses and praxis are typologies, for example, conservative, neofundamentalist, reformist, secularist (Monshipouri 2009: 247–54), which are used to organize and illuminate the diversity of Islamic experiences with and reactions to modernity. An alternative framework, focusing on rising levels of religiosity as manifested in one of four forms, for example, popular Islam, political Islam, intellectual Islam (further demarcated into conservative and reformist strands), and Islamic fundamentalism, was proposed by Mehran Kamrava (2006), who notes that they are often mutually reinforcing. For example, popular Islam, characterized by growing piety and religious observance, can facilitate the rise of political Islam, "a political means and a political end in itself," which can in turn manifest in extremist and violent forms (fundamentalist Islam) when emergent in repressive political environments (Kamrava 2006: 6). Yet another approach is that of Bassam Tibi, who rejects the notion of multiple modernities ("there exists only one modernity, shared by the whole of humanity … consonant with the heritage of Islamic rationalism") (2009: 7). He calls for the revival of Islamic rationalism, which he links with secularization, and for religious pluralism.[1] In contemplating the above, it is useful to recall, to borrow from Wael Hallaq (2009: 279), that applying standards from "a secularized modern Europe" to Islam is fraught with difficulty; moreover, distinguishing between seemingly contrasting ideologies such as secularism and Salafism, the Egyptian philosopher Ḥasan Ḥanafī has cautioned, may represent "a false dualism" (Wahyudi 2006).

Democracy and Constitutionalism in the Muslim World

In the debates on Islam and modernity, two themes stand out: the relationship between the Sharia and modern constitutionalism and that between Islam and democracy. As with Islamic responses to modernity, there is a spectrum of approaches to religion and governance. Clinton Bennett (2005: 44–5) classifies these ideologically from left to right in the following manner: secular Muslims (advocate separation of religion and state, although Islam can inform the values and public ethics of the state);[2] progressives (embrace an Islamic state with an elected executive, a liberal view of gender and minorities, and alternative punishments for theft); revivalists (seek an Islamic state with elected executives, but with different rights for non-Muslims and women, limited pluralism, and traditional approaches to punishment); and fundamentalists (insist upon a non-elected executive with a traditional interpretation of Islamic law, and possibly even the violent overthrow of existing regimes and violent jihad with America and Israel). The diversity of views represented indicates the weakness of monolithic accounts of the debate over Islam and democracy (Voll 2005: 86). This is compounded by differences in religious, ethnic, and national identities of Muslims, and by complex political and economic histories of Muslim states, as well as the need to differentiate between electoral democracy (for example) and genuine constitutional liberalism (Zakaria 2004).

The debate as to whether Islam is compatible with democracy enjoys as well a plurality of voices. Some who advocate the idea that Islam is compatible with or enjoins democracy argue that

1 Tibi's project is not without controversy; some argue that it rests on a caricature of the West and Islam and on a homogenized, one-sided treatment of Islam as Islamic or Muslim fundamentalism (Farouk-Alli 2006: 288–91).

2 Representing the emerging sub-discipline of comparative political theory, Hashemi 2009 and March 2009 explore the compatibility of Islam with secularism and liberal democracy.

the Islamic embrace of democratic principles did not originate in the modern age. These scholars trace it back to the Quran and the Prophet, drawing in part on the exegesis of the eleventh-century Shafiʿi jurist al-Māwardī. They identify the so-called Constitution of Medina as democratic, citing its promulgation of standing laws defining the rights and duties of all members of the state, arrangements for impartial decisions on matters of right, and unfailing protection of the members of the community in the enjoyment of these rights. The purposes of this "early model of an Islamic state" were, among others, to fashion citizens into a new unity, "to maintain peace and cooperation, to protect the life and property of all citizens, to eliminate aggression and injustice regardless of tribal or religious affiliations, and to ensure freedom of religion and movement" (Khatab and Bouma 2007: 34).

The credal principle of *tawḥīd* ("oneness"), which stipulates that sovereignty over all belongs to God and authority exercised by people falls within divinely set limits, is also referenced in the assertion that specific democratic values are enshrined in the Quran. Although it would seem to be the opposite of the principle of popular sovereignty, a threefold argument is put forth for the co-existence of divine sovereignty and democracy within the Islamic tradition: first, political power has been delegated by God to the people; second, this delegation serves as a moral check on the power of those who exercise it, as they must acknowledge its divine source; and third, such power can only be used for the creation of a just society (otherwise, orders may be annulled and leaders removed) (Jillani 2006: 734–6). This and related principles, such as consensus and *ijtihād*, as well as a pluralistic tradition,[3] are taken to indicate that Islam is not "the chief encumbrance to the development of democracy in Muslim states"; rather, other factors such as complacency, ruthless suppression of dissent, and a de-emphasis on education and scientific research combined with colonial rule, postcolonial authoritative rule, and the development of fascism in the Middle East to erode democratic ideals in the modern Muslim world (Jillani 2006: 745–8).

It is nearly impossible to separate an analysis of Islam and democracy from considerations of jurisprudence. Mohammad Fadel suggests a clarifying distinction between Islamic law as a system of moral reasoning and Islamic law as a separate system of positive law. Insofar as it is a system of moral reasoning, Muslims are morally and religiously bound to the rules of Islamic law. Non-Muslims, however, are not bound and thus questions of jurisdiction arise (Fadel 2012: 234). Moreover, applied Islamic law is the product of both the jurists and the state, whereby the two main issues become: who has the authority to reform the Sharia and how can the Sharia comply with the rule of law and constitutional principles? Some argue that law in the Muslim world should be interpreted primarily via the state's legal system, with Islamic law understood within the context of that system (Hamoudi 2009: 813), or that the state (and only the state) can secure a revival of Islamic law (Hallaq 2004: 47). For others, because in Muslim states "religious authorities—individuals—have a special status and may be beyond the law," a limited rule of law system based on "reformed and rationalized principles" of Sharia may be established provided it is developed from within and gradually (Esmaeili 2011: 344, 366). What would such a development require?

Noah Feldman attributes the absence of political justice in much of the Muslim world to the failure of modern Muslim states to "establish themselves as legal states in the twin senses of being legitimated by law and governing through it" (2008: 8). Historically, through their interpretation and administration of Islamic law, the jurists balanced the power of executive authorities. In Feldman's view, a proper interpretation of the present call for Sharia is a call for a return to the rule of law, which can only be restored if effective human institutions emerge and are "reinforced by regular practice and the recognition of the actors within the system that they have more to gain by remaining faithful to its dictates than by deviating from them" (2008: 149). Localized self-interest (rather than episodic

3 For the innateness and importance of pluralism in the Islamic tradition, see also Sachedina 2001; Yilmaz 2005: 31.

external pressure) is essential to the adoption and sustainability of constitutional rights such as liberty and equality in Muslim states, he asserts (2005: 885–9).[4]

Feldman's account has not gone unchallenged. Mohammad Fadel frames the constitutional dilemma of the modern Islamic state in different terms, asking "how to square the normative assumptions implicit in the Islamic constitution, whether modern or classical, with the explicit constitutional assumptions of the modern state, in which the state is not the representative of only Muslims but of the 'people,' at least some of whom will be non-Muslims." This suggests that the democratic Islamic constitution cannot depend for its coherence upon a sectarian definition of the body politic, but that Muslims will need to agree to respect a constitution that applies as well to non-Muslims "on the basis of equality" (2009: 122–3). Elsewhere, Fadel (2008) has approached this problem by distinguishing philosophical conceptions from political ones, adopting a Rawlsian framework to assess Islam's compatibility with constitutional principles. For Sherman Jackson, Feldman's conclusion that only an Islamist interpretation of Islam—not Islam itself—threatens the achievement of democracy in the Muslim world would benefit by the elaboration of two additional considerations: first, the scope of the interpretive authority of Muslim jurists (and, by extension, whether a state governed by Sharia must give priority to the views of religious scholars); and second, the need to avoid conflating the framework of democracy (for example, the nation state) with the spirit and essence of democratic rule. Jackson concludes that "neither Islamic law nor Muslim jurists need to be viewed as enemies of democracy or harbingers of theocratic tyranny," nor should the nation state, with its "secular tyranny" be identified exclusively "as democracy's inseparable friend" (2004: 107). In a democracy that is embraced by Muslims, Islamic law and thus Muslim jurists must play an integral role.

Supplemental to discussions of jurisprudence, it is useful to recall that laws—state and Islamic—are embedded in societies, and when those societies are deeply religious, it can be difficult to achieve the goals of liberal democracy. Democracy can be curtailed by "ideological constitutions and judicial activism," while "constitutions that empower majorities and weaken judicial control pose a threat to the rights of individuals and minorities" (Tezcür 2007: 497). Judicial review can help sustain liberal rights in Muslim societies, but three conditions must be met: (1) constitutions must be built on popular consensus and contain unambiguous definitions of political and civil rights; (2) courts must be neither allied with nor controlled by other powerful institutions like the military; and (3) presidents or parliamentary majorities must not control the judicial appointment and promotion process, and vulnerable groups and individuals must have direct access to courts (Tezcür 2007: 498–500). Additionally, to counter the use of Sharia as a determinate anchor in contests over political identity, Anver Emon advocates that governments and the private sector join together to cultivate a Muslim civil society capable of facilitating debate within the religious community, but also between the religious community and the state. In this way, civil society "can empower competing voices … undermine conceptions of religious absolutism, and foster a mutual accommodation between religious commitment and national values" (Emon 2006: 354–5).

Illustrative of these debates are the writings of three prominent Muslim scholars, Khaled Abou El Fadl, Abdullahi Ahmed An-Na'im, and Abdolkarim Soroush, whose ideas are central to strategies of change and accommodation, including those aimed at reconciling Western and Islamic notions of freedom, democracy and human rights.[5] Brief summaries of their thought follow.

The Kuwaiti-born Abou El Fadl—at the time of writing professor at UCLA School of Law—identifies the real challenge confronting Muslim intellectuals as the displacement of moral investigation and thinking in Islam by the political interests that dominate public discourse. This "theology of power," which renders the "normative imperatives and intellectual subtleties of the Islamic moral tradition …

4 For case studies of Islamic constitutionalism, see Rabb 2008 on Iraq; Brown and Sherif 2004 on Egypt.

5 There are, of course, many other important thinkers, of whom one is Tariq Ramadan (2006, 2009; cf. Sonn 2005: 76–9); see also Freamon 2008.

subservient to political expedience," has contributed directly to the emergence of highly radicalized Islamic groups and is fully a by-product of colonialism and modernity (2005b: 183). By returning to Islam's fundamental moral values, he claims, it is possible to discover interpretive and practical possibilities that could be developed into a democratic system (2004a).[6] This type of serious, nuanced discourse is necessary, Abou El Fadl asserts, "if democracy is to become a systematic normative goal of large numbers of Muslims in Muslim countries" (2004b: 128). Repeatedly throughout his writings, Abou El Fadl cites the nature of religious discourse in a liberal democracy, emphasizing the importance of rendering legal decisions, for example, in fair, impartial, non-exclusive and accessible terms (1996, 1998). Nevertheless, "religion can legitimately play a role in the public sphere as long as it is not dismissive or oppressive toward others" (2005a: 202). Within Islam, this can be accomplished by interpreting Quranic verses in accordance with the moral imperatives of the text, including mercy, justice, kindness, and goodness (2002: 13–4), and by deconstructing and rejecting interpretations that perpetuate intolerance and violence (2002: 97–104).[7] It seems to Abou El Fadl that "serving God means serving justice, and serving justice necessarily means engaging in the search for the just, moral and humane" (2009: 144).

Emory University School of Law professor An-Na'im, Sudanese by birth and schooling, maintains that the future of Islamic law "lies among believers and their communities, and not in the enforcement of its principles by the coercive powers of the state" (2009b: 145). When enforcement depends upon such coercive authority, the rule ceases to be religious—in succumbing to political authority, it loses its moral authority. Applying the public law aspects of historical Sharia in public life would be problematic, yet Sharia principles can and should be relevant to Muslims wherever they live, and thus an alternative and modern conception of Islamic public law is needed. "[W]hat must be done is to clarify and specify the relationship between Islam and political authority on the basis of an Islamic approach to secularism"; from this perspective, "the protection of human rights, especially freedom of belief, expression and association, is an Islamic imperative ... because these rights are prerequisites for the necessary discourse" (1999: 120). Elaborating his vision of secularism, An-Na'im argues, among other things, that while a secular state must preclude an institutional link between Islam and state institutions, faith should play a role in society.[8] Additionally, Muslims should act upon their right to engage in consensus-building around a transformative reinterpretation of Sharia that incorporates citizenship, constitutionalism, and human rights (An-Na'im 1990, 2005, 2008, 2009a, 2011; and Chapter 22, below).

Finally, the Iranian dissident Soroush, living outside of Iran in voluntary exile, asserts that those who criticize an Islamic form of democracy make three "dark and dangerous" errors: they equate democracy with extreme liberalism; they sever Sharia from its foundations; and they equate religious democratic government with religious jurisprudential (*fiqhī*) government (Sadri and Sadri 2000: 134; Kalanges 2012: 99–101). Soroush advocates for democracy in the Muslim world based on two related principles: true belief requires freedom (including freedom to leave a chosen faith), and religious understanding must continue—of necessity—to evolve, for while sacred texts do not change, their interpretation is subject to the influence of the age and the conditions in which believers live. Correspondingly, everyone is entitled to his or her own understanding and no interpretation is automatically more authoritative than others. Furthermore, "given his belief in the unity of truth," Soroush asserts "the necessity of religious toleration in societies claiming to uphold human rights" and the requirement of a plurality of voices if justice is to prevail (Oh 2007: 103; Wright 1996: 67–8).

6 While largely in agreement with Abou El Fadl's conclusions, Fadel 2004 is uncertain whether the latter's specific arguments for democracy are ultimately persuasive in Islamic terms.

7 For a challenge to Abou El Fadl's emphasis on theological issues to explain the actions of peoples and societies, see Ali 2002; for the argument that Islamic "intolerance" is the principled resistance of Muslims standing up for justice, see Jan 2002.

8 For a criticism of this perspective, which he identifies with an exclusionary model of the relationship between law and Islam, see Fadel 2013.

In practical terms, Soroush calls for the end of financial support for religious leaders, from the state in most Sunni countries and from the people in Shiʿi communities, so that they will no longer be compelled to propagate official or popular interpretations of Islamic law (Wright 1996: 70; see also Heyking 2006). Criticized for not taking into account such factors as the form of the state, the existence of civil institutions, the presence of a tolerant political culture, or discrepancies in the socio-economic and political status of various groups (Boroujerdi 2001), Soroush nevertheless succeeds in demonstrating how innovative interpretations of Islam might engender its compatibility with freedom, democracy, and human rights.

Islam and Human Rights

Generally, Islam rejects the formal separation of religion from law and politics (for a more extensive presentation of this history, see Kalanges 2012: 140–67); hence, many Muslim scholars, states, and social movements have favored Islamic formulations of human rights even after modernizing (Entelis 1996).[9] Unlike Western interpretations of human rights, which have been heavily influenced by the primacy of the individual in liberal political thought, Islamic law is largely communitarian, more likely to be concerned with public morality, order, and social justice (Mayer 2007; Monshipouri 1998). Despite these differences of emphasis, Islam contains principles that resonate with international human rights law, such as good governance and human welfare. Even so, "human rights as they are presently formulated in international law lack precise equivalents in the Islamic legal heritage" (Mayer 1994: 321). Indeed, it was not until the nineteenth century that the concept of human rights (*ḥuqūq al-insān*) was introduced in the Arabic language by the Egyptian intellectual and translator Rifāʿa Rāfiʿ al-Ṭahṭāwī (d. 1873).[10] Al-Ṭahṭāwī's European-inspired writings on civil rights, especially *Takhlīṣ al-ibrīz fī talkhīṣ bārīz*, contained ideas that were subsequently developed by local, Muslim and Christian secularist writers, particularly those educated in institutions run by missionaries or colonial powers. Unsurprisingly, these ideas were consistent with European political thought, contributing to the perception that Muslim countries largely accepted the international consensus on human rights[11] in the decades immediately following the Second World War (Haddad 2008; Mayer 2007: 20, 102).

By the late 1960s and 1970s, however, amid the postcolonial reaction against the West, secular Arab nationalism was increasingly displaced by political Islam (Esposito 2000). With the latter emerged a new assertion that international human rights law (characterized variously as Judeo-Christian, Western, or secular) was incompatible with Islam and must be rejected by Muslim states. Islamists used their newfound political power to institutionalize alternate models of governance, at the domestic level by changes to state constitutions (granting Islam official status and formulating rights with reference to Islamic law), and at the international level by developing religiously based alternatives to human rights law (for example, the 1981 Universal Islamic Declaration of Human Rights and the 1990 Cairo Declaration on Human Rights in Islam) (Lombardi and Brown 2006).

Whether these declarations represent authentic Islamic teachings is greatly disputed. This discordance has been attributed to the internal struggles of Muslim societies, as they seek to resist "the dominant global economic and political power" while also engaging it "in order to restore some level of political and economic power to the Muslim world" (Hamoudi 2008: 423–4). If the call for a return to Sharia is interpreted from within this struggle, as Haider Hamoudi says it must be, Islamic human

9 One noteworthy exception is ʿAlī ʿAbd al-Rāziq, whose treatise (1925) has been utilized by Muslim modernists and realists arguing for the separation of mosque and state (Samuelson 1995; and see An-Naʿim 2008).

10 Cf. Mohsen Kadivar's assertion (2009: 54) that historical Islam did not face a conflict with the notion of human rights because the human rights system belongs to the modern age.

11 With the exception of religious liberty rights, about which more below.

rights declarations appear both to participate in global legal norms and also to agitate against them (2008: 463–70). This is part of a larger debate over the method and substance of Islamic interpretations of human rights. Ebrahim Moosa (2000–1) cautions that establishing a credible discourse within Muslim jurisprudence requires a more careful parsing of methodological issues, juridical theology, and legal philosophy. He identifies multiple problems with the present human rights debate in Islam. For example, talking of Islamic rights as if it presented as one undiversified category is erroneous, when diverse theological traditions (for example, Muʿtazilis, Ashʿaris, Hanbalis) yield different assumptions about what constitutes a right and how it ought to be implemented in law; similarly, assuming the medieval expression of the law to be sacrosanct and permanent "denies the historical evolution of the legal system over centuries." Moosa laments the contemporary trend of reducing the rich history of jurisprudential development and practice to simplistic slogans for purposes of Sharia revival, and urges a fundamental rethinking directed toward producing a credible version of human rights in dialogue with both the tradition and the present (2000–1: 193–5).[12]

Ahmad Moussalli links premodern Islamic thought with contemporary religious and political debates to argue that the concepts of democracy, pluralism, and human rights have been absorbed and "Islamized" (2001: 3). To illustrate, he highlights the text of a pact published and distributed by the Tunisian Islamist Muḥammad al-Hāshim al-Ḥāmidī to other Islamists, in which the success of the Islamic movement, once it took power, would hinge on establishing "a just and democratic system," guaranteeing basic rights for women and minorities, justice, free and fair trials, freedom of belief, expression, religion, etc. (2001: 156–7). Abdulaziz Sachedina, who has published a book called *The Islamic Roots of Democratic Pluralism* (2001), argues for the importance of dispelling doubts about the universality of human rights. He asserts that Islam, along with other religious traditions, shares with the Declaration a common moral purpose, which is to protect inalienable human rights (2009: 8).

Other scholars are more hesitant about relying on Islam to defend human rights in the Muslim world. Some therefore call for the inclusion not just of "new traditionalists" who, like An-Naʿim, emphasize the reinterpretation of Islamic tradition to bring it into closer alignment with international norms, but also of secular voices (Afshari 1994), as well as for collaboration between those working from within secular and religious perspectives (Rohe 2012). Contra Sachedina, Fadel (2007) draws upon the overlapping political consensus of John Rawls, hopeful that public reason can free the debate from controversial metaphysical foundations and serve as a useful strategy for the principled reconciliation of Sharia and international human rights law.

These tensions at play in the general debate about Islam and human rights are brought into sharp relief by two related areas of specific contestation: religious freedom and freedom of expression.

Religious Freedom and Freedom of Expression

Article 18 of the 1948 Universal Declaration of Human Rights (UDHR) recognizes religious liberty as a human right and imposes a moral obligation on signatory states to uphold it. It is noteworthy for addressing issues that became more problematic when the 1966 International Covenant on Civil and Political Rights (ICCPR) and the 1981 United Nations Declaration on the Elimination of All Forms of Intolerance and of Discrimination Based on Religion or Belief (1981 Declaration) were negotiated, namely, conversion and proselytizing. Several religions were uncomfortable with the language, but it was most problematic for Muslims (see generally, Kalanges 2012: 56–70). The Saudi Arabian representative was especially persistent in his dissent to the right to change religion, claiming that conversion from Islam is forbidden in Islamic law and rallying other Islamic countries to his position; ultimately the Pakistani diplomat and Ahmadi Muslim, Muhammad Zafrullah Khan (d. 1985), succeeded in securing all but Saudi Arabia's consent to the UDHR's language by presenting

12 For a critique of some human rights scholarship, see Peters 1999; Ali 1997.

an Islamic defense of freedom of conscience on the basis of the Quranic *lā ikrāha fī l-dīn*, "there is no compulsion in religion" (Q 2:256) (Little et al. 1988).

Matters became more complicated in subsequent decades. Article 18 of the ICCPR similarly addresses religious liberty, and efforts to incorporate a right to change one's religion or belief were met with opposition from Muslim-majority countries such as Egypt, Saudi Arabia, Yemen, and Afghanistan, which agitated for its deletion (Baderin 2003: 118–9). As Mashood Baderin notes, a compromise clause was adopted, but the net result is that the ICCPR (the only binding treaty that contains a coherent articulation of religious liberty rights, Lerner 2000: 914) does not explicitly refer to the right to change religion. While most specialists interpret Article 18 of the ICCPR as fully recognizing that right, signatory Islamic states have not formally accepted this understanding of their obligations under the Covenant and uniformly remain outside of the international consensus on this central feature of religious liberty rights (Boyle 2007: 40–1). References to the right to change one's religion were also deleted from the text of both the preamble and Article 1 of the 1981 Declaration, in response to Muslim objections (Davis 2002: 229). Moreover, in a study of 44 predominantly Muslim countries, the US Commission on International Religious Freedom found that despite the ratification by many of them of the UDHR and the ICCPR, several nonetheless maintain constitutional provisions that limit the freedom to manifest a religion or belief, in contradiction to their treaty obligations (Stahnke and Blitt 2005).

Contrary to what this modern history (which is bound up with the rise of political Islam) might suggest, Muslims point to traditional Islamic teachings in support of religious liberty, such as the above-mentioned Quranic verse 2:256, along with other verses supporting faith as a free and voluntary act, establishing guidelines for preaching, and responding to religious pluralism peacefully. To the extent that Islam granted Muslims religious liberty in the seventh century, it was a new idea, one grounded, according to the Tunisian religious historian Mohamed Talbi (1986), in the divinely ordered nature of humanity and the unique capabilities and obligations of human beings (Kalanges 2012: 90–6). Even so, Muslim scholars and policymakers disagree as to the proper interpretation of these precepts, and there is no consensus on matters such as conversion, blasphemy, tolerance, and the treatment of Muslim minorities or non-Muslims. Unsurprisingly, Sharia is used to justify both sides of the debate. On one reading, Islamic law constitutes "an eternal, correct and immutable truth" and "any allegation that Islam is less than ideal would inevitably be perceived as a disloyal act of treason against Allah and the values of the believing community" (Arzt 1996: 373). In response, defenses of religious freedom have been crafted from within the tradition (Kalanges 2012: 174–8). Sachedina, for example, employs exegesis to argue that various theological and philosophical roots of Western principles of religious freedom have counterparts in Quranic teachings (Little et al. 1988: 53–90). Synthesizing old and new, Abou El Fadl suggests that Sharia's historic purpose of fulfilling the welfare of the people could ground a systematic theory of individual rights based on the five basic values (that is, protection of the basic value of religion could be achieved by religious liberty rights) (2003: 332–3).

One additional issue at the intersection of religious freedom and other civil and political liberties is the extent to which freedom of speech should be limited by religious sensibilities or concerns that it unduly targets particular groups. To take a recent example, when a Danish newspaper published multiple editorial cartoons depicting the Prophet Muḥammad, violent protests erupted among Muslim communities in Europe and throughout the world. Some interpreted the controversy as representative of the "incommensurable divide in democratic societies" between liberal values and religious taboos (for example, blasphemy), others as a civilizational clash between the West and Islam centered on Muslim minority communities in Europe, and still others as reflecting rising Islamophobia and discrimination against Muslims in the West in the wake of 9/11 (Danchin 2010: 6; see also Kahn 2010, 2011).

Those concerned about such publications and other expressions that are deemed by some, but not others, as hate speech argue that abusive language is unnecessary to furnish effective criticism of public policies. Thus, the growing international legal consensus prohibiting hate speech that incites violence, hostility, and discrimination is a positive development, whereas jurisprudence that does not preclude all forms of hate speech (for example, US First Amendment jurisprudence), "even if it causes emotional harm to groups of people or degrades prophets and holy books," is to be criticized (Khan 2008: 851–2). There are equally strong critics of calls to limit freedom of expression in these ways, with an emphasis on the Islamic influence. One critic remarks that while old blasphemy laws have lost their legal significance in the West, new blasphemy laws are being introduced in the guise of anti-incitement laws at the national and international levels. He characterizes this as a larger process of Islamization wherein society's institutions are made to conform to the requirements of Sharia (Durie 2012). Others describe the process as lawfare, specifically "Islamist lawfare," designed to counter the human rights of citizens of the West so as to make it difficult to freely transmit information about radical Islam (Goldstein and Meyer 2008; and see Blitt 2011). Instructively, Peter Danchin concludes that the real significance of the Danish cartoon controversy is not so much what it reveals about Islamic norms and values, but rather how it raises "unsettling questions regarding core features of secular modernity and the place of religion in liberal democratic orders" (2010: 9).

Concluding Remarks

As a final matter, debates about the encounter between Sharia and modernity highlight the importance of interdisciplinary research for a proper understanding of challenges facing the Muslim world and possible responses to them. For example, as I have noted elsewhere, explanations that ignore history and politics risk conflating religious teachings and traditions with the political agendas of country elites. Likewise, explanations that minimize the influence of Islam in favor of purely legal and political strategies underestimate the extent to which religion conditions institutional possibilities. Well-informed debates and sustainable laws and policies thus require the insights of many disciplines. Moreover, getting the theory right is not enough to produce workable institutions. The battle for hearts and minds must be won in the public square, and while arguments may come from a variety of perspectives, it appears for the foreseeable future that arguments made from within Islam will be essential. This is an important reality that should not be disregarded by those who would seek to promote democracy, development, and human rights in Muslim-majority states.

References

ʿAbd al-Rāziq, ʿAlī. 1925. *Al-Islām wa-uṣūl al-ḥukm: Baḥth fī l-khilāfa wa-l-ḥukūma fī l-islām*. Cairo: Maṭbaʿat Miṣr; Eng. trans. *Islam and the Foundations of Political Power*, London: Edinburgh University Press, 2012.

Abou El Fadl, Khaled. 1996. Muslim Minorities and Self-Restraint in Liberal Democracies. *Loyola of Los Angeles Law Review* 29(4): 1525–42.

———. 1998. Muslims and Accessible Jurisprudence in Liberal Democracies: A Response to Edward B. Foley's Jurisprudence and Theology. *Fordham Law Review* 66(4): 1227–32.

———. 2002. The Place of Tolerance in Islam; and Reply. In *The Place of Tolerance in Islam*, ed. J. Cohen and I. Lague, pp. 3–23, 93–111. Boston: Beacon Press.

———. 2003. The Human Rights Commitment in Modern Islam. In *Human Rights and Responsibilities in the World Religions*, ed. J. Runzo et al., pp. 301–64. Oxford: Oneworld.

———. 2004a. Islam and the Challenge of Democracy. In *Islam and the Challenge of Democracy*, ed. J. Cohen and D. Chasman, pp. 3–46. Princeton: Princeton University Press.

———. 2004b. Reply. In *Islam and the Challenge of Democracy*, ed. J. Cohen and D. Chasman, pp. 109–28. Princeton: Princeton University Press.
———. 2005a. *The Great Theft: Wrestling Islam from the Extremists*. New York: HarperCollins.
———. 2005b. The Orphans of Modernity and the Clash of Civilisations. In *Islam and Global Dialogue: Religious Pluralism and the Pursuit of Peace*, ed. R. Boase, pp. 179–88. Aldershot, UK: Ashgate.
———. 2009. Islamic Authority. In *New Directions in Islamic Thought: Exploring Reform and Muslim Tradition*, ed. K. Vogt et al., pp. 129–44. London: I.B. Tauris.
Afshari, Reza. 1994. An Essay on Islamic Cultural Relativism in the Discourse of Human Rights. *Human Rights Quarterly* 16(2): 235–76.
Ali, Shaheen S. 1997. Conceptual Foundations of Human Rights: A Comparative Perspective. *European Public Law* 3(2): 261-82.
Ali, Tariq. 2002. Theological Distractions. In *The Place of Tolerance in Islam*, ed. J. Cohen and I. Lague, pp. 37–41. Boston: Beacon Press.
An-Na'im, Abdullahi A. 1990. *Toward an Islamic Reformation: Civil Liberties, Human Rights, and International Law*. Syracuse, NY: Syracuse University Press.
———. 1999. Political Islam in National Politics and International Relations. In *The Desecularization of the World: Resurgent Religion and World Politics*, ed. P.L. Berger, pp. 103–21. Grand Rapids, MI: W.B. Eerdmans.
———. 2005. Globalization and Jurisprudence: An Islamic Law Perspective. *Emory Law Journal* 54(5): 25–51.
———. 2008. *Islam and the Secular State: Negotiating the Future of Shari'a*. Cambridge, MA: Harvard University Press.
———. 2009a. Religion, the State, and Constitutionalism in Islamic and Comparative Perspectives. *Drake Law Review* 57(4): 829–50.
———. 2009b. A Theory of Islam, State, and Society. In *New Directions in Islamic Thought: Exploring Reform and Muslim Tradition*, ed. K. Vogt et al., pp. 145–62. London: I.B. Tauris.
———. 2011. *Muslims and Global Justice*. Philadelphia: University of Pennsylvania Press.
Arzt, Donna E. 1996. Heroes or Heretics: Religious Dissidents under Islamic Law. *Wisconsin International Law Journal* 14: 349–421.
Baderin, Mashood A. 2003. *International Human Rights and Islamic Law*. Oxford: Oxford University Press.
Bennett, Clinton. 2005. *Muslims and Modernity: An Introduction to the Issues and Debates*. London: Continuum.
Berger, Peter L. 1999. The Desecularization of the World: A Global Overview. In *The Desecularization of the World: Resurgent Religion and World Politics*, ed. P.L. Berger, pp. 1–18. Grand Rapids, MI: W.B. Eerdmans.
Blitt, Robert C. 2011. Defamation of Religion: Rumors of Its Death are Greatly Exaggerated. *Case Western Reserve Law Review* 62(2): 347–98.
Boroujerdi, Mehrzad. 2001. Review of *Reason, Freedom, and Democracy in Islam: Essential Writings of Abdolkarim Soroush. Middle East Journal* 55(3): 519–20.
Boyle, Kevin. 2007. Freedom of Religion in International Law. In *Religion, Human Rights and International Law: A Critical Examination of Islamic State Practices*, ed. J. Rehman and S.C. Breau, pp. 23–51. Leiden: Martinus Nijhoff.
Brown, Nathan J., and Adel Omar Sherif. 2004. Inscribing Islamic Shari'a in Arab Constitutional Law. In *Islamic Law and the Challenges of Modernity*, ed. Y.Y. Haddad and B.F. Stowasser, pp. 55–81. Walnut Creek, CA: AltaMira Press.
Casanova, Jose. 1994. *Public Religions in the Modern World*. Chicago: University of Chicago Press.
Danchin, Peter G. 2010. Defaming Muhammad: Dignity, Harm, and Incitement to Religious Hatred. *Duke Forum for Law and Social Change* 2(1): 5–38.

Davis, Derek. 2002. The Evolution of Religious Freedom as a Universal Human Right. *Brigham Young University Law Review* 2002(2): 217–36.
Durie, Mark. 2012. Sleepwalking into Sharia: Hate Speech Laws and Islamic Blasphemy Strictures. *International Trade and Business Law Review* 15: 394–407.
Eickelman, Dale. 2000. Islam and the Languages of Modernity. *Daedalus* 129(1): 119–35.
Emon, Anver M. 2006. Conceiving Islamic Law in a Pluralist Society: History, Politics and Multicultural Jurisprudence. *Singapore Journal of Legal Studies* 2006(2): 331–55.
Entelis, Joelle. 1996. International Human Rights: Islam's Friend or Foe? Algeria as an Example of the Compatibility of International Human Rights Regarding Women's Equality and Islamic Law. *Fordham International Law Journal* 20(4): 1251–1305.
Esmaeili, Hossein. 2011. Nature and Development of Law in Islam and the Rule of Law Challenge in the Middle East and the Muslim World. *Connecticut Journal of International Law* 26: 329–66.
Esposito, John L. 2000. Introduction: Islam and Secularism in the Twenty-First Century. In *Islam and Secularism in the Middle East*, ed. A. Tamimi and J.L. Esposito, pp. 1–12. New York: New York University Press.
Euben, Roxanne. 1997. Premodern, Antimodern or Postmodern? Islamic and Western Critiques of Modernity. *The Review of Politics* 59(3): 429–59.
Fadel, Mohammad H. 2004. Too Far from Tradition. In *Islam and the Challenge of Democracy*, ed. J. Cohen and D. Chasman, pp. 81–6. Princeton: Princeton University Press.
———. 2007. Public Reason as a Strategy for Principled Reconciliation: The Case of Islamic Law and International Human Rights Law. *Chicago Journal of International Law* 8(1): 1–20.
———. 2008. The True, the Good and the Reasonable: The Theological and Ethical Roots of Public Reason in Islamic Law. *Canadian Journal of Law and Jurisprudence* 11(1): 5–69.
———. 2009. Back to the Future: The Paradoxical Revival of Aspirations for an Islamic State. *Review of Constitutional Studies* 14(1): 105–23.
———. 2012. Islamic Law and American Law: Between Concordance and Dissonance. *New York Law School Law Review* 57(2): 231–44.
———. 2013. Seeking an Islamic Reflective Equilibrium: A Response to Abdullahi A. An-Na'im's Complementary, Not Competing, Claims of Law and Religion. An Islamic Perspective. *Pepperdine Law Review* 39: 1257–72.
Farouk-Alli, Aslam. 2006. The Second Coming of the Theocratic Age? Islamic Discourse after Modernity and Postmodernity. In *The Blackwell Companion to Contemporary Islamic Thought*, ed. I.M. Abu-Rabi', pp. 285–301. Malden, MA: Blackwell.
Feldman, Noah. 2005. Imposed Constitutionalism. *Connecticut Law Review* 37: 857–89.
———. 2008. *The Fall and Rise of the Islamic State*. Princeton: Princeton University Press.
Freamon, Bernard K. 2008. The Emergence of a New Qur'anic Hermeneutic. In *Law Applied: Contextualizing the Islamic Shari'a*, ed. P. Bearman et al., pp. 342–59. London: I.B. Tauris.
Goldstein, Brooke, and Aaron E. Meyer. 2008. Legal Jihad: How Islamist Lawfare Tactics are Targeting Free Speech. *ILSA Journal of International and Comparative Law* 15(2): 395–410.
Haddad, Yvonne Y. 2008. *Muslims and Human Rights*. Washington, DC: Georgetown University.
Hallaq, Wael B. 2004. Can the Shari'a Be Restored? In *Islamic Law and the Challenges of Modernity*, ed. Y.Y. Haddad and B.F. Stowasser, pp. 21–53. Walnut Creek, CA: AltaMira Press.
———. 2009. Groundwork of the Moral Law: A New Look at the Qur'ān and the Genesis of Sharī'a. *Islamic Law and Society* 16(3–4): 239–79.
Hamoudi, Haider A. 2008. The Muezzin's Call and the Dow Jones Bell: On the Necessity of Realism in the Study of Islamic Law. *American Journal of Comparative Law* 56(2): 423–70.
———. 2009. Dream Palaces of Law: Western Constructions of the Muslim Legal World. *Hastings International and Comparative Law Review* 32(2): 803–14.
Hashemi, Nader. 2009. *Islam, Secularism, and Liberal Democracy: Toward a Democratic Theory for Muslim Societies*. New York: Oxford University Press.

Hefner, Robert W. 1998. Multiple Modernities: Christianity, Islam, and Hinduism in a Globalizing Age. *Annual Review of Anthropology* 27: 83–104.

Heyking, John von. 2006. Mysticism in Contemporary Islamic Political Thought: Orhan Pamuk and Abdolkarim Soroush. *Humanitas* 19: 71–96.

Jackson, Sherman. 2004. Shari'ah, Democracy, and the Modern Nation-State: Some Reflections on Islam, Popular Rule, and Pluralism. *Fordham International Law Journal* 27(1): 88–107.

Jan, Abid U. 2002. The Limits of Tolerance. In *The Place of Tolerance in Islam*, ed. J. Cohen and I. Lague, pp. 42–50. Boston: Beacon Press.

Jillani, Tassaduq H. 2006. Democracy and Islam: An Odyssey in Braving the Twenty-First Century. *Brigham Young University Law Review* (2006)3: 727–54.

Kadivar, Mohsen. 2009. Human Rights and Intellectual Islam. In *New Directions in Islamic Thought: Exploring Reform and Muslim Tradition*, ed. K. Vogt et al., pp. 47–73. London: I.B. Tauris.

Kahn, Robert. 2010. Flemming Rose, the Danish Carton Controversy, and the New European Freedom of Speech. *California Western International Law Journal* 40(2): 253–90.

———. 2011. A Margin of Appreciation for Muslims? Viewing the Defamation of Religions Debate through Otto-Preminger-Institut v. Austria. *Charleston Law Review* 5(3): 401–56.

Kalanges, Kristine. 2012. *Religious Liberty in Western and Islamic Law: Toward a World Legal Tradition*. New York: Oxford University Press.

Kamrava, Mehran. 2006. Introduction: Reformist Islam in Comparative Perspective. In *The New Voices of Islam: Rethinking Politics and Modernity. A Reader*, ed. M. Kamrava, pp. 1–27. Berkeley and Los Angeles: University of California Press.

Khalil, Mohamed I. 2004. Islam and the Challenges of Modernity. *Georgetown Journal of International Affairs* 85(2): 495–520.

Khan, Liaquat A. 2008. The Immutability of Divine Texts. *Brigham Young University Law Review* 2008(3): 807–76.

Khatab, Sayed, and Gary D. Bouma. 2007. *Democracy in Islam*. London: Routledge.

Lapidus, Ira. 1997. Islamic Revival and Modernity: The Contemporary Movements and the Historical Paradigms. *Journal of the Economic and Social History of the Orient* 40(4): 444–60.

Lerner, Natan. 2000. The Nature and Minimum Standards of Freedom of Religion or Belief. *Brigham Young University Law Review* 2000(3): 905–32.

Little, David et al. 1988. *Human Rights and the Conflict of Cultures: Western and Islamic Perspectives on Religious Liberty*. Columbia: University of South Carolina Press.

Lombardi, Clark B., and Nathan J. Brown. 2006. Do Constitutions Requiring Adherence to Shari'a Threaten Human Rights? How Egypt's Constitutional Court Reconciles Islamic Law with the Liberal Rule of Law. *American University International Law Review* 21(3): 379–435.

March, Andrew F. 2009. *Islam and Liberal Citizenship: The Search for an Overlapping Consensus*. New York: Oxford University Press.

Masud, Muhammad Khalid. 2009. *Islamic Modernism*. In *Islam and Modernity: Key Issues and Debates*, ed. M.K. Masud et al., pp. 237–60. Edinburgh: Edinburgh University Press.

Mayer, Ann E. 1994. Universal Versus Islamic Human Rights: A Clash of Cultures or a Clash with a Construct? *Michigan Journal of International Law* 15: 307–404.

———. 2007. *Islam and Human Rights: Tradition and Politics*. 4th ed. Boulder: Westview.

Monshipouri, Mahmood. 1998. *Islamism, Secularism, and Human Rights in the Middle East*. Boulder: Lynne Rienner.

———. 2009. *Muslims in Global Politics: Identities, Interests, and Human Rights*. Philadelphia: University of Pennsylvania Press.

Moosa, Ebrahim. 2000-1. The Dilemma of Islamic Rights Schemes. *Journal of Law and Religion* 15: 185–215.

Moussalli, Ahmad S. 2001. *The Islamic Quest for Democracy, Pluralism, and Human Rights*. Gainesville: University Press of Florida.

Oh, Irene. 2007. *The Rights of God: Islam, Human Rights, and Comparative Ethics*. Washington, DC: Georgetown University Press.
Peters, Ruud. 1999. Islamic Law and Human Rights: A Contribution to an Ongoing Debate. *Islam and Christian-Muslim Relations* 10(1): 5–14.
Rabb, Intisar A. 2008. We the Jurists: Islamic Constitutionalism in Iraq. *University of Pennsylvania Journal of Constitutional Law* 10(3): 527–80.
Ramadan, Tariq. 2006. The Way (*Al-Sharia*) of Islam. In *The New Voices of Islam: Rethinking Politics and Modernity. A Reader*, ed. M. Kamrava, pp. 65–98. Berkeley and Los Angeles: University of California Press.
———. 2009. *Radical Reform: Islamic Ethics and Liberation*. Oxford: Oxford University Press.
Rohe, Mathias. 2012. On the Foundations of Human Rights: Religious and Secular Approaches in the West and in Islam. In *Tensions within and between Religions and Human Rights*, ed. J.A. van der Ven and H.G. Ziebertz, pp. 67–93. Leiden: Brill.
Rubin, Barry. 1994. Religion and International Affairs. In *Religion, the Missing Dimension of Statecraft*, ed. D. Johnston and C. Sampson, pp. 20–34. New York: Oxford University Press.
Sadri, Mahmoud, and Ahmad Sadri, tr. and ed. 2000. *Reason, Freedom, and Democracy in Islam: Essential Writings of Abdolkarim Soroush*. New York: Oxford University Press.
Sachedina, Abdulaziz. 2001. *The Islamic Roots of Democratic Pluralism*. New York: Oxford University Press.
———. 2009. *Islam and the Challenge of Human Rights*. Oxford: Oxford University Press.
Samuelson, Peter A. 1995. Pluralism Betrayed: The Battle between Secularism and Islam in Algeria's Quest for Democracy. *Yale Journal of International Law* 20: 309–58.
Sonn, Tamara. 2005. Islam and Modernity: Are They Compatible? In *Modernization, Democracy and Islam*, ed. S.T. Hunter and H. Malik, pp. 65–81. Westport, CT: Praeger.
Stahnke, Tad, and Robert C. Blitt. 2005. The Religion-State Relationship and the Right to Freedom of Religion or Belief: A Comparative Textual Analysis of the Constitutions of Predominantly Muslim Countries. *Georgetown Journal of International Law* 36: 947–1078.
Talbi, Mohamed. 1986. Religious Liberty: A Muslim Perspective. In *Religious Liberty and Human Rights in Nations and in Religions*, ed. L. Swidler, pp. 175–87. Philadelphia: Ecumenical Press and Hippocrene Books.
Tezcür, Güneş M. 2007. Constitutionalism, Judiciary, and Democracy in Islamic Studies. *Polity* 39(4): 479–501.
Tibi, Bassam. 2009. *Islam's Predicament with Modernity: Religious Reform and Cultural Change*. London: Routledge.
Voll, John O. 2005. Islam and Democracy: Is Modernization a Barrier? In *Modernization, Democracy and Islam*, ed. S.T. Hunter and H. Malik, pp. 82–97. Westport, CT: Praeger.
Wahyudi, Yudian. 2006. Hassan Hanafi on Salafism and Secularism. In *The Blackwell Companion to Contemporary Islamic Thought*, ed. I.M. Abu-Rabi', pp. 257–70. Malden, MA: Blackwell.
Wright, Robin. 1996. Islam and Democracy: Two Visions of Reformation. *Journal of Democracy* 7(2): 64–75.
Yilmaz, Ihsan. 2005. *Muslim Laws, Politics and Society in Modern Nation States: Dynamic Legal Pluralisms in England, Turkey and Pakistan*. Aldershot, UK: Ashgate.
Zakaria, Fareed. 2004. Islam, Democracy, and Constitutional Liberalism. *Political Science Quarterly* 119(1): 1–20.

Sharia and Medical Ethics

Birgit Krawietz

Problematizing Medical Ethics

Since the age of colonial expansion, industrialization, and widespread travel, modern forms of the natural sciences, medical education, and general healthcare have been introduced to the Islamic world and turned by state actors into full-fledged biopolitics. This development has generated enhanced normative assessment not only on the level of state law (*qānūn*) but also from the viewpoint of Islamic jurisprudence (*fiqh*). Reactions to it are expressed in fatwas, studies (*buḥūth*), conference discussions (*nadawāt*) among experts (including physicians), and debates in mass media—in Arabic as well as other languages relevant to Muslims around the globe. No Muslim regime can dare to ignore pious scholarly voices and their potential criticisms; indeed, a number of states structurally incorporate them in their law-making process and medical policies. The period from the mid-twentieth century on has witnessed a surge of scholarly monographs on specific medico-jurisprudential questions (not least in university theses and conference proceedings), in contrast to the comprehensive manuals that dominated premodern Islamic jurisprudence, and such knowledge is now spreading widely among the broader public in the form of popular booklets, fatwa-style snippets, and new media discussions, sparking at times political repercussions.

This chapter elucidates—with a Middle Eastern focus—how Muslim Sharia scholars discuss measures that create, uphold, improve, or threaten human life. From a historical perspective, the term "medical ethics" cannot be taken as an originally Islamic understanding of the topic. Further, it needs to be problematized in relation to Sharia or, rather, to what is understood as Islamic normativity from the following modern perspectives: (1) medical ethics excludes some traditional Islamic jurisprudence that treats the body, such as physical aspects of jihad (wartime atrocities, torture and other treatment of prisoners, martyrdom, and suicide attacks) and penal law with its variety of corporal punishments; (2) the care for animals and, more generally, environmental concerns are largely marginalized; (3) the psychological dimensions of ritual purity, spiritual healing, or somatized forms of norm control can be addressed here only insofar as medical experts are involved; (4) the wider debate on sexuality, which Islamic jurisprudence covers only to a certain extent, intersects also only partly with the medical sphere;

Birgit Krawietz is Professor at the Institute for Islamic Studies at the Freie Universität, Berlin. She is the author of *Die Ḥurma: Schariatrechtlicher Schutz vor Eingriffen in die körperliche Unversehrtheit nach arabischen Fatwas des 20. Jahrhunderts* (1991) and *Hierarchie der Rechtsquellen im tradierten sunnitischen Islam* (2002), and of numerous chapters and articles, including "Brain Death and Islamic Traditions: Shifting Borders of Life?" (2003), and has co-edited, with Helmut Reifeld, *Islam und Rechtsstaat: Zwischen Scharia und Säkularisierung* (2008; Eng. trans, *Islam and Rule of Law: Between Sharia and Secularization*, 2008), with Katrin Bromber and Joseph Maguire, *Sport across Asia* (2013), and, with Georges Tamer, *Islamic Theology, Philosophy and Law: Debating Ibn Taymiyya and Ibn Qayyim al-Jawziyya* (2013).

and (5) the demands of medical ethics represent just one segment of the much broader tapestry in which Islamic normativity prescribes how to shape gender roles somatically, emotionally, and performatively.

There is no distinct genre of medical ethics in premodern Islamic scholarship. Identifying ethics with the Arabic term *adab* (exemplary behavior) does not agree with what Western observers are looking for today (Sachedina 2004: 153). Although *adab* reflects an overall moral, intellectual, and professional etiquette (Fähndrich 1990: 326, 329, 331), the traditional issue of the rules of conduct of the physician (*adab al-ṭabīb*) or pharmacist (Chipman 2002) is quite narrow and does not represent a solely legal topic even if its practical application became monitored by the public space control of the *ḥisba*. In 1981 an official "Islamic Code of Medical Ethics" was published in Kuwait. By making use of selected views taken from Islamic jurisprudence modern authors have begun to write monographs that discuss the responsibility of the medical doctor both broadly and in detail (for example, al-Bārr and al-Sibāʿī 1997), in line with global expectations. However, neither in the revealed sources of Quran and hadith (apart from entries on treatment, *ṭibb*, or on ill people, *marḍā*) nor in premodern manuals of Islamic jurisprudence do we encounter a full-fledged medical section assembling the majority of pertinent doctrines. There, relevant remarks tend to be scattered throughout the chapters on, for example, ritual purity, funerals, dietary rules, family law, civil liability of physicians, and the role of slaves (whose bodies are traditionally less valorized). Furthermore, Islamic jurisprudence evaluates medical treatment in complementary cooperation with theology; thus "Sharia" in this chapter's title should be understood as a shortcut to both of these disciplines and their sub-genres.

Nowadays many observers favor the expression "Islamic bioethics" or "biomedical ethics" (Sachedina 2009). However it is called, a burst of writings in Western languages has appeared since the genesis of modern bioethics in the early 1970s, which very much dictates the agenda (Ach and Runtenberg 2002: 13–4). Islamic Studies scholarship, which had begun reflecting on pertinent debates decades earlier, has become increasingly joined if not partly sidelined by medical experts. On behalf of the latter, some authors explicitly demand "applied Islamic bioethics" as defined by the needs of their "consumers" (Padela et al. 2011: 54–6, who depict this discipline as "devotional" and even advocate a best practice model of how to approach bioethical questions): "Many medical schools in countries with Muslim majorities have bioethics curricula. There are established mechanisms for addressing emerging biomedical and bioethics issues, and curricula are updated accordingly" (Daar and Al-Khitamy 2010: 122). This development decisively restructures the object under discussion and the ways it is presented. That is to say, while state-of-the-art medical concerns are addressed with growing expertise and specific Islamic problems that are dealt with by hospital ethical committees are being increasingly globally streamlined, Islamic religious (including philosophical) implications and the intricacies of Islamic jurisprudence are partly marginalized or glossed over. Hence, we encounter not only a growing knowledge about Muslim debates on medical or bioethics, but also a correlated process of forgetting. However, there is good reason not to leave medical ethics to medical doctors and medical ethicists and to be cautiously aware of the systemic merits as well as the shortcomings of the very mixed bag of writings that is being produced by the various disciplines involved in the analysis of Islamic medical ethics. For instance, representatives of state law (*qānūn*) closely follow the logic of their own discipline and usually do not address broader audiences; medical anthropologists have been very helpful in turning attention to local settings of norm negotiation, but have often downplayed historical developments and ignored the scriptural great tradition;[1] in turn, scholars of Islamic Studies are often not anthropologically informed and pay little attention to appropriations on the ground and even less to long-winded emic accounts of life stories as medical case studies; medical

1 This term was introduced by Robert Redfield (1956: 70): "The great tradition is cultivated in schools or temples; the little tradition works itself out and keeps itself going in the lives of the unlettered in their village communities." And see http://www.ifeas.uni-mainz.de/workingpapers/desplat.pdf (accessed 24 February 2013). To avoid Redfield's hierarchical division, Talal Asad (1986: 7, 15–7) proposed rather to study Islam as a "discursive tradition"—a framework within which the multiple versions of normative Islam and also the contexts in which they are suggested should be perceived.

practitioners who participate in committees on medical ethics at times selectively mix bits and pieces taken from secondary literature or mimic a familiarity with Islamic normativity by referring only to the Quran and Sunna, instead of turning to the important interface of fiqh controversies; experts on modern developments tend to bypass the importance of, for example, Islamic doctrines of the soul or turn a blind eye to the strong Sufi tradition when examining the topic of medical treatment; and Western scholars of Islamic jurisprudence may neglect theology with its eschatological anxieties and expectations. Finally, many scholars regard it as an atavistic nuisance to even consider the impact of the widespread and scripture-based belief in demons (*jinn*) as a weighty health-related factor.

In addition, the wider and more subtle mechanisms of power politics and the difficulties of non-ideological discussion of such medical questions as circumcision or HIV/AIDS must also be acknowledged. As a consequence, while the subtopics presented below do touch on some hotly debated problems, this chapter also tries to point to some issues that are affected by a certain structural amnesia, although they must be confined to a weak spotlight backed by a necessarily limited selection of publications. Generally speaking, however, analysis of the perception of relevant medical fiqh positions among the community members of 57 Islamic states, of their integration into state law, their influence on the public health sector with its various institutions and practitioners, and the degree to which such fiqh versions are contested or taken up by NGO activities, as also a reflection on bioethics as civilizing mission (De Vries and Rott 2011), must remain outside the scope of this chapter.

Fatalism Versus Agency

Derivatives of the Arabic root *w-k-l*, which connotes complete trust in someone or something, appear a number of times in the Quran and are also present in hadith literature (on the concept of *tawakkul* as reliance on God, see chapter 35 of al-Ghazālī's *Iḥyā' 'ulūm al-dīn*; Reinert 1968). Concerning the question whether medical treatment is compatible with doctrines of faith, Islamic theology conceded final causality only to God and came up with the formula that without His willing, no healing (*shifā'*) can be expected. Some early Muslims were anxious to avoid medical treatment (*tark al-tadāwī*), which attitude became the subject of scholarly discussion in some detail. The related concept of steadfastness (*ṣabr*) likewise has a long intellectual tradition, ranging from the story of the Prophet Job (*Ayyūb*) in the Quran to comprehensive accounts such as Ibn Qayyim al-Jawziyya's (d. 751/1350) *'Uddat al-ṣābirīn*. Nevertheless, it is a persistent orientalist stereotype that Muslims have a fatalistic attitude toward grievances; and although "redemptive suffering" is discussed as one of the means to mitigate the impact of one's evil deeds on the day of judgment, the majority opinion in theology and jurisprudence has always opted in favor of (plausible) treatment. Moreover, according to the medical anthropologist Sherine Hamdy (2009), even religiously articulated, seemingly fatalistic statements of terminally ill patients can be understood as agency on the part of the individual Muslim (that is, not a passive attitude but an active embrace of God's will). However, the assurance of the Prophet that there is a remedy for every ill (or illness), attested by hadith literature, has never been taken as a blanket license to accept and test just anything as a potential cure. Hence, since earliest times there has been an ongoing debate on the permissibility of treatment with forbidden things (*al-tadāwī bi-l-muḥarram*), such as medicines containing narcotic drugs (*mukhaddirāt*). As a rule of thumb, it is held that they should only be used if no permitted alternative is available. New medication and measures of treatment need to be checked systematically for compatibility with the demands of the Sharia, with their potential violation of ritual duties (such as the administering of injections or suppositories during fasting) of especial concern. The dispensation (*rukhṣa*) usually accorded by Islamic jurisprudence in cases of a precarious health situation, such as managing diabetes during the fast of Ramadan (Ababou et al. 2008), is not always accepted by Muslims, eager to comply with the demands of the religion; hence, it may be advisable for medical staff to involve Sharia scholars (Atighetchi 2007: 273–4).

With the contemporary expansion of Muslim consumer culture and overall insistence on "Halalisation" (Fischer 2008: 29), the debate about impure substances (*mawādd najisa*) has acquired increasing symbolic value and, especially in Southeast Asia, has led to the setting up of authoritative chemical test laboratories. Originally intended to certify ritually slaughtered meat, halal certificates have become a visible marketing strategy to advertise all sorts of Islamically approved products to Muslim consumers, especially in diasporic contexts. Also acting as an agent is the genre of Prophetic medicine (*al-ṭibb al-nabawī, al-ṭibb al-rūḥī, al-ṭibb al-rūḥānī*; in Shiʿi rendering *ṭibb al-aʾimma*), which despite its containing many Greek elements and a hybrid structure from its beginnings in the ninth century (Perho 1995: 53–4) is nevertheless regarded as belonging to the broader realm of Islamic normativity. Prophetic medicine distinguishes between black magic (*siḥr*), which it forbids, and white magic (*ruqya*, including exorcism of jinn), which it allows or even recommends; further, it presents various sorts of traditional medication and treatment with Prophetically approved substances, as well as certain spiritual measures that are suitable against the evil eye and other sources of affliction. Today, related publications that are advertised as, for instance, "healing through the Quran" explicitly promise assistance in cases of psychological distress, but also to avoid—if not cure—AIDS (*aydz*), cancer, or rheumatism (Ḥasan 2009). They increasingly merge how-to manuals with ecological or other lifestyle orientations and advocate self-medication as well as—with more of a Sufi flavor—self-monitoring devices. In recent decades, an ever-growing market has developed for such spiritual consumption, buttressed by the huge reservoir of Islamic normativity. On the psychological level, not only traditional healers but also some postmodern medical experts have begun to relate to and integrate their Muslim patients' belief in demons as a means to objectify and challenge what is tormenting them.

Especially since the twentieth century, with its many scientific advancements and social upheavals, Islamic acceptance of modern medicine (with some provisos and preconditions) has become much more evident (Krawietz 1991); this process correlates with a rekindled emphasis on personal effort and creativity in legal evaluation (*ijtihād*), surmounting ready-made prior solutions (*taqlīd*) and jurisprudential gaps. Discussions of medical necessity and need (*ḍarūra*) and their plausible public interest (*maṣlaḥa*) are already prominent in the first decades of the twentieth century in Muḥammad Rashīd Riḍā's fatwas published in the reformist periodical *al-Manār*. These and, in particular, the contemporaneous debates on the all-pervasive basic values (*maqāṣid*) of the Islamic Sharia attest not only to the modern relevance of Islamic jurisprudence, but also to the profound revival of its theoretical bases, *uṣūl al-fiqh*. For some decades now, scholars of Islamic jurisprudence have begun systematically expanding their medical knowledge while medical specialists are becoming increasingly informed about Islamic law; without actually achieving the historical example of some very renowned classical jurists who also practiced as physicians, there is a growing number of publications that cross established jurisprudential or medical genre boundaries or that at least integrate the findings of the other genre to a certain degree—for instance, by comparing religious to medical fasting (Muḥammad 2007) or by addressing questions of ritual transfer, such as whether Muslims may use fasting practices for hunger strikes (Āl Sayf 2006). In general, there has been an upsurge of writings that reflect the growing importance of somatic technologies of the self to check and actively enhance one's attitudes, beliefs, and practices. In this sense, the normative realm of Sharia and medical ethics today is only secondarily about official application in the form of state law, despite the many contested cases of highly invasive medical interventions.

The Beginning of Life

The most prominent debates about new medical methods revolve around the early phase of pregnancy and the final phase of dying (see below). This is mainly because two closely intertwined Islamic paradigms are then severely challenged, namely, the understanding and the sanctity of human life (*ḥurma*).

The clear Islamic answer as to what exactly constitutes human life is ensoulment (*nafḫ al-rūḥ*, via the angel Gabriel who breathes life into the embryo). However, the exact timeline for such an occurrence is contested, even within the schools of law, which discuss a period between 40 and 120 days after conception (for premodern debates, see Katz 2003) and try to pinpoint a specific number of days as a cut-off point.[2] Although a few Islamic countries have enacted legislation that accepts non-medical reasons for abortion (*ijhāḍ, isqāṭ al-ḥaml*), this intervention is usually illegal after 120 days of pregnancy unless the life of the mother is endangered; before the 120th day, it is regarded at a minimum as reprehensible (*makrūh*) and needs to be justified in medical terms.

The Quran offers only a rudimentary embryology (22:5, 23:12–4), which is complemented by hadith materials; its three distinct phases of development[3] are expanded upon in exegetical literature (*tafsīr*). The evolution of Islamic intellectual history in this field is greatly complicated by the mixing of two conflicting concepts, namely, the Quran-inspired narrative of ensoulment and one that is very much influenced by later translations of Greek Neoplatonic texts into Arabic and is based on the idea of an entelechy of the soul and its specific faculties. The latter concept may be used to argue in favor of protection before the fortieth day, even from conception onward.[4] While some classical scholars referred in their normative writings explicitly to non-Islamic—above all Greek—sources, especially Ibn Sīnā (d. 428/1037), others seem not to be aware of these influences. Up to today, abortion is—in practice as well—often shrouded in ambiguity; thus, a number of medical doctors speak of "menstrual regulation" or "cleansing" of the womb as a pretext to conceal abortive measures. The traditional assistance of the midwife (*qābila*) in such matters has been considerably devalued since abortion has been turned into a clinical intervention (Kozma 2011: 25–49). The advancement of testing procedures (non-invasive and invasive) opened up new avenues for prenatal screening and prenatal diagnosis (PND), which inform parents and doctors about potential physical disabilities of the fetus (*janīn*)—however, these tend to be conducted later than the time frame during which abortion is regarded as less problematic, namely, the first 40 days of pregnancy. In the 1970s abortion on such grounds was vehemently opposed by Sharia scholars, but in 1990, after considerable criticism, the Islamic Fiqh Academy of the Muslim World League in Mecca approved its practice within a period lasting up to the 120th day (Eich 2006a: 168–70). For this decision the Academy made use of the permissive potential of certain premodern fiqh doctrines, such as Ibn Qayyim al-Jawziyya's support of a 120-day period before ensoulment (Fischer 2012: 74–6). In the wake of the Kosovo War (1998–99) a global discussion of abortion was set off, triggered by the systematic Serbian mass rape (*ightiṣāb*) of Bosnian Muslim women, who were often held in captivity beyond the 120-day window of opportunity for abortion. Nevertheless, scenarios of rape that feature Muslim perpetrators (the understanding of "political rape" in Pakistan as reshaped from "feudal honor rape" is pointed out by Haeri 1999: 56) cannot yet be publicly addressed, although some scholars have begun moving away from the allegation of illegitimate intercourse (*zinā*) or its false accusation (*qadhf*) and are taking the emotional and psychic distress of raped women into consideration, thereby allowing late abortion as an exception (Hilālī 2000: 312–3).

Other topics of reproductive health emerged to be a forceful component in medical ethics in the course of the twentieth century, the first being contraception (*taḥdīd al-nasl, tanẓīm al-nasl*) with demographic and economic developments demanding family planning since the 1960s. Some Muslim religious scholars have severely criticised such a strategy of population policy, calling it an imperialist conspiracy designed to undermine the world of Islam. A vigorous spokesman of this camp was Abul Ala

2 The decisive criterion was that a person who induced a miscarriage or aborted a fetus prior to the fourth month of pregnancy was only obliged to pay compensation (*ghurra*) equal to one-tenth of the blood money (*diya*) required for an adult since the embryo did not yet represent human life. After the 120th day more serious consequences are in play.

3 Viz., the stage of a drop (*nuṭfa*), then of a clot (*ʿalaqa*), and then of a lump of flesh (*muḍgha*), as recited in Q 22:5.

4 The Catholic Church has tried time and again to close ranks with Muslims and have both advocate a more rigid position toward abortion (Bowen 1997: 161).

Mawdudi (d. 1979), leader of the Islamist party Jamaat-e-Islami, who in his bestseller on birth control denounced the decadence and cheap pleasures resulting from the intermingling of the sexes that prevail in Western societies (Maudoodi 2001). Defenders of birth control based their argument on the Prophet's condoning of (temporary) coitus interruptus (*ʿazl*), and regarded more modern forms of contraceptives as equally permissible on the basis of analogy (*qiyās*). The Quranic recommendation for a two-year period of breastfeeding (2:233; 31:14), too, was taken as encouragement to practice spacing between pregnancies. Today, outspoken opponents of family planning seem to be fighting an uphill battle in many Islamic countries against the increasing number of prominent supporters, although irreversible measures such as sterilization (*taʿqīm*) are still considered forbidden (Amanullah 2003). There has recently been a surge in the promotion of neo-traditional values, including of their psychological aspects, by way of, for example, publications extolling the normative forms of motherhood (*umūma*) on the hand of Islamic jurisprudence (Ḥasan 2011), or guides to halal dating and how-to manuals for a successful marriage in accordance with religious tenets, while the idea of romance and of choosing one's own spouse without family intermediaries is increasingly promoted by the media. On the more medical and jurisprudential level, a series of dense interdisciplinary and multinational conferences have been organized to explore and discuss the whole scale of problems related to embryology and demographic engineering, including gender and quality of life issues (Fischer 2012: 82–109).

Artificial insemination (*al-talqīḥ al-ṣināʿī, al-talqīḥ al-iṣṭināʿī*) and test tube babies (*aṭfāl al-anābīb*) became a topic of note since the birth of Louise Brown in 1978. Childless couples are often stigmatized in Muslim societies, and since Islamic law does not view adoption (*tabannin*, see Quran 33:4–5) as an alternative, such new possibilities have been enthusiastically welcomed by many people.[5] After an initial phase of reproductive tourism to Western countries, IVF-centers, often privately run, mushroomed in the Middle East—for example, Egypt, Iran, Lebanon, and Saudi Arabia—a phenomenon that the anthropologist Marcia Inhorn has dealt with in considerable detail (including patterns of secrecy, expectations, and endangered masculinity). Although a variety of technical models of assisted reproductive technologies (ARTs) exists, using different combinations of sperm and egg donors, all suffer from the overriding legal insistence on the preservation of relations of filiation (*nasab*) (Clarke 2009: 94–6), which under no circumstances may become confused or mixed up (*ikhtilāṭ*), as would happen in the case of a surrogate mother (*muṭawwiʿa*), even if she was a second wife. This is in sharp distinction to recent voices in Iran, where some Shiʿi jurists "have invoked *mutʿa* to make egg donation legal within the parameters of marriage; they argue that the husband should contract a *mutʿa* marriage with the egg donor for the period of time in which the whole procedure" is carried out (Moinifar and Vaghefi 2010: 254); other Shiʿi jurists do not even require such a contract. Besides the insistence on only married couples receiving treatment, a concern is that in vitro fertilization (IVF) entails exposure of private body parts (*kashf al-ʿawra*) in front of medical staff. The handling of semen is also an issue and must be evaluated within the framework of two of the five basic values (*maqāṣid*) that pervade the entire Sharia, namely, descent (*nasab*) and life (*nafs*). For in-depth information concerning the jurisprudential evaluation of the various distinct forms of artificial insemination and related issues, one needs to turn to sources other than often too succinct fatwas. Spontaneous, apodictic answers are not possible when it comes to complicated medical procedures. In the second half of the twentieth century, some international Islamic committees were therefore established, for example, *Majmaʿ al-Fiqh al-Islāmī* of the Muslim World League in Mecca, the Fiqh Academy of the Organization of Islamic Conference (since renamed Organization of Islamic Cooperation) in Jedda, the *Majmaʿ al-Buḥūth al-Islāmiyya* of Azhar University, and the Islamic Organisation of Medical Sciences. Together they represent a regular institutional framework that in cooperation enables preparatory conferences and counseling with natural science experts, whereby necessary detail and distinctions are taken into account; hence, they provide structured

5 Arguments against the general *fiqhī* prohibition of masturbation (*istimnāʾ*) are grounded in the concern for legitimate offspring.

collective processes of creative legal interpretation (*ijtihād*). The preliminary steps and outcomes are often no longer called fatwas, but resolutions (*qarārāt*) or recommendations (*tawṣiyāt*), and relevant publications make the course of the discussions transparent.

IVF has created successive problems, such as the procedure of preimplantation genetic diagnosis (PGD), which analyzes the harvested and extracorporally fertilized eggs in order to exclude those with genetic or chromosomal defects from implantation (Eich 2008). It also provides a means for gender selection that is all the more tempting in patriarchal societies (with excesses especially in Bangladesh, India, and Pakistan, known as the "missing girls" phenomenon), so that most Muslim jurists insist on gender selection only for medical reasons. Furthermore, the dilemmas of designer babies and intentional conception of a genetically compatible stem-cell donor for an afflicted sibling represent a challenge to the value of life as such. The regulations allowing medical interventions in the first 120 days of pregnancy also entail the danger of attracting international biomedical companies that may turn parts of the Islamic world into an ethical dumping site. Although the availability of genetic counseling on risks of genetic disorders is quite widespread in richer Arab states, the advisability of paternal cousin marriages still remains a bone of contention, mainly between Muslims in Middle Eastern countries and the West (Eich 2006a).

With regard to cloning (*istinsākh*), another contested topic, we must distinguish between two basic types—reproductive cloning, by splitting a fertilized egg, that is, induced identical twinning, and therapeutic cloning, which is at the core of the more recent debates. The latter is a euphemism for the creation, medical use, and final destruction of the cytoplasm of an egg without nucleus that is combined with the DNA of another person. Muslim scholars had debated cloning even before Dolly, the first cloned sheep, was born in 1996. The main unease stemmed from questions as to whether the individuality of a human being is challenged by this procedure and whether cloning is an infringement on a divine monopoly—dangers that were both negated by the majority of jurists (Eich 2006b: 296–7). Yūsuf al-Qaraḍāwī and the late Lebanese Shiʿi scholar Muḥammad Ḥusayn Faḍl Allāh (d. 2010) are often quoted as being in support of cloning, but this qualification necessitates some caveats and closer reading of their statements. However, other problems are highly contested and have engaged state muftis and high-ranking conference participants (Eich 2006b: 297–302). The wider debate about embryonic stem cell research, for example, is too complex to relate here, but it is connected to cloning and the same discussion of abortion and the definition of life not beginning until weeks after fertilization.

Once Western medical science acknowledged the existence of HIV/AIDS, Muslim ethicists began discussing it officially as late as the mid-1980s. The tone that has been set in pronouncements by Sharia scholars has mostly been one of criticism of the Western "Other" and of attribution of the phenomenon to "homosexual or extramarital relations and drug addiction," identifying its occurrence as a "divine punishment" (Atighetchi 2007: 200–1)[6] predominantly applicable to indecent Western societies. Such prevailing bias hampers safe-sex campaigns, although there are some initiatives, such as the Pink Triangle in Malaysia or the Naz Project in several South Asian and other communities. In the first decade of the twenty-first century, the now formally dissolved or transformed non-governmental organization "Positive Muslims," a support group in South Africa for those suffering from HIV/AIDS, was very influential under Farid Esack as its most prominent spokesman (for a critical evaluation of the organization's proposed "theology of compassion," see Svensson 2012). There are some, such as Jāsim ʿAlī Sālim (1996: 170–8, 229), who strongly advocate AIDS tests before marriage and call on the legal guardian (*walī*) of the bride to withdraw his consent if either spouse tests positive. Whether a wife is entitled to demand a divorce on the basis of her husband's affliction and several other issues are open to debate.[7]

Advancements in life sciences have rendered many assumptions and procedures of traditional Islamic jurisprudence and of customary law obsolete (and may even call for a revision of earlier

6 Atighetchi's chapter includes information on various Islamic countries; see also http://www.islamset.com/bioethics/aids1/index.html (accessed 24 February 2013).

7 See Islamic Fiqh Academy (India) 2009; http://www.fiqhacademy.org.sa/, under *Nadwat al-jawānib al-fiqhiyya li-marḍā al-aydz* (accessed 24 February 2013).

positions). Modern law codes have restricted, for instance, the maximum period of pregnancy to about one year only—the doctrine of the dormant fetus (*rāqid*) that was applicable in Maliki law, allowing for protracted pregnancies of up to five or even more years (Bosaller 2004) which thus provided an opportunity to cover up (illicit) sexual relationships between two marriages or ascribe a child to a prior husband, is no longer tenable. Similar inroads are being made into the classical Islamic law of evidence, which is predicated on the ritualized testimony of respected Muslim individuals (Johansen 2002: 169, 171, 180). The efficacy of this bias had already been questioned by renowned postclassical authors such as Ibn Qayyim al-Jawziyya and Ibn Farḥūn (d. 799/1397) (Idrīs 2010: 85–90), who argued in favor of greater liberties for the qadi and other law enforcement personnel and for the inclusion of circumstantial evidence (*qarā'in*), and modern science now offers a whole new array of means that represent an even greater challenge. Technologies such as paternity tests (Shaham 2010, 2011), fingerprints (*baṣamāt jildiyya*), genetic fingerprints (*baṣamāt wirāthiyya*),[8] and generally the analysis of blood, urine, sperm, and hair (Idrīs 2010: 118–31) have turned traditional claims of Islamic jurisprudence upside down. This affects both penal and family law, as well as demographic engineering via, for example, premarital screening procedures; theoretically it could portend even a potential rewriting of Islamic history in light of its lineage claims.

Organ Transplants, Human Inviolability, and End-of-life Debates

Developments in the natural sciences have shaken up the domain of Sharia scholars in accompanying and explaining death and dying. In general, many of the Sharia's established ritual practices have been placed under a critical light, as hygienic, medical, or other reservations present reasons to frown upon them. In succession, the colonial regimes, Western influences, and "the modern state and its new tools of control, e.g. vaccination, post-mortem examination, registration of new-born babies, and regular check-ups of school children and army soldiers" (Fahmy 1999: 245) forced ordinary Muslims to submit to new regulations that challenged their familiar lives. The widespread practice of pilgrimage to holy places—and not only the hajj to Mecca and Medina—was hampered by quarantines when national borders began to be crossed, while the transportation of corpses to the holy cities of Karbala, Mashhad, and Qom—paramount in the Shi'i tradition, so as to bury them in the close vicinity of the Imams or special friends of God (*mujāwara*)—was seen as horrific and generated biting commentary. In his study of public health in nineteenth- and early twentieth-century Iran, Willem Floor (2004) conveys a sense of the mocking tone used by commentators who portrayed religion as backward. Although many of the ulema refused to abandon their religious arguments despite being increasingly challenged by the evolving world of life science and secular scientists, a not inconsiderable number engaged in renewed *ijtihād*, which is most evident in the complex and multifaceted phenomenon of organ transplantation (*naql al-a'ḍā', zar' al-a'ḍā'*) (Krawietz 1991: 169–202).

The first cornea transplants in the Islamic world were performed in Egypt in the 1960s; in the following decades more complicated operations entailing other organs, such as kidneys in the beginning of the 1970s, followed suit. For medical transplantations such as these, organs are harvested from either the living or the dead. Both categories endanger the paradigm of the inviolability and sanctity of the human body (*ḥurma*) that is constructed by both prescriptions and interdictions—not as a zone of autonomy for the individual, but rather as a thereby indirectly constituted protective shield.[9] As stated above, this principle guards the living, including that of the fetus, as well as the dead body,

8 See also http://www.islamset.com/bioethics/genetics/index.html (accessed 24 February 2013).

9 The Algerian legal scholar Bilḥāj al-'Arabī uses the expression *ma'ṣūmiyyat al-juththa* ("the inviolability of the corpse") in the title of his survey of the whole range of modern-day procedures that have evolved around dying and death but switches in the text itself to *ḥurma* (2009: for example, 140).

and is extended to the ground in which the corpse is buried. Since the body is regarded as something entrusted (*amāna*) to man by God, but not human property, it must be handed back to the Creator immediately upon death; and it may not be sacrificed by cremation, suicide (*intiḥār*), or euthanasia (*qatl al-raḥma*) (Krawietz 1991: 91–108). Early Islamic burial prescriptions express an overall concern with preserving and cherishing (*karāma*) the integrity of the deceased with reference to a Prophetic saying that breaking (*kasr*) the bones of the dead is like breaking the bones of the living. The abhorred early example of corpse mutilation of the Prophet's uncle by Hind, the wife of Abū Sufyān, the leader of the Quraysh and a staunch opponent of Muḥammad, is an integral part of Islamic cultural memory. Even in jihad, the mutilation of a dead person is forbidden. However, exceptions have been granted in special situations: when a valuable item belonging to a third person is to be rescued from the belly of the corpse or when a child is to be removed from his deceased mother's womb. Emilie Savage-Smith (2011: esp. 229, 309, 328) tests the widespread assumption that anatomical dissection (*tashrīḥ*) was prohibited in Islam, and presents textual evidence seemingly in favor of a postmortem opening, but in the end she affirms that Muslim religious scholars of the premodern period showed "no forensic impetus to engage in dissection." Nevertheless, it became accepted practice, and is regarded today even as a collective duty (*farḍ kifāya*) that medical doctors carry out on behalf of the whole community. The standard answer is that the transplantation of regenerative body parts is permitted if there are sound medical reasons, even with regard to blood (*naql al-dam*) although this substance is seen by Islamic law as principally impure. Paired organs like kidneys may also be donated; however, altruism may not lead to death of the donor or even serious health risks. It is permissible to extract organs when brain death has been established (for a quick answer, see Van den Branden and Broeckaert 2011).

Apart from this outline in a nutshell, there are a host of problems related to organ transplantation, some of which follow: since—as a complement to the beginning of life—death is defined by Islamic religious scholars as the departure of the soul from the body, this again raises the problem of ascertainment. In accordance with the demands of Islamic law and theology, "Muslims have always paid great attention to the phases of dying and the exact moment of death" and even used to identify certain characteristics or signs of death (Krawietz 2003: 198–9). However, the idea of brain death (*mawt al-dimāgh*) or of the death of the brain stem (*mawt jidh' al-dimāgh*), which enables the harvesting of organs while the functions of the organs are maintained by machines in intensive care units (*al-'ināya al-murakkaza*), posed a fundamental challenge to this understanding. In 1986 the Third International Conference of Islamic Jurists in Amman embraced brain-stem death in their catalogue of death criteria, although details remain debated. There is no need to maintain the vegetative state by artificial machines, but the death of the brain is a process; medical doctors distinguish between different key parts of the brain (Padela et al. 2011: 65–72) and complain about the lack of medical precision and the gaps in pertinent statements of the Islamic Fiqh Academy of the Organization of the Islamic Conference (OIC) and the Islamic Medical Association of North America (IMANA). Although organ transplantation after brain death is now widely accepted, at least in principle, opponents as well as proponents have criticized the dark side of organ transplantation: corneas illegally taken from the dead, the trade in organs to the detriment of the poor, and dubious medical tourism, without it leading to straightforward national state law solutions (Hamdy 2012). In the wake of a policy shift in the last decade of the twentieth century, "Iran became the only country in which the compensation of living organ donors is not only legal, but also facilitated by the government" (which is quite unusual among Islamic countries), nevertheless "private arrangements for compensation between donors and recipients do exist" (Tober 2007: 157). Diane Tober points to the paradox that in Iran "the use of cadaveric donors has been far more controversial than the living donor program" (2007: 161). Theoretically, every Muslim is—within the divinely ordained limits—entitled to the same beneficial use of the body; however, Farhat Moazam stresses that "Western conceptions of autonomous decisions of a self-responsible individual who makes his personal choices do not apply to current Pakistan society at large" (2006: 45, 74, 220) and that weaker family members, usually women, become "volunteers" for organ donation because "the best medicinal-biological match as a potential donor is often someone who does not feel obliged to donate—given his social status within the family hierarchy" (2006: 66, 163–4). Furthermore, controversies about whether non-Muslims are entitled to organs from Muslim donors or only the other way round have stirred unrest (Atigetchi 2007: 164–8), as have discussions about transplants from animals to humans (Atigetchi 2007: 181–3) and among people of different nationalities.

Medical Necessities of Sorts

Many medical operations do not represent procedures that are a matter of life and death; others do not even seem to be dictated by health necessities. The assumption that gender rectification is needed compels important invasive measures on the human body, such as circumcision, sex change surgery, and hymen repair. The most widespread and accepted bodily mutilation in Islam is certainly male circumcision (*khitān*), which is usually regarded as a duty and established life cycle ritual: "The rate of circumcision in Muslim nations is between 90 and 100 percent. This includes the Christians who form a significant part of some Arab states" (Alahmad and Dekkers[10] 2012: 2). A growing movement against it in the West—as seen in the recent court ruling outlawing it in Germany in 2012[11]—has stirred tensions and evoked harsh criticism, also from Jewish circles. The Swiss scholar Sami Aldeeb Abu-Sahlieh, of Christian Palestinian background, explicitly condemned it already in the 1990s, along with female circumcision (*ṭahāra, khitān al-unthā, khifāḍ*; or female genital mutilation, FMG), which has been much more widely criticized.

Muslim legal scholars regard FMG only as recommended (*mandūb, sunna*), not as prescribed (*wājib*); it is not unanimously practiced throughout the Islamic world nor is Islam the driving force behind its most invasive forms, especially in sub-Saharan Africa (FGM-types II–IV), against which it even warns. Nevertheless, the general acquiescence in this operation from fiqh, which helps to legitimize it, the downplaying of medical objections, and the prevailing lack of guilt or empathy toward the young girls and women who undergo it, combined with a vivid imagination about female sexuality, considerably block jurisprudential flexibility on the issue (Krawietz 1991: 228). Many campaigns and NGO initiatives have tried to curb female circumcision; in November 2006, for instance, under the auspices of the then Egyptian Grand Mufti ʿAlī Jumʿa, the German NGO "TARGET" co-organized a pioneering conference on FGM at al-Azhar University. Medical doctors as well as Egyptian and other Muslim Sharia scholars, such as Yūsuf al-Qaraḍāwī, participated and signed a resolution against FGM, in what was intended to be a breakthrough.[12] However, like previous initiatives, it was of little avail, seemingly more a show of symbolic politics, and not enough to bring about the desired paradigm shift. The extremely complicated and persistent nature of the practice is shown by a meticulous and painstaking study of the mindset of migrant Sudanese women in the USA who had undergone FGM (Abdel Halim 2006).

Apart from the above, the ulema are often suspicious of operations that are not medically required, and they habitually refer to the Quran's teaching: "When Shaitân (Satan) was dismissed from Paradise, he threatened that he would urge the human beings to make changes in their own bodies and to the bodies of animals by piercing their ears, which are considered a violation of bodily integrity" (Alahmad and Dekkers 2012: 4). Their reproach is aimed especially at cosmetic surgery and other changes to one's appearance, with regard to which the dicta of the Sharia scholars oscillate between insistence on a clear-cut binary gender identity and encouragement of women to please their spouses with beauty-enhancing measures, which contrasts with the general prohibition of deception

10 Ghiath Alahmad and Wim Dekkers do not convincingly manage to explain the compatibility of male circumcision with the Islamic principle of inviolability.

11 After virulent public debate, legislation was then passed allowing the procedure providing certain criteria were met.

12 See the online link http://www.target-human-rights.com/HP-02_target/u1-2_alAzha_kairo/index.php?p=gelehrtenkonferenz (accessed February 24, 2013).

and delusion (Krawietz 1991: 242–77). Although it cracks down harshly on homosexuals, Iran is very forthcoming about sex-change surgery in cases of medically proven psychological distress. In 1983 the transsexual Maryam Molkara, who was born a man but identified as a woman, managed under adventurous but brutal circumstances to obtain permission in the form of a quasi-fatwa from Ayatollah Khomeini to undergo such surgery. Hymen repair surgery (*ratq ghishāʾ al-bakāra*) has been debated since the late 1980s. This intervention is mainly sought shortly before marriage to eliminate any suspicion of premarital sex or to rectify an involuntary loss of virginity. The different approaches to this topic in the secondary literature reveal assumptions about sexuality, gender roles, and social values (for their pros and cons, see Rispler-Chaim 2007: 332–9).

The respective necessity (*ḍarūra*) or legitimate public interest (*maṣlaḥa*) of today's broad range of operations needs to be questioned more thoroughly. Although the trend started earlier, after September 11, 2001, large sums of money have been shifted from the USA and Western countries to the Arab Gulf region, where complete medical cities have been set up that are designed to make medical trips to Western destinations superfluous and that attract patients from all parts of the globe. What is regarded as a medical necessity or as desirable may therefore also be considerably influenced by the availability of medical infrastructure.

General Remarks and Outlook

Sharia scholars have been challenged, competed against, and cornered—to the point of being in danger of marginalization—by the many changes that have shaped the modern Middle East and beyond. Instead of relying solely on the option of participating in the drafting of state law, which option was quite limited in most cases, they vigorously catered to the expanding book market, and with the backing of many newly institutionalized faculties of Islamic jurisprudence, comparative law, and Islamic religion, were co-opted in medical institutions as ethical voices. Certain figures were even employed to represent their respective nation, above all in the capacity—however nominal the authority—of the Grand Mufti. A related trend of presenting Islamic teachings in the form of international conferences, workshops, and symposia further weakened the influence of many imported Western doctrines, while the flow of Muslim migrants enhanced the discursive power of Islamic normativity. The same is true of the new media and especially the counseling opportunities that the Internet provides—a global source at the fingertips of Muslims everywhere.

With their emphasis on orthopraxis and an overly somatic orientation, a potential pitfall for advice-seekers is that the experts in Islamic jurisprudence will neglect the many advancements in medical and other life sciences. Nevertheless, these scholars generally have managed to develop and publicize thoughtful positions, first through the increased use of fatwas, the most successful Sharia genre of the twentieth century, and further by their employment in institutions that enable state-of-the-art normative counseling.[13] A whole series of fatwas can be assembled in which muftis clearly display that they are out of their depth or are overwhelmed by medical developments. But in general, they have tried to do their homework—whether one agrees on an ideological level with the doctrinal outcomes or not. They have not relinquished their privilege of warning against practices that are not in accordance with Sharia, and they still insist on defining ultimate questions, such as the meaning of life or the concept of death, even when brain death has been adopted as a criterion.

Despite the myriad of Islamic voices and plurality of actors, institutions, and movements, some general trends can be identified that characterized Islamic medical ethics in the twentieth century, such

13 The article "Medical Experts and Islamic Scholars Deliberating over Brain Death: Gaps in the Applied Islamic Bioethics Discourse" (Padela et al. 2011), written by three medical scholars, is critical of shortcomings in the discourse, but not without hope.

as the (majoritarian) position against surrogate motherhood and for female circumcision, and an open attitude toward a variety of medical novelties, such as organ transplantation. Another characteristic, however, which is often underrated because of the many media-hyped topics of concern, is that most fatwas do not deal with questions on the level of principle, but with fine-tuning in individual cases. They also largely address ritual concerns. Religious anxieties about medical treatment are still dominated by more or less traditional topics; they mostly refer to everyday life and the fulfillment of common religious practices, such as the use of toothpaste and toothbrush during Ramadan.[14] Worth mentioning is also the intermediary function of Sharia experts with regard to the (re-)construction of the normative heritage that is often rendered as a "revival." Moreover, with their ability to confidently navigate the realm of substantive Sharia (*furūʿ al-fiqh*), these scholars have come up with new formats or presented fiqh positions in newly arranged norm clusters, thereby managing to fit them into upcoming developments, as exemplified by the appearance of Disability Studies in the beginning of the 1980s. Neither the term nor the concept existed in traditional Islamic law and only "with regard to marriage do medieval fiqh scholars speak in a generalized manner" of the defects (*ʿuyūb*) of both spouses (Rispler-Chaim 2006: 4). Yet several fiqh studies have been composed since on either disability (*iʿāqa*) or disabled people (*muʿāqūn*) that assemble a cross-section of materials from classical fiqh manuals, from the writings of a specific author, or from fatwas.

It is burdensome for Sharia scholars to share in frontline medical ethics decisions that necessitate new terminology and thinking as well as to fit into organizational infrastructures in order to pave the way for sufficiently informed decisions. At the same time, however, consumers of normativity are no longer content with only asking questions (or "shopping" for favorable fatwas), but have themselves started to turn into semi-educated or grass-roots "prosumers" who use the enhanced research possibilities of the internet to cruise the reservoir of Islamic normativity to come to their own conclusions. Although there is a growing movement that invokes human rights (*ḥuqūq al-insān*) or postulates their compatibility with normative Islam, as well as others that advocate cross-cultural/cross-religious convergences, systematic and especially feminist bioethics in the sense of liberation jurisprudence (Abou El Fadl 2001) are quite rare—especially in Muslim "core" countries. Nevertheless, one must acknowledge that the flexibility of Islamic jurisprudence finds its most lively expression in medical ethics. Contemporary edicts prove not only the scholars' familiarity with the "hidden treasures" of Islamic law, but represent even more creative readings influenced by global developments. Being less hampered than Christianity by the Cartesian dichotomy between body and mind, Islamic jurisprudence is well equipped for the future.

References

Ababou, Mohammed et al. 2008. Le jeûne du Ramadan au Maroc: Un dilemme pour les patients diabétiques et les soignants. *Sciences Sociales et Santé* 26(2): 79–104.

Abdel Halim, Asma M. 2006. *Sudanese Women in the United States: The Double Problem of Gender and Culture*. Lewiston, NY: Edwin Mellon Press.

Abou El Fadl, Khaled. 2001. *Speaking in God's Name: Islamic Law, Authority and Women*. Oxford: Oneworld.

Ach, Johann S., and Christa Runtenberg. 2002. *Bioethik: Disziplin und Diskurs. Zur Selbstaufklärung angewandter Ethik*. Frankfurt: Campus.

Āl Sayf, ʿAbd Allāh b. Mubārak. 2006. *Ḥukm al-iḍrāb ʿan al-ṭaʿām fī l-fiqh al-islāmī*. Riyadh: Wizārat al-Taʿlīm al-ʿĀlī, Jāmiʿat al-Imām Muḥammad Ibn Saʿūd al-Islāmiyya.

14 See, for example, http://alifta.net/Fatawa/FatawaChapters.aspx?View=Tree&NodeID=35&PageNo=1&BookID=17 and http://www.dar-alifta.org/ViewMindFatawa.aspx?ID=171&LangID=1 (both accessed February 24, 2013).

Alahmad, Ghiath, and Wim Dekkers. 2012. Bodily Integrity and Male Circumcision: An Islamic Perspective. *Journal of the Indian Medical Association* 44: 1–9.
Amanullah, Muhammad. 2003. Opinions of Modern Egyptian Scholars about Family Planning in Islam. *Arab Law Quarterly* 18: 184–96.
al-ʿArabī, Bilḥāj. 2009. *Maʿṣūmiyyat al-juththa fī l-fiqh al-islāmī ʿalā ḍawʾ al-qawānīn al-ṭibbiyya l-muʿāṣira*. Amman: Dār al-Thaqāfa.
Asad, Talal. 1986. *The Idea of an Anthropology of Islam*. Washington, DC: Center for Contemporary Arab Studies, Georgetown University.
Atighetchi, Dariusch. 2007: *Islamic Bioethics: Problems and Perspectives*. Dordrecht: Springer.
al-Bārr, ʿAlī, and Zuhayr Aḥmad al-Sibāʿī. 1997. *Al-Ṭabīb adabuhu wa-fiqhuhu*. 2nd ed. Beirut: al-Dār al-Shāmiyya, and Damascus: Dār al-Qalam.
Bosaller, Anke. 2004. *"Schlafende Schwangerschaft" in islamischen Gesellschaften: Entstehung und soziale Implikationen einer weiblichen Fiktion*. Würzburg: Ergon.
Bowen, Donna Lee. 1997. Islam, Abortion and the 1994 Cairo Population Conference. *International Journal of Middle East Studies* 29: 161–84.
Chipman, Leigh. 2002. The Professional Ethics of Medieval Pharmacists in the Islamic World. *Medicine and Law* (Haifa) 21: 321–38.
Clarke, Morgan. 2009. *Islam and New Kinship: Reproductive Technology and the Shariah in Lebanon*. New York: Berghahn Books.
Daar, Abdallah, and Ahmed Al-Khitamy. 2010. Health Care. In *A Companion to Muslim Ethics*, ed. A.B. Sajoo, pp. 119–30. London: I.B. Tauris.
De Vries, Raymond, and Leslie Rott. 2011. Bioethics as Missionary Work: The Export of Western Ethics to Developing Countries. In *Bioethics around the Globe*, ed. C. Myser, pp. 3–18. New York: Oxford University Press.
Eich, Thomas. 2006a. Die Diskussion islamischer Rechtsgelehrter um *pre-marital screening* und die Abtreibung behinderter Embryonen. In *Kulturübergreifende Bioethik: Zwischen globaler Herausforderung und regionaler Perspektive*, ed. T. Eich and T. Hoffmann, pp. 152–78. Freiburg and Munich: Karl Alber.
———. 2006b. The Debate about Cloning among Muslim Religious Scholars since 1997. In *Cross-Cultural Issues in Bioethics: The Example of Human Cloning*, ed. H. Roetz, pp. 291–309. Amsterdam: Rodopi.
———. 2008. Decision-Making Process among Contemporary *ʿUlamaʾ*: Islamic Embryology and the Discussion of Frozen Embryos. In *Muslim Medical Ethics: From Theory to Practice*, ed. J.E. Brockopp and T. Eich, pp. 61–77. Columbia: The University of South Carolina Press.
Fahmy, Khaled. 1999. The Anatomy of Justice: Forensic Medicine and Criminal Law in Nineteenth-Century Egypt. *Islamic Law and Society* 6(2): 224–71.
Fähndrich, Hartmut. 1990. Der Begriff "adab" und sein literarischer Niederschlag. In *Orientalisches Mittelalter*, ed. W. Heinrichs, pp. 326–45. Wiesbaden: AULA.
Fischer, Johan. 2008. *Proper Islamic Consumption: Shopping among the Malays in Modern Indonesia*. Copenhagen: NIAS Press.
Fischer, Nils. 2012. *Islamische Positionen zum pränatalen Leben*. Freiburg and Munich: Karl Alber.
Floor, Willem M. 2004. *Public Health in Qajar Iran*. Washington, DC: Mage.
Haeri, Shahla. 1999. Woman's Body, Nation's Honor: Rape in Pakistan. In *Hermeneutics and Honor: Negotiating Female "Public" Space in Islamic/ate Societies*, ed. A. Afsaruddin, pp. 55–69. Cambridge, MA: CMES, Harvard University.
Hamdy, Sherine F. 2009. Islam, Fatalism, and Medical Intervention: Lessons from Egypt on the Cultivation of Forbearance (*Sabr*) and Reliance on God (*Tawakkul*). *Anthropological Quarterly* 82: 173–96.
———. 2012. *Our Bodies Belong to God: Organ Transplants, Islam, and the Struggle for Human Dignity in Egypt*. Berkeley and Los Angeles: University of California Press.

Ḥasan, ʿAlī Maḥmūd. 2009. *Al-Shifāʾ bi-l-Qurʾān wa-ʿulūm al-anbiyāʾ*. Beirut: Dār Iḥyāʾ al-Turāth al-ʿArabī li-l-Ṭibāʿa wa-l-Nashr wa-l-Tawzīʿ.

Ḥasan, Ḥāmid Aḥmad Muḥammad. 2011. *Aḥkām al-umūma fī l-fiqh al-islāmī*. Alexandria: Maktabat al-Wafāʾ al-Qānūniyya.

Hilālī, Saʿd al-Dīn. 2000. Ijhāḍ janīn al-ightiṣāb fī ḍawʾ al-aḥkām al-islāmiyya. *Majallat al-Sharīʿa wa-l-Dirāsāt al-Islāmiyya* 41: 247–322.

Idrīs, ʿAbd al-Qādir. 2010. *Al-Ithbāt bi-l-qarāʾin fī l-fiqh al-islāmī*. Amman: Dār al-Thaqāfa.

Islamic Fiqh Academy (India). 2009. *Islamic Shariah Guidance on Aids*. Beirut: Dār al-Kutub al-Islāmiyya.

Johansen, Baber. 2002. Signs as Evidence: The Doctrine of Ibn Taymiyya (1263–1328) and Ibn Qayyim al-Jawziyya (d. 1351) on Proof. *Islamic Law and Society* 9(2): 168–93.

Katz, Marion H. 2003. The Problem of Abortion in Classical Sunni *fiqh*. In *Islamic Ethics of Life*, ed. J.E. Brockopp, pp. 25–50. Columbia: University of South Carolina Press.

Kozma, Liat. 2011. *Policing Egyptian Women: Sex, Law, and Medicine in Khedival Egypt*. Syracuse: Syracuse University Press.

Krawietz, Birgit. 1991. *Die Ḥurma: Schariatrechtlicher Schutz vor Eingriffen in die körperliche Unversehrtheit nach arabischen Fatwas des 20. Jahrhunderts*. Berlin: Duncker & Humblot.

———. 2003. Brain Death and Islamic Traditions: Shifting Borders of Life? In *Islamic Ethics of Life*, ed. J.E. Brockopp, pp. 194–213. Columbia: University of South Carolina Press.

Maudoodi, Syed Abul ʿAla. 2001. *Birth Control: Its Social, Political, Economic, Moral and Religious Aspects*, tr. K. Ahmad and M.I. Faruqi. Delhi: Markazi Maktaba Islami Publications.

Moazam, Farhat. 2006. *Bioethics and Organ Transplantation in a Muslim Society: A Study in Culture, Ethnography, and Religion*. Bloomington: Indiana University Press.

Moinifar, Heshmat S., and Amir Ashraf Vaghefi. 2010. Gamete Donation and the Role of Religious Leaders in Iran. *Hawwa* 8: 247–73.

Muḥammad, Ḥusayn Najīb. 2007. *Al-Shifāʾ bi-l-ṣiyām: Muqārana bayn al-ṣawm al-dīnī wa-l-ṣawm al-ṭibbī*. Beirut. Dār al-Hādī.

Padela, Aasim I. et al. 2011. Medical Experts and Islamic Scholars Deliberating over Brain Death: Gaps in the Applied Islamic Bioethics Discourse. *The Muslim World* 101: 53–72.

Perho, Imerli. 1995. *The Prophet's Medicine: A Creation of Muslim Traditionalist Scholars*. Helsinki: Finnish Oriental Society.

Redfield, Robert. 1956. *Peasant Society and Culture: An Anthropological Approach*. Chicago: University of Chicago Press.

Reinert, Benedikt. 1968. *Die Lehre vom* tawakkul *in der klassischen Sufik*. Berlin: De Gruyter.

Rispler-Chaim, Vardit. 2006. *Disability in Islamic Law*. Springer: Dordrecht.

———. 2007. The Muslim Surgeon and Contemporary Ethical Dilemmas Surrounding the Restoration of Virginity. *Hawwa* 5: 324–45.

Sachedina, Abdulaziz. 2004. Islamic Bioethics. In *Religious Perspectives in Bioethics*, ed. J.F. Peppin et al. Pp. 153–71. London: Taylor and Francis.

———. 2009. *Islamic Biomedical Ethics: Principles and Application*. New York: Oxford University Press.

Sālim, Jāsim ʿAlī. 1996. Al-Iṣāba bi-maraḍ faqd al-manāʿa al-muktasab wa-aḥkām al-muʿāmalāt. *Journal of Shariʿa and Islamic Studies* (Kuwait University) 11(28): 165–231.

Savage-Smith, Emilie. 2011. Attitudes toward Dissection in Medieval Islam. In *Islamic Medical and Scientific Tradition*, ed. P.E. Pormann. Vol. 1: 299–342. London: Routledge. Reprint from *Journal of the History of Medicine and Allied Sciences* 50 (1995): 67–110.

Shaham, Ron. 2010. *The Expert Witness in Islamic Courts: Medicine and Crafts in the Service of the Law*. Chicago: Chicago University Press.

———. 2011. Law versus Medical Science: Competition between Legal and Biological Paternity in an Egyptian Civil Court. *Islamic Law and Society* 18: 219–49.

Svensson, Jonas. 2012. Islam, HIV/AIDS and Activism: A Critical Analysis of Some Themes in Positive Muslims' "Theology of Compassion". *Islam and Christian–Muslim Relations* 24: 1–19.

Tober, Diane M. 2007. Kidneys and Controversies in the Islamic Republic of Iran: The Case of Organ Sale. *Body and Society* 13(3): 151–70.

Van den Branden, Stef, and Bert Broeckaert. 2011. The Ongoing Charity of Organ Donation: Contemporary English Sunni Fatwas on Organ Donation and Blood Transfusion. *Bioethics* 25(3): 167–75.

Epilogue: The Normative Relevance of Sharia in the Modern Context

Abdullahi Ahmed An-Na'im

In this chapter I propose to take a comparative legal approach to modern conceptions of constitutionalism and the rule of law, human rights, and pluralism. I have a clear position on this issue, which I have attempted to present and clarify since the early 1980s (An-Na'im 1990, 2008) so I will refrain from tinkering with prevalent views among scholars and opinion makers; for the assumptions, analysis, and findings of standard scholarship in Islamic studies, see Chapter 20, above. In any case I believe we need a paradigm shift in the interpretation of Sharia in the modern context.[1] Why waste an opportunity for fresh thinking by repeating what audiences already know or believe they know? This is not to suggest that I will be inventing new facts to feed my fantasies for social and political transformation in Islamic societies, because that is not helpful for any cause or purpose. Rather, I see my task as to theorize for the actual reality of struggles for individual freedom and social justice throughout the Muslim world. The vast majority of Muslim-majority countries are, in fact, secular states, where there are no demands for the enforcement of Sharia as state law. I prefer not to focus on the re-enactment of an imaginary historical conception of Sharia as law of the state that is being attempted in vain in a few countries (Afghanistan, Iran, Pakistan, Saudi Arabia, and Sudan) and ignore the reality of secular states and their law in some 40 Muslim-majority countries.[2]

In my view, the position of the proponents of Sharia as positive law of the state is untenable because the idea of an Islamic state to enforce Sharia norms as such is conceptually incoherent, historically unprecedented, and practically unworkable today. At the same time, I find the position of the opponents of Sharia unwise, and probably dangerous, because pushing Sharia out of the public domain does not negate its powerful cultural and political role in the lives of Islamic societies. Since it is not possible to force such distinctions on the psyche and internal motivation of the political

Abdullahi Ahmed An-Na'im is Charles Howard Candler Professor of Law, and Director of the Center for International and Comparative Law, at Emory University School of Law in Atlanta, Georgia. A prominent human rights activist and renowned scholar, he is the author of *Muslims and Global Justice* (2011); *Islam and the Secular State* (2008); *African Constitutionalism and the Role of Islam* (2006); and *Toward an Islamic Reformation: Civil Liberties, Human Rights and International Law* (1990). His edited books include *Human Rights under African Constitutions* (2003); *Islamic Family Law in a Changing World: A Global Resource Book* (2002); *Cultural Transformation and Human Rights in Africa* (2002); and *Human Rights in Cross-Cultural Perspectives: Quest for Consensus* (1992).

1 I prefer the term Sharia over Islamic law to avoid confusing the religious normative system of Muslims with the legal system of positive state law. For Sharia vs fiqh, see Chapter 1, above.

2 These comprise more than 50 percent of the world's population. A total of 1.2 billion Muslims live in these countries, representing 74 percent of the global Muslim population of 1.6 billion. In 2010, more than one-fifth of the world's Muslims (23.3 percent) lived in non-Muslim-majority, less-developed countries.

behavior of believers, the so-called private role of Sharia is bound to encroach on what the opponents of Sharia see as the secular public domain. This apparent deadlock can be mediated, I argue, through the internal transformation of the interpretation of Sharia by Muslims, instead of seeking to suppress it through the coercive constraints of the secular law of the state.

A related proposition I wish to emphasize from the outset is that it is misleading to assume that there is an "exemplary Islam" that is represented by what we call the Arab world, by which all other Islamic experiences should be judged. The idea of an exemplary Islam represented by any one community or region is inconsistent with the essence of religious belief and practice, which must necessarily be personal in communal context. The most significant spiritual and intellectual experiences of Muslims throughout history were not confined to any particular region of the world. Demographically speaking, about 88 percent of the total Muslim population of the world today lives outside what is now called the Arab world. The second largest Muslim population in the world today is totally integrated in the social and political life of the secular democratic state of India—indeed, more Muslims live in India than in any other country except Indonesia.[3] The point I wish to emphasize here is that the plausibility of what I am proposing below should not be judged by what is seen in the popular media about the Middle East and North Africa. Even regarding this region, the media are covering events for Western audiences and not from the perspective of the region's Muslim population.

A Note on Modernity

Before I set forth my position and argument about Sharia and modernity, I would like to briefly sketch a working definition of modernity for the purposes of this chapter, without getting into debates about modernity, modernization, and postmodernism. In particular, I wish to avoid being identified with any specific theory or discourse that assumes my consequential commitment to one position or another in those debates.

It is interesting that the first noted use of the term "modern" is attributed to the Christian Church of the fifth century, in contrast to the assumption of some participants in current debates that religion is inherently anti-modern. The contradiction may be resolved, however, by recalling the quality of Christianity that was seen as modern in that early historical context. The term modern was used in the fifth century "to distinguish the Christian era from the pagan age. Arising from this was an association of modernity with the renunciation of the recent past, which was rejected in favour of a new beginning and a reinterpretation of historical origins" (Delanty 2007: 3068). Thus, the notion of modernity was seen as marked by the quality of being able to renounce the past in favor of reinterpreting historical origins, and that quality is exactly what I am advocating in relation to the role of Sharia in the present context today.

I am also renouncing the recent colonial past that asserted a Eurocentric view of what it means to be modern to justify European colonialism.[4] I do not accept notions of modernity as "meaning, most simply, those modes of social life or organization which emerged in Europe from the seventeenth century onwards and which subsequently became more or less world-wide in their influence" (Harris 2000: 325, quoting Giddens 1991: 1). Instead, I accept the idea of multiple modernities, to shift away from "exclusive concern with western modernity to a more cosmopolitan perspective.

3 According to the Pew Research Center report of 2011, Pakistan is expected to surpass both Indonesia and India by 2030, making India the third largest Muslim country.

4 Famously called "The White Man's Burden" by Rudyard Kipling in a poem first published in *McClure's Magazine* 12,4 (February 1899): 290–1 (accessible at http://www.unz.org/Pub/McClures-1899feb-00290?View=PDF). The poem addressed the United States regarding its conquest of the Philippine Islands, and was commonly seen at the time as strong justification of the expansionist policies of the United States. See *International Herald Tribune* (February 4, 1999), "In Our Pages: 100, 75 and 50 Years Ago. 1899: Kipling's Plea."

Modernity is not westernization and its key processes and dynamics can be found in all societies" (Delanty 2007: 3070; see generally, Eisenstadt 2003).

However, what I see as two perspectives on the way modernity is defined are frequently fused into one. For instance, one author defines modernism as "marked by change, ambiguity, doubt, risk, uncertainty and fragmentation," and goes on to define modernity as a "post-traditional, post-medieval historical period marked by the rise of industrialism, capitalism, the nation-state and forms of surveillance [i.e., control of information and social supervision]" (Barker 2003: 443–4). While I find aspects to do with "change, ambiguity, doubt, risk, uncertainty and fragmentation" useful, I find the rest of this definition too narrow and exclusive. A modernity that is identified as post-traditional does not tell us what is wrong with the traditional, in which context or regarding which issues; and to say that modernity is post-medieval is meaningless for the rest of humanity that did not experience European medievalism, failing to take account of the actual histories of non-European societies. This notion of modernity has no criteria for evaluating the human costs of industrialism, capitalism, and surveillance, no standard for judging the quality of the state. To assume that the territorial state as such is a hallmark of modernity fails to distinguish a totalitarian fascist state from a constitutional democratic state.[5]

Such contextually and historically conditioned definitions of modernity can only lead to endless debates about the concept in the limited context or political history of some societies, without accounting for the same features in other societies (Toulmin 1990). I am not suggesting that factors such as scale and complexity of economic activities and political institutions like the territorial state are irrelevant to modernity. Rather, I am suspicious of narrowly defining such factors to fit European and North American societies to the exclusion of the rest of the world, because that sort of exclusive modernity was used to justify colonialism and continues to underlie neo-colonial relations of domination and exploitation.

From my perspective, therefore, I have no use for a concept that has no place for me and my community on our own terms, instead of by analogy to other persons and communities taken as the norm by which the experience and consciousness of humanity everywhere is evaluated. At the same time I am not rejecting European experiences with modernity simply because they are European, and do find some of them relevant to my experiences as an African Muslim. For instance, I find the sense of modernity as "the transitory, the fugitive, the contingent" (Baudelaire 1964: 13) appropriate for my sense of being a Muslim.

In light of these remarks on my working definition of modernity, I will now turn to the subject of this chapter. I will begin this by briefly clarifying the premise and objectives of my argument in the first section, and then attempt in the second section to clarify the formulation and establishment of Sharia norms and institutions through human interpretation and experience in historical context. In the third section I will try to briefly explain why Sharia norms cannot be enacted as state law and retain their religious quality.

The Illusion of an Islamic State

The discourse initiated by Islamist ideologues since the 1940s, such as Abul Ala Mawdudi in the Indian subcontinent and Sayyid Quṭb in Egypt, is based on the premise that the foundational Islamic religious texts are interpreted within that tradition in order to be enacted and enforced by the postcolonial territorial state. The idea is that now that we are politically independent from European colonial rule, we should "return" to the pristine Islam of the precolonial era where "Islamic states" enforced

5 I prefer "territorial" state over "nation" state because territorial sovereignty and jurisdiction are more universally accurate features of all modern states, while the notion of nation is a myth or fiction that is often manipulated to exclude or oppress some segments of the population.

Sharia norms as the law of the land. The revivalist puritanical dimension of this discourse—the idea of returning to pure and totalistic Islam—is not new in the Islamic tradition (Voll 1982). What is conceptually false and historically unprecedented in Islamic history, as I have argued elsewhere (An-Na'im 2008), is the notion that a centralized, hierarchical, bureaucratic European model of a territorial state can and should now coercively enforce Sharia as positive law of the state. Sharia has had a strong influence at the level of community-based compliance or implementation (Hallaq 2004), but that was never through systematic and coercive centralized administration of justice by the state.

Paradoxically, by the 1980s the fallacy of the Islamist claim seems to have dominated public discourse in a few countries, such as Iran, Pakistan, Sudan, and Yemen by default. In other words, Islamists seem to be gaining the upper hand in public discourse due to the failure of other perspectives to assert their counterpoint of view or to challenge the Islamist discourse on its own terms. The problem is that once a Muslim concedes the plausibility of the Islamists' model, he or she will be locked into a normative straightjacket from which there is no way to affirm freedom of religion, equality for women, and non-Muslims within that framework (An-Na'im 1990).

To advance an alternative discourse about the role of Islam and Sharia in the Muslim world today, let me begin with a few clarifications. First, the generality of Muslims believe the Quran to be the direct and immediate speech of God to all humanity, and most Muslims take the Sunna of the Prophet Muḥammad to be divinely inspired, if not revelation in a different form. Since discussion, interpretation, and implementation of a religious text is always a human endeavor, the outcome cannot be immutable or divine. This includes the methodology of interpretation, and the authority of those engaged in the process. We are dealing with actions undertaken by fallible human beings which can therefore be challenged and changed by other human beings (Ibn Rushd 2001: 8–10). As a Muslim, I accept these general propositions and related concepts and practices; I do not see any possibility of human understanding or practice of the Quran and Sunna except through the human agency of believers.

Moreover, the exclusively human nature of this process means that there is no possibility of independent, impartial "adjudication" of which method of interpretation is valid or more authoritative than other methods, or which view should prevail over other views. In the final analysis, every believer is personally responsible for her or his own choices and action, and cannot abdicate responsibility by deferring to another human being. This is the honor and advantage God has bestowed on every human being, and not only believers in any particular religion or a class or segment of those believers. Quran 17:70 can be translated as follows: "We have honored the children of Adam [all human beings], and conveyed them by land and sea, and granted them good living, and preferred them over many of our creation."[6]

Despite the apparent plausibility of these propositions, we find that the interpretation of Sharia by Muslim scholars of the eighth and ninth centuries CE have come to be assumed by the generality of Muslims up to the present time to be immutable, which precludes possibilities of significant reinterpretation. I believe it necessary to challenge this assumption, as well as the more recent call by Islamists to establish Islamic states that will enforce Sharia as positive state law, in order to overcome common inhibitions of creative discourse about the role of Islam and Sharia today. To this end, I am arguing against the fallacy of a so-called "Islamic state" that can enforce Sharia as the positive law of the state. As the product of human interpretation of the Quran and Sunna, Sharia norms are not immutable and remain subject to differing interpretations in various contexts.

This view does not question the religiously binding authority of Sharia norms on Muslims as believers everywhere, but that authority works only according to their personal acceptance of what they believe to be Sharia norms. There is simply no way to impose religious authority on believers against their will. This is true not only with regard to differences between Sunni and Shi'i Muslims, but also among and within

6 Since every translation of the Quran in fact an interpretation, I prefer to offer my own translation and readers can verify how reasonable it is.

each side of this historical broad sectarian divide. If a believer is coerced into compliance with what he or she does not accept as a valid interpretation of Sharia, the outcome will not be religious.

For example, one and the same conduct, such as stealing, may be a sin and a crime, but the source, authority, and process by which the characterization is established are fundamentally different. A crime is not a crime because it is a sin and a sin is not a sin because it is a crime. Sharia norms and state law are two fundamentally different normative systems, Sharia being religious and state law being political, regardless of which one is more influential in shaping human behavior.

To avoid confusion due to the use of the term "law" in different meanings, we should speak of the normativity of Sharia and the legality of state law. A parliament, for instance, is the source of legally binding authority of a statute of state law, but it cannot be the source of authority of a Sharia norm. Conversely, the Quran and Sunna as interpreted through the established methodology of the Islamic tradition are the source of the authority of a Sharia norm, but they cannot be the source of a statute of state law. This difference in the source of authority means that all state law is secular because it is dependent on the political authority of the state, even when it claims to "enforce" a Sharia norm.

If that is true, then there is no religious obligation on Muslims to enforce Sharia norms as the positive law of the state. That realization, I believe, will be profoundly liberating for Muslims everywhere, enabling them to see that any effort to enforce a Sharia norm through state law is political and not religious. If there is a religious obligation in this field at all, it is to reject any effort to manipulate the religious piety of Muslims in the service of a political end. The political project of so-called Islamists, as explained below, should be evaluated as a good or a bad political program, and not as a religious mandate. I believe this approach is the best response to Islamist politics because it exposes and explains its true political nature.

To conclude this section, the clarification I am seeking to advance is consistent with the historical nature of Sharia and how it evolved through human methodology and consensus. At the same time, I am arguing for a revision of the traditional methodology through modern consensus among present and future generations of Muslims. For this methodological shift to be taken seriously, I believe that I need to challenge what I see as a false assumption about the relationship between normative and legal systems, and challenge the immutability of Sharia.

Regarding the methodology question, Sharia norms have always been established through what I call inter-generational consensus among communities of Muslims, rather than through formal enactment by the state. This means that Sharia norms cannot be immutable for all Muslims, let alone non-Muslims, because they are the product of human interpretation and consensus. A norm is religiously binding only on Muslims who accept the particular interpretation of relevant provisions of the Quran and Sunna. This quality of Sharia defies legal enforcement by the state because Muslims disagree about what they accept as Sharia norms to be and to mean. I will now turn to a brief explanation of these remarks.

The Nature and Development of Sharia

The term Sharia is often used in present discourse as if it were synonymous with Islam itself, as the totality of Muslim obligations in both the private, personal religious sense and vis-à-vis social, political, and legal norms and institutions. However, it is important to distinguish between the *concept* of Sharia, as the totality of the duty of Muslims, and any particular interpretation of the *content* of Sharia through a specific human methodology of interpretation of the Quran and Sunna in a particular *context*.

But even as a concept, Sharia is only the door and passageway into being Muslim, and does not exhaust the possibilities of experiencing Islam. There is more to Islam than Sharia, though knowing and complying with the dictates of Sharia is the way to realize Islam in the daily lives of Muslims. Since religious compliance is necessarily a personal matter for individual believers, it bears repeating that it does not include coercive enforcement of religious principles as state law. It is, of course, legitimate for Muslims to strive for their religious values to be reflected in state policies and legislation, but that is a matter of politics and should be sought through civic reason and the democratic process (An-Na'im 2008: 7–8), and not as a matter of religious imperative.

For the following historical narrative, I present only the briefest of background information. I refer the reader to Chapters 2 through 8, above, for a detailed exposition.

The primary sources of Sharia are the Quran and Sunna, as understood in the context of early Muslim communities throughout the region known now as the Middle East. Other sources in common discourse are said to include consensus (*ijmā'*) and reasoning by analogy (*qiyās*), but these are methodological tools rather than substantive sources as such. Independent juridical reasoning (*ijtihād*) was more accepted as a method in the early development of Sharia norms and institutions than in subsequent stages when the main concepts and norms were already established. It was apparently assumed that *ijtihād* should be exercised when the Quran and Sunna were silent and there was no pre-existing consensus or rule that might apply through reasoning by analogy. As Sharia norms and institutions developed and became better established, the perceived need for *ijtihād* was believed to have declined.

While it may be true that there were some juridical adaptations that may be described as *ijtihād* (Hallaq 1984), it is certainly true that no interpretation of Sharia sources was accepted beyond the boundaries established by traditional jurisprudence, *uṣūl al-fiqh*, since the ninth century. It is therefore necessary to challenge the presumed immutability of *uṣūl al-fiqh* itself in order to open up possibilities of a fresh reinterpretation of the Quran and Sunna.

As some general principles began to emerge through the growing influence of the leading scholars in the eighth and ninth centuries, prototype schools of Islamic jurisprudence (sg. *madhhab*) began to emerge among early generations of Muslims in Medina, southern Iraq, and Syria. The systemic development of Sharia law began during the eighth and ninth centuries with the emergence of the major schools of Islamic jurisprudence, the gathering and verification of what came to be accepted as authoritative records of the Prophetic custom, and the development of the juridical methodology of Sharia. The formulation of *uṣūl al-fiqh* and the gathering and verification of Sunna sources used by the scholars continued into the tenth century.

The principle of consensus apparently acted as a unifying force during the ninth century in drawing the methodologies and substantive content of Sunni schools together by drastically diminishing the role of creative juridical thinking since the tenth century. Whatever the degree of reform and practical adaptation achieved over time in different parts of the Muslim world, they were always done within the framework of the methodology and parameters of *uṣūl al-fiqh* as established by the tenth century. While that historical rigidity may have played a stabilizing role in times of great political turmoil and external invasion, there is nothing to prevent the revival and active exercise of creative juridical thinking in the modern era. In fact, many Muslim scholars and community leaders have called for this for at least two centuries now, but few have actually attempted to do so in order to develop coherent methodologies of reform, or to produce concrete reform proposal. While critically important, this aspect of the issues is not the subject of this chapter.

What came to be known among Muslims as Sharia was therefore the product of a very slow, gradual, and spontaneous process of interpretation of the Quran, and collection, verification, and interpretation of Sunna during the first three centuries of Islam. That process took place among scholars who developed their own methodology for the classification of sources, derivation of specific rules from general principles, and so forth. For our purposes here, it is enough to confirm that the framework and main principles of Sharia were developed as an ideal normative system by scholars who were clearly independent of the state and its institutions. The fact that the founding jurists were not employed by the state or subject to its control, which is beyond dispute, may partly explain their drive to elaborate the normative system of Islam as they believed it ought to be, regardless of pragmatic factors that may diminish its practical application.

The religious nature of Sharia means that there is no person or institution authorized to decide for all believers what the Sharia rule is on any subject, as each believer is responsible for his or her own belief in the matter. This has always been the case for Sunni Muslims, who make up about 90 percent of the total Muslim population of the world today—hence the diversity of opinions among, and within, the Sunni schools of Islamic jurisprudence. For Shiʿi Muslims,[7] the Imam may declare or change established principles of Sharia, but that has not been a practical possibility for Twelvers, the majority of Shiʿis today, since their last Imam Ḥasan al-ʿAskarī disappeared (went into occultation) in Samarra, Iraq, in 874, and will reappear as the Messiah. Although present-day Twelvers uphold a hierarchy of religious leaders, there are significant disagreements on the ranking and personal following of those leaders (Esposito 2004a, 3: 41–2; 2004b: 192).

With no central authority, how did any principle of Sharia get established in the first place? That happened through what I call inter-generational consensus among the members of each community or group of Muslims who accepted a principle of Sharia as binding from a religious point of view. In other words, every principle accepted today as part of Sharia among any group of Muslims has achieved that status only by virtue of the fact that succeeding generations of Muslims have personally accepted it as valid and binding. It is logically impossible for Muslims to have a legislative authority that can enact a single principle of Sharia. Even if the total Muslim population of the world were to meet in a single time and place and agree to adopt a principle as part of Sharia, that principle would not necessarily continue to be binding, either on those who agreed on it, because they are entitled to change their minds, or on subsequent generations, because they did not accept it for themselves.

In regard to reaching consensus among scholars who are accepted as authoritative, Ibn Rushd (2001: 8–10) explained that the conditions for the validity of a claim of consensus are so difficult to establish that the claim cannot be more than suppositional (*ẓannī*), that is, never a certainty. It is equally suppositional, if not completely unrealistic, to expect any group of Muslims of any place, however small, to agree on a principle of Sharia that can be enacted as state law. Like any community, Muslims are unlikely to agree on what to enact as Sharia. But in the event this highly unlikely scenario arises, it should still remain possible from a religious point of view for a Muslim to change his or her mind about what has been agreed. This slow and mysterious, contingent and contestable manner of "Sharia formation" is a good safeguard against the imposition of any one view of Sharia on a believer without her voluntary acceptance.

The nature of the process also means that it is difficult to accelerate it or influence its outcome in a particular direction. By the nature and history of the process, all one can do is to abide by what one believes to be Sharia and wait to see whether over time consensus emerges among Muslims in favor of one proposition or another. The issue cannot be resolved by the democratic principle of majority rule for that has no validity in matters of religion, in which a single person can be right and the rest of humanity can be wrong. Otherwise, all prophets would have been "overruled" by the majority of their communities, thereby ending their mission. Majority rule can decide matters of secular legislation, but never matters of religious principles.

This reality is liberating, on the one hand, because it means that no human being can legitimately impose a religious position on another human being. Of course, people can be coerced to conform outwardly, but they can never be compelled to accept any view within their inner moral conscience. On the other hand, however, this nature of the process of Sharia formation means that one cannot ensure that desirable change will happen, at least within a specific period of time. For example, I believe it is necessary and theoretically possible within Islam to achieve complete equality for women and non-Muslims, to secure freedom of religion, and to abolish aggressive jihad from a Sharia point

7 There are several different Shiʿi sects distinguished by the exact historical line of Imams (supreme religious leader) each of them accepts as legitimate, though they all share certain general principles and practices. The most influential sects today are the Twelvers, Zaydis, and the Ismaʿilis (Seveners). See also Chapter 7, above.

of view (Ṭāhā 1987: 139–45; An-Na'im 1990: 52–60). Yet it is difficult to see how and when this theoretical possibility might be confirmed as established reality among the Muslims of a particular place or of the world at large.

At the same time, however, any Muslim can decide that what I am calling for is in her or his view the correct view of Sharia on the subject, and act accordingly. Thus, each and every Muslim is, in fact, bound to determine what Sharia is on any issue and to act accordingly, in the knowledge that she or he is accountable before God. For that to happen, however, Muslims must have the freedom to freely think, study, debate with others, and decide for themselves, in order to act according to the best of their judgment, without fear of suppression or other retaliation by the state. In other words, the state must remain neutral in all matters of religion for believers to follow their own convictions and accept religious responsibility for their actions and omissions.

While our appreciation of the ways in which Sharia worked in practice at different stages of its history continues to grow (al-Azmeh 1988: 250–61; Hallaq 1997), it is clear that the core content of the system still reflects the social, political, and economic conditions of the eighth to tenth centuries, thereby placing it increasingly out of touch with subsequent developments and realities of society and state, especially in the modern context. This conceptual and methodological deficit has been mitigated in the precolonial context by the ability of judges and legal practitioners to maintain nominal allegiance to the classical theory of Sharia with minimal observance of it in their daily practice. But such expedient strategies have increasingly become untenable, especially in the present globally interdependent context of Islamic societies. The requirements of sustainable economic development, international investment, and trade with other countries, as well as political stability and democratic governance at home, demand much greater predictability and consistency of legal norms and practice throughout predetermined territorial jurisdictions.

The essentially religious nature of Sharia, which focuses on regulating the relationship between God and humankind, was probably one of the main reasons for the persistence and growth of parallel rulers' courts to adjudicate a wide range of practical matters in the administration of justice and government in general. The distinction between the jurisdiction of the various state and Sharia courts under different imperial states came very close to the philosophy of a division between secular and religious courts (Coulson 1964: 122). The early acceptance of a "division of labor" between different kinds of courts has probably contributed to the eventual confinement of Sharia jurisdiction to family law matters in the modern era.

Another aspect of the legal history of Islamic societies that is associated with the religious nature of Sharia is the development of private legal consultation, or fatwa-issuing (*iftā'*). Scholars who were independent of the state issued legal opinions, fatwas, at the request of provincial governors and state judges, in addition to providing advice for individual persons, from the very beginning of Islam (see Chapter 6, above). This type of private advice persisted through subsequent stages of Islamic history, and became institutionalized during the period of the Ottoman empire, but there is a significant difference between this sort of moral and social influence of independent scholars and the enforcement of Sharia by the state as such.

As explained by Bernard Weiss, "Shari'a law is the product of legislation (*shar'*), of which God is the ultimate subject (*shāri'*). Fiqh law consists of legal understanding, of which the human being is the subject (*faqīh*)" (Weiss 1998: 120). But this distinction does not mean that those principles that are taken to be Sharia rather than fiqh are the direct product of revelation, because the Quran and Sunna can neither be understood nor have any influence on human behavior except through the comprehension and action of fallible human beings. Again, as Weiss observes, "[a]lthough the law is of divine provenance, the actual construction of the law is a human activity; and its results represent the law of God *as humanly understood.* Since the law does not descend from heaven ready-made, it is the human understanding of the law—the human fiqh—that must be normative for society" (1998: 116, emphasis in original).

As noted earlier, the founding jurists and scholars of Sharia accepted diversity of interpretations and resisted imposing their views, which could be wrong, while seeking to enhance consensus among themselves and their communities. That position may have in fact provided valuable flexibility in local legal practices under highly decentralized imperial states. For present-day legal systems, however, the obvious question is how and by whom can reasonable and legitimate difference of opinion among premodern schools and scholars be settled in order to determine what is the law to be applied by state courts and other authorities? The basic dilemma is that, on the one hand, there is the paramount importance of a minimum degree of certainty in the determination and enforcement of positive law for any society, and the nature and role of positive law in the modern state require the interaction of a multitude of actors and complex factors that cannot possibly be contained by an Islamic religious rationale. On the other hand, a religious rationale is imperative for the binding force of Sharia for Muslims.

Thus, given the diversity of opinion among Muslim jurists, whatever the state elects to enforce as positive law would be the personal preference of ruling elites, which might well be contrary to the view of some Muslims in the country. We can see this in Saudi Arabia, for instance, where Wahhabi views of Sharia are imposed on Shiʿi citizens, in addition to likely disagreement among the Sunni population as well. The imperative of certainty and uniformity in national legislation requires the enactment of one view over others, but the outcome can only be the political will of the state and not the religious belief of Muslims. The Sharia view that Muslims can accept as a matter of religious belief and practice can only be outside the framework of state law and policy, where there is freedom of religious choice. I will now close with highlighting this dialectic of the normative relevance of Sharia within communities of believers, and its irrelevance to the legal system and institutions of the modern state.

The Normativity of Sharia in the Secular State

The framework I am proposing for the religious normative role of Sharia—a modern secular one, whether Muslims are the predominant majority or not—is premised on the need to ensure the institutional separation of Islam and the state, despite the organic and unavoidable connection between Islam and politics. The challenge is to maintain the neutrality of the state regarding all Islamic doctrine, although religion will continue to influence the political behavior of Muslims. The first part of this proposition sounds like "secularism" as commonly understood today, but the second part indicates the opposite. The relationship between Islam, state, and society is always the product of a constant and deeply contextual negotiation rather than the subject of a fixed formula of either total separation or complete fusion of religion and the state.

The paradox of separation of Islam and the (religiously neutral) state and the connection of Islam and politics can be mediated through practice over time rather than completely resolved by theoretical analysis or stipulation. The challenge is therefore how to create the most conducive conditions for this mediation to continue in a constructive fashion, instead of hoping to resolve it once and for all. The two poles of this mediation can be clarified as follows. First, the modern territorial state should neither seek to enforce Sharia as positive law or public policy nor claim to interpret its doctrine and general principles for Muslim citizens. Second, Sharia principles can and should be a source of public policy and legislation, subject to the constitutional and human rights of all citizens—men and women, Muslims and non-Muslims—equally and without discrimination. In other words, Sharia principles are neither privileged or enforced as such nor necessarily rejected as a source of state law and policy simply because they are derived from Sharia.

I am proposing that the rationale of all public policy and legislation always be based on what might be called "civic reason," whereby Muslims and others should be able to propose policy and legislative initiatives emanating from their (religious) beliefs, provided they can support what they are proposing in a public, free, and open debate with reasons that are accessible and convincing to the generality of citizens. But since such decisions will in practice be made by majority vote in accordance with democratic principles, all state action must also conform to basic constitutional and human rights safeguards against the tyranny of the majority.

Allowing Sharia principles to play a positive role in public life without permitting them to be implemented as such through law and policy is a delicate balance that each society must strive to maintain for itself over time. For example, such matters as dress style and religious education will normally remain in the realm of free choice, but can also be the subject of public debate, even constitutional litigation, to balance competing claims. This process can happen, for instance, regarding dress requirements for safety in the work place or the need for comparative and critical religious education in state schools to enhance religious tolerance and secularism. I am not suggesting that the context and conditions of free choice of dress or religious education will not be controversial. In fact, such matters are likely to be very complex at a personal and societal level. Rather, my concern is with ensuring, as far as humanly possible, fair, open, and inclusive social, political, and legal conditions for the negotiation of public policy in such matters. Those conditions, for instance, are to be secured through the entrenchment of such fundamental rights of the persons and communities as the right to education and freedom of religion and expression, on the one hand, and due consideration for legitimate public interests or concerns, on the other. There is no simple or categorical formula to be prescribed for automatic application in every case, although general principles and broader frameworks for the mediation of such issues will emerge and continue to evolve within each society.

To reiterate, my call for recognizing and regulating the political role of Islam is untenable without significant Islamic reform. I believe that it is critically important for Islamic societies today to invest in the rule of law and protection of human rights in their domestic politics and international relations. This investment is unlikely to happen if historical interpretations of Sharia that support such principles as male authority over women (*qiwāma*), legal superiority of Muslims over non-Muslims (*dhimma*), and aggressive jihad are not reformed. Significant reform of such views is necessary because of their powerful influence on social relations and political behavior of Muslims, even when Sharia principles are not directly enforced by the state.[8]

Recalling the core issue of how to mediate competing claims, I highlight below some specific modalities of mediation available to Muslims in democratic pluralistic states. That is, how can the competing claims of normative systems and the legal system of the state be mediated at different levels of social and political life, without undermining the peace and stability of society and the state, or violating social justice for all segments of the population? In my view, there are three main elements to this framework:

1. Private social practice of Sharia within the framework of state law and subject to its constitutional safeguards;
2. Consideration of Sharia as jurisprudential resource for state law through scholarly and judicial legal analysis or civic reason in the democratic political process, without claiming that Sharia as such can be state law;
3. Religious discourse and cultural transformation to mediate tensions between historical interpretations of Sharia and modern constitutional and human rights principles.

As to the first, Muslims can in fact behave in conformity with the vast majority of Sharia principles without coming into conflict with state law in a democratic society. For example, Muslims can refrain from taking or charging interest (ribā), which is prohibited by Sharia, and can establish financial institutions that enable them to do so, within the framework of existing state law that permits charging interest. Muslims can also observe Sharia requirements about marriage and divorce voluntarily—within the parameters allowed by the applicable law—without having those requirements imposed by state law. However, private voluntary compliance should not affect the rights of others. For instance, the exclusive preference that traditional views of Sharia grant fathers in matters of custody of children

8 For the approach I find most promising in achieving the necessary degree of reform, see An-Na'im 1990.

is subject to the principle of state law that all determinations affecting children must be made in the "best interest of the child."[9]

The premise of the second element is that the law and administration of justice of any state should reflect the ethical values, priorities, and interests of the majority, subject to the constitutional/human rights of the minority or minorities, however small, including members of the Muslim majority who disagree with other Muslims. Muslims (and other religious or cultural communities) have the right to organize to act collectively in contributing to the formulation and implementation of public policy and legislation through civic reason and the political process, provided they do not claim to have a monopoly or veto power over such matters, even when acting in the name of the predominant majority of the population.

For instance, judges and legal scholars can incorporate some of the jurisprudential thinking of early Muslim scholars in the definition of property, principles of contracts, or the finer points of specific types of contracts. The key point here is that such resources are examined, incorporated, or left untouched as human legal theory and jurisprudence, not as the binding word of God. This qualification is necessary because other citizens may not accept or care for our God, or our interpretation of God's word. Even those who do accept have no way of knowing whether their understanding of it is valid, and they might want to change their mind in the future but cannot if that would be violating what they already affirmed as the word of God.

So, Sharia jurisprudence should be considered just as one might consider Roman law, English common law, or German legal theory. Once approached in this way, we will find truly superb legal theory, definitions and distinctions, varieties of legal wrongs and their remedies (Hallaq 2009: 239–70, 296–306), which can be instructive in the interpretation and application of the secular law of the state, without affecting its secular nature. This jurisprudential approach is also recommended by its appeal to popular consciousness of state law and its legitimacy. After all, Sharia jurisprudence is the source of common understanding and resonance of the same terms and concepts used in modern legislation and judicial practice.

The possibility of consideration of Sharia jurisprudence through civic reason and democratic process enables Muslims to lobby for legislation consistent with their religious beliefs without asserting that belief as the rationale of state law enforcement. A plausible example of this is that Muslims can lobby for a legal ban on charging interest by trying to persuade other citizens of the economic or social benefits of such a ban through reason and reasoning that all citizens can debate freely, rather than asserting their own religious conviction or cultural affiliation as categorical justification. Another example is that Muslims can also propose legislation based on Sharia principles of child custody, family maintenance, or testate and intestate succession (inheritance), through the same process and subject to constitutional or human rights of all citizens. This possibility does not mean that Sharia as such can co-exist as a parallel legal system competing with state law of any country, or that it retains its religious authority when incorporated into state law. In view of the centralized, bureaucratic, and coercive nature of the modern territorial state, the secular legislative organs of the state must have exclusive monopoly on enacting state law, and secular judicial administrative organs must also have exclusive authority to interpret and apply state law.

The third and critically important element noted above is that of open and free discourse on the interpretation of Sharia in the modern context. Since all principles accepted by Muslims as Sharia norms today were the product of human interpretation of the Quran and Sunna, any of those principles can be modified through reinterpretation of the same sources. If accepted by present-day Muslims as reasonable or valid, the outcome would be as legitimate from an Islamic point of view as any earlier

9 Article 3.1 of the Convention on the Rights of the Child of 1989 provides: "In all actions concerning children, whether undertaken by public or private social welfare institutions, courts of law, administrative authorities or legislative bodies, the best interests of the child shall be a primary consideration." This principle is therefore legally binding on all states that ratified this Convention, which means every country in the world except Somalia and the United States of America.

interpretation of the Quran and Sunna. Such popular consensus was the only manner in which any principle of Sharia was established in the past, or remains valid today. There is no possibility of a human institution that can "declare or amend Islamic doctrine" on behalf of the general Muslim population of the world (An-Na'im 2008).

It must be emphasized that none of these approaches would permit Muslims to opt out of the application of secular state law, or have Sharia principles enacted as state law, except through the regular democratic process and subject to constitutional safeguards. Neither would Muslims be entitled to plead Sharia as justification of violation of state law. Rather, the object is to enable Muslims to exercise their right to religious/cultural self-determination within the framework of state law and its constitutional safeguards, like any other religious/cultural community. The same or equivalent approaches are equally available to other religious/cultural communities to exercise their right to self-determination within the same framework and subject to the same safeguards.

In conclusion, the core idea presented in this chapter is that coercion negates the quality of piety in religious practice which must be voluntary and deliberate. In other words, the integrity and validity of religious experience itself requires the religious neutrality of the state, which is my definition of a secular state. By showing that enforcement of Sharia norms as state law is counterproductive for the religious purpose and rationale of those norms, I hope to dispel the myth that Islam mandates or requires the establishment of a so-called Islamic state. I am therefore proposing to keep the practice of Sharia norms as such in the realm of voluntary and deliberate behavior outside state institutions. At the same time, I believe that Sharia norms can influence secular state law through the democratic political process and public discourse and subject to constitutional safeguards for equal citizenship for all, men and women, Muslims and non-Muslims. I must emphasize that the outcome of the influence of Sharia is always secular law and not the enforcement of Sharia as such. No religious outcome can result from enactment or enforcement by the state.

My proposal is already the reality of the vast majority of Muslim societies around the world. The paradigm Sharia as legally binding is presumed to exist today in Iran and Saudi Arabia, and to extend in two or three more countries such as Pakistan and Sudan. As of today, this paradigm is not applied in more than 35 out of 40 Muslim-majority countries in the world. I am therefore theorizing the reality of the normativity of Sharia as it is generally practiced today, and rejecting the pretence that Sharia principles are ever legally binding as state law.

References

An-Na'im, Abdullahi Ahmed. 1990. *Toward an Islamic Reformation: Civil Liberties, Human Rights, and International Law*. Syracuse: Syracuse University Press.

———. 2008. Islam and the Secular State: Negotiating the Future of Shari'a. Cambridge, MA: Harvard University Press.

al-Azmeh, Aziz. 1988. Islamic Legal Theory and the Appropriation of Reality. In idem, ed., *Islamic Law: Social and Historical Contexts*. London: Routledge.

Barker, Chris. 2003. *Cultural Studies: Theory and Practice*. London: Sage Publications.

Baudelaire, Charles. 1964. *The Painter of Modern Life and Other Essays*, tr. and ed. J. Mayne. London: Phaidon Press.

Coulson, Noel. 1964. *A History of Islamic Law*. Edinburgh: Edinburgh University Press.

Delanty, Gerard. 2007. Modernity. In *The Blackwell Encyclopedia of Sociology*, ed. G. Ritzer. Malden, MA: Blackwell.

Eisenstadt, S.N. 2003. *Comparative Civilizations and Multiple Modernities*. 2 vols. Leiden: Brill.

Esposito, John L., ed. 2004a. *The Islamic World: Past and Present*. 3 vols. New York: Oxford University Press.

———, ed. 2004b. *The Oxford Dictionary of Islam*. 2nd ed. New York: Oxford University Press.
Giddens, Anthony. 1991. *The Consequences of Modernity*. Cambridge: Polity Press.
Hallaq, Wael B. 1984. Was the Gate of Ijtihad Closed? *International Journal of Middle Eastern Studies* 16: 3-41.
———. 1997. *A History of Islamic Legal Theories: An Introduction to Sunnī* uṣūl al-fiqh. Cambridge: Cambridge University Press.
———. 2004. Can the Shari'a Be Restored? In *Islamic Law and the Challenges of Modernity*, ed. Y.Y. Haddad and B.F. Stowasser, pp. 21-53. Walnut Creek, CA.: AltaMira Press.
———. 2009. *Shari'a: Theory, Practice, Transformations*. Cambridge: Cambridge University Press.
Harris, John. 2000. The Second 'Great Transformation'? Capitalism at the End of the Twentieth Century. In *Poverty and Development into the 21st Century*, ed. T. Allen and A. Thomas, pp. 325–42. Oxford: Open University with Oxford University Press.
Ibn Rushd, Abū l-Walīd Muḥammad. 2001. *Faṣl al-maqāl fī mā bayna l-sharī'a wa-l-ḥikma min al-ittiṣāl* (The Decisive Treatise Determining the Connection between the Law and Wisdom), tr. C.E. Butterworth. Provo, UT: Brigham Young University Press.
Masud, M. Khalid, Brinkley Messick, and David S. Powers. 1996. Muftis, Fatwas, and Islamic Legal Interpretation. In *Islamic Legal Interpretation: Muftis and Their Fatwas*, ed. M.K. Masud et al., pp. 3–32. Cambridge, MA: Harvard University Press.
Newby, Gordon D. 2002. *A Concise Encyclopedia of Islam*. Oxford: Oneworld.
Pew Research Center. 2011. The Future of the Global Muslim Population: Projections from 2010 to 2030. Accessible at http://www.pewforum.org/Global-Muslim-Population.aspx.
Ṭāhā, Maḥmūd Muḥammad. 1987. *The Second Message of Islam*, tr. A.A. An-Na'im. Syracuse: Syracuse University Press.
Toulmin, Stephen. 1990. *Cosmopolis: The Hidden Agenda of Modernity*. New York: The Free Press.
Voll, John Obert. 1982. *Islam, Continuity and Change in the Modern World*. Boulder: Westview Press.
Weiss, Bernard G. 1998. *The Spirit of Islamic Law*. Athens, GA: University of Georgia Press.

Glossary

adab al-muftī	a genre of literature on the comportment and culture of the mufti
adab al-qāḍī	a genre of literature concerned with the culture or "etiquette" of the judgeship
ahl al-ḥadīth	lit. the people of the hadith; traditionalist scholars who denounced personal opinion in the formation of the law
ahl al-raʾy	lit. the people of personal opinion; religio-legal scholars who allowed personal opinion to shape their legal doctrine alongside the Quran and hadith
ʿamal	judicial practice, accepted as a legal source in the Maliki school of law
aṣḥāb	(Ar., sg. *ṣāḥib*) companions (of the Prophet Muḥammad); proponents
dār al-Islām	lit. the abode of Islam; territory governed by Muslims and by Sharia law
dhimma	protection granted to a non-Muslim (dhimmi) living under Islamic rule
dhimmi	(Ar. *dhimmī*) a non-Muslim resident on Islamic territory, granted protection, *dhimma*
diya	blood money, financial compensation paid to the heirs of a murder victim
faqīh	(Ar., pl. *fuqahāʾ*) jurist
fatwa	(Ar. *fatwā*) non-binding legal opinion of a learned scholar (mufti)
fiqh	(Islamic) jurisprudence
furūʿ al-fiqh	lit. the branches of jurisprudence; the substantive law, as opposed to *uṣūl al-fiqh*, legal theory
ḥadd	see *ḥudūd*, below
hadith	(Ar. *ḥadīth*; pl. *aḥādīth*) (Prophetic) tradition; the sayings and actions of the Prophet Muḥammad passed down as canonical wisdom; syn. *khabar* (pl. *akhbār*)
hijra	emigration; specifically, the emigration of the Prophet and the early Muslims from Mecca to Medina in 622
ḥudūd	(sg. *ḥadd*) fixed Quranic punishments for a specific crime
ḥukm	rule, ruling, or (depending on context) judicial decision

ʿibādāt	the acts of worship, ritual matters; one of two divisions in Islamic law, the other being civil obligations, *muʿāmalāt*
ijmāʿ	consensus, one of the non-textual sources of Islamic rulings
ijtihād	the personal legal reasoning of the jurist
ikhtilāf	difference, controversy
ʿilla	ratio legis, the reason behind a legal rule
isnād	the chain of transmitters of a hadith
istiḥsān	lit. deeming something good; a legal method to determine the law if there is no applicable text, as, for example, preferring one of two analogies that is the better for society
istiṣlāḥ	lit. deeming something in the public interest; a legal method to determine the law for the good of society if there is no applicable text, a term used mainly by Malikis
jihad	(Ar. *jihād*) struggle, fight; spiritual striving to combat evil; holy war
jizya	poll tax, to be paid by dhimmis, the protected People of the Book, when residing in the abode of Islam
kalām	theology
kanun	(T., < Ar. *qānūn*) sultanic decree(s)
khabar	see hadith, above
kharāj	land tax
madhhab	(Ar. *madhhab*) lit. path one takes; method; school of jurisprudence
mahr	dower, bride price; the amount, either in cash or property, given by the groom to the bride in consideration of the marriage
maqāṣid	lit. aims; used in the phrase *maqāṣid al-sharīʿa* to imply the objectives, as opposed to the letter, of the Sharia
maṣlaḥa	common good; public interest
matn	text or content, one of two components of a hadith, the other being the *isnād*
maẓālim	ruler's court; state court of grievances
miḥna	the inquisition that took place from 833–48, initiated by the Abbasid caliph al-Maʾmūn, testing scholars as to their belief that the Quran was created and imprisoning those, such as traditionalists, who did not publicly proclaim this belief
muʿāmalāt	civil obligations, social conduct; one of two divisions in Islamic law, the other being worship, *ʿibādāt*

mufti	(Ar. *muftī*) a jurist or religious scholar who issues an authoritative but non-binding opinion on a legal matter to either a private individual, a judge, or the state
muḥtasib	a legal official, appointed by the ruler to police the markets for fraudulent commercial practices and to oversee public places for illicit behavior
mujtahid	a jurist deemed qualified to practice independent reasoning, *ijtihād*
mutawātir	a term of hadith scholarship to indicate a hadith that has been transmitted by a number of people independently of one another, as opposed to an isolated hadith, *khabar wāḥid*
naṣṣ	revealed text; written law
naskh	abrogation (for example, of an earlier Quranic verse by a later one)
qadhf	unfounded accusation of unlawful sexual intercourse
qāḍī	(Sharia court) judge
qānūn	(< Gk, T. *kanun*) a state decree or directive; administrative law
qāṭiʿ	clear-cut (*qaṭʿī*) rule, as opposed to *ẓann*, an inferred rule
qawāʿid	(Ar., sg. *qāʿida*) legal maxims
qiṣāṣ	talionic punishment; retaliation
qiyās	analogy, analogical reasoning
raʾy	opinon, personal view
riba	(Ar. *ribā*) banking interest; unearned gain
şeyhülislam	(T., Ar. *shaykh al-islām*) in the Ottoman empire, a title for the Grand Mufti of Istanbul
shurāt	lit. sellers [of themselves to God] (sg. *shārī*) a (self-employed) designation for a seccessionist group in early Islam that withdrew its support for ʿAlī
shurūṭ	(Ar., sg. *sharṭ*) lit. conditions, stipulations; notarial legal formularies, model documents
sijill	(Ar., T. *sicill*) court register, court record
siyāsa	governance, ruling; policy
siyāsa sharʿiyya	ruler's law
sunna	custom, either pre-Islamic or Prophetic; when capitalized, for example, Sunna, the term refers to the corpus of Prophetic traditions that is considered the second revealed source alongside the Quran
sura	(Ar. *sūra*) Quranic chapter

ṭalāq	unilateral repudiation of the wife by the husband
taʿzīr	discretionary punishment issued by the qadi or ruler for unlawful or sinful behavior or for *ḥadd*
tafsīr	genre of exegetical literature; Quranic commentary
taqlīd	the following of a school's, or a particular jurist's, doctrine, as opposed to determining one's own legal reasoning, *ijtihād*
ulema	(Ar. *ʿulamāʾ*, sg. *ʿālim*) religious scholars
uṣūl al-fiqh	lit. the bases of jurisprudence; legal epistemology; legal theory, as contrasted to *furūʿ al-fiqh*,
uṣūlī	(Ar.) an adjective to denote one engaged in legal theory
waqf	charitable trust
zakāt	alms-giving, one of the five pillars of Islam; tax paid on personal wealth
ẓann	(adj. *ẓannī*) a rule based on inference that can be subject to discussion
zinā	unlawful sexual intercourse

Index